# SERVICES MARKETING:
## CONCEPTS, STRATEGIES, & CASES

Third Edition

**K. Douglas Hoffman**
*Professor of Marketing*
*Colorado State University*

**John E. G. Bateson**
*Group Chief Executive Officer*
*SHL Group plc*

**THOMSON**
————— ✦ —————™
**SOUTH-WESTERN**

Australia · Brazil · Canada · Mexico · Singapore · Spain · United Kingdom · United States

**THOMSON**
™
**SOUTH-WESTERN**

Services Marketing: Concepts, Strategies, & Cases, Third Edition
K. Douglas Hoffman & John E. G. Bateson

**VP/Editorial Director:**
Jack W. Calhoun

**VP/Editor-in-Chief:**
Dave Shaut

**Senior Publisher:**
Melissa Acuña

**Executive Editor:**
Neil Marquardt

**Developmental Editor:**
Mary Draper

**Marketing Manager:**
Nicole Moore

**Production Project Manager:**
Margaret M. Bril

**Manager of Technology, Editorial:**
Vicky True

**Technology Project Editor:**
Pam Wallace

**Web Coordinator:**
Karen Schaffer

**Senior Manufacturing Coordinator:**
Diane Lohman

**Production House:**
Pre-Press Company, Inc.

**Printer:**
RR Donnelley
Crawfordsville, Indiana

**Art Director:**
Stacy Shirley

**Internal Designer:**
Design Matters – Diane & Nick Gliebe

**Cover Designer:**
Design Matters – Diane & Nick Gliebe

**Cover Images:**
© Getty Images

**Photography Manager:**
Deanna Ettinger

**Photo Researcher:**
Terri Miller

Library of Congress Control Number:
2005934852

For more information about our
products, contact us at:

Thomson Learning Academic
Resource Center
1-800-423-0563

**Thomson Higher Education**
5191 Natorp Boulevard
Mason, OH 45040
USA

*To Brittain, Emmy, Maddy and my parents*
**Doug Hoffman**

*For Dori, Lorna, and Jonathan*
**John E. G. Bateson**

# Preface

The primary objective of *Services Marketing: Concepts, Strategies, and Cases* is to provide materials that not only introduce you to the field of services marketing but also acquaint you with specific customer service issues. The business world now demands, in addition to traditional business knowledge, increasing employee competence in customer satisfaction, service quality, and customer service, skills that are essential in growing and sustaining the existing customer base.

## > APPROACH OF SERVICES MARKETING: CONCEPTS, STRATEGIES, AND CASES

The third edition of *Services Marketing: Concepts, Strategies, and Cases* purposely examines the use of services marketing as a competitive weapon from a broader perspective. Consequently, we view services marketing not only as a marketing tool for service firms, but also as a means of competitive advantage for those companies that market products on the tangible dominant side of the continuum. As a result, business examples used throughout the text reflect a wide array of firms representing the nine service economy supersectors including education and health services, financial activities, government, information, leisure and hospitality, professional and business services, transportation and utilities, wholesale and retail trade, and other services.

Ultimately, the *service sector* is one of the three main categories of a developed economy—the other two being *industrial* and *agricultural*. Traditionally, economies throughout the world tend to transition themselves from an *agricultural economy* to an *industrial economy* (e.g, manufacturing,and mining) to a *service economy*. The United Kingdom was the first economy in the modern world to make this transition. Several other countries including the U.S., Japan, Germany, and France have made this transition and many more are expected to do so at an accelerated rate.

We live in interesting times! The increased rate of transformation from an agricultural to a manufacturing to a service-based economy has generally been caused by a highly competitive international marketplace. Simply stated, goods are more amenable to international trade than services, making them more vulnerable to competitive actions. In other words, countries that industrialized their economies first eventually come under competitive attack by other countries that are newly making the transition from an agricultural to an industrial economy. These newcomer countries offer lower production costs (especially labor), which is attractive to industry. Consequently, as industrial sectors flow from one country to the next, the countries they abandon begin to more heavily rely on the growth of their service sectors as the mainstay of their economies. This whole process repeats itself over and over again as other less developed countries enter the fray; consequently, facilitating the transformation from agriculture to industrial to service-based economies.

> ## STRUCTURE OF THE BOOK

*Services Marketing: Concepts, Strategies, and Cases* is divided into four main parts. The first part, "An Overview of Services Marketing," concentrates on defining services marketing and discusses in detail the fundamental concepts and strategies that differentiate the marketing of services from the marketing of tangible goods. The primary objective of Part 1 is to establish a core knowledge base that will be built upon throughout the remainder of the text.

Chapter 1 provides an introduction to the field of services marketing. It establishes the importance of the service sector in the world economy and the need for services marketing education. Chapter 2 focuses more deeply on the fundamental differences between goods and services and their corresponding managerial implications. Chapter 3 provides an overview of the service sector and focuses on the nine service industry supersectors and the most substantial changes taking place within the service sector. New concepts such as the "graying of America" and the "outservicing of America" are presented, and predicted keys to success within the service encounter are also discussed. Chapter 4 focuses on consumer purchase decision issues as they relate to the services field. Consumers often approach service purchases differently from the way they approach the purchase of goods. The first part of the book concludes with Chapter 5, which takes an in-depth look at ethics in the service sector. Because of the differences between goods and services, unique opportunities arise that may encourage ethical misconduct.

The second part of the book, "Service Strategy: Managing the Service Experience," is dedicated to topics that concern the management of the service encounter. Due to the consumer's involvement in the production of services, many new challenges are presented that do not frequently occur within the manufacturing sector. The primary topics in Part 2 are strategic issues related to the marketing mix as well as the Servuction Model including process, pricing, promotion, physical evidence, and people (employee and customer) issues.

Chapter 6 provides an overview of service operations, pinpointing the areas where special managerial attention is needed in the construction of the service process. In addition, the importance of balancing operations and marketing functions in service operations is discussed. Chapters 7 and 8 focus on pricing and communication issues as they relate specifically to service firms. Chapter 9 examines the development and management of the service firm's physical environment. Chapter 10 discusses the many challenges associated with managing employees within the service experience. The service business, by its very definition, is a people business and requires talented managers who can navigate the thin line between the needs of the organization, its employees, and its customers. Part 2 concludes with Chapter 11 where the art of managing service consumers is explored. Due to the impact of inseparability, the consumer's role in service production can both facilitate and hinder the exchange process. Hence, developing a strategic understanding of how the consumer can be effectively managed within the service encounter is critical. Chapter 11 also introduces the fundamental components as well as the advantages and disadvantages associated with customer relationship management (CRM) systems.

Part 3, "Assessing and Improving Service Delivery," focuses on customer satisfaction and service quality issues. Methods are presented for tracking service failures and employee recovery efforts, as well as customer retention strategies. Ideally, assessing and improving the service delivery system will lead to "seamless service"—provided without interruption, confusion, or hassle to the customer.

Chapter 12 presents an overview of the importance and benefits of customer satisfaction and the special factors to consider regarding measurement issues. Chapter 13 builds from the materials presented in Chapter 12 and discusses conceptual and measurement issues pertaining to service quality and service quality information systems. Chapter 14 presents methods for tracking service failures and employee service recovery efforts. Chapter 15 focuses on the often forgotten benefits of customer retention and discusses strategies that maximize a firm's customer retention efforts. Chapter 16 concludes this section of the text as well as the entire text with "Putting the Pieces Together: Creating the Seamless Service Firm." Chapter 16 is dedicated to pulling the ideas in the book together in a manner that demonstrates the delivery of flawless customer service.

Part 4 of the book consists of cases that are specifically relevant to each of the chapters and also integrates other topics discussed throughout the text. The cases are to be used at the instructor's discretion to give students realistic practice in using the concepts presented in the textbook. Many of these cases have been purposely written to include an international and/or e-business flavor to reflect the changing business climate and the wide variety of issues that face service marketers today.

## > WHAT'S NEW IN THE THIRD EDITION?

- New Opening Vignettes in every chapter represent a variety of firms and relevant customer service issues from the nine service economy supersectors. These firms include the following:

| | |
|---|---|
| Private Escapes | Westin's Heavenly Bed |
| GEICO | Wegman's Grocery Store |
| UPS | "Yours is a Very Bad Hotel" |
| Skype | American Customer Satisfaction Index |
| Vail Resorts | Malcolm Baldrige National Quality Award |
| Build-A-Bear Workshop | Wendy's International Inc. |
| Airline Pricing | Loyalty Gadgets |
| Aflac | The Katitche Point Great House |

- New Global Services in Action features in every chapter provide international examples of service marketing concepts and strategies. Companies and topics featured in Global Services in Action boxes include the following:

| | |
|---|---|
| Service Exports | Hong Kong Disneyland |
| Importing American Standards | Dell Offshore Technical Support |
| Cuba's Hotel Industry | Cultural Expectations |
| Finland Tourism | Global Customer Satisfaction |
| Global Health Care Perceptions | The Global Communication Gap |
| Delighting Global Customers | Mitsubishi Motors |
| Ethnic Pricing | BMO Bank of Montreal |
| Marriott International Inc. | Ethnic Marketing |

- New B2B Services in Action features in every chapter provide B2B business examples of service marketing concepts and strategies. Companies and topics featured in B2B Services in Action boxes include the following:

| | |
|---|---|
| IBM | Airbus A380 |
| Hotel Business Customers | Private Banks |
| Business Class Travelers | Customer Relationship Management |
| Citigroup | J. D. Power and Associates |
| American Nursing Services | ISO 9000 |
| Verizon Enterprise Solutions Group | Service Recovery Audit |
| Private Jet Service | B2B Customer Loyalty |
| Law Practice Marketing | State Farm Insurance |

- New E-Services in Action features in every chapter provide eBusiness examples of service marketing concepts and strategies. Companies and topics featured in E-Services Services in Action boxes include the following:

| | |
|---|---|
| Self-service Technologies | Google.com |
| Cellular Service | Online Complaint Sites |
| Hewlett-Packard | The 7Cs of Customer Interface |
| E-Consumer Decision Process | Humanizing the Net |
| Confidentiality Issues on the Net | Dimensions of E-Qual |
| E-Returns | E-failures Online |
| E-Pricing | Online Customer Retention |
| Online Advertising | RateMyProfessor.com |

- Expanded coverage of e-business, global service, and B2B issues
- Updated service industry examples
- Expanded test bank
- Redesigned PowerPoint slides

## > INSTRUCTOR RESOURCES

The instructor resources for *Services Marketing: Concepts, Strategies, and Cases*, 3e provide a variety of valuable resources for leading effective classroom discussions and assessing student learning. The following instructor resources are available for this text.

## > INSTRUCTOR'S RESOURCE CD-ROM

The Instructor's Resource CD-ROM includes the Instructor's Manual, the Test Bank, PowerPoint Lecture Slides, and Examview.

- The Instructor's Manual for *Services Marketing: Concepts, Strategies, and Cases*, 3e includes a summary of the goals of each chapter, detailed lecture outlines, key terms

and definitions, answers to discussion questions, case teaching notes, and other resources to reduce lecture preparation time. This new edition also includes a list of suggested Harvard Business School cases.
- The Test Bank has been expanded to include an abundant number of multiple-choice questions and new short-answer essay questions.
- PowerPoint lecture slides highlight the key concepts of each chapter.
- Examview (Windows/Macintosh) Computerized Testing allows you to create, deliver, and customize tests in minutes with this easy-to-use assessment and tutorial system. Using ExamView's complete word processing capabilities, you can enter an unlimited number of new questions or edit existing questions.

## > PREMIER BUSINESS CASE PROGRAM

Creating the perfect casebook is now simpler than ever. Thomson Customer Solutions serves as your single point of contact, while allowing you to select and arrange content from a variety of business case libraries to develop a customized casebook for your course. You may browse the content available in each collection by visiting any of the following providers:

- NACRA
- Harvard Business School of Publishing
- Darden
- The Kennedy School at Harvard University
- NYU Salomon Center
- Arthur M. Blank Center for Entrepreneurship at Babson College
- University of Denver Daniels College of Business

If you are interested in ordering or learning more about Thomson's Premier Business Case Program, please contact your local Thomson sales representative.

## > WEBTUTOR TOOLBOX

Available free with the purchase of a new textbook, WebTutor ToolBox provides students with links to the rich content from our book companion websites. Available for WebCT and Blackboard only. Your sales representative will provide you with additional information about WebTutor Toolbox.

## > INSTRUCTOR SUPPORT WEBSITE

The Instructor Support website provides access to downloadable supplements (Instructor's Manual, Test Bank, and PowerPoint Slides), and a variety of marketing resources including "Marketing in the News," summaries of the latest marketing-related news stories, indexed by topic for your convenience. Each Marketing News summary contains a headline, subject category, key words, a three- to five-paragraph summary of a news article, article source line, and questions to spur further thought. The URL for the Instructor Support Web site is http://hoffman.swlearning.com.

## > STUDENT RESOURCES

### STUDENT SUPPORT WEBSITE

The Student Support Website (http://hoffman.swlearning.com) enriches the learning experience with a variety of interactive tools and Web resources:

- Flash Cards
- Crossword Puzzles
- Interactive Quizzes
- PowerPoint Slides
- Marketing in the News
- Marketing Resources
- Marketing Careers

## > ACKNOWLEDGMENTS

We would like to extend are heart-felt thanks to the many good folks at South-Western, many of whom we have had the pleasure of knowing for many years through our other text projects. Special thanks to Jack Calhoun, VP/Editorial Director; Dave Shaut, VP/Editor-in-Chief; Neil Marquardt, Executive Editor; and Nicole Moore, Marketing Manager for generating and maintaining the level of support and enthusiasm associated with this project throughout the entire process.

We would especially like to thank Mary Draper—Developmental Editor beyond compare. Mary, as always, thank you so much for your professionalism and dedication to our projects.

Additional thanks are extended to Jan Turner, Project Manager, Marge Bril, Production Editor; Stacy Shirley, Art Director; and Deanna Ettinger, Photo Manager for putting the project together... no small task!

We would also like to thank Holly Hapke for revising the Instructor's Manual, Test Bank, and PowerPoint Slides. Thank you, Holly!

In addition, we would like to thank our case contributors: Jochen Wirtz, Stephan Martin, S. Mohan, Brian Wansink, Jeanette Ho Pheng Theng, Aliah Hanim M. Salleh, Eric Cannell, Richard A. Engdahl, and Judy Siguaw.

Finally, we would also like to thank the Thomson sales force for supporting this project. We truly appreciate your efforts in bringing this package to the marketplace and offer our assistance in support of your efforts.

We are very appreciative of the insightful comments made on the earlier editions of this text by the following colleagues:

Kenneth D. Bahn, James Madison University
Julie Baker, University of Texas at Arlington
Ronald E. Goldsmith, Florida State University
Scott Kelley, University of Kentucky
Rhonda Walker Mack, College of Charleston
Gene W. Murdock, University of Wyoming
Susan Stites-Doe, SUNY-Brockport
Louis Turley, Western Kentucky University

In closing, we hope that you enjoy the book and your services marketing class. It will likely be one of the most practical courses you will take during your college career. Education is itself a service experience. As a participant in this service experience, you are expected to participate in class discussions. Take advantage of the opportunities provided you during this course, and become an integral component of the education production process. Regardless of your major area of study, the services marketing course has much to offer.

We would sincerely appreciate any comments or suggestions you would care to share with us. We believe that this text will heighten your sensitivity to services, and because of that belief, we leave you with this promise: We guarantee that after completing this book and your services marketing course, you will never look at a service experience in the same way again. This new view will become increasingly frustrating for most of you, as you will encounter many experiences that are less than satisfactory. Learn from these negative experiences, relish the positive encounters, and use this information to make a difference when it is your turn to set the standards for others to follow. As evangelists of services marketing, we could ask for no greater reward.

K. Douglas Hoffman (Doug)
Professor of Marketing
Marketing Department
Colorado State University
Fort Collins, Colorado 80523
(970) 491-2791 (office)
(970) 491-5956 (fax)
doug.hoffman@colostate.edu

John E. G. Bateson
SHL Group plc
The Pavilion
Thames Ditton
Surrey KT7 One
United Kingdom
+44(020) 8335 8000 (office)
+44(020) 8335 7000 (fax)
john.bateson@shlgroup.com

# About the Authors

*K. Douglas Hoffman* is a Professor of Marketing at Colorado State University. He received his B.S. from The Ohio State University, and his M.B.A. and D.B.A. from the University of Kentucky. Over the last twenty years, Doug has taught courses such as Principles of Marketing, Services Marketing, E-Marketing, Retail Management, and Marketing Management. His primary teaching and research passion is in the Services Marketing area where he has started the first Services Marketing classes at Mississippi State University, The University of North Carolina at Wilmington, and Colorado State University. He has also taught courses as a visiting professor at the Helsinki School of Economics and Business Administration in Helsinki, Finland; The Institute of Industrial Policy Studies in Seoul, South Korea; and Thammasat University in Bangkok, Thailand.

Doug has been formally recognized for teaching excellence at Colorado State University and the University of North Carolina at Wilmington. In addition, he has served as the Education Coordinator for the Services Marketing Special Interest Group of the American Marketing Association. Doug has published a variety of articles in academic and practitioner journals and is the co-author of three textbooks:

*Services Marketing: Concepts, Strategies, and Cases,* Third Edition, Thomson South-Western

*Managing Services Marketing,* Fourth Edition, Thomson South-Western

*Marketing Principles and Best Practices*, Third Edition, Thomson South-Western

Doug's current research and consulting activities are primarily in the areas of customer service/satisfaction, service failure and recovery, and services marketing education.

*John E.G. Bateson* is the Group Chief Executive Officer, SHL Group, plc. He was Associate Professor of Marketing at the London Business School, England, and a visiting associate professor at the Stanford Business School. Prior to teaching, he was a brand manager with Lever Brothers and marketing manager with Philips.

Dr. Bateson holds an undergraduate degree from Imperial College, London, a master's degree from London Business School, and a Ph.D. in marketing from the Harvard Business School. He has published extensively in the services marketing literature, including the *Journal of Marketing Research*, *Journal of Retailing*, *Marketing Science*, and *Journal of Consumer Research*. He is also the author of *Managing Services Marketing: Text and Readings* (South-Western) and *Marketing Public Transit: A Strategic Approach* (Praeger).

Dr. Bateson was actively involved with the formation of the services division of the American Marketing Association. He served on the Services Council for four years and has chaired sessions of the AMA Services Marketing Conference. He also serves on the steering committee of the Marketing Science Institute. Dr. Bateson consults extensively in the services sector.

# Contents in Brief

# Contents

# PART | 1

# AN OVERVIEW OF SERVICES MARKETING

*Services Marketing: Concepts, Strategies, and Cases* is divided into three main parts.

Part I, An Overview of Services Marketing, concentrates on defining services marketing

and discusses in detail the fundamental concepts and strategies that differentiate the

marketing of services from the marketing of tangible goods. The primary objective for

Part I is to establish a core knowledge base that will be built upon throughout the

remainder of the text.

# CHAPTER 1

# AN INTRODUCTION TO SERVICES

## CHAPTER OBJECTIVES

*This chapter provides an introduction to the field of services marketing. The chapter discusses the basic differences between goods and services and the factors necessary for the creation of the service experience. In addition, the chapter establishes the importance of the service sector in the world economy and the need for services marketing education.*

After reading this chapter, you should be able to:

- Understand the basic differences between goods and services.
- Appreciate the factors that create the customer's service experience.
- Comprehend the driving forces behind the increasing demand for services marketing knowledge.
- Understand the two organization models used in service firms: the industrial management model and the market-focused management model.

*"Economic value, like the coffee bean, progresses from commodities to goods to services to experiences."*

Joseph B. Pine II &
James H. Gilmore
*The Experience Economy*

## > PRIVATE ESCAPES

© AP / WIDE WORLD PHOTOS

The service sector consists of a number of industries but perhaps none more compelling than the hospitality industry. The hospitality industry comprises a variety of segments including lodging, travel, and tourism with worldwide employment expected to reach 338 million people by 2005. Within the lodging segment of the hospitality industry, today's success stories include those firms that are truly creative in the manner in which they conduct business. One of the most creative firms today would have to include Destination Clubs by Private Escapes.

Private Escapes is a worldwide destination club with a business model similar to a private country club where a limited number of members have virtually unlimited access to a global portfolio of exquisitely maintained, luxurious vacation homes complete with five-star concierge services. This is done by maintaining a member-to-property ratio of no more than 6:1, thereby purposely underutilizing each property to ensure high availability.

Private Escapes' properties are in the finest resort locations with property values averaging $550,000. Locations include numerous beach, mountain, leisure, and city destinations selected throughout the United States, Mexico, Western Europe, and the Caribbean. For example, the La Buscadora, an 80-foot motor yacht in the British Virgin Islands, provides an all-inclusive vacation experience for groups up to eight people, featuring an on-board steward and gourmet cook in addition to activities such as scuba diving, snorkeling, waterskiing, and ocean kayaking. Other destinations provide access to their own unique variety of activities such as golfing, shopping, theatres, spas, beaches, skiing, hunting, hiking, fishing, sailing, and horseback riding.

While in residence, Private Escapes' members and their guests are treated to outstanding amenities and services. Amenities typically include two- and three-bedroom homes, condominiums, and town homes with fully equipped kitchens, luxury baths, and elegantly furnished dining and living areas. In addition, other special touches are thoughtfully included such as Stearns and Foster™ bedding with luxurious high thread-count linens; plasma screen television with full theatre surround sound; DVD players and state-of-the-art stereo systems; video game entertainment, such as Sony Playstation™ and X-Box™; private-label bath amenities; and thick terrycloth bathrobes and towels.

Private Escapes is committed to delivering five-star concierge services for all members and their guests. Guest services include travel arrangements; the development of an "Escape Plan" including reservations for selected activities such as dining, golfing, or show tickets; shopping services that ensure that the kitchen is stocked when guests arrive; cleaning services; and in-residence concierge services. In addition, Private Escapes also offers (at additional cost) air travel to members through an optional private jet service.

Clearly, Private Escapes understands the bundle of benefits provided to its members through the effective management of the member's service experience. Furthermore, it does so at a price point lower than its competitors.

Private Escapes is currently enjoying phenomenal membership growth and satisfaction.

---

Source: Private Escapes Web site:
http://www.private-escapes.com accessed 30 January 2005.

> ## INTRODUCTION

Services are everywhere we turn, whether it be travel to an exotic tourism destination, a visit to the doctor, a church service, a meal at our favorite restaurant, or a day at school. More and more countries, particularly the so-called industrialized countries, are finding that the majority of their gross national products are being generated by their service sectors, as shown in the table found on the inside back cover of the textbook. However, the growth of the service sector does not just lie within traditional service industries such as leisure and hospitality services, education and health services, financial and insurance services, and professional and business services. Traditional goods producers such as automotive, computer, and numerous other manufacturers are now turning to the service aspects of their operations to establish a differential advantage in the marketplace as well as to generate additional sources of revenue for their firms. In essence, these companies, which used to compete by marketing "boxes" (tangible goods), have now switched their competitive focus to the provision of unmatched, unparalleled customer services.

Ample evidence exists that documents this transition from selling "boxes" to service competition. Traditional goods-producing industries such as the automotive industry are now emphasizing the service aspects of their businesses such as low APR financing, attractive lease arrangements, bumper-to-bumper factory warranties, low maintenance guarantees, and free shuttle service for customers. Simultaneously, less is being heard about the tangible aspects of vehicles such as gas mileage, acceleration, and vehicle styling. Similarly, the personal computer industry promotes in-home repairs, 24-hour customer service, and leasing arrangements; and the satellite television industry is now boasting the benefits of digital service, pay-per-view alternatives, and security options to prevent children from viewing certain programming.

Overall, this new "global services era" is characterized by:

- economies and labor force figures that are dominated by the service sector;
- more customer involvement in strategic business decisions;
- products that are increasingly market-focused and much more responsive to the changing needs of the marketplace;
- the development of technologies that assist customers and employees in the provision of services;
- employees who have been provided with more discretionary freedom to develop customized solutions to special customer requests and solve customer complaints on-the-spot with minimal inconvenience;
- and the emergence of new service industries and the **"service imperative"** where the intangible aspects of the product are becoming more and more the key features that differentiate products in the marketplace.

**service imperative**
Reflects the view that the intangible aspects of products are becoming the key features that differentiate the product in the marketplace.

It is clear that the service sectors in many countries are no longer manufacturing's poor cousin. Services provide the bulk of the wealth and are an important source of employment and exports for many countries. In addition, there are countless examples of firms using the service imperative to drive their businesses forward to profit and growth. Many of these are highlighted in the *Services in Action* boxes located throughout the remainder of the text. In the near future, the service boom is expected to continue.

## > WHAT IS A SERVICE?

Admittedly, the distinction between goods and services is not always perfectly clear. In fact, providing an example of a pure good or a pure service is very difficult, if not impossible. A pure good would imply that the benefits received by the consumer contained no elements supplied by service. Similarly, a pure service would contain no elements of goods.

In reality, many services contain at least some goods elements, such as the menu selections at a Rain Forest Café, the bank statement from the local bank, or the written policy from an insurance company. Also, most goods at least offer a delivery service. For example, simple table salt is delivered to the grocery store, and the company that sells it may offer innovative invoicing methods that further differentiate it from its competitors.

The distinction between goods and services is further obscured by firms that conduct business on both sides of the fence. For example, General Motors, the "goods" manufacturing giant, generates a significant percentage of its revenue from its financial and insurance businesses, and the car maker's biggest supplier is Blue Cross–Blue Shield, not a parts supplier for steel, tires, or glass as most people would have thought.[1] Other examples include General Electric and IBM, generally thought of as major goods producers, who now generate more than half of their revenues from services. The transition from goods producer to service provider can be found to varying degrees throughout much of the industrial sector. One of the world's largest steel producers now considers its service-related activities to be the dominate force within its overall business strategy.[2]

Despite the confusion, the following definitions should provide a sound starting point in developing an understanding of the differences between goods and services. In general, **goods** can be defined as objects, devices, or things, whereas **services** can be defined as deeds, efforts, or performances.[3] Moreover, we would like to note that when the term **product** is mentioned, it refers to both goods and services and is used in such a manner throughout the remainder of this text. Ultimately, the primary difference between goods and services is the property of *intangibility*. By definition, intangible products lack physical substance. As a result, intangible products face a host of services marketing problems that are not always adequately solved by traditional goods-related marketing solutions. These differences are discussed in detail in Chapter 2, Fundamental Differences Between Goods and Services.

### THE SCALE OF MARKET ENTITIES

An interesting perspective regarding the differences between goods and services is provided by the scale of market entities.[4] The **scale of market entities** presented in Figure 1.1 displays a continuum of products based on their tangibility where goods are **tangible dominant** and services are **intangible dominant**. The core benefit of a tangible dominant product typically involves a physical possession that contains service elements to a lesser degree. For example, an automobile is a tangible dominant product that provides transportation. As the product becomes more and more tangible dominant, fewer service aspects are apparent (e.g., salt). In contrast, intangible dominant products do not involve the physical possession of a product and can only be

**goods**
Objects, devices, or things.

**services**
Deeds, efforts, or performances.

**product**
Either a good or a service.

**scale of market entities**
The scale that displays a range of products along a continuum based on their tangibility.

**tangible dominant**
Goods that possess physical properties that can be felt, tasted, and seen prior to the consumer's purchase decision.

**intangible dominant**
Services that lack the physical properties that can be sensed by consumers prior to the purchase decision.

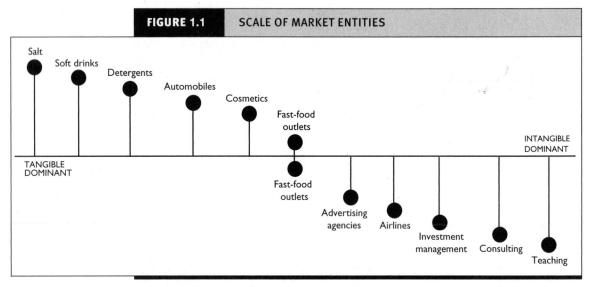

**FIGURE 1.1    SCALE OF MARKET ENTITIES**

Source: Adapted from G. Lynn Shostack, "Breaking Free from Product Marketing," *The Journal of Marketing* (April 1977), p. 77.

experienced. Like the automobile, an airline provides transportation, but the customer does not physically possess the plane. The airline customer experiences the flight; consequently, service aspects dominate the product's core benefit and tangible elements are present to a lesser degree. In comparison, fast food businesses, which contain both a goods and service component, fall in the middle of the continuum.

The scale of market entities reveals two important lessons. First, there really may be no such thing as a pure product or pure service. Products seemingly are a bundle of tangible and intangible elements that combine to varying degrees. Second, the tangible aspects of an intangible dominant product and the intangible aspects of a tangible dominant product are an important source of product differentiation and new revenue streams. For example, businesses that produce tangible dominant products and ignore, or at least forget about, the service (intangible) aspects of their product offering are overlooking a vital component of their businesses. By defining their businesses too narrowly, these firms have developed classic cases of **marketing myopia**. For example, the typical family pizza parlor may myopically view itself as being in the pizza business and primarily focus on the pizza product itself. However, a broader view of the business recognizes that it is providing the consumer with a reasonably priced food product in a convenient format surrounded by an experience that has been deliberately created for the targeted consumer. Interestingly, adding service aspects to a product often transforms the product from a commodity into an experience, and by doing so, increases the revenue-producing opportunities of the product dramatically.

For example, when priced as a raw *commodity,* coffee beans are worth little more than $1 per pound.[5] When processed, packaged, and sold in the grocery store as a *good,* the price of coffee jumps to between 5 and 25 cents a cup. When that same cup is sold in a local restaurant, the coffee takes on more *service* aspects and sells for $1 to $2 per cup. However, in the ultimate act of added value, when that same cup of coffee is sold

**marketing myopia**
Condition of firms that define their businesses too narrowly.

within the compelling *experience* of a five-star restaurant or within the unique environment of a Starbucks, the customer gladly pays $4 to $5 per cup. In this instance, the whole process of ordering, creation, and consumption becomes "a pleasurable, even theatrical" experience. Hence, economic value, like the coffee bean, progresses from *commodities* to *goods* to *services* to *experiences*. In the previous example, coffee was transformed from a raw commodity valued at approximately $1 per pound to $4–$5 per cup—a markup as much as 5,000 percent!

## THE MOLECULAR MODEL

Molecular models further expand our understanding of the basic differences between goods and services. A **molecular model** is a pictorial representation of the relationship between the tangible and intangible elements of a firm's operation.[6] One of the primary benefits obtained from developing a molecular model is that it is a management tool that offers the opportunity to visualize the firm's entire bundle of benefits that its product offers customers. Figure 1.2 depicts two molecular models, which continues our earlier discussion concerning the differences between automobile ownership (tangible dominant) and purchasing an airline ticket (intangible dominant). Airlines differ from automobiles in that typically consumers do not physically possess the airline. Consumers

*molecular model*
A conceptual model of the relationship between tangible and intangible components of a firm's operations.

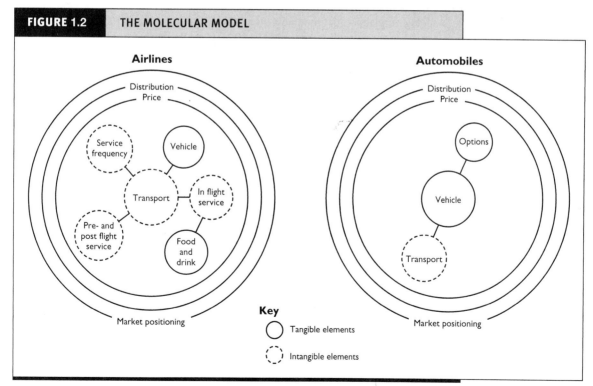

**FIGURE 1.2    THE MOLECULAR MODEL**

Source: Adapted from G. Lynn Shostack, "Breaking Free from Product Marketing," *The Journal of Marketing* (April 1977), p. 76.

in this case purchase the core benefit of transportation and all of the corresponding tangible (denoted by solid-lined circles) and intangible benefits (denoted by dashed-lined circles) that are associated with flying. In contrast, a consumer who purchases an automobile is primarily benefited by the ownership of a physical possession that renders a service—transportation.

The diagrams provided in Figure 1.2 are oversimplifications of the bundle of benefits that ultimately comprise the airline experience and car ownership. From a managerial perspective, an elaboration of these models would identify the tangible and intangible product components that need to be effectively managed. For example, the successful airline experience is not just determined by the safe arrival of passengers to their selected destinations. The airline molecular model could easily be expanded to include:

- long-term and short-term parking (intangible element)
- shuttle services (intangible element)
- rental car availability (intangible element)
- flight attendants (tangible elements)
- gate attendants (tangible elements)
- baggage handlers (tangible elements)

Similarly, the automobile model could be expanded to include:

- salespersons on the showroom floor (tangible element)
- financing arrangements (intangible element)
- finance manager (tangible element)
- maintenance and repair services (intangible element)
- mechanics and service representatives (tangible elements)

The overriding benefit obtained by developing molecular models is the appreciation for the intangible and tangible elements that comprise most products. Once managers understand this broadened view of their products, they can do a much better job of understanding customer needs, servicing those needs more effectively, and differentiating their product-offering from competitors. The molecular model also demonstrates that consumers' service "knowledge" and goods "knowledge" are not obtained in the same manner. With tangible dominant products, goods "knowledge" is obtained by focusing in on the physical aspects of the product itself. In contrast, consumers evaluate intangible dominant products based on the experience that surrounds the core benefit of the product. Hence, understanding the importance and components of the service experience is critical.

## > FRAMING THE SERVICE EXPERIENCE: THE SERVUCTION MODEL

Because of the intangible nature of service products, service knowledge is acquired differently than knowledge pertaining to goods. For example, consumers can sample tangible dominant products such as soft drinks and cookies prior to purchase. In contrast, a consumer cannot sample an intangible dominant product such as a haircut, a surgical procedure, or a consultant's advice prior to purchase. Hence, service knowledge is gained through the experience of receiving the actual service itself. Ultimately, when a consumer purchases a service, he or she is actually purchasing an experience!

All products, be they goods or services, deliver a bundle of benefits to the consumer.[7] The **benefit concept** is the encapsulation of these tangible and intangible benefits in the consumer's mind. For a tangible dominant good such as Tide laundry detergent, for example, the core benefit concept might simply be cleaning. However for other individuals, it might also include attributes built into the product that go beyond the mere powder or liquid, such as cleanliness, whiteness, and/or motherhood (it's a widely-held belief in some cultures that the cleanliness of children's clothes is a reflection upon their mother). The determination of what the bundle of benefits comprises—the benefit concept purchased by consumers—is the heart of marketing, and it transcends all goods and services.

*benefit concept*
The encapsulation of the benefits of a product in the consumer's mind.

In contrast to goods, services deliver a bundle of benefits through the experience that is created for the consumer. For example, most consumers of Tide will never see the inside of the manufacturing plant where Tide is produced; they will most likely never interact with the factory workers who produce the detergent nor with the management staff that directs the workers; and they will also generally not use Tide in the company of other consumers. In contrast, restaurant customers are physically present in the "factory" where the food is produced; these customers do interact with the workers who prepare and serve the food as well as with the management staff that runs the restaurant. Moreover, restaurant customers consume the service in the presence of other customers where they may influence one another's service experience. One particularly simple but powerful model that illustrates factors that influence the service experience is the **servuction model** depicted in Figure 1.3. The servuction model consists of four factors that directly influence customers' service experiences:

*servuction model*
A model used to illustrate the factors that influence the service experience, including those that are visible to the consumer and those that are not.

1. servicescape (visible)
2. contact personnel/service providers (visible)
3. other customers (visible)
4. organizations and systems (invisible)

The first three factors are plainly visible to customers. In contrast, organization and systems, although profoundly impacting the customer's experience, are typically invisible to the customer.

## THE SERVICESCAPE

The term **servicescape** refers to the use of physical evidence to design service environments. Due to the intangibility of services, customers often have trouble evaluating the quality of service objectively. As a result, consumers rely on the physical evidence that surrounds the service to help them form their evaluations. Hence, the servicescape consists of *ambient conditions* such as room temperature and music; *inanimate objects* that assist the firm in completing its tasks, such as furnishings and business equipment;

*servicescape*
All the nonliving features that comprise the service environment.

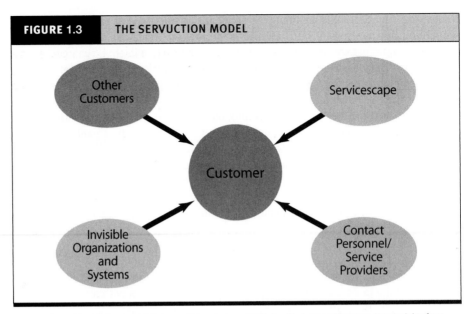

**FIGURE 1.3     THE SERVUCTION MODEL**

Source: Adapted from E. Langeard, J. Bateson, C. Lovelock, and P. Eiglier, *Marketing of Services: New Insights from Consumers and Managers,* Report No 81-104, Cambridge, MA: Marketing Sciences Institute, 1981.

and *other physical evidence, for example,* signs, symbols, and personal artifacts such as family pictures and personal collections. The use of physical evidence varies by the type of service firm. Service firms such as hospitals, resorts, and child-care centers often use physical evidence extensively as they design facilities and other tangibles associated with the service. In contrast, service firms such as insurance agencies and express mail drop-off locations use limited physical evidence. Regardless of the variation in usage, all service firms need to recognize the importance of managing the servicescape, because of its role in:

- packaging the service
- facilitating the service delivery process
- socializing customers and employees
- differentiating the firm from its competitors

## CONTACT PERSONNEL/SERVICE PROVIDERS

**contact personnel**
Employees other than the primary service provider who briefly interact with the customer.

**service providers**
The primary providers of a core service, such as a waiter or waitress, dentist, physician, or college instructor.

**Contact personnel** are employees other than the primary service provider who briefly interact with the customer. Typical examples of contact personnel are parking attendants, receptionists, and hosts and hostesses. In contrast, **service providers** are the primary providers of the core service, such as a waiter or waitress, dentist, physician, or college instructor.

Unlike the consumption of goods, the consumption of services often takes place where the service is produced (e.g., dentist's office, restaurant, and hair salon) or where the service is provided at the consumer's residence or workplace (e.g., lawn care, house painter, janitorial service). Regardless of the service delivery location, interactions between consumers and contact personnel/service providers are commonplace. As a result, service providers have a dramatic impact on the service experience. For example, when asked what irritated them most about service providers, customers have noted seven categories of complaints:

- *Apathy:* What comedian George Carlin refers to as DILLIGAD—Do I look like I give a damn?
- *Brush-off:* Attempts to get rid of the customer by dismissing the customer completely . . . the "I want you to go away" syndrome.
- *Coldness:* Indifferent service providers who could not care less what the customer really wants.
- *Condescension:* The "you are the client/patient, so you must be stupid" approach.
- *Robotism:* When the customers are treated simply as inputs into a system that must be processed.
- *Rulebook:* Providers who live by the rules of the organization even when those rules do not make good sense.
- *Runaround:* Passing the customer off to another provider, who will simply pass them off to yet another provider.[8]

Service personnel perform the dual functions of interacting with customers and reporting back to the internal organization. Strategically, service personnel are an important source of product differentiation. It is often challenging for a service organization to differentiate itself from other similar organizations in terms of the benefit bundle it offers or its delivery system. For example, many airlines offer similar bundles of benefits and fly the same types of aircraft from the same airports to the same destinations. Therefore, their only hope of a competitive advantage is from the service level—the way things are done. Hence, the factor that often distinguishes one airline from another is the poise and attitude of its service providers. Singapore Airlines, for example, enjoys an excellent reputation due in large part to the beauty and grace of its flight attendants. Other firms that hold a differential advantage over competitors based on personnel include the Ritz Carlton, IBM, and Disney Enterprises. Given the importance of service providers and other contact personnel, Chapter 10 is devoted to hiring, training, and empowering personnel.

## OTHER CUSTOMERS

Ultimately, the success of many service encounters depends on how effectively the service firm manages its clientele. A wide range of service establishments such as restaurants, hotels, airlines, and physicians' offices serve multiple customers simultaneously. Hence, other customers can have a profound impact on an individual's service experience. Research has shown that the presence of other customers can enhance or detract from an individual's service experience.[9] The influence of other customers can

Hertz is addressing travelers' needs and minimizing the impact of "other customers" with programs such as Hertz #1 Club Gold ® and Instant Return. Hertz #1 Club Gold ® and Hertz Instant Return programs improve customers' travel experiences by reducing the time it takes to pick up and return a car.

be *active* or *passive.* For instance, examples of other customers actively detracting from one's service experience include unruly customers in a restaurant or a night club, children crying during a church service, or theatergoers carrying on a conversation during a play. Some passive examples include customers who show up late for appointments, thereby delaying each subsequent appointment; an exceptionally tall individual who sits directly in front of another customer at a movie theater; or the impact of being part of a crowd, which increases the waiting time for everyone in the group.

Though many customer actions that enhance or detract from the service experience are difficult to predict, service organizations can attempt to manage the behavior of customers so that they coexist peacefully. For example, firms can manage waiting times so that customers who arrive earlier than others get first priority, clearly target specific age segments to minimize potential conflicts between younger and older customers, and provide separate dining facilities for smokers and customers with children.

## INVISIBLE ORGANIZATION AND SYSTEMS

Thus far, the servuction model suggests that the benefits derived by Customer A are influenced by the interaction with (1) the servicescape, (2) contact personnel and/or service providers, and (3) other customers. The benefits are therefore derived from an interactive process that takes place throughout the service experience. Of course, the visible components of service firms cannot exist in isolation, and indeed, they have to be supported by invisible components. For example, UPS attributes much of the firm's success to the behind-the-scenes activities that the customer seldom sees including 12 mainframes capable of computing 5 billion bits of information every second; 90,000 PCs; 80,000 hand-held computers to record driver deliveries; the nation's largest private cellular network; and the world's largest BD-2 database designed for package tracking and other customer shipping information.[10]

The **invisible organization and systems** reflect the rules, regulations, and processes upon which the organization is based. As a result, although they are invisible to the customer, they have a very profound effect on the consumer's service experience. The invisible organization and systems determine factors such as information forms to be completed by customers, the number of employees working in the firm at any given time, and the policies of the organization regarding countless decisions that may range from the substitution of menu items to whether the firm accepts AARP (American Association of Retired Persons) identification cards for senior citizens' discounts.

*invisible organization and systems*
That part of a firm that reflects the rules, regulations, and processes upon which the organization is based.

The four components of the servuction model combine to create the experience for the consumer, and it is the experience that creates the bundle of benefits for the consumer. Creating "experiences" for customers is not a new idea. The entertainment industry and venues such as Disney have been doing it for years. Others, particularly in the hospitality sector, have recently picked up on the idea and have introduced "experience" product concepts such as the Hard Rock Café, Planet Hollywood, and the Rainforest Café. The question facing many other types of service providers is how to transform their own operations into memorable experiences for the customer. One unique example involves a computer repair firm based in Minneapolis, Minnesota. This team of crack technicians, formally called the "Geek Squad," are purposely dressed in white shirts, thin black ties, pocket protectors, and badges. In this instance, a mundane service has been transformed into a memorable event that's fun for the customer. Other profit opportunities have opened up for the firm as demand for "Geek memorabilia" increases.

Perhaps the most profound implication of the servuction model is that it demonstrates that consumers are an integral part of the service process. Their participation may be active or passive, but they are always involved in the service delivery process. This has a significant effect on the nature of the services marketing task and provides a number of challenges that are not typically faced by goods' manufacturers.

## > WHY STUDY SERVICES?

Over the last 35 years, substantial changes have taken place in the global business environment. Emerging service sectors (profit and nonprofit) are now dominating economies that were once known for their industrial manufacturing strength. Coinciding with the tremendous growth in the global service economy, the demand for individuals who command services marketing expertise is also greatly expanding. Currently, all but 1 of the 50 highest paying jobs in the service economy require a college degree (air traffic controller is the exception).[11] Practitioners in the services field have quickly learned that traditional marketing strategies and managerial models, with roots based in the goods-producing manufacturing sector, do not always apply to their unique service industries. More specifically, the demand for services marketing knowledge has been fueled by the following:

- the tremendous growth in service-sector employment;
- increasing service-sector contributions to the world economy;
- and a revolutionary change of managerial philosophy in how service firms should organize their companies.

## SERVICE SECTOR EMPLOYMENT

Throughout the industrialized world, the growth and shifting of employment from manufacturing to services is evident (see Figure 1.4). The service industries have not only grown in size, but along the way they have absorbed all the jobs shed by traditional industries, such as agriculture, mining, and manufacturing. The Bureau of Labor Statistics expects service occupations to account for more than 96 percent of all new job growth for the period 2002–2112.[12] And the same pattern is being repeated in the European Community and Japan. In 1990, services accounted for 58 percent of GDP in Japan and 60 percent of total GDP in the European Community. In 2004, services had grown to 73 percent of GDP in Japan and 70 percent of GDP in the European Community.[13] The service sector employs 144 million persons, or 65 percent of the workforce,

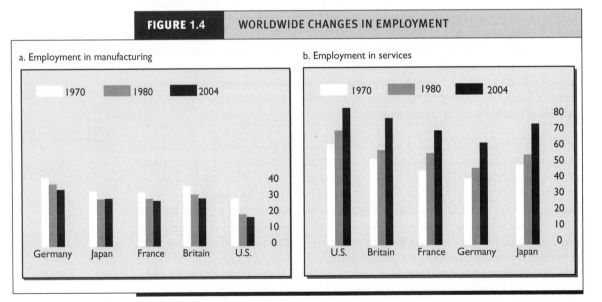

| FIGURE 1.4 | WORLDWIDE CHANGES IN EMPLOYMENT |

a. Employment in manufacturing

b. Employment in services

in the European Community, whereas industrial employment has declined steadily to approximately 28 percent.[14]

In 1900, 30 percent of the United States' workforce was employed in the service sector; by 1984, service industries employed 74 percent of the workforce; and by 2004, that figure had risen to just over 81 percent. At the same time, the proportion of the workforce engaged in agriculture declined from 42 percent to just 2.4 percent.[15] In 1948, 20.9 million persons were employed in goods production of all kinds in America, and 27.2 million persons were employed in services; by the mid-1990s, employment in goods production was 19.9 million (with no increase in more than two decades), whereas service employment had risen to 81.1 million, far more than the total number of persons employed in all sectors 30 years earlier.[16]

Even these numbers conceal the true contribution of services to economic growth, because service employees on direct payroll of goods companies are counted as industrial employees. The service division of IBM, one of the largest worldwide service organizations, is counted as being in the goods, not the service sector because the government views IBM's core business as computers and electronics. In contrast, IBM views itself as a major service provider in the "business solutions" industry (see B2B Services in Action). A truer picture can be obtained by looking at the combination of persons formally employed in the services sector—such as independent architectural or accounting firms—and the persons employed in those same jobs but working for firms based in the goods sector.[17]

One of the consequences of this change has been a change in the shape of the workforce itself. For example, the bulk of new jobs created in America over the last 30 years have been white-collar jobs, in higher-level professional, technical, administrative, and sales positions. Experts monitoring the American economy note that as services have replaced goods as the most dominant force in the economy, "human capital" has replaced physical capital as the important source of investment. "Americans must unshackle themselves from the notion that goods alone constitute wealth, whereas services are nonproductive and ephemeral. At the same time, they should act on Adam Smith's understanding that the wealth of a nation depends on the skill, dexterity, and knowledge of its people."[18]

## ECONOMIC IMPACT

Worldwide economic growth has fueled the growth of the service sector, as increasing prosperity means that companies, institutions, and individuals increasingly have become willing to trade money for time and to buy services rather than spend time doing things for themselves. New technology has led to considerable changes in the nature of many services and in the development of new services. Higher disposable incomes have led to a proliferation of personal services, particularly in the entertainment sector. Growth has meant an increase not only in the overall volume of services, but in the variety and diversity of services offered.

The result has been phenomenal growth in service industries, shown clearly in economic and trade statistics (see Figure 1.5). All developed economies now have large service sectors, and Japan, France, and Great Britain have service economies at least as

## B₂B SERVICES *IN ACTION*

### > IBM: FROM BOXES TO SERVICES

Traditional manufacturing firms are increasingly reorienting themselves around services. In these cases, the manufacturing firm is basing its marketing strategy on the philosophy that by serving customers well through supplementary services, the value of the tangible core product ("the box") is enhanced. IBM is an example of such a firm.

When most people think about IBM, they think about its celebrated history as the manufacturer of tangible products such as the typewriter, personal computers, workstations, notebooks, desktops, servers, printing systems, and other assorted accessories. However, in recent years IBM has transitioned itself from a manufacturer to a provider of business solutions. For example, IBM and its corporate partners offer a number of services to both small and large business customers that are designed to:

- boost workplace efficiency
- build a flexible infrastructure
- enhance financial management
- enhance security, privacy and compliance
- improve the customer experience
- increase business innovation
- manage human capital
- optimize IT investments
- optimize supply chains and operations
- streamline business processes

Essentially, IBM has spent over 100 years in the business of information handling as nearly all of its products were designed and developed to record, process, communicate, store, and retrieve information. By focusing on customer-oriented service solutions in combination with the innovation and development of new products, IBM differentiates itself from the competition, enhances the value of its core products, and establishes new revenue streams for the company.

Source: http://www-03.ibm.com/ibm/history/history/history_intro.html; http://www1.ibm.com/services/us/index.wss/gen_bt accessed 31 January 2005; John R. Delaney, "IBM Corp." *PC Magazine* (April 9, 2002), Vol. 21, Issue 7.

developed as that of the United States. In addition, many service firms now operate internationally, and exports of services are also increasing (see Global Services In Action).

Despite the growth of the service sector, the idea that an economy cannot survive without relying on manufacturing to create wealth continues to dominate business and political thinking in the West. *The Economist* magazine noted in 1992: "That services

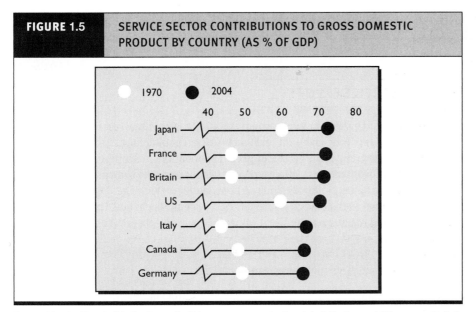

**FIGURE 1.5**    SERVICE SECTOR CONTRIBUTIONS TO GROSS DOMESTIC PRODUCT BY COUNTRY (AS % OF GDP)

cannot thrive without a strong manufacturing 'base' is a claim rarely challenged. The opposite argument—that manufacturing needs services—is hardly ever put."[19] Today, it is hard to avoid the conclusion that it is services, not manufacturing, that are the real creators of wealth in many countries. Case in point, without demand for transportation services there would be little need for airplanes, trucks, buses, and ships. Moreover, without demand for information and entertainment services, the need for theatre complexes, printing presses, televisions, and radios would collapse.[20]

> ## THE SERVICES REVOLUTION: A CHANGE IN PERSPECTIVE

Without a doubt, the world economy is experiencing the most substantial period of change in its economic history since the industrial revolution. Accompanying this change has been a shift in the philosophy of how service firms should organize their businesses. Many feel that the management model currently in place, the *industrial management model,* needs to be replaced by a *market-focused management model* if service companies are to survive and thrive.[21] Service marketing professionals who understand the pros and cons of both models will be needed to make the necessary changes.

### THE INDUSTRIAL MANAGEMENT MODEL

The industrial management model, which has its roots in the manufacturing sector, is still employed today by many service organizations. Organizations that follow the **industrial management model** believe that (1) location strategies, sales promotions, and advertising

*industrial management model*
An approach to organizing a firm that focuses on revenues and operating costs and ignores the role personnel play in generating customer satisfaction and sustainable profits.

## GLOBAL SERVICES *IN ACTION*

### > OBSTACLES TO SERVICE EXPORTS

Given the dominance of services in most economies, the share of total world exports attributed to services is relatively low—approximately 20 percent. Motivations for engaging in service exporting are plentiful including profit motivations, escaping saturated domestic markets, tax advantages, and discovering new ideas and new sources of supply. However, service growth in international trade has been hindered by several factors many of which can be attributed to the unique properties of service products (i.e., intangibility, inseparability, heterogeneity, and perishability). Obstacles to exporting services include:

- Many services are difficult to inventory and transport (e.g., legal advice or surgery).
- Service delivery is often a face-to-face encounter and requires the customer and the provider to be in the same physical location (e.g., hairstylist or dentist).
- Service providers are often small firms and lack the resources and expertise needed to conduct business at an international level (e.g., landscaper or accountant).
- Services are often customized. Cultural differences and product variations may limit demand in international marketplaces.
- Trade barriers such as ownership, control issues, and limitations on physical establishments may also hinder service exports.
- Restrictions on local establishments and operations; for example, most countries restrict the cross-border provision of one of more professional services. Doctors, lawyers, and accounts who are qualified in one country will most likely have to be recertified in order to provide services in another country.

Reducing barriers to service trade is a complex matter. Services cross a wide spectrum of business activities (e.g., surgery vs. lawncare); therefore, it is difficult to address service trade in terms of generalizations. Removing service trade barriers must be approached one service sector at a time. The good news is that service exports are increasing and currently outpacing the annual growth rate of their tangible goods counterparts.

Source: Organization for Economic Co-Operation and Development (OECD) (2000), *The Service Economy, STI: Business and Industry Policy Forum Series*, pp.24–27

drive sales revenue; and that (2) labor and other operating costs should be kept as low as possible. In sum, the industrial model focuses on revenues and operating costs and ignores (or at least forgets) the role personnel play in generating customer satisfaction and sustainable profits. Given the role that people play throughout the service encounter, it is sadly ironic how the industrial model continues to be embraced by many of today's companies.

## E - S E R V I C E S  *IN  ACTION*

> ### > THE PROS AND CONS OF SELF-SERVICE TECHNOLOGIES

Over the years, consumers have been increasingly exposed to a vast variety of self-service technologies (SSTs). SSTs include websites, kiosks, automated telephone systems, and ATMs, just to name a few. These marvels of technological development allow customers to book their own flights, manage their own finances, prepurchase movie tickets, and track shipped packages without ever talking to a real live human being.

In theory, self-service technologies are a win-win proposition. The customer is the recipient of faster, reliable, and more convenient service at a lower price. Similarly, the company benefits from lower operating costs and a greater supply of labor that is now able to conduct tasks other than servicing customers face-to-face. Self-service is to the service sector what mass production is to manufacturing—a process used to develop products more cheaply and on a massive scale.

Despite the apparent advantages associated with self-service technologies not everyone is thrilled. Many are beginning to question the true motivations of companies that utilize self-service technologies. Is the primary goal to provide improved customer service or simply to lower operating costs and distance the company from its high-maintenance consumers? If you ever waited an inordinate amount of time in an automated telephone queue or found that the telephone menu selections are not organized in a manner that addresses your particular question, you are not alone.

In response to customer frustrations, some service firms are now guaranteeing access to "live" customer service representatives. However, the price for such service is typically higher than those firms that use SSTs. The end result is that people who prefer personal service or who cannot effectively utilize SSTs (the elderly) will be forced to pay higher prices for their services. Ultimately, the effectiveness of an SST, whether it's a website or a tracking service, will be determined by the benefit it provides to the customer. SSTs that truly benefit only the company will motivate customers to defect to more fulfilling alternative providers.

Source: "Do it yourself," *The Economist,* (September 18, 2004), Vol. 372 (Issue 8393), p. 16, 1/2p.

Followers of the industrial model believe that good employees are difficult to find and support the view that "all things being equal, it is better to rely on technology, machines, and systems than on human beings" (see E-Services in Action).[22] Followers of this approach believe that most employees are indifferent, unskilled, and incapable of fulfilling any duties beyond performing simple tasks. Consequently, jobs under the industrial model are specifically narrowly defined to leave little room for employees to exercise judgment. Moreover, employees are held to low job performance expectations, their wages are kept as low as possible, and few opportunities for advancement are available.

As opposed to valuing front-line employees, the industrial model places a higher value on upper and middle managers while viewing the people who deliver service to the customer as the "bottom of the barrel." The industrial approach assumes that only managers can solve problems; consequently, resolving customer problems quickly becomes almost impossible as additional steps are built into the service delivery process.

In sum, the industrial model by definition guarantees a cycle of failure as service failures are designed directly into the system. Due to its lack of support for front-line personnel, the industrial approach, albeit unintentionally, actually encourages front-line employees to be indifferent to customer problems. In essence, the system prohibits the front-line employee from taking any action even if the employee wants to assist in correcting the problem. Customer reactions to this type of treatment are not surprising. Two-thirds of customers who now defect from their former suppliers do so not because of the product, but because of the indifference and unhelpfulness of the person providing the service.[23]

In further attempts to reduce operating costs, many firms that embrace the industrial model have replaced their full-time personnel with less experienced and less committed part-time personnel. These individuals are paid less than full-time personnel and receive few, if any, company benefits. In some instances, companies routinely release workers before mandatory raises and other benefits begin, in an attempt to keep operating costs down. Managerial practices such as this have created a new class of migrant worker in the United States—16 million people now travel from one short-term job to another.

The consequences associated with the industrial model in regard to service organizations have been self-destructive. The industrial model has produced dead-end front-line jobs, poor pay, superficial training, no opportunity for advancement, and little, if any, access to company benefits. Moreover, the industrial approach has led to customer dissatisfaction, flat or declining sales revenues, high employee turnover, and little or no growth in overall service productivity. In summary, many believe that the industrial approach is bad for customers, employees, shareholders, and the countries in which this philosophy continues to be embraced.

### THE MARKET-FOCUSED MANAGEMENT MODEL

*market-focused management model*
A new organizational model that focuses on the components of the firm that facilitate the firm's service delivery system.

In contrast to the industrial management model, proponents of the **market-focused management model** believe that the purpose of the firm is to serve the customer.[24] Consequently, logic suggests that the firm should be *organized in a manner that supports the people who serve the customer*. By following this approach, service delivery becomes the focus of the system and the overall differential advantage in terms of competitive strategy.

The framework that supports this change in philosophy is based on the services triangle presented in Figure 1.6.[25] The services triangle depicts six key relationships. First, the firm's service strategy must be communicated to its customers. If superior service is the focus of the organization and the key point of differentiation on which it distinguishes itself from competitors, the customer needs to be made aware of the firm's commitment to excellence. Second, the service strategy also needs to be communicated to the firm's employees. Good service starts at the top, and management must

---

**FIGURE 1.6**    **THE SERVICES TRIANGLE**

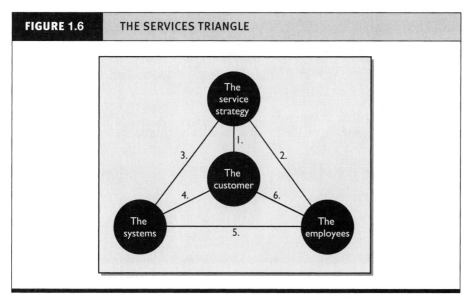

Source: Adapted from Karl Albrecht and Ron Zemke, *Service America* (Homewood, IL: Dow Jones-Irwin, 1985), pp. 31–47.

lead by example. If top management is not committed to the process, front-line employees who interact with the firm's customers will be ineffective at best.

The third relationship depicted within the triangle focuses on the consistency of the service strategy and the systems that are developed to run the day-to-day operations. The systems, like those discussed as the invisible components of the servuction model, should flow logically from the service strategy and enhance the service encounter for employees and customers alike. The fourth relationship involves the impact of organizational systems upon customers. Interactions with the firm's systems should facilitate the customer's service experience. Too often, systems are designed for the sole purpose of keeping a small minority of customers from taking advantage of the company. Meanwhile, the majority of honest customers are forced to suffer through systems and policies that treat them as suspects instead of valued assets.

The fifth relationship within the services triangle pinpoints the importance of organizational systems and employee efforts. Organizational systems and policies should not be obstacles in the way of employees wishing to provide good service. For example, a frustrated Sam's Club (a division of Wal-Mart Stores) employee informed a customer that policy dictated that he was not permitted to help customers load merchandise into their vehicles. His frustration stemmed from the firing of an employee who, a week earlier, turned down a woman's request for assistance. It later became apparent that the employee was fired not so much for his refusal, but due to the content of his response: "Hey, lady, this ain't Food Lion (a grocery store)!" Finally, the last relationship is perhaps the most important of them all—the customer/service provider interaction. These interactions represent critical incidents or "moments of truth." The quality of this interaction is often the driving force in customer satisfaction evaluations.

The market-focused management model, supported by the services triangle, is based on the belief that employees, in general, want to do good work. Hence,

Proponents of the market-focused management model believe that employee satisfaction is directly linked to customer satisfaction. Better-trained and better-paid flight attendants are likely to provide better service.

© PAULA BRONSTEIN / GETTY IMAGES

proponents of this model are more optimistic regarding their faith in human nature. As such, the market-focused management approach encourages investing in people as much as it does investing in machines. For example, the primary purpose of technology is viewed as a means to assist front-line personnel, not to replace them or monitor and control their activities. In addition, data once collected and controlled by middle managers is now made readily available to front-line personnel.

## A COMPARISON OF THE TWO APPROACHES

In contrast to the industrial management model, the market-focused management model recognizes that employee turnover and customer satisfaction are clearly related. Consequently, the market-focused management model emphasizes the recruitment and training of front-line personnel and ties pay to performance at every level throughout the organization. The benefits of superior training and compensation programs are clear. For example, the turnover rate for employees not participating in training programs at Ryder Truck Rental is 41 percent. In comparison, employees who did participate in training turned over at the rate of 19 percent.[26] Better-trained and better-paid employees provide better service, need less supervision, and are more likely to stay on the job. In turn, their customers are more satisfied, return to make purchases more often, and purchase more when they do return.

Past studies have also indicated that the correlation between customer satisfaction and employee turnover is also affected by the proportion of full-time to part-time employees.[27] As you might expect, the higher the proportion of full-time to part-time employees, the more satisfied the customers. Full-time employees tend to be more knowledgeable, more available, and more motivated to satisfy customers.

In further contrast to the industrial management model philosophy, proponents of the market-focused management model refuse to sacrifice competent and motivated full-time personnel in the name of lower operating costs. The benefits of maintaining a highly motivated full-time staff are clear. As evidence, companies that pay their employees more than competitors pay often find that as a percent of sales, their labor costs are actually lower than industry averages.

One final difference between the industrial management model and the market-focused management model is that the latter attempts to utilize innovative data to examine the firm's performance by looking beyond generally accepted accounting principles. Traditional accounting principles reflect the sales orientation of the old industrial management model. New accounting measures that reflect the focus on customer orientation need to be developed and refined. The new measures of interest include the value of customer retention as opposed to obtaining new customers, the costs of employee turnover, the value of employee training, and the monetary benefits associated with service recovery—making amends with the customer when the service delivery system fails.

Given what has been presented thus far, it should be clear that the field of services marketing is much broader than what is discussed in a traditional marketing class. As such, many of the concepts and strategies presented in this text have their origins in management science, human resources, and psychology as well as marketing. Ultimately, services marketing is about managing the compromising relationships that must exist among marketing, operations, and human resources.

## ✳ SUMMARY

Services permeate every aspect of our lives; consequently, the need for services marketing knowledge is greater today than ever before. When defining services, the distinction between goods and services is often not perfectly clear. In general, goods are defined as objects, devices, or things, whereas services are defined as deeds, efforts, or performances. Very few, if any, products can be classified as pure services or pure goods. The scale of market entities and the molecular model presented in Figures 1.1 and 1.2 illustrate how various goods and services vary according to their tangibility.

When a consumer purchases a service, he or she purchases an experience. The four components of the servuction model create the experience for the consumer—the servicescape, service providers/contact personnel, other customers, and the invisible organization and systems. In turn, the service experience that is created delivers a bundle of benefits to the consumer. In contrast to the production of goods, the servuction model demonstrates that service consumers are an integral part of the service production process.

Recent developments have fueled the demand for services marketing knowledge. First, tremendous growth has occurred in service-sector employment and in the service sector's contribution to many countries' gross domestic product. For example, experts suggest that by the year 2020, 90 percent of the United States labor force will be employed in service or service-related industries. The demand for services marketing knowledge has also been fueled by a change in perspective in how service firms should manage their companies. Organizations that follow the traditional industrial management model believe that (1) location strategies, sales promotions, and advertising drive sales revenue; and (2) labor and other operating costs should be kept as low as possible. The industrial management model focuses on revenues and operating costs and ignores, or at least forgets, the role personnel play in generating customer satisfaction and sustainable profits.

In contrast, proponents of the market-focused management model believe that the purpose of the firm is to serve the customer. Consequently, logic suggests that the firm should organize itself in a manner that supports the people who serve the customer. By following this approach, service delivery becomes the focus of the system and the overall differential advantage in terms of competitive strategy. The basic concepts and outcomes associated with the market-focused management model are illustrated in the services triangle depicted in Figure 1.6.

## ✱ KEY TERMS

service imperative, 4
goods, 5
services, 5
product, 5
scale of market entities, 5
tangible dominant, 5
intangible dominant, 5
marketing myopia, 6
molecular model, 7

benefit concept, 9
servuction model, 9
servicescape, 9
contact personnel, 10
service providers, 10
invisible organization and systems, 13
industrial management model, 17
market-focused management
   model, 20

## ✱ DISCUSSION QUESTIONS

1. Define the following terms: goods, services, and products.
2. Why is it difficult to distinguish between many goods and services? Use the scale of market entities and the molecular model concept to explain your answer.
3. Discuss the relevance of the scale of market entities to marketing myopia.
4 Develop a molecular model for your College of Business.
5. Utilizing the servuction model, describe your classroom experience. How would your servuction model change as you describe the experience at a local restaurant?
6. Discuss the consequences of the industrial-management model.
7. What benefits are associated with better-paid and better-trained personnel?
8. Discuss the relevance of the services triangle to the market-focused management model.

# ✳ NOTES

1. "The Final Frontier," *The Economist,* February 20th, 1993, p. 63.
2. Organization for Economic Co-Operation and Development (OECD) (2000), *The Service Economy, STI: Business and Industry Policy Forum Series,* p. 10
3. Leonard L. Berry, "Services Marketing Is Different," *Business Magazine* (May–June 1980), pp. 24–29.
4. This section adapted from G. Lyn Shostack, "Breaking Free from Product Marketing," *Journal of Marketing* 41 (April 1977), pp. 73–80.
5. Joseph B Pine II and James H. Gilmore, *The Experience Economy* (1999). Harvard Business School Press: Boston, MA.
6. This section adapted from G. Lyn Shostack, "Breaking Free from Product Marketing,"*Journal of Marketing* 41 (April 1977), pp. 73–80.
7. This section adapted from John E. G. Bateson, *Managing Services Marketing,* 2nd ed. (Fort Worth, TX: The Dryden Press, 1992), pp. 8–11.
8. Ron Zemke and Kristen Anderson, "Customers from Hell," *Training* (February 1990): 25–29.
9. For more information, see Charles L. Martin, "Consumer-to-Consumer Relationships: Satisfaction with Other Consumers' Public Behavior," *Journal of Consumer Affairs* 30, no. 1 (1996): 146–148; and Stephen J. Grove and Raymond P. Fisk, "The Impact of Other Customers on Service Experiences: A Critical Incident Examination of Getting Along," *Journal of Retailing* 73, no. 1 (1997): 63–85.
10. Jim Kelley, "From Lip Service to Real Service: Reversing America's Downward Service Spiral," *Vital Speeches of the Day,* 64(10), 1998, pp. 301–304.
11. Chuck Jenrich, "It's a Service Economy! What and Where Are the Jobs?" *Business—The Inside Scoop* (October 3, 2004).
12. http://www.starnespapers.com/star/spbiz/ sccop/x03scp.htm accessed 9 November, 2004.
13. Ibid.
14. http://www.cia.gov/cia/publications/ factbook/geos/ja.html#Econ and http://www.cia.gov/cia/publications/ factbook/geos/ee.html#Econ accessed 18 February 2005.
15. Peter Mills, *Managing Service Industries* (Cambridge, MA: Ballinger, 1986), 3.
16. *Statistical Abstract of the United States,* 1993.
17. Eli Ginzberg and George J. Vojta, "The Service Sector of the U.S. Economy," *Scientific American* 244, no. 3 (March 1981): 31–39.
18. Ibid.
19. "The Manufacturing Myth," *The Economist* (March 19, 1994), p. 91.
20. Organization for Economic Co-Operation and Development (OECD) (2000), *The Service Economy, STI: Business and Industry Policy Forum Series,* p. 9
21. Leonard A. Schlesinger and James L. Heskett, "The Service-Driven Service Company," *Harvard Business Review* (September–October 1991), pp. 71–75.
22. "Do it yourself," in *The Economist,* September 18, 2004, vol. 372, no. 8393, p.16. Copyright © The Economist Newspaper Limited, London 2004. All rights reserved. Reproduced by permission.
23. Schlesinger and Heskett, "The Service-Driven Service Company," p. 71.
24. Schlesinger and Heskett, "The Service-Driven Service Company," p. 77.
25. Karl Albrecht and Ron Zemke, *Service America* (Homewood, IL: Dow Jones-Irwin, 1985), pp. 31–47.
26. Schlesinger and Heskett, "The Service-Driven Service Company," p. 76.
27. Ibid.

## CHAPTER 2

# FUNDAMENTAL DIFFERENCES BETWEEN GOODS AND SERVICES

## CHAPTER OBJECTIVES

*This chapter discusses the basic differences between goods and services, the marketing problems that arise due to these differences, and possible solutions to the problems created by these differences.*

After reading this chapter, you should be able to:

- Understand the characteristics of intangibility, inseparability, heterogeneity, and perishability.
- Discuss the marketing problems associated with intangibility and their possible solutions.
- Describe the marketing problems associated with inseparability and their possible solutions.
- Explain the marketing problems associated with heterogeneity and their possible solutions.
- Identify the marketing problems associated with perishability and their possible solutions.
- Consider the impact of intangibility, inseparability, heterogeneity, and perishability on marketing's relationship to other functions within the service organization.

*"It is wrong to imply that services are just like goods 'except' for intangibility. By such logic, apples are just like oranges, except for their 'appleness'."*

G. Lynn Shostack

COURTESY OF: GEICO

Service companies are unique from manufacturers in that they do not produce anything tangible from scratch. Consequently, service firms often face challenges such as how do you market a product that no one can see; price a product that has no cost of goods sold; inventory a product that cannot be stored; or distribute a product that seems inextricably linked to its provider? One company that has excelled at all of these challenges in the insurance sector is GEICO.

Although it seems for many of us that GEICO is a relatively new addition to the major players in the insurance sector such as State Farm, Prudential, and Allstate, the company has actually been around since the 1930s. Founded in 1936 by Leo and Lillian Goodwin, the company originally marketed auto insurance to its primary target markets of federal employees and the top three grades of non-commissioned military officers (hence, the name GEICO—the Government Employees Insurance Company). The company was based on the idea that if it could lower costs by focusing on specific target markets, the company could charge lower premiums and still be profitable. The idea caught on quickly and by the end of 1936 the company had sold 3,700 auto policies and had 12 employees. Approximately, 30 years later, GEICO passed the 1 million policyholder mark in 1964.

Today, GEICO is a subsidiary of one of the most profitable organizations in the country—Warren Buffet's Berkshire Hathaway investment firm. Buffet's investment firm provided the financial backing necessary in 1996 that led to GEICO's explosive growth over the past decade. National advertising and direct mail campaigns were launched on an enormous scale and consumers responded en masse. GEICO now boasts more than 6 million auto policyholders and insures more than 10 million vehicles. GEICO is now the fifth largest private-passenger auto insurer in the United States with $13.7 billion in assets; 22,000 associates; and 12 major offices around the country. The company's product mix includes auto insurance; motorcycle insurance; boat insurance; umbrella insurance; and home, condo, and renter's insurance.

Contributing to the company's success has been the introduction of the GEICO "gecko." GEICO's gecko became an instant advertising phenomenon when introduced during the 1999–2000 television season. Developed by the Martin agency in Richmond, Virginia, the gecko was the result of the mispronunciation of the GEICO name. The gecko with his English voice has become a recognizable tangible symbol and an advertising icon for the company. The gecko makes special appearances at community events around the country. Gecko merchandise can be purchased by visiting the Gecko Store Online. Items for sale include bobble heads, tattoos, pens, visors, die-cast racing cars, and polo shirts, among a plethora of other items for the gecko enthusiast.

In addition to the gecko, GEICO has strengthened its organizational image by supporting a number of driver safety programs including the Insurance Institute for Highway Safety, National Commission Against Drunk and Drugged Driving (NCADD), Highway Insurance Loss Data Institute (HLDI), the National Highway Transportation Safety Agency (NHTSA), and the Insurance Information Institute (III). GEICO also holds an annual National Safety Belt Poster contest for students ages 6 to 15 that focuses on the importance of safety belt use. Winning posters are featured in GEICO's national promotions. GEICO also provides tips for teens and parents of new drivers on the company's Web site.

For those interested in pursuing a career with GEICO, The GEICO Web site provides an abundance of information. Career opportunities at GEICO include best-in-the-industry training, continued education, and opportunity for growth in such fields as actuary, auto damage adjusting, claims, controllers, information technology, marketing, sales, and service.

Source: http://www.geico.com/ accessed 22 February 2005.

## > INTRODUCTION

In the beginning the work toward accumulating services marketing knowledge was slow. In fact, not until 1970 was services marketing even considered an academic field. It then took 12 more years before the first international conference on services marketing was held in the United States, in 1982.[1] One of the reasons the field of services marketing was slow to grow within the academic community was that many marketing educators felt that the marketing of services was not significantly different from the marketing of goods. Markets still needed to be segmented, target markets still needed to be sought, and marketing mixes that catered to the needs of the firm's intended target market still needed to be developed. However, since those early days, a great deal has been written regarding specific differences between goods and services and their corresponding marketing implications. The majority of these differences are primarily attributed to four unique characteristics—intangibility, inseparability, heterogeneity, and perishability.[2]

**intangibility**
A distinguishing characteristic of services that makes them unable to be touched or sensed in the same manner as physical goods.

Services are said to be **intangible** because they are performances rather than objects. They cannot be touched or seen in the same manner as goods. Rather, they are experienced, and consumers' judgments about them tend to be more subjective than objective. **Inseparability** of production and consumption refers to the fact that whereas goods are first produced, then sold, and then consumed, services are sold first and then produced and consumed simultaneously. For example, an airline passenger first purchases a ticket and then flies, consuming the in-flight service as it is produced.

**inseparability**
A distinguishing characteristic of services that reflects the interconnection among the service provider, the customer involved in receiving the service, and other customers sharing the service experience.

**Heterogeneity** refers to the potential for service performance to vary from one service transaction to the next. Services are produced by people; consequently, variability is inherent in the production process. This lack of consistency cannot be eliminated as it frequently can be with goods. Finally, **perishability** means that services cannot be saved; unused capacity in services cannot be reserved, and services themselves cannot be inventoried.[3] Consequently, perishability leads to formidable challenges relating to the balancing of supply and demand.

**heterogeneity**
A distinguishing characteristic of services that reflects the variation in consistency from one service transaction to the next.

This chapter focuses on each of these four unique characteristics that differentiate the marketing of services from the marketing of goods. Because services fall in many places along the continuum that ranges from tangible dominant to intangible dominant, as described by the scale of market entities in Chapter 1, the magnitude and subsequent impact that each of these four characteristics has on the marketing of individual services will vary.

**perishability**
A distinguishing characteristic of services in that they cannot be saved, their unused capacity cannot be reserved, and they cannot be inventoried.

## > INTANGIBILITY: THE MOTHER OF ALL UNIQUE DIFFERENCES

Of the four unique characteristics that distinguish goods from services, intangibility is the primary source from which the other three characteristics emerge. As discussed in Chapter 1, services are defined as performances, deeds, and efforts; whereas, goods are defined as objects, devices, and things. As a result of their intangibility, services cannot be seen, felt, tasted, or touched in the same manner as physical goods can be sensed.

 For example, compare the differences between purchasing a movie ticket and purchasing a pair of shoes. The shoes are tangible goods, so the shoes can be objectively evaluated before the actual purchase. You can pick up the shoes, feel the quality of materials from which they are constructed, view their specific style and color, and actually put them on your feet and sample the fit. After the purchase, you can take the shoes home, and you now have ownership and the physical possession of a tangible object.

In comparison, consider the purchase of a service such as a movie to be enjoyed at a local cinema. In this instance, the customer purchases a movie ticket, which entitles the consumer to an experience. Because the movie experience is intangible, it is subjectively evaluated; that is, consumers of services must rely on the judgments of others who have previously experienced the service for prepurchase information. Because the information provided by others is based on their own sets of expectations and perceptions, opinions will differ regarding the value of the experience. For example, if you ask five movie-goers what they thought about the film *Million Dollar Baby,* they are likely to express five different opinions ranging from "I loved it!" to "I hated it!" After the movie the customer returns home with a memory of the experience and retains the physical ownership of only a ticket stub.

## MARKETING PROBLEMS CAUSED BY INTANGIBILITY

As a result of the intangibility of services, a number of marketing challenges arise that are not normally faced when marketing tangible goods. More specifically, these challenges include the lack of service inventories, the lack of patent protection, the difficulties involved in displaying and communicating the attributes of the service to its intended target market, and the special challenges involved in the pricing of services. The following sections address these challenges and offer possible solutions to minimize their effects.

### Lack of Service Inventories
Because of their intangibility, services cannot be inventoried. As a result, supplies of services cannot be stored as buffers against periods of high demand. For example, physicians cannot produce and store physical exams to be used at a later date; movie seats that are not sold for the afternoon matinee cannot be added to the theater for the evening show; and the auto club cannot inventory roadside service to be distributed during peak periods. Consequently, customers are commonly forced to wait for desired services, and service providers are limited in how much they can sell by how much they can produce. The bottom line is that the inability to maintain an inventory translates into constant supply and demand problems. In fact, the lack of service inventories presents so many challenges to marketers that it has earned its own name—perishability. Specific problems associated with perishability and the strategies associated with minimizing its effects are discussed in much greater detail later in the chapter.

### Lack of Patent Protection
Because of the property of intangibility, services are not patentable. What is there to patent? Human labor and effort are not protected. Firms sometimes advertise that their processes are patented; however, the reality is that the tangible machinery involved in the process is protected, not the process itself. One challenge faced by the lack of patent protection is that new or existing services may be easily copied. Consequently, it is difficult to maintain a firm's differential service advantage over attentive competitors for long periods.

### Difficulty in Displaying or Communicating Services

The promotion of services presents yet another set of special challenges to the service marketer and is discussed in greater detail in Chapter 8, Developing the Service Communications Mix. The root of the challenge is this: How do you get customers to take notice of your product when they cannot see it? For example, consider the insurance industry. Insurance is a complicated product for many people. As customers, we cannot see it, we are unable to sample it prior to purchase, and many of us do not understand it. Insurance seems to cost an awful lot of money, and the benefits of its purchase are not realized until some future time, if at all. In fact, if we do not use it, we are supposed to consider ourselves lucky. Why should spending thousands of dollars a year on something the customer never uses make them feel lucky? To say the least, due to intangibility the task of explaining your product's merits to consumers is highly challenging.

### Difficulty in Pricing Services

Typically products' prices are based on cost-plus pricing. This means that the producing firm figures the cost of producing the product and adds a predetermined markup to that figure. The challenge involved in the pricing of services is that there is no cost of goods sold! The primary cost of producing a service is labor.

For example, let's say you are very competent in the field of mathematics. Taking notice of your expertise in the field, a student who is struggling with his math assignments wants to hire you as a tutor. What would you charge per hour? What are the costs involved?

Based on feedback from other services marketing classes faced with this example, students usually begin laughing and indicate that they would engage in price-gouging and charge the student $100 per hour. After reality sets in, students quickly realize that it is very difficult to place a value on their time. Specific considerations usually emerge, such as how much money the tutor could make doing something else and the opportunity costs associated with not being able to lie around the apartment and enjoy free time. Typically the consensus is that the tutor should charge something comparable to the fees charged by other tutors. The problem with this response is that it still does not answer the original question, that is, how was this competitive-based price originally calculated?

## POSSIBLE SOLUTIONS TO INTANGIBILITY PROBLEMS

Marketing practitioners have implemented a number of strategies in the attempt to offset or minimize the marketing challenges posed by intangibility. These strategies include the use of tangible clues to help "tangibilize" the service, the use of personal sources of information to help spread the word about service alternatives, and the creation of strong organizational images to reduce the amount of perceived risk associated with service purchases. Although marketers may not be totally capable of eliminating the affects of intangibility, strategies such as these have provided innovative solutions for many service industries.

**physical evidence/ tangible clues**
The physical characteristics that surround a service to assist consumers in making service evaluations, such as the quality of furnishings, the appearance of personnel, or the quality of paper stock used to produce the firm's brochure.

### The Use of Tangible Clues

Given the absence of tangible properties, services are evaluated differently from goods. In many instances, consumers look at the **physical evidence** or **tangible clues** that surround the service to assist them in making service evaluations. Tangible clues may include such evidence as the quality of furniture in a lawyer's office, the appearance of the personnel in a bank, and the quality of paper used for an insurance policy.

Tangible clues are also often used in services advertising. As previously discussed, because of intangibility, firms often find it difficult to effectively communicate their service offerings to consumers. Returning to the insurance example, the major challenge of an insurance firm is to communicate to consumers in a 30-second television commercial what the specific firm has to offer and how the firm is different from every other insurance firm. One strategy embraced by many service firms is to use some form of tangible clues in advertising. Prudential uses "the rock" and promises "rock-solid protection." Allstate shows us "helping hands" and promises that "you're in good hands with Allstate." The list goes on and on—Merrill Lynch has "the bull," Nationwide promotes "blanket-wide protection," Kemper has "the cavalry," Travelers utilizes "the umbrella," Geico has the "gecko," and Transamerica promotes the shape of its office building as "the power of the pyramid." The lesson that all these companies have learned over time is that the services they sell are abstract to the consumer and therefore difficult for the average consumer to understand. The answer to this challenge was to provide tangible clues that were easily understood by the public and directly related to the bundle of benefits the services provided. For example, State Farm's credo of "Like a good neighbor, State Farm is there" reinforces the firm's commitment to looking after its customers when they are in need.

### The Use of Personal Sources of Information

Because consumers of services lack any objective means of evaluating services, they often rely on the subjective evaluations relayed by friends, family, and a variety of other opinion leaders. For example, when moving to a new town and seeking a family physician, consumers will often ask co-workers and neighbors for referrals. Hence, in purchasing services, **personal sources** of information become more important to consumers than **nonpersonal sources** such as the mass media (e.g., television, radio, and the Yellow Pages).

Personal sources of information such as friends, family, and other opinion leaders are sources of word-of-mouth advertising that consumers use to gather information about services. One strategy often used to stimulate word-of-mouth advertising is to offer incentives to existing customers to tell their friends about a firm's offerings. Apartment complexes often use the incentive of a free month's rent to encourage tenants to have their friends rent vacant units. Service firms sometimes simulate personal communication while using the mass media. Mass advertising that features customer testimonials simulates word-of-mouth advertising and can be very effective. Examples include hospital advertisements featuring former patients who have successfully recovered from major surgery and are now living normal and happy lives. Other examples include insurance companies that feature victims of hurricanes, fires, and earthquakes who were satisfied with their insurance protection when they needed it most.

*personal sources*
Sources such as friends, family, and other opinion leaders that consumers use to gather information about a service.

*nonpersonal sources*
Sources such as mass advertising that consumers use to gather information about a service.

### Creation of a Strong Organizational Image

Another strategy utilized to minimize the effects of intangibility is to create a strong organizational image. Because of intangibility and the lack of objective sources of information to evaluate services, the amount of perceived risk associated with service

| TABLE 2.1 | INTANGIBILITY: MARKETING PROBLEMS AND POSSIBLE SOLUTIONS | |
|---|---|---|
| **Characteristic** | **Marketing problems** | **Possible solutions** |
| Intangibility | Lack of service inventories | Use of tangible clues |
| | Lack of patent protection | Use of personal sources of information |
| | Difficulty in displaying or communicating services | Creation of a strong organizational image |
| | Difficulty in pricing services | |

**organizational image**
The perception an organization presents to the public; if well known and respected, lowers the perceived risk of potential customers making service provider choices.

purchases is generally greater than their goods counterparts. In an attempt to combat the higher levels of perceived risk, some service firms have spent a great deal of effort, time, and money in developing a nationally known **organizational image.** A well-known and respected corporate image lowers the level of perceived risk experienced by potential customers and, in some instances, lowers the reliance on personal sources of information when making service provider choices. For example, the consumer who is moving to a new town may bypass personal referrals and automatically seek out the nearest Nationwide Insurance agent for home and auto insurance needs based on the firm's organizational image. In this case, the national firm, through image development and subsequent brand awareness, has developed a differential advantage over small, local firms of which the consumer is unaware. Table 2.1 summarizes the marketing problems and possible solutions for minimizing the challenges of intangibility.

## > INSEPARABILITY

One of the most intriguing characteristics of the service experience involves the concept of inseparability. Inseparability reflects the interconnection among the service provider, the customer involved in receiving the service, and other customers sharing the same experience. Unlike the goods manufacturer, who may seldom see an actual customer while producing the good in a secluded factory, service providers are often in constant contact with their customers and must construct their service operations with the customer's physical presence in mind. This interaction between customer and service provider defines a **critical incident.** Critical incidents represent the greatest opportunity for both gains and losses in regard to customer satisfaction and retention.

**critical incident**
A specific interaction between a customer and a service provider.

### MARKETING PROBLEMS CAUSED BY INSEPARABILITY

The inseparable nature of services poses a number of unique challenges for marketing practitioners. First, in many instances, the execution of the service often requires the physical presence of the service provider. As a result, service providers require

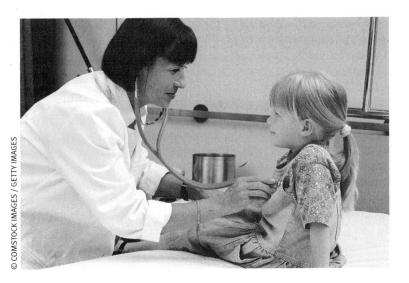

Medical services provide a prime example of the interconnectivity between service provider and the customer receiving the service. In most cases, the physician and patient have to be physically present for the service to occur.

different skill sets than a manufacturer who may never actually interact with a customer. Second, customer involvement in the service delivery process presents a number of other challenges. Customers often dictate the type of service to be delivered, the length of the service delivery process, and the cycle of service demand. Quite frankly, customer involvement often jeopardizes the efficiency of the service operation. Third, services are often a shared experience among a number of customers. Consequently, problems arise as customers adversely influence one another's service experience. Finally, inseparability presents a number of challenges pertaining to the mass production of services. A single service provider can produce only a finite amount of service. In addition, only so many customers can travel to one physical location to consume a service.

### Physical Connection of the Service Provider to the Service

For the production of many services to occur, the service provider must be physically present to deliver the service. For example, dental services require the physical presence of a dentist or hygienist, medical surgery requires a surgeon, and in-home services such as carpet cleaning require a service provider to complete the work. Because of the intangibility of services, the service provider becomes a tangible clue on which at least part of the customer's evaluation of the service experience becomes based.

As tangible clues, service providers are particularly evaluated based on their use of language, clothing, personal hygiene, and interpersonal communication skills. Many service firms have long appreciated the impact that public contact personnel have on the firm's overall evaluation. For example, wearing uniforms or conforming to dress codes is often required of service employees to reflect professionalism. Other service firms, such as restaurants, often place their most articulate and attractive personnel in public contact positions such as wait staff, host/hostess, and bartender. Personnel who do not have these skills and traits are often employed in areas that are invisible to the consumer, such as the kitchen and dish room areas.

Face-to-face interactions with customers make employee satisfaction crucial. Without a doubt, employee satisfaction and customer satisfaction are directly related. Dissatisfied employees who are visible to customers will translate into lower consumer perceptions of the firm's performance. The importance of employee satisfaction within service firms cannot be overemphasized. Customers will never be the number one priority in a company where employees are treated poorly. Employees should be viewed and treated as internal customers of the firm. This issue is discussed in much greater detail in Chapter 10, People Issues: Managing Service Employees.

### Involvement of the Customer in the Production Process

The second defining characteristic of inseparability is that the customer is involved in the production process. The customer's involvement in the production process may vary from (1) a requirement that the customer be physically present to receive the service, such as in dental services, a haircut, or surgery; (2) a need for the customer to be present only to start and stop the service, such as in dry cleaning and auto repair; and (3) a need for the customer to be only mentally present, such as in participation in college courses that are transmitted via the Internet. Each scenario reflects different levels of customer contact, and as a result each service delivery system should be designed differently.

Unlike goods, which are produced, sold, and then consumed, services are first sold and then produced and consumed simultaneously because of inseparability. For example, a box of breakfast cereal is produced in a factory, shipped to a store where it is sold, and then consumed by customers at a place and time of the customer's choosing. In contrast, services are produced and consumed simultaneously, so consumption takes place inside the service factory. As a result, service firms must design their operations to accommodate the customer's presence (see B2B Services in Action).

Hospitals provide a good example of how the unique service characteristic of inseparability affects everyday operations.[4] Generally, when someone from the healthcare industry starts talking about rapid response programs, most of us would think that it pertained to how fast the ambulance could get to the scene of the accident. However, in this instance, "rapid response" refers to how quickly the healthcare institution can identify customer service problems and resolve them. The University of Chicago as well as other healthcare institutions have learned much from the patient satisfaction surveys that illustrates the interconnection between the patients and their healthcare providers. Some of the improvements that have been implemented in these various healthcare institutions include the following:

- Outdoor bike racks were added.
- More wheelchairs were made available.
- Clerical staff were trained in telephone etiquette.
- Patient parking prices were reduced.
- Efforts to reduce waiting time were implemented.
- Employee award programs were started to reward extra kindness to patients.
- A noisy nurses' station was moved away from patient rooms.
- Room service was started for a maternity ward.
- Patients were given prepaid phone cards to encourage them to complete customer satisfaction forms.

## B 2 B   S E R V I C E S   *IN ACTION*

> **GETTING DOWN TO BUSINESS IN THE HOTEL INDUSTRY**

Leading Hoteliers such as Best Western, Holiday Inn, Hilton InterConntinental and Langham Place Hotels are stepping up their efforts to attract the business traveler by creating fully-functioning office environments for guests. In essence, hotels are rein-venting themselves as offices away from the office. This change is in direct response to changing customer needs. According to Naill Mackin, head of American Express's new business-travel service, "We've definitely seen a swing toward customers wanting the business side of the hotel more than the entertainment side."

Transforming hotels into offices is particularly occurring at the mid-level chains where high-speed Internet access and Wi-Fi capabilities are becoming the norm. In addi-tion, some hotels are now offering guests the option of booking rooms wirelessly using their PDAs or BlackBerrys. The check-in process is getting easier as well. Hilton's OnQ service allows gold and diamond Hilton HHonors members to check in online up to 24 hours in advance of arrival. Hilton is also expanding its supply of check-in kiosks and equipping hotel personnel with wireless PCs that are capable of checking guests in anywhere on the hotel property. Poolside and lounge check-ins should increase exponentially.

More innovative services are currently being offered by upscale hotels such as 24-hour "e-butlers" or "technology concierges" who are available to serve guests' every communication need. London's Dorchester Hotel equips every room with a computer, wireless keyboard, scanner/fax machine, and color printer. As one might expect, a room at the Hotel@MIT includes ergonomically designed furniture, robotic sculptures, and workspaces equipped with high-speed Internet access, data ports, and dual telephone lines.

Industry observers predict that the most innovative advances in the hotel/office concept will occur in Asia, which is currently undergoing a boom in hotel construction. For example, one-third of the cost to build the five-star Langham Place Hotel in Hong Kong went to technology—an investment of $4.5 million. Amenities include high-speed access everywhere (including elevators), cordless room phones, email touch screens, and Internet telephony technology. Not to be outdone, the Peninsula Group of Hong Kong equips its rooms with telephones that automatically edit out the sound of running water (e.g., shower, bath, etc.). Other proprietary innovations are currently being kept quiet. According to one Peninsula officer, "It's quite top secret."

---

Source: Chuck Gonzales/www.artscounselinc.com

The bottom line for many of these institutions is that "clinical or technical excellence" is not enough to succeed in a competitive healthcare market. Listening and responding to customer feedback and recognizing the customer as an integral part of the service delivery process often points to improvements in areas other than their medical needs.

Overall, as customer contact increases, the efficiency of the operation decreases. The customer's involvement in the production process creates uncertainties in the scheduling of production. More specifically, the customer has a direct impact on the type of service desired, the length of the service delivery process, and the cycle of service demand. Attempting to balance consumer needs with efficient operating procedures is a delicate art.

Regarding the cycle of demand, restaurants would be more efficient if consumers would smooth their demands for food throughout the day as opposed to eating primarily during breakfast, lunch, and dinner hours. As one frustrated, senior-citizen McDonald's employee told a customer, "These people would get better service if they all didn't show up at the same time!" Further complications arise as consumers also dictate the nature or type of service needed. This is particularly frustrating for healthcare workers who provide services to waiting emergency-room patients. Every patient has a different need, some needs are more immediate than others, and you never know what the next ambulance will deliver. Obviously, this scenario is frustrating for waiting patients as well as for the healthcare providers. Finally, even when consumer needs are the same, some consumers ask more questions and/or need more attention than others, thereby affecting the length of demand. As a result, fixed schedules are difficult to adhere to without delays.

During the customer's interaction with the service provider, the customer provides inputs into the service production process. As such, the customer often plays a key role in the successful completion of the service encounter. For example, a patient who feels ill must be able to accurately describe his or her symptoms to a physician to receive proper treatment. Not only must the symptoms be described accurately, but the patient must also take the recommended dosage of medicines prescribed. In this case, the customer (the patient) becomes a key player in the service production process and can directly influence the outcome of the process itself. Failure of the patient to follow recommended instructions will likely lead to a dissatisfactory service experience. The customer will probably blame the service provider, even though the service provider fulfilled his or her part of the transaction.

Another issue directly related to the consumer's presence in the service factory concerns the appearance of the service factory itself. Service factories must be built with consumers' presence in mind. Consequently, the service factory not only provides the service, but in and of itself becomes a key tangible clue in the formation of consumer perceptions regarding service quality. The design and management of the service factory is discussed in much greater detail in Chapter 9, Managing the Firm's Physical Evidence.

### Involvement of Other Customers in the Production Process

The presence of other customers during the service encounter is the third defining characteristic of inseparability. Because production and consumption occur simultaneously, several customers often share a common service experience. This "shared experience" can be negative or positive.

The marketing challenges presented by having other customers involved in the production process generally reflect the negative aspects of their involvement. Restaurants once again provide an ideal setting for examples of negative events, including smokers violating the space of nonsmokers and vice versa, families with young children sharing the same space with adult couples seeking a quiet dining experience, drunk customers interacting with sober patrons, and the occasional lovers' quarrel that spills over into the aisles. Overall, the primary challenge concerns effectively managing different market segments with different needs within a single service environment. Such will be the case if cell phone use is eventually approved on airlines. Some passengers will see the addition of this service as overwhelmingly positive while others will view it as noise pollution (see E-Services in Action).

## E-SERVICES *IN ACTION*

> **THE REAL STORY BEHIND CELLULAR SERVICE IN THE AIR**

Contrary to popular belief, the real story behind the prohibition of cell phones on airlines has little to do with interfering with the plane's avionics. This is a big relief for most of us. Did you truly believe that all of your co-passengers were disciplined enough to turn off their cell phones stowed away in their briefcases and luggage? As it turns out, the real problem is what 300 "in use" cell phones in the air moving at several hundred miles an hour does to mobile networks on the ground. Apparently as the plane is moving across the sky, phone signals on board quickly hop from one base-station to the next, which totally befuddles a ground-based mobile network.

A solution to this problem is currently being tested by a consortium of companies including Airbus, Siemens, and Ericsson. The primary idea is to install a laptop-size base-station, called a "picocell" in the plane's cabin area. In turn, the picocell is connected to a telephone network via a satellite link. Since the picocell is located so close to passenger cell phones, very little transmission power is needed to establish and maintain contact. As a result, low transmission power does not interfere with the planes avionics or with existing networks on the ground. This system will not only support typical cell phones but will also provide support for laptop-based Internet services via the popular Wi-Fi protocol. It is projected that the use of wireless devices in-flight will first become available in mid-2005.

The question remains whether the airlines themselves will become network operators or whether they will team up with existing mobile and satellite operators. There is some speculation that roaming rates may be linked to the customer's frequent flyer status. For example, premier flyers talk for free while economy class pays per minute charges. Another issue of concern is "user etiquette." Who really wants to sit next to someone who talks incessantly on the phone during a three-hour flight? Airlines may be forced to consider "phoning" and "non-phoning" sections within their cabins.

Source: "Cleared for take-off?," *The Economist*, April 2, 2004, Vol. 371, Issue 8369, p. 68, 1/2p.

The impact of "other customers" is not always negative. On the positive side, audience reaction in the form of laughter or screams of terror often enhances the show at a movie theater. Similarly, a crowded pub may facilitate the opportunity for social interaction, and a happy crowd may make a concert an even more pleasurable event. As social creatures, humans tend to frequent places of business and feel more comfortable in places that have other customers in them. In fact, the lack of other customers may act as a tangible clue that the impending experience may be less than satisfactory. For example, if given the choice of dining at one of two new restaurants, would you select a restaurant that had no cars in the parking lot, or would you choose a restaurant down the street with a full parking lot? In the absence of other information, which restaurant would most potential customers believe would be the better dining experience?

### Special Challenges in Mass Production of Services

One final obstacle presented by inseparability is how to successfully mass produce services. The problems pertaining to mass production are twofold. First, because the service provider is directly linked to the service being produced, an individual service provider can produce only a limited supply. Consequently, the question arises: How does one provide enough service product to meet the demand of the mass market? The second problem directly relates to the consumer's involvement in the production process. Consumers interested in a particular provider's services would have to travel to the provider's location. In comparison, if goods were constrained by inseparability, every consumer in the world who was interested in purchasing a Chevrolet Corvette would have to travel to the production facility in Bowling Green, Kentucky, to purchase a vehicle. Hence, one of the problems associated with inseparability is how to sell intangible products to a geographically widespread target market.

## POSSIBLE SOLUTIONS TO INSEPARABILITY PROBLEMS

Similar to the solutions proposed for intangibility, marketing practitioners have developed a number of strategies in the attempt to offset or minimize the marketing challenges posed by inseparability. These strategies include (1) an increased emphasis placed on the selection and training of public contact personnel to ensure that the right types of employees are in the right jobs; (2) the implementation of consumer management strategies that facilitate a positive service encounter for all consumers sharing the same service experience; and (3) the use of multi-site locations to offset the mass production challenges posed by inseparability.

### Selecting and Training Public Contact Personnel

Contact personnel, unlike goods, are not inanimate objects, and being human, they exhibit variations in behavior that cannot be controlled by the service process. Moreover, the attitudes and emotions of contact personnel are visible to the customer and can affect the service experience for better or worse (see Global Services in Action). Surly or unhappy employees can affect both customers with whom they come into direct contact and other employees. On the other hand, a bright, highly motivated employee can create a more pleasant service experience for everyone who comes into contact with that person.[5]

## GLOBAL SERVICES *IN ACTION*

### > THE IMPORTING OF AMERICAN SERVICE STANDARDS

The public face of a service firm is its contact personnel. Since services are intangible, contact personnel become the service in the eyes of many consumers. As a result, the customer's first impression of the service provider is of paramount importance. First impressions are believed to often establish or deny relationships within the first four minutes of contact. Perhaps then, it comes as no surprise that many European cities are now trying to change their surly customer service image through the training of their public contact personnel.

It may seem like common sense to be nice to customers, but not everyone is on the same page when it comes to establishing friendly customer relationships. For example, the Russian airline, Aeroflot, actually ran an ad campaign that attempted to justify its poor customer service: "We don't smile because we are serious about making you happy." However, even in Russia times are changing. In May of 2004, Russian border guards, known for their stoicism, were ordered to smile. The annual Bienvenue en France campaign that urges cab drivers to be friendlier to tourists is another example of the efforts being made to improve European customer service.

One of the most ambitious programs aimed at importing American service standards is currently occurring in London where a $6.4 million, four-year program has been launched to improve restaurant and hotel staff behavior. However, unlike French and Russian efforts, the English effort is about improving actual service standards and not just the image of its service providers. Training includes, the proper way to carve meat, serve cigars, pour champagne, improve spoken English, and handle complaints. Programs are specifically targeting improving customer service for business travelers who account for one out of three travel dollars spent in London. London businesses, who are contributing to pay for the cost of the program, generally welcome the program that is being implemented by the London Development Agency. The thinking is "what's good for customers is good for business"!

Source: "Don't mention the War," *The Economist*, (August 21, 2004), Vol. 372, Issue 8389, p. 47, 1/3p, 1c.

**selection and training**
A strategy that minimizes the impact of inseparability by hiring and educating employees in such a way that the customer's service experience is positive and the employees are properly equipped to handle customers and their needs.

As a result of the frequency and depth of interactions between service providers and consumers, **selection** of service personnel with superior communication and interpersonal skills is a must. In addition, **training** personnel once they are on the job is also necessary. A case in point is UPS. UPS handles more than 3 billion packages and 5.5 percent of the United States' GNP annually. The behind-the-scenes activities of hiring, training, and rewarding employees is directly related to how well customers are served. UPS believes in building trust and teamwork and making employees loyal to the company's mission. The company spends more than $300 million a year on training, paying full-time drivers (on average) more than $50,000 a year, and surveying its employees for suggestions. The company is virtually 100 percent employee owned.[6]

Too often, newly hired employees are often left to fend for themselves. A large percentage of consumer complaints about service focuses on the action or inaction of employees. Critics of service quality have focused on "robotic" responses by staff who have been trained in using the technology associated with the business but not in dealing with different types of customers. Experts in service quality believe that employees must also be trained in "soft" management skills such as reliability, responsiveness, empathy, assurance, and managing the tangibles that surround the service.

### Consumer Management

**consumer management**
A strategy service personnel can implement that minimizes the impact of inseparability, such as separating smokers from nonsmokers in a restaurant.

The problems created by inseparability can also be minimized through effective **consumer management.** Separating smokers from nonsmokers is an example of one way to minimize the impact on other customers. Sending a patient insurance forms and information about office procedures before the patient arrives may help control the length of the service encounter. Restaurant reservation systems may help smooth out demand created by traditional cycles. Providing delivery services may eliminate the need for many consumers to be physically present within a service factory, thereby increasing the firm's operating efficiencies. Finally, isolating the technical core of the business from the consumer allows for consumer involvement but limits the customer's direct impact on the firm's operations. For example, the typical neighborhood dry cleaning business is designed so that customers are attended to at the front counter; meanwhile, the core operation is located in an area of the building where customer contact is not permitted. The management of service consumers is discussed in much greater detail in Chapter 11, People Issues: Managing Service Customers.

### Use of Multi-Site Locations

**multi-site locations**
A way service firms that mass produce combat inseparability, involving multiple locations to limit the distance the consumers have to travel and staffing each location differently to serve a local market.

**factories in the field**
Another name for multi-site locations.

To offset the effects of inseparability on centralized mass production, service firms that mass produce do so by setting up multiple locations. Typical examples include H & R Block accounting services, Hyatt Legal Services, and LensCrafters (an eye-care service firm). **Multi-site locations** serve at least two purposes. First, because the consumer is involved in the production process, multi-site locations limit the distance the consumer must travel to purchase the service. Second, each multi-site location is staffed by different service providers, each of whom can produce their own supply of services to serve their local market. Multi-site locations act as **factories in the field.** Without them, every consumer who desired legal services would have to travel to a single location that housed all the lawyers in the country plus all their clients for that day. Obviously, this is not practical or realistic.

The use of multi-site locations is not without its own set of special challenges. Each site is staffed by different service providers who have their own personalities and their own sets of skills. For example, every H & R Block tax representative does not have the same personality and the same set of skills as the founder, Henry Block. The differences in personnel are particularly troublesome for service firms attempting to establish a consistent image by providing a standardized product. The variability in performance

| TABLE 2.2 | INSEPARABILITY: MARKETING PROBLEMS AND POSSIBLE SOLUTIONS | |
|-----------|----------------------------------------------------------|---|
| **Characteristic** | **Marketing problems** | **Possible solutions** |
| Inseparability | Physical connection of the service provider to the service | Selecting and training public contact personnel |
| | Involvement of the customer in the production process | Consumer management |
| | Involvement of other customers in the production process | Use of multi-site locations |
| | Special challenges in mass production of services | |

from one multi-site location to another and even from one provider to another within a single location leads us to the next special characteristic of services—heterogeneity. Table 2.2 identifies the marketing problems and strategies for overcoming the challenges of inseparability.

## > HETEROGENEITY

*Heterogeneity*

One of the most frequently stressed differences between goods and services is heterogeneity—the variation in consistency from one service transaction to the next. Service encounters occur in real time, and consumers are already involved in the factory, so if something goes wrong during the service process, it is too late to institute quality-control measures before the service reaches the customer. Indeed, the customer (or other customers who share the service experience with the primary customer) may be part of the quality problem. If, in a hotel, something goes wrong during the night's stay, the lodging experience for a customer is bound to be affected; the manager cannot logically ask the customer to leave the hotel, re-enter, and start the experience from the beginning.

Heterogeneity, almost by definition, makes it impossible for a service operation to achieve 100 percent perfect quality on an ongoing basis. Manufacturing operations may also have problems achieving this sort of target, but they can isolate mistakes and correct them over time, since mistakes tend to reoccur at the same points in the process. In contrast, many errors in service operations are one-time events; the waiter who drops a plate of food in a customer's lap creates a service failure that can be neither foreseen nor corrected ahead of time.[7]

Another challenge heterogeneity presents is that not only does the consistency of service vary from firm to firm and among personnel within a single firm, but it also varies when interacting with the same service provider on a daily basis. For example, some McDonald's franchises have helpful and smiling employees, whereas other McDonald's franchises employ individuals who act like robots. Not only can this be said for different

The corporate name may be the same from one location to the next, but is the quality of service? Service standardization and quality control are difficult to achieve among employees.

franchises, but the same is true within a single franchise on a daily basis because of the mood swings of individuals.

## MARKETING PROBLEMS CAUSED BY HETEROGENEITY

The major obstacles presented by heterogeneity translate into the fact that service standardization and quality control are difficult to achieve. Why is this so? Because of the inseparability characteristic previously discussed, you now know that in many instances the service provider must be present to provide the service. Firms such as financial institutions employ a multitude of front-line service providers. As an individual, each employee has a different personality and interacts with customers differently. In addition, each employee may act differently from one day to the next as a result of mood changes as well as numerous other factors. For example, many students who work as wait staff in restaurants frequently acknowledge that the quality of interaction between themselves and customers will vary even from table to table. Hotel desk clerks, airline reservationists, and business-to-business service personnel would respond similarly.

The marketing problems created by heterogeneity are particularly frustrating. A firm could produce the best product in the world, but if an employee is having a "bad day," a customer's perceptions may be adversely affected. The firm may never have another opportunity to serve that customer. Returning to our McDonald's example, the franchisee may pay $1,000,000 for the franchise and the right to sell a "proven product." However, the real secret to each individual franchise's success is the 16-year-old behind the counter who is interacting with customers and operating the cash register. Can you imagine the franchisee who has just spent $1,000,000 for the franchise trying to sleep at night while thinking that his or her livelihood depends on the "kid" behind the counter? It does!

## POSSIBLE SOLUTIONS TO HETEROGENEITY PROBLEMS

Solutions proposed to offset the challenges posed by heterogeneity could be considered complete opposites of one another. On one hand, some service firms use the heterogeneous nature of services to provide customized services. In this case, the service offering is tailored to the individual needs of the consumer. The second possible solution is to develop a service delivery system that standardizes the service offering—every consumer receives essentially the same type and level of service. Each of these opposing strategies encompasses a different set of advantages and disadvantages.

### Customization

One possible solution to the problems created by heterogeneity is to take advantage of the variation inherent in each service encounter and customize the service. **Customization** develops services that meet each customer's individual needs. Producers of goods typically manufacture the good in an environment that is isolated from the customer. As such, mass-produced goods do not meet individual customer needs. However, because both the customer and the service provider are involved in the service delivery process, it is easier to customize the service based on the customer's specific instructions.

*customization*
Taking advantage of the variation inherent in each service encounter by developing services that meet each customer's exact specifications.

Note that there are tradeoffs associated with a customized service. On one hand, if everything is provided exactly to the customer's specifications, the customer ends up with a service that meets his or her specific needs; however, the service will take longer to produce. Consequently, the provider can obtain higher prices, which lead to higher profit margins for the provider. Providers pursuing a customization strategy focus on profit margins on a per-customer basis as opposed to achieving profits through a mass volume or turnover strategy.

The downside of providing customized services is threefold. First, customers may not be willing to pay the higher prices associated with customized services. Second, the speed of service delivery may be an issue. Customized services take extra time to provide and deliver, and the customer may not have the luxury of waiting for the final product. Finally, customers may not be willing to face the uncertainty associated with customized services. Each customized service is different, so the customer is never sure exactly what the final product will be until it is delivered. So, do customers prefer customized services over standardized services? Intuitively, most believe that customers would prefer customized products; however, the answer is, "it depends." If price, speed of delivery, and consistency of performance are issues, the customer will probably be happier with a standardized service.

### Standardization

Standardizing the service is a second possible solution to the problems created by heterogeneity. The goal of **standardization** is to produce a consistent service product from one transaction to the next. Service firms can attempt to standardize their service through intensive training of their service providers. Training certainly helps reduce extreme variations in performance. However, despite all the training in the world,

*standardization*
To produce a consistent service product from one transaction to the next.

| TABLE 2.3 | HETEROGENEITY: MARKETING PROBLEMS AND POSSIBLE SOLUTIONS | |
| --- | --- | --- |
| Characteristic | Marketing problems | Possible solutions |
| Heterogeneity | Difficult to standardize service and quality control | Customization Standardization |

employees ultimately will continue to vary somewhat from one transaction to the next. One way to eliminate this variance is to replace human labor with machines.

A financial institution's automatic teller machine (ATM) and an automated car wash are prime examples of standardized services that appeal to consumers' convenience-oriented needs. In both instances, consumers key in their service request by answering a series of predetermined automated prompts and the service is then provided accordingly. This type of system minimizes the amount of customer contact and variations in quality during the order and delivery processes.

On the positive side, standardization leads to lower consumer prices, consistency of performance, and faster service delivery. However, some consumer groups believe that standardization sends the message that the firm does not really care about individual consumer needs and is attempting to distance itself from the customer. Perceived distancing is particularly an issue as organizations are increasingly replacing human labor with machines such as automated phone services. In many instances, customers are becoming increasingly frustrated when forced to select from a menu of phone messages. Of course, standardization and customization do not have to be all-or-nothing propositions. Numerous companies, particularly in the travel and tourism arena, provide a standardized core product and allow consumers to select options to semi-customize their final outcome. Table 2.3 lists the special marketing challenges posed by heterogeneity and possible solutions to those challenges.

# > PERISHABILITY

The fourth and final unique characteristic that distinguishes goods from services is perishability. Perishability refers to the fact that services cannot be saved, their unused capacity cannot be reserved, and they cannot be inventoried. Unlike goods that can be stored and sold at a later date, services that are not sold when they become available cease to exist. For example, hotel rooms that go unoccupied for the evening cannot be stored and used at a later date; airline seats that are not sold cannot be inventoried and added on to aircraft during the holiday season, when airlines seats are scarce; and service providers such as dentists, lawyers, and hairstylists cannot regain the time lost from an empty client appointment book.

Some service firms find it possible to inventory part of their service process. McDonald's, for example, can inventory hamburgers for a limited period; however, a

McDonald's outlet cannot inventory the entire service experience. Spare capacity in the system on a Thursday evening cannot be saved for the Friday evening peak, nor can the hamburgers.

The inability to inventory creates profound difficulties for marketing services. When dealing with tangible goods, the ability to create an inventory means that production and consumption of the goods can be separated in time and space. In other words, a good can be produced in one locality in Europe and transported for sale in another. Similarly, a good can be produced in January and not released into the channels of distribution until June. In contrast, most services are consumed at the point of production. From a goods-marketing manager's point of view, concerns about when and where the customer consumes the product are important in understanding consumer behavior and motivation but are largely irrelevant in day-to-day operations.

The existence of inventory also greatly facilitates quality control in goods-producing organizations. Statistical sampling techniques can be used on warehouse stock to select individual items for testing, to the point of destruction if necessary (e.g., automobile crash tests). The sampling process can be set up to ensure minimum variability in the quality of product released for distribution. Quality-control systems also provide numerical targets against which managers can work. It is thus possible for Procter & Gamble to produce tens of millions of packages of Tide laundry detergent that are essentially identical. In contrast, when you purchase a room at a hotel, you are likely to experience a wide range of factors that may influence your good night's sleep. Issues such as air conditioning, plumbing, and noisy neighbors factor into the hotel guest's experience.

Finally, in goods-producing businesses, inventory performs the function of separating the marketing and the production departments. In many organizations, stock is actually sold at a transfer price from one department to another. The two parts of the firm have what amounts to a contract for quality and volumes. Once this contract has been negotiated, each department is able to work relatively independently of the other. In service firms, however, marketing and operations constantly interact with each other—because of the inability to inventory the product.[8]

## MARKETING PROBLEMS CAUSED BY PERISHABILITY

Without the benefit of carrying an inventory, matching demand and supply within most services firms is a major challenge. In fact, because of the unpredictable nature of consumer demand for services, the only way that supply matches demand is by accident! For example, as a manager, try to imagine scheduling cashiers at a grocery store. Although we can estimate the times of the day that the store will experience increased demand, that demand may fluctuate widely within any 15-minute interval. Now try to imagine forecasting demand for a hospital's emergency ward, an entertainment theme park, or a ski resort. Demand can be "guesstimated" but will rarely be exact. Simply stated, consumer demand for many services at any given time is unpredictable. The lack of inventories and the need for the service provider to provide the service leads to several possible demand and supply scenarios. In contrast to their service-producing counterparts, manufacturers of goods could more easily adapt to these scenarios through selling or creating inventories.

### Higher Demand Than Maximum Available Supply

Within this scenario, consumer demand simply outpaces what the firm can supply, which results in long waiting periods and, in many cases, unhappy customers. Business may be lost to competitors as waiting times become too excessive for consumers to endure. Ironically, in cases of consistent excess consumer demand, consumers may continue to attempt to patronize a firm out of curiosity and/or the social status obtained by telling others of their experience: "We finally got in to see the show!"

### Higher Demand Than Optimal Supply Level

In many instances, the consequences associated with demand exceeding optimal supply may be worse than when demand exceeds maximum available capacity. By accepting the customer's business, the firm implicitly promises to provide the same level of service that it always provides, regardless of the quantity demanded. For example, it seems that airlines typically staff flights with the same number of flight attendants regardless of the number of tickets actually sold. However, when demand exceeds optimal levels, the service provided is generally at inferior levels. As a result, customer expectations are not met, and customer dissatisfaction and negative word-of-mouth publicity results.

When demand exceeds optimal supply levels, the temptation is to accept the additional business. However, in many instances the firm's personnel and operations are not up to the task of delivering service effectively beyond optimal demand levels. For example, suppose that a landscaper became very successful in a short time by providing high-quality services to upscale customers. As the word spread to other potential clients, demand for the landscaper's time dramatically increased. As the firm expanded to serve new clients via the purchase of new equipment and the hiring of new personnel, the landscaper quickly found that he was losing control over the quality of service delivered by his firm. His new personnel simply did not provide the same level of service that his original customer base had grown accustomed to receiving. Over time the landscaper lost his new clients as well as his old clients, and he eventually filed for bankruptcy. In this case the service traits of perishability, inseparability, and heterogeneity all took their toll on the business.

### Lower Demand Than Optimal Supply Level

As we discussed earlier, providing the exact number of grocery store cashiers needed at any given time is a challenge for most store managers. One solution would be to staff each line with a full-time cashier; however, this strategy would result in an inefficient deployment of the firm's resources. During times when demand is below optimal capacity, resources are underutilized (e.g., cashiers are standing around), and operating costs are needlessly increased.

### Demand and Supply at Optimal Levels

The optimal scenario is to have demand match supply. This scenario describes the situation in which customers do not wait in long lines and in which employees are utilized to their optimal capacity. Because services cannot be stored, a buffer to ease excess demand cannot be developed. Moreover, service providers are not machines and cannot produce a limitless supply. Consequently, service demand and supply rarely balance.

Customers do at times experience lengthy waits, and service providers are sometimes faced with no one to serve.

## POSSIBLE SOLUTIONS TO PERISHABILITY PROBLEMS

Because service demand and supply balance only by accident, service firms have developed strategies that attempt to adjust supply and demand to achieve a balance. The strategies presented here are possible solutions to overcome the difficulties associated with the perishability of services.[9] The first group of strategies concerns the management of the firm's demand. This discussion is followed by a second group of strategies that focuses on managing supply.

### Demand Strategy: Creative Pricing

**Creative pricing** strategies are often used by service firms to help smooth demand fluctuations. For example, offering price reductions in the form of "earlybird specials" and "matinees" have worked well for restaurants and movie theaters, respectively. Price-conscious target markets, such as families with children, are willing to alter their demand patterns for the cost savings. At the same time, service firms are willing to offer price reductions to attract customers during nonpeak hours, thereby making their operations more efficient. By shifting demand to other periods, the firm can accommodate more customers and provide better service during periods in which demand in the past has been (1) turned away because of limited supply, and (2) not served as well as usual because demand surpasses optimal supply levels.

Creative pricing has also been used to target specific groups such as senior citizens, children and their parents (families), and college students. This type of pricing strategy has not only helped smooth fluctuating demand but has also aided in separating diverse target markets from sharing the same consumption experience at the same time. For example, by providing family-type specials during late afternoon and early evening hours, a restaurant significantly reduces the amount of potential conflict between its "family customers" and its "adult-only customers," who generally dine later in the evening.

Price incentives have also been used recently to persuade customers to use the company's Web site. Customers who are willing to place their orders on the Internet may do so 24 hours a day, 7 days a week. Increasing Web site usage reduces demand for personal service during regular business hours.

*creative pricing*
Pricing strategies often used by service firms to help smooth demand fluctuations, such as offering "matinee" prices or "earlybird specials" to shift demand from peak to nonpeak periods.

### Demand Strategy: Reservation Systems

Another common strategy used to reduce fluctuations in demand is to implement a **reservation system** by which consumers ultimately reserve a portion of the firm's services for a particular time slot. Typical service firms that use reservation systems include restaurants, doctors of all varieties, golf courses (tee times), and day spas. On the plus side, reservations reduce the customer's risk of not receiving the service and minimize the time spent waiting in line for the service to be available. Reservation systems also allow service firms to prepare in advance for a known quantity of demand. Consequently, the customer and the firm benefit from improved service.

*reservation system*
A strategy to help smooth demand fluctuations in which consumers ultimately request a portion of the firm's services for a particular time slot.

Despite the advantages of a reservation system, a host of disadvantages also accompanies this strategy. First, someone must maintain the reservation system, which adds additional cost to the operation. Next, customers do not always show up on time or sometimes fail to show up at all. As a result, the operation ends up with unused services and lost revenues. For example, a common strategy for some golfers (particularly young and single) is to reserve a tee time at two or three different golf courses at two or three different times on the same day. Depending on their whims and which golf course they decide to play that particular day, the golfers choose which tee time to use, leaving the other two golf courses holding the tee for a foursome that is not going to show up. Given that the greens fee for an 18-hole round with riding cart averages at least $50, the golf course has just lost $200 that it could have otherwise collected by filling the spot with another foursome.

Another drawback of reservation systems is that they offer to the customer an implied guarantee that the service will be available at a specified time, thereby increasing the customer's expectation. All too often, this implied guarantee is not met. For example, customers with early appointments may show up late, causing a chain reaction of delayed appointments for the rest of the day. Similarly, the rate at which restaurant tables turn over is difficult to determine and is further compounded by the size of the party sitting at a table compared with the size of the party waiting for a table. In addition, medical doctors schedule as many as four patients at the same appointment time in an attempt to serve patient demand. Despite the use of reservation systems, customers may still end up waiting and become even more unhappy (compared with a "first come, first serve" system) because of the implied promise made by the reservation system.

### Demand Strategy: Development of Complementary Services

**complementary services**
Services provided for consumers to minimize their perceived waiting time, such as driving ranges at golf courses, arcades at movie theaters, or reading materials in doctors' offices.

The trials and tribulations associated with perishability can also be buffered by developing **complementary services** that directly relate to the core service offering. A lounge in a restaurant is a typical example of a complementary service that not only provides the space to store customers while they wait but also provides the restaurant with an additional source of revenue. Similarly, golf courses often provide putting greens for their customers as a form of complementary service. Although free of charge to customers, the putting green occupies the customers' time, thereby minimizing their perceived waiting time. The result is more satisfied customers. Other complementary services that have been developed to help manage demand include driving ranges at golf courses, arcades at movie theaters, reading materials in doctors' offices, and televisions in the waiting areas of hospital emergency rooms.

### Demand Strategy: Development of Nonpeak Demand

**nonpeak demand development**
A strategy in which service providers use their downtime to prepare in advance for peak periods or by marketing to a different segment that has a different demand pattern than the firm's traditional market segment.

The effects of perishability can also be modified by developing nonpeak demand. **Nonpeak demand development** utilizes service downtime to prepare in advance for peak periods, and/or to market to different market segments with different demand patterns. Consequently, nonpeak demand development can reduce the effects of perishability in two ways. First, employees can be cross-trained during nonpeak demand periods to perform a variety of other duties to assist fellow personnel (e.g., dishwashers may be trained to set up and clear tables) during peak demand periods. In addition, although services cannot be stored, the tangibles associated with the service (such as salads at a restaurant) can be premade and ready prior to the service encounter. Advance preparation activities such as these free personnel to perform other types of service when needed.

Second, nonpeak demand can also be developed to generate additional revenues by marketing to a different market segment that has a different demand pattern than the firm's traditional segment. For example, golf courses have filled nonpeak demand by marketing to housewives, senior citizens, and shift workers (e.g., factory workers, nurses, students, and teachers) who use the golf course during the morning and afternoon hours, which are traditionally slow periods during weekdays. These groups exhibit different demand patterns than traditional golfers, who work from 8:00 am to 5:00 pm and demand golf course services in the late afternoons, early evenings, and on weekends.

### Supply Strategy: Part-Time Employee Utilization

In addition to managing consumer demand, the effects of perishability can also be minimized through strategies that make additional supply available in times of need. One such supply strategy is the use of **part-time employees** to assist during peak demand periods. For many years, retailers have successfully used part-time employees to increase their supply of service during the holidays.

The advantages of employing part-time workers as opposed to adding additional full-time staff include lower labor costs and a flexible labor force that can be employed when needed and released during nonpeak periods. On the negative side, using part-time employees sometimes causes consumers to associate the firm with lower job skills and lack of motivation and organizational commitment. Such traits subsequently lead to dissatisfied customers. However, these disadvantages appear most commonly in organizations that staff their operations with part-time workers on a full-time basis as opposed to employing part-time employees only during peak demand periods.

*part-time employees*
Employees who typically assist during peak demand periods and who generally work fewer than 40 hours per week.

### Supply Strategy: Capacity Sharing

Another method of increasing the supply of service is **capacity sharing,** forming a type of service co-op with other service providers, which permits the co-op to expand its supply of service as a whole. For example, many professional service providers are combining their efforts by sharing the cost and storage of expensive diagnostic equipment. By sharing the cost, each service firm is able to supply forms of service it may not otherwise be able to provide because of the prohibitive costs associated with such equipment. In addition, the funds saved through cost sharing are freed to be spent on additional resources such as equipment, supplies, and additional personnel, thereby expanding the supply of service to consumers even further. Surgery centers and other medical group practices offer typical examples of capacity sharing in application.

*capacity sharing*
Strategy to increase the supply of service by forming a type of co-op among service providers that permits co-op members to expand their supply of service as a whole.

### Supply Strategy: Advance Preparation for Expansion

Although the strategy of **expansion preparation** does not provide a "quick fix" to the supply problems associated with perishability, it may save months in reacting to demand pressures, not to mention thousands of dollars in expansion costs. In an effort to prepare in advance for expansion, many service firms are taking a long-term orientation with regard to constructing their physical facilities.

*expansion preparation*
Planning for future expansion in advance and taking a long-term orientation to physical facilities and growth.

For example, one local airport was built with future expansion in mind. This facility was built on a isolated portion of the airport property, where no adjoining structure would interfere with future growth. All plumbing and electrical lines were extended to the ends on both sides of the building and capped, making "hook-ups" easier when expansion becomes a reality. Even the road leading to the terminal was curved in the expectation that new terminal additions will follow along this predetermined pattern.

### Supply Strategy: Utilization of Third Parties

A service firm can also expand its supply of a service through use of third parties. Service organizations frequently use **third parties** to service customers and thereby save on costs and personnel. Travel agencies are a typical example. Travel agents provide the same information to customers as an airline's own representatives. This third-party arrangement, however, enables the airline to reduce the number of personnel it employs to make flight reservations and lets it redirect the efforts of existing personnel to other service areas. The cost savings associated with using third parties is evidenced by the airlines' willingness to pay commissions to travel agencies for booking flights.

Note that although the use of third parties increases the supply of service, this type of arrangement may expose customers to competitive offerings as well. As a result, a tradeoff does exist. Many third parties, such as travel agents, represent a variety of suppliers. A customer who intended to book a flight on British Airways may end up taking a Lufthansa flight because of a more compatible flight schedule and/or a less expensive fare. This type of competitive information would not have been available if the customer had called British Airways directly to make the flight reservation.

### Supply Strategy: Increase in Customer Participation

Another method for increasing the supply of service available is to have the customer perform part of the service. For example, in many fast-food restaurants, **customer participation** means giving customers a cup and expecting them to fill their own drink orders. In other restaurants, customers make their own salads at a "salad bar," dress their own sandwiches at the "fixings bar," prepare plates of food at the "food bar," and make their own chocolate sundaes at the "dessert bar."

Without a doubt we are performing more and more of our own services every day. We pump our own gas, complete our own bank transactions at automatic teller machines, and bag our own groceries at wholesale supermarkets. In fact, one of the major advantages of a Web site is that it enables customers to help themselves, or at least be more prepared when they request help from service personnel. However, although self-service does free employees to provide other services, a number of advantages and disadvantages are associated with customer participation. The willingness of customers to provide their own service is generally a function of convenience, price, and customization. For example, automatic teller machines offer the customer the convenience of 24-hour banking, bagging groceries is generally accompanied by lower grocery prices, and Dell Computers provides customers the opportunity to configure their own personal computer order to their own individual specifications.

*third parties*
A supply strategy in which a service firm uses an outside party to service customers and thereby save on costs and personnel.

*customer participation*
A supply strategy that increases the supply of service by having the customer perform part of the service, such as providing a salad bar or dessert bar in a restaurant.

In contrast, customer participation may also be associated with a number of disadvantages that predominantly concern loss of control. In many instances, the more the customer becomes a major player in the production of the service, the less control the service firm is able to maintain over the quality of the service provided. For example, the physician who instructs a patient to administer his own medicine relinquishes control over the outcome of the prescribed care. Quality control may also suffer as a result of confused customers who decrease the efficiency of the operating system. Customer confusion in a self-service environment is likely to affect not only the outcome of the confused customer's service, but also the delivery process of other customers who are sharing that customer's experience. For example, customers who are standing in line behind a customer who is using an ATM for the first time experience the effects of the new customer's learning curve.

The loss of quality control may also be accompanied by the loss of control over operating costs. Self-service, particularly in the food industry, is associated with waste as a result of abuse of the system. Customers may take more food than they would normally order and then consume or share food with nonpaying friends.

Finally, increasing customer participation may be interpreted by some customers as the service firm's attempt to distance itself from the customer. As a result, the image of an uncaring, unresponsive, and out-of-touch firm may develop, driving many customers away to full-service competitors. Hence, the tradeoff is apparent. While increasing customer participation frees service providers to provide additional services and may provide the customer with increased convenience, opportunities for customization, and reduced prices, this strategy may also create unhappy customers who are forced to fend for themselves. Table 2.4 provides a list of possible solutions to the various marketing problems posed by perishability.

| TABLE 2.4 | PERISHABILITY: MARKETING PROBLEMS AND POSSIBLE SOLUTIONS | |
| --- | --- | --- |
| **Characteristic** | **Marketing problems** | **Possible solutions** |
| Perishability | Higher demand than maximum available supply | Demand strategy: Creative pricing |
| | Higher demand than optimal supply level | Demand strategy: Reservation systems |
| | Lower demand than optimal supply level | Demand strategy: Development of complementary services |
| | | Demand strategy: Development of nonpeak demand |
| | | Supply strategy: Part-time employee utilization |
| | | Supply strategy: Capacity sharing |
| | | Supply strategy: Advance preparation for expansion |
| | | Supply strategy: Utilization of third parties |
| | | Supply strategy: Increase in customer participation |

## THE ROLE OF MARKETING IN THE SERVICE FIRM

This chapter has outlined some of the factors that characterize services marketing in general, and some of the problems that service marketers face. Because of the effects of intangibility, inseparability, heterogeneity, and perishability, marketing plays a very different role in service-oriented organizations than it does in pure goods organizations. As a result of the effects of intangibility, inseparability, heterogeneity, and perishability, this chapter has shown how closely the different components of the service organization are interwoven. The invisible and visible parts of the organization, the contact personnel and the physical environment, the organization and its customers, and indeed the customers themselves are all bound together by a complex series of relationships. Consequently the marketing staff must maintain a much closer relationship with the rest of the service organization than is customary in many goods businesses. The concept of the operations department being responsible for producing the product and the marketing department being responsible for selling it cannot work in a service firm.

## ✳ SUMMARY

The major differences between the marketing of goods and the marketing of services are most commonly attributed to four distinguishing characteristics—intangibility, inseparability, heterogeneity, and perishability. This chapter has discussed the marketing challenges presented by these four characteristics and possible solutions that minimize their impact on service firms.

Intangibility means that services lack physical substance and therefore cannot be touched or evaluated like goods. The marketing challenges associated with intangibility include difficulties in communicating services to consumers, pricing decisions, patent protection, and storage of services for future use. Strategies developed to offset the challenges posed by intangibility include the use of tangible clues, organizational image development, and the development of personal sources of information that consumers access when selecting service providers.

Inseparability reflects the interconnection between service providers and their customers. Unlike the producers of goods, service providers engage in face-to-face interactions with their customers, who are directly involved in the service production process. Strategies developed to minimize the challenges of inseparability include the selective screening and thorough training of customer contact personnel, the implementation of strategies that attempt to manage customers throughout the service experience, and the use of multi-site facilities to overcome the inseparability difficulties associated with centralized mass production.

Heterogeneity pertains to the variability inherent in the service delivery process. The primary marketing problem associated with heterogeneity is that standardization and quality control are difficult for a service firm to provide on a regular basis. Service firms typically react to heterogeneity in two diverse directions. Some firms try to standardize performance by replacing human labor with machines. In contrast, other firms take advantage of the variability by offering customized services that meet individual customer needs. Neither strategy is universally superior, because customer preference for customization versus standardization is dependent on price, speed of delivery, and consistency of performance.

Perishability refers to the service provider's inability to store or inventory services. Services that are not used at their appointed time cease to exist. Moreover, because services cannot be inventoried, the few times that supply matches demand often occur by accident. A variety of strategies have been developed to try to offset the potential problems created by perishability. Some strategies attack the problems by attempting to manage demand, while others attempt to manage supply. Demand management strategies include creative pricing strategies, reservation systems, staging demand through complementary services, and developing nonpeak demand periods. Supply management strategies include using part-time employees, capacity sharing, third-party utilization, increasing customer participation in the production process, and preparing in advance for future expansion to reduce the response time in reaction to demand increases.

Because of the challenges posed by intangibility, inseparability, heterogeneity, and perishability, marketing plays a very different role in service-oriented organizations than it does in pure goods organizations. Traditional management practices, which work under the premises that the operations department is solely responsible for producing the product and that the marketing department is solely responsible for selling it, cannot work in a service firm. The four characteristics presented in this chapter that distinguish the marketing of goods from the marketing of services provide ample evidence that the invisible and visible parts of the organization, the contact personnel, the physical environment, and the organization and its customers are bound together by a complex set of relationships. As a result, marketing must maintain a much closer relationship with the rest of the service organization than is customary in a traditional goods manufacturing plant.

## ✱ KEY TERMS

intangibility, 28
inseparability, 28
heterogeneity, 28
perishability, 28
physical evidence/tangible clues, 30
personal sources, 31
nonpersonal sources, 31
organizational image, 32
critical incident, 32
selection and training, 39
consumer management, 40
multi-site locations, 40

factories in the field, 40
customization, 43
standardization, 43
creative pricing, 47
reservation system, 47
complementary services, 48
nonpeak demand development, 48
part-time employees, 49
capacity sharing, 49
expansion preparation, 49
third parties, 50
customer participation, 50

## ✳ DISCUSSION QUESTIONS

1. Briefly describe how the unique service characteristics of intangibility, inseparability, heterogeneity, and perishability apply to your educational experience in your services marketing class.
2. Why is the pricing of services particularly difficult in comparison with the pricing of goods?
3. What strategies has the insurance industry utilized in its attempt to minimize the effects of intangibility? Of the companies that have actively attempted to minimize the effects, have some companies done a better job than others? Please explain.
4. Discuss the implications of having the customer involved in the production process.
5. Discuss the reasons that centralized mass production of services is limited.
6. Why are standardization and quality control difficult to maintain throughout the service delivery process?
7. Which is better for consumers: (1) a customized service or (2) a standardized service? Explain.
8. What are the limitations associated with a service firm's inability to maintain inventories?

## ✳ NOTES

1. Leonard L. Berry and A. Parasuraman, "Building a New Academic Field—The Case of Services Marketing," *Journal of Retailing* 69 (Spring 1993), 1, 13.
2. The framework for this chapter was adapted from Figures 2 and 3 in Valerie A. Zeithaml, A. Parasuraman, and Leonard L. Berry, "Problems and Strategies in Services Marketing," *Journal of Marketing* 49 (Spring 1985), 33–46. For a more in-depth discussion of each of the problems and strategies associated with services marketing, consult Figures 2 and 3 in this article for the appropriate list of references.
3. Adapted from John E. G. Bateson, *Managing Services Marketing,* 3rd ed. (Fort Worth, TX: The Dryden Press, 1995), 9.
4. Adapted from Dave Carpenter, "Fast Fixes for Bad Service," *Hospitals & Health Networks* 16, no. 74 (March 2000), 16.
5. Adapted from John E. G. Bateson, *Managing Services Marketing,* 3rd ed. (Fort Worth, TX: The Dryden Press, 1995), 9.
6. Jim Kelley, "From Lip Service to Real Service: Reversing America's Downward Service Spiral," *Vital Speeches of the Day* 64, no. 10 (1998), 301–304.
7. Bateson, *Managing Services Marketing,* p. 18.
8. Ibid., 11–13.
9. The framework and materials for this section were adapted from W. Earl Sasser, "Match Supply and Demand in Service Industries," *Harvard Business Review* (November/December 1976), 133–140.

# CHAPTER 3

# AN OVERVIEW OF THE SERVICES SECTOR

## CHAPTER OBJECTIVES

*This chapter provides an overview of the service economy by introducing the nine service supersectors. Although on the surface many of these supersectors seem quite diverse, service classification schemes are discussed that assist in our understanding of the commonalities among service industries. Trends and concerns pertaining to the growth of service industries are presented, which further our understanding of the service economy. Finally, this chapter explores the predicted keys to success within the service sector.*

After reading this chapter, you should be able to:

- Describe the nine supersectors that comprise the service economy.
- Discuss how classification schemes that identify commonalities among service industries can be used as learning tools.
- Identify the trends and concerns pertaining to the growth of the service economy.
- Address the keys to operating a successful service firm.

*"The scientist who pauses to examine every anomaly he notes will seldom get significant work done."*

Thomas S. Kuhn

## > WHAT CAN BROWN DO FOR YOU?

The United Parcel Service (UPS), also commonly known as "Brown," originally started in the U.S. as a messenger service company in 1907. Nearly 100 years later, the company is currently the world's largest package delivery company serving over 200 countries and territories worldwide and generates over $30 billion in revenue annually. The sheer scope and array of UPS activities is truly amazing as UPS provides services to household as well as business-to-business (B2B) customers. Employing over 357,000 workers worldwide, the company delivers some 3.4 billion packages and documents a year with an average daily delivery volume of 13.6 million packages and documents. The busiest delivery day of the year is traditionally December 21st when shipping Christmas packages is at its peak. On Peak Day, UPS delivers an astounding 20 million packages, averaging 230 package deliveries a second!

Within the service economy, "critical incidents" reflect the interaction between the customer and the organization and represent the greatest opportunity for gains/losses in terms of customer satisfaction and customer loyalty. UPS directly interacts with 7.9 million customers on a daily basis consisting of 1.8 million pick-ups and 6.1 million deliveries—many of which ship and/or receive more than one package. The company's Web site, UPS.com, receives 115 million hits a day, of which 9.1 million are tracking requests (on a peak day, online package tracking requests soar to 16 million!). Clearly, "critical incidents" are plentiful at UPS.

Much of UPS' success can be attributed to the company's infrastructure, which most customers never see. On the retail side of the business, the company maintains 3,400 UPS stores; 1,100 Mail Boxes Etc.; 1,000 UPS customer centers; 17,000 authorized outlets; and 45,000 UPS drop boxes. Packages and documents collected at these retail sites are then funneled to 1,748 operating facilities where they are distributed to a delivery fleet consisting of 88,000 package cars, vans, tractors, and motorcycles; 270 UPS jet aircraft; and 304 chartered aircraft. UPS serves 385 domestic and 466 international airports with major distribution hubs located in the United States, Europe, and Asia Pacific.

Today, UPS is one of the most recognized and admired brands in the world. In addition to claiming the #1 spot in package delivery, UPS is now a global leader in providing specialized transportation and logistic services to its B2B customers. According to UPS' portfolio of services found on its corporate Web site (http://www.ups.com), the answer to the question often posed by the firm's advertisements "What can Brown do for you?" is "Quite a lot!" UPS offers a vast array of B2B services including (1) global transportation services consisting of integrated freight and package delivery (utilizing road, ocean, and air freight) and reverse logistics (handling returns); (2) business technology solutions such as wireless, electronic data interchange, and billing solutions; (3) supply chain services including design and planning, post-sales support, and international trade management; and (4) financial services where UPS helps its B2B customers enhance their cash flow. Including B2B services in its product portfolio has allowed UPS to expand its profit-earning potential and cement its reputation as a world leader in the field of distribution.

Source: UPS Web site: http://www.ups.com accessed 30 January 2005; "Only Santa Delivers More in One Day than UPS," Press Release (December 13, 2004) http://pressroom.ups.com/ups.com/us/press_releases/accessed 30 January 2005.

## INTRODUCTION

Thus far, we have discussed the basic differences between goods and services in Chapters 1 and 2. The focus of this chapter is the service economy. We take an in-depth look into the service economy by providing an overview of the service economy super-sectors including education and health services, financial activities, government, information, leisure and hospitality, professional and business services, transportation and utilities, wholesale and retail trade, and other services. The nine service supersectors illustrate the diversity of activities within the service sector. Service classification schemes are presented, which highlight the commonalities among these service industries. For example, you might wonder what a bank teller and an airline ticket agent have in common. The answer is quite a lot! This chapter also discusses the major influences and concerns pertaining to the growth of the service economy. Clearly, technological, socio-cultural, and competitive forces impact the economy's direction and rate of growth. Concerns about the economy's reliance on its service sector and the continued decline of its industrial sector are also discussed. Finally, we conclude with a summary of the predicted key factors that many believe lead to success within the service sector.

## WHAT IS THE SERVICE ECONOMY?

It is generally accepted that the **service economy** includes the "soft parts" of the economy consisting of nine industry supersectors—education and health services, financial activities, government, information, leisure and hospitality, professional and business services, transportation and utilities, wholesale and retail trade, and other services (see Table 3.1).[1] The *service sector* is one of the three main categories of a developed economy—the other two being *industrial* and *agricultural*. Traditionally, economies throughout the world tend to transition themselves from an *agricultural economy* to an *industrial economy* (e.g, manufacturing and mining) to a *service economy*. The United Kingdom was the first economy in the modern world to make this transition. As presented in Chapter 1, several other countries including the U.S., Japan, Germany, and France have made this transition and many more are expected to do so at an accelerated rate. The increased rate of transformation has generally been caused by a competitive marketplace. Simply stated, goods are more amenable to international trade than services, thereby making them more vulnerable to competitive actions. Countries that industrialize their economies first eventually come under attack by other countries that are newly making the transition from an agricultural to an industrial economy. These "newcomer" countries offer lower production costs (especially labor), which is attractive to industry. Consequently, as industrial sectors flow from one country to the next, the countries they abandon begin to rely more heavily on the growth of their service sectors as the mainstay of their economies. This whole process repeats itself over and over again as other less developed countries enter the fray; consequently, facilitating the transformation from agriculture to industrial to service-based economies.

*service economy*
Includes the "soft parts" of the economy consisting of nine industry supersectors.

| TABLE 3.1 | THE SERVICE ECONOMY |
|-----------|---------------------|

| Service Sector | Related Activities | Employment Projections* |
|----------------|--------------------|-------------------------|
| **Wholesale and Retail Trade** | | |
| Wholesale trade | Sales to businesses | +11.3% |
| Retail trade | Sales to individuals | +13.8% |
| **Transportation and Warehousing and Utilities** | | |
| Transportation and warehousing | Transportation or storage. Modes of transportation include air, rail, water, road, and pipeline. | +21.7% |
| Utilities | Establishments that provide electricity, natural gas, steam, water, and sewage removal. | -5.7% |
| **Information** | Establishments that produce and distribute information and cultural products, provide the means to distribute or transmit these products, and/or process data. | +18.5% |
| **Financial Activities** | | |
| Finance and insurance | Engaging in financial transactions including pooling or risks. | +12.3% |
| Real estate, rental, and leasing | Selling or allowing the use of assets. | |
| **Professional & Business Services** | | |
| Professional, scientific, and technical | Legal advice, accounting, architectural, engineering, computer services, consulting, health care, research, and others. | +30.4% |
| Management of companies and enterprises | Undertake a decision-making role in the company or enterprise. | |
| Administrative and support, and waste management | Performing routine support activities for other organizations. | |
| **Education & Health Services** | | |
| Education | Provide instruction and training. | +31.8% |
| Health care and social assistance | Provide medical care and social assistance. | |
| **Leisure & Hospitality** | | |
| Arts, entertainment, and recreation | Providing services to meet cultural, entertainment, and recreational interests. | +17.8% |
| Accommodation and food services | Accommodation, and food service establishments. | |
| **Government** | | |
| Public administration | Federal, state, and local agencies. | +0.4% |
| **Other Services** | Providing services including repair, personnel care, dating, grantmaking, advocacy, pet services, and parking. | +15.7% |

*Projections are expected growth through year 2012. Combined projected industries growth including manufacturing is 14.8 %.

The U.S. Bureau of Labor Statistics (http://www.lbs.gov) provides an overview of each of these supersectors as well as a career guide. The career guide contains a description of the industries in each supersector as well as information about working conditions, current and projected employment, occupations, and wages. A brief description of each supersector as classified in the United States (service sectors in other countries may be classified differently based on government recordkeeping practices) is provided next.

## EDUCATION AND HEALTH SERVICES

The education and health services sector consists of two parts: (1) the educational services subsector and (2) the healthcare and social assistance subsector. The educational services sector includes schools, colleges, universities, and training centers. One in four Americans is currently enrolled in educational institutions. Accordingly, educational services, including both public and private institutions, is the second largest employment industry, accounting for 12.7 million jobs. The healthcare and social assistance sector is comprised of health services such as hospitals, nursing care facilities, physicians' offices, and home healthcare services. In turn, social assistance includes individual and family services, vocational rehabilitation services, community food and housing, and emergency and other relief services. Healthcare and social assistance accounts for about 10.4 percent of all employment and about 7.9 percent of all establishments. Health services is currently the largest industry in the private sector, providing 12.9 million jobs. Overall, employment projections for the education and health services supersector forecast employment will increase by 31.8 percent over the period 2002–2012, making it the highest projected growth of any industry supersector.

## FINANCIAL ACTIVITIES

The financial activities supersector consists of the finance and insurance subsector and the real estate and rental and leasing subsector. The finance and insurance subsector is comprised of establishments primarily engaged in financial transaction such as commercial banking, savings institutions, credit unions, securities and commodities brokers, as well as insurance carriers. Due to numerous mergers and acquisitions within the finance and insurance subsector, job growth is limited. However, job openings are expected due to retirement and people leaving the industry. The finance and insurance subsector represents about 4.4 percent of all employment and 5.2 percent of all establishments. Real estate and rental and leasing consists of establishments that manage real estate, sell, rent, or buy real estate for others, and real estate appraisals. Real estate and rental and leasing represents 1.6 percent of all employment and 3.9 percent of all establishments. Projected employment growth for the financial activities supersector for the period 2002–2012 is 12.3 percent.

## THE GOVERNMENT

The government supersector consists of publicly-owned establishments of federal, state, and local agencies that administer, oversee, and manage public programs. Examples of such agencies include those that set policies, create laws, adjudicate civil and criminal legal cases, provide public safety and national defense. Public schools and public hospitals are also included in the government supersector. The federal government represents approximately 2.2 percent of all employment and 0.6 percent of all establishments. Interestingly, four out of five federal employees work outside Washington D.C. Employment in the newly created Department of Homeland Security will drive most of the new hires. State government accounts for about 3.5 percent of all employment and 0.8 percent of all establishments. Local government claims 10.5 percent of all employment and 1.8 percent of all establishments. Local government employs more than three times as many workers as state government; most are firefighters and law enforcement. Government supersector employment projections for the period 2002–2012 are the lowest rate of increase of any other supersector with a projected increase of 0.4 percent.

## INFORMATION

The information supersector consists of establishments that produce and distribute information and cultural products, provide the means to distribute or transmit these products, and/or process data. Major players in this supersector include publishing industries (both traditional and Internet publishing), the motion picture and sound recording industries, the broadcasting industries, the telecommunication industries, Internet service providers and Web search portals, data processing industries, and information services industries. Although wide in scope, the information supersector modestly employs about 2.6 percent of all employment and accounts for 1.9 percent of all establishments. However, within the information supersector, software publishers are currently the fastest growing industry in the economy with a projected growth rate of 68 percent for the period 2002–2012. Overall, projected growth for the information supersector for the period 2002–2012 is forecasted at 18.5 percent.

## LEISURE AND HOSPITALITY

The leisure and hospitality sector is comprised of two subsectors—the arts, entertainment, and recreation subsector; and the accommodation and food services subsector (see Global Services in Action). The arts, entertainment, and recreation sector includes establishments that (1) produce, promote, or participate in live performances, events, or exhibits intended for public viewing; (2) preserve and exhibit objects and sites of historical, cultural, or educational interest; and (3) operate facilities that provide amusement, hobby, and leisure-time interests. The arts, entertainment, and recreation subsector represents approximately 1.4 percent of all employment and accounts for about 1.3 percent of all establishments. More than 40 percent of the workforce within this subsector has no formal education beyond high school. In comparison, the accommodation and food services subsector includes establishments providing lodging and/or meal, snack, or beverage preparation for immediate consumption. Hotels, food services, and drinking places provide many young people with their first job. Twenty-two percent of employees within the food service and drinking establishments are between the ages of 16 and 19. Compared to all other industries, this is a fivefold increase. In addition, two out of five employees work part time—twice the proportion of other industries.

**MILITARY TAKING COMMAND AND CONTROL OF CUBA'S HOTEL INDUSTRY**

In its purest form, marketing strategy involves target market selection, tailoring of the marketing mix, and reinforcing the firm's positioning strategy in the minds of consumers. Marketing strategy evolves over time to offset changes in the marketing environment—consisting of political and legal, competitive, economic, technological, natural, and socio-cultural forces. The Cuban government's latest move to regain control of its hotel industry offers a prime example of how political and legal forces impact marketing strategy.

Cuba's tourism industry provides almost half of the country's hard currency revenues with industry annual sales of over $2 billion. Over the past decade, tourism has averaged double-digit growth and 25 percent profit on sales. However, not all is well, as the Cuban government has retaken control of the industry, particularly hotels, in an apparent move to combat corruption and to reinforce respect for the government and the Communist Party. Apparently, money that was supposed to end up in government coffers was winding up in individuals' pockets. In addition, it was felt that the tourism reforms were weakening the grip of government control over life in Cuba.

Cuba's hotel industry and tourism began to flourish in the 1990s, as reforms were put into place to offset the country's economic dependence on the former Soviet Union. Tourism was said to be "the standard bearer of a move towards a less monolithic and more decentralized economy in Cuba." However, Cuba's president, Fidel Castro, has never much cared for his country's dependence on tourism. The president's brother and current Defense Minister, 74-year-old Raul Castro, has compared the industry to "a tree born twisted that must be uprooted and planted anew." No less than 12 government committees are now examining how to recentralize the industry. In the meantime, hotel operations that were once joint ventures with foreign hotel firms have been centralized and are now under the control of Gaviota—a hotel company set up by the armed forces in the early 1990s. Joint ventures have been relinquished of their quasi-independent status under which they could compete and make decisions. As a result, foreign investment in Cuba's hotel industry is expected to decline.

Interpretations of what is really happening with Cuba's tourism industry vary. One very possible explanation is that the political maneuvering by Raul Castro to take control over the country's main industry is to position himself as Fidel's successor. The former front-runner, Carlos Lage, presided over the economic reforms of the 1990s that originally led to the tourism boom.

Source: "Tourists: by the left, march." *The Economist*, (July 31, 2004) Vol. 372 Issue 8386, p33, 2/3p, 1c.

The average earnings for hotel workers are lower than most other industries. However, jobs are plentiful. The accommodation and food services subsector accounts for about 8 percent of all employment and represents 6.7 percent of all establishments. Projected employment growth for the supersector is 17.8 percent for the 2002–2012 period.

## PROFESSIONAL AND BUSINESS SERVICES

Professional and business services are projected to have the second highest employment growth rate of all sectors—30.4 percent for the period 2002–2012. This supersector consists of three subsectors including (1) professional, scientific, and technical services (5.2 percent of all employment, 10.5 percent of all establishments); (2) management of companies and enterprises (1.3 percent of all employment, 0.5 percent of all establishments); and (3) administration and support and waste management and remediation services (5.9 percent of all employment, 5.0 percent of all establishments). Professional, scientific, and technical services is one of the highest paying industries across all supersectors. The professional and business services supersector includes a multitude of activities such as legal advice and representation, accounting, bookkeeping, payroll services, engineering, research services, advertising services, veterinary services, office administration, hiring and placement of personnel, clerical services, security and surveillance services, cleaning, and waste disposal services.

## TRANSPORTATION AND WAREHOUSING AND UTILITIES

As its name implies, the transportation and warehousing and utilities supersector consists of two subsectors—(1) transportation and warehousing and (2) utilities. The transportation and warehousing subsector includes the transportation of passengers and cargo (see B2B Services in Action), warehousing and storage, scenic and sightseeing

Today, networks are an essential part of business, education, government, and home communications, and Cisco Internet Protocol-based (IP) networking solutions are the foundation of these networks. Cisco hardware, software, and service offerings are used to create Internet solutions that allow individuals, companies, and countries to increase productivity, improve customer satisfaction, and strengthen competitive advantage.

© PHOTODISC RED / GETTY IMAGES

## B 2 B   S E R V I C E S   *IN  ACTION*

> ## BUSINESS TRAVELERS PREFER OLD-LINE CARRIERS

As discount airlines such as Southwest, JetBlue, and Frontier continue to make strides in the nonbusiness airline travel market, it appears that when it comes to loyalty, business travelers prefer the old-line carriers. In a recent *BusinessWeek* survey, approximately 1,250 of its readers revealed their favorite and least favorite airlines. Some may find the results surprising.

| What is your favorite airline? | | What is your least favorite airline? | |
|---|---|---|---|
| United | 19.2% | Southwest | 15.9% |
| American | 18.9% | United | 14.7% |
| Southwest | 12.6% | US Airways | 13.5% |
| Continental | 12.4% | Northwest | 12.7% |
| Delta | 11.2% | Delta | 11.2% |

According to the survey, respondents traveled and average 12.5 business trips a year and booked their flights online 54 percent of the time. However, only 36 percent purposely selected cheaper flights when on business. Key selection criteria for business travelers include flight schedules, fewer stops, assigned seats, early boarding privileges, and generous frequent flyer programs. In addition, business travelers also mentioned the power of little touches such as friendly flight attendants and gate agents who were willing to be flexible in changing flight schedules when necessary.

It is interesting to note that while United was listed as the favorite airline, it was also mentioned as one of the least favorite. One reason for this contradiction is that the old-line carriers still dominate the industry. Seven out of every ten passengers in the U.S. fly an old-line carrier or one of their regional affiliates. However, it is interesting to note that while price is a major consideration for the nonbusiness traveler, nonprice criteria continue to drive business demand.

Source: Michael Arndt, "The Big Airlines' Loyal Fans," *Business Week*, (October 25, 2004), Issue 3905, p112, 2p, 3charts, 1c.

transportation, and other support activities related to the primary modes of transportation (air, rail, water, road, and pipeline). Transportation and warehousing account for approximately 3.1 percent of all employment and 2.6 percent of all establishments. The utility subsector comprises establishments that provide the following services: electricity, natural gas, steam, water, and sewage removal. Utilities represent approximately 0.5 percent of all employment and 0.2 percent of all establishments. Employment projections for this service supersector are mixed. Employment projections forecast a 21.7 percent increase for the transportation and warehousing subsector for the 2002–2012 period. In contrast, overall utility employment projections indicate a 5.7 percent decrease during the same timeframe.

## WHOLESALE AND RETAIL TRADE

The wholesale and retail trade supersector consists of the wholesale trade subsector and the retail trade subsector. Wholesale trade includes establishments that wholesale merchandise (generally without transformation) and provide services related to the sale of merchandise. Most wholesalers are small, employing fewer than 50 workers of which two-thirds work in office and administrative support, sales, or transportation and material-moving occupations. Wholesale trade represents about 4.4 percent of all employment and 7.2 percent of all establishments. Similarly, the retail trade subsector includes establishments that retail merchandise (generally without transformation) and provide services related to the sale of merchandise. Most retail trade jobs (83 percent) consist of sales and administrative support positions. Retail trade represents about 11.7 percent of all employment and 12.9 percent of all establishments. Employment projections for the period 2002–2012 include an 11.3 percent increase for wholesale trade and a 13.8 percent increase for retail trade.

## OTHER SERVICES

The other services supersector is a "catch-all" for all of the services that do not neatly fit into the preceding eight supercenter categories. Consequently, the other services supersector includes a myriad of establishments that are engaged in a variety of activities including equipment and machinery repair, promoting or administering religious activities, grantmaking, advocacy, drycleaning and laundry service, personal care, death care, pet care, photofinishing, temporary parking services, and dating services. The other services supersector accounts for approximately 3.3 percent of all employment and 12.6 percent of all establishments. Employment projections for the 2002–2012 period indicate a 15.7 percent increase.

## SERVICE CLASSIFICATION SCHEMES: WHAT CAN SERVICE INDUSTRIES LEARN FROM ONE ANOTHER?

The nine service supersectors illustrate the diversity of activities within the service economy. Our next objective is to determine what service firms in different sectors can learn from one another. Clearly, there will be exceptions. However, as the opening quote in this chapter states, "The scientist who pauses to examine every anomaly he notes will seldom get significant work done."[2] Consequently, one of the major themes of this text is to convey the message that service sectors should not be studied as separate entities (such as banking, transportation, business services, healthcare, and food service firms). Seemingly too often companies diminish their own chances to develop truly innovative ideas by examining only the practices of competitors within their own industries. Many service industries share common service delivery challenges and therefore would benefit from sharing their knowledge with each other. Unfortunately, many service firms look only to firms within their own industry for guidance. For example, banks look to other banks, insurance companies look to other insurance companies, and so on. This myopic approach slows the progress of truly unique service innovations within each of the respective industries. One needs only to consider the advances that hospitals could make if they borrowed concepts from restaurants and hotels instead of relying only on other hospitals for innovative service ideas.

Marketing has traditionally developed classification schemes to facilitate our managerial understanding of how different products share similar characteristics. For example, the consumer products classification scheme of *convenience, shopping,* and *specialty* products taught in introductory marketing classes aids in our understanding of how consumers spend their time shopping and their information requirements for various products. Similarly, the industrial products classification scheme of *raw materials, supplies, accessories, component parts and materials,* and *installations* has led to numerous implications concerning promotion mix strategies, types of goods purchased, evaluation processes, usage behavior, and purchasing procedures, to name a few.

Classification schemes applied solely to services have also been developed to facilitate our understanding of what different types of service operations have in common. Early attempts at developing classification categories are presented in Table 3.2 and include the following:

- degree of tangibility
- skill level of the service provider
- labor intensiveness
- degree of customer contact
- goal of the service provider

Although somewhat helpful in developing our understanding of what different services have in common, early service classification schemes failed to provide meaningful managerial implications to marketers. Subsequent classification schemes have been developed, which have proven to be more useful.[3] Presented in Tables 3.3 through 3.7, these classification categories include the following:

- Understanding the nature of the service
  - Is the nature of the service a tangible action or intangible action?
  - Is the direct recipient of the service a person or a thing?
- Relationships with the customer
  - Is the nature of the service delivery continuous or discrete?
  - Does the service firm have a membership relationship with its customers or no formal relationship?

| TABLE 3.2 | TRADITIONAL SERVICE CLASSIFICATIONS |
|---|---|

**Degree of Tangibility**
- Owned goods
- Rented goods
- Nongoods

**Labor Intensiveness**
- People-based
- Equipment-based

**Goal of the Service Provider**
- Profit
- Nonprofit

**Skill Level of the Service Provider**
- Professional
- Nonprofessional

**Degree of Customer Contact**
- High
- Low

- Customization and judgment in service delivery
  - Is the extent to which customer contact personnel exercise judgment in meeting customer needs high or low?
  - Is the extent to which service characteristics are customized high or low?
- The nature of demand relative to supply
  - Can peak demand usually be met without a major delay or does peak demand regularly exceed capacity?
  - Is the extent to which demand fluctuates over time wide or narrow?
- Method of service delivery
  - What is the nature of the interaction between the customer and the organization? Does the customer go to the service organization? Does the service organization come to the customer? Do customer and service organization transact business at arms length?
  - Is service available at a single site or multiple sites?

Services marketing classes may want to discuss each of these classification schemes and their marketing implications. For example, many service jobs such as a bank teller and an airline gate agent, who on the surface seem quite different, actually perform similar tasks and experience many of the same customer-related challenges throughout a typical day. Consequently, lessons that have been learned in the front lines of banking operations may be of value to those who work the front lines of the airline industry.

| **TABLE 3.3** | **UNDERSTANDING THE NATURE OF THE SERVICE** | |
|---|---|---|
| | **Who or What Is the Direct Recipient of the Service?** | |
| **What Is the Nature of the Service Act?** | **People** | **Things** |
| **Tangible Actions** | Services directed at people's bodies:<br>• Health care<br>• Passenger transportation<br>• Beauty salons<br>• Exercise clinics<br>• Restaurants<br>• Haircutting | Services directed at goods and other physical possessions:<br>• Freight transportation<br>• Industrial equipment repair and maintenance<br>• Janitorial services<br>• Laundry and dry cleaning<br>• Landscaping/lawn care<br>• Veterinary care |
| **Intangible Actions** | Services directed at people's minds:<br>• Education<br>• Broadcasting<br>• Information services<br>• Theaters<br>• Museums | Services directed at intangible assets:<br>• Banking<br>• Legal services<br>• Accounting<br>• Securities<br>• Insurance |

Source: Christopher H. Lovelock, "Classifying Services to Gain Strategic Marketing Insights," *Journal of Marketing* 47 (Summer 1983), pp. 9–20. Reprinted by permission of the American Marketing Association.

**TABLE 3.4**    **RELATIONSHIPS WITH CUSTOMERS**

| Nature of Service Delivery | Type of Relationship between the Service Organization and Its Customers | |
| --- | --- | --- |
| | "Membership" Relationship | No Formal Relationship |
| Continuous Delivery of Service | Insurance<br>Telephone subscription<br>College enrollment<br>Banking<br>American Automobile Association | Radio station<br>Police protection<br>Lighthouse<br>Public highway |
| Discrete Transactions | Long-distance phone calls<br>Theater series subscriptions<br>Commuter ticket or transit pass | Car rental<br>Mail service<br>Toll highway<br>Pay phone<br>Movie theater<br>Public transportation<br>Restaurant |

Source: Christopher H. Lovelock, "Classifying Services to Gain Strategic Marketing Insights," *Journal of Marketing* 47 (Summer 1983), pp. 9–20. Reprinted by permission of the American Marketing Association.

**TABLE 3.5**    **CUSTOMIZATION AND JUDGMENT IN SERVICE DELIVERY**

| Extent to Which Customer Contact Personnel Exercise Judgment in Meeting Individual Customer Needs | Extent to Which Service Characteristics Are Customized | |
| --- | --- | --- |
| | High | Low |
| High | Legal services<br>Health care/surgery<br>Architectural design<br>Executive search firm<br>Real-estate agency<br>Taxi service<br>Beautician<br>Plumber<br>Education (tutorials) | Education (large classes)<br>Preventive health programs |
| Low | Telephone service<br>Hotel services<br>Retail banking<br>  (excluding major loans)<br>Good restaurant | Public transportation<br>Routine appliance repair<br>Fast-food restaurant<br>Movie theater<br>Spectator sports |

Source: Christopher H. Lovelock, "Classifying Services to Gain Strategic Marketing Insights," *Journal of Marketing* 47 (Summer 1983), pp. 9–20. Reprinted by permission of the American Marketing Association.

| TABLE 3.6 | THE NATURE OF DEMAND FOR THE SERVICE RELATIVE TO SUPPLY | |
|---|---|---|
| | **Extent of Demand Fluctuations over Time** | |
| **Extent to Which Supply Is Constrained** | **Wide** | **Narrow** |
| **Peak Demand Can Usually Be Met without a Major Delay** | Electricity<br>Natural gas<br>Telephone<br>Hospital maternity unit<br>Police and fire emergencies | Insurance<br>Legal services<br>Banking<br>Laundry and dry cleaning |
| **Peak Demand Regularly Exceeds Capacity** | Accounting and tax preparation<br>Passenger transportation<br>Hotels and motels<br>Restaurants<br>Theaters | Services similar to those above but that have insufficient capacity for their base level of business |

Source: Christopher H. Lovelock, "Classifying Services to Gain Strategic Marketing Insights," *Journal of Marketing* 47 (Summer 1983), pp. 9–20. Reprinted by permission of the American Marketing Association.

| TABLE 3.7 | METHOD OF SERVICE DELIVERY | |
|---|---|---|
| **Nature of Interaction between Customer and Service Organization** | **Availability of Service Outlets** | |
| | **Single Site** | **Multiple Site** |
| **Customer goes to service organization** | Theater<br>Barbershop | Bus service<br>Fast-food chain |
| **Service organization comes to customer** | Lawn care service<br>Pest control service<br>Taxi | Mail delivery<br>AAA emergency repairs |
| **Customer and service organization transact at arms length (mail or electronic communications)** | Credit card company<br>Local TV station | Broadcast network<br>Telephone company |

Source: Christopher H. Lovelock, "Classifying Services to Gain Strategic Marketing Insights," *Journal of Marketing* 47 (Summer 1983), pp. 9–20. Reprinted by permission of the American Marketing Association.

> ## SERVICE ECONOMY GROWTH: KEY INFLUENCES AND CONCERNS

Several key forces continue to influence the growth of the service sector. These forces include the emergence of technologically-based e-services, socio-cultural forces derived from an aging population, and the competitive force of "outservicing," which involves the *offshoring, outsourcing,* and *industrialization* of many services. The continued growth and dominance of the service sector has been met with some criticism. *Materialismic* individuals believe that without manufacturing, there will be little for people to service.

## TECHNOLOGICAL INFLUENCES: THE EMERGENCE OF E-SERVICE[4]

One of the most profound changes driving the growth of the service economy and the way service firms conduct business has been the phenomenal advance in technology, in particular the Internet. Sometime around 1996, the obsession with the Internet began. Thousands of businesses, customers, employees, and partners got wired to one another and began conducting business processes online ("e-business"). Eventually, more and more customers (B2B and final) became wired and formed a critical mass. Through repeated usage, customer trust dramatically increased, and the Net became a viable means for revenue production and economic growth ("e-commerce").

### E-Service Defined

What exactly is an e-service? According to Hewlett-Packard (http://www.e-service. hp.com), "an **e-service** is an electronic service available via the Net that completes tasks, solves problems, or conducts transactions. E-services can be used by people, businesses, and other e-services and can be accessed via a wide range of information appliances." Figure 3.1 provides an overview of an e-service. E-services that are available today include your local bank's online account services, UPS package tracking service, and Schwab's stock trading services. In essence, an e-service is any asset that is made available via the Net that creates new efficiencies and new revenue streams (see E-Services in Action). In an Internet context, the term *asset* can include any software application that is placed on the Net and made available as an *ap-on-tap*.

*e-service*
An electronic service available via the Net that completes tasks, solves problems, or conducts transactions.

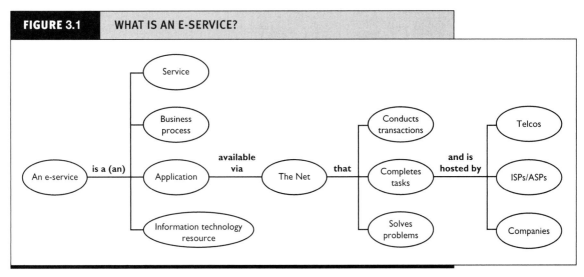

| **FIGURE 3.1** | **WHAT IS AN E-SERVICE?** |
| --- | --- |

**applications-on-tap**
E-service that is available
for rent on the Internet.

**ASPs**
Application service
providers—those who
provide aps-on-tap.

**Applications-on-tap** refer to e-services that are available for rent on the Internet. Those who provide aps-on-tap are known as **ASPs** (application service providers). One of the many intriguing aspects of e-services is that they apparently overcome many of the traditional challenges faced by service marketers—namely, intangibility, inseparability, heterogeneity, and perishability. This is particularly true of information-based services.[5]

### Managing Intangibility

Perhaps the main problem associated with intangibility is that service marketers have nothing to show the customer. E-services can overcome some of the challenges provided by intangibility by using the Web to provide evidence of service. For example, an innovative Ford Motor Company dealership is planning to install video cameras in its service bays to provide a live feed to the dealership's Web site. This strategy will enable customers to visit the service bay (without actually being there) and check on their vehicle's progress throughout the day. Other Web sites such as the Royal Automobile Club (RAC) in Europe provide tangible evidence by emailing new members who join online almost instantaneously with the new member's membership number and policy document. E-services also make tangible the intangible by providing additional evidence such as the appearance of the site, the frequency of information updates, the accuracy of information, the speed of the server, and ease of navigation. Customers are also able to sample information-based e-services prior to purchase, which is not true of traditional physical-based services such as hairstyling, surgical procedures, and dental services.

### Managing Inseparability

Inseparability reflects the simultaneity of service production and consumption. Inseparability also describes services as a shared experience in which, in many cases, the producer and the consumer both have to be present in order for the transaction to be completed. In addition, other customers are often involved in the service delivery process and the mass production of services is difficult if not impossible. E-services minimize the impact of inseparability in numerous ways. First, the service provider and the customer no longer need to occupy the same physical space to complete the transaction. Customers submit their requests from one location and the order is received and processed by the provider at another location. Second, the customer can initiate and consume the transaction in their own home or office; consequently, consumption is no longer a shared experience with other customers. In addition, e-services enable the mass production of information-based services. For example, customers wishing to download music are able to do so 24 hours a day 7 days a week.

### Managing Heterogeneity

The characteristic of heterogeneity reflects the variability in quality of service provided from one transaction to the next. When services are provided by people, variations are going to occur and mistakes will happen in real time. Service providers are human and they have good days and bad days. In contrast, e-services are electronically based; variations in quality provided from one customer to the next should be minimal. The airline's Web site, the bank's automated teller machine, and the credit card company's automated telephone system provide the same level of consistent service day-in and day-out. In addition, other e-services that perhaps monitor customer service conversations

## E-SERVICES *IN ACTION*

> ### HEWLETT-PACKARD'S CHAPTER TWO OF THE INTERNET

"Okay, everyone knows that the Net is changing everything . . . that's old news. The savvy companies are already asking themselves: *what comes next?* Chapter Two of the Internet will be about the mass proliferation of e-services."

An E-Services Strategy Book,
The Hewlett-Packard Company

Hewlett-Packard believes that e-services could easily become the dominant entity on the Net. In fact, HP refers to e-services as "Chapter Two of the Internet." "Chapter One" was about building the infrastructure and providing access. "Chapter Two" is about what the Internet can do for you–the customer. HP forecasts that entire ecosystems or e-services will be built around specific industries (insurance, travel), specific types of customers (physicians, attorneys), specific processes (buying a house, procurement), specific problems (too few computers and too much demand for processing), and specific transaction chains (new product development).

Product lines in HP's current e-service product mix include employee portals, trading portals, consumer portals, printing and imaging, general business, IT infrastructure, vertical industries, and publishing. As an example of what is available, e-service selections falling under the printing and imaging product category include the following:

- Dazel–An HP document router featuring Dazel technology that ensures delivery of important business documents.
- Encryptix.com–Turns your printer into a ticket office.
- IIPS–A print appliance that provides IT managers with a cost-effective way to manage print queues by using a browser. In addition, this category also includes a color pocket PC that can beam color images to color printers with the tap of a stylus.
- InternetShip–Turns your printer into a personal shipping station.
- ImageTag–Stores, retrieves, and sends important documents using uniquely barcoded labels called Post-it eFlags.
- Mimeo.com–Securely receives documents via the Internet to be printed, bound, and sent overnight anywhere in the United States and Canada.
- NewspaperDirect–Prints international newspapers locally on demand.
- PrintCafe–E-procurement solutions for corporate print buyers and commercial printers.
- Stamps.com–Turns your printer into a post office.

Source: http://www.e-services.hp.com/solutions/ips_solutions.html

may assist future customer service training sessions as typical problems are identified, resolved, and appropriate responses to customer complaints are formalized.

As discussed in Chapter 2, one of the possible solutions to minimize the challenges presented by heterogeneity is to provide customized solutions. Because of the modularity of e-services, solutions to individual customer requests can be more easily customized. For example, an airline passenger can easily book departure and return flights online that best meet their individual schedules. E-services help customers help themselves, thereby transferring the service production process into the hands of consumers. Information that is requested on Web sites requires that consumers become active participants in the process to the point where the customers themselves are actually becoming "partial employees." For example, if a customer places an order over the phone, the service firm has a paid employee who answers that phone, records the order, and requests billing and shipping information. By providing an access portal on the Web, that same company can reduce its labor costs by having customers input that same information on the company's Web site. In essence, the customer is now working for the service provider.

Another suggested method to reduce the negative effects of heterogeneity is to standardize (or industrialize) the service. Once again, e-services can be very effective. Because e-services are accessed at a distance (e.g., Web, cell phone, and PDA), customer involvement in the actual production process is minimized. Customers are often purposely led step by step to control the flow of the process. Because one-third of customer complaints are related to problems caused by the customers, a number of companies are instituting fail-safe procedures into their online operations. Examples include informing customers what information they are going to need prior to the encounter, providing online map services so that customers will not get lost driving to physical locations, requesting that customers enter email addresses twice to cut down on data entry errors, and having customers "click" as opposed to type in choices and information whenever possible.

### Managing Perishability

Perishability reflects the challenges faced by service marketers as a result of the inability to inventory services. Supply and demand problems are rampant. Services that are not consumed at their appointed time cease to exist. Hotel rooms that are not sold on Thursday night cannot be added to the supply of rooms available for occupancy on Friday night. E-services are not faced with these same problems. E-services are available 24 hours a day, 7 days a week. Applications not purchased one day are available for sale the next. E-services such as online auctions can help airlines fill unused capacity. On the demand side of the equation, if ten customers want to rent the same e-service application on the same day, this is not a problem. Although not perfect, information-based e-services can handle supply and demand fluctuations with much greater ease than most other types of physical-based services, such as restaurants, hospitals, and hotels.

E-services are able to overcome many of the traditional challenges faced by service marketers as a result of three main properties—*quantization,* the ability to *search,* and the ability to *automate.* Traditional service firms often bundle their offerings to the customer. For example, a hotel may bundle the room, breakfast and dinner, and a show for one price. **Quantization** (the breaking down of services [modularity] into component parts) allows opportunities for unparalleled mass customization. In addition, **search**—the ability and ease in which information can be sought, facilitates ultra-efficient information markets. As such, supply and demand can be more carefully monitored and matched. Finally, by offering consumers choices on a 24/7 basis, **automation**—replacing tasks that require human labor with machines, overcomes the traditional limitations of time and space.

*quantization*
The breaking down of monolithic services into modular components.

*search*
The ability and ease in which information can be sought.

*automation*
Replacing tasks that required human labor with machines.

## SOCIO-CULTURAL INFLUENCES: THE GRAYING OF AMERICA

A second key trend influencing the growth of the service economy involves the many demographic changes that are taking place throughout the world.[6] In essence, a type of chain reaction is occurring that facilitates the growth of the service sector. Consumers have less time than ever to accomplish their various roles. The growth in the number of time-pressured consumers has led to an increase in time-saving services such as restaurants, housekeeping services, laundry services, hairstyling shops, and tax preparation services. The time saved through the use of these services is now being spent on entertainment, travel, and recreation services.

The continued growth of the service sector throughout the world will be influenced by each area's demographic make-up. For example, on average the population of the United States is becoming older. By the year 2008 the median age of the U.S. labor force is projected to rise to nearly 41 years. This will exceed the previous high of 40.5 set in 1962.[7] In addition, advances in healthcare and more health-conscious consumers have led to a dramatic growth in "older" market segments. Although the immediate implication is an increase in demand for healthcare-related services, other service sectors stand to benefit from an aging population. The over-50 age group controls 77 percent of the nation's assets and 50 percent of the country's discretionary income.[8] In fact, the term **woofs**, which stands for "well-off older folks," has been coined to represent this group's purchasing power. It has also been noted that this particular group is engaged in "down aging"—acting younger than one's years. As a result, amusement and recreation services are one of the fastest employment growth industries within the service sector. In addition, personal services that assist older age groups in accomplishing everyday activities are also experiencing increases in demand.

*woofs*
"Well-off older folks," that segment of the population that controls 77 percent of the nation's assets and 50 percent of its discretionary income.

## COMPETITIVE INFLUENCES: THE OUTSERVICING OF AMERICA

Service sector growth is also being impacted by "outservicing," which involves the *offshoring, outsourcing,* and *industrialization* of many services. When Americans hear the term **offshoring,** they typically think of manufacturing jobs being moved from the U.S. to less developed countries that are able to produce products at a lower cost, primarily due to lower labor costs.[9] Today, however, more and more service jobs are at risk to suffer the same fate. It is estimated that 10 percent of American service sector jobs have the potential to be lost to other sources. The loss of service jobs will not just be an American phenomenon. Other developed countries such as the UK, Germany, and Sweden are also feeling the crunch, both economically and politically.

*offshoring*
The migration of domestic jobs to foreign host countries.

The migration pattern of service jobs should be somewhat predictable. In many cases it is based on economic diversity and a common language. For example, the English-speaking world consists of some of the most developed economies (U.S., U.K., and Australia) and some of the poorest (India and Pakistan). Consequently, India and Pakistan offer a competitive advantage (wage structure) to host service jobs that serve the more developed English-speaking economies. Case in point, the U.S. is experiencing somewhat of a mass exodus of its service call centers to India. In contrast, much of the worldwide Spanish-speaking population has roughly the same income distribution. As a result, one would expect less offshoring of service jobs within Spanish-speaking economies. Similarly, isolated languages such as Italian should spare Italy from the offshoring phenomenon.

**outsourcing**
The purchase and use of labor from a source outside the company.

**industrialization**
Mechanized or automated services that replaced human labor with machines.

The loss of corporate service jobs is fueled by other sources as well—*domestic outsourcing* and the *industrialization* of services. Because of **outsourcing**, many middle-class corporate jobs are now undertaken by independent contractors. Although this phenomenon has fueled the growth of the professional business service sector, wages and benefits for these jobs are often lower. Technological advances have **industrialized** (automated) many services, further taking its toll on the service sector workforce. Information-based services are most at risk for automation. We have already experienced the transition of automated simple services (e.g., data entry and credit card processing) to more complex services (e.g., market research, tax returns, billing, and customer service). Experts predict that the automation of engineering, management, publishing, financial services, and education are not far behind. Worldwide, 10 million service jobs could be lost to offshoring, outsourcing, and automation. Interestingly, not all service sectors are necessarily vulnerable. The physical services such as nursing, construction workers, hairstyling, restaurant and hotel workers, which require the physical presence of the service worker and customer, seem to be the most protected.

### SERVICE SECTOR GROWTH CONCERNS: MATERIALISMO SNOBBERY

According to the U.S. Bureau of Labor Statistics workforce projections for the years 1998 to 2008, the service sector is expected to account for more than 90 percent of all job growth. Although the service economy is growing in leaps and bounds, not everyone is rejoicing.[10] **Materialismo snobbery** reflects the attitude that only manufacturing can create real wealth and that all other sectors of the economy are parasitic and/or inconsequential. Materialismic individuals believe that without manufacturing, there will be little for people to service. As a result, more people will be available to do less work, driving wages down and subsequently decreasing the standard of living in the United States. Ultimately, materialismo snobbery supports the belief that the continued shift to a service economy will jeopardize the American way of life.

**materialismo snobbery**
Belief that without manufacturing there will be less for people to service and so more people available to do less work.

Similar concerns were voiced in the United States more than 140 years ago, when the economy was shifting from agriculture to manufacturing. In 1850, 50 years after industrialization, 65 percent of the population was connected to farming. During this period, many experts voiced great concern over workers leaving the farms to work in the factories. The concerns centered on the same type of logic: If the vast majority of the population left the farms, what would the people eat? Today, less than 2 percent of the

U.S. labor force is involved in farming operations.[11] This small but mighty workforce provides such a surplus of food that the federal government provides price supports and subsidies to keep the farms in business. Apparently, the concerns regarding the shift to manufacturing were unwarranted. In fact, the shift lead to economic growth.

Similarly, with advances in technology and new management practices, the need no longer exists to have as many people in manufacturing as we had in the mid-1900s. Manufacturing is not superior to services. The two are interdependent. In fact, half of all manufacturing workers perform service-type jobs.[12]

Another criticism of the service economy pertains to the dichotomization of wealth among service workers. In the United States, 60 percent of the population has experienced a decrease in real income over the past 15 years. In contrast, the wealthiest 5 percent has seen an increase of 50 percent, and the top 1 percent has seen a doubling in income.[13] Although experts disagree, some believe that because of the poor wages paid by some service industries, the shift of the economy away from manufacturing will lead to a further **dichotomization of wealth**—the rich will get richer and the poor will get poorer. Without a doubt, the service sector has many low-paying jobs.[14] For individuals under the age of 30, service jobs pay 25 percent less than manufacturing jobs. Some experts believe that as the manufacturing sector continues to decline, the supply of labor available for service jobs will increase, driving wages even lower.

*dichotomization of wealth*
The rich get richer and the poor get poorer.

However, not everyone in services is poorly paid. For example, in the finance and wholesale trade, salaries are much closer to manufacturing wages. Moreover, an increasing number of service personnel are highly skilled and employed in knowledge-based industries. In fact, more than half the U.S. labor force is currently employed in either the production, storage, retrieval, or dissemination of knowledge. Furthermore, the fastest-growing service sector employment opportunities are in finance, insurance, property, and business services, occupations that require educated personnel.[15] Overall, service wages seem to be catching up with wages obtained via manufacturing employment. According to one recent report, service worker pay has risen from a pay disadvantage of 18 to 1 percent below the average of all private sector workers.[16]

The concern over wages associated with service employment is real, and continued acceptance of the industrial management model (presented in Chapter 1) within service industries will do nothing but perpetuate the problem. "Most service enterprises consist of a well-paid brain trust and poorly paid support staff—$500-an-hour lawyers and $5-an-hour secretaries."[17] As a result of the democratic election process in most service economies, a multitude of workers unable to feed and support their families could substantially alter the make-up and direction of future governments. Only time will tell.

> ## > PREDICTED KEYS TO SUCCESS WITHIN THE SERVICE SECTOR

Several common themes to success become clear when examining the growth of the service sector. First, many of the successful firms excel at niche marketing. Niche marketing strategies include focusing on particular consumer groups and/or filling voids in specific locations. For example, the U.S. areas currently experiencing the fastest service firm growth are the small Southern metro areas, where competition is scarce and the population base is rapidly expanding.

The second key to success seems to be directly related to the firm's ability to master technological change. The impact of technology on the worldwide service sector is undeniable. Firms that view technology as a source of innovation as opposed to a "necessary evil" are particularly successful. Improvements in technology have enabled successful service firms to open new avenues of communication between them and their customers. Other technological innovations have led to improved services that permit more customer involvement in the service delivery process, offering the dual advantages of decreasing customer-handling costs while providing customers with convenient services. Automatic teller machines (ATMs) and a variety of online services are prime examples.

**customer retention**
Focusing the firm's marketing efforts toward the existing customer base.

Other keys to success are the service firms' abilities to excel at customer service and develop compelling service experiences. Because of the absence of a tangible product, successful service firms must look to their customer service delivery systems to differentiate themselves from competitors. In 1898, Caesar Ritz, the founder of Ritz Hotels, became the manager of the struggling Savoy Hotel in London. Ritz understood men and women and their desire for beautiful things, and he went to great lengths to achieve the atmosphere he desired. First, he turned the Savoy into a center of cultural activity by introducing an orchestra to the dining room and extending the dining period. Proper evening attire was made compulsory, and unescorted women were prohibited from the premises. Ritz also understood his guests' need for romance. For a time, the lower dining room of the Savoy was converted into a Venetian waterway, complete with gondolas and gondoliers who sang Italian love songs. So it seems that regardless of the industry involved, one common thread connects all service firms that are successful—service excellence, the ability to continuously provide courteous, professional, and caring service to customers.[18]

The final key to success, which differentiates successful service firms from mediocre ones, is an understanding of the value of **customer retention**—focusing the firm's marketing efforts toward the existing customer base. Successful service firms understand the multiple benefits of retaining existing customers: (1) the marketing costs associated with retaining customers are much lower than the costs associated with acquiring new customers; (2) existing customers tend to purchase more services more frequently; (3) current customers are more familiar with the firm's personnel and procedures and are therefore more efficient in their service transactions; and (4) reducing customer

© THE IMAGE BANK / GETTY IMAGES

Service excellence, the ability to continuously provide courteous, professional, and caring service to customers, is the one common thread that connects all service firms that are successful.

defections by 5 percent in some industries can increase profits by as much as 50 percent. Businesses commonly lose 50 percent of their customers every 5 years.[19] However, most companies have no idea how many customers are lost or the reasons for their defections.[20] Consequently, companies that do not excel at customer retention are destined to make the same mistakes over and over. The lack of attention paid to customer retention can be explained by the time-honored tradition of **conquest marketing**—the pursuit of new customers as opposed to the retention of existing ones.

*conquest marketing*
The pursuit of new customers as opposed to the retention of existing ones.

## ✳ SUMMARY

This chapter has provided an overview of the service sector by discussing the following:

- the nine supersectors that comprise the service economy
- service classification schemes that identify commonalities among diverse service industries
- the trends and concerns that pertain to the growth of the service economy
- the predicted keys to success within the service sector

It is generally accepted that the service economy includes the "soft parts" of the economy consisting of nine industry supersectors—education and health services, financial activities, government, information, leisure and hospitality, professional and business services, transportation and utilities, wholesale and retail trade, and other services. The *service sector* is one of the three main categories of a developed economy—the other two being *industrial* and *agricultural*. Traditionally, economies throughout the world tend to transition themselves from an *agricultural economy* to an *industrial economy* (e.g., manufacturing and mining) to a *service economy*.

The nine service supersectors illustrate the diversity of activities within the service economy. Many service industries share common service delivery challenges and therefore would benefit from sharing their knowledge with each other. Classification schemes applied solely to services have also been developed to facilitate our understanding of what different types of service operations have in common. Services marketing classes may want to discuss each of these classification schemes and their marketing implications.

Several key forces continue to influence the growth of the service sector. These forces include the emergence of technologically-based e-services, socio-cultural forces derived from an aging population, and the competitive force of "outservicing," which involves the *offshoring, outsourcing*, and *automation* of many services. The continued growth and dominance of the service sector has been met with some criticism. *Materialismic* individuals believe that without manufacturing, there will be little for people to service.

Several guidelines to success become clear when examining the growth and dominance of the service sector across industries. These strategies include excelling at niche marketing; providing customer service and developing compelling service experiences far superior to that offered by competitors; mastering technological change; and excelling at customer retention.

## ✳ KEY TERMS

service economy, 57
e-service, 69
application-on-tap, 70
ASPs, 70
quantization, 73
search, 73
automation, 73
woofs, 73

offshoring, 73
outsourcing, 74
industrialization, 74
materialismo snobbery, 74
dichotomization of wealth, 75
customer retention, 76
conquest marketing, 77

## ✳ DISCUSSION QUESTIONS

1. Rank and discuss the projected growth rates of the nine service supersectors. What do you believe is driving the growth of the three most highly ranked supersectors?
2. What is an e-service?
3. Go to http://www.bls.gov/iag/leisurehosp.htm and click on the Hotel and Other Accommodations Career Guide link found at the bottom of the scrolled page. Discuss working conditions, current and projected employment, occupations, and earnings as they relate to the hotel industry.
4. Service firms can learn a great deal from other firms in other industries. What strategies appear to be linked with success across the service spectrum?
5. Discuss the marketing implications of Table 3.2, "Understanding the Nature of the Service Act."
6. Define and discuss the term *materialismo snobbery.*
7. Compare changing from an agricultural economy to an industrial economy with moving from an industrial economy to a service economy.
8. Discuss the possible political consequences associated with the dichotomization of wealth in the United States.
9. Discuss why the offshoring of services phenomenon is somewhat predictable.
10. How can an e-service minimize the problems caused by inseparability that traditionally impact other types of traditional service firms?

## ✳ NOTES

1. http://www.bls.gov accessed 25 February 2005; http://encyclopedia.thefreedictionary.com accessed 25 February 2005.
2. Thomas S. Kuhn, *The Structure of Scientific Revolutions,* 2nd ed. (Chicago: University of Chicago Press, 1970).
3. Christopher H. Lovelock, "Classifying Services to Gain Strategic Marketing Insights," *Journal of Marketing* 47 (Summer 1983), 9–20.
4. This section was developed from materials obtained from http://www.e-services.hp.com.

5.  Christopher Lovelock and Evert Gummesson, "Whither Services Marketing? In Search of a New Paradigm and Fresh Perspectives," *Journal of Service Research* 7, no. 1 (2004), 20–41. Leyland F. Pitt, Pierre Berthon, and Richard T. Watson, "Cyberservice: Taming service marketing problems with the World Wide Web," *Business Horizons* 42, no. 1 (1999), 11–18.

6.  "Millennial themes: age, education, services," *MLR: The Editor's Desk,* http://stats.bls.gov/opub/ted/1999/nov/wk5/art03.htm.

7.  Robert W. Van Geizen, "Occupational pay in private goods- and service-producing industries," *Compensation and Working Conditions Online* 1, no. 1 (June 1996).

8.  Philip Kotler, *Marketing Management,* 8th ed. (New York: Prentice-Hall, 1995).

9.  Uday Karmarkar, "Will You Survive the Services Revolution?" *Harvard Business Review,* June 2004, Vol. 82, Issue 6, pp. 100–108.

10. Michael E. Raynor, "After Materialismo . . . ," *Across the Board* (July–August 1992), pp. 38–41.

11. http://www.cia.gov/cia/publications/factbook/geos/us.html#Econ accessed 25 February 2005.

12. "Wealth in Services," *The Economist,* February 20, 1993, p. 16.

13. Raynor, "After Materialismo . . . ," p. 41.

14. "The Manufacturing Myth," *The Economist,* March 19, 1994, p. 92.

15. "The Final Frontier," *The Economist,* February 20, 1993, p. 63.

16. Van Giezen, "Occupational Pay."

17. Raynor, "After Materialismo . . . ," p. 41.

18. Richard L. Brush and Teresa Schulz, "Pioneers and Leaders in the Hospitality Industry," in *Hospitality Management,* 7th ed., Robert A. Brymer, ed. (Dubuque, Iowa: Kendall/Hunt Publishing, 1995), 24–34.

19. Frederick F. Reichheld, "Learning from Customer Defections," *Harvard Business Review* (March–April 1996), 56–69.

20. Gabriel R. Gonzalez, K. Douglas Hoffman, and Thomas N. Ingram, "Improving Relationship Selling through Failure Analysis and Recovery Efforts: A Framework and Call to Action," *Journal of Personal Selling and Sales Management* (forthcoming 2005).

# CHAPTER 4

## THE CONSUMER DECISION PROCESS IN SERVICES MARKETING

### CHAPTER OBJECTIVES

*In this chapter we discuss consumer decision process issues as they relate to the purchase of services.*

After reading this chapter, you should be able to:

- Discuss the six steps that comprise the consumer decision process model.
- Understand the special considerations of service purchases as they pertain to the prepurchase, consumption, and postpurchase stages of the consumer decision process model.
- Describe models that attempt to explain the consumer's postpurchase evaluation.

*"The consumer's mind is still closed to us; it is a 'black box' that remains sealed. We can observe inputs to the box and the decisions made as a result, but we can never know how the act of processing inputs (information) truly happens."*

John E. G. Bateson

## > SKYPEOUT: TWO CENTS A MINUTE TO ANYWHERE IN THE WORLD

© PHOTODISC RED / GETTY IMAGES

The Internet revolution has made a tremendous impact on consumer decision-making processes. The Web has acted as a new source of stimuli that has opened consumer eyes to whole new sets of unforeseen needs and wants. Information search is now available at a click of a button, and chat groups and other online third-party sources provide additional insight into evaluating alternatives. Once a choice has been selected, the Web provides a plethora of purchase avenues and allows us to share our own insights pertaining to the product after purchase and use. Clearly, the Web has revolutionized consumer decision making.

In addition to transforming consumer decision making, the Web has offered a number of service offerings that are new to the world. Skype is one such product that may very well transform the telecommunications industry forever. According to Michael Powell, FCC Chairman, "I knew it was over when I downloaded Skype. The world will change now inevitably." Over the years, communications have come a long way—we have beat drums, sent smoke signals, used human messengers, wrote letters that were sent by Pony Express, tapped out telegraph messages, made phone calls, sent email, communicated through the use of cell phones, and now perhaps we may just use the Web to talk. The best news of all is that calls on Web-based services such as Skype are free or at least very close to it! How will the likes of Verizon, AT&T, T-Mobile, and Sprint ever compete?

Not so long ago, using your computer's voice-enabled capabilities to talk to someone else on the Net was best left to geeks. Quality was poor, connections were spotty, and you had to be somewhat of a technology whiz-kid to figure it all out. Today, however, much has changed. Thanks to advances in technology, the spread of broadband connections around the world, and free Internet telephony services, quality calls can be made from one computer to another, absolutely free! If you would like to connect to a land-line, users of "SkypeOut" can talk to anyone in the world for roughly two cents a minute. Leading the charge in this free-for-all include service firms such as Skype (http:// www.skype.com), Free World Dialup (http://www.freeworlddialup.com), and Babble (htpp://www.babble.com).

Skype receives the highest marks in terms of ease of use. Users simply download free software from the company's website and select a name and password. Calls are easily dialed from an on-screen dial pad or from the caller's call list. Recipients of the call simply click on a receiver icon that appears on their screen and the call is then connected. Call quality is typically excellent and calls generally go through quickly and easily. The service does require that users have their own headsets equipped with earpieces and microphones. According to Skype, anyone with a PC, Mac, or Pocket PC can make free calls to any other Skype user in the world. To date, the number of Skype users is approximately 25 million people, and that number is growing at a rate of 140,000 people a day.

Skype is similar to Voice Over Internet Protocol (VOIP) that is rapidly eroding the profits of traditional land-line companies as well as the giants of the mobile-phone industry. Skype becomes even more appealing with the expansion of Wi-Fi hot spots and the ever increasing availability of Wi-Fi devices that currently provide very cheap voice services over the Internet. The industry is still in the early growth stages but companies such as Cisco, Vonage, and T-Mobile are scrambling to include voice over Wi-Fi to their service mix.

Sources: Mark Halper, "What Worries Mobile Operators," *Fortune (Europe)*, 150, no. 9 (November 15, 2004), 18–19; Ronalee R. Roha and Elizabeth Kountze, "Free Global Calls," *Kiplinger's Personal Finance*, 59, no. 4 (April 2005), 92; Dan Sweeny, "Sum of All Fears," *America's Network*, (November 15, 2004), 16–20.

> ## INTRODUCTION

Consumer orientation lies at the heart of the marketing concept.[1] As marketers, we are required to understand our consumers and to build our organizations around them. This requirement is particularly important for services, which in many instances still tend to be operations dominated rather than customer oriented (see Figure 4.1). Hence, today it is more important than ever to understand consumers, how they choose among alternative services offered to them, and how they evaluate these services once they have received them.

Throughout the three stages of *prepurchase, consumption, and postpurchase evaluation,* the consumer must be using a process or model to make his or her decision. Although a variety of models have been developed and are discussed in this chapter, it is important to point out that no model is wholly accurate. As the quote at the beginning of the chapter says, "The consumer's mind is still closed to us; it is a 'black box' that remains sealed. We can observe inputs to the box and the decisions made as a result, but we can never know how the act of processing inputs (information) truly happens."

Why, then, bother with such models? Whether marketing managers like it or not, every time they make marketing decisions, they are basing their decisions on some model of how the consumer will behave. Quite often these models are implicit and seldom shared with others, representing, in effect, the marketing manager's own experience. However, every time a price is changed, a new product is launched, or advertising appears, some assumption has been made about how the consumer will react.

The purpose of this chapter is to discuss the consumer decision process as it relates to the purchase of services. Due to the unique characteristics of services, differences exist between the way consumers make decisions regarding services versus goods. This chapter has been constructed in two sections. The first section is a broad overview of the consumer decision-making process. It provides a summary of the process and its applications to marketing decisions. The second section of the chapter is dedicated to specific considerations about the consumer decision-making process as it relates to services.

> ## THE CONSUMER DECISION PROCESS: AN OVERVIEW

**consumer decision process**
The three-step process consumers use to make purchase decisions; includes the prepurchase stage, the consumption stage, and the postpurchase evaluation stage.

To market services effectively, marketing managers need to understand the thought processes used by consumers during each of the three stages of the **consumer decision process:** the prepurchase choice among alternatives, the consumer's reaction during consumption, and the postpurchase evaluation of satisfaction (see Figure 4.2). Although we can never truly know the thought process used by the individual when making that choice, the consumer decision process helps to structure our thinking and to guide our marketing research regarding consumer behavior. Let's begin this discussion by focusing on the prepurchase stage of the model, which includes the stimulus, problem awareness, information search, and evaluation of alternatives.

---

**FIGURE 4.1**      **EXAMPLE OF OPERATIONS-DOMINATED COMMUNICATIONS**

1700 EASTWOOD RD
PO BOX 1110
WILMINGTON NC 28402

# Customer Bill

page 1 of 2

| Account | 872 675 5229 |
|---|---|
| Date mailed | Oct 3, 1996 |
| Usage period | Sep 4 - Oct 2 |
| Payment received - Sep 30 | $197.22 |
| **Total due** | **$146.86** |
| **Payment due** | **Oct 28** |

*Thank you for your last payment!*

00011606  1 AC  0.230  00  **AUTOCR **C064

Hurricane Fran has made things tough for many of us by bringing financial hardship and inconvenience. In addition to restoring your power, we are here to answer billing questions and to find a payment option that will work for you. If you have questions, or face a financial hardship due to Fran, please call 1-800-228-8485.

## Usage

| Meter number | R71133 |
|---|---|
| Readings: Oct  2 | 60947 |
| Sep  4 | - 58872 |
| Kwh usage | 2075 |

*Total Peak Registration*

| On-peak KW | Sep 11 at  8:15 pm | 13.35 |
|---|---|---|
| On-peak KW | Oct  1 at  8:00 am | 7.50 |
| Off-peak KW | Sep 29 at  7:30 pm | 13.72 |
| Off-peak KW | Oct  1 at 10:15 pm | 5.98 |

**Billing**
Residential-
Time of Use
Demand rate

| | | | | 28 Days |
|---|---|---|---|---|
| Basic customer charge | | | | 9.85 |
| *Summer, September 04 - September 30* | | | | |
| On-peak KWH | 777 kwh | x | $0.04301 | 33.4188 |
| Off-peak KWH | 1,226 kwh | x | $0.02927 | 35.8850 |
| On-peak KW at .9361 proration | 13.35 kw | x | $5.02000 | 62.7346 |
| *Non-summer, October 1 - October 02* | | | | |
| On-peak KWH | 53 kwh | x | $0.04301 | 2.2795 |
| Off-peak KWH | 19 kwh | x | $0.02927 | 0.5561 |
| On-peak KW at .0639 proration | 7.50 kw | x | $3.73000 | 1.7876 |
| Energy conservation discount | | | | -6.8331 |
| Total R-TOUD Rate Billing | | | | 139.68 |

*On-peak kw proration factor*

| Non-summer  on-peak kwh | 53 kwh / | 830 kwh | .0639 |
|---|---|---|---|
| Summer  on-peak kwh | 777 kwh / | 830 kwh | .9361 |
| Total on-peak kwh | 830 | | |

**SLR rate**

| | | | 28 Days |
|---|---|---|---|
| *Sodium vapor lights,    8 kwh,   9500 lumens, enclosed* | | | |
| Residential lighting | 1 Light  x | $2.90 | 2.90 |
| 3% North Carolina sales tax | | | 4.28 |
| Total due | | | $146.86 |

The first page of a typical electric bill is dominated by operations-oriented information. Company bills are often the only form of communication with customers, yet most fail to communicate with customers effectively.

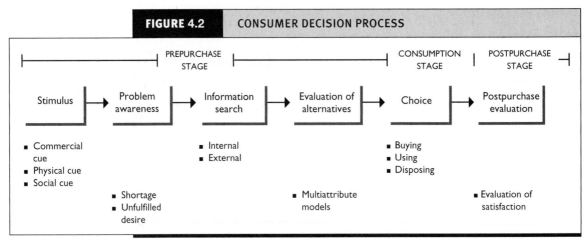

**FIGURE 4.2     CONSUMER DECISION PROCESS**

## THE PREPURCHASE STAGE: THE STIMULUS

*stimulus*
The thought, action, or motivation that incites a person to consider a purchase.

The prepurchase stage of the consumer decision process refers to all consumer activities occurring before the acquisition of the service. This stage begins when an individual receives a **stimulus** that may incite the person to consider a purchase.[2] The stimulus may be a commercial cue, a social cue, or a physical cue. **Commercial cues** are the result of promotional efforts. For example, a consumer may be exposed to a commercial about a local college. As a result, the individual may begin to assess his or her current situation and the possibility of enrolling at a university to pursue a degree. Similarly, **social cues** are obtained from the individual's peer group or from significant others. For example, watching friends leave for college in the fall may incite an individual to consider furthering his or her own education. The stimulus may also be the result of a **physical cue** such as thirst, hunger, or various other biological cues. Hypothetically, an individual may enroll in a university as a response to a biological need to find a suitable partner for marriage and to begin a family.

*commercial cue*
An event or motivation that provides a stimulus to the consumer and is a promotional effort on the part of the company.

*social cue*
An event or motivation that provides a stimulus to the consumer, obtained from the individual's peer group or from significant others.

*physical cue*
A motivation, such as thirst, hunger, or another biological cue, that provides a stimulus to the consumer.

## THE PREPURCHASE STAGE: PROBLEM AWARENESS

*problem awareness*
The second phase of the prepurchase stage, in which the consumer determines whether a need exists for the product.

Once the consumer has received the stimulus, the next phase of the process is problem awareness. During the **problem awareness** phase, the consumer examines whether a need or want truly exists for the product. The need may be based on a **shortage** (a need) or on an **unfulfilled desire** (a want). For example, if the consumer is incited by a commercial cue for a university and is not currently enrolled in any other university, then a shortage exists. In contrast, if the consumer is currently enrolled in a college but in one that he or she no longer values, then an unfulfilled desire exists. If the consumer does not recognize a shortage or unfulfilled desire, the decision process stops at this point. Otherwise, the decision process continues on to the information search stage.

*shortage*
The need for a product or service due to the consumer's not having that particular product or service.

COMPLIMENTS OF THE CAYMAN ISLANDS DEPARTMENT OF TOURISM

Consumers may encounter a commercial cue like this advertisement for American Express, which may kindle a desire to purchase a vacation package using an American Express Card.

**unfulfilled desire**
The need for a product or service due to a consumer's dissatisfaction with a current product or service.

**information search**
The phase in the prepurchase stage in which the consumer collects information on possible alternatives.

**evoked set**
The limited set of "brands" that comes to the consumer's mind when thinking about a particular product category from which the purchase choice will be made.

**internal search**
A passive approach to gathering information in which the consumer's own memory is the main source of information about a product.

**external search**
A proactive approach to gathering information in which the consumer collects new information from sources outside the consumer's own experience.

**evaluation of alternatives**
The phase of the prepurchase stage in which the consumer places a value or "rank" on each alternative.

## THE PREPURCHASE STAGE: INFORMATION SEARCH

The recognition of a problem demands a solution from the individual, and it usually implies that a potential purchase will ensue. The individual searches for alternatives during the information search phase of the prepurchase stage (see E-Services in Action). As the name implies, during the **information search** phase, the consumer collects information regarding possible alternatives. It is clear that in all consumer decision making, consumers seldom consider all feasible alternatives. Instead, they have a limited list of options chosen on the basis of past experience, convenience, and knowledge. This list is often referred to by theorists as the **evoked set**—the set of "brands" that comes to the consumer's mind when thinking about a particular product category and from which the choice will be made.

Returning to our college selection example, when considering alternatives, the consumer may first engage in an internal search. An **internal search** accesses the consumer's own memories about possible alternative colleges. In this example, the previous knowledge may be based on the proximity to a local college, information obtained while watching local sporting events, or listening to older family members reminisce about their own college experiences. An internal search is a passive approach to gathering information.

The internal search may be followed by an **external search,** which would involve the collection of new information obtained via campus visits, talking to friends, and/or reading *U.S. News & World Report*, which rates universities on an annual basis.

## THE PREPURCHASE STAGE: EVALUATION OF ALTERNATIVES

Once relevant information has been collected from both internal and external sources, the consumer arrives at a set of alternative solutions to the recognized problem. The possible solutions are considered in the **evaluation of alternatives** phase of the

## E - S E R V I C E S  *IN ACTION*

> **THE CONSUMER DECISION PROCESS AS IT RELATES TO E-COMMERCE**

The Internet revolution has made a tremendous impact on consumer decision making. Information search, evaluation of alternatives, and purchase processes have been particularly impacted. The following checklist maximizes the effectiveness of e-marketers in each of these areas.

*Information Search:*

1. Ease of navigation—is it easy to move throughout the website?
2. Speed of page downloads—does each page load quickly enough?
3. Effectiveness of search features—are search features returning the information users are looking for?
4. Frequency of product updates—is product information updated often enough to meet user needs?

*Evaluation of Alternatives:*

1. Ease of product comparisons—is it easy to compare the different products the website offers?
2. Product descriptions—are product descriptions accurate, clear, and comprehensive enough to allow customers to make informed decisions?
3. Contacting customer service representatives—are customer service phone numbers easy to locate?
4. In-stock status—are out-of-stock products flagged before the customer proceeds to the checkout process?

*Purchase:*

1. Security and privacy issues—do users feel comfortable transmitting personal information?
2. Checkout process—are users able to move through the checkout process in a reasonable amount of time?
3. Payment options—are payment options offered that non-buyers desire?
4. Delivery options—are delivery options offered that non-buyers desire?
5. Ordering instructions—are ordering instructions easy to understand?

---

Source: Adopted from Jody Dodson, "What's Wrong with Your Website," *Target Marketing*, 23 (2), (February 2000), pp. 135–139.

consumer decision process. This phase may consist of a **nonsystematic evaluation** of alternatives, such as the use of intuition—simply choosing an alternative by relying on a "gut-level feeling"—or it may involve a **systematic evaluation** technique, such as a multiattribute model. Such systematic models utilize a set of formalized steps to arrive at a decision.

Marketing theorists have made extensive use of multiattribute models to simulate the process of evaluating products.[3] According to these models, consumers employ a number of attributes or criteria as basic references when evaluating a service. For example, consumers may compare alternative colleges based on entrance requirements, tuition, academic reputation, and location. Consumers compute their preference for the service by combining the scores of the service on each individual attribute.

Within the evaluation of alternatives phase of the decision process, consumers are assumed to create a matrix similar to the one shown in Table 4.1 to compare alternatives. The example in the table is the choice of a college for an undergraduate degree. Across the top of the table are two types of variables. The first is the evoked set of brands to be evaluated. As previously mentioned, this evoked set will, for various reasons, be less than an exhaustive list of all possible choices; in this example it includes UNT, ETU, SCSU, and SCG. The second type of variable is the importance rating with which the consumer ranks the various attributes that constitute the vertical axis of the table. For example, in Table 4.1, the consumer rates location as the most important attribute, followed by tuition, and so on. To complete the table, the consumer rates each brand on each attribute based on his or her expectations of each attribute. For example, this particular consumer gives UNT top marks for location, tuition, and admission requirements but perceives the university to be not as strong on academic reputation.

Given such a table, various choice processes have been suggested with which the consumer can use the table to make a decision. The **linear compensatory approach** proposes that the consumer creates a global score for each brand by multiplying the rating of the brand on each attribute by the importance attached to the attribute and adding the scores together. UNT would score 10 x 10 (location) plus 10 x 9 (tuition) plus 10 $\times$ 8 (admission requirements), and so on. The university with the highest score, in this example UNT, is then chosen.

*nonsystematic evaluation*
Choosing among alternatives in a random fashion or by a "gut-level feeling" approach.

*systematic evaluation*
Choosing among alternatives by using a set of formalized steps to arrive at a decision.

*linear compensatory approach*
A systematic model that proposes that the consumer creates a global score for each brand by multiplying the rating of the brand on each attribute by the importance attached to the attribute and adding the scores together.

| **TABLE 4.1** | **A TYPICAL MULTIATTRIBUTE CHOICE MATRIX** | | | | |
|---|---|---|---|---|---|
| | Evoked Sets of Brands | | | | |
| Attributes | UNT | ETU | SCSU | SCG | Importance Weights |
| Location | 10 | 10 | 10 | 9.9 | 10 |
| Tuition | 10 | 10 | 9 | 9 | 9 |
| Admission requirements | 10 | 10 | 10 | 10 | 8 |
| Academic reputation | 8 | 9 | 9 | 9 | 7 |
| Degree programs | 10 | 8 | 8 | 10 | 6 |

*lexicographic approach*
A systematic model that proposes that the consumer makes a decision by examining each attribute, starting with the most important, to rule out alternatives.

Another type of multiattribute approach that has been suggested is the **lexicographic approach**. This approach describes so-called "lazy decision makers" who try to minimize the effort involved. They look at each attribute in turn, starting with the most important, and try to make a decision. The individual whose preferences are shown in Table 4.1 would look first at location and rule out SCG. Next, tuition would rule out SCSU. At this stage, the choice is reduced to UNT and ETU, but admission requirements produces a tie in the scoring. Finally, the choice would be made in favor of ETU based on the next attribute, academic reputation. Thus, a different decision rule results in a different choice: ETU under the lexicographic model and UNT under the linear compensatory model.

Given the popularity of multiattribute models, it is no surprise that they have been used to describe and explain the consumer's service decision processes. The merit of these models lies in their simplicity and explicitness. The attributes identified cover a wide range of concerns related to the service experience, and they are easily understood by service managers. For example, analyzing consumer multiattribute models provides the following:

- a list of alternatives that are included in the evoked set
- the list of criteria that consumers consider when making purchase decisions
- the importance weights attached to each criteria
- performance beliefs associated with a particular firm
- performance beliefs associated with the competition

The tasks for management when using these models are relatively straightforward. For example, advertising can be used to stress a particular attribute on which the firm's service appears to be weak in the mind of consumers. A college may have had a poor academic reputation in the past, but advertising may change consumer perceptions by featuring the school's accomplishments. If necessary, competitive advertising can also be used to try and reduce the attribute scores obtained by competitors. For example, many regional universities are attracting students by comparing the student/instructor ratio of large universities to their own ratios.

## THE CONSUMPTION STAGE: CHOICE

Thus far, we have discussed the prepurchase stage of the consumer decision process, which described the stimulus, problem awareness, information search, and evaluation of alternatives phases. An important outcome of the prepurchase stage is a decision to buy a certain brand of the product category. During this consumption stage, the consumer may make a *store choice*—deciding to purchase from a particular outlet, or a *nonstore choice*—deciding to purchase from a catalog, the Internet, or a variety of mail-order possibilities. This decision is accompanied by a set of expectations about the performance of the product. In the case of goods, the consumer then uses the product and disposes of any solid waste remaining. The activities of buying, using, and disposing are grouped together and labeled the **consumption process**.[4]

*consumption process*
The activities of buying, using, and disposing of a product.

Maintaining a long-term relationship with the same service provider, such as going to the same hairstylist everytime; reduces the perceived risk associated with the purchase. In a sense, customers are "brand loyal" to their service providers as well as to the products they buy.

## THE POSTPURCHASE STAGE: POSTPURCHASE EVALUATION

Once a choice has been made and as the product is being consumed, postpurchase evaluation takes place. During this stage, consumers may experience varying levels of cognitive dissonance—doubt that the correct purchase decision has been made. Marketers often attempt to minimize the consumer's **cognitive dissonance** by reassuring the customer that the correct decision has been made. Strategies to minimize cognitive dissonance include aftersale contact with the customer, providing a reassuring letter in the packaging of the product, providing warranties and guarantees, and reinforcing the consumer's decision through the firm's advertising. For example, learning through the college's advertising that the school has been nationally recognized by *U.S. News & World Report* would positively reinforce the consumer's enrollment decision. Simply stated, postpurchase evaluation is all about customer satisfaction, and customer satisfaction is the key outcome of the marketing process. Customer satisfaction is achieved when consumers' perceptions meet or exceed their expectations (see Global Services in Action). Customer satisfaction is an end in itself, but is also the source of word-of-mouth recommendations and can thus stimulate further purchases.

*cognitive dissonance*
Doubt in the consumer's mind regarding the correctness of the purchase decision.

During the evaluation process of the postpurchase stage, multiattribute models can once again be utilized. For this process, the choice of schools is replaced by two columns. The first is the score expected by the consumer on each attribute. The second is the perceived score on each attribute obtained by the consumer after enrollment. The satisfaction score is then derived by creating a global score of the comparisons between perceptions and expectations weighted by the importance of each attribute. This is shown in Table 4.2.

In this example, the customer chose UNT by using the multiattribute choice matrix shown in Table 4.1 and based on the linear compensatory approach. The expected levels on each attribute are, therefore, taken from that matrix. In reality, the tuition was

## GLOBAL SERVICES *IN ACTION*

### > MANAGING VISITOR EXPECTATIONS: FINLAND—WHAT IT IS NOT

Customer satisfaction is commonly measured as a comparison between customer perceptions ("what customers think they received") and customer expectations ("what customers thought they were going to receive"). As such, service marketers can increase customer satisfaction by lowering expectations or by enhancing perceptions. In an attempt to manage tourist expectations about the country and people of Finland, the *Helsinki Guide* publishes the following list in its visitor publications:

1. Finland is not a small country nor is it close to the North Pole.
2. Finland is not awfully cold all the time, and polar bears do not roam the streets of Helsinki.
3. Finnish is not a Slavic language, and only very few Finns speak Russian which, of course, is a pity.
4. Finland did not suffer too badly from any war-time occupation.
5. Finns and Lapps are not the same thing.
6. Finland is not, and has never been a member of the Eastern Block—if there is one anymore.
7. Finns don't drink as much as the rumors say.
8. Finns don't eat just fish.
9. Finland is not the country of limitless sex that it is made out to be.
10. Finland is not in a very uncomfortable position between East and West.

Visitors flying to Finland on Finnair receive an extra dose of "expectation management." During the last hour of flight, a 30-minute film titled "The Finnish Way" is shown to passengers.

Source: virtual.finland.fi/People/way_of_life.asp accessed 15 April 2005; *Helsinki Guide* (2000), Karprint Publishers (Jan–Feb), 16.

| TABLE 4.2 | COLLEGE SELECTION: A POSTPURCHASE EVALUATION FOR UNT | | |
|---|---|---|---|
| Attributes | Expected Score (from Table 4.1) | Perceived Score | Importance Weights |
| Location | 10 | 10 | 10 |
| Tuition | 10 | 9.5 | 9 |
| Admission requirements | 10 | 10 | 8 |
| Academic reputation | 8 | 6 | 7 |
| Degree programs | 10 | 10 | 6 |

increased, and the school did not live up to its academic reputation. The consumer, therefore, downgraded his evaluation on those attributes. The smaller the gap between expectations and perceptions, the more positive the postpurchase evaluation.

> ## SPECIAL CONSIDERATIONS PERTAINING TO SERVICES

Although the consumer decision process model applies to both goods and services, unique considerations arise with respect to service purchases. Many of these special considerations can be directly attributed to the unique service characteristics of intangibility, inseparability, heterogeneity, and perishability. The considerations addressed in this part of the chapter help in developing a deeper understanding of the challenges faced when marketing services.

### PREPURCHASE STAGE CONSIDERATIONS: PERCEIVED RISK

In comparison with goods consumers, consumers of services tend to perceive a higher level of risk during the prepurchase decision stage. The concept of perceived risk as an explanation for customer purchasing behavior was first suggested in the 1960s.[5] The central theory is that consumer behavior involves risk in the sense that any action taken by a consumer will produce consequences that he or she cannot anticipate with any certainty, and some of which are likely to be unpleasant. Perceived risk is proposed to consist of two dimensions:

- *Consequence*—the degree of importance and/or danger of the outcomes derived from any consumer decision.
- *Uncertainty*—the subjective possibility of the occurrence of these outcomes.

Surgery provides an excellent example of how consequence and uncertainty play a major role in service purchases. With respect to uncertainty, the consumer may have never undergone surgery before. Moreover, even though the surgeon has performed the operation successfully in the past, the patient is not guaranteed that this particular surgery will end with the same successful outcome. In addition, uncertainty is likely to increase if the patient lacks sufficient knowledge prior to the operation concerning details of the surgery and its aftereffects. The consequences of a poor decision regarding surgery could be life threatening.

#### Types of Risk

As the idea of consumer-perceived risk developed, five types of perceived risk were identified, based on five different kinds of outcomes: financial, performance, physical, social, and psychological.[6] **Financial risk** assumes that financial loss could occur if the purchase goes wrong or fails to operate correctly. **Performance risk** relates to the idea that the item or service purchased will not perform the task for which it was purchased. The **physical risk** of a purchase can emerge if something does go wrong and injury is inflicted on the purchaser.

**financial risk**
The possibility of a monetary loss if the purchase goes wrong or fails to operate correctly.

**performance risk**
The possibility that the item or service purchased will not perform the task for which it was purchased.

**physical risk**
The possibility that if something does go wrong, injury could be inflicted on the purchaser.

In the competitive cell phone industry, consumers frequently choose a wireless service based on the wireless carrier's performance claims such as coverage area and voice clarity. Wireless carriers vigorously promote performance claims to reduce consumers' perceived performance risk.

© STOCKBYTE PLATINUM / GETTY IMAGES

**social risk**
The possibility of a loss in personal social status associated with a particular purchase.

**psychological risk**
The possibility that a purchase will affect an individual's self-esteem.

**Social risk** suggests that there might be a loss of personal social status associated with a particular purchase (e.g., a fear that one's peer group will react negatively—"You bought this?"). **Psychological risk** pertains to the influence of the purchase upon the individual's self-esteem. For example, you will not consider wearing certain clothes, or you will refuse to own certain cars because they are not consistent with your self-image.

### Risk and Standardization

Much of the heightened level of perceived risk can be attributed to the difficulty in producing a standardized service product. In Chapter 2, we introduced the concept of heterogeneity. Because a service is an experience involving highly complex interactions, it is, not surprisingly, very difficult to replicate the experience from customer to customer or from day to day.[7] As a result, the customer may find it difficult to predict precisely the quality of service he or she will be buying. The fact that Brown's Auto Repair Shop did a good tune-up for your neighbor does not mean that it will perform on the same level for you. Perceived risk, therefore, tends to be higher for purchasing services in contrast to the purchase of goods.

### Co-Producer Risk

The involvement of the consumer in the "production process of services" is another source of increased perceived risk. Co-producer risk is directly related to the concept of inseparability. Once again, surgery is a good example of the consumer's involvement in the production process. Unlike goods, which can be purchased and taken away, services cannot be taken home and used in private, where the buyer's mistakes will not be visible. Instead, the consumer must take part in the ritual of the service itself. To be part of such a process and not to know exactly what is going on clearly increases the uncertainty about the consequences, particularly the physical consequences of being involved in a service encounter such as surgery, or the social consequences of doing the "wrong" thing, such as wearing the wrong type of clothing to an important dinner party.

### Risk and Information

Others have argued that the higher levels of risk associated with service purchases are due to the limited information that is readily available before the purchase decision is made. For example, the economics literature suggests that goods and services possess three different types of attributes:[8]

- *Search attributes*—attributes that can be determined prior to purchase.
- *Experience attributes*—attributes that can be evaluated only during and after the production process.
- *Credence attributes*—attributes that cannot be evaluated confidently even immediately after receipt of the good or service.

Because of the intangible nature of services, it is often extremely difficult for consumers to objectively evaluate a service before it is bought. Services thus have very few search attributes. In contrast, goods can be touched, seen, smelled, heard, and, in some instances, tasted prior to purchase and are therefore predominantly characterized by search attributes.

A large proportion of the properties possessed by services (e.g., the friendliness of the flight attendants of a particular airline or the skill level of a hairstylist) can be discovered by consumers only during and after the consumption of the service; these are thus experience attributes. Moreover, some of the properties of many services (e.g., how well a car has been repaired by a body shop or how well your doctor performs services) cannot be assessed even after the service is completed; these are called credence attributes. All in all, due to the properties of intangibility (which limits search attributes), inseparability (which increases credence attributes), and the variation in quality provided by service personnel, services tend to be characterized by experience and credence attributes.

### Risk and Brand Loyalty

If we start with the premise that consumers do not like taking risks, then it would seem obvious that they will try, whenever possible, to reduce risk during the purchase process. One strategy is to be brand- or store-loyal.[9] Brand loyalty is based on the degree to which the consumer has obtained satisfaction in the past. If consumers have been satisfied in the past with their supplier of service, they have little incentive to risk trying someone or something new. For example, satisfied clients of Citigroup may see little reason to switch their loyalty to another insurance and financial service provider (see B2B Services in Action).

Having been satisfied in a high-risk purchase, a consumer is less likely to experiment with a different purchase. Maintaining a long-term relationship with the same service provider, in and of itself, helps to reduce the perceived risk associated with the purchase. This is why it is common to observe consumers acquiring services from the same physician, dentist, and hairstylist over long periods of time.

Brand loyalty may also be higher in purchasing services due to the limited number of alternative choices available. This is particularly true of professional services, where acceptable substitutes may not be available. In contrast, consumers of goods generally have more substitutes available in a given area. Moreover, purchasing alternative goods does not represent the same level of increased risk as purchasing alternative services.

## B 2 B  S E R V I C E S  *IN ACTION*

> ### CITIGROUP: BUSINESS-TO-BUSINESS FINANCIAL SERVICES

Citigroup provides world-class global business-to-business financial services for small business, corporate clients, and government agencies. Citigroup provides many services to small business customers, including: small business banking, leasing, brokerage services, cash management, retirement solution, credit card merchant services, and business as well as travel credit cards. For small business banking, Citigroup allows their clients free access to customizable online banking systems to manage all their financial business. Citigroup credit card services provide free downloadable credit card transaction history that integrates with Quicken, QuickBooks and Microsoft Money. Citigroup also provides retirement solutions for businesses big and small. Citigroup financial consultants can tailor a retirement plan specific to each company's needs.

In addition to small business solutions, Citigroup also provides a variety of services for their corporate clients. Stock plan services include an integrated family of stock plan services such as employee stock options and stock purchase plan administration. In addition, Citigroup offers an online program called Benefit Access. Benefit Access allows clients to view employer-paid benefit account information such as 401K, 529 college savings plans, stock option plans, and deferred compensation plans. Treasury and cash management services provide solutions that help businesses manage their working capital more effectively. Citibank electronic accounts simplify payment processes. Citigroup also offers numerous fund and service securities to its corporate clients.

In addition to serving small businesses and corporate clients, Citigroup takes a consultative approach to government services by designing programs to fit their individual needs. Government services help streamline transaction, accounting, reporting, and payment processes. Citigroup government services also include analysis and control of purchasing and travel-related expenses. Citigroup prides itself on providing the best business-to-business services to its respective markets. Citigroup is the end result of the Citicorp and Travelers merger that occurred in 1998. Citigroup has 275,000 employees working in more than 100 countries and territories.

Source: www.citigroup.com accessed 13 April 2005. Original draft provided by Rhianna Bain, Sean Bruner, Jamie Fisher, and Christina Manweiler.

**switching costs**
Costs that accrue when changing vendors.

Finally, brand loyalty may also be higher for services due to the **switching costs** that can accrue when changing from one service provider to another. A wide array of switching costs can be accrued, depending on the product involved. Consider, for example, the switching costs involved in changing from one brand of canned vegetables to another compared with the costs involved in changing banks. Typical switching costs include the following:

- *Search costs*—the time it takes to seek out new alternatives.
- *Transaction costs*—the costs associated with first-time visits, such as new x-rays when changing dentists.
- *Learning costs*—costs such as time and money that are associated with learning new systems, such as new versions of software packages.
- *Loyal customer discounts*—discounts that are given for maintaining the same service over time, such as accident-free auto insurance rates. Such discounts are sacrificed when switching from one supplier to the next.
- *Customer habit*—costs associated with changing established behavior patterns.
- *Emotional costs*—emotional turmoil that one may experience when severing a long-term relationship with a provider. Emotional costs are particularly high when a personal relationship has developed between the client and the provider.
- *Cognitive costs*—costs in terms of the time it takes simply thinking about making a change in service providers.

## PREPURCHASE STAGE CONSIDERATIONS: THE IMPORTANCE OF PERSONAL SOURCES OF INFORMATION

Another special consideration during the prepurchase stage is the importance of personal sources of information. Research has shown that in the area of communications, personal forms such as word-of-mouth references and information from opinion leaders are often given more importance than company-controlled communications. A reference from a friend becomes more important when the purchase to be made has a greater risk. For example, a visit to a new hairdresser can be stressful since the outcome of the service will be highly visible. That stress can be reduced by a recommendation from someone whose judgment the consumer trusts. The consumer will then feel more confident about the outcome.

Similarly, evidence suggests that opinion leaders play an important role in the purchase of services. An opinion leader in a community is an individual who is looked to for advice. Within the perceived-risk framework, an opinion leader can be viewed as a source of reduced social risk. A woman who visits a hairdresser for the first time may feel uncertain about the quality of the outcome. However, she might be reassured by the fact that the friend who recommended the service is widely known to have good judgment in such matters and will convey this to others in their mutual social group. In this way, the opinion leader's judgment partially substitutes for the consumer's own.

In addition to reducing perceived risk, the importance of personal sources of information to service consumers is relevant for a number of other reasons. Due to the intangibility of services, mass media is not as effective in communicating the qualities of the service compared with personal sources of information. For example, would you feel comfortable purchasing services from a surgeon who is featured in television advertising? Moreover, would it be feasible for the physician to adequately describe the surgical procedure during a 30-second television spot? Overall, personal sources of information become more important as objective standards for evaluation decrease and as the complexity of the product being marketed increases.

Other reasons that consumers rely to such a great extent on personal sources of information is that nonpersonal sources may simply not be available because of professional restrictions or negative attitudes regarding the use of advertising. Alternatively, many service providers are small and may lack the resources or knowledge to advertise. How many marketing or communications classes do you suppose your dentist or physician enrolled in while attending college? Most have no idea what a target market is, what a marketing mix is for, or what a marketing plan entails. Regardless of their training and subsequent status, professional service providers are operating businesses and must effectively compete in order to maintain their livelihoods. The bottom line is that many professional service providers either lack the knowledge or feel uncomfortable marketing their services.

## PREPURCHASE STAGE CONSIDERATIONS: FEWER ALTERNATIVES TO CONSIDER

In comparison with goods, consumers of services tend to evaluate a smaller number of alternative sources of supply during the prepurchase stage for a variety of reasons. First, each service provider tends to offer only one brand. For example, State Farm Insurance sells only one brand of insurance—State Farm. Similarly, your dentist provides only one brand of dental care. In contrast, consumers shopping for a blender generally have many brands to consider at each retail location.

The second reason the evoked set tends to be smaller pertains to the number of establishments providing the same service. The tendency in services is to have a smaller number of outlets providing the same service. For example, a market area can support only so many psychologists, dentists, and medical doctors. In comparison, similar goods tend to be available in many locations. The difference between the distribution of goods and services relates directly to the diversification of the product mix. Retailers of goods sell many products under many brand names, thereby earning their revenues through many different sources. Due to the diversified product mix, the same goods are available at many locations. In contrast, the survival of the service firm is dependent upon selling only one brand of service.

A third reason consumers consider fewer service alternatives relates to the lack of available prepurchase information. Consumers of services simply are not aware of as many service substitutes and/or choose not to undertake the time-consuming task of obtaining information from competing service providers. In contrast, consumers of goods often simply look at what is on the store's shelves and are able to compare prices as well as a number of other factors such as ingredients, construction quality, feel, and scent.

## PREPURCHASE STAGE CONSIDERATIONS: SELF-SERVICE AS A VIABLE ALTERNATIVE

Another difference between goods and services in the prepurchase choice stage of the consumer decision process is that self-provision often becomes a viable alternative for such services as lawn care, fence installation, housekeeping, painting, and a number of other services. In comparison, consumers rarely consider building a refrigerator over purchasing one from a local retailer. For obvious reasons, many professional service providers are not generally competing against the self-service alternative. However, some self-service solutions such as homeopathic medicines do exist.

## CONSUMPTION STAGE CONSIDERATIONS

The consumption of goods can be divided into three activities: buying, using, and disposing. The three activities occur in a definite buy-use-dispose order and have clear boundaries between them. The customer buys a box of detergent at a supermarket, uses it at home in the washing machine, and disposes of the empty box after the detergent is used up.

This scenario does not apply to the consumption of services, however. First of all, no clear-cut boundary or definite sequence exists between the acquisition and the use of services because there is no transfer of ownership. Because of the prolonged interactions between the customer and the service provider, the production, acquisition, and use of services become entangled and appear to be a single process.[10] Furthermore, the concept of disposal is irrelevant because of the intangibility and experiential nature of services.

Without a doubt, the consumption stage is more complex for services in comparison with that of goods. The servuction system concept introduced in Chapter 1 suggests that the benefits bought by a customer consist of the experience that is delivered through an interactive process. Even when a service is rendered to something that the consumer owns, such as a car, rather than to the individual's person, the service production/consumption process often involves a sequence of personal interactions (face to face or by telephone) between the customer and the service provider.[11]

Interactions between the customer and the company's facilities and personnel are inevitable. It is from these interpersonal and human-environment interactions that the service experience is acquired.[12] Perhaps the most important outcome of these interactions is the contradiction of the idea that postchoice evaluation occurs only at a certain point in time after use.[13] The use of goods is essentially free from any kind of direct marketer influence. For example, the manufacturer of the breakfast cereal that you ate this morning had no interaction with you whatsoever. Hence, consumers of goods can choose when, where, and how they will use a good. On the other hand, service firms play an active role in customer consumption activities because services are produced and consumed simultaneously.

No service can be produced or used with either the consumer or the service firm absent. Due to the extended service delivery process, many believe that the consumer's postchoice evaluation occurs both during and after the use of services, rather than only afterward. In other words, consumers evaluate the service while they are experiencing the service encounter during the consumption stage as well as during the postpurchase stage.

From a marketer's point of view, this opens up the prospect of being able to directly influence that evaluation. Hence, the restaurant manager who visits diners' tables and asks, "How is your dinner this evening?" is able to catch problems and change evaluations in a way that the manufacturer of a packaged good cannot.

## POSTCHOICE CONSIDERATIONS

The postpurchase evaluation of services is a complex process. It begins soon after the customer makes the choice of the service firm he or she will be using and continues throughout the consumption and postconsumption stages. The evaluation is influenced by the unavoidable interaction of a substantial number of social, psychological, and situational variables. Service satisfaction relies not only on the properties of the four elements of the servuction system—contact personnel, servicescape, other customers, and internal organization systems—but also on the synchronization of these elements in the service production/consumption process.

The success or failure of a service firm can be at least partly attributed to management's ability or inability to manipulate the customer experience as the output of a collection of interpersonal interactions (client versus client, client versus employee) and human-environment interactions (employee versus working environment and supporting facilities, customer versus service environment and supporting facilities). A number of proposed models attempt to describe the process by which consumers evaluate their purchase decisions.

### Postchoice Models: The Expectancy Disconfirmation Model

*expectancy disconfirmation model* The model in which consumers evaluate services by comparing expectations with perceptions.

How does service satisfaction arise during the consumption and postpurchase stages? A number of approaches have been suggested, but perhaps the simplest and most powerful is the **expectancy disconfirmation model**. The concept of this model is straightforward. Consumers evaluate services by comparing expectations with perceptions. If the perceived service is better than or equal to the expected service, then consumers are satisfied. Hence, ultimately customer service is achieved through the effective management of customer perceptions and expectations.

It is crucial to point out that this entire process of comparing expectations with perceptions takes place in the mind of the customer. It is the perceived service that matters, not the actual service. One of the best examples that reinforces this issue involves a high-rise hotel. The hotel was receiving numerous complaints concerning the time guests had to wait for elevator service in the lobby. Realizing that from an operational viewpoint, the speed of the elevators could not be increased, and that attempting to schedule the guests' elevator usage was futile, management installed mirrors in the lobby next to the elevator bays. Guest complaints were reduced immediately—the mirrors provided a means for the guests to occupy their waiting time. Guests were observed using the mirror to observe their own appearance and that of others around them. In reality, the speed of the elevators had not changed; however, the perception was that the waiting time was now acceptable.

It is also feasible to manage expectations in order to produce satisfaction without altering in any way the quality of the actual service delivered. Motel Six, for example, by downplaying its service offering in its cleverly contrived advertising, actually increases consumer satisfaction by lowering customer expectations prior to purchase. The firm's advertising effectively informs consumers of both what to expect and what not to expect: "A good clean room for $39.99 . . . a little more in some places . . . a little less in some others . . . and remember . . . we'll leave the light on for you." Many customers simply do not use services such as swimming pools, health clubs, and full-service restaurants, which are associated with the higher-priced hotels. Economy-minded hotels, such as Motel Six, are carving out a niche in the market by providing the basics. The result is that customers know exactly what they will get ahead of time and are happy not only with the quality of the service received but also with the cost savings.

### Postchoice Models: The Perceived-Control Perspective

Another model that assists in describing the postpurchase stage is the **perceived-control perspective**. The concept of control has drawn considerable attention from psychologists. They argue that in modern society, in which people no longer have to bother about the satisfaction of primary biological needs, the need for control over situations in which one finds oneself is a major force driving human behavior.[14] Rather than being treated as a service attribute, as implied by multiattribute models, perceived control can be conceptualized as a superfactor—a global index that summarizes an individual's experience with a service. The basic premise of this perspective is that during the service experience, the higher the level of control over the situation perceived by consumers, the higher their satisfaction with the service. A similar positive relationship is proposed between service providers' experience of control and their job satisfaction.

In a slightly different way, it is equally important for the service firm itself to maintain control of the service experience. If the consumer gets too much control, the economic position of the firm may be affected as consumers tip the value equation in their favor, even to an extent that the firm may begin to lose money. On the other hand, if the service employees take complete control, consumers may become unhappy and leave. Even if this does not happen, the operational efficiency of the firm may be impaired. This three-cornered struggle among the service firm, its employees, and consumers is described in Figure 4.3.

*perceived-control perspective*
A model in which consumers evaluate services by the amount of control they have over the perceived situation.

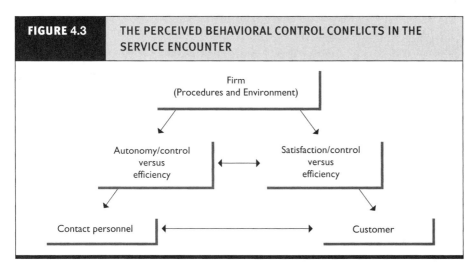

**FIGURE 4.3    THE PERCEIVED BEHAVIORAL CONTROL CONFLICTS IN THE SERVICE ENCOUNTER**

Source: Adapted from John E. G. Bateson, "Perceived Control and the Service Encounter," in John A. Czepiel, Michael R. Solomon, and Carol F. Suprenant, eds., *The Service Encounter* (Lexington, MA: Heath, 1985), pp. 67–82.

Services can be thought of as a consumer's giving up cash and control in exchange for benefits, with each party seeking to gain as much advantage as possible. But it would appear that no one can truly win in such a "contest." In fact, the concept of control is much broader than implied. Behavioral control, the ability to control what is actually going on, is only part of the idea. Research shows that cognitive control is also important. Thus, when consumers perceive that they are in control, or at least that what is happening to them is predictable, the effect can be the same as that achieved by behavioral control. In other words, it is the perception of control, not the reality, that is important.

Managerially, this concept raises a number of interesting ideas. The first idea raised is the value of the information given to consumers during the service experience in order to increase their sense that they are in control and that they know what will happen next. This is particularly important for professional service firms, which often assume that simply doing a good job will make their clients happy—they forget that their clients may not have heard from them for more than a month and might be frantic due to the lack of contact and little or no information. It is equally important to an airline that delays a flight after passengers have boarded but fails to let them know what is happening or how long the delay will be.

Similarly, if a firm is due to make changes in its operation that will have an impact on consumers, it is important that those consumers be forewarned. If they are not, they may perceive themselves to be "out of control" and become dissatisfied with the service received to the extent that they change suppliers.

The control perspective raises interesting issues about the trade-off between predictability and choice. Operationally, one of the most important strategic issues is the amount of choice to give the consumer. Because both choice and predictability (standardization) can contribute to a sense of control, it is crucial to determine which is the more powerful source of control for the consumer.

### Postchoice Models: The Script Perspective—All the World's a Stage and All the People Players

A number of theories in psychology and sociology can be brought together in the ideas of a *script* and a *role*. A role is defined as "a set of behavior patterns learned through experience and communication, to be performed by an individual in a certain social interaction in order to attain a maximum effectiveness in goal accomplishment."[15] The principal idea proposed is that in a service encounter, customers perform roles, and their satisfaction is a function of **role congruence**—whether the actual behaviors by customers and staff are consistent with the expected roles.

*role congruence*
The property of actual behaviors by customers and staff being consistent with their expected roles.

This role congruence thus focuses on the postpurchase phases of a service encounter. The described interaction is two-way, so role congruence is expected to exert an impact on the customer as well as on the service provider. In other words, satisfaction of both parties is likely when the customer and the service provider engage in behaviors that are consistent with each other's role expectation; otherwise, both performers may be upset by the interaction.

The key managerial tasks implied by role theory perspectives are (1) to design roles for the service encounter that are acceptable and capable of fulfilling the needs of both the customers and the service providers and (2) to communicate these roles to both customers and employees so that both have realistic perceptions of their roles as well as those of their partners in their interactions.

Role is assumed to be *extra-individual*. Hence, every individual is expected to display the same predetermined set of behaviors when he or she takes up a certain role, either as a customer or as a service provider. Because role theory originally was not directly concerned with the perception of participants in the service encounter, it is incompatible with the concepts of service evaluation and customer satisfaction. For example, consider that two customers, one an introvert and one an extrovert, may have completely different perceptions and evaluations of interactions with the same chatty service provider. In this case, *intra-individual* variables must be employed in order to explain the differences in customer evaluation and satisfaction.

The role idea can, however, be adapted for use in service situations. This adaptation draws on the psychological idea of a script. The script theory and role theory perspectives appear on the surface to be similar. **Script theory** argues that rules, mostly determined by social and cultural variables, exist to facilitate interactions in daily repetitive events, including a variety of service experiences.[16] These rules shape the participants' expectations in these types of interactions. Furthermore, the rules must be acknowledged and obeyed by all participants if satisfactory outcomes are to be generated. For example, patrons of a fine dining restaurant will have behavioral expectations of their waiter that are consistent with the service setting. Similarly, the waiter will have expectations of the patron's behavior as well. If one participant deviates from the rules, the other co-actors in the service setting will be uncomfortable. Therefore, a satisfied customer is unlikely given a dissatisfied service provider, and a dissatisfied customer is unlikely given a satisfied service provider.

Despite the similarity of the role theory and script theory perspectives, basic differences exist between them. First, the script theory perspective has a wider range of concerns (including the impact of the service setting) and hence is concerned with the whole service experience rather than with only the interpersonal service encounter. Second, scripts are by definition intra-individual and are a function of an individual's experience and personality. Finally, consumer scripts can be revised by service providers who educate consumers about the service process.

The expectancy disconfirmation model, the perceived-control perspective, and the script perspective may not totally reflect reality, but because they are the result of much research in marketing and psychology, they at least allow us to make logical deductions about consumer behavior when making marketing decisions. Moreover, since all the models described here have both strengths and weaknesses, they should be considered complementary rather than mutually exclusive. Managerial insights can be developed more effectively through a combination of these various perspectives as we continue to learn about consumer decision processing.

*script theory*
Argues that rules, mostly determined by social and cultural variables, exist to facilitate interactions in daily repetitive events, including a variety of service experiences.

## * SUMMARY

This chapter has presented consumer decision process issues as they relate to service consumers. The consumer decision process model consists of three main stages: the pre-purchase stage, the consumption stage, and the postpurchase stage. The prepurchase stage consists of the events that occur prior to the consumer's acquisition of the service and includes stimulus reception, problem awareness, information search, and evaluation of alternatives. The outcome of the prepurchase stage is a choice that takes place during the consumption stage. The consumption stage includes the activities of buying, using, and disposing of the product. The postpurchase stage refers to the process by which the consumer evaluates his or her level of satisfaction with the purchase.

Although the consumer decision process model applies to both goods and services, unique considerations arise with respect to services in each of the three stages. Compared with their considerations when purchasing goods, consumers of services during the prepurchase stage of the decision process (1) perceive higher levels of risk to be associated with the purchase; (2) tend to be more brand loyal; (3) rely more on personal sources of information; (4) tend to have fewer alternatives to consider; and (5) often include self-provision as a viable alternative.

The consumption stage is more complex for services in comparison with that of goods as the production, acquisition, and use of services become entangled in a single process. Moreover, due to the extended service delivery process, many believe that the consumer's postchoice evaluation occurs both during and after, rather than only after, the use of services. From a marketer's point of view, this provides the opportunity to directly influence the consumer's evaluation during the service delivery process. Because of the client/company interface, the service provider is able to catch problems and change evaluations in a way that the manufacturer of a packaged good cannot.

Similarly, the postpurchase evaluation of services is also a complex process. The evaluation process begins soon after the customer makes the choice of the service firm he or she will be using and continues throughout the consumption and postconsumption stages. The evaluation is influenced by the unavoidable interaction of a substantial number of social, psychological, and situational variables. Service satisfaction relies not only on the technical quality of the service and the four elements of the servuction system (contact personnel, servicescape, other customers, and internal organizational systems), but also on the synchronization of these elements in the service production/consumption process.

Models that assist in our understanding of the consumer's postpurchase evaluation process include the expectancy disconfirmation model, the perceived-control perspective, and the script perspective. In short, the expectancy disconfirmation model defines satisfaction as meeting or exceeding customer expectations. The perceived-control perspective proposes that during the service experience, the higher the level of control over the situation perceived by consumers, the stronger will be their satisfaction with the service. The script perspective proposes that in a service encounter, customers perform roles, and their satisfaction is a function of role congruence—whether or not the actual behaviors by customers and staff are consistent with the expected roles. Models such as these help us understand how consumer evaluations are processed and indicate areas where service marketers can focus their efforts in pursuit of the ultimate goal of providing customer satisfaction.

## ✳ KEY TERMS

consumer decision process, 82
stimulus, 84
commercial cue, 84
social cue, 84
physical cue, 84
problem awareness, 84
shortage, 84
unfulfilled desire, 85
information search, 85
evoked set, 85
internal search, 85
external search, 85
evaluation of alternatives, 85
nonsystematic evaluation, 87
systematic evaluation, 87

linear compensatory approach, 87
lexicographic approach, 88
consumption process, 88
cognitive dissonance, 89
financial risk, 91
performance risk, 91
physical risk, 91
social risk, 92
psychological risk, 92
switching costs, 94
expectancy disconfirmation model, 98
perceived-control perspective, 99
role congruence, 100
script theory, 101

## ✳ DISCUSSION QUESTIONS

1. In general terms, discuss the value of consumer behavior models.
2. Why do consumers of services perceive higher levels of risk associated with their purchases?
3. Discuss the different types of risk.
4. Define and discuss the following terms: search attributes, experience attributes, and credence attributes. Which type(s) of attributes most accurately apply to services? Explain.
5. Regarding multiattribute models, what is the difference between the linear compensatory approach and the lexicographic approach?
6. Explain why consumers of services tend to be more brand loyal.
7. Why do personal sources of information tend to be more important for consumers of services?
8. Discuss the managerial implications of the client/company interface during the consumption stage.
9. What is the difference between a role and a script?
10. Explain the relevance of the perceived-control model as it relates to the postconsumption stage.

## ✱ NOTES

1. John E. G. Bateson, *Managing Services Marketing: Text and Readings*, 2nd ed. (Fort Worth, TX: The Dryden Press, 1992), p. 93.

2. Adapted from Michael Levy and Barton A. Weitz, *Retailing Management* (Homewood, IL: Irwin, 1992), pp. 117–154.

3. Adapted from John E. G. Bateson, *Managing Services Marketing*.

4. F. Nicosia and R. N. Mayer, "Toward a Sociology of Consumption," *Journal of Consumer Research* 3, 2 (1976), pp. 65–75.

5. D. Guseman, "Risk Perception and Risk Reduction in Consumer Services," in *Marketing of Services*, eds. J. Donnelly and William R. George (Chicago: American Marketing Association, 1981), pp. 200–204; and R. A. Bauer, "Consumer Behavior as Risk Taking," in *Dynamic Marketing for a Changing World,* ed. R. S. Hancock (Chicago: American Marketing Association, 1960), pp. 389–398.

6. L. Kaplan, G. J. Szybilo, and J. Jacoby, "Components of Perceived Risk in Product Purchase; A Cross-Validation," *Journal of Applied Psychology* 59 (1974): pp. 287–291.

7. D. Guseman, "Risk Perception," pp. 200–204.

8. Adapted from John E. G. Bateson, *Managing Services*.

9. Zeithaml, Valerie A., "How Consumer Evaluation Processes Differ between Goods and Services," in *Marketing of Services*, eds. J. Donnelly and William R. George (Chicago: American Marketing Association, 1981), pp. 191–199.

10. Bernard Booms and Jody Nyquist, "Analyzing the Customer/Firm Communication Component of the Services Marketing Mix," in *Marketing of Services*, eds. J. Donnelly and W. George (Chicago: American Marketing Association, 1981), p. 172; and Raymond Fisk, "Toward a Consumption/Evaluation Process Model for Services," in *Marketing of Services*, eds. J. Donnelly and W. George (Chicago: American Marketing Association, 1981), p. 191.

11. Christopher H. Lovelock, "Classifying Services to Gain Strategic Marketing Insights," *Journal of Marketing* 47 (Summer 1983), pp. 9–20.

12. Alan Andrasen, "Consumer Research in the Service Sector," in *Emerging Perspectives on Services Marketing*, eds. L. Berry, G. L. Shostack, and G. Upah (Chicago: American Marketing Association, 1982), pp. 63–64.

13. Raymond Fisk, "Toward a Consumption/ Evaluation Process Model for Services," in *Marketing of Services*, eds. J. Donnelly and W. George (Chicago: American Marketing Association, 1981), p. 191.

14. John E. G. Bateson, "Perceived Control and the Service Encounter," in *The Service Encounter*, eds. John A. Czepiel, Michael R. Solomon, and Carol F. Suprenant (Lexington, MA: Lexington Books, 1984), pp. 67–82.

15. Michael R. Solomon, Carol F. Suprenant, John A. Czepiel, and Evelyn G. Gatman, "A Role Theory Perspective on Dyadic Interactions: The Service Encounter," *Journal of Marketing* 1, 49 (Winter 1985), pp. 99-111.

16. Ruth A. Smith and Michael Houston, "Script-Based Evaluations of Satisfaction with Services," in *Emerging Perspectives in Services Marketing*, eds. L. Berry, G. L. Shostack, and G. Upah (Chicago: American Marketing Association, 1982), pp. 59–62.

# CHAPTER 5

# ETHICAL ISSUES IN SERVICES MARKETING

## CHAPTER OBJECTIVES

*The primary purpose of this chapter is to introduce you to a variety of ethical issues as they pertain to services marketing issues.*

After reading this chapter, you should be able to:

- Describe the difference between ethical decisions and ordinary decisions.
- Understand the reasons that consumers are particularly vulnerable to ethical misconduct within the service sector.
- Describe the moral philosophies upon which individuals base their ethical decisions.
- Appreciate the types of ethical issues that often arise in the business sector.
- Examine factors, other than moral philosophies, that may influence ethical decision making.
- Discuss the consequences of ethical misconduct.
- Explain strategies that attempt to control ethical behavior.

*"Always do right. This will gratify some people, and astonish the rest."*

Mark Twain

© TAXI/GETTY IMAGES

Service marketers have an ethical and social responsibility to enhance society's welfare—including the welfare of its customers, employees, stockholders, and surrounding communities. Many leading service companies actively embrace their responsibility to society and conduct business in an ethical manner. Vail Resorts is an example of such a company.

Like many other service encounters, winter skiing on the Colorado slopes is a shared experience where skiers enhance and detract from one another's skiing experience. Vail Resorts, the owners and operators of Vail, Beaver Creek, Keystone, Breckenridge, and Heavenly ski resorts recognizes the potential threat that skiers pose to one another. Consequently, Vail Resorts has recognized its responsibility to its guests and is aggressively promoting skier safety.

There are many different kinds of winter sports enthusiasts enjoying the ski slopes of the Rocky Mountains. In addition to traditional alpine skiers, the slopes are shared by snowboarders, telemark skiers, blade skiers, ski bikers, cross-country skiers, skiers with disabilities, and skiers with specialized equipment. The needs and abilities within and among each group often differ greatly. In addition to showing courtesy to one another and using good common sense, Vail Resorts has developed "Your Responsibility Code." Vail Resorts hopes that by its guests following the code and sharing the responsibility for safety, everyone will have a great experience.

The Responsibility Code is highly visible in and around Vail Resorts properties. Posted prominently in lodges, on ski maps, and even the support posts of ski lifts, the code reads as follows:

**Your Responsibility Code**

Always stay in control and be able to stop or avoid persons or objects.
People ahead of you have the right of way; it's your responsibility to avoid them.
Do not stop where you obstruct a trail or are not visible from above.
Whenever starting downhill or merging on a trail, look uphill and yield to others.
Always use devices to help prevent runaway equipment.
Observe all posted signs and warnings. Keep off closed trails and out of closed areas.
Prior to using any lift, you must have the knowledge and ability to load, ride, and unload safely.

In addition to skier safety programs, Vail Resorts demonstrates its commitment to social responsibility in a number of other ways that protect the surrounding environment including waste reduction, recycling, chemical management, and educational programming. Keystone Resort's environmental statement typifies Vail Resorts' commitment to the environment:

Keystone resort is entrusted with the stewardship of lands in the beautiful Rocky Mountains and the White River National Forest. We promote renewable energy, resource conservation, recycling, wildlife habitat preservation, and environmental education. Please help us by sharing in this responsibility:

Pack it in, pack it out.
Carpool and use public transportation.
Reduce, Reuse, and Recycle.
Share the mountain. Respect all posted closures.
Spread the word.

Sources: http://mediaguide.sonw.com/info/k.saftey.asp accessed April 11, 2005; and http://mediaguide.snow.com/info/k.env.asp accessed April 11, 2005.

## > INTRODUCTION

The opening vignette provides an example of how Vail Resorts conducts business in a responsible manner. In general terms, *social responsibility* is the collection of marketing philosophies, policies, procedures, and actions intended to enhance society's welfare.[1] Ethics are embedded within a firm's social responsibility. Over the past decade, integrating ethics into the business curriculum has reemerged as an important topic of discussion among marketing educators and practitioners. Originally, business ethics was generally taught as a single course; however, many business schools now believe that business ethics should be taught across the curriculum and that ethical issues as they relate to each topic area should be discussed in greater detail.[2]

Because of the unique opportunities that exist for ethical misconduct in service fields, students of the services marketing course in particular should be made aware of the issues surrounding ethical decision making. Although the majority of service providers fulfill their duties ethically, infamous service providers such as Enron and WorldCom, have provided recent evidence that not all service providers may be trustworthy.

Unique circumstances in the service sector create an ethical environment worth examination and discussion. This chapter presents a variety of ethics-related topics as they pertain to the service sector, including (1) methods of ethical decision making, (2) issues that create ethical conflict, (3) factors influencing ethical decision making, (4) the effects of ethical misconduct, and (5) strategies for controlling ethical behavior.

Note that in this chapter, we do not intend to "preach" what we think is right or wrong. Such a decision is left to your discretion. Unfortunately, as you will live to learn, the appropriateness and/or public acceptance of your decision is usually decided on the evening news or even popular talk shows such as "Oprah" or "Ellen DeGeneres." Our objective is primarily to provide you with food for thought, to encourage **ethical vigilance**—paying close attention to whether one's actions are right or wrong, and to facilitate class discussions about an important subject that is often overlooked. Overall, we hope that the information provided in this chapter will aid in your understanding of ethics and perhaps have an impact on the decisions with which you will be faced as you pursue your career.

*ethical vigilance*
Paying close attention to whether one's actions are "right" or "wrong," and if ethically "wrong" asking why you are behaving in that manner.

## > WHAT ARE ETHICS?

In general, **ethics** are commonly defined as (1) "a branch of philosophy dealing with what is good and bad and with moral duty and obligation" and (2) "the principles of moral conduct governing an individual or group."[3] **Business ethics** comprises moral principles and standards that guide behavior in the world of business.[4] The distinction between an ordinary decision and an ethical one is that values and judgments play a critical role in ethical decisions. In contrast, ordinary decisions are generally decided utilizing a set of preordained acceptable rules.

The field of business ethics is particularly intriguing. On one hand, businesses must make a profit in order to survive. The survival of the firm provides employees salaries with

*ethics*
A branch of philosophy dealing with what is good and bad and with moral duty and obligations; the principles of moral conduct governing an individual or group.

*business ethics*
The principles of moral conduct that guide behavior in the business world.

which employees feed their families and educate their children, thereby leading to the betterment of society. In addition, company profits and employee salaries are taxed, the funds from which furnish the support for various governmental programs. On the other hand, business profits should not be obtained by any means necessary. A trade-off must exist between the firm's desire for profits and what is good for individuals and society.

Sears Auto Centers found themselves in a controversial position as they pondered such trade-offs. It is generally agreed that the marketing concept states that the goal of most for-profit organizations is to recognize and satisfy customer needs while making a profit. Such was the goal of Edward Brennan, chairman of Sears, Roebuck and Company. Under his leadership, market research studies were conducted on customer automotive repair needs. Subsequently, Sears established a preventive maintenance program that instructed the auto repair centers to recommend repair/replacement of parts based on the mileage indicated on the odometer. Concurrently, sales quotas were established for Sears' 850 auto repair centers. Meeting or exceeding these quotas earned bonus money for the service personnel and provided management with an objective means of evaluating employee performance.

The new sales incentive program required the sale of a certain number of repairs or services, including alignments, springs, and brake jobs, every eight hours. Service employees were also able to qualify for bonus money by selling a specified number of shock absorbers or struts for every hour worked. The objective of this program was to meet customer needs while increasing the profits of the auto service centers.

After the program was put into place, the automotive unit became the fastest growing and most profitable unit in recent Sears history. However, a growing number of consumer complaints were lodged against Sears. These complaints sparked investigations by the states of California, New Jersey, and Florida into practices at Sears auto service centers. The state of California alleged that Sears consistently overcharged its customers an average of $223 for unnecessary repairs or work that was never done. Sears contends that its auto centers were merely servicing vehicles based on the manufacturer's suggested maintenance schedule. Moreover, Sears maintains that its failure to make these suggestions for improvements would neglect the safety of the consumer. Consequently, the dilemma for Sears employees concerning what is good for customers and what is good for the company became muddled.[5] Ethical issues as they relate to Sears Auto Centers are discussed throughout the remainder of the chapter.

In general, the public's view about business ethics is not overwhelmingly positive.[6] According to a Business Week/Harris poll, 46 percent of respondents believed that the ethical standards of businesspeople were only average. In addition, 90 percent of respondents believed that white-collar crime was somewhat or very common.

Another survey reported that the majority of Americans believe that many businesspeople regularly engage in ethical misconduct. In fact, 76 percent of respondents in yet another study believe that the decline in moral standards in the United States is a direct result of the lack of business ethics practiced daily. Perhaps even more damaging are the results of a survey of business practitioners themselves: 66 percent of executives surveyed believe that businesspeople will occasionally act unethically during business dealings, while another 15 percent believe that ethical misconduct occurs often in the business sector.

> ## THE OPPORTUNITY FOR ETHICAL MISCONDUCT IN SERVICES MARKETING

Opportunities for ethical misconduct within the service sector can be attributed predominantly to the intangibility, heterogeneity, and inseparability dimensions inherent in the provision of services.[7] As introduced in Chapter 2, intangibility complicates the consumer's ability to objectively evaluate the quality of service provided; heterogeneity reflects the difficulty in standardization and quality control; and inseparability reflects the human element involved in the service delivery process. All three dimensions contribute to consumer vulnerability to and reliance upon the service provider's ethical conduct during the service encounter.

In more specific terms, consumer vulnerability to ethical misconduct within the service sector can be attributed to several sources:[8]

- Services are characterized by few search attributes.
- Services are often specialized and/or technical.
- Some services have a significant time lapse between performance and evaluation.
- Many services are sold without guarantees and warranties.
- Services are often provided by boundary-spanning personnel.
- Variability in service performance is somewhat accepted.
- Reward systems are often outcome-based as opposed to behavior-based.
- Customers are an active participant in the production process.

### *FEW SEARCH ATTRIBUTES*

As discussed in Chapter 4 (on the consumer decision process), search attributes can be determined prior to purchase and include such attributes as touch, smell, visual cues, and taste. However, due to the intangibility of services, consumers lack the opportunity to physically examine a service before purchasing it. Consequently, consumers have little prepurchase information available to help them make an informed, intelligent decision. Hence, consumers of services often must base their purchase decisions on information provided by the service provider.

Using Sears Auto Centers as an example, the dilemma a consumer faces due to the lack of search attributes is clear. The car may look fine on the outside, but the mechanic provides information about parts and systems that may not be visible to the consumer. The consumer now must rely on the advice of the mechanic. In addition, even though price is a search attribute that can be obtained prior to purchasing an auto repair service, the price is only an estimate. The final price is not calculated until after the service is performed.

### *TECHNICAL AND SPECIALIZED SERVICES*

Many services are not easily understood and/or evaluated; consequently, the opportunity exists to easily mislead consumers. Evaluating the performance of professional service providers is particularly intriguing. As a consumer, how do you know whether your doctor, lawyer, broker, priest, or minister is competent at his or her job? Often, our evaluations of these people are based on their clothing, the furniture in their offices, and whether they have pleasant social skills. In other words, in the absence of information that they can understand, customers often resort to evaluating information that surrounds the service as opposed to the core service itself when forming evaluations.

The auto repair industry is also characterized by services that are technical, specialized, and not easily understood or evaluated by the average consumer. Again, the consumer must rely on the service provider for guidance. As a result, unethical service providers can easily mislead consumers, perform unnecessary services, or charge for services that are never performed. Do you check your oil when it's changed? How do you know that the mechanic really did rotate and balance your tires?

## TIME LAPSE BETWEEN PERFORMANCE AND EVALUATION

The final evaluation of some services such as insurance and financial planning is often conducted only at a time in the distant future. For example, the success or failure of retirement planning may not be realized until 30 years after the original service transaction is conducted. Hence, service providers may not be held accountable for their actions in the short run. This could lead to a scenario where unethical service providers may maximize their short-term gains at the expense of consumers' long-term benefits.

Unethical auto mechanics may also benefit from the time lapse between service performance and service evaluation. The discovery of low-quality work may happen via mechanical problems 30 days after repairs have been made or by having a future mechanic question the previous mechanic's work. In either case, the consumer is left to deal with the situation and generally experiences little success in convincing the original mechanic that the inferiority of past efforts is at the root of present problems.

When purchasing home insurance, consumers trust that the insurance company will quickly and thoroughly process their claims after tragedy strikes. However, the time lapse that occurs between the purchase of home insurance and the time a need arises creates a situation where ethical misconduct may occur.

© NAJLAH FEANNY/CORBIS SABA

## SERVICES SOLD WITHOUT GUARANTEES AND WARRANTIES

Another opportunity for ethical misconduct in the service sector results from few meaningful guarantees and warranties. Consequently, when the consumer experiences difficulties with an unscrupulous provider, there are few or no means of seeking quick retribution. For example, what are your options if you get a bad haircut—wear a hat?

Although the auto repair industry is famous for its 90-day guarantee on all parts, the guarantee generally fails to cover the labor required to reinstall the part that failed. Moreover, the 90-day guarantee does little to help the consumer who experiences failure 120 days after the repair. One of the authors had the experience of paying more than $400 to replace the rear-window motor of a Chrysler LeBaron twice within a 16-month period. The 90-day guarantee did little but indicate that the company that built the replacement motor had little faith in its product—and rightly so!

## SERVICES PERFORMED BY BOUNDARY-SPANNING PERSONNEL

Many service providers deliver their services outside their firm's physical facilities. In doing so, these types of service providers expand the boundary of a firm beyond the firm's main office. Service providers such as painters, lawn-care specialists, paramedics, and carpet cleaners are typical examples.

Because of the physical distance from the main office inherent in the role of **boundary-spanning personnel**, these particular service providers often are not under direct supervision and may act in a manner inconsistent with organizational objectives. Hence, the opportunity to engage in ethical misconduct without repercussions from upper management increases.

*boundary-spanning personnel*
Personnel who provide their services outside the firm's physical facilities.

## ACCEPTED VARIABILITY IN PERFORMANCE

Another opportunity for ethical misconduct within the service sector is provided via the heterogeneity inherent in the provision of services. Due to heterogeneity, standardization and quality control are difficult to maintain throughout each individual service delivery transaction. Many services are customized, requiring different skills of the service provider, and often consumers are exposed to different providers within the same firm (see B2B Services in Action). The bottom line is that variability in performance is unavoidable.

Variability in performance is evident in the auto repair industry. Automobiles develop a variety of problems that require an array of skills from the service provider, who may not be equivalently skilled to undertake each task. Moreover, consumers often receive services from a number of different mechanics. Each mechanic's performance is likely to vary from the next. Due to consumer acceptance of variability in service performance, unethical service providers may attempt to broaden the window of acceptable performance through slightly increasing gaps in performance quality.

## B 2 B   S E R V I C E S   *IN  ACTION*

### > | AMERICAN NURSING SERVICES

The modern hospital is a dynamic environment that is a prime example of the variability that can exist within a service encounter. Patients are constantly cycling in and out, and so are the healthcare providers. Inside this ever changing environment, the nurses are depended on by doctors to keep a variety of hospital operations moving and patients satisfied. With this much responsibility in the hands of nurses, what happens when one or two call in sick? The hospital cannot just stop operating. A replacement must be found and this is where American Nursing Services Inc. (http://www.american-nurse.com) has found its niche.

American Nursing Services Inc. (ANS) is a nurse-owned and -operated nurse staffing company and home care agency founded in 1982 and headquartered in the greater New Orleans metropolitan area. ANS has a large employment inventory of certified nurses in all areas of hospital operations. Nursing skills range from critical care to labor and delivery, psychiatry to medical/surgery. By placing a call to the nearest ANS staffing center, a hospital can request a certified nurse who can be supplied immediately and prepared to take on all responsibilities needed. American Nursing Services are in high demand. Hospitals cannot operate without a quality supply of nurses, and with the ever-shrinking number of available nurses, ANS is providing healthcare organizations with this very important business-to-business service.

In addition to meeting hospitals' on-call needs, American Nursing Services also provides full staffing services. ANS is capable of taking on an entire hospital's nursing needs from supplying staff to managing staffing activities. ANS promises to provide hospitals with standardized nursing rates and contracts, accurate and timely invoices, and excellent accountability. ANS allows hospitals to concentrate on other parts of their organization and leave the nursing to ANS. ANS guarantees each client hospital a full staff at all times at a cost savings to the hospital.

Patient satisfaction is crucial within the healthcare industry. Nurses are key to patient satisfaction. The on-call and full staffing services provided by ANS have proven to be a very useful service to many healthcare organizations.

Source: www.American-nurse.com accessed 13 April 2005. Original draft provided by Jenny Bowes, Jake Fear, and Clint Strait.

## OUTCOME-BASED REWARD SYSTEMS

The reward system of an organization often dictates the behavior of its employees, and it does not take employees long to figure out the shortest route to the most money. Hence, the reward system of an organization may encourage, albeit unintentionally, the unethical conduct of its employees.

Straight commissions and quotas reinforce activities that are directly linked to making the sale while discouraging nonselling activities such as maintaining the store, stocking shelves, and spending an inordinate amount of time fielding customer questions.

Looking at the reward structure at Sears Auto Centers, the impact that it likely had on employee behavior is clear. Employees were indeed rewarded for making repairs regardless of whether they were needed.

## CONSUMER PARTICIPATION IN PRODUCTION

On the surface, one would think that the more the consumer is involved in the service encounter, the less the opportunity exists for the service provider to engage in ethical misconduct. However, service exchanges may be jeopardized by coercive influence strategies used by the service provider.

The consumer's involvement in the service delivery process enables a service provider to try to influence the consumer through fear or guilt to agree to a purchase the consumer would otherwise decline. An auto mechanic who makes a statement such as, "I wouldn't want my family riding around in a car that has brakes like these," is a typical example of the type of influence a service provider can have on a customer. Moreover, due to the consumer's input into the production process, the consumer often accepts much of the responsibility for less-than-satisfactory service transactions. Consumers often feel that they didn't explain themselves clearly enough and will accept much of the blame to avoid a confrontation with the service provider. In fact, conflict avoidance is one of the major reasons customers do not complain to service providers (see Chapter 13 for a more complete discussion of customer complaining behavior). This situation further removes service providers from taking responsibility for their own actions and provides yet another opportunity to engage in unethical behavior.

## > METHODS FOR ETHICAL DECISION MAKING

The behavior of service providers engaged in ethical decision making reflects the **moral philosophies** in which they believe.[9] Moral philosophies are the principles or rules service providers use when deciding what is right or wrong. For example, if for economic reasons a company is forced to lay off workers, does it notify the workers ahead of the actual layoff? On one hand, notifying employees provides them with time to seek other employment before they are out of a job. On the other hand, disgruntled employees, after learning of the layoff, may not work as hard, and the quality of subsequent service delivery suffers.

*moral philosophies*
The principles or rules service providers use when deciding what is right or wrong.

As you consider the practices of Sears Auto Centers discussed earlier in this chapter, you should ponder the moral philosophies and decision-making processes embraced by the parties involved. Methods for ethical decision making include teleology, deontology, and relativism. Again, note that we are not proposing that one moral philosophy is better than another. We are merely providing you with alternative schools of thought regarding the way decisions are made.

## TELEOLOGY

**teleology**
A type of ethical decision making in which an act is deemed morally acceptable if it produces some desired result.

Followers of **teleology** believe an act is morally right or acceptable if the act produces some desired result. Teleology is referred to as a type of **consequentialism.** As such, followers of teleology assess the morality of their decisions based on the consequences. If the decision leads to some desired result, such as increased pay, promotion, or recognition, then the decision is acceptable.

**consequentialism**
A type of ethical decision making that assesses the morality of decisions based on their consequences.

For example, consider the following. Most persons would agree that robbery is an unethical behavior. Let's say that a drug is available at the drugstore, and the pharmacist is charging $1000 for it. Meanwhile, you have a family member who desperately needs the drug in order to survive. A problem arises when you have only $900 and the pharmacist refuses to sell you the drug. Would you steal from the drugstore in order to save a family member? If your answer is yes, then the consequences of your behavior are dictating the morality of your actions.

Teleology is further broken down into two subclasses, *egoism* and *utilitarianism*, which reflect the beneficiary of the decision's consequences. **Egoists** define acceptable actions as those that benefit an individual's self-interest as defined by that individual. Benefits can take the form of fame, personal wealth, recognition, and other self-gratifying consequences. Egoists believe that they should "do the act that promotes the greatest good for oneself."[10]

**egoist**
An individual who subscribes to a subclass of teleology in which acceptable actions are defined as those that benefit the individual's self-interest as defined by the individual.

Returning to the example of Sears Auto Centers, employees who act as egoists may choose a number of alternative behaviors. First, if the employee wants to increase his own personal wealth, he may engage in activities that lead to greater commissions, such as suggesting repairs that do not need to be made. On the other hand, if the employee believes that reporting the unethical behavior of others would lead to a promotion, the egoist may notify upper management of a problem. Further, as another alternative, an egoist who notifies the press of the problem may be looking for personal recognition.

**utilitarianist**
An individual who follows a subclass of teleology in which acceptable behavior is defined as that which maximizes total utility—the greatest good for the greatest number of people.

In contrast to the egoist, the **utilitarianist** defines acceptable behavior as that which maximizes the **principle of utility**—the greatest good for the greatest number of people. This philosophy of promoting "the needs of the many over the needs of the few" has led to some interesting decisions. Cuba, for example, isolated all its HIV-positive citizens from the general population. The decision was made to sacrifice the personal freedoms of these people for the health and well-being of the remainder of the Cuban population.

**principle of utility**
The behavior that produces the most good for the most people in a specific situation.

Referring back to the Sears example, the mechanic who engages in ethical misconduct to make a sale in order to benefit the company, so that all concerned can keep their jobs, may be classified as a utilitarianist. The utilitarianist may also believe that although not every customer's car may need a specific type of repair, many will benefit from the repairs made over time.

## DEONTOLOGY

**deontology**
A type of ethical decision making in which the inherent rightness or wrongness of an act guides behavior, regardless of the outcome.

In contrast to teleology, a deontologist believes that the inherent rightness or wrongness of an act should guide behavior regardless of the outcome. Hence, **deontology** is not a form of consequentialism since it does not focus on the consequences of an action. In contrast, deontology focuses on individual rights and the intentions associated with a particular behavior. Deontologists believe that the rights of the individual should prevail over what is better for society as a whole, thereby differentiating itself from the utilitarian philosophy.

Deontologists believe that there are some things people should never do, regardless of the consequences. If recalling a product to save lives means bankrupting the company, then the company should go bankrupt. Deontologists further believe that moral standards are permanent. They do not alter over time, and are based on the **categorical imperative**. "Simply put, if you feel comfortable allowing everyone in the world to see you commit an act and if your rationale for acting in a particular manner is suitable to become a universal principle guiding behavior, then committing that act is ethical."[11]

*categorical imperative*
Asks whether the proposed action would be right if everyone did it.

Returning again to the Sears example, a deontological mechanic would probably never make repairs that were not needed. Making an unnecessary repair would be a form of lying, and based on the deontological perspective, lying is inherently wrong. On the other hand, it could also be argued based on the deontological perspective that Sears felt it was inherently wrong not to do the preventive maintenance as suggested by manufacturers. The deontological mechanic might believe that not conducting the maintenance as suggested by the manufacturer could possibly lead to the harm of an individual customer.

## *RELATIVISM*

In contrast to deontology and teleology, people practicing **relativism** are prone to believe that the correctness of ethical decisions may change over time. Relativists evaluate ethical decisions subjectively on a case-to-case basis based on past individual or group experiences. As such, relativists observe the actions of their relevant group to determine the consensus of opinion concerning decisions. The consensus reflects whether the decision is "right" or "wrong."

*relativism*
A type of ethical decision making in which the correctness of ethical decisions is thought to change over time.

Because relativists use themselves or the people around them to judge the ethicality of decisions, they may follow one set of ethical guidelines at work and a different set at home. Consequently, service providers, as relativists, working within an unethical work environment (from an outsider's viewpoint) may eventually come to adopt these behaviors as their own. Sears mechanics who made unnecessary repairs may have simply adopted the actions of their co-workers and supervisors. Co-worker and supervisor opinions can particularly influence the decisions made by new employees. An overview of methods for ethical decision making is presented in Table 5.1.

## > | ISSUES THAT CREATE ETHICAL CONFLICT

The types of ethical issues service providers encounter are not always unique to the service sector. This can be accounted for by the mix of products and customer service involved in a multitude of different businesses. Table 5.2 contains a sample of the many types of ethical issues that are encountered in the business world. Through surveying

| TABLE 5.1 | METHODS FOR ETHICAL DECISION MAKING |
|-----------|--------------------------------------|
| Teleology | Acts are morally right or acceptable if they provide some desired result. |
| Egoism | Acceptable actions are those that maximize a particular person's self-interest as defined by the individual. Egoism is a form of teleology. |
| Utilitarianism | Acceptable actions are those that maximize total utility—the greatest good for the greatest number of people. Utilitarianism is a form of teleology. |
| Deontology | Acceptable actions are those that focus on the preservation of individual rights and on the intentions associated with a particular behavior rather than on its consequences. |
| Relativism | Acceptable actions are determined by the actions of some relevant group. A relativist evaluates ethicalness on the basis of individual and group experiences. |

their personnel, individual companies can determine the specific ethical issues that pertain to their firm. The most typical issues that managers and/or employees will face while conducting business include the following:[12]

- conflict of interest
- organizational relationships
- honesty
- fairness
- communication

## CONFLICT OF INTEREST

**conflict of interest**
The situation in which a service provider feels torn between the organization, the customer, and/or the service provider's own personal interest.

Service providers are often in close proximity to customers during the provision of services. Consequently, the service provider may experience **conflicts of interest** as the service provider/customer relationship develops and friendships are formed. In such a situation, the service provider may feel torn between the organization, the customer, and/or the service provider's own personal interest.

For example, insurance personnel may coach friends and family members on how to complete the necessary forms in order to obtain a less expensive rate. In this situation, the customer benefits (via lower rates), the employee benefits (via "the sale"), but the organization suffers (by failing to obtain the proper premium amount). Likewise, Sears employees may have felt torn between what was best for the customer, what was best for the company, and what was best for their own personal finances.

## ORGANIZATIONAL RELATIONSHIPS

**organizational relationships**
Working relationships formed between service providers and various role partners such as customers, suppliers, peers, subordinates, supervisors, and others.

Service providers form working **organizational relationships** with a variety of role partners, including customers, suppliers, peers, subordinates, supervisors, and others. The information gained via these relationships is often highly sensitive. For example, most

| **TABLE 5.2** | **TYPES OF ETHICAL ISSUES ENCOUNTERED BY BUSINESSES** |
|---|---|
| Honesty | Accuracy of books and records |
| Conflict of interest | Privacy of employee records |
| Marketing and advertising issues | Political activities and contributions |
| Environmental issues | Misuses of company assets |
| Discrimination by age, race, or sex | Corporate governance |
| Product liability and safety | Issues |
| Codes of ethics and self-governance | Ethical theory |
| Relations with customers | Ethics in negotiation |
| Bribery | Relations with local communities |
| Rights of and responsibilities to shareholders | Plant closing and layoffs |
| Whistleblowing | Employee discipline |
| Kickbacks | Use of others' proprietary information |
| Insider trading | Relations with U.S. government represen- |
| Antitrust issues | tatives |
| Issues facing multinationals | Relations with competitors |
| Relations with foreign governments | Employee benefits |
| Ethical foundations of capitalism | Mergers and acquisitions |
| Workplace health and safety | Drug and alcohol abuse |
| Managing an ethical environment | Drug and alcohol testing |
| Relations with suppliers and subcontractors | Intelligence gathering |
| Use of company proprietary information | Leveraged buyouts |

Source: Lynn Sharp Paine, "Report on Ethics Issues Covered in the Undergraduate Curriculum," in *Ethics Education in American Business Schools,* 1988, p. 17. Copyright © 1988 Ethics Resource Center. Used with permission of the Ethics Resource Center, 1747 Pennsylvania Avenue NW, Suite 400, Washington, DC. 20006, www.ethics.org.

people would not want their priest to reveal the contents of their confession or their doctor telling others of their medical problems. Because of the sensitivity of information, ethical service providers are required to maintain confidentiality in relationships to meet their professional obligations and responsibilities (see E-Services in Action ). In contrast, unethical service providers may use the information acquired from organizational relationships for their own personal gain. Ivan Boesky, one of Wall Street's top arbitragers, was charged with insider trading activities by the Securities and Exchange Commission (SEC). Boesky allegedly made millions from obtaining information concerning company takeovers before the public announcements of the takeovers were made. Once Boesky learned of a takeover, he would purchase large blocks of stock that he later sold at huge profits. In exchange for the names of other inside traders, Boesky plead guilty to one charge of criminal activity and agreed to pay $100 million in penalties. He also served three years in jail. The old adage that "knowledge is power" is often embraced by those who engage in ethical misconduct.

The structure of the organizational relationship may also provide an opportunity for an unethical firm to place undue influence on its employees. In particular, the relationship between supervisor and subordinate comes to mind. Regarding the Sears example, the mechanics could argue that they felt they would lose their jobs or suffer large decreases in pay if they did not make the repairs required by the quota system that was put into place by upper management.

## E-SERVICES *IN ACTION*

### > | CONFIDENTIALITY ISSUES ON THE NET

One of the biggest obstacles that keeps consumers from purchasing products on the Internet is concern about confidentiality. Customers must trust that the sensitive financial and personal information that is transmitted to Web merchants is kept confidential. In turn, businesses must be certain that payment information collected from consumers over Web storefronts is indeed valid. Additional precautions must be taken by merchants to ensure that confidential consumer databases are not compromised by hackers or misused by malicious employees.

Netscape summarizes security threats as follows:

- *Unauthorized access*: accessing or misusing a computer system to intercept transmissions and steal sensitive information;
- *Data alteration*: altering the content of a transaction—user names, credit card numbers, and dollar amounts—during transmission;
- *Monitoring*: eavesdropping on confidential information;
- *Spoofing*: a fake site pretending to be yours to steal data from unsuspecting customers or just disrupt your business;
- *Service denial*: an attacker shuts down your site or denies access to visitors;
- *Repudiation*: a party to an online purchase denies that the transaction occurred or was authorized.

Source: Bruce Kratofil, "Is Surfing the Web a Walk on the Wild Side?" *Bug Net* http://www.bugnet.com/analysis/0005/ftbrowsers.html accessed 15 April 2005; and http://www.ecommerce.ncsu.edu accessed 13 April 13, 2005.

## *HONESTY*

**honesty**
The characteristics of truthfulness, integrity, and trustworthiness.

**Honesty** is a partner of truthfulness, integrity, and trustworthiness. Examples of dishonesty in customer service include promising to do something for a customer but having no intention of delivering on the promise or stating that a service has been performed when, in fact, it has not. Honesty issues may also cover selected business strategies utilized by service firms to manage consumer expectations. For example, a typical practice at some restaurants today is to purposely estimate waiting times in excess of the actual expected waiting times. If customers are seated before expected, they feel they are getting better service. Do you think this practice is ethical?

Other honesty issues involve (1) respecting the private property of clients while services are provided in the clients' homes and places of business; (2) performing services as promised at the designated time; (3) providing accurate billing for services delivered; and (4) providing clients accurate information even if it means the loss of a sale.

## FAIRNESS

**Fairness** is an outcome of just treatment, equity, and impartiality. Clients should be treated equitably, and deals based on favoritism should be avoided. In addition, service discrimination issues should also be addressed. Do men receive better service than women, or vice versa? Are well-dressed persons served better than blue jean–clad clients? Does a client's race or general appearance affect the level of service provided?

*fairness*
The characteristics of just treatment, equity, and impartiality.

## COMMUNICATION

Ethical issues also arise through the communication that the service organization releases to the public. Communication may range from mass advertising to warranty information to interpersonal communication between the service provider and the customer. Ethical misconduct stemming from communication may include making false claims about the superiority of the company's services, making false claims about competitive offerings, and/or making promises the company knowingly understands it cannot keep.

## > FACTORS THAT INFLUENCE ETHICAL DECISION MAKING

Different people make different decisions in similar ethical situations. Some individuals make consistent ethical decisions over time, while others evaluate each ethical decision on a case-by-case basis. The reasons that we make different ethical decisions are functions of a variety of factors that may influence our judgments. Factors influencing ethical decision making include the following:[13]

- stage of cognitive moral development
- personal values
- corporate culture
- cultural differences
- organizational structure
- opportunity
- reward systems
- significant others
- competitive environment
- changes in technology

| TABLE 5.3 | STAGES OF COGNITIVE MORAL DEVELOPMENT |
|---|---|

**Stage 1:**
"Right" is based on rules and authority.

**Stage 2:**
"Right" is based on one's own needs or another's in terms of what is fair.

**Stage 3:**
"The individual focuses more on others as opposed to personal gains.

**Stage 4:**
"Right" is based on the individual's duty to society.

**Stage 5:**
"Right" is based on basic rights, values, and legal contracts.

**Stage 6:**
"Right" is a set of universal ethical principles that everyone should adhere to.

## COGNITIVE MORAL DEVELOPMENT

**cognitive moral development**
A model of ethical development that proposes individuals progress through six stages of ethical development.

The model of **cognitive moral development** proposes that individuals progress through six stages of ethical development (see Table 5.3). As the individual develops, ethical decisions are evaluated differently. In the first stage, the stage of punishment and obedience, a person defines what is right based on rules and authority. Consequently, when faced with making an ethical decision, the individual bases the decision on a set of rules or instructions provided by an authority figure. In the second stage, the stage of individual instrumental purpose and exchange, decisions are based on fulfilling one's own needs or another's in terms of what is fair. During the third stage, the stage of mutual interpersonal expectations, relationships, and conformity, the individual focuses more on others as opposed to personal gains.

As the individual progresses to the fourth stage, the stage of social system and conscience maintenance, the individual defines what is right based on his or her duty to society. In the fifth stage, the stage of prior rights, social contract, or utility, the individual begins to more narrowly define what is right based on basic rights, values, and legal contracts. The sixth and final stage, the stage of universal ethical principles, reflects the individual's belief that right is determined by a set of universal ethical principles that everyone should adhere to when confronted with ethical decisions.

## PERSONAL VALUES

**personal values**
The standards by which each person lives in both a personal and professional life.

Ethical decisions are also influenced by an individual's **personal values**. In general, personal values are not necessarily static. Hence, as the person matures, personal values may change. Furthermore, individuals may apply one set of personal values to their personal life and another set to their business life. Incidentally, this explains why, when television tabloids interview the neighbors of a suspected embezzler, the neighbors always say: "He was just a regular guy, a good family man, and a great neighbor . . . we had no idea he was a crook!"

## CORPORATE CULTURE

Another factor that impacts individual ethical decision making is the **corporate culture** within the firm. Corporate cultures guide decisions, actions, and policies of organizations and are functions of (1) the personal values of those employed by the organization, (2) the procedures used to carry out the daily business, and (3) the policies that are put in place to guide decision making. Overall, procedures and policies play a more important role in corporate culture than do personal values.

*corporate culture*
The general philosophy of a company that guides decisions, actions, and policies of the company.

## CULTURAL DIFFERENCES

In addition to corporate cultures, service firms may have **cultural differences** because of their own nationality-based cultures (see Global Services in Action).[14] For example, although considered unethical in the United States, bribes are common business practice in some countries. Some further argue that ethical behaviors should not be regionally generalized. Accordingly, Asian countries, such as Japan, South Korea, Thailand, China, and Singapore should not be viewed as a single, homogeneous entity with respect to business conduct.[15] Service firms who engage in international operations should consider developing policies that help guide ethical decision making in different cultural climates.

*cultural differences*
Differences in standards of behavior from one culture to another.

## ORGANIZATIONAL STRUCTURE

The **organizational structure** of a service firm may also impact the ethical decision making of its employees. Traditional organizational structures are characterized as *centralized* or *decentralized*. Service providers employed by decentralized firms, where authority is spread throughout the firm, have more latitude when making decisions. In contrast, centralized firms, where authority is concentrated in one area, tend to place stricter controls over employees. Past studies have proposed that centralized organizations tend to be more ethical due to the development and implementation of rigid controls such as codes of ethics and other similar corporate policies.[16] Service firms wishing to implement the concept of empowerment need to consider and discuss with front-line personnel the decentralizing effects of this philosophy as it may create new opportunities for ethical misconduct.

*organizational structure*
The way an organization is set up regarding hierarchy of authority and decision making.

## OPPORTUNITY

As discussed earlier in the chapter, service organizations often operate within a business environment, where ethical misconduct is not easily detected. Hence, the

## GLOBAL SERVICES *IN ACTION*

### > | CULTURAL PERCEPTIONS

Customer expectations and perceptions are psychological phenomena and are not necessarily based on reality. For example, individual customers can experience the same service situation and walk away with different impressions of the same event. This inherent variation in customer expectations and perceptions makes managing service operations particularly challenging. One cultural group may feel their treatment was ethical while another may not.

According to a recent study, it appears that in addition to individual differences, cultural background also influences customer expectations and perceptions. A study of more than 10,000 Kaiser Permanente HMO patients, consisting of 7,747 Caucasians, 836 African Americans, 710 Latinos, and 1,007 Asians requested information pertaining to healthcare-related outcomes such as overall satisfaction with the care provided; accessibility; willingness to recommend their physician to a friend; the technical competence of their healthcare provider; the physician's focus on health promotion; the physician's communication style; adequacy of explanations; time spent with patient; and concern, courtesy, and respect for patient.

In terms of what each cultural group found most important, all groups rated technical competence and adequacy of explanation as the most important outcomes. Higher proportions of nonCaucasian groups indicated that the physician's display of concern, courtesy, and respect were more important than anything else. Other interesting findings indicated that for 7 of the 10 performance measures, Asians rated overall physician performance lower than Caucasian groups. Within the Asian group, Chinese and Filipino patients were the least satisfied, and Japanese patients were least likely to recommend their doctor. African Americans rated technical competence and focus on health promotion higher than did Caucasians. Latinos and Caucasians reported the most comparable ratings; however, Latinos rated the accessibility of physicians significantly lower.

Source: Anonymous, "Ethnicity Defines Patient Satisfaction," *Trustee*, 53 (5), (May 2000), p. 5.

**opportunity**
An occasion in which a chance for unethical behavior exists.

**opportunity** to engage in and benefit from unethical behavior within the service sector is fairly prevalent. Opportunity acts as temptation and has been proposed to be a better predictor of behavior than an individual's own personal moral beliefs.[17] Moreover, opportunity is said to increase along with title and status. Recent history has taught us via savings and loan scandals, insider trading schemes, and corrupt governmental officials that professional service providers may be particularly tempted by the opportunities that arise with a higher title and status.

## REWARD SYSTEMS

Ethical misconduct may further be encouraged if rewarded (or not punished) by a firm's **reward system**. As with many types of employees, service providers are often rewarded according to outcome-based control measures (e.g., sales and number of calls handled). The major problem associated with outcome-based control systems is that employees are evaluated and compensated based on results (outcomes) rather than on behaviors utilized to achieve results. In other words, what you accomplish is judged, and how you accomplished it is seldom examined. Under this system, if a behavior (ethical or unethical) leads to outcomes valued by the organization (sales), then the employee should be rewarded (salary plus commissions). Thus, outcome-based control systems tend to focus employee efforts on activities with immediate payoffs rather than on behaviors that build long-term relationships between the service provider and the client. Service firms wishing to enhance the ethical behavior of their employees should consider implementing a behavior-based control system that monitors employees' activities and evaluates employees on the aspects of their jobs in which they exercise control.[18] Compared with outcome-based reward systems, behavior-based reward systems are more harmonious with a long-term relationship marketing approach.

*reward systems*
The methods used by an organization to evaluate and compensate employees.

## SIGNIFICANT OTHERS

As proposed by the theory of **differential association**, ethical decision making is greatly influenced by **significant others** (e.g., supervisors, peers, subordinates, and customers) with whom the service provider interacts. The more frequent the contact with the significant other, the more likely the employee will adopt similar ethical (or unethical) beliefs. "Association with others who are unethical, combined with the opportunity to act unethically oneself, is a major influence on ethical decision making."[19]

*differential association*
A theory that proposes ethical decision making is greatly influenced by significant others.

*significant others*
Supervisors, peers, subordinates, customers, and others who influence a service provider's behavior.

## COMPETITIVE ENVIRONMENT

Past research also indicates that the competitive environment in which the individual operates has an impact upon ethical behavior.[20] Pressures from business superiors and ethical climate in the industry are cited as reasons for ethical conflict. Furthermore, it has been suggested that when individuals feel the pressure to succeed and realize what must be done in order to compete, they tend to compromise their own personal standards to reach corporate goals.

## CHANGES IN TECHNOLOGY

As science has advanced, many products and services have been developed that carry with them an array of ethical considerations (e.g., abortion, euthanasia, cloning, and fertility clinics). And in handling consumer information, advances in direct marketing techniques (e.g., database technology that allows greater storage and access to consumer information and purchase histories) have given service marketers powerful tools to "identify" their optimal customer profiles and track customer purchase/service histories.[21] For example, when a customer calls Sears to check a catalog order, the service representative has instant access (via an order number) to the customer's previous sales/service transactions. This data can be used to sell other products and service warranties as well as enable more efficient order processing. However, the availability of this information and ease of access to it creates the opportunity to utilize the data in an unethical manner and may violate the customer's right to privacy.

### FACTORS CONTRIBUTING TO SEARS EMPLOYEE BEHAVIOR

Returning to the Sears example, factors contributing to the decisions made by Sears Auto Center employees may have included the following: (1) corporate culture—employees were apparently following company procedures and policies; (2) opportunity—due to the difficulty involved in consumer evaluation of service quality, the situation existed where consumers could be easily misled; (3) reward systems—the quota/bonus system rewarded outcomes (sales) rather than ethical behavior; (4) significant others—supervisors and co-workers were engaging in and/or encouraging the method of operation; (5) competitive environment—employees may have felt the pressure to succeed and tended to compromise their own personal standards to reach corporate goals; and (6) technology—the technological advances in the production of automobiles makes it very difficult these days to be one's own mechanic. Hence, technology contributed to the consumer's vulnerability.

## > THE EFFECTS OF ETHICAL MISCONDUCT

Service organizations should stress the importance of ethical conduct by employees for several reasons. First, in terms of social responsibility, service organizations should be required to act in a manner that is in the best interests of society. Secondly, employees forced to deal with ethical issues on a continuing basis frequently suffer from job-related tension, frustration, anxiety, ineffective performance (i.e., reduced sales and reduced profits), turnover intentions, and lower job satisfaction.[22] One only needs to witness Firestone's and Ford's dilemma regarding the recall of millions of tires to see first-hand the impact of covering up mistakes.

In addition to the personal effects of ethical misconduct, the organization as a whole suffers. Ethical improprieties have also been linked to customer dissatisfaction (loss of sales), unfavorable word-of-mouth publicity for the organization, and a negative public image for the entire industry.[23]

The effects of the Sears Auto Centers policies were damaging. Some of the consequences included loss of consumer trust, lost sales due to the publicity surrounding the charges, and an increase in legal actions filed against the company. It could also be argued that employees suffered as well, via increased anxiety, job-related tensions, and low job satisfaction.

> ## > CONTROLLING ETHICAL DECISION MAKING

The adverse effects of unethical decision making may lead service firms to try to control the ethical behavior of their employees in a number of ways. Suggestions for controlling and managing ethical behavior include the following:[24]

- employee socialization
- standards of conduct
- corrective control
- leadership training
- service/product knowledge
- monitoring of employee performance
- building long-term customer relationships

## EMPLOYEE SOCIALIZATION

**Employee socialization** refers to the process through which an individual adapts and comes to appreciate the values, norms, and required behavior patterns of an organization. Ethical issues such as cheating, payment of bribes, and lying may be defined through socialization of organizational values and norms. These values and norms may be transmitted via new employee orientation sessions and subsequent formal meetings to address new issues and reinforce past lessons.

*employee socialization*
The process through which an individual adapts and comes to appreciate the values, norms, and required behavior patterns of an organization.

Service organizations can also convey organizational values and norms through communications such as company newsletters and advertising. For example, Delta Airlines has been commended for its advertising that depicts very helpful, friendly, and happy employees who exert discretionary effort to assist the airline's customers. The ads not only appeal to customers but also help define for Delta employees their role within the company and the types of behavior the company expects and rewards.

## STANDARDS OF CONDUCT

As part of the socialization process, formal standards of conduct can be presented to service employees through a **code of ethics**. Research indicates that employees desire codes of ethics to help them define proper behavior, thereby reducing role conflict and role ambiguity.[25] Although developing a code of ethics does not guarantee subsequent employee ethical behavior, it is an important early step in the process of controlling ethical decision making.

*code of ethics*
Formal standards of conduct that assist in defining proper organizational behavior.

## CORRECTIVE CONTROL

For the service firm's code of ethics to be effective, the conditions set forth in it must be enforced. Enforcement of the code of ethics may be accomplished through **corrective control**, the use of rewards and punishments. Service providers who are rewarded (or not punished) for unethical behavior will continue practicing it. Interestingly, research

*corrective control*
The use of rewards and punishments to enforce a firm's code of ethics.

Fidelity employees are required to review their Code of Ethics annually and to acknowledge in writing that their personal investing has been conducted in compliance with it. This is an important step in the process of controlling ethical decision making.

© STONE/GETTY IMAGES

indicates that employees of firms that have codes of ethics are more prone to believe that violators of ethical codes should be punished.

## LEADERSHIP TRAINING

Due to the apparent effects of differential association upon ethical decision making, service organizations need to stress to their leaders the importance of those leaders' own behavior and its influence upon subordinates. Leaders must be examples of the standards of ethical conduct. They need to understand that employees faced with ethical decision making often emulate the behavior of their supervisors. This is particularly true of young employees, who tend to comply with their supervisors to demonstrate loyalty.

## SERVICE/PRODUCT KNOWLEDGE

Service firms need to constantly train all employees concerning the details of what the service product can and cannot provide. Due to the complex nature of many service offerings and an ever-changing business environment, service firms cannot afford to assume that employees completely understand the ramifications of new service/product developments. A few service industries understand the social responsibility of keeping employees informed. For example, the insurance industry now requires continuing education of its sales agents.[26]

## MONITORING OF EMPLOYEE PERFORMANCE

Another possible method of controlling ethical decision making is the measurement of employee ethical performance. This approach involves comparing behaviors utilized in obtaining performance levels against organizational ethical standards. Service firms may monitor employee performance by either observing employees in action or by utilizing employee questionnaires regarding ethical behavior. Results obtained from monitoring should be discussed with the employees to alleviate any ambiguities in the employees' minds about the appropriate actions to take when questionable situations arise.

## STRESS LONG-TERM CUSTOMER RELATIONSHIPS

Service providers must build trusting relationships between themselves and their customers to promote a long-term, mutually beneficial relationship.[27] Ethical marketing practices provide the basis from which such trust-based relationships are formed. Many unethical decisions that are made emphasize the short-run benefits that the decision provides. For example, a service provider may mislead a customer in order to make a quick sale. Service firms that properly socialize their employees should stress the importance of building long-term relationships. Service firms whose employees are oriented toward a long-term customer relationship should be able to minimize the frequency of unethical decision making.

## STRATEGIES FOR CONTROLLING THE ETHICAL BEHAVIOR AT SEARS AUTO CENTERS

Strategies for controlling the future ethical behavior of Sears Auto Centers employees might include the following: (1) employee socialization—orientation sessions regarding ethics for new employees; (2) standards of conduct—a code of ethics needs to be developed or reviewed; (3) corrective control—violations of the code of ethics need to be enforced; (4) leadership training—supervisors need to understand that subordinates emulate their behavior and that they are role models, particularly to new employees; (5) service/product training—all employees must be required to have adequate skills so that mechanical problems are not misdiagnosed or unnecessary repairs made; (6) employee performance monitoring—assess and discuss behavior utilized to obtain results as well as the results themselves; (7) long-term customer relationships stressed—emphasize that long-term satisfaction is more important than meeting the company's short-term (monthly) sales quota.

## ✳ SUMMARY

This chapter has presented an overview of ethics as they apply to the service sector. Service consumers are particularly vulnerable to ethical misconduct for a variety of reasons. For example, services possess few search attributes and therefore are difficult to evaluate before the purchase decision has been made; services are often technical and/or specialized, making evaluation by the common consumer even more difficult; many services are sold without warranties and/or guarantees and are often provided by unsupervised boundary-spanning personnel. In addition, reward systems that compensate service personnel are often based on results as opposed to the behaviors utilized to achieve those results. Other factors contributing to consumer vulnerability include the time lapse that occurs for some services between service performance and customer evaluation (e.g., financial planning and life insurance), the inherent variation in service performance, and the consumer's willingness to accept the blame for failing to effectively communicate his or her wishes to the service provider.

The most common ethical issues involve conflict of interest, confidentiality in organizational relationships, honesty, fairness, and the integrity of the firm's communications efforts. The behavior of service providers engaged in ethical decision making reflects the moral philosophies in which they believe. Moral philosophies are the principles or rules service providers use when deciding what is right or wrong and include philosophies such as teleology, deontology, and relativism.

Different service personnel may make different decisions under similar ethical situations due to their cognitive moral development and a variety of other factors, including personal values, cultural differences, corporate culture, organizational structure, opportunity, reward systems, significant others, and the pressures of conducting business in a competitive environment.

Employees forced to deal with ethical issues on a continuous basis frequently suffer from job-related tension, frustration, anxiety, ineffective performance, turnover intention, and low job satisfaction. In addition to the personal effects of ethical misconduct, the organization as a whole is likely to suffer as well. Ethical improprieties have been linked to customer dissatisfaction, unfavorable word-of-mouth publicity, and negative public images for an entire industry.

Organizations have utilized a number of strategies that attempt to control the ethical behavior of employees, including employee socialization, the development and enforcement of codes of ethics, leadership training, service/product knowledge training, monitoring employee performance, and education of employees regarding the benefits of long-term customer relationships.

## ✳ KEY TERMS

ethical vigilance, 107
ethics, 107
business ethics, 107
boundary-spanning personnel, 111
moral philosophies, 113
teleology, 114
consequentialism, 114
egoist, 114
utilitarianist, 114
principle of utility, 114
deontology, 114
categorical imperative, 115
relativism, 115
conflict of interest, 116
organizational relationships, 116

honesty, 118
fairness, 119
cognitive moral development, 120
personal values, 120
corporate culture, 121
cultural differences, 121
organizational structure, 121
opportunity, 122
reward systems, 123
differential association, 123
significant others, 123
employee socialization, 125
code of ethics, 125
corrective control, 125

# ✳ DISCUSSION QUESTIONS

1. Discuss the difference between ethics and social responsibility.
2. How does the public feel about the ethical behaviors of businesspeople?
3. What are boundary-spanning personnel? What provides these employees with the opportunity to engage in ethical misconduct?
4. Does consumer participation in the service delivery process increase or decrease the service provider's opportunity to engage in unethical behavior? Explain.
5. Which moral philosophies best describe your own personal ethical behavior? Explain.
6. Discuss the difference between an egoist and a utilitarianist.
7. Discuss the primary difference between a teleologist and a deontologist.
8. Discuss the theory of differential association.

# ✳ NOTES

1. K. Douglas Hoffman, et al., *Marketing Principles & Best Practices*, 3rd ed. (Mason, OH: Thomson South-Western, 2006), p. 68.
2. Mary L. Nicastro, "Infuse Business Ethics into Marketing Curriculum," *Marketing Educator* 11, 1 (1992), p. 1.
3. *Webster's New Ideal Dictionary* (Springfield, MA: G. & C. Merriam Co., 1973), p. 171.
4. O. C. Ferrell and John Fraedrich, *Business Ethics* (Boston, MA: Houghton Mifflin, 1991), p. 5.
5. Lawrence M. Fisher, "Sears Auto Centers Halt Commissions After Flap," *The New York Times*, 1992, pp. D1, D2; Gregory A. Patterson, "Sears' Brennan Accepts Blame for Auto Flap," *The Wall Street Journal*, 1992, p. B1; "Systematic Looting," *Time*, June 22, 1992, pp. 27, 30; and Tung Yin, "Sears Is Accused of Billing Fraud at Auto Centers," *The Wall Street Journal*, June 12, 1992, pp. B1, B5.
6. Gene R. Laczniak and Patrick E. Murphy, *Ethical Marketing Decisions* (Needham Heights, MA: Allyn and Bacon, 1993), p. 3.
7. Valerie A. Zeithaml, A. Parasuraman, and Leonard L. Berry, "Problems and Strategies in Services Marketing," *Journal of Marketing* 49, 2 (1985), pp. 33–46.
8. K. Douglas Hoffman and Judy A. Siguaw, "Incorporating Ethics into the Services Marketing Course: The Case of the Sears Auto Centers," *Marketing Education Review* 3, 3 (1993), pp. 26–32.
9. Ferrell and Fraedrich, *Business Ethics*, pp. 40–48.
10. Ferrell and Fraedrich, *Business Ethics*, p. 42.
11. Ferrell and Fraedrich, *Business Ethics*, p. 45.
12. Ferrell and Fraedrich, *Business Ethics*, pp. 22–29.
13. Ferrell and Fraedrich, *Business Ethics*, pp. 68–133.
14. David J. Fritzsche and Helmet Becker, "Linking Management Behavior to Ethical Philosophy: An Empirical Investigation," *Academy of Management Journal* 27 (1984), pp. 166–175.
15. Alan J. Dubinsky, Marvin A. Jolson, Masaaki Kotabe, and Chae Un Lim, "A Cross-National Investigation of Industrial Salespeople's Ethical Perceptions," *Journal of International Business Studies* 4 (1990), pp. 651–671.
16. Sandra Pelfrey and Eileen Peacock, "Ethical Codes of Conduct Are Improving," *Business Horizons* (Spring 1991), pp. 14–17.
17. O. C. Ferrell and Larry G. Gresham, "A Contingency Framework for Understanding Ethical Decision Making in Marketing," *Journal of Marketing* (Summer 1985), pp. 87–96.
18. Gilbert A. Churchill, Jr., Neil M. Ford, Steven W. Hartley, and Orville C. Walker, Jr., "The Determinants of Salesperson Performance: A Meta-Analysis," *Journal of Marketing Research* 22, 2 (1985), pp. 103–118.
19. Ferrell and Fraedrich, *Business Ethics*, p. 110.
20. K. Douglas Hoffman, Vince Howe, and Don Hardigree, "Selling of Complex Others and Competitive Pressures," *Journal of Personal Selling and Sales Management* 11, 4 (1991), pp. 13–25.

21. David Shepard, *The New Direct Marketing: How to Implement a Profit-Driven Database Marketing Strategy* (Homewood, IL: Business One Irwin, 1990).

22. Orville C. Walker, Gilbert A. Churchill, and Neil M. Ford, "Where Do We Go from Here: Selected Conceptual and Empirical Issues Concerning the Motivation and Performance of the Industrial Sales Force," in *Critical Issues in Sales Management: State-of-the-Art and Future Research Needs*, G. Albaum and G. A. Churchill, eds. (Eugene, OR: College of Business Administration, University of Oregon, 1979).

23. Ronald W. Vinson, "Industry Image Stuck in Downcycle," *National Underwriter Property & Casualty-Risk & Benefits Management*, January 7, 1991, pp. 25–29.

24. Ferrell and Fraedrich, *Business Ethics*, pp. 137–150.

25. Sandra Pelfrey and Eileen Peacock, "Ethical Codes of Conduct Are Improving," *Business Horizons* (Spring 1991), pp. 14–17.

26. C. King, "Prof. Challenges Industry to Face Ethical Issues," *National Underwriter Life & Health-Financial Services*, August 16, 1990, pp. 15–16.

27. Lawrence A. Crosby, Kenneth R. Evans, and Deborah Cowles, "Relationship Quality in Services Selling: An Interpersonal Influence Perspective," *Journal of Marketing* (July 1990), pp. 68–81.

# PART | 2

## SERVICE STRATEGY: MANAGING THE SERVICE EXPERIENCE

Part 2 is dedicated to topics that pertain to managing the service experience. Due to consumer involvement in the production of services, many challenges for management occur that rarely, if ever, need to be considered in the production of goods. In this part, you will learn about the strategic issues that affect both the marketing mix and the components of the servuction model including process, pricing, promotion, physical evidence, and people (employee and customer) issues.

## CHAPTER 6

# SERVICE DELIVERY PROCESS

## CHAPTER OBJECTIVES

*The main objective in this chapter is to familiarize you with operations concepts and explain the importance of balancing operations and marketing functions in service operations.*

After reading this chapter, you should be able to:

- Discuss the stages of operational competitiveness.
- Appreciate the relationship between operations and marketing as it pertains to developing service delivery systems.
- Describe the types of operational models that facilitate operational efficiency.
- Consider the challenges associated with applying peak efficiency models to service organizations and recommend strategies that overcome some of these difficulties.
- Explain the art of service blueprinting as it relates to the design of service delivery systems.

*"Choose Me, Hear Me, Stuff Me, Stitch Me, Fluff Me, Name Me, Dress Me, Take Me Home"*

Build-a-Bear Workshop's World-Class Service Process

© GETTY IMAGES

Service firms can strategically view their operations along a continuum ranging from necessary evil to the other extreme, where operations are viewed as a key source of competitive advantage. Clearly, Build-a-Bear Workshop have used their world-class service delivery systems to create a compelling service experience for its customers. Build-a-Bear Workshops offer an experience-based business model where customers and their children or grandchildren can make and accessorize their own teddy bears. Given the option of purchasing a bear off the shelf at the local discount toy store or accompanying a child to a Build-a-Bear Workshop where they can be personally involved in creating the bear as a family, many customers are enthusiastically opting for the latter choice.

Build-a-Bear Workshop is the only national company that provides a make-your-own stuffed animal, interactive-entertainment retail experience. The company opened its first store in St. Louis in 1997 and as of January 2005 operated 170 stores in 40 states and Canada. The company opened international stores in 2003 and 2004 in England, Japan, Denmark, and Australia. Since 1997, the company has sold over 25 million stuffed animals, making Build-a-Bear Workshop the global leader in the teddy bear business.

Build-a-Bear's competitive advantage has been its service delivery system consisting of the clever process of *Choose Me, Hear Me, Stuff Me, Stitch Me, Fluff Me, Name Me, Dress Me, and Take Me Home*. As described by the company's website (http://www.buildabear.com), the process of making a teddy bear flows as follows:

Choose Me—guests select from a variety of bears, dogs, cats, bunnies, monkeys, and a series of limited edition offerings.

Hear Me—guests are then able to select from several sound choices that are placed inside their new stuffed friend. Examples of sounds include giggles, growls, barks, meows, and recorded messages such as "I Love You" and songs like "Let Me Call You Sweetheart."

Stuff Me—guests, with the help of master Bear Builder associates, fill their new stuffed friends with just the right amount of stuffing for customized huggability. Each guest then selects a satin heart, makes a wish, and places the heart inside their new furry friend.

Stitch Me—stuffed friends are stitched up but not before a store associate places a barcode inside the stuffed animal so that if lost, the furry friend can be reunited with its owner. The company believes that thousands of bears have been returned to their owners through their exclusive Find-a-Bear ID tracking program.

Fluff Me—guests are now able to fluff their new friends to perfection with the use of cool-air hair dryers and brushes at the purposely designed bear spa.

Name Me—guests stop at the Name Me computer where they enter their names, and the birth date and name of their new friend. Guests can then select between customized birth certificates or a story that incorporates the owner's name and the stuffed animal's name. Guests can select either English or Spanish.

Dress Me—guests are now directed to the bear apparel boutique where Pawsonal Shoppers help guests select from hundreds of choices the perfect outfit and accessories for their new friend.

Take Me Home—guests end their experience at the Take Me Home station where they are given their customized birth certificate or story and a Buy Stuff Club Card to apply toward future purchases. Finally, each new furry friend is placed within a Club Condo carrying case that is specifically designed as a handy travel carrier and new home.

As testament to the effectiveness of Build-a-Bear Workshop's extraordinary delivery system, the company has received numerous awards such as *ICSC "2004 Hot Retailer Award"* and was named *National Retail Federation's International 2001 Retail Innovator of the Year—Global Winner*. The company has also been profiled in books such as *Revolutionize Your Customer Experience* and *Customer Service Excellence 2004: Exemplary Practices in Retail*.

Source: http://www.buildabear.com accessed 11 April, 2005.

## > INTRODUCTION

The servuction model introduced in Chapter 1 clearly demonstrates that consumers are an integral part of the service process. Their participation may be active or passive, but they are always there. If the consumer is an active participant in the service factory, it is clear that if the factory is changed, consumer behavior will have to be changed. Moreover, changes to the visible part of the service firm will be apparent to the consumer.

For example, when convenience stores first opened, gasoline was not part of the product offering. The introduction of gasoline to the product mix presented two new challenges to consumers. First, from a psychological standpoint, the initial thought of buying gasoline at the same location as food products was resisted. Gasoline stations at the time were generally dirty, grimy places staffed by burly men who had years of grit built up under their fingernails. A gasoline station was hardly the place one wanted to buy food. The second challenge, having customers pump their own gas, created a change in operations that required a change in consumer behavior. Consumers had to learn how to work a gas pump, and the convenience store and gasoline pump manufacturers had to develop gas pumps and monitoring procedures for this new type of self-service operation.

Managers of service firms must understand the interactive nature of services and the involvement of the consumer in the production process. As we discussed in Chapter 4, consumers appear to develop a script for frequently used services. This script is similar to a theatrical script in that it helps guide the consumer through the service experience. Changes in the service factory process will imply changes in the consumer script—the way in which the consumer participates in the process.

New developments coming from either the service factory or the consumer imply major changes in the consumer script as well as changes in the scripts of contact personnel. This chapter highlights the trade-offs between the search for operational efficiency and the need to create marketing effectiveness. In the service factory, many of the traditional methods for increasing operational effectiveness cannot be implemented behind closed doors. In fact, changes made to increase the service operation's efficiency can often downgrade the final service product. This chapter focuses on the positive things marketing can achieve to help improve the efficiency of service operations.

> ## STAGES OF OPERATIONAL COMPETITIVENESS

Without a successful operation, the firm is out of business, because it will have nothing to offer the customer. However, firms setting out to construct a service operation can choose from a large range of operational options. Strategically, the service firm can choose to use its operations as the key component of its competitive strategy or view its operations as a necessary evil. The manner in which "operational competitiveness" is embraced by various service firms can be described by four stages:[1]

> Stage 1: Available for service
> Stage 2: Journeyman
> Stage 3: Distinctive competencies achieved
> Stage 4: World-class service delivery

### STAGE 1: AVAILABLE FOR SERVICE

Operations for a firm with this level of competitiveness are viewed as a "necessary evil." Operations are at best reactive to the needs of the rest of the organization and deliver the service as specified. As its mission, the operations department attempts primarily to avoid mistakes. Back-office support is minimized to keep costs down. Technological investment is also minimized, as is investment in training for front-line personnel. Management designs the skill out of work done by these personnel and pays them the minimum wage whenever possible.

### STAGE 2: JOURNEYMAN

This level of competitiveness is often provided by the arrival of competition. It is no longer enough just to have an operation that works. The firm must now seek feedback from its customers on the relative costs and perceived qualities of the service. At this point, the operations department becomes much more outward-looking and often becomes interested in benchmarking.

Technology for firms at this stage tends to be justified based on the cost savings possible. The back office is now seen as a contributor to the service but tends to be treated as an internal service function. In the management of front-line employees, the emphasis shifts from controlling workers to managing processes. Employees are often given procedures to follow, and management consists of ensuring that these procedures are followed.

### STAGE 3: DISTINCTIVE COMPETENCE ACHIEVED

By this stage, operations have reached a point where they continually excel, reinforced by the personnel management function and systems that support the customer focus (see Global Services in Action). By this time, the firm has mastered the core service and understands the complexity of changing such operations. The back office is now seen to be as valuable as the front-of-house personnel. Technology is no longer seen as a source of cost advantage alone, but also as a way of enhancing the service to customers.

Perhaps the biggest changes come about in the workforce and in the nature of front-line management. Front-line workers are allowed to select from alternative procedures and are not tied down in the same way. The role of front-line management is to listen to customers and become coaches to the front-line workers.

### STAGE 4: WORLD-CLASS SERVICE DELIVERY

To sustain this level of performance, operations not only have to continually excel but also become a fast learner and innovator. The back office, once seen as a second-class citizen, now must be proactive, develop its own capabilities, and generate opportunities. Technology is seen as a way to break the paradigm— to do things competitors cannot do.

The workforce itself must be a source of innovators, not just operators. To achieve this, the front-line supervisors must go beyond coaching to mentoring. As mentors, they need to be accountable for the personal development of the workforce so that employees can develop the skills necessary for them to innovate for the firm.

Overall, the purpose of this chapter is to highlight the fact that operations management problems in services cannot be solved by the operations function alone. As pointed out by the four stages noted earlier, the search for operations efficiency can be crucial to long-term competitiveness. However, efficiency must be balanced against the effectiveness of the system from the customer's point of view. Table 6.1 provides a quick glimpse into the major trade-offs between efficiency and effectiveness when developing operations for low-customer-contact versus high-customer-contact services.

Frequently, it is too easy to view the customer as a constraint: "If we could get rid of all these customers, we could run a good service operation!" Such a negative perspective ignores a golden opportunity. Customers in a service operation can be used to help operations. Such a positive view, does, however, require that operations personnel recognize the importance of their marketing counterparts.

More importantly, such a view also requires that marketing personnel have an intimate knowledge of the operations system and its problems. It is not enough to propose new products that can be delivered through the system. The impact of such products on the whole system must be considered.[2]

> ### MARKETING AND OPERATIONS: BALANCE IS CRITICAL

In a broad sense, one way of viewing the relationship between marketing and operations is to think of it as the marrying of consumers' needs with the technology and

## GLOBAL SERVICES *IN ACTION*

### DELIGHTING THE GLOBAL CUSTOMER: ORDERING, FULFILLMENT, AND RETURNS

When operating globally, the manner in which core processes such as ordering, fulfillment, and handling returns are designed and implemented can lead to significant competitive advantages. A few key areas to pay close attention to include the following:

*Ordering* should be made as easy as possible and forms should be adapted where necessary such as:

Name and address—plenty of room should be provided since many addresses are much longer than U.S. addresses.

Instructions—clothing merchandisers should provide size conversion charts to increase customer confidence and reduce the number of returns.

Product descriptions—should be provided using the local language to reduce confusion.

Response channels—provide customers with a variety of choices in which to place their orders including phone, mail, fax, and the Web. In America, the vast majority of orders are taken over the phone. In Japan, phone calls are expensive and most orders are taken by mail. The majority of business-to-business transactions are received by fax.

Fulfillment switch—if orders are collected by phone, language, culture, time, and costs are four good reasons why it makes sense to set up an overseas call center.

Payment options—preferred methods of payment often vary by country. For example, German customers are typically billed after their purchases are delivered. Options such as cash on delivery, check, payment by invoice, direct debit, credit card, and bank transfers should be considered.

*Fulfillment* pertains to the actual delivery of goods and services:

Distribution centers—establishing overseas distribution centers makes sense when overseas sales represent a high rate of return or when the company is fully vested in its global operations.

Delivery—cost savings are often offset by lengthy delivery timetables. Shipping from local warehouses obviously saves time. For example, if shipped from the U.S., a package can take ten days to reach its destination in Japan. If sent from a local warehouse, that same package can reach its destination in less than 24 hours.

*Returns*, *exchanges*, and *refunds* must be managed:

Refunds—currency fluctuations should not impact a customer's refund. The customer should be reimbursed at the same rate as the original payment.

Postage—postage is always to be refunded when specifically asked by the customer to do so. Otherwise, experts suggest that refunding postage is dependent upon the profit margin of the sale. When affordable, postage should be refunded.

Source: Lisa A. Yorgey, "Delighting the Global Customer," *Target Marketing*, 23 (2), (February 2000), pp. 104–106.

| TABLE 6.1 | MAJOR DESIGN TRADE-OFFS IN HIGH- AND LOW-CONTACT SYSTEMS | |
|---|---|---|

| Decision | High-Contact System | Low-Contact System |
|---|---|---|
| Facility location | Operations must be near the customer. | Operations may be placed near supply, transportation, or labor. |
| Facility layout | Facility should accomodate the customer's physical and psychological needs and expectations. | Facility should enhance production. |
| Product design | Environment as well as the physical product define the nature of the service. | Customer is not in the service environment so the product can be defined by fewer attributes. |
| Process design | Stages of production process have a direct immediate effect on the customer. | Customer is not involved in the majority of processing steps. |
| Scheduling | Customer is in the production schedule and must be accommodated. | Customer is concerned mainly with completion dates. |
| Production planning | Orders cannot be stored, so smoothing production flow will result in loss of business. | Both backlogging and production smoothing are possible. |
| Worker skills | Direct workforce makes up a major part of the service product and so must be able to interact well with the public. | Direct workforce need have only technical skills. |
| Quality control | Quality standards are often in the eye of the beholder and, hence, variable. | Quality standards are generally measurable and, hence, fixed. |
| Time standards | Service time depends on customer needs, so time standards are inherently loose. | Work is performed on customer surrogates (e.g., forms), and time standards can be tight. |
| Wage payments | Variable output requires time-based wage systems. | "Fixable" outputs permits output-based wage systems. |
| Capacity planning | To avoid lost sales, capacity must be set to match peak demand. | Storable output permits setting capacity at some average demand level. |
| Forecasting | Forecasts are short term, time oriented. | Forecasts are long term, output oriented. |

Source: Richard C. Chase, "Where Does the Customer Fit in a Service Operation?" *Harvard Business Review* (November–December 1978), pp. 137–142. Reprinted by permission of *Harvard Business Review.* Copyright © 1978 by the President and Fellows of Harvard College.

manufacturing capabilities of the firm (see B2B Services in Action). Such a marriage will obviously involve compromises since the consumers' needs can seldom be met completely and economically. In a goods firm, this partnership requires marketing's understanding of the capabilities of manufacturing and of research and development. The task of marketing goods is made somewhat easier because the different functions can be separated by means of an inventory.

In a service firm, this marketing problem is magnified. Significant aspects of the operation are the product because they create the interactive experience that delivers the bundle of benefits to the consumer. For example, a restaurant experience is not based solely on the quality of the food. The physical environment and interactions with contact personnel throughout the experience also affect consumer perceptions of the quality of service delivered. A successful compromise between operations efficiency and marketing effectiveness is, therefore, that much more difficult to achieve. Success

**B2B SERVICES** *IN ACTION*

> ### VERIZON ENTERPRISE SOLUTIONS GROUP: TEAMING UP WITH HEALTHCARE

Verizon Enterprise Solutions Group provides network solutions for large businesses, government, and education customers across the United States. As a business entity, the solutions group employs more than 7,800 employees and generated approximately $6 billion in 2004 business unit revenues. Verizon Enterprise Solutions Group products and services include voice services, voice and data customer premises equipment, managed network services, and a vast array of data services. Key target markets include finance, education, healthcare, and government.

One of the more intriguing solutions projects has been Verizon's interaction with UMass Memorial Healthcare, the largest healthcare system in Massachusetts. Thanks to a recent $9.6 million agreement between the healthcare system and Verizon, medical specialists will now collaborate in the diagnosis and care of patients through the use of high-speed, broadband services. Managed SONET Services allow patient histories and diagnostic data to be viewed simultaneously at the healthcare system's three campuses, four community hospitals, and other care facilities. SONET Services provides the hospital with the ability to communicate with physicians and healthcare professionals without being in the same place at the same time. Patient privacy is also ensured.

Verizon Enterprise Solutions Group also offers Telemedicine Solutions to the healthcare industry. Telemedicine Solutions can literally place physicians and other key medical personnel in patient homes and other critical places. Physicians can now communicate with paramedics while en route to the hospital and oversee procedures in an operating room while not being physically present. Telemedicine Solutions utilize picture archiving and communications systems that provide information to multiple users at the same time, regardless of their locations.

The ultimate goal of all Verizon healthcare solutions is to increase patient access to healthcare services, provide faster service delivery, improve patient outcomes, and reduce healthcare costs. In the meantime, Verizon Enterprise Solutions Group generates an increasingly significant amount of revenue for the firm.

Source: http://www22.verizon.com/enterprisesolutions/Default/Index.jsp accessed 13 April 2005.

in services marketing demands a much greater understanding of the constraints and opportunities posed by operations.

To introduce these complexities, we will first adopt the perspective of an operations manager and ask, "What would be the ideal way to run the system from an operations perspective?" The impact on marketing and the opportunities for marketing to assist in the creation of this ideal are then developed.

As pointed out in Chapter 1, the key distinctive characteristic of services is that the product is an experience. That experience is created by the operating system of the firm's interaction with the customer. Thus, the operating system of the firm, in all its complexity, is the product. For a marketing manager, this imposes constraints on the strategies that can be employed, but it also presents new and challenging opportunities for improving the profitability of the firm.

Chapter 4 provided one base on which to build an understanding of the product design problem for services. An understanding of consumer behavior has always been a necessary condition for successful marketing. One way of viewing the product design process is to think of it as the process of combining such an understanding with the technological and manufacturing skills of the organization. To be an effective services marketer, a knowledge of consumer behavior is not sufficient in itself to produce economically successful products. Successful managers also need a keen understanding of operations and human resource concepts and strategies.

As we discussed in Chapter 2, it is possible for goods producers to separate the problems of manufacturing and marketing by the use of inventory. Even so, there are many areas of potential conflict, as shown in Table 6.2. Although the issues are characterized as conflicts, they can be reconceptualized as opportunities. In each area it is clear that a better integration of marketing and manufacturing plans could yield a more efficient and profitable organization. For example, the determination of the extent of the product line should be seen as a compromise between the heterogeneous demands of consumers and the manufacturing demand of homogeneity. If marketing managers have their way, too many products will probably be developed, and the operation will become inefficient. As long as this is compensated for by higher prices, then a successful strategy can be implemented. In contrast, if the operations people have their way, everyone would be driving the same model of car, painted the same color, which is less attractive for consumers. As long as this is compensated for by lower costs, and hence lower prices, a successful strategy can emerge.

Marketing and operations are in a tug of war that should be resolved by compromise. In the service sector, the possible areas of conflict or compromise are much broader because the operation itself is the product. Again, there is no single solution since operational efficiency and marketing effectiveness may push in opposite directions.

To polarize the issues, the perspective adopted in this chapter is that of the operations manager, just as in Chapter 4 the consumer's position was presented. The focus is on the requirements for operational efficiency and the ways that marketing can help achieve those requirements. We stress that in the drive for competitive advantage in the marketplace, marketing demand may in the end mean less operational efficiency. As the level of customer contact increases, the likelihood that the service firm will operate efficiently decreases. Customers ultimately determine:

- the type of demand,
- the cycle of demand,
- and the length of the service experience.

Meanwhile, the service firm loses more and more control over its daily operations. This is the nature of the service business.

| TABLE 6.2 | SOURCES OF COOPERATION/CONFLICT BETWEEN MARKETING AND OPERATIONS | |
|---|---|---|
| **Problem Area** | **Typical Marketing Comment** | **Typical Manufacturing Comment** |
| 1. Capacity planning and long-range sales forecasting | "Why don't we have enough capacity?" | "Why didn't we have accurate sales forecasts?" |
| 2. Production scheduling and short-range sales forecasting | "We need faster response. Our lead times are ridiculous." | "We need realistic customer commitments and sales forecasts that don't change like wind direction." |
| 3. Delivery and physical distribution | "Why don't we ever have the right merchandise in inventory?" | "We can't keep everything in inventory." |
| 4. Quality assurance | "Why can't we have reasonable quality at reasonable costs?" | "Why must we always offer options that are too hard to manufacture and that offer little customer utility?" |
| 5. Breadth of product line | "Our customers demand variety." | "The product line is too broad—all we get are short, uneconomical runs." |
| 6. Cost control | "Our costs are so high that we are not competitive in the marketplace." | "We can't provide fast delivery, broad variety, rapid response to change, and high quality at low cost." |
| 7. New product introduction | "New products are our lifeblood." | "Unnecessary design changes are prohibitively expensive." |
| 8. Adjunct services such as spare parts, inventory support, installation, and repair | "Field service costs are too high." | "Products are being used in ways for which they weren't designed." |

Source: Reprinted by permission of Harvard Business Review. An exhibit from "Can Marketing and Manufacturing Coexist?" by Benson P. Shapiro (September/October 1977), p. 105. Copyright © 1977 by the President and Fellows of Harvard College; all rights reserved.

## > IN A PERFECT WORLD, SERVICE FIRMS WOULD BE EFFICIENT

Operating a service firm at peak efficiency would be an ideal situation. Thompson's *perfect-world model* provides us the direction needed to achieve this ultimate goal. However, in reality, peak efficiency is often unattainable. The *focused factory* and *plant-within-a-plant* concepts provide managers with alternative strategies that enhance the efficiency of the firm while taking into consideration marketing effectiveness.

### THOMPSON'S PERFECT-WORLD MODEL

The starting point for this discussion is the work of J. D. Thompson.[3] Thompson, who started from an organizational perspective, introduced the idea of a **technical core**—the place within the organization where its primary operations are conducted. In the service sector, the technical core consists of kitchens in restaurants, garages in auto service stations, work areas at dry cleaners, and surgical suites in a hospital. Thompson proposed

**technical core**
The place within an organization where its primary operations are conducted.

By isolating the technical core, such as not letting customers into a restaurant's kitchen, the efficiency of the operation increases. In this instance, the kitchen becomes a focused factory.

© JOUANNEAU THOMAS / CORBIS SYGMA

**perfect-world model**
J. D. Thompson's model of organizations proposing that operations' "perfect" efficiency is possible only if inputs, outputs, and quality happen at a constant rate and remain known and certain.

in his **perfect-world model** that to operate efficiently, a firm must be able to operate *"as if the market will absorb the single kind of product at a continuous rate and as if the inputs flowed continuously at a steady rate and with specified quality."* At the center of his argument was the idea that uncertainty creates inefficiency. In the ideal situation, the technical core is able to operate without uncertainty on both the input and output side, thereby creating many advantages for management.

The absence of uncertainty means that decisions within the core can become programmed and that individual discretion can be replaced by rules; the removal of individual discretion means that jobs are "de-skilled" and that a lower quality of labor can be used. Alternatively, the rules can be programmed into machines and labor replaced with capital. Because output and input are fixed, it is simple to plan production and to run at the high levels of utilization needed to generate the most efficient operations performance.

All in all, a system without uncertainty is easy to control and manage. Performance can be measured using objective standards. And since the system is not subject to disturbances from the outside, the causes of any problems are also easy to diagnose.

## THE FOCUSED FACTORY CONCEPT

**focused factory**
An operation that concentrates on performing one particular task in one particular part of the plant; used for promoting experience and effectiveness through repetition and concentration on one task necessary for success.

Obviously, such an ideal world as proposed by Thompson is virtually impossible to create, and even in goods companies the demands of purchasing the inputs and marketing's management of the outputs have to be traded off against the ideal operations demands. In goods manufacturing, this trade-off has been accomplished through the **focused factory**.[4] The focused factory focuses on a particular job; once this focus is achieved, the factory does a better job because repetition and concentration in one area allow the workforce and managers to become effective and experienced in the task required for success. The focused factory broadens Thompson's perfect-world model in that it argues that focus generates effectiveness as well as efficiency. In other words, the focused factory can meet the demands of the market better whether the demand is low cost through efficiency, high quality, or any other criterion.

## THE PLANT-WITHIN-A-PLANT CONCEPT

The idea of a focused factory can be extended in another direction by introducing the **plant-within-a-plant (PWP)** concept. Because there are advantages to having production capability at a single site, the plant-within-a-plant strategy introduces the concept of breaking up large, unfocused plants into smaller units buffered from one another so that they can each be focused separately.

In goods manufacturing, the concept of **buffering** is very important. "Organizations seek to buffer environmental influences by surrounding their technical core with input and output components."[5] A PWP can thus be operated in a manner close to Thompson's perfect-world model if buffer inventories are created on the input and output sides. On the input side, the components needed in a plant can be inventoried and their quality controlled before they are needed; in this way, it can appear to the PWP that the quality and flow of the inputs into the system are constant. In a similar way, the PWP can be separated from downstream plants or from the market by creating finished goods inventories. Automobile manufacturers are good examples. Finished goods are absorbed downstream by an established retail dealership system who purchases and holds the manufacturer's inventory in regional markets until sold to the final consumer.

The alternatives proposed by Thompson to buffering are smoothing, anticipating, and rationing. Smoothing and anticipating focus on the uncertainty introduced into the system by the flow of work; **smoothing** involves managing the environment to reduce fluctuations in supply and/or demand, and **anticipating** involves mitigating the worst effects of those fluctuations by planning for them. Finally, **rationing** involves resorting to triage when the demands placed on the system by the environment exceed its ability to handle them. Successful firms preplan smoothing, anticipating, and rationing strategies so that they can be more efficiently implemented in times of need.

> ## APPLYING THE EFFICIENCY MODELS TO SERVICE FIRMS

The application of operations concepts to services is fraught with difficulty. The problem can be easily understood by thinking about the servuction model presented in Chapter 1. From an operational point of view, the key characteristics of the model are that the customer is an integral part of the process and that the system operates in real time. Because the system is interactive, it can be (and often is) used to customize the service for each individual.

To put it bluntly, the servuction system itself is an operations nightmare. In most cases it is impossible to use inventories and impossible to decouple production from the customer. Instead of receiving demand at a constant rate, the system is linked directly to a market that frequently varies from day to day, hour to hour, and even

**plant within a plant**
The strategy of breaking up large, unfocused plants into smaller units buffered from one another so that each can be focused separately.

**buffering**
Surrounding the technical core with input and output components to buffer environmental influences.

**smoothing**
Managing the environment to reduce fluctuations in supply and/or demand.

**anticipating**
Mitigating the worst effects of supply and demand fluctuations by planning for them.

**rationing**
Direct allocations of inputs and outputs when the demands placed on a system by the environment exceed the system's ability to handle them.

## E-SERVICES *IN ACTION*

### > THE REAL Y2K NIGHTMARE: E-RETURNS

There is little doubt that the Internet is here to stay and that many opportunities in the field of e-service lay ahead. However, as more consumers order products on the Web, more problems for e-tailers emerge. One of those problems pertains to the customer service issue of processing exchanges and returns. Termed, "The Season of E-Returns," ordering online during the 1999 holiday season turned out to be the real Y2K nightmare.

Extraprise, an e-business market research firm located in Boston, notes of the 50 sites that it researched, the vast majority had polices that penalized the customer for returns and exchanges. The company's most notable findings included the following:

- Few standard practices exist for returning purchases that were made online.
- It's the customer's responsibility to sift through the fine print to determine how exchanges and returns are to be conducted.
- In most cases, the consumer has to pay the shipping cost of the returned item.
- In some cases, consumers must pay shipping cost even if the item is delivered broken or in error.
- Many sites charge return-related expenses via hidden fees that are charged to customers.
- Dot.coms, as opposed to "click-and-mortar stores," are three times as likely to charge a restocking fee (Buy.com charges a $35 "reboxing fee") if the returned item's packaging is damaged.
- Two out of three dot.coms do not explicitly state whether it's the seller or the buyer who is responsible for the shipping costs associated with returned items.

Overall, "click-and-mortar" stores far outperformed dot.coms when it came to stating return policies and providing the customer with more friendly policies regarding exchanges and returns. Extraprise noted: "retail brands with a reputation for providing excellent service tend to carry this trait over to their websites."

minute to minute (see E-Services in Action). This creates massive problems in capacity planning and utilization. In fact, in many instances supply and demand match up purely by accident.

It is clear from this simplified model that services, by their very nature, do not meet the requirements of the perfect-world model. The closest the servuction model comes to this ideal state is the part of the system that is invisible to the customer. Even here, however, the customization taking place may introduce uncertainty into the system. Providing that all customization can take place within the servuction system itself, then the part invisible to the customer can be run separately. It can often be located in a place different from the customer-contact portion of the model.[6] However, when customization cannot be done within the servuction system, uncertainty can be introduced into the back office.

Instead of "the single kind of product" desired by the perfect-world model, the service system can be called upon to make a different "product" for each customer. Indeed, one could argue that since each customer is different and is an integral part of the process, and since each experience or product is unique, the uncertainty about the next task to be performed is massive.

The Thompson model requires inputs that flow continuously, at a steady rate, and at a specified quality. Consider the inputs to the servuction system: the physical environment, contact personnel, other customers, and the individual customer. The environment may remain constant in many service encounters, but the other three inputs are totally variable, not only in their quality, but also in their rate of arrival into the process.

Moreover, contact personnel are individuals, not inanimate objects. They have emotions and feelings and, like all other people, are affected by things happening in their lives outside of the work environment. If they arrive in a bad mood, this can influence their performance throughout the day. And that bad mood directly affects the customer, since the service worker is a visible part of the experience being purchased.

Customers can also be subject to moods that can affect their behavior toward the service firm and toward one another. Some moods are predictable, like the mood when a home team wins and the crowds hit the local bars. Other moods are individual, specific, and totally unpredictable until after the consumer is already part of the servuction system.

Finally, customers arrive at the service firm at unpredictable rates, making smoothing and anticipation of incoming demand difficult. One minute a restaurant can be empty, and in the next few minutes, it can be full. One need only consider the variability of demand for cashiers in a grocery store to understand the basics of this problem. Analysis of demand can often show predictable peaks that can be planned for in advance; but even this precaution introduces inefficiency into the firm since the firm would ideally prefer the customers to arrive in a steady stream. Worse still are the unpredictable peaks. Planning for these peaks would produce large amounts of excess capacity at most times. The excess would strain the entire system, undermining the experience for customer and contact personnel alike.

Within the operations management and marketing literatures of the past decade, a growing list of strategies has emerged regarding overcoming some of the problems of service operations. These strategies can be classified into six broad areas:

1. isolating the technical core;
2. minimizing the servuction system;
3. production-lining the whole system;
4. creating flexible capacity;
5. increasing customer participation; and
6. moving the time of demand.

## *ISOLATING THE TECHNICAL CORE*

Isolating the technical core of the service firm and minimizing the servuction system have been combined because they are closely related from an operations viewpoint and because their marketing implications are similar. This approach proposes the clear separation of the servuction system, which is characterized by a high degree of customer contact, from the technical core. Once separation is achieved, different management philosophies should be adopted for each separate unit of operation. In other words, let's divide the service firm into two distinct areas—high customer contact and no/low customer contact, and operate each area differently.

In the servuction system, management should focus on optimizing the experience for the consumer. Conversely, once the technical core (no/low contact area) has been isolated, it should be subjected to traditional production-lining approaches.[7] In summary, high-contact systems should sacrifice efficiency in the interest of the customer, but low-contact systems need not do so.[8]

Isolating the technical core argues for minimizing the amount of customer contact with the system. "Clients . . . pose problems for organizations . . . by disrupting their routines, ignoring their offers for service, failing to comply with their procedures, making exaggerated demands, and so forth."[9] Operating efficiency is thus reduced by the uncertainty introduced into the system by the customer.[10]

*decoupling*
Disassociating the technical core from the servuction system.

Examples of **decoupling** the technical core from high contact areas of the servuction system include suggestions from operations experts such as handling only exceptions on a face-to-face basis, with routine transactions as much as possible being handled by telephone or, even better, by mail—mail transactions have the great advantage of being able to be inventoried.[11] In addition, the degree of customer contact should be matched to customer requirements, and the amount of high-contact service offered should be the minimum acceptable to the customer.[12] Overall, operational efficiency always favors low-contact systems, but effectiveness from the customer's point of view may be something completely different.

At this point, the need for marketing involvement in the approach becomes clear, as a decision about the extent of customer contact favored by the customer is clearly a marketing issue. In some cases, a high degree of customer contact can be used to differentiate the service from its competitors; in such cases, the operational costs must be weighed against the competitive benefits. Consider the competitive advantages that a five-star restaurant has over a fast-food franchise.

Conversely, in some situations, the segment of the firm that the operations group views as the back office is not actually invisible to the customer. For example, in some financial services, the teller operation takes place in the administrative offices. Operationally, this means that staff members can leave their paperwork to serve customers only when needed. Unfortunately, customers view this operationally efficient system negatively. A customer waiting to be served can see a closed teller window and observe staff who apparently do not care because they sit at their desks without offering to assist the customer. However, the reality is that these tellers may be very busy, but the nature of the administrative work is such that they may not give this impression to customers.

Even if it is decided that part of the system can be decoupled, marketing has a major role in evaluating and implementing alternative approaches. Any change in the way in which the servuction system works implies a change in the behavior of the customer. A switch from a personal service to a combined mail and telephone system clearly requires a massive change in the way the customer behaves in the system.

Sometimes decoupling the system to become more efficient does not go over well with customers. For example, in its effort to make its tellers use their time more efficiently, First National Bank of Chicago made national news when it started charging customers with certain types of accounts a $3.00 fee for speaking with a bank teller. The bank's Chicago competition had a field day with promotions, featuring "live tellers" and giving away "free" money at their teller windows. Even Jay Leno, from NBC's "The Tonight Show" got in on the act: "Nice day isn't it? . . . That'll be $3.00 please. Huh? What? Who? . . . That'll be another $9.00 please."[13]

## PRODUCTION-LINING THE WHOLE SYSTEM

The **production-line approach** involves the application of hard and soft technologies to both the "front" and "back" of the service operation.[14] **Hard technologies** involve hardware to facilitate the production of a standardized product. Similarly, **soft technologies** refer to rules, regulations, and procedures that should be followed to produce the same result. This kind of approach to increasing operational efficiency is relatively rare, and, indeed, fast-food firms provide a classic example in which customization is minimal, volume is large, and customer participation in the process is high.

Generating any kind of operational efficiency in such a high-contact system implies a limited product line. In the case of fast food, the product line is the menu. Moreover, customization must be kept to a minimum since the whole operating system is linked straight through to the consumer. The primary problem is how to provide efficient, standardized service at some acceptable level of quality while simultaneously treating each customer as unique.[15] Past attempts to solve this problem illustrate its complexity. Attempts at forms of routine personalization such as the "have-a-nice-day" syndrome have had positive effects on the perceived friendliness of the service provider but have had adverse effects on perceived competence. Consequently, an apparently simple operations decision can have complex effects on customer perceptions.

The servuction system applied to fast food also depends for its success on a large volume of customers being available to take the standardized food that is produced. Since the invisible component is not decoupled and food cannot be prepared to order, the operating system has to run independently of individual demand and assume that, in the end, aggregate demand will absorb the food produced. This is why pre-made sandwiches are stacked in bins as they wait to be absorbed by future demand in the marketplace.

Such an operating system is extremely demanding of its customers. They must preselect what they want to eat. They are expected to have their order ready when they reach the order point. They must leave the order point quickly and carry their food to the table. Finally, in many cases, these same customers are expected to bus their own tables.

*production-line approach*
The application of hard and soft technologies to a service operation in order to produce a standardized service product.

*hard technologies*
Hardware that facilitates the production of a standardized product.

*soft technologies*
Rules, regulations, and procedures that facilitate the production of a standardized product.

Although the production-line approach to increasing service operational efficiency is rare, fast-food firms provide a classic example in which customization is minimal, volume is large, and customer participation in the process is high.

© MICHAEL NEWMAN / PHOTO EDIT

## *CREATING FLEXIBLE CAPACITY*

As pointed out in Chapter 2, the few times that supply matches demand during service encounters occur primarily by accident. One method used to minimize the effects of variable demand is to create flexible capacity (supply).[16] However, even in this area, strategies that start as common-sense operational solutions have far-reaching marketing implications as these new initiatives come face to face with the service firm's customer base. For example, a few of the strategies to create flexible capacity mentioned in Chapter 2 included (1) using part-time employees; (2) cross-training employees so that the majority of employee efforts focus on customer-contact jobs during peak hours; and (3) sharing capacity with other firms.

Although these strategies are fairly straightforward from an operational point of view, consider their marketing implications. Part-time employees appear to be a useful strategy because they can be used to provide extra capacity in peak times without increasing the costs in off-peak times. There are, however, a number of marketing implications. For example, part-time employees may deliver a lower-quality service than full-time workers; their dedication to quality may be lower, and their training probably less comprehensive. They are used at times when the operation is at its busiest, such as Christmas or during tourist seasons, when demand is fast and furious, and this may be reflected in their attitudes of frustration, which can be highly visible to customers and negatively influence customer perceptions of the quality of service delivered.[17]

In a similar way, the other two possible solutions for creating flexible capacity also have major marketing implications. First, focusing on customer-contact jobs during peak demand presupposes that it is possible to identify the key part of the service from the customer's point of view. Secondly, the dangers of sharing capacity are numerous. For example, the television show "Cheers" provided ample examples of the problems associated with the upscale and upstairs customers of Melville's Restaurant as they mixed with Cheers' everyday clientele such as Norm and Cliff. Confusion may be produced in the customer's mind over exactly what the service facility is doing, and this could be particularly critical during changeover times when customers from two different firms are in the same facility, each group with different priorities and different scripts.

## *INCREASING CUSTOMER PARTICIPATION*

The essence of increasing customer participation is to replace the work done by the employees of the firm with work done by the customer.[18] Unlike the other strategies discussed, which focus on improving the efficiency of the operation, this approach focuses primarily on reducing the costs associated with providing the service to the customer. This strategy, too, has its trade-offs.

Consider for a moment our earlier discussions about consumer scripts. Increasing consumer participation in the service encounter requires a substantial modification of the consumer's script. Moreover, the customers are called upon to take greater responsibility for the service they receive. For example, the automatic teller machine (ATM) is seen by many operations personnel as a way of saving labor. In fact, the substitution of human labor with machines is a classic operations approach, and the ATM can definitely be viewed in that light. From a customer's point of view, such ATMs provide added convenience in terms of the hours during which the bank is accessible. However, it has been shown that for some customers, an ATM represents increased risk, less control of the situation, and a loss of human contact.[19]

Such a switching of activities to the customer clearly has major marketing implications since the whole nature of the product received is changing. Such changes in the customer's script, therefore, require much customer research and detailed planning.

Increasing customer participation, such as customers scanning their own groceries at the check-out counter, decreases the cost of providing the service and generally provides added convenience and/or cost savings to the customer.

## MOVING THE TIME OF DEMAND TO FIT CAPACITY

Finally, yet another strategy utilized to optimize the efficiency of service operations is the attempt to shift the time of demand to smooth the peaks and valleys associated with many services. Perhaps the classic example of this problem is the mass transit system that needs to create capacity to deal with the rush hour and, as a consequence, has much of its fleet and labor idle during nonrush hours. Many mass transit authorities have attempted to reduce the severity of the problem by inducing customers through discounts and give-aways to travel during nonrush periods. Once again, operations and marketing become intertwined. Smoothing demand is a useful strategy from an operations point of view; however, this strategy fails to recognize the change in consumer behavior needed to make the strategy effective. Unfortunately, because much of the travel on the mass transit system is derived from demand based on commuter work schedules, little success in the effort to reallocate demand can be expected.[20]

## > THE ART OF BLUEPRINTING

One of the most common techniques used to analyze and manage complex production processes in pursuit of operational efficiency is flowcharting. Flowcharts:

- identify the directions in which processes flow,
- the time it takes to move from one process to the next,
- the costs involved with each process step,
- the amount of inventory build-up at each step, and
- the bottlenecks in the system.

*blueprinting*
The flowcharting of a service operation.

The flowcharting of a service operation, commonly referred to as **blueprinting**, is a useful tool not only for the operations manager but for the marketing manager as well.[21]

Because services are delivered by an interactive process involving the consumer, the marketing manager in a service firm needs to have detailed knowledge of the operation. Blueprinting provides a useful systematic method for acquiring that knowledge. Blueprints enable the marketing manager to understand which parts in the operating system are visible to the consumer and hence part of the servuction system—the fundamental building blocks of consumer perceptions.

Identifying the components of an individual firm's servuction system turns out to be more difficult than it first appears. Many firms, for example, underestimate the number of points of contact between them and their customers. Many forget or underestimate the importance of telephone operators, secretarial and janitorial staff, or accounting personnel. The material that follows describes the simple process of flowcharting these numerous points of contact. Service flowcharts, in addition to being useful to the operations managers, allow marketing managers to better understand the servuction process.

The heart of the service product is the experience of the consumer, which takes place in real-time. This interaction can occur in a building or in an environment created by the service firm, such as the complex environments that are created at Disney World, Epcot Center, and Universal Studios. In some instances, such as lawncare, the service interaction takes place in a natural setting. It is the interactive process itself that creates the benefits desired by the consumer. Designing that process, therefore, becomes key to the product design for a service firm.

The interactive process that is visible to consumers develops their perception of reality and defines the final service product. However, as the servuction model discussed in Chapter 1 demonstrated, the visible part of the operations process, with which the consumer interacts, must be supported by an invisible process.

The search for operational efficiency is not unique to service firms, but it does pose some interesting problems. A change in the service operation may be more efficient, but it may also change the quality of interaction with the consumer. For example, students at many universities are now able to register for classes through automated telephone services. This type of operation offers increased efficiency but sometimes minimizes the quality of the student/advisor interaction. A detailed blueprint provides a means of communications between operations and marketing and can highlight potential problems on paper before they occur in real-time.

## AN EXAMPLE OF A SIMPLE BLUEPRINT[22]

Figure 6.1 shows a simple process in which, for now, it is assumed that the entire operation is visible to the customer. It represents the blueprint of a cafeteria-style restaurant and specifies the steps involved in getting a meal. In this example, each process activity is represented by a box. In contrast to a goods manufacturer, the "raw materials" flowing through the process are the customers. Due to the intangibility of services, there are no inventories in the process, but clearly, inventories of customers form at each step in the process while they wait their turn to proceed to the next counter. A restaurant run in this manner would be a single long chain of counters with customers progressing along the chain and emerging after paying, such as a Western Sizzlin' or Golden Corral. In Figure 6.1, the cost calculation by each stage represents the cost of providing personnel to service each counter.

To calculate the **service cost per meal**, or the labor costs associated with providing the meal on a per-meal basis, the following calculations are made. First, the **process time** is calculated by dividing the **activity time** (the time required to perform the activity) by the number of **stations**, or locations performing the activity. In our example, the process and activity times are the same because only one station is available for each activity.

Second, the **maximum output per hour** for each location is calculated based on the process time. Simply stated, the maximum output per hour is the number of people that can be served at each station in an hour's time. For example, the process time at the salad counter is 30 seconds. This means that two people can be processed in a minute, or 120 people (2 people x 60 minutes) in an hour. Another easy way to calculate the maximum output per hour is to use the formula: 60(60/process time). In our example, the salad counter calculation would be 60(60/30) = 120.

---

**service cost per meal**
The labor costs associated with providing a meal on a per-meal basis (total labor costs/maximum output per hour).

**process time**
Calculated by dividing the activity time by the number of locations at which the activity is performed.

**activity time**
The time required to perform one activity at one station.

**stations**
A location at which an activity is performed.

**maximum output per hour**
The number of people that can be processed at each station in one hour.

| FIGURE 6.1 | BLUEPRINT FOR CAFETERIA-STYLE RESTAURANT |
|---|---|

|  | Appetizer counter | Salad counter | Hot-food counter | Dessert counter | Drinks counter | Cashier |
|---|---|---|---|---|---|---|
|  | $8/hr | $8/hr | $8/hr | $8/hr | $8/hr | $10/hr |
| Number of stations | 1 | 1 | 1 | 1 | 1 | 1 |
| Activity time | 15 sec | 30 sec | 60 sec | 40 sec | 20 sec | 30 sec |
| Process time | 15 sec | 30 sec | 60 sec | 40 sec | 20 sec | 30 sec |
| Maximum output/hr | 240 | 120 | 60* | 90 | 180 | 120 |

*Bottleneck      Service cost per meal = $\dfrac{50}{60}$ = $0.83

Finally, to calculate the service cost per meal, total labor costs per hour of the entire system are divided by the maximum output per hour for the system (total labor costs/maximum output per hour). Total labor costs per hour are calculated by simply adding the hourly wages of personnel stationed at each counter. In our example, total labor cost per hour equals $50.00 (8 + 8 + 8 + 8 + 8 + 10). Maximum output per hour is determined by selecting the lowest maximum output calculated in the second step. Hence, the service cost per meal in our example is $50.00/60 customers, or $0.83 per meal.

Why would you use the lowest maximum output per hour? This step is particularly confusing for some students. The lowest maximum output in the system is the maximum number of people who can be processed through the entire system in an hour. In our example, 240 customers can be processed through the appetizer counter in an hour; however, only 120 customers can be processed through the salad counter in the same amount of time. This means that after the first hour, 120 customers (240 – 120) are still waiting to be processed through the salad counter. Similarly, only 60 customers can be processed through the hot-food counter in an hour's time. Since 60 is the lowest maximum output per hour for any counter in the system, only 60 customers can actually complete the entire system in an hour.

## THE SERVICE OPERATIONS MANAGER'S PERSPECTIVE

The first thing the blueprint does is provide a check on the logical flow of the whole process. Clearly, a service blueprint makes it immediately apparent if a task is being performed out of sequence. At this point, we shall place a constraint on our example system that the cashier's station is fixed and cannot be moved to another point in the process. All other stations can be moved and resequenced.

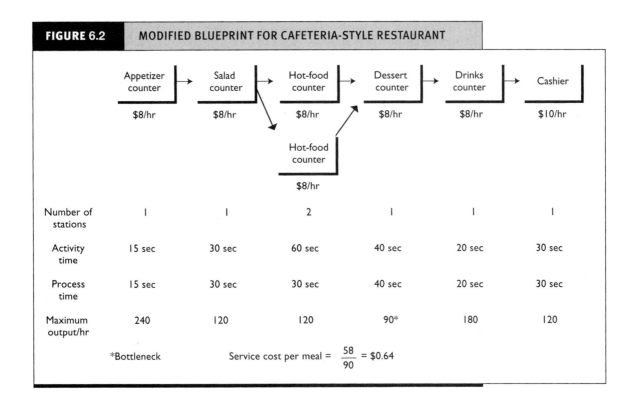

| **FIGURE** 6.2 | **MODIFIED BLUEPRINT FOR CAFETERIA-STYLE RESTAURANT** |
|---|---|

|  | Appetizer counter | Salad counter | Hot-food counter | Dessert counter | Drinks counter | Cashier |
|---|---|---|---|---|---|---|
|  | $8/hr | $8/hr | $8/hr | $8/hr | $8/hr | $10/hr |
|  |  |  | Hot-food counter |  |  |  |
|  |  |  | $8/hr |  |  |  |
| Number of stations | 1 | 1 | 2 | 1 | 1 | 1 |
| Activity time | 15 sec | 30 sec | 60 sec | 40 sec | 20 sec | 30 sec |
| Process time | 15 sec | 30 sec | 30 sec | 40 sec | 20 sec | 30 sec |
| Maximum output/hr | 240 | 120 | 120 | 90* | 180 | 120 |

*Bottleneck       Service cost per meal = $\dfrac{58}{90}$ = $0.64

Once the different steps have been identified, it is relatively easy to identify the potential **bottlenecks** in the system. Bottlenecks represent points in the system where consumers wait the longest periods of time. In Figure 6.1, the hot-food counter is an obvious bottleneck since it represents the longest process time—the time to process one individual through that stage. A balanced production line is one in which the process times of all the steps are the same and inventories or, in our case, consumers flow smoothly through the system without waiting for the next process.

To solve this particular bottleneck problem, we could consider adding one extra station, in this case an extra counter, to the hot-food stage. The process time would drop to 30 seconds (60 seconds divided by 2). The bottleneck would then become the dessert counter, which has a process time of 40 seconds and a maximum turnover rate of 90 persons per hour. Costs would go up by $8.00 per hour; however, the service cost per meal would go down to $0.64 per meal. These changes are illustrated in Figure 6.2.

The creative use of additional counters and staff may produce a model such as that shown in Figure 6.3, which combines certain activities and uses multiple stations. This particular layout is capable of handling 120 customers per hour compared with the original layout presented in Figure 6.1. Although labor costs rise, the service cost per meal falls because of the increase in the number of consumers that are processed through the system in a shorter period of time. Further changes to this particular setup would be fruitless. Adding counters at the bottlenecks created by both the dessert/drinks and cashier counters would actually increase the service cost per meal from $0.48 ($58.00/120 meals) to $0.50 ($68.00/137.14 meals).

*bottlenecks*
Points in the system at which consumers wait the longest periods of time.

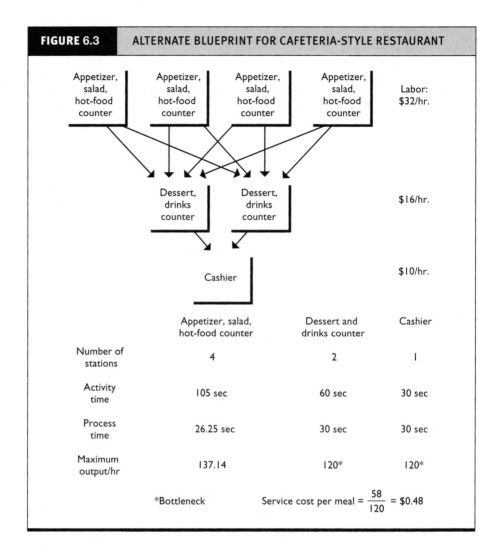

**FIGURE 6.3    ALTERNATE BLUEPRINT FOR CAFETERIA-STYLE RESTAURANT**

|  | Appetizer, salad, hot-food counter | Dessert and drinks counter | Cashier |
|---|---|---|---|
| Number of stations | 4 | 2 | 1 |
| Activity time | 105 sec | 60 sec | 30 sec |
| Process time | 26.25 sec | 30 sec | 30 sec |
| Maximum output/hr | 137.14 | 120* | 120* |

*Bottleneck      Service cost per meal = $\dfrac{58}{120}$ = $0.48

## THE SERVICE MARKETING MANAGER'S PERSPECTIVE

A marketing manager dealing with the process illustrated in Figure 6.1 has some of the same problems as the operations manager. The process as defined is designed to operate at certain production levels, and these are the service standards that customers should perceive. But if the process is capable of processing only 60 customers per hour, there may be a problem. For example, lunch customers who need to return to work quickly might purchase their lunches at a competing restaurant that serves its customers more efficiently. Also, it is clear that the bottleneck at the hot-food counter will produce lengthy, possibly frustrating, waits within the line.

The marketing manager should immediately recognize the benefits of changing the system to process customers more effectively. However, the blueprint also shows the change in consumer behavior that would be required in order for the new system to operate. In Figure 6.1, the consumer goes from counter to counter, has only one choice at each counter, will probably have to wait in line at each counter, and will definitely have to wait longer at the hot-food counter. Moreover, the wait at each stage will certainly exceed the time spent in each activity. In the process proposed in Figure 6.3, the consumer visits fewer stations but is frequently faced with a choice between different stations. Clearly, depending on the format chosen, the script to be followed by consumers will be different. In addition, the restaurant itself will look completely different.

The use of the blueprinting approach allows the marketing and operations personnel to analyze in detail the process that they are jointly trying to create and manage. It can easily highlight any conflict between operations and marketing managers and provide a common framework for their discussion and a basis for the resolution of their problems.

## USING SERVICE BLUEPRINTS TO IDENTIFY THE SERVUCTION PROCESS

Blueprints may also be used for a different purpose. Consider Figure 6.4, which shows a much more detailed blueprint for the production of a discount brokerage service. This chart is designed to identify the points of contact between the service firm and the customer. The points above the line are visible to the consumer, and those below are invisible. In assessing the quality of service received, according to the servuction model, the customer refers to the points of contact when developing perceptions regarding the value of service quality received.

To illustrate, consider the customers to be proactive rather than reactive. Consider them as worried individuals looking for clues that they have made the right decision rather than as inanimate raw materials to which things are done. The points of contact are the clues that develop the servuction process.

Besides illustrating a more complicated process, Figure 6.4 has a number of added features. First, each of the main features is linked to a target time. In the top-right corner, for example, the time to mail a statement is targeted as five days after the month's end. In designing a service, these target times should initially be set by marketing, and they should be based on the consumers' expected level of service. If the service is to be offered in a competitive marketplace, it may be necessary to set standards higher than those of services currently available. Once the standards have been set, however, the probability of achieving them must be assessed. If the firm is prepared to invest enough, it may be feasible to meet all of the standards developed by marketing; doing so, however, affects the costs and, therefore, the subsequent price of the service. The process should, then, be an interactive one.

Figure 6.4 also highlights the potential **fail points**, "F." Fail points have three characteristics:

1. the potential for operations malfunction is high;
2. the result of the malfunction is visible to consumers; and
3. a system malfunction is regarded by consumers as particularly significant.

**fail points**
Points in the system at which the potential for malfunction is high and at which a failure would be visible to the customer and regarded as significant.

**FIGURE 6.4**    **FLOWCHART OF A DISCOUNT BROKERAGE SERVICE**

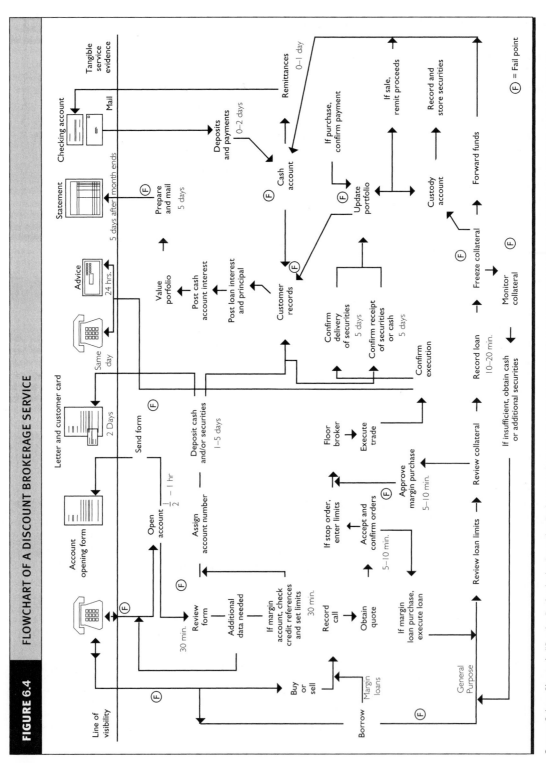

Source: G. Lynn Shostack, "Service Design in the Operating Environment," pp. 27–43. 1984, reprinted with permission from *Developing New Services*, William R. George and Claudia Marshall, eds., published by American Marketing Association, Chicago, IL 60606.

## *A MARKETING OR AN OPERATIONS BLUEPRINT?*

Although the idea of a blueprint is attractive to both marketing and operations, it may well be that a marketing blueprint should be prepared in a different way. The blueprints we have discussed so far have an internal focus—although they identify clearly the tangible points of contact with the client, they start from the organization and look outward.

An alternative way to develop a blueprint would be to start from consumer scripts. Consumers, individually or in groups, would be asked to describe the process or steps they follow in using a service. Obviously, such an approach cannot cover the invisible part of the service firm, but it can provide a much better understanding of the points of contact. The process as described by the consumer may differ greatly from that perceived by the firm.

Consumers asked to describe a flight on USAir, for example, might start with their experience with the travel agent. They might then describe the process of getting to the airport, parking, and entering the terminal. If the signs for USAir and the entrance to its specific terminal are confusing, this will be reflected in consumers' perceptions of the airline. A parking lot that is littered, poorly lit, and inhabited by vagrants will also deter customers. Although the airline may not have direct control over these points of contact, it could be a wise investment for the airline to use its own staff to improve the parking lot. McDonald's long ago learned the value of removing the litter not only from its own property but also from the adjoining roadways. McDonald's recognized that their customers' experiences began long before they entered the actual restaurant.

## *CONSTRUCTING THE SERVICE BLUEPRINT[23]*

The first step in the design of a service blueprint is to elicit scripts from both employees and consumers. The primary objective of this task is to break down the service system into a sequence of events followed by both parties. Too often, management makes the mistake of developing a **one-sided blueprint** based on its own perception of how the sequence of events should occur. This one-sided approach fails to recognize that consumer perceptions, not management's, define the realities of the encounter. Similarly, employee scripts are equally important in identifying those parts of the service system not observable to the consumer. Hence, both scripts are necessary to develop a successful blueprint.

Script theory suggests that consumers possess purchasing scripts that guide their thinking and behavior during service encounters. The scripts contain the sequence of actions that consumers follow when entering a service interaction. Experts believe that "these action sequences, or cognitive scripts, guide the interpretation of information, the development of expectations, and the enactment of appropriate behavior routines."[24]

Similarly, service employees also have scripts that dictate their own behavior during interactions with the customer. **Convergent scripts**, those that are mutually agreeable, enhance the probability of customer satisfaction and the quality of the relationship between the customer and the service operation. **Divergent scripts** point to

*one-sided blueprint*
An unbalanced blueprint based on management's perception of how the sequence of events *should* occur.

*convergent scripts*
Employee/consumer scripts that are mutually agreeable and enhance the probability of customer satisfaction.

*divergent scripts*
Employee/consumer scripts that "mismatch" and point to areas in which consumer expectations are not being met.

areas that need to be examined and corrected because consumer expectations are not being met and evaluations of service quality could decline.

Obtaining consumer and employee scripts is a potentially powerful technique for analyzing the service encounter. Scripts provide the dialogue from which consumer and employee perceptions of the encounter can be analyzed and potential or existing problems identified. Overall, scripts provide the following:

- the basis for planning service encounters;
- goals and objectives;
- development of behavioral routines that maximize the opportunities for a successful exchange; and
- evaluation of the effectiveness of current service delivery systems.

**two-sided blueprint**
A blueprint that takes into account both employee and customer perceptions of how the sequence of events actually occurs.

**script norms**
Proposed scripts developed by grouping together events commonly mentioned by both employees and customers and then ordering those events in their sequence of occurrence.

The procedure used to develop a **two-sided blueprint** is to present employees and customers with a script-relevant situation, such as the steps taken to proceed through an airline boarding experience. Respondents are requested to note specific events or activities expected in their involvement in the situation. In particular, employees and consumers are asked to pay special attention to those contact activities that elicit strong positive or negative reactions during the service encounter. **Script norms** are then constructed by grouping together commonly mentioned events and ordering the events in their sequence of occurrence.

To facilitate the process of identifying script norms, the blueprint designer can compare the frequency of specific events mentioned by each of the groups. The value of this process is the potential recognition of gaps or discrepancies existing between employee and consumer perceptions. For example, consumers may mention the difficulties associated with parking, which employees may not mention since many report to work before the operation is open to customers.

The second step of the blueprint development process is to identify steps in the process at which the system can go awry. By asking employees and customers to further focus on events that are important in conveying service satisfaction and dissatisfaction, fail points can be isolated. The consequences of service failures can be greatly reduced by analyzing fail points and instructing employees on the appropriate response or action when the inevitable failure occurs.

After the sequence of events/activities and potential fail points have been identified, the third step in the process involves specifying the timeframe of service execution. The major cost component of most service systems relates to the time required to complete the service; consequently, standard execution time norms must be established.

Once the standard execution times of the events that make up the service encounter have been specified, the manager can analyze the profitability of the system, given the costs of inputs needed for the system to operate. The resulting blueprint allows the planner to determine the profitability of the existing service delivery system as well as to speculate on the effects on profitability when changing one or more system components. Consequently, the service blueprint allows a company to test its assumptions on paper and to minimize the system's shortcomings before the system is imposed on customers and employees. The service manager can test a prototype of the delivery system with potential customers and use the feedback to modify the blueprint before testing the procedure again.

## BLUEPRINTING AND NEW-PRODUCT DEVELOPMENT: THE ROLES OF COMPLEXITY AND DIVERGENCE

Blueprints may also be used in new-product development. Once the process has been documented and a blueprint has been drawn, choices can be made that will produce "new" products. Although the processes in Figures 6.1, 6.2, and 6.3 are for the same task, from the consumer's point of view they are very different. The two blueprints define alternatives that are operationally feasible; the choice between which of the two to implement is for marketing.

Strategically, the decision may be to move the line separating visibility and invisibility. Operationally, arguments have been made for minimizing the visible component by isolating the technical core of the process. From a marketing point of view, however, more visibility may create more differentiation in the mind of the consumer. For example, a restaurant can make its kitchen into a distinctive feature by making it visible to restaurant patrons. This poses constraints on the operations personnel, but it may add value in the mind of the consumer.

New-product development within service firms can be implemented through the introduction of complexity and divergence.[25] **Complexity** is a measure of the number and intricacy of the steps and sequences that constitute the process—the more steps, the more complex the process. **Divergence** is defined as the degrees of freedom service personnel are allowed when providing the service. As an example, Figures 6.5 and 6.6 illustrate the blueprints for two florists who differ dramatically in their complexity and divergence. Although they perform equivalent tasks from an operations viewpoint, they can be very different from a marketing viewpoint and, therefore, constitute new products.

Figure 6.5 presents a traditional florist. The process, as in our restaurant example in Figure 6.1, is linear and involves a limited number of steps and so is low in complexity. However, the generation of flower arrangements under such a system calls for considerable discretion or degrees of freedom to be allowed the florist at each stage—in the choice of vase, flowers, and display—and produces a heterogeneous final product. The system is, therefore, high in divergence.

Figure 6.6 provides the blueprint for a second florist that has attempted to standardize its final product. Because the objective of this system is to deskill the job, the system is designed to generate a limited number of standardized arrangements. The divergence of the system is therefore reduced, but to achieve this, the complexity of the process is increased significantly.

In developing products in the service sector, the amount of manipulation of the operation's complexity and divergence are the two key choices. Reducing divergence creates the uniformity that can reduce costs, but it does so at the expense of creativity and flexibility in the system. Companies that wish to pursue a **volume-oriented positioning strategy** often do so by reducing divergence. For example, a builder of swimming

**complexity**
A measure of the number and intricacy of the steps and sequences that constitute a process.

**divergence**
A measure of the degrees of freedom service personnel are allowed when providing a service.

**volume-oriented positioning strategy**
A positioning strategy that reduces divergence to create product uniformity and reduce costs.

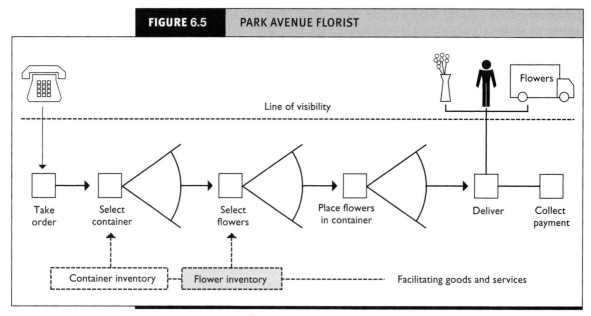

**FIGURE 6.5    PARK AVENUE FLORIST**

Line of visibility

Take order → Select container → Select flowers → Place flowers in container → Deliver → Collect payment

Container inventory — Flower inventory — Facilitating goods and services

Source: G. Lynn Shostack, "Service Positioning through Structural Change," *Journal of Marketing* 51 (January 1987), pp. 34–43. Reprinted by permission of the American Marketing Association.

pools who focuses on the installation of prefabricated vinyl pools has greatly reduced the divergence of his operations. In addition to lowering production costs, reducing divergence increases productivity and facilitates distribution of the standardized service. From the customer's perspective, reducing divergence is associated with improved reliability, availability, and uniform service quality. However, the downside of reduced divergence is the lack of customization that can be provided individual customers.

On the other hand, increasing divergence creates flexibility in tailoring the experience to each customer, but it does so at increased expense, and consumer prices are subsequently higher. Companies wishing to pursue a **niche positioning strategy** do so through increasing the divergence in their operations. For example, our pool builder may increase the divergence of his operation by specializing in the design and construction of customized pools and spas that can be built to resemble anything from a classical guitar to an exclamation point! Profits, under this scenario, depend less on volume and more on margins on each individual purchase. The downside of increasing divergence is that the service operation becomes more difficult to manage, control, and distribute. Moreover, customers may not be willing to pay the higher prices associated with a customized service.

Reducing complexity is a **specialization positioning strategy** often involving the **unbundling** of the different services offered. Hence, our hypothetical pool builder may restrict himself to the installation of a single type of prefabricated pool and divest operations that were focused on supplemental services such as maintenance and repair as well as the design of pools and spas. The advantages associated with reduced complexity

*niche positioning strategy*
A positioning strategy that increases divergence in an operation to tailor the service experience to each customer.

*specialization positioning strategy*
A positioning strategy that reduces complexity by unbundling the different services offered.

*unbundling*
Divesting an operation of different services and concentrating on providing only one or a few services in order to pursue a specialization positioning strategy.

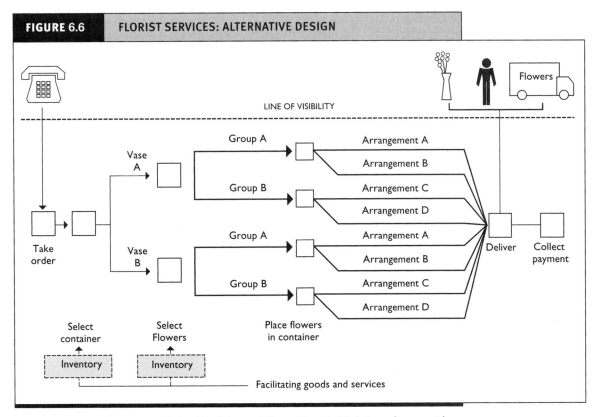

**FIGURE 6.6    FLORIST SERVICES: ALTERNATIVE DESIGN**

Source: G. Lynn Shostack, "Service Positioning through Structural Change," *Journal of Marketing* 51 (January 1987), pp. 34–43. Reprinted by permission of the American Marketing Association.

include improved control over the final product and improved distribution. However, risks are involved if full-service competitors, offering one-stop convenience, continue to operate. The full-service competitor appeals to consumers wishing to work with a provider that offers a number of choices.

Increasing complexity is utilized by companies that pursue a mass market or **penetration strategy**. Increasing complexity translates into the addition of more services to the firm's offering as well as the enhancement of current ones. Within this scenario, our pool builder would offer customized pools and spas and a wide variety of prefabricated vinyl pools. In addition to installation, other services such as general pool maintenance and repair would be offered. Firms pursuing a penetration strategy often try to be everything to everybody and often gloss over individual consumer needs. Moreover, when providing such a broad range of services, the quality of the provider's skills are bound to vary depending upon the task being performed, leaving some customers less than satisfied. Hence, firms that increase complexity of their operations by offering enhanced and/or additional services run the risk of becoming vulnerable to companies that pursue more specialized types of operations.

*penetration strategy*
A positioning strategy that increases complexity by adding more services and/or enhancing current services to capture more of a market.

## ✳ SUMMARY

The primary objective of this chapter was to highlight the idea that for a service firm to be successful, its marketing and operations departments must work together. In a broad sense, one could view the functions of marketing and operations as the marriage of consumers' needs with the technology and manufacturing capabilities of the firm. This marriage entails many compromises that attempt to balance operational efficiency with the effectiveness of the system from the consumer's point of view. To be effective, operations personnel must recognize the importance of their marketing counterparts, and vice versa.

Firms operating at peak efficiency are free from outside influences and operate as if the market will consume the firm's production at a continuous rate. Uncertainty creates inefficiency. Hence, in an ideal situation, the technical core of the firm is able to operate without uncertainty on either the input or output side. Although the attempt to operate at peak efficiency is a worthy goal, it likely represents an unrealistic objective for most service firms. The production of most services is an operations nightmare. Instead of receiving demand at a constant rate, service firms are often linked directly to a market that frequently varies from day to day, hour to hour, and even minute to minute. Service customers frequently affect the time of demand, the cycle of demand, the type of demand, and the duration of many service transactions.

Plans to operate at peak efficiency must be altered to cope with the uncertainties inherent in service operations. Strategies that attempt to increase the efficiency of the service operation by facilitating the balance of supply and demand include minimizing the servuction system by isolating the technical core; production-lining the whole system utilizing hard and soft technologies; creating flexible capacity; increasing customer participation; and moving the time of demand to fit capacity.

Service blueprints can be developed that identify the direction in which processes flow and the parts of a process that may both increase operational efficiency and enhance the customer's service experience. Operational changes made to the service blueprint often require changes in consumer behavior and, in some instances, lead to new service products. New service development is achieved through the introduction of complexity and divergence. Reducing divergence standardizes the service product and reduces production costs, whereas increasing divergence enables service providers to tailor their products to individual customers. Similarly, reducing complexity is consistent with a specialization positioning strategy, while increasing complexity is appropriate for firms pursuing a penetration strategy.

## ✳ KEY TERMS

technical core, 141

perfect-world model, 142

focused factory, 142

plant within a plant (PWP), 143

buffering, 143

smoothing, 143

anticipating, 143

rationing, 143

decoupling, 146

production-line approach, 147

## ✱ DISCUSSION QUESTIONS

1. Explain how the inability to inventory services affects the operational efficiency of most service firms.
2. Compare Thompson's perfect-world model to the focused factory and plant-within-a-plant concepts.
3. What is buffering? How do the strategies of anticipating, smoothing, and rationing relate to buffering?
4. Discuss some specific examples of how the customer's involvement in the service encounter influences the operational efficiency of the average service firm.
5. What does it mean to isolate the technical core of a business?
6. Provide examples of hard and soft technologies and explain their relevance to this chapter.
7. Discuss the steps for developing a meaningful blueprint.
8. What are the trade-offs associated with increasing/decreasing divergence and increasing/decreasing complexity?

## ✱ NOTES

1. Richard B. Chase and Robert H. Hayes, "Beefing Up Operations in Service Firms," *Sloan Management Review* (Fall 1991), pp. 15–26.
2. Much of this chapter is adopted from Chapters 3 and 4 of John E. G. Bateson, *Managing Services Marketing*, 2nd ed. (Fort Worth, TX: The Dryden Press, 1992), pp. 156–169, 200–207.
3. J. D. Thompson, *Organizations in Action* (New York: McGraw-Hill, 1967).
4. W. Skinner, "The Focused Factory," *Harvard Business Review* 52, 3 (May-June 1974), pp. 113–121.
5. Thompson, *Organizations in Action*, p. 69.
6. R. J. Matteis, "The New Back Office Focuses on Customer Service," *Harvard Business Review* 57 (1979), pp. 146–159.
7. Matteis, "The New Back Office."
8. These extensions of the customer contact model are developed in Richard B. Chase, "The Customer Contact Approach to Services: Theoretical Base and Practical Extensions," *Operations Research* 29, 4 (July-August 1981), pp. 698–706; and Richard B. Chase and David A. Tansik, "The Customer Contact Model for Organization Design," *Management Service* 29, 9 (1983), pp. 1037–1050.

9. B. Danet, "Client-Organization Interfaces," in *Handbook of Organization Design*, 2nd ed., P. C. Nystrom and W. N. Starbuck, eds. (New York: Oxford University Press, 1984), p. 384.

10. These studies employed the critical incident technique to look at service encounters that fail. See Mary J. Bitner, Jody D. Nyquist, and Bernard H. Booms, "The Critical Incident Technique for Analyzing the Service Encounter," in *Service Marketing in a Changing Environment*, Thomas M. Block, Gregory D. Upah, and Valerie A. Zeithaml, eds. (Chicago: American Marketing Association, 1985), pp. 48–51.

11. Chase, "The Customer Contact Approach."

12. For a detailed description, see Richard B. Chase and Gerrit Wolf, "Designing High Contact Systems: Applications to Branches of Savings and Loans," Working Paper, Department of Management, College of Business and Public Administration, University of Arizona.

13. Chad Rubel, "Banks Should Show that They Care for Customers," *Marketing News*, July 3, 1995, p. 4.

14. T. Levitt, "Production-line Approach to Services," *Harvard Business Review* 50, 5, (September–October 1972), pp. 41–52.

15. Carol F. Suprenant and Michael Solomon, "Predictability and Personalization in the Service Encounter," *Journal of Marketing* 51 (April 1987), pp. 86–96.

16. W. Earl Sasser, "Match Supply and Demand in Service Industries," *Harvard Business Review* 54, 5 (November-December 1976), pp. 61–65.

17. Benjamin Schneider, "The Service Organization: Climate Is Crucial," *Organizational Dynamics* (Autumn 1980), pp. 52–65.

18. See also J. E. G. Bateson, "Self-Service Consumer: An Exploratory Study," *Journal of Retailing* 61, 3 (Fall 1986), pp. 49–79.

19. Ibid.

20. Christopher H. Lovelock and Robert F. Young, "Look to Consumers to Increase Productivity," *Harvard Business Review* (May–June 1979), pp. 168–178.

21. G. Lynn Shostack, "Service Positioning through Structural Change," *Journal of Marketing* 51 (January 1987), pp. 34–43.

22. Bateson, *Managing Services*, pp. 200–207.

23. K. Douglas Hoffman and Vince Howe, "Developing the Micro Service Audit via Script Theoretic and Blueprinting Procedures," in *Marketing Toward the Twenty-First Century*, Robert L. King, ed. (University of Richmond: Southern Marketing Association, 1991), pp. 379–383.

24. Thomas W. Leigh and Arno J. Rethans, "Experience with Script Elicitation within Consumer Making Contexts," in *Advances in Consumer Research*, Volume Ten, Alice Tybout and Richard Bagozzi, eds. (Ann Arbor, MI: Association for Consumer Research, 1983) pp. 667–672.

25. Shostack, "Service Positioning," pp. 34–43.

# CHAPTER 7

## THE PRICING OF SERVICES

### CHAPTER OBJECTIVES

*The purpose of this chapter is to familiarize you with the special considerations needed when pricing services.*

After reading this chapter, you should be able to:

- Describe how consumers relate value and price.
- Understand the special considerations of service pricing as they relate to demand, cost, customer, competitor, profit, product, and legal considerations.
- Discuss the circumstances under which price segmentation is most effective.
- Explain satisfaction-based, relationship, and efficiency approaches to pricing.

*"Only by reducing their costs can any of the major airlines rationally afford to reduce their prices. If airlines reform pricing first, it will be a financial disaster."*

Scott Gillespie, CEO
Travel Analytics

# PRICING WOES CONTINUE FOR U.S. AIRLINES

© FLYING COLOURS LTD / GETTY IMAGES

Many services are characterized by a high fixed/variable cost ratio. The airline industry is a typical example. The three major costs to an airline are the fleet, labor, and jet fuel. Fleet and labor costs are primarily fixed, whereas fuel costs are variable. Perhaps more importantly, fuel costs are beyond an airline's control; however, the airline has some influence over the other two expenses.

The traditional airline business model bases its economic vitality on its high-fare business travelers. Business travelers generally account for three-quarters of an airline's revenues but only half of the passenger total. Business travelers who book last-minute fares pay on average five times the price of the lowest leisure ticket price. Says Paul Tate, CFO of Frontier Airlines, "Big carriers need that high-yield, close-in traffic in order to support their high costs structures." However, many business travelers are angry and confused by this pricing structure. "The price variation is so significant that it just doesn't make sense. It doesn't make sense to the travelers, the [travel] agency community, or to the airline themselves," says Alex Wasilov, president and COO of Rosenbluth International. Ironically, the major airlines agree. According to Donald J. Carty, CEO of American Airlines, "Everybody knows the industry's current pricing model is badly broken. Many of our best customers feel as though they're being cheated. It's clear that something dramatic has to be done."

What that "something" is, hasn't been easy to figure out or to implement. In order to increase profits, airlines can sell more tickets, reduce costs, or both. In the attempt to sell more tickets, airlines engage in price discounting, which is virtually always matched by their competition. The net result is that the airline cost structure has stayed the same while industry revenues steadily decrease. In other words, the net result is a greater loss. Consequently, the winner of any price war will be the airlines with the lowest cost structures. For example, Frontier Airlines break-even load factor is approximately 55 percent—55 percent of available seats need to be filled on average of every flight for the airline to break even. In contrast, United Airlines break-even load factor is approximately 91 percent. Clearly, Frontier and other discount airlines are better positioned to withstand the competitive pressures of a price war.

Reducing the cost structures of an airline is no easy task. Fuel prices are largely uncontrollable and fleet costs are directly tied to available seating capacity. Obviously, airlines need the fleet to fly and reducing the fleet means giving up market share, which is precisely what the airlines are loathe to consider. As a result, short-term cost reductions are being achieved primarily by means of labor concessions. Differences in break-even load factors can be largely explained by labor costs. Labor costs account for 25 percent of total expenses at Frontier Airlines while at American Airlines that number is closer to 40 percent. It seems that the major airline's labor contracts are perpetually renegotiated and one wonders when employee morale will eventually take its toll on the big carriers. Commenting on United's most recent cost reduction move to terminate its workers' pension plans, Robert Roach, Jr., general vice-president of the International Association of Machinists states, "People would be so demoralized that the carrier couldn't survive."

Despite the combined wisdom of the airline industry, Delta Airlines announced a simplified pricing structure in January of 2005 that lowers and places a cap on its top fares. Delta's strategy, which has already identified

$5 billion in cost cuts, is predicted to "sink an airline or three" accounting for nearly 10 percent of domestic capacity. Industry experts believe Delta's move will accelerate the pace of cost restructuring at other airlines. The airline industry is expected to lose at least $2 billion in 2005 on top of 2004's loss of $5.4 billion. Who will be left in the end? No one knows for sure.

Sources: Wendy Zellner and Brain Grow, "Waiting for the First Bird to Die," *Business Week*, Issue 3917 (January 24, 2005), 38; and Lori Calabro, "Making Fares Fairer," *CFO*, 18 no. 9 (September 2002), 105–107.

> ## INTRODUCTION

Of the traditional marketing mix variables that are utilized to influence customer purchase decisions, the development of effective pricing strategies perhaps remains the most elusive. Pricing is often a perplexing issue for practitioners and researchers alike. Consider the following sample of expressed opinions regarding pricing practices over the last fifty years that reflect both the confusion and frustration associated with pricing decisions:

> . . . Pricing policy is the last stronghold of medievalism in modern management. [Pricing] is still largely intuitive and even mystical in the sense that the intuition is often the province of the big boss.[1]

> [P]erhaps few ideas have wider currency than the mistaken impression that prices are or should be determined by costs of production.[2]

> For marketers of industrial goods and construction companies, pricing is the single judgment that translates potential business into reality. Yet pricing is the least rational of all decisions made in this specialised field.[3]

> Many managing directors do not concern themselves with pricing details; some are not even aware of how their products are priced.[4]

> Pricing is approached in Britain like Russian roulette—to be indulged in mainly by those contemplating suicide.[5]

> Perhaps it is reasonable that marketers have only recently begun to focus seriously on effective pricing. Only after managers have mastered the techniques of creating value do the techniques of capturing value become important.[6]

Today, price remains one of the least researched and mastered areas of marketing. Research and expertise pertaining to the pricing of services is particularly lacking. Many of the concepts developed for goods apply equally to services. This chapter focuses on how the pricing approaches apply and on how, to a greater or lesser extent, service pricing policies differ from those of goods.

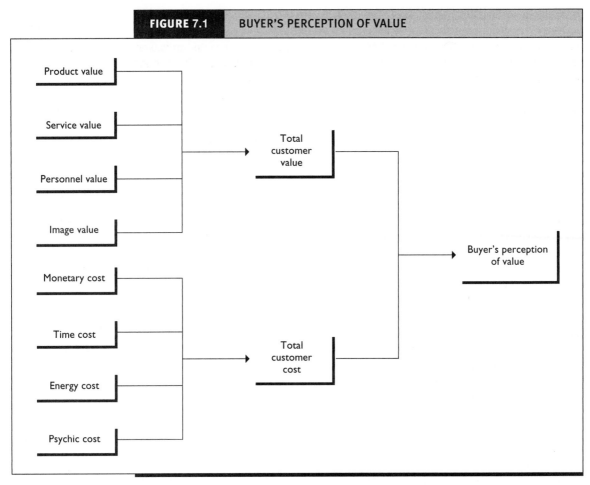

**FIGURE 7.1    BUYER'S PERCEPTION OF VALUE**

Source: Kotler, Philip; Keller, Kevin Lane, *Marketing Management,* 12th Edition, © 2006, p. 141. Adapted by permission of Pearson Education, Inc., Upper Saddle River, NJ.

## > PERCEPTIONS OF VALUE

Buyers' perceptions of value represent a trade-off between the perceived benefits of the service to be purchased and the perceived sacrifice in terms of the costs to be paid (see Figure 7.1). Total customer costs include more than simply the **monetary price** paid for the service. Other costs include **time costs, energy costs,** and **psychic costs,** which reflect the time and trouble the customer has to endure to acquire the service. Similarly, total customer value extends beyond **product value** and includes **service value, personnel value,** and **image value.**[7]

For example, a customer who wishes to purchase an 18-inch satellite dish system must pay the monetary price for the dish and receiver plus the monthly charges for the

**monetary price**
The actual dollar price paid by the consumer for a product.

**time costs**
The time the customer has to spend to acquire the service.

video services received. In this example, the customer chose a Sony system due to its hardware and software advantages (product value) over those of competitors and the quality associated with the Sony name (image value). In addition, Sony's warranty (service value) was competitive with leading alternatives. The customer bought the system at Sears Department Store because of the sales representative's superior product knowledge (personnel value) compared with the dismal quality of information received at alternative purchase locations.

In addition to the monetary cost, the customer incurred time and energy costs while shopping at various locations and questioning sales representatives about the various brands of satellite systems. Additional time costs were incurred waiting for the installer to actually install the system. The installation, which should have taken two hours, took six hours. In addition, the installer's truck leaked vast amounts of oil onto the customer's driveway, the installer's ladder scraped paint off the outside of the house, and the installer accidentally dropped the satellite receiver from the large screen TV onto the floor. Each of these events added to the psychic cost (e.g., worry and aggravation) of the whole experience.

Overall, if the signal sent by total customer cost is an indicator of sacrifice relative to value, then price will have a negative or repelling effect and may reduce demand. If the signal sent by the price is an indicator of benefit or value, then price will be an attractor and may increase demand. Because of the perceived connection between cost and benefit, buyers have both lower and upper price thresholds. For example, buyers might be discouraged from buying when the price is perceived to be too low simply because they see a low price as an indicator of inferior quality.

Consumers exchange their money, time, and effort for the bundle of benefits the service provider offers. Economic theory suggests that consumers will have a reservation price that captures the value they place on these benefits. As long as the total cost to the consumer is less than the reservation price, he or she will be prepared to buy. If the consumer can purchase the service for less than the reservation price, a consumer's surplus will exist. The eight dimensions of value described here and shown in Figure 7.1 provide direction for how service firms can differentiate themselves from competitors.

*energy costs*
The physical energy spent by the customer to acquire the service.

*psychic costs*
The mental energy spent by the customer to acquire the service.

*product value*
The worth assigned to the product by the customer.

*service value*
The worth assigned to the service by the customer.

*personnel value*
The worth assigned to the service-providing personnel by the customer.

*image value*
The worth assigned to the image of the service or service provider by the customer.

> | **SPECIAL CONSIDERATIONS OF SERVICE PRICING**

The ultimate pricing challenge faced by most firms is determining a price that sells the service while at the same time offering a profitable return. When pricing services, many of the same market conditions that are considered for pricing goods should be examined. "The difference between price setting and strategic pricing is the difference between reacting to market conditions and proactively managing them." [8] The literature suggests that price determination should be based on demand, cost, customer, competitive, profit, product, and legal considerations. [9] While these market conditions are the same for goods and services, the content of the considerations differ. The discussion that follows highlights these key differences (see Table 7.1).

| TABLE 7.1 | UNIQUE DIFFERENCES ASSOCIATED WITH SERVICE PRICES |
|---|---|

**Demand Considerations**

D1:    The demand for services tends to be more inelastic than the demand for goods.

D2:    Due to the implicit bundling of services by consumers, cross-price elasticity considerations need to be examined.

D3:    Price discrimination is a viable practice to manage demand and supply challenges.

**Cost Considerations**

D4:    With many professional services (and some others), the consumer may not know the actual price they will pay for the service until the service is completed.

D5:    Cost-oriented pricing is more difficult for services.

D6:    Services tend to be characterized by a high fixed/variable cost ratio.

D7:    Economies of scale tend to be limited.

**Customer Considerations**

D8:    Price tends to be one of the few cues available to consumers during prepurchase.

D9:    Service consumers are more likely to use price as a cue to quality.

D10:    Service consumers tend to be less certain about reservation prices.

**Competitive Considerations**

D11:    Comparing prices of competitors is more difficult for service consumers.

D12:    Self-service is a viable competitive alternative.

**Profit Considerations**

D13:    Price bundling makes the determination of individual prices in the bundle of services more complicated.

D14:    Price bundling is more effective in a services context.

**Product Considerations**

D15:    Compared to the goods sector, there tend to be many different names for price in the service sector.

D16:    Consumers are less able to stockpile services by taking advantage of discount prices.

D17:    Product-line pricing tends to be more complicated.

**Legal Considerations**

D18:    The opportunity for illegal pricing practices to go undetected is greater for services than goods.

## DEMAND CONSIDERATIONS

There are a number of demand considerations that differentiate the pricing of services from the pricing of goods. First, demand for services tends to be more inelastic. Cost increases are often simply passed along to consumers. Second, consumers of services often implicitly bundle prices. For example, the demand for food services at a theme park are impacted by the price of the theme park's hotel and ticket prices. Consequently, the cross-price elasticity of services should be taken into careful consideration. Finally, due to the supply and demand fluctuations inherent in services, price discrimination strategies should also be investigated.

| TABLE 7.2 | FACTORS INFLUENCING CUSTOMERS' PRICE SENSITIVITY |
|---|---|

| Price Sensitivity Factors | Proposed Relationship |
|---|---|
| Perceived Substitute Effect | Price sensitivity increases when the price for Service A is higher than the price of perceived substitutes. |
| Unique Value Effect | Price sensitivity increases as the unique value of Service A is perceived to be equal to or less than the unique value of perceived substitutes. |
| Switching Costs Effect | Price sensitivity increases as switching costs decrease. |
| Difficult Comparison Effect | Price sensitivity increases as the difficulty in comparing substitutes decreases. |
| Price-Quality Effect | Price sensitivity increases to the extent that price is not used as a quality cue. |
| Expenditure Effect | Price sensitivity increases when the expenditure is large in terms of dollars or as a percentage of household income. |
| End-Benefit Effect | The more price sensitive consumers are to the end benefit, the more price sensitive they will be to services that contribute to the end benefit. |
| Shared-Cost Effect | Price sensitivity increases as the shared-costs with third parties decreases. |
| Fairness Effect | Price sensitivity increases when the price paid for similar services under similar circumstances is lower. |
| Inventory Effect | Price sensitivity increases as the customers' ability to hold an inventory increases. |

*Demand for services tends to be more inelastic.* In general, consumers of services are more willing to pay higher prices if doing so reduces their level of perceived risk. Perceived risk is a function of consequence (the degree of importance and/or danger associated with the purchase) and uncertainty (the variability in service performance from customer to customer or from day to day). The service characteristics of intangibility, inseparability, heterogeneity, and perishability contribute greatly to heightened levels of perceived risk.

Experts in the field suggest ten factors that influence customer price sensitivity (see Table 7.2). In short, price sensitivity decreases as:[10]

1. the perceived number of substitutes decrease;
2. the perceived unique value of the service increases;
3. switching costs increase;
4. the difficulty in comparing substitutes increases;
5. the extent to which price is used as a quality cue increases;
6. the expenditure is relatively small in terms of dollars or as a percentage of household income;
7. the less price sensitive consumers are to the end-benefit;
8. shared-costs for the expenditure increase;
9. the price is perceived as fair compared to similar services purchased under similar circumstances; and
10. the customer's ability to build an inventory decreases.

*inelastic demand*
The type of market demand when a change in price of service is greater than a change in quantity demanded.

Clearly, price sensitivities will vary across different types of services, but in general the demand for services tends to be **inelastic**. Different groups of consumers will likely weigh the importance of each price sensitivity factor differently (see B2B Services in Action). Service firms must assess which of the factors are more salient to their target market's purchasing decisions.

*Cross price elasticity considerations need to be examined*. Consumers of services often implicitly bundle prices. In other words, consumers may figure that the total cost of going to the movies includes the tickets and refreshments. Therefore, total revenues may be maximized by carefully considering the cross-price elasticities of the total product offering. This is particularly true in cases where the price of the core service offering influences the demand of supplemental services. **Cross-price elasticity** of demand measures the responsiveness of demand for a service relative to a change in price for another service. If this relationship is negative, then the two services are said to be **complementary**. For example, if movie ticket prices increase substantially, consumers are likely to purchase less popcorn. If the relationship is positive, however, then the two services are called **substitutes,** and consumption of one is at the expense of the consumption of the other. For example, the increase in movie theatre tickets will likely increase the demand for DVD rentals. Multi-product considerations dominate many service industries such as business services, personal services, professional services, and the hospitality industry. The golf industry provides a prime example of the effects of cross-price elasticities. Consumers have different price sensitivities for greens fees, cart fees, range fees, and food and beverage expenses. If consumers perceive the price of admission (greens fees) as a good value, they are likely to purchase additional revenue-generating products in the form of riding carts, practice range balls, and food and beverages. In contrast, if the price of admission is perceived as low in value, consumer price sensitivities for supplemental services are likely to increase. Consumers often forgo some or all of these additional services in order to keep their total expenses in line. In effect, the higher price of admission often leads to overall lower consumer expenditures and reduces the revenue stream for the firm.

*cross-price elasticity*
A measure of the responsiveness of demand for a service relative to a change in price for another service.

*complementary*
The result of negative cross-price elasticity in which the increasing price of one service decreases the demand for another service.

*substitutes*
The result of positive cross-price elasticity in which the increasing price of one service increases the demand for another service.

*Price discrimination is a viable practice to manage demand and supply challenges.* **Price discrimination** involves charging customers different prices for essentially the same service (see Global Services in Action). This unique aspect of service pricing relates to both the perishability and simultaneous production and consumption of services. Price discrimination is a viable practice in service industries due in part to differences in the demand elasticities held by customers and the need of the organization to balance demand and supply for its service products.

*price discrimination*
Charging customers different prices for essentially the same service.

The viability of price discrimination is enhanced by the fact that in some services customers readily accept that prices often drop significantly before the opportunity to sell the service passes completely (e.g., last minute concert tickets). In other service settings, consumers have become quite accustomed to different customers paying different amounts for the same service (e.g., airfares). In addition, online services such as priceline.com have now emerged that allow consumers to name their own price for airline tickets and car rentals. Service providers accept these proposals in order to cover at least some portion of their fixed costs. Some revenue is deemed better than no revenue in these situations.

# B 2 B   S E R V I C E S   *IN   ACTION*

## > | FRACTIONAL JET OWNERSHIP

Price sensitivity decreases as the shared cost for a service expenditure increases. Consequently, one way businesses can lower their price sensitivity to business travel is to purchase a fractional ownership of an aircraft. Fractional jet ownership occurs when a company purchases a fractional interest in one aircraft, much like a customer might acquire part ownership in a condominium. The buyer typically purchases at least $1/8^{th}$ interest of an aircraft, which may include as many as 100 hours of usage time per year. Buyers can use their own aircraft for travel or if not available another similar aircraft is made available. The cost of fractional ownership is dependent upon the fraction purchased and the type of aircraft desired. Purchases prices vary from approximately $275,000 for a $1/16^{th}$ interest in a BeechJet that seats 7 people and has a range of 1,750 miles to about $20,000,000 for 1/2 ownership for a Boeing Business Jet. Typical costs are approximately $3,000,000 for $1/8^{th}$ ownership, which includes management fees, hourly usage fees, insurance, and finance costs over a 5-year period. Fractional ownership includes the aircraft, crews, scheduling, and maintenance on demand.

The primary advantages of fractional jet ownership are convenience and cost. In fact, statistical studies indicate that business jet service is more economical than commercial service even when commercial services are available between the cities involved. The following are provided as advantages of fractional jet ownership (aka: business jet service):

- On average business jet service saves four hours of travel time and eight hours of productive time per trip.
- Business jet service saves on hotel bills and overnight time spent away from home.
- Smoking is permitted on business jet service, which is a real benefit for smokers.
- Business jet services have access to 5,500 U. S. airports compared to approximately 500 for commercial jets.
- Business jet service usage is not mutually exclusive. Different company personnel can be taken to different locations at the same time.

Given the economics of fractional jet ownership, it is not for everyone. The most likely business customers are those who need to fly 101 to 399 hours per year. Those businesses flying more than 400 hours a year are recommended to operate their own fleet.

---

Source: http://www.fractionaljetownership.com accessed 19 April 2005.

## GLOBAL SERVICES *IN ACTION*

### > ETHNIC PRICING . . . IS THIS ETHICAL?

The practice of *ethnic pricing*, giving discounts to people of certain nationalities, has long been routine in countries such as India, China, and Russia. Other countries also offer ethnic pricing but are not very public about it due to ethical and legal ramifications. According to a recent *Wall Street Journal* article, airline passengers throughout Europe can obtain discount fares on airline tickets based on the origin of their passport or those of their employers. Brenden McInerney, a passenger attempting to book a Lufthansa flight to Japan, accidently learned of the practice and was not too happy about it. His wife could fly to Japan for 1,700 marks; however, Mr. McInerney's ticket was priced at 2,700 marks! The reason given by the airline: Mr. McInerney is an American, while his wife is Japanese. The airline eventually capitulated and Mr. McInerney was finally given the same fare after he complained.

**EXAMPLES OF SOME ETHNIC DISCOUNTS**

| Airline | Route | Normal Price | "Ethnic Price" |
|---|---|---|---|
| Lufthansa | Frankfurt–Tokyo | 1,524 | 960 |
| Lufthansa | Frankfurt–Seoul | 1,524 | 903 |
| British Airways | Istanbul–London | 385 | 199 |

Note: Taxes and landing fees not included
Source: Travel Agents

Lufthansa does not deny its involvement with ethnic pricing. Dagmar Rotter, a spokesperson for the airline, states that the airline is only reacting to the competition from the national carrier of Japan that also flies out of Germany. "The others started it . . .we only offer it [ethnic pricing] after the market forced us to do so."

Other European airlines such as Swissair, and Air France also practice ethnic pricing. Swissair offers "guest-worker" fares to passengers from Turkey, Portugal, Spain, Greece, and Morocco flying to these same destinations. However, it does not offer discount fares to Japanese flying to Japan. A Swissair spokesperson argues that if the discounts were not provided to the "guest-workers" from Southern Europe and the Mediterranean rim, they would never be able to afford to go home to visit their families. Similarly, Air France offers discounted rates to citizens of Vietnam, China, South Korea, and Japan, but only for its flights that are departing from Germany. An Air France spokesperson notes: "In Germany everybody seems to be doing it . . . it seems to be something very specific to the German market."

British Airway's involvement was readily apparent when it offered its travel package: "Ho, Ho, Ho" for British citizens in Turkey. "Short of stuffing, need some pork sausages, fretting about Christmas pud? Not to worry—show your British passport and you can take 48 percent of normal fares to Britain."

U.S. airlines were quietly involved in ethnic pricing until the practice was barred in 1998. A spokesperson for Lufthansa in New York noted that ethnic pricing could not occur in the U.S. "because it is discriminatory."

Source: "Ethnic Pricing Means Unfair Air Fares," *Wall Street Journal*, December 5, 1997, pp. B1, B14.

Effective price segmentation benefits consumers and providers alike. Consumers often benefit from options that offer lower prices, and providers are often able to manage demand and increase capacity utilization. The interaction that creates the service experience, which is what the consumer buys, takes place in real-time. Since consumers must, in most cases, come to the service setting to be part of the experience, capacity utilization depends on when they arrive. For most services, consumers tend to arrive unevenly and unpredictably, such as at a grocery store or restaurant. The result is often periods of low utilization of capacity because of the impossibility of matching capacity to demand.

If you don't want to spend $90 to see *The Producers*, you can purchase a discount ticket at the famous TKTS booths in Time Square. By selling these tickets on the same day as the performance at a reduced price, theatres create demand for unused capacity.

© AP / WIDE WORLD PHOTOS

Capacity, in turn, represents the bulk of the costs for a service. The restaurant has to be open, staffed, and resourced even at times when it has no customers. The result is a very low level of variable costs for services and a high value attributable to incremental customers, even at discount prices. As a result, pricing is called upon to try to smooth demand in two ways:

- Creating new demand in off-peak, low-capacity utilization periods.
- Flattening peaks by moving existing customers from peaks to less busy times.

The following are several criteria for effective price segmentation:[11]

1. ***Different groups of consumers must have different responses to price***. If different groups of consumers have the same response to price changes, then the price segmentation strategy becomes counterproductive. For example, for years movie theaters have offered afternoon matinees at a reduced fee. This strategy helped the theater create demand for unused capacity during the day and also helped to smooth demand during the evening shows. Moreover, this approach has attracted market segments such as families with children and individuals on

fixed incomes, who may not otherwise attend the higher-priced evening shows. This strategy has been effective because the price change did not create the same response for everyone. If most consumers had shifted their demand to the afternoon shows at lower rates, the movie theater would have overutilized capacity in the afternoons and would be generating lower total revenues for the firm.

2. *The different segments must be identifiable, and a mechanism must exist to price them differently.* Effective price segmentation requires that consumer segments with different demand patterns be identifiable based on some readily apparent common characteristic such as age, family-life cycle stage, gender, and/or educational status. Discriminating based on a convoluted segmentation scheme confuses customers and service providers, who must implement the strategy. Common forms of segmentation identification include college ID card holders, AARP card holders, and drivers' licensees.

3. *No opportunity should exist for individuals in one segment who have paid a low price to sell their tickets to those in other segments.* For example, it does the movie theater little good to sell reduced-price seats in the afternoon to buyers who can turn around and sell those tickets that evening in the parking lot to full-paying customers. Sometimes you just can't win! A local municipal golf course was trying to do "the right thing" by offering its senior citizen customers coupon books for rounds of golf priced at a reduced rate. Soon after the promotion began, some senior citizen customers were seen in the parking lot selling their coupons at a profit to the golf course's full-price customers.

4. *The segment should be large enough to make the exercise worthwhile.* The time and effort involved in offering a price segmentation scheme should be justified based on the return it brings to the business. Having little or no response to the firm's effort signals that either consumers are uninterested, eligible customers are few, or the firm's price segmentation offer is off its mark.

5. *The cost of running the price segmentation strategy should not exceed the incremental revenues obtained.* The objectives of engaging in price segmentation efforts may be to reduce peak demand, fill periods of underutilized capacity, increase overall revenues, or achieve nonprofit issues, such as making your service available to individuals who otherwise may not be able to take advantage of the services the firm offers. If the cost of running the price segmentation strategy exceeds the returns produced, management needs to reconsider the offering.

6. *The customers should not be confused by the use of different prices.* Phone companies and electric utilities often offer customers reduced rates that are based on the time of usage. Frequently, however, these time-related discounts change as new promotions arise. Customers caught unaware of the change often end up paying higher rates than expected, which negatively impacts customer satisfaction. Other pricing strategies such as the one discussed in the opening vignette may simply frustrate the customer. Recently, phone companies such as AT&T have attempted to utilize "simple pricing" as a point of differentiation in their advertising. Other firms are offering higher-priced "peak rates" and lower-priced "nonpeak" rates that vary throughout the day, and customers must be aware at all times which rate they will be paying in order to take advantage of this particular type of pricing strategy.

## COST CONSIDERATIONS

Cost considerations should also be taken into account when formulating service pricing strategy. First, service pricing is often not finalized until after provision. Consequently, the consumer experiences greater price uncertainty. Second, since services have no cost of goods sold (nothing tangible was produced), cost-based pricing is more difficult for services. Third, many service industries, such as the airlines discussed in the opening vignette, are often characterized by a high fixed/variable cost ratio, which leads to further pricing challenges. Finally, the mass production of services leads to limited economies of scale.

*Consumers may not know the actual price they will pay for a service until after the service is completed.* Although consumers can usually find a base price to use as a comparison during prepurchase evaluation, many services are customized during delivery. Consumers may not know the exact amount they will be charged until after the service is performed. For example, a patient may know what a doctor's office visit costs, but may not know what she charges for lab work or an x-ray. Similarly, a client may know how much an attorney charges for an hour of work but may not know how many hours it will take to finalize a will. In contrast to goods that are produced, purchased, and consumed, services are purchased (implied), produced and consumed simultaneously, and then actually paid for when the final bill is presented. The final price is sometimes the last piece of information revealed to the customer.

*Cost-based pricing is more difficult for services.* Many service managers experience difficulties accurately estimating their costs of doing business. This difficulty arises for several reasons. First, when producing an intangible product, cost of goods sold is either a small or nonexistent portion of the total cost. Second, labor needs are difficult to accurately forecast in many service settings due in part to fluctuating demand. Third, workforce turnover is typically high in many service industries. This, coupled with the fact that finding good personnel is an ongoing challenge, leads to further difficulty in estimating the costs associated with a particular service encounter. These factors make what is often considered the most common approach to pricing, cost-oriented pricing, difficult at best for service firms. Consequently, the difficulties associated with controlling and forecasting costs are a fundamental difference between goods and services pricing.

Unfortunately, traditional cost accounting practices, which were designed to monitor raw material consumption, depreciation, and labor, offer little in helping service managers understand their own cost structures. A more useful approach, **activity-based costing** (ABC), focuses on the resources consumed in developing the final product.[12] Traditionally, overhead in most service firms has been allocated to projects based on the amount of direct labor charged to complete the customer's requirements. However, this method of charging overhead has frustrated managers of specific projects for years. Consider the following example:

Let's say that ABC Company charges $2.00 for overhead for every dollar of direct labor charged to customers. As the manager of ABC Company, you have just negotiated with a customer to provide architectural drawings of a deck for $1,000. The customer wants the drawing in three days. Realizing that using your best architect, whom you pay $20 an hour, will result in a loss for the project, you assign the architect's apprentice, who makes $7 an hour. The results of the project are as follows:

*activity-based costing* Costing method that breaks down the organization into a set of activities, and activities into tasks, which convert materials, labor, and technology into outputs.

Time Required       40 hours
Apprentice's Rate   $7 per hour
Direct Labor        $280
Overhead @ $2       $560
Project Cost        $840
Revenue             $1000
Profit              $160

If the firm's best architect had completed the job, the following results would have been submitted:

Time Required       20 hours
Architect's Rate    $20 per hour
Direct Labor        $400
Overhead @ $2       $800
Project Cost        $1200
Revenue             $1000
Profit              ($200)

This traditional approach used in service firms makes little sense. Intuitively, it does not make sense that a job that took a shorter period of time should be charged more overhead. Moreover, this type of system encourages the firm to use less-skilled labor, who produce an inferior product in an unacceptable period of time as specified by the customer. The firm produces a profit on paper but will most likely never have the opportunity to work for this customer again (or his/her friends, for that matter). Even more confusing is that raises and promotions are based on profits generated, so the manager is rewarded for using inferior labor. Something is definitely wrong with this picture!

Activity-based costing focuses on the cost of activities by breaking down the organization into a set of activities, and activities into tasks, which convert materials, labor, and technology into outputs. The tasks are thought of as "users" of overhead and identified as **cost drivers**. The firm's past records are used to arrive at cost-per-task figures that are then allocated to each project based on the activities required to complete the project. In addition, by breaking the overall overhead figure into a set of activities that are driven by cost drivers, the firm can now concentrate its efforts on reducing costs and increasing profitability.

*cost drivers*
The tasks in activity-based costing that are considered to be the "users" of overhead.

For example, one activity in the firm's overall overhead figure is ordering materials. Ordering materials is driven by the number of purchase orders submitted. Company records indicate that overhead associated with ordering materials cost the firm $10,400 during the period. During this same period, 325 purchase orders were submitted. Hence, the activity cost associated with each purchase order is $32.00. Similar calculations are made for other overhead items. Overhead is then allocated to each project based on the activities undertaken to complete the project. Table 7.3 presents examples of overhead items and their cost drivers.

*Services are typically characterized by a high fixed/variable cost ratio.* The United Parcel Service (UPS) is a prime example. On the retail side of the business, the company maintains 3,400 UPS stores; 1,100 Mail Boxes Etc.; 1,000 UPS customer centers; 17,000 authorized outlets; and 45,000 UPS drop boxes. Packages and documents collected at

| TABLE 7.3 | ACTIVITY-BASED COSTING |
|-----------|------------------------|

| Activity Pools | Cost Driver |
|----------------|-------------|
| General administration | Direct Labor $ |
| Project costing | No. of timesheet entries |
| Accounts payable/receiving | No. of vendor invoices |
| Accounts receivable | No. of client invoices |
| Payroll/mail sorting and delivery | No. of employees |
| Recruiting personnel | No. of new hires |
| Employee insurance processing | Insurance claims processed |
| Proposals/RFPs | No. of proposals |
| Client sales meeting/sales aids | Sales $ |
| Shipping | No. of project numbers |
| Ordering | No. of purchase orders |
| Copying | No. of copies |
| Blueprinting | No. of blueprints |

| Cost Driver | Fixed Overhead Cost | Total Base | Cost per Driver |
|-------------|---------------------|------------|-----------------|
| Direct labor $ | 73 | 1,016,687 | 0.07 |
| No. of time entries | 10 | 13,300 | 0.78 |
| No. of vendor invoices | 29 | 2,270 | 12.60 |
| No. of client invoices | 10 | 1,128 | 9.22 |
| No. of employees | 18 | 67 | 271.64 |
| No. of new hires | 8 | 19 | 410.53 |
| Insurance claims filed | 3 | 670 | 3.88 |
| No. of proposals | 29 | 510 | 56.08 |
| Sales $ | 42 | 3,795,264 | 0.01 |
| No. of project numbers | 5 | 253 | 20.55 |
| No. of purchase orders | 10 | 325 | 32.00 |
| No. of copies | 16 | 373,750 | 0.04 |
| No. of blueprint sq. ft. | 8 | 86,200 | 0.09 |
|  | 260 |  |  |

Source: Adapted from Beth M. Chapman and John Talbott, "Activity-Based Costing in a Service Organization," *CMA Magazine* (December 1990/January 1991), 15–18.

these retail sites are then funneled to 1,748 operating facilities where they are distributed to a delivery fleet consisting of 88,000 package cars, vans, tractors, and motorcycles; 270 UPS jet aircraft; and 304 chartered aircraft. As a result of this infrastructure, the company handles more than 3 billion packages and 5.5 percent of the United States' GDP annually.[13]

In comparison to UPS' massive **fixed costs,** the **variable costs** associated with handling one more package are practically nil. The challenges faced by businesses that have a high fixed/variable cost ratio are numerous. First, what prices should be charged to individual customers? How should the firm sell off unused capacity? For example, should an airline sell twenty unsold seats at a reduced rate to customers who are willing to accept the risk of not reserving a seat on the plane prior to the day of departure? Does selling unused capacity at discounted rates alienate full-fare paying customers?

*fixed costs*
Costs that are planned and accrued during the operating period regardless of the level of production and sales.

*variable costs*
Costs that are directly associated with increases in production and sales.

How can companies offer reduced prices to sell off unused capacity without full-fare paying customers shifting their buying patterns?

*Service economies of scale tend to be limited.* Due to inseparability and perishability, the consumption of services is not separated by time and space. Inventory cannot be used to buffer demand, and the physical presence of customers and providers is frequently necessary for a transaction to take place. Consequently, service providers often produce services on demand rather than in advance. Therefore, it is difficult for service providers to achieve the cost advantages traditionally associated with economies of scale. Some services are also more likely than goods to be customized to each customer's specifications and/or needs. Customization limits the amount of work that can be done in advance of a customer's request for service.

## CUSTOMER CONSIDERATIONS

Customer considerations take into account the price the customer is willing to pay for the service. In comparison to goods, the price of the service tends to be one of the few search attributes available to consumers for alternative evaluation purposes. As a result, the price of the service is often used as a quality cue—the higher the price, the better the perceived quality of the service. Services that are priced too low may very well be perceived as inferior in quality and bypassed for more expensive alternatives. Finally, service customers tend to be less certain about reservation prices.

*Price tends to be one of the few cues available to consumers during prepurchase.* Due to the intangible nature of services, services are characterized by few search attributes. Search attributes are informational cues that can be determined prior to purchase. In contrast, the tangibility of goods dramatically increases the number of search attributes available for consumers to consider. For example, the style and fit of a suit can be determined prior to purchase. In contrast, the enjoyment of a dinner is not known until after the experience is complete.

Service providers, including those who offer scuba diving lessons, are unable to achieve cost advantages associated with economies of scale because they are unable to use inventory to buffer demand.

© BILC BACHMANN / INDEX STOCK IMAGERY

Pricing research has noted that the informational value of price decreases as the number of other informational cues increase. Similarly, others have found consumer reliance on price to be U-shaped. Price is heavily used if few cues are present, loses value as more cues become present, and then increases in value if consumers are overwhelmed with information.[14]

*Service consumers are more likely to use price as a cue to quality.* Service providers must also consider the message the service price sends to customers. Much work has been devoted to understanding whether price can be an indicator of quality. Some studies that have been performed seem to imply that consumers can use price to infer the quality of the product they are considering. Conflicting studies seem to indicate that they cannot. For example, classic studies in the field have presented customers with identical products, such as pieces of carpet, priced at different levels. The respondents' judgment of quality seemed to indicate that quality followed price. However, very similar studies later found little relationship between price and perceived quality.[15]

Price plays a key informational role in service consumer decision processes. Decision theory suggests that consumers will use those cues that are most readily available in the alternative evaluation process to assess product quality. Due to the importance of its role, price should be a dominant cue for consumers attempting to evaluate service quality prior to purchase. Studies suggest that price is more likely to be used as a cue to quality under the following conditions:

- when price is the primary differential information available;
- when alternatives are heterogeneous; and
- when comparative price differences are relatively large.

Clearly, these conditions exist in many service purchase scenarios.

*Service consumers tend to be less certain about reservation prices.* A consumer's **reservation price** is the maximum amount that the consumer is willing to pay for a product. Ultimately, a consumer's reservation price for a service determines whether a purchase or no purchase decision is made. If the reservation price exceeds the price charged for the service, the consumer is more inclined to purchase that particular service. However, if the reservation price is lower than the actual price charged, then the consumer is precluded from purchasing that particular service offering.

Research has noted the lack of service consumer certainty regarding reservation prices. Consumers' reservation prices are determined in part by their awareness of competitive prices in the market. For some services, the lack of pricing information available and the lack of purchasing frequency may lead to less certainty regarding the reservation price of the service under consideration.[16]

*reservation price*
The price a consumer considers to capture the value he or she places on the benefits.

## COMPETITIVE CONSIDERATIONS

Service pricing strategy is affected by two unique competitive considerations. First, comparing prices of service alternatives is often difficult, which may make competitive-based pricing less of an important consideration for services compared to goods. In addition, a unique competitor must be considered when pricing services—the self-service consumer. Consumers are often willing to provide self-service to save money and customize the end result among other perceived advantages.

*Comparing prices of competitors is more difficult for service consumers.* Actual price information for services tends to be more difficult for consumers to acquire than it is for goods. Further, when service price information is available to consumers, it also tends to be more difficult to make meaningful comparisons between services (see E-Services in Action). For example, although base service prices can sometimes be determined in advance, competing services are not sold together in retail stores the way that many competing goods are in supermarkets, discount, or department stores. Consumers have to either individually visit geographically-separated service firms or contact them to compare prices. Comparative shopping requires more time and effort.

*Self-service is a viable competitive alternative.* One result of the inseparability of production and consumption for services is the possibility of the customer actively participating in the service delivery process, commonly referred to as self-service options. The availability of self-service options has an effect on customer perceptions of the service. Initially, self-service options invariably provided the service customer with some form of price reduction (e.g., self-service gasoline). Today, the literature suggests that service customers often are seeking other benefits besides lower prices when purchasing self-service options. These benefits might include greater convenience, more control, less human contact, faster service time, greater efficiency, and greater independence. Self-service options must be considered in the formation of pricing strategy.

## PROFIT CONSIDERATIONS

Price bundling often increases the profit opportunities for service firms. Compared to goods, services are more amenable to price bundling; however, price bundling makes the determination of individual prices in the bundle of services more complicated. *Price bundling* involves pricing a group of services at a price that is below their cost if bought separately. In general, price bundles are perceived as a better value for the customer and typically generate additional revenues for the selling firm.

*Price bundling makes the determination of individual prices in the bundle of services more complicated.* Bundling, the practice of marketing two or more goods and/or services for a single price, is a useful strategic pricing tool that can help services marketers achieve several different strategic objectives. However, it also complicates the alternative evaluation process for consumers. Consumers experience difficulty when attempting to calculate how much each component of the bundle is contributing to the total cost. For example, a consumer evaluating available alternatives for a trip to Jamaica might have a hard time comparing the costs associated with an all-inclusive hotel package bundled with airfare and transfers to a traditional pay-as-you-go vacation alternative.

*Price bundling is more effective in a service context.* A wide variety of services make use of price bundling as a strategic approach to pricing. Many service organizations bundle their own service offerings together, as when a doctor combines diagnostic tests with physical examinations. Other service organizations choose to form strategic alliances with other firms and bundle services that each provides. For example, the

## E - S E R V I C E S *IN ACTION*

### > PRICING ON THE INTERNET

The Internet allows for price transparency—the idea that both buyers and sellers can view all competitive prices for items sold online. Price transparency would tend to make commodities out of products sold online and offline. In other words, customer service really doesn't matter. All that really matters in the minds of many e-customers is that products can always be purchased cheaper from an Internet provider than a bricks-and-mortar retailer.

Are e-tailers really less expensive? Let's consider the trade-offs. Internet technology allows e-tailers to save costs in a number of ways:

*Order processing—self service.* Customers fill their own orders and submit their requests electronically saving e-tailers lots of money. For example, the average online banking transaction costs $0.15 to $0.20 compared to $1.50 offline.

*Just-in-time inventory.* Electronic data interchange (EDI) systems coordinate value chain activities and allow some e-tailers not to carry inventory at all. Products are simply drop-shipped from third parties.

*Overhead.* E-tailers seldom see customers face to face. Consequently, money is not spent on creating lavish retailing environments. Most e-tailers are operating out of warehouse-type facilities.

*Customer service.* Customers can help themselves and answer their own questions through Web-based services. Offline customer service averages $15 to $20 per request. In contrast, online customer service costs $3 to $5.

*Printing and mailing.* E-mail promotions and Web-based catalogs cost little compared to traditional mail distributing and printing costs.

*Digital product distribution costs.* Distribution costs for digital products such as music, airline tickets, and financial activities are extremely low compared to the shipping of tangible products.

Although the Internet lowers many operating costs, it also adds operating costs as well. Consider the following:

*Online customer service.* Once a luxury, now customers expect online firms to have top-notch online customer support. Customer service has become an expensive necessity for many e-tailers.

*Distribution costs.* The shipping of tangible products to separate destinations is costly. E-tailers pass shipping costs on to their customers, thereby, increasing the customer's overall costs. Some inflate shipping costs to offset the discounts advertised online.

*Affiliate programs.* Web storefronts often pay a 7 to 15 percent commission for each referral that results in a sale.

*Site development and maintenance.* The costs involved to develop and maintain a "conservative" site are estimated to be $10,000 to $100,000 a year. In comparison, the costs associated with an "aggressive" site can exceed $1,000,000.

*Customer acquisition costs.* The downfall of many previous e-tailers, the cost of acquiring an online customer averages $82. In addition, online customers are less brand loyal than their offline counterparts.

The bottom line is that when it comes to Internet pricing, prices are not necessarily always lower on the Net!

Source: Judy Strauss, Adel El-Ansary, and Raymond Frost, *E-Marketing*, 4e (Upper Saddle River, NJ: Pearson Prentice Hall), 2006, p. 268–270.

travel industry bundles hotel charges, airline tickets, and transfer services into a single price. Regardless of the form or type of bundling, this strategy essentially creates a new service that can be used to either attract new customers, cross-sell existing customers, or retain current customers. Bundling has proliferated in the service sector primarily because of high fixed/variable cost ratios, the degree of cost sharing, and the high levels of interdependent demand. For example, the demand for a hotel restaurant is directly related to the demand for hotel rooms.

## PRODUCT CONSIDERATIONS

Service pricing strategy recognizes three unique service product considerations. First, price is called by many different names in the service sector. As a result, price may be perceived differently in some sectors compared to others. Second, since service products are unable to be inventoried, service consumers should be less price sensitive and less prone to delay their purchases until a better price is offered some time in the future. Finally, the common practice of price lining used for tangible products makes less sense to service consumers.

*Compared to the goods sector, there tend to be many different names for price in the service sector.* One of the interesting aspects of pricing in a service context involves the many different names that are used to express price in different service industries. For example, in the financial services industry the term *price* is rarely if ever used. Instead, customers pay service charges, points, and commissions. Similarly, travelers pay airfares or bus fares, apartment dwellers pay rent, hotel occupants are charged a room rate, and the list goes on and on.

Upon further examination, many of the terms used for price in the service sector incorporate the benefit(s) customers receive. For instance, customers pay fares for the benefit of transportation, rents and room rates for occupancy, and service charges for processing requests. Is price by any other name still a price, or does incorporating the benefit into the term used for price alter consumer perceptions and affect price sensitivities?

Consumers are less able to stockpile services by taking advantage of discount prices. Retail pricing researchers note that pricing policies and strategies can have a direct impact on inventory decisions and planning. [17] Goods are often discounted to reduce over-abundant inventories. Consumers take advantage of the discounts and often engage in forward buying. **Forward buying** enables consumers to build their own inventories of goods and reduces the amount of defections to competitive brands. In contrast, services cannot be stored. Consequently, service consumers cannot stockpile service offerings. When consumers need or want a service, they must pay the prevailing price.

*Product-line pricing tends to be more complicated.* **Product-line pricing,** the practice of pricing multiple versions of the same product or grouping similar products together, is widely used in goods marketing. For example, beginner, intermediate, and expert level tennis racquets are generally priced at different price points to reflect the different levels of quality construction. Consumers of goods can more easily evaluate the differences among the multiple versions offered since tangibility provides search attributes. Search attributes assist consumers in making objective evaluations. In contrast, consider the difficulty of real estate consumers when faced with the choices offered by Century 21 Real Estate. The company offers home sellers three levels of service that are priced at increasing commission rates of six, seven, and eight percent. Customers, particularly those who sell homes infrequently, lack the expertise to make an informed decision. The performance levels associated with the three levels of service offered cannot be assessed until after the contract with the real estate agent has been signed and the customer has committed to the commission rate.

Traditionally, product-line pricing provides customers with choices and gives managers an opportunity to maximize total revenues. However, the product-line pricing of services more often than not generates customer confusion and alienation. Industries struggling with the price lining of their services include telecommunications (e.g., AT&T, MCI, and Sprint calling plans), healthcare (e.g., multiple versions of Blue Cross/Blue Shield plans and HMOs), and financial services (e.g., multiple types of checking and savings accounts and investment options).

*forward buying*
When retailers purchase enough product on deal to carry over until the product is being sold on deal again.

*product-line pricing*
The practice of pricing multiple versions of the same product or grouping similar products together.

## LEGAL CONSIDERATIONS

When developing pricing strategy, marketers must not only consider what is profitable but also what is legal. In general, the opportunity to engage in and benefit from illegal pricing practices in the service sector is predominantly attributed to intangibility, inseparability, and heterogeneity. As discussed in Chapter 5, intangibility decreases the consumer's ability to objectively evaluate purchases, while inseparability reflects the human element of the service encounter that can potentially expose the customer to coercive influence techniques.

*The opportunity for illegal pricing practices to go undetected is greater for services than goods.* Is it legal for a physician to charge excessive prices for vaccinations during an influenza epidemic, or for repair services to triple their hourly rate to repair homes in neighborhoods damaged by severe weather? In some states there are gouging laws to protect consumers from such practices during special circumstances. However, the special circumstances (e.g., epidemics and severe weather) draw attention to such practices. In contrast, identifying excessive service pricing practices is not as clear for "everyday" types of purchase occasions.

Service consumers are more vulnerable to illegal pricing practices. The pricing implications of service consumer vulnerability are twofold. First, consumer vulnerability and perceived risk are directly related. Consumers feeling particularly vulnerable are willing to pay higher prices for a service if it lowers their perceived risk. Second, dubious service providers that abuse the customer's trust by taking advantage of vulnerable consumers through excessive prices may benefit in the short term, but once they are discovered, the long-term success of their firms is doubtful. To consumers, the issue is one of fairness and **dual entitlement**. Cost-driven price changes are perceived as fair because they allow sellers to maintain their profit entitlement. In contrast, demand-driven prices are often perceived as unfair. They allow the seller to increase their profit margins purely at the expense of the increasing consumer demand.[18]

*dual entitlement*
Cost-driven price increases are perceived as fair, whereas, demand-driven price increases are viewed as unfair.

> ## EMERGING SERVICE PRICING STRATEGIES

Traditional pricing strategies such as penetration pricing, competitive pricing, and premium pricing offer little benefit to service customers or service providers. For example, competitive pricing has led to disappearing profit margins in industries such as car rental and health insurance and to customer confusion and mistrust in industries such as long distance telephone service. At the core of the pricing problem is a lack of understanding of the special considerations in the pricing of intangibles and how consumers use and benefit from the services they are purchasing. Service marketers should create pricing strategies that offer a compromise between the overly complex and the too simplistic, both of which neglect the variations in consumer needs.[19]

To effectively price services, the service firm must first understand what its target market truly values. Three alternative pricing strategies that convey value to the customer include satisfaction-based, relationship, and efficiency pricing (see Table 7.4).[20]

### SATISFACTION-BASED PRICING

*satisfaction-based pricing*
Pricing strategies that are designed to reduce the amount of perceived risk associated with a purchase.

The primary goal of **satisfaction-based pricing** is to reduce the amount of perceived risk associated with the service purchase and appeal to target markets that value certainty. Satisfaction-based pricing can be achieved through offering guarantees, benefit-driven pricing, and flat-rate pricing.

Service guarantees are becoming a popular way of attracting customers.[21] The guarantee assures customers that if they are less than satisfied with their purchase, they can invoke the guarantee, and a partial or full refund will occur. Offering guarantees signals to customers that the firm is committed to delivering quality services and is confident in its ability to do so. In instances where competing services are priced similarly, the service guarantee offers a differential advantage.

*benefit-driven pricing*
A pricing strategy that charges customers for services actually used as opposed to overall "membership" fees.

**Benefit-driven pricing** focuses on the aspects of the service that customers actually use. The objective of this approach is to develop a direct association between the price of the service and the components of the service that customers value. For example,

| TABLE 7.4 | SATISFACTION-BASED, RELATIONSHIP, AND EFFICIENCY PRICING STRATEGIES | |
|---|---|---|
| **Pricing Strategy** | **Provides Value by . . .** | **Implemented as . . .** |
| Satisfaction-based pricing | Recognizing and reducing customers' perceptions of uncertainty, which the intangible nature of service magnifies. | Service guarantees<br>Benefit-driven pricing<br>Flat-rate pricing |
| Relationship pricing | Encouraging long-term relationships with the company that customers view as beneficial. | Long-term contracts<br>Price bundling |
| Efficiency pricing | Sharing with customers the cost saving that the company has achieved by understanding, managing, and reducing the costs of providing the service. | Cost-leader pricing |

Source: Leonard L. Berry and Manjit S. Yadav, "Capture and Communicate Value in the Pricing of Services," *Sloan Management Review* (Summer 1996), 41–51.

online computer services typically do not use benefit-driven pricing strategies. This is evident by their practice of charging customers for the amount of time spent online as opposed to billing for services they actually use. Innovative online services, such as ESA-IRS and its "pricing for information" program, have introduced benefit-driven pricing and have shifted their marketing focus from keeping customers online to marketing information that is beneficial to their customers.

The concept of **flat-rate pricing** is fairly straightforward. Its primary objective is to decrease consumer uncertainty about the final price of the service by agreeing to a fixed price before the service transaction occurs. With flat-rate pricing, the provider assumes the risk of price increases and overruns. Flat-rate pricing makes the most sense when:

*flat-rate pricing*
A pricing strategy in which the customer pays a fixed price and the provider assumes the risk of price increases and cost overruns.

- the price is competitive;
- the firm offering the flat rate has its costs under control and operates efficiently; and
- the opportunities to engage in a long-term relationship and to generate additional revenues with the customer is possible.

## RELATIONSHIP PRICING

The primary objective of **relationship pricing** is to enhance the firm's relationship with its targeted consumers. For example, in the banking industry, relationship pricing strategies can be utilized to further nurture the relationship between the bank and its existing checking account customers by offering special savings accounts, deals on safe-deposit boxes, and special rates on certificates of deposit. Two types of relationship pricing techniques include long-term contracts and price bundling.

*relationship pricing*
Pricing strategies that encourage the customer to expand his/her dealings with the service provider.

**long-term contracts**
Offering prospective customers price and non-price incentives for dealing with the same provider over a number of years.

**Long-term contracts** offer prospective customers price and non-price incentives for dealing with the same provider over a number of years. UPS recently entered into long-term shipping contracts with Land's End and Ford Motor Company. Because of its customers' long-term commitments, UPS has been able to transform its business with these clients from discrete to continuous transactions. UPS now has operations and personnel dedicated solely to providing services to these specific customers. Since transactions are now continuous, economies of scale have developed, and cost savings that can be passed to the customer plus opportunities for improving the firm's profit performance have emerged.

**price bundling**
The practice of marketing two or more products and/or services in a single package at a single price.

Since most service organizations provide more than one service, the practice of bundling services has become more common.[22] **Price bundling,** broadly defined, is the practice of marketing two or more products and/or services in a single package at a single price. Common examples include hotels putting together weekend packages that include lodging, meals, and sometimes entertainment at an inclusive rate. Airlines routinely price vacation packages that include air travel, car rental, and hotel accommodations.

Price bundling flows logically from the issues discussed earlier in the chapter. Individual services have low marginal costs and high shared costs. Moreover, the services offered by most businesses are generally interdependent in terms of demand. For example, the demand for the hotel's food service is directly related to the demand for hotel rooms.

**mixed bundling**
Price-bundling technique that allows consumers to either buy Service A and Service B together or purchase one service separately.

Generally, services are concerned with **mixed bundling,** which enables consumers to buy either Service A and Service B together or purchase one service separately. The simplest argument for bundling is based on the idea of consumer surplus: Bundling makes it possible to shift the consumer surplus from one service to another service that otherwise would have a negative surplus (i.e., would not be purchased). Thus, the combined value of the two services is less than the combined price, even though separately, only one service would be purchased.

Three reasons have been suggested for why the sum of the parts would have less value than the whole. First, information theory would argue that the consumer finds value in easy access to information. Consumers of one financial service institution have a lower information cost when buying another service from the same institution than when buying that service from a different institution. A second case argues that the bundling of Service B with Service A can enhance a consumer's satisfaction with Service A, for example, a ski resort that offers a ski-rental-and-lessons package. The reservation price for the lessons is likely to be the same whether or not the skis are rented because the value of the lessons depends on the skills and needs of the skier. However, the reservation price of the ski rental will be enhanced, at least for novices, by lessons. The final argument is that the addition of Service B to Service A can enhance the total image of the firm. A financial-planning service offering both investment advice and tax advice enhances its credibility in both services.

**efficiency pricing**
Pricing strategies that appeal to economically minded consumers by delivering the best and most cost-effective service for the price.

## EFFICIENCY PRICING

The primary goal of **efficiency pricing** is to appeal to economically minded consumers who are looking for the best price. "Efficiency pricers almost always are industry heretics, shunning traditional operating practices in search of sustainable cost advantages."[23]

Southwest Airlines and its relentless efforts to reduce costs is one such example. Southwest reduces costs by flying shorter, more direct routes to less congested, less expensive airports. No meals are served, passengers are seated on a first-come, first-served basis, and the airline was the first to offer "ticketless" travel on all flights.

Efficiency pricing is focused on delivering the best and most cost-effective service available for the price. Operations are streamlined, and innovations that enable further cost reduction become part of the operation's culture. The leaner the cost structure, the more difficult it is for new competitors to imitate Southwest's success. Understanding and managing costs are the fundamental building blocks of efficiency pricing.

## SOME FINAL THOUGHTS ON PRICING SERVICES

Pricing services is a difficult task. Consumers are purchasing an experience and often feel uneasy about or do not understand what they are paying for. Similarly, service providers do not have a cost-of-goods-sold figure upon which to base their prices. Confused and bewildered, many providers simply look to what the competition is charging, regardless of their own cost structures and competitive advantage. In contrast, successful service providers tend to abide by the following pricing guidelines:[24]

- The price should be easy for customers to understand.
- The price should represent value to the customer.
- The price should encourage customer retention and facilitate the customer's relationship with the providing firm.
- The price should reinforce customer trust.
- The price should reduce customer uncertainty.

## ✳ | SUMMARY

Successful service pricing depends on recognizing the value that a customer places on a service and pricing that service accordingly. Customer perceptions of value represent a trade-off between the perceived benefits obtained from purchasing the product and the perceived sacrifice in terms of cost to be paid. Total customer costs extend beyond monetary costs and include time, energy, and psychic costs. Similarly, total customer value extends beyond product value and includes service, personnel, and image value.

When developing service pricing strategies, managers should take into account a number of considerations including demand, cost, customer, competitive, profit, product, and legal considerations. Table 7.1 provides a summary of each of these considerations.

Overall, traditional pricing strategies and cost accounting approaches offer little benefit to either service consumers or service providers. Three alternative pricing strategies that convey value to the customer include satisfaction-based, relationship, and efficiency pricing. The primary goal of satisfaction-based pricing is to reduce the perceived risk associated with the purchase of services and to appeal to target markets that value certainty. Satisfaction-based pricing strategies include offering guarantees, benefit-driven pricing, and flat-rate pricing. The goal of relationship pricing is to enhance the firm's relationship with its targeted consumers. Relationship pricing techniques include offering long-term contracts and price bundling. In comparison, efficiency pricing appeals to economically-minded consumers and focuses on delivering the best and most cost-effective service for the price. Understanding and managing costs are the fundamental building blocks of efficiency pricing.

## ✳ KEY TERMS

| | |
|---|---|
| monetary price, 168 | fixed costs, 179 |
| time costs, 168 | variable costs, 179 |
| energy costs, 169 | reservation price, 181 |
| psychic costs, 169 | forward buying, 185 |
| product value, 169 | product-line pricing, 185 |
| service value, 169 | dual entitlement, 186 |
| personnel value, 169 | satisfaction-based pricing, 186 |
| image value, 169 | benefit-driven pricing, 186 |
| inelastic demand, 172 | flat-rate pricing, 187 |
| cross-price elasticity, 172 | relationship pricing, 187 |
| complementary, 172 | long-term contracts, 188 |
| substitutes, 172 | price bundling, 188 |
| price discrimination, 172 | mixed bundling, 188 |
| activity-based costing, 177 | efficiency pricing, 188 |
| cost drivers, 178 | |

## ✳ REVIEW QUESTIONS

1. What factors comprise consumer perceptions of value?
2. Discuss the role of price as an indicator of quality to consumers.
3. Describe the trade-offs associated with taking hotel reservations from customers who pay lower rates than same-day customers.
4. Discuss the differences between traditional methods of allocating overhead expenses and activity-based costing.
5. Should self-service always be rewarded with lower prices? Please explain.
6. Under what conditions is price segmentation most effective?
7. Discuss the basic concepts behind satisfaction-based, relationship, and efficiency pricing.

# ✱ NOTES

1. J. Dean, "Research Approach to Pricing," in *Planning the Price Structure*, Marketing Series No. 67, American Marketing Association (1947).

2. J. Backman, *Price Practices and Price Policies* (New York: Ronald Press, 1953).

3. Walker A.W. (1967), "How to Price Industrial Products," *Harvard Business Review*, 45, 38–45.

4. A. Marshall, *More Profitable Pricing* (London, McGraw-Hill, 1979).

5. Chief Executive, "Finding the Right Price Is No Easy Game to Play," *Chief Executive* (September 1981), 16–18.

6. Thomas T. Nagle and Reed K. Holden, *The Strategy and Tactics of Pricing*, (Englewood Cliffs, NJ: Prentice Hall, 1995).

7. Philip Kotler, *Marketing Management*, 8th ed. (Englewood Cliffs, NJ: Prentice-Hall, 1994), p. 38.

8. Thomas T. Nagle and Reed K. Holden, *The Strategy and Tactics of Pricing*, 3rd ed. (Upper Saddle River, Prentice Hall, 2002), p. 1.

9. Dale Lewison, *Retailing*, 6th ed. (Upper Saddle River, Prentice Hall, 1997).

10. K. Douglas Hoffman and L. W. Turley, "Toward an Understanding of Consumer Price Sensitivity for Professional Services," in *Developments in Marketing Science*, Charles H. Noble, ed., (Miami, FL: Academy of Marketing Science, 1999), 169–173.

11. Adapted from John E. G. Bateson, *Managing Services Marketing*, 2nd ed. (Fort Worth, TX: The Dryden Press, 1992), pp. 357–365.

12. Beth M. Chaffman and John Talbott, "Activity-Based Costing in a Service Organization," *CMA Magazine* (December 1990/January 1991), pp. 15–18.

13. UPS Web Site: http://www.ups.com accessed 30 January 2005. "Only Santa Delivers More in One Day than UPS," Press Release (December 13, 2004); http://pressroom.ups.com/ ups.com/us/press_releases/ accessed 30 January 2005; and John Alden, "What in the World Drives UPS?" *International Business* (1998), 11(2), pp. 6–7; and Jim Kelley, "From Lip Service to Real Service: Reversing America's Downward Service Spiral," *Vital Speeches of the Day* (1998), 64(10), pp. 301–304.

14. Kent B. Monroe, "Buyers Subjective Perceptions of Price," *Journal of Marketing Research*, 10 (February 1973), pp. 70–80.

15. Bateson, Managing Services Marketing, pp. 338–339

16. Joseph P. Guiltinan, "The Price Bundling of Services: A Normative Framework," *Journal of Marketing* (1987), 51 (2), pp. 74–85.

17. Saroja Subrahmanyan and Robert Shoemaker, "Developing Optimal pricing and Inventory Policies for Retailers Who Face Uncertain Demand," *Journal of Retailing*, (1996) 72 (1), pp. 7–30.

18. Czinkota, et al. *Marketing: Best Practices* (Fort Worth, TX: The Dryden Press, 2000).

19. Leonard L. Berry and Manjit S. Yadav, "Capture and Communicate Value in the Pricing of Services," *Sloan Management Review* (Summer 1996), pp. 41–51.

20. Ibid.

21. Christopher W. L. Hart, Leonard A. Schlesinger, and Dan Maher, "Guarantees Come to Professional Service Firms," *Sloan Management Review* (Spring 1992), pp. 19–29.

22. Joseph P. Guiltinan, "The Price Bundling of Services: A Normative Framework," *Journal of Marketing* (April 1987), pp. 51, 74–85.

23. Berry and Manjit, "Capture and Communicate Value," p. 49.

24. Ibid.

# CHAPTER 8

## DEVELOPING THE SERVICE COMMUNICATIONS MIX

### CHAPTER OBJECTIVES

*The purpose of this chapter is to provide an overview of communications mix strategies as they apply to the marketing of services.*

After reading this chapter, you should be able to:

- Discuss factors that influence the development of the firm's communications mix.
- Describe the goals of the communications mix during prepurchase, consumption, and postpurchase stages.
- Appreciate the special problems associated with developing the service communications mix.
- Understand the basic guidelines for advertising services.
- Explain the special problems encountered by professional service providers.

*"I know half of my advertising is wasted, I just don't know which half."*

John Wanamaker

## > AFLAC: THE MAKING OF AN AMERICAN ADVERTISING ICON

Given the intangible nature of services, service products are often abstract in the minds of potential customers. Consequently, one of the principal guidelines for advertising a service is to make it more concrete. Insurance companies are faced with this challenge on a daily basis—how to make tangible the intangible? One possible solution for many companies has been to utilize tangible symbols to represent their companies. Prudential has "The Rock," Merrill Lynch has "The Bull," and GEICO has "The Gecko." However, no insurance icon has ever been as successful as the Aflac Duck!

According to Aflac Inc., "The duck has done more for the life and disability insurer's brand recognition in less than five years than most advertising symbols have done for their brand over decades." The Aflac Duck campaign was created by Linda Kaplan Tahler, CEO/chief creative officer and Robin Koval, chief marketing officer/general manager of The Kaplan Thaler Group (KTG) Ltd. Their charge was to increase the public's awareness of the Aflac brand. Aflac's Chair and CEO told Thaler, "I don't care what you do, as long as you get people to know the name of this company." The impetus behind the duck campaign was based on KTC's "big bang" theory—"If we allow a little illogic into our thoughts...we can break through the prison of current convention." When pronounced audibly, Aflac sounds like a duck, so why not create a slightly annoying waterfowl (who hates to be ignored) to represent a company that is trying to make a splash in the marketplace?

The Aflac Duck campaign has been an unparalleled success. To begin, Aflac's name recognition has grown from 12 percent in January of 2000 to over 90 percent in 2005. Aflac is now the number-one provider of guaranteed-renewable insurance in the United States and Japan. Aflac has a presence in all 50 United States and U.S. territories. The company employs 56,000 licensed agents and insures more than 40 million people worldwide. Aflac is actively involved in a number of philanthropic endeavors and has been nationally recognized in "The 100 Best Companies to Work For in America" for seven consecutive years; "100 Best Places to Work in IT" for six consecutive years; the "50 Best Companies for Latinas" to work for the last six consecutive years; "America's Most Admired Companies" for five consecutive years; and "100 Best Companies for Working Mothers" for four consecutive years. Although founded in Georgia by three brothers, today Aflac insures one in four Japanese households and is the fourth most profitable foreign company operating in any industry in Japan.

The Aflac Duck's fame has become legendary. In 2004, the Aflac Duck beat out Ronald McDonald, the Michelin Man, Charlie the Tuna, and many other popular advertising symbols to join the Advertising Walk of Fame, which selected America's top five favorite icons. The Aflac Duck was the youngest contender nominated for the award. The M&M talking candies came in first, the Aflac Duck placed second, followed by Mr. Peanut, The Pillsbury Doughboy, and Tony the Tiger, respectively. Winners of the Walk of Fame were honored with an image-enshrined plaque that was installed at the corner of 50th Street and Madison Avenue in New York City. In its never ending task of increasing Aflac's name recognition, the duck has appeared on CNBC, "The Tonight Show with Jay Leno," "Saturday Night Live," and "Lemony Snickett's—A Series of Unfortunate Events." The Duck's popularity continues overseas. Aflac U.S.A and Aflac Japan's advertisements can be viewed on http://www.aflac.com/us/ en/aboutaflac/aflac-commercials.aspx. In 2005, the Aflac Duck was incorporated into the firm's logo to symbolize Aflac's strengthening commitment to its consumers. The Aflac Duck truly represents one of service marketing's great advertising success stories!

---

Sources: http://www.aflac.com accessed 26 April 2005; Jerry Fisher, "Duck Season," *Entrepreneur*, 33, Issue 1 (January 2005), 67; and Fran Matso Lysiak, "Aflac's Quacking Duck Selected One of America's Favorite Ad Icons," *BEST'S REVIEW*, 105, Issue 6, (October 2004), 119.

## > INTRODUCTION

Communications strategy is one of the key components of the service marketing mix.[1] In general, the primary role of a service firm's communications strategy is to inform, persuade, or remind consumers about the service being offered. Consumers cannot be expected to use a service they do not know about; therefore, a primary objective of communications strategy is to create consumer awareness and position the firm's service offering in the consumer's evoked set of alternatives. Moreover, even when awareness of the service product exists, consumers may need additional encouragement to try it and information about how to obtain and use the service. Finally, people forget. Just because they have been told something once does not mean that they will necessarily remember it over the course of time.

*nonpersonal sources*
Communication channels that are considered impersonal, such as television advertising or printed information.

Communicating the firm's service offering may be accomplished through **nonpersonal sources**, such as television advertising or printed information in magazines and newspapers, or through **personal sources** on a face-to-face basis through all the individuals who come into contact with the consumer in the prepurchase, consumption, and postpurchase stages. In addition, the communications mix can be designed to influence customer expectations and perceptions of the service.

*personal sources*
Communication channels that are considered personal, such as a face-to-face encounter.

Communications objectives and strategies vary, depending upon the nature of the target audience. Separate communications strategies are necessary for current users of a service in order to influence or change their patterns of service use, and for nonusers in order to attract them to the service.

## > DEVELOPING A COMMUNICATIONS STRATEGY: THE BASICS

The development of a sound communications strategy is based on the fundamentals of marketing strategy—identifying a target market, selecting a positioning strategy, and tailoring a communications mix to the targeted audience that reinforces the desired positioning strategy. The threefold objectives of communications strategy—*inform, persuade,* and *remind*—change in priority over the course of the product's life cycle and whether the company is targeting current users or nonusers. Communications mix elements will also change under the same considerations.

### SELECTING TARGET MARKETS

*target markets*
The segments of potential customers that become the focus of a firm's marketing efforts.

Developing a communications strategy follows a common pattern whether the firm is producing goods or services. The service firm must first analyze the needs of consumers and then categorize consumers with similar needs into market segments. Each market segment should then be considered based on profit and growth potential and the segment's compatibility with organizational resources and objectives. Segments that become the focus of the firm's marketing efforts become **target markets.**

With this ad, Carnival is trying to convey the wide variety of choices available to its target market as part of its "Today's Carnival" product enhancement strategy.

## DEVELOPING THE FIRM'S POSITIONING STRATEGY

Once the target market is selected, successful service firms establish a **positioning strategy**, which differentiates them from competitors in consumers' eyes. Effective positioning is particularly critical for service firms where intangibility clouds the consumer's ability to differentiate one service provider's offering from the next. For example, competing airlines that fly the same routes may stress operational elements such as the percentage of "on-time" arrivals, while others stress service elements such as the friendliness and helpfulness of the flight crew and the quality of the food served.

*positioning strategy*
The plan for differentiating the firm from its competitors in consumers' eyes.

Ultimately, positioning involves a strategic manipulation of the firm's marketing mix variables: *product, price, promotion, place, physical facilities, people,* and *processes.* Each of these marketing mix variables is controllable. When effectively combined, the marketing mix can offset the effects of the uncontrollable factors that exist in every firm's operating environment such as technological advances, consumer needs, new and existing competitors, governmental regulations, economic conditions, and the effects of seasonality that are constantly changing the environment in which the firm operates. Firms that fail to alter their positioning strategy to reflect environmental changes in order to differentiate themselves from competitors often falter in the long run (see Table 8.1).[2]

| TABLE 8.1 | DIFFERENTIATION APPROACHES FOR EFFECTIVE POSITIONING |
|---|---|

**Product Differentiation**
Features
Performance
Conformance
Durability
Reliability
Repairability
Design (integrates the above)

**Personnel Differentiation**
Competence
Courtesy
Credibility
Reliability
Responsiveness
Communication Style

**Image Differentiation**
Symbols
Written, audio/visual media
Atmosphere
Events

**Service Differentiation**
Delivery (speed, accuracy)
Installation
Customer training
Consulting service
Repair
Miscellaneous service

Source: Adapted from Philip Kotler, *Marketing Management,* 9th ed. (Englewood Cliffs, NJ: Prentice-Hall, 1997), p. 283.

**communications mix**
The array of communications tools available to marketers.

**personal selling**
The two-way element of the communications mix in which the service provider influences a consumer via direct interaction.

**media advertising**
A one-way communications tool that utilizes such media as television and radio to reach a broadly defined audience.

**publicity/public relations**
A one-way communications tool between an organization and its customers, vendors, news media, employees, stockholders, the government, and the general public.

**sales promotions**
A one-way communications tool that utilizes promotional or informational activities at the point of sale.

## DEVELOPING THE COMMUNICATIONS BUDGET AND MIX

The firm's promotion, or communications mix, communicates the firm's positioning strategy to its relevant markets, including consumers, employees, stockholders, and suppliers. The term **communications mix** describes the array of communications tools available to marketers. Just as marketers need to combine the elements of the marketing mix (including communications) to produce a marketing program, they must also select the most appropriate communication vehicles to convey their message (see E-Services in Action).

The elements of the communications mix fall into four broad categories: **personal selling, media advertising, publicity and public relations,** and **sales promotions**— promotional or informational activities at the point of sale. Only personal selling is a two-way form of communication. The remainder are one-way communications, going only from the marketer to the customer. Using more than one communications tool or using any one tool repeatedly increases the chances that existing and potential customers will be exposed to the firm's message, associate it with the firm, and remember it. By reinforcing its message, the firm can ensure that existing customers as well as potential ones become more aware of "who" the firm is and what it has to offer. The firm's communications mix often lays the foundation for subsequent contact with potential consumers, making discussions with consumers easier for the provider and more comfortable for the consumers.

It is important at this stage of developing the firm's communications mix to determine the communications budget. Budget-setting techniques typically covered in

# E-SERVICES *IN ACTION*

## > | THE TEN-YEAR ANNIVERSARY OF ONLINE ADVERTISING

The ten-year anniversary of online advertising occurred in 2004. Examples of online advertising include permission email, keyword-targeted search engine advertising, floating animated page takeovers, interactive on-page rich media ads, streaming audio and video, and viral marketing to name a few. It is almost hard to imagine that a decade ago the Internet was virtually unknown. Today, consumers can't seem to live without it. According to DoubleClick, "No medium since black-and-white television has penetrated 50 percent of U.S. households as quickly as the internet; both did so in eight years." In comparison, radio took 9 years, 10 years for VCRs, 39 years for cable TV, and 70 years for the telephone.

The first Internet advertisements appeared on HotWired in October of 1994. The advetisements were banner ads and promoted the brands Zima, Club Med, and AT&T. In 2004, U.S. advertisers spent $9.6 billion on Internet ads. As a point of comparison, the money spent on Internet advertising in 2004 is larger than the whole outdoor advertising industry (e.g., billboards), accounts for 80% of the magazine ad industry, and 50 percent of the size of the radio ad industry. Internet ads increased 31.5 percent between 2003 and 2004. During this same time period, broadcast TV ads grew by 10 percent and the entire ad industry grew by 7.4 percent.

Four major trends seem to be emerging in online advertising. First, online advertising is becoming a seller's market. Many premium online publishers sold out of ad space for perhaps the first time ever in 2004. Sellers of product categories such as automobiles, telecom, travel, technology, and healthcare are now buying ad space a full year in advance. Second, marketers are demanding more accountability for the return on advertising spending. The return on online advertising dollars spent is often more measurable than offline expenditures. Common metrics include post-click conversions, cost per conversion, ad exposure time, and view-through rate just to name a few. Third, consumers are demanding more control. Technological advances such as pop-up blockers, MP3s podcasting, TiVo, and ReplayTV are limiting advertisers' access to consumers. Permission marketing may very well become the wave of the future. Finally, the fourth major trend is that rich media is becoming the communication method of choice for many Internet advertisers. Advertisements incorporating rich media include high-quality animation, streaming audio and video, and other software-life features such as games, registration forms, and expanded marketing information.

Based on DoubleClick's review of the first ten years of online advertising, "The new face of advertising is almost certain to be more entertaining, more informative, more timely, more relevant, more authentic and more in tune with customers."

Source: Rick E. Bruner, "The Decade in Online Advertising: 1994–2004, DoubleClick website, http://www.doubleclick.com accessed 27 April 2005.

most introductory marketing classes include the percentage-of-sales technique, the incremental technique, the all-you-can-afford approach, competitive parity, and the objective-and-task method.[3] After the budget has been established, the target audience or audiences, objectives, and budgets are divided among the different areas of the communications mix. Each area does not have to be assigned the same task or audience as long as they collectively meet the overall objectives of the firm's communications strategy. Once they do, information delivery can be planned and executed and the results monitored.

## DEFINING COMMUNICATIONS OBJECTIVES

The objectives of a firm's communications mix often relate directly to the service offering's stage within the product life cycle (PLC) (see Table 8.2). In general, the major communications objectives within the introduction and growth stages of the PLC are to inform the customer. Informational communications introduce the service offering and create brand awareness for the firm. Informational communications also encourage trials and often prepare the way for personal selling efforts to be conducted later.

As professional service providers slowly begin to advertise, informational communications objectives tend to be the first step. Informational communications tend to be less obtrusive than other forms of communication, and in many ways, the information being conveyed often provides a public service to consumers who otherwise might not have access to or knowledge of the range of services available. Legal and medical referral services that advertise are typical examples. Although many of us poke fun at many of the ads that lawyers place on the airways, they do serve their purpose (see B2B Services in Action). Many of the clients who contact these services are lower-income, lower-educated clients who, by their own admission, have stated that if it were not for the advertisements,

| TABLE 8.2 | COMMUNICATION CONTENT AND OBJECTIVES | |
|---|---|---|
| **Product Life Cycle Stage** | **Communication Content** | **Communication Objectives** |
| Introduction | Informational | Introduce the service offering |
| | | Create brand awareness |
| | | Prepare the way for personal selling efforts |
| | | Encourage trial |
| Growth and maturity | Informational and persuasive | Create a positive attitude relative to competitive offerings |
| | | Provoke an immediate buying action |
| | | Enhance the firm's image |
| Maturity and decline | Persuasive and reminder | Encourage repeat purchases |
| | | Provide ongoing contact |
| | | Express gratitude to existing customer base |
| | | Confirm past purchase decisions |

**B₂B  SERVICES  *IN ACTION***

> ### RAINMAKER MARKETING:MARKETING YOUR LAW PRACTICE WITH TELEVISION

If you don't particularly like the way lawyers are portrayed on television advertisements, there is probably a good reason—you're not their target market. According to Greg Norton, Vice President of Rainmaker Marketing, Inc. located in Wilmington, North Carolina, "Over one half of the attorney advertisers on television nationwide are sending the wrong message to the wrong audience. In markets all over the country, attorney advertisers are turning off the people they wish to reach." Rainmaker Marketing offers its services to law clients to keep them from making the same mistakes.

Who responds to lawyers who advertise on television? The results may surprise you. For example, research indicates that women make the initial calls to lawyers 60 to 70 percent of the time for automobile injuries (regardless of whether it's a male or female that is injured in the accident). Clearly, attorney advertisements should be created to speak to that female audience and the message should be "trust." Women are looking for a relationship based on trust when selecting an attorney.

The typical respondents to attorney advertising are blue collar, aged 21–54, with a 9th to 12th grade education. Younger callers tend to be single wage earners with families consisting of small children. This target audience is very connected to their television as they obtain 90 percent of their current information from this medium. Women tend to respond immediately to attorney advertising viewed in the morning, but will delay responses in the afternoon until after their favorite shows have ended.

The timing of attorney advertising is an interesting science. Based on automobile accident statistics, 50 to 60 percent of all injury-causing accidents occur between Friday morning and Sunday midnight. Two-thirds of all injuries are soft tissue damage that begins to show symptoms 24–72 hours after the accident. Consequently, prime time for attorney advertising begins Monday morning and extends through Wednesday afternoon.

According to Rainmaker Marketing, this target audience will call if the attorney communicates what they do and makes it easy for prospective clients to contact the attorney's office. Advertising spots should be appropriately paced, the music appropriately selected, and the copy pertinent and confidently voiced. As the company name indicates (i.e., a rainmaker is someone who achieves outstanding results in business or politics), it's Rainmaker Marketing's job to help their legal clients sell more legal services.

Source: Gregory Norton, "Marketing Your Practice with Television," *FindLaw*, http://marketing.lp.findlaw.com/articles/oherron2.html, accessed 26 April 2005.

they would not know where to turn.[4] Information-based communications are also ruling the Web. By 2005, it is predicted that U.S. online consumers will spend more than $632 billion in offline channels due to information that is obtained through websites. In comparison, actual online purchases are forecasted to be $199 billion.[5]

Communications objectives during the growth and maturity stages of the PLC tend to lean toward informational and persuasive content. Objectives during this stage include creating a positive attitude toward the service offering relative to competitive alternatives, attempting to provoke an immediate purchase action, and enhancing the firm's image. Professional service organizations often discourage the use of persuasive advertising among their members as it often pits one professional member of the organization against another. Many in professional organizations believe that members engaged in persuasive communications ultimately cheapen the image of the entire industry. As a result, promotional messages that are primarily information based are viewed as a more acceptable and tasteful method of promotion.

Finally, communications objectives during the maturity and decline stages of the PLC tend to utilize persuasive and reminder communications. The communications objectives during this phase of the PLC are to influence existing customers to purchase again, to provide ongoing contact with the existing client base in order to remind clients that the firm still values their relationship, and to confirm clients' past purchase decisions, thereby minimizing levels of felt cognitive dissonance. As with informational communications, reminder communications tend to be less obtrusive and more acceptable to professional organizations than persuasive communications.

## DIVIDING THE COMMUNICATIONS OBJECTIVES AND TARGET AUDIENCES

Once the overall objectives and target audiences for the entire communications mix have been set, it is necessary to divide the tasks among advertising, selling, publicity and public relations, and sales promotions. This is a process of matching the tasks to the capabilities of the different communications channels.

### Targeting Nonusers
If the objective is to reach nonusers of the service, then the choice of communications channel is reduced to media advertising, selling performed by a sales force rather than a service provider, and publicity and public relations.

One way of assigning tasks across the array of communications channels is to consider the degree to which the message can be targeted at specific audiences. Media advertising itself varies along this dimension. At the broadcast, "shotgun" level, television can reach a very wide audience but is not especially selective except in the variation of audiences across channels by time of day. National print media such as newspapers and magazines offer more selective focus, as they themselves tend to be targeted at more specific segments of consumers. Trade magazines are even more specific in their readership. Direct mail offers the most focused of the impersonal media. The choice among these media must be based on the cost per thousand members of the target audience and the risk and cost of reaching the wrong segments.

When the service provider has a broadly defined audience and little to lose in reaching the wrong segments, television advertising may work out to be the least expensive vehicle on a cost per person basis. However, television and other forms of mass media are unlikely to be efficient for a specialty service such as an upscale restaurant with a tightly defined target audience and a high cost associated with attracting the wrong segment.

Public relations and publicity can be either broad or tightly focused, depending on how they are used. Editorial comment can be solicited in broad or narrow media. Public relations carries with it the advantages and disadvantages of not being paid advertising. On the positive side, it is given more credence by the consumer; on the negative side, it is much more difficult to control. The content may not be designed, or the coverage may be limited.

Both media advertising and public relations and publicity are one-way forms of communication. They cannot respond to consumers' inquiries or tailor the message to the particular characteristics of the receiver. Personal or telemarketing is far more expensive per member of the target audience, but it does offer the flexibility of altering the message during the presentation. If the message is difficult to communicate or a great deal of persuasion is needed, personal communication may be most appropriate. A sales force can be highly targeted and trained to make complex arguments interactively, responding to the inputs of consumers during the process.

### Targeting Users

Users can be reached through all the channels we have discussed, and they can be further reached by communications through the service provider. The role of the service provider is multifaceted. Different providers are called upon to perform different communication functions. The classifications of these providers and functions are described next.[6]

**Type 1 service staff** are required to deal with customers quickly and effectively in "once only" situations where large numbers of customers are present. The exchanges consist of simple information and limited responses to customer requests. Effective communication requires the ability to establish customer relationships very quickly, deal efficiently with customer problems, and convey short, rapid messages that customers can easily understand. Typical examples include front-line personnel at fast-food restaurants or dry cleaners and patient representatives whose job is to obtain and process insurance information.

*type 1 service staff*
Service staff that are required to deal with customers quickly and effectively in "once only" situations where large numbers of customers are present.

**Type 2 service staff** deal with numerous, often repeat customers in restricted interactions of somewhat longer duration. The information provided is mixed—partly simple and partly more complex—and requires some independent decision making on the part of the staff member. Communication in this category requires effective listening skills, the ability to establish trust, interpreting customer information, and making decisions in customer relationships that are often ongoing over a period of time. Communications are generally more intense than in type 1 situations. Typical examples include relationships with suppliers or customer relationships such as with a customer who requests floral designs from a florist on a regular basis, a loyal customer of a seamstress/tailor, or an effective wait staffperson at a fine dining establishment.

*type 2 service staff*
Service staff that deal with numerous, often repeat customers in restricted interactions of somewhat longer duration.

*type 3 service staff*
Service staff required to have more highly developed communication skills because of more extended and complex interactions with customers.

**Type 3 service staff** are required to have more complex communication skills. Interactions with consumers are repeated over time, extensive flow of communication is

Type 1 service staff, such as a ticket booth employee at an amusement park, deal with customers quickly and effectively in "once only" situations.

© BILL BACHMANN / PHOTO EDIT

required, and communication tasks are complicated and often nonrepeatable. Effective communication requires the ability to listen and process complicated information, to think creatively in face-to-face interactions with consumers, and to provide information in a clear and understandable manner. Typical examples include staff members who are likely to be qualified as professionals.

Any service organization may have employees in one, two, or all three of these categories. Thus, a bank may have tellers performing type 1 communications, a loan officer engaged in type 2, and a commercial loan officer engaged in type 3. A travel company may have an agent engaged in both type 2 (when writing tickets and booking arrangements) and type 3 communications (when planning trips) and a receptionist handling type 1 communications.

Each type of communication requires a different set of skills from the providers and places different levels of stress on them. It is clearly important that the correct communications role be assigned to the correct person within the organization. Type 1 is predominantly an operations role, whereas type 3 is a mixed selling and operations role.

When a communications mix that includes the service provider is developed, the final objectives for the staff will probably fall within one of the three service categories. However, it is important to recall the position of the employee providing the service. The service provider is not simply a salesperson; he or she is an integral part of the operations process and a part of the experience purchased by the customer. An apparently simple decision—for example, to have a bank teller sell services—can have profound negative consequences. It could well be that the decision produces role conflict for the teller. Role/self-conflict could be caused by the tellers' wanting to see themselves not as salespeople but as bankers. Direct conflict between the two roles can arise when the operations role demands fast service and minimization of the time spent with each customer but the selling role demands the opposite. In addition, the script may break down for both the service provider and the customer as the teller tries to do something new. The customer may be expecting a brisk, businesslike transaction when suddenly, the teller wants to build rapport by talking about the weather (before starting the sell).

Potentially, such a decision can also diminish operational efficiency as the transaction time per customer rises. This problem is illustrated by the experiences of FedEx before it centralized its telephone customer contact system. In times of peak demand, especially if those times were unpredicted, everyone in the FedEx depots answered telephones, including the field salespersons based at the depots. The result was that the various depot employees changed the service communication from type 1 to type 3. It also meant that calls took much longer than usual, and the telephone bottleneck consequently worsened.

> ## THE COMMUNICATIONS MIX AS IT RELATES TO CONSUMER BEHAVIOR CONSIDERATIONS[7]

Consumer behavior is important because it imposes constraints on the objectives set for services. It is perhaps best to consider behavior during the three phases discussed in Chapter 4—prepurchase, consumption, and postpurchase.

### THE PRECONSUMPTION CHOICE STAGE

Consumers will try to minimize risk taken in the purchase phase. Risk is some combination of consequences and uncertainty, so these are the two dimensions that the firm's communications objectives can attempt to minimize. In each case, the objective must be to ensure that the company's service is the one perceived to be the least risky alternative. For example, an Internet company can reduce consumer fears of ordering by taking the lead and communicating customer-friendly return policies. However, in a recent survey of dot.com sites, two out of three do not explicitly state whether it's the seller or the buyer who is responsible for shipping costs associated with returned items.

Communication can obviously impart information that is a key factor in reducing the uncertainty in all risky decisions. It can also offer reassurance. Consequences are generally of three basic types: financial, social, and performance. **Financial consequences** can be reduced by communications that ensure that consumers correctly understand the likely financial consequences of a purchase, particularly if a money-back guarantee is offered. Concerns about **social consequences** can be reduced by highlighting for consumers that other people are using the service and that it would not be embarrassing for them to use it. **Performance consequences** need to be made explicit and clearly communicated to ensure that consumers understand what would happen if the performance were not 100 percent successful. Clearly, most services are perceived as more risky on the social and performance dimensions, and communications have a key role to play in reassuring customers.

The communications mix can, for example, be based on generating positive word-of-mouth references. This key communications area for services can be managed using public relations and publicity. It has also been shown to be a key method in reducing consumers' perceived risk.

*financial consequences*
The perceived monetary consequences of a purchase decision by a consumer.

*social consequences*
The perceived consequences of a consumer's purchase decision among the consumer's peers or the public in general.

*performance consequences*
The perceived consequences of a consumer's purchase decision should the service perform less than 100 percent effectively.

*rational mathematician model*
A model that assumes consumers are rational decision makers using a choice matrix of attributes, brand or company scores, and importance weights.

The **rational mathematician model** assumes that consumers are rational decision makers using a choice matrix of attributes, brand or company scores, and importance weights like those described in the college selection example presented in Chapter 4. Services in the evoked set are scored using the matrix, and the one with the highest score is chosen. Communications can be used to try to influence the choice in the following ways:

- To ensure that the firm's service offering is in the evoked set.
- To alter the weights consumers attach to different attributes to favor those in which the company is strong.
- To alter the score on a given attribute for the company, particularly if a gap exists between performance and consumers' perceptions.
- To alter the score on a given attribute given to a competitor, again, particularly if a gap exists between performance and consumers' perceptions.
- If the company is not in the evoked set, to build enough awareness of the offering to stimulate inclusion.

It is important to remember the difference between actual and perceived performance. If actual performance is higher than perceived performance, communications may be more effective than if the reverse were the case. Alternatively, advertising can be used to maintain a situation that is favorable to the firm. Consumers need to be reminded that a firm does well on particular attributes and that those attributes are important.

## THE CONSUMPTION STAGE

During the consumption stage, the service consumer is more or less an active participant in the production process. It is important that consumers perform that production role successfully. From the firm's point of view, successful performance will improve the efficiency of the operation and the satisfaction of other customers. From the consumer's point of view, successful performance will ensure a high level of perceived control and, in all probability, a high level of satisfaction in the postconsumption phase.

Communications, in the broadest sense, can be used to ensure successful performance by giving the consumer a clear script (see Figure 8.1). Although this can be done through advertising, the presence of the consumer in the actual service setting creates the opportunity for a much broader range of communications channels. Point-of-sale signs, service providers, and the environment itself can all be used to teach the consumer the script.

In times of operational change, managing the consumer's script takes on even more importance. An example can be seen in a bank that is changing from multiple-line queuing to single-line queuing. No longer may consumers wait in front of a specific teller window. Instead, they must form a single line and go to the first free window available to them when they arrive at the head of the line. Operationally, this offers shorter and more predictable waiting times.

However, such a shift requires a script change. Arriving at the bank without prior warning of the change, the consumer finds a new experience, one that no longer

| FIGURE 8.1 | TEACHING THE CONSUMER THE SCRIPT: WENDY'S HAMBURGERS |
|---|---|

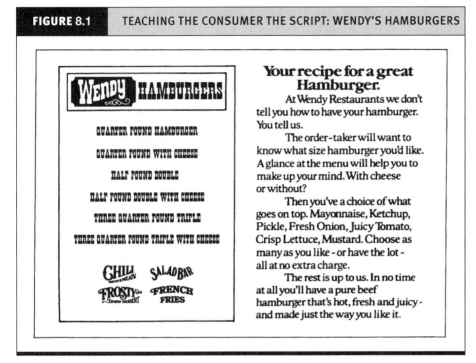

Source: Bateson and Hoffman, *Managing Services Marketing*, 4th ed., Page 170.

conforms to the existing script. Because it is not immediately obvious how the new system works, the customer may feel a loss of control. The line seems to be extremely long, and worse still, it is no longer possible to choose a specific, favorite teller. Clearly, the script needs to be modified.

It is fairly obvious how elements of the communications mix can be used to achieve script modification. The bank can use media advertising or leaflets to describe the new process. Contact personnel outside the bank can explain the new system to customers before they enter. Public relations can be used to generate consumer comment about the benefits of the new system. Inside the building, the layout and signs displayed can clearly signal the desired customer behavior. Finally, service providers can personally reassure customers and reinforce the new script.

## THE POSTCONSUMPTION EVALUATION STAGE

Chapter 4 also introduced the disconfirmation model of consumer satisfaction. This model hypothesizes that consumers determine satisfaction by comparing their prior expectations of performance with the perceived actual performance.

Consumer expectations come from a number of sources, some within the control of the service firm, and some beyond its control. Expectations arise either from previous experience with the firm and/or its competitors or from some form of communication. The latter can encompass all aspects of the communications mix. Advertising, designed to influence prepurchase choice behavior, can set expectations in the customer's mind about the quality of service that will be received. Indeed, setting such expectations may be a key aspect of a firm's advertising strategy.

In Chapter 4, you learned that, based on studies of consumer behavior, word-of-mouth communication can be expected to have an increased role in the service industry because of the high levels of perceived risk associated with the purchase of many services. Such word-of-mouth communication can be random, or it can be orchestrated through the public relations component of the communications mix. Service firms often strategically place customer testimonials in their promotional campaigns for this very reason.

## > SPECIAL PROBLEMS OF THE SERVICE COMMUNICATIONS MIX[8]

Intangibility and inseparability present special challenges that should be considered when developing a communications strategy. First, since services are often consumed as a shared experience, mistargeted communications are likely to result in unanticipated consequences. Second, a firm's communications are often interpreted as an explicit service promise that consumers use to base their initial expectations. Third, since employees often produce the service in close proximity to customers, employees should be considered as much a target audience as customers. Finally, service providers produce the service and also must sell the service. When the service provider is engaged in selling activities, production halts. When the service provider is producing services, future customers are not being cultivated. How should service providers balance the activities of selling and operations?

### *MISTARGETED COMMUNICATIONS*

Segmentation is one of the basic concepts of marketing. In essence, it suggests that a firm's marketing efficiency can be improved by targeting marketing activities at discrete groups of consumers who behave differently in some way toward the firm. Although segmentation is applied in both goods and service companies, the consequences of reaching an inappropriate segment with a part of the communications mix are far less serious for goods companies than for services. If the wrong group of consumers buys a particular brand of detergent, for example, it does not really affect the company making the detergent; sales are still being generated. Or a product may have been developed for the youth market, but through some quirk of the advertising execution, the product has attracted some senior citizens. For example, take the Pepsi advertisement that portrayed the youthful effects of Pepsi being delivered to a senior citizen's home by error instead of to the college fraternity house. Let's say that the ad is interpreted by senior citizens that Pepsi will make them feel young again. Clearly, this was not Pepsi's (who targets the younger generation) original intent. Members of this group who misinterpreted the message visit the supermarket, buy the product, and use it in their homes. The negative consequences associated with the elder segment's use of the product are nil.

Suppose, however, that some of the wrong segment decides to buy the services of a restaurant. An upscale concept has been developed, but to launch the restaurant, management decides to have a price promotion, and the advertising agency develops inappropriate advertising. Or, through poor management, publicity activity is unfocused and produces feature articles in the wrong media. The result is that the restaurant gets two types of customers: upscale, middle-aged couples and price-conscious groups of students. The former were the original target, and the latter were attracted by inappropriate marketing tactics. Unfortunately for the restaurant and for many other services, the other customers are part of the product. The result is that neither segment enjoys the experience because of the presence of the other, and neither type of customer returns. Hence, the consequences of **mistargeted communications** for service firms, because of the shared consumption experience, are clearly more significant than the consequences experienced by traditional goods-producing firms.

*mistargeted communications*
Communications methods that affect an inappropriate segment of the market.

## MANAGING EXPECTATIONS[9]

The service firm's communications strategy can play a key role in formulating customer expectations about its services (see Global Services in Action). Firms may reinforce pre-existing ideas or they may dramatically alter those ideas. Expectations can be set by something as explicit as a promise ("Your food will be ready in five minutes") or as implicit as a behavior pattern that sets a tone. Often such expectations are created unwittingly, as when a server promises to "be right back." Such a statement can be viewed both as a binding contract by a customer and as a farewell salutation by the service provider.

Perceived service also has many service sources. **Technical service quality** is an objective level of performance produced by the operating system of the firm. It is measurable with a stopwatch, temperature gauge, or other measuring instrument. Unfortunately, this is not the level of performance the customer perceives. Perception acts as a filter that moves the perceived service level up or down.

*technical service quality*
An objective, measurable level of performance produced by the operating system of the firm.

Perception is itself influenced by the same factors that dictate expectations. For example, communications can create warm feelings toward the organization that raises perceived service levels. Inappropriately-dressed and ill-behaving staff can deliver high levels of technical service quality but be poorly perceived by the consumer, who will downgrade the perceived service level.

Many sources of expectations are under the direct control of the firm. Only past experience and competitors' activities cannot be directly influenced in one way or the other. Given such control, the firm must determine the objectives of the communications mix.

In the absence of competition, reduced expectations will result in higher satisfaction levels, provided that levels of perceived service are maintained. Therefore, one strategy would be to reduce expectations as much as possible. Regardless of the service actually delivered, the customer would then be satisfied.

Unfortunately, communications must also play the more traditional role of stimulating demand. It is inconsistent to think of achieving this by promising average service, even if doing so might minimize customers' expectations (for the few customers who use the service!).

## GLOBAL SERVICES *IN ACTION*

### > | MARRIOTT INTERNATIONAL, INC.

Believe it or not, Marriott International, Inc., one of the world's leading hospitality companies, started out as a root beer stand in Washington D.C. in 1927. Over the years, the proud owners of that root beer stand, J. Willard and Alice S. Marriott, have done very well. Today, Marriott International is comprised of 2,600 properties located in 66 countries and territories. The hospitality giant opened its first international hotel in Acapulco, Mexico in 1969.

One of the challenges faced by international service marketers is developing promotional campaigns that meet the needs of local clientele. In order to customize the promotional plan for the international market, the international marketer should consider issues related to positioning and advertising copy. The most important category of adaptations is based on local behavior, tastes, attitudes, and traditions—all reflecting the marketer's need to gain customers' approval. The product itself may not change at all but its positioning may need to be adjusted. For example, a Marriott property in one location may be positioned as a weekend getaway for adults, while another location in a more conservative country may stress family values in its communication strategy.

Frequently, the copy in advertisements needs to be adjusted to appeal to the international customer. While some advertisements may share common graphic elements, the copy in the ad will be customized for the local culture. Marriott used similar ads to reach the business traveler in the U.S., Saudi Arabia, Latin America, and German-speaking Europe. However, the copy was modified based on needs of the local consumer. While the common theme, "When You Are Comfortable, You Can Do Anything," was used worldwide, local emphases in the creative varied; for example, the Latin version stressed comfort, the German version focused on results.

Similarly, ads for hotel properties marketed in countries such as Saudi Arabia need to be sensitive to local moral standards. While a global creative approach can be used, the copy and the images used in promotions may require some adjusting. For example, if a western-based Marriott advertisement showed a man and a women embracing with bare arms visible, this version used around the world may be adjusted for Saudi Arabia to show the man's arm clothed in a dark suit sleeve, and the woman's hand merely brushing his hand. In the end, international service promotions should be carefully tailored to fit the needs and expectations of local markets.

Source: http://www.marriott.com accessed 27 April 2005; Adapted from K. Douglas Hoffman et al., *Marketing Principles & Best Practices*, (Mason, OH: Thomson South-Western, 2006), 121–122.

In competitive terms, firms make promises and strive to build expectations that will differentiate them in the marketplace and cause customers to come to them and not to their competitors. The temptation is, therefore, to promise too much and to raise expectations to an unrealistic level. It is perhaps fortunate that the variability in services is well known to most consumers and that they consequently discount many of the promises made by service firms. When the promises are taken seriously, however, the result is often dissatisfied customers.

It is probably more effective to attempt to match customers' expectations to the performance characteristics of the service delivery system. In such a scenario, the behavior of the customer is most likely to conform to the script required by the operating system. There is little point, for example, in encouraging McDonald's customers to specify how well they want their hamburgers done. Not only would the customers be disappointed, but any attempt to meet their demands would destroy the efficiency of the operating system.

## ADVERTISING TO EMPLOYEES

The staff of service firms frequently forms a secondary audience for any firm's advertising campaign. Clearly, communications seen by the staff, if they empathize with it, can be highly motivating. However, if communications are developed without a clear understanding of the operational problems, it can imply service performance levels that are technically or bureaucratically impossible; that is, it can set expectation levels unrealistically high. This has a doubly detrimental effect on the staff since (1) it shows that people who developed the communications (the marketing department) did not understand the business and (2) it raises the prospects that customers will actually expect the service to operate that way, and the staff will have to tell them that the reality differs from the level of service portrayed in the firm's communications. In both cases, the impact will be a negative influence on staff motivation, which will in turn, negatively influence customer satisfaction. A classic example involved American Airlines. The company ran an ad that featured a flight attendant reading a young child a story during the flight. As a result, passengers expected the flight attendants to tend to their children, and flight attendants were miffed by the implication that they were supposed to be babysitters in addition to all of their other duties.

The bottom line is that in order for service firms to succeed, they must first sell the service job to the employee before they sell the service to the customer.[10] For years, communications from Southwest Airlines have shown smiling employees going to great lengths to please the customer. Although the communications are clearly targeted toward customers, they also send a message to employees regarding appropriate role behavior. In the end, service communications not only provide a means of communicating with customers, but also serve as a vehicle to communicate, motivate, and educate employees.[11]

## SELLING/OPERATION CONFLICTS

Another consideration unique to the service sector is that the individuals who sell the service are often the same people who provide the service. In many instances, the service provider is much more comfortable providing the service than marketing his or her own abilities. However, in some cases, providers become so involved in the communications aspects of their firm that they no longer actively participate in the operations end of the business.

The conflicts associated with selling versus operations are at least two-fold. First are the economic considerations. Typically, service providers are paid for providing services and are not paid for time spent on communications activities. Clearly, the provider must engage in marketing activities in order to generate future customers, but the time spent on marketing does not generate revenues for the provider at that particular moment. Moreover, the time spent on communications activities is often while an ongoing project is being conducted. This means that the time dedicated to communications activities must be considered when estimating completion dates to customers. Often the firm's communications efforts must occur while previously sold services are being processed in order to avoid shut-down periods between customer orders.

The second conflict that arises is often role related. Many professional service providers believe that communications activities such as personal selling are not within their areas of expertise. Consequently, some providers feel uncomfortable with communications activities, and, even more disturbing, some providers feel that this type of activity is beneath them. The healthcare field in particular has been plagued by this problem through the years. However, increased competition in the healthcare arena has lead to a recognition of the need for marketing training directed at technical specialists. Many healthcare institutions, particularly the good ones, now embrace the importance of the firm's communications efforts.

> ## GENERAL GUIDELINES FOR DEVELOPING SERVICE COMMUNICATIONS

After a review of the literature that directly examines the specifics of advertising services, several common themes emerge that create guidelines for advertising services. Many of these guidelines have developed directly as a result of the intangibility, inseparability, heterogeneity, and perishability inherent in service products.

### DEVELOP A WORD-OF-MOUTH COMMUNICATIONS NETWORK

Consumers of services often rely on personal sources of information more than nonpersonal sources to reduce the risk associated with a purchase. Given the importance of nonpersonal sources, communications should be developed that facilitate the development of a word-of-mouth network. Advertising that features satisfied customers and promotional strategies that encourage current customers to recruit their friends are typical. Other communications strategies such as presentations for community and professional groups and sponsorship of community and professional activities have also been effective in stimulating word-of-mouth communications.

## PROMISE WHAT IS POSSIBLE

In its most basic form, customer satisfaction is developed by customers' comparing their expectations to their perceptions of the actual service delivery process. In times of increasing competitive pressures, firms may be tempted to overpromise. Making promises the firm cannot keep initially increases customer expectations and then subsequently lowers customer satisfaction as those promises are not met.

Two problems are associated with overpromising. First, customers leave disappointed, and a significant loss of trust occurs between the firm and its customers. Moreover, disappointed customers are sure to tell others of their experience, which increases the fallout from the experience. The second problem directly affects the service firm's employees. Working for firms that make false promises places employees in compromising and often confrontational positions. Front-line personnel are left to repeatedly explain to customers why the company cannot keep its promises. Given the link between employee satisfaction and customer satisfaction, creating expectations that cannot be met can have devastating long-term effects.

## MAKE TANGIBLE THE INTANGIBLE[12]

In Chapter 1, we discussed that the distinction between goods and services is unclear and presented the scale of market entities—a continuum that assesses the tangible properties of the market entity, ranging from tangible dominant to intangible dominant. Interestingly, tangible dominant market entities, such as perfume, utilize image development in their advertising schemes. From a basic viewpoint, perfume is simply liquid scent in a bottle. The customer can pick it up, try it on, and smell the fragrance. Hence, the perfume is tangible dominant. As with many tangible dominant products, the advertising tends to make them more abstract in order to differentiate one product from another. For example, when you think of the fragrance Calvin Klein, what images come to mind? The company uses these images to differentiate its product from competitive offerings.

In contrast, services, being intangible dominant are already abstract. Hence, one of the principal guidelines for advertising a service is to make it more concrete. This explains why corporations utilize tangible symbols to represent their companies. For example, Meryll Lynch has "The Bull," Prudential uses "The Rock," and of course as the opening vignette discussed Aflac has "The Duck." Insurance products are already abstract, so it becomes the advertisement's objective to explain the service in simple and concrete terms. In addition to tangible symbols, other firms have made tangible their service offerings by using numbers in their advertisements, such as, "We've been in business since 1925,"or "Nine out of ten customers would recommend us to a friend."

In making tangible the intangible, the scale of market entities should be turned on its end (see Figure 8.2). The advertising of tangible dominant products tends to make them more abstract in order to differentiate them from one another. In contrast, the advertising of intangible dominant products should concentrate on making them more

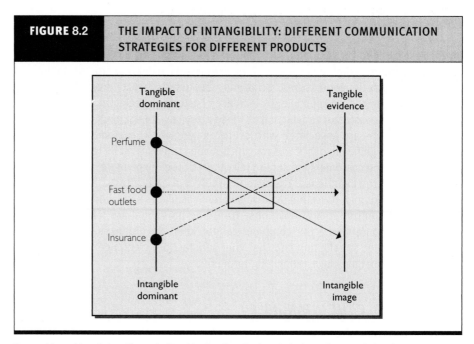

**FIGURE 8.2    THE IMPACT OF INTANGIBILITY: DIFFERENT COMMUNICATION STRATEGIES FOR DIFFERENT PRODUCTS**

Source: Adapted from G. Lynn Shostack, "Breaking Free from Product Marketing," *The Journal of Marketing* (April 1977).

concrete through the use of physical cues and tangible evidence. The advertising of products in the middle of the continuum often utilizes both approaches. McDonald's, for example, promotes "food, folks, and fun" in its advertisement. Food and folks are concrete, and fun is abstract.

### FEATURE THE WORKING RELATIONSHIP BETWEEN CUSTOMER AND PROVIDER

As you should well understand by now, service delivery is an interactive process between the service provider and the customer. Because of inseparability, it is appropriate in the firm's advertising to feature a company representative and a customer working together to achieve a desired outcome. H&R Block advertising commonly shows a company representative and a customer interacting in a friendly and reassuring manner. Many financial institutions, legal firms, and insurance companies also follow this same model. The advertising of services, in particular, must concentrate not only on encouraging customers to buy, but also on encouraging employees to perform. Clearly, advertising that illustrates the inseparability of the service delivery process should target both the customer and the firm's service providers.

## REDUCE CONSUMER FEARS ABOUT VARIATIONS IN PERFORMANCE

The firm's advertising can also minimize the pitfalls of heterogeneity in the customer's mind. To enhance the perception of consistent quality, the firm's advertising should provide some form of documentation that reassures the customer. Typical examples include stating the firm's performance record through numbers as opposed to qualitative testimonials. The use of "hard" numbers in advertisements reduces the consumer's fear of variability and also tangibilizes the service, as mentioned earlier.

## DETERMINE AND FOCUS ON RELEVANT SERVICE QUALITY DIMENSIONS

The reasons customers choose among competing services are often closely related to the five dimensions of service quality—reliability, responsiveness, assurance, empathy, and the quality of the tangibles associated with the service. However, it is common that some features are more important to customers than others. For example, 30 percent of today's airline customers list "safety" as one of their top five considerations when choosing an airline.[13] Consequently, it would be appropriate for airlines to emphasize the assurance dimension of service quality by featuring the airline's safety record, maintenance and training programs, as well as any certified aspects of their particular airline operation. One advertising campaign that backfired promoted a hotel as one of the tallest hotels in the world. Although this reinforced the tangible dimension of service quality, this particular tangible component was not very important to customers in choosing hotels. In fact, many customers who had even the slightest fear of heights avoided the hotel for fear of being placed on an upper floor.

## DIFFERENTIATE THE SERVICE PRODUCT VIA THE SERVICE DELIVERY PROCESS

A dramatic difference exists between what the service provides and how it is provided. Identifying the various inputs into the process, which contributes to a competitive or quality advantage, and stressing these inputs in the firm's advertising is likely to be a successful approach. On the surface, it appears somewhat difficult to differentiate one tax accountant from the next. However, if we consider the process of obtaining a consultation, which consists of calling to make an appointment, interacting with staff at the front desk, the appearance of the office in the reception area where the client is waiting, the appearance of the accountant's office, the interaction between the client and the accountant, and the payment procedures, several potential areas for differentiation arise. Outlining the various inputs within the service delivery process may indicate key competitive and/or quality advantages that traditionally have been overlooked.

## MAKE THE SERVICE MORE EASILY UNDERSTOOD

Services can be more fully explained to potential customers via the communications mix by presenting the service as a series of events. When questioned, consumers often break down the service experience into a series of sequential events. Understanding the sequence permits the service provider to view the service from the customer's perspective. For example, bank customers may first view the external building, parking facilities, landscaping, and cleanliness of the grounds. When entering the bank, customers notice the interior furnishings, odors, music, temperature, and service personnel. While conducting bank transactions, the appearance and demeanor of specific contact personnel become additional quality cues. Hence, perceptions of quality are assessed at each stage of the service encounter. Advertising developed from the sequence-of-events perspective considers the customer throughout the process and highlights the firm's strengths in each area.

> ## SPECIAL CONSIDERATIONS OF PROFESSIONAL SERVICE PROVIDERS

Professional service providers often experience distinct challenges that may be tempered by the development of an effective communications program.[14] Specifically, the ten most frequent problems encountered include the following:

1. *Third-party accountability.* Investors, insurance companies, banks, governmental agencies, and even members of their own professions often hold professional service providers accountable for their actions or at least monitor those actions. Creating credibility and projecting the image of a quality firm to third parties can be accomplished through the firm's communications mix, thereby minimizing excessive scrutiny by outside parties. Communication strategies that come to mind include conducting business seminars, giving speeches, and writing trade articles.[15]

   Business seminars in the professional's area of specialization demonstrate the provider's expertise not only to potential and existing clients, but also to interested third parties, particularly other industry members. Speeches to local civic organizations as well as national conventions spotlight the firm's talents and further enhance the firm's image. Reprints of articles should be included in company newsletters and sent to appropriate audiences.

2. *Client uncertainty.* Many professional services are costly, are associated with danger or importance, and are, in some cases, technical and specialized, making them difficult for the customer/client to understand. Effective communications can communicate the procedures involved, show the likely outcomes (which manages consumer expectations), answer consumers' common questions, and/or minimize consumers' areas of concern. For example, many surgical centers send patients informational pamphlets that describe surgical procedures prior to the patient's scheduled appointment.

3. *Experience is essential.* Communications must be effective in attracting and maintaining the customer base. The opening of a new doctor's office is not greeted

with nearly the enthusiasm as that of a new restaurant. Once again, the value of offering seminars, membership in local organizations, speaking at civic functions or on talk-radio programs, and writing articles for local consumption are great icebreakers.

4. *Limited differentiability.* As the level of competition increases among professional service providers, differentiation among providers decreases as they match one another's offerings with comparable alternatives. Communications that differentiate the provider on factors beyond the mere service product itself, such as personnel, customer service, and image, must be communicated to the marketplace to set the provider apart from the crowd (see Table 8.1).

5. *Maintaining quality control.* Because the consumer is part of the service production process, he or she ultimately has a large amount of control over the quality of the final outcome. Communications that stress the importance of following the professional's advice and its relationship to positive outcomes educates the consumer about the importance of his or her own role in the service delivery system.

6. *Turning doers into sellers.* In many instances, the employment of outside sales representatives to market professional services to clientele is inappropriate and ineffective. Client uncertainty dictates that the professional provider him/herself must become actively involved in the sales process to reassure clients and minimize their fears. Ultimately, no one should be able to sell the available service better than the provider. However, while some providers thrive on making sales, many other providers feel uncomfortable when thrust into the sales spotlight.

7. *The challenge of dividing the professional's time between marketing and providing services.* Directly related to the previous point are the problems associated with the professional's becoming too involved in the personal selling component of the firm's communications mix. Professionals generate revenues by billing for the time that they are servicing existing customers. Marketing activities not only consume a portion of the professional's billable hours, but the professional does not get paid directly for the time spent conducting marketing efforts. As a result, the professional must make decisions about how much personal time to allocate to marketing activities and also how to divide that time among cultivating new prospects, maintaining relationships with existing clients, and involvement in more general public relations work.

8. *Tendencies to be reactive rather than proactive.* The pressure of everyday business cuts into the amount of time the professional can devote to marketing activities. Existing customers demand the attention of the provider in the short-run by expecting services to be delivered in an expedient manner. As a result, many professionals find themselves in a reactive mode as they search out new business while existing business transactions end. This creates the unenviable position of attempting to run a business while moving from one client to the next. Often, slack time develops between clients, which negatively affects the cash flow of the operation, not to mention placing increased pressure on the desperate provider looking for new clients.

The communications mix should not be based solely on the professional's personal selling efforts. Ongoing communications must work for the provider in a proactive manner while the provider performs everyday activities with existing clientele. The professional can make better use of the time devoted to marketing efforts by focusing on closing the sale, not starting from scratch.

9. *The effects of advertising are unknown.* In the not-so-distant past, many professional organizations such as those for U.S. lawyers forbade their members to engage in marketing communication activities. However, in 1978, the courts ruled that the ban on marketing communications was unconstitutional, based on the case *Bates v The State Bar of Arizona.* Despite the ruling, some members of professional societies still frown upon the use of certain communications methods such as traditional advertising.

Consumer groups are particularly advocating that professional service providers engage in active marketing communications. Consumer advocates believe that an increase in communication efforts will provide consumers with much-needed information and increase the level of competition among providers. They also believe that as a result of the increase in competition, prices will fall, and the quality of service will improve. However, service providers such as those in the healthcare arena do not agree. Healthcare providers quickly point to the legal profession and state that increasing communications will likely have a negative impact on their profession's image, credibility, and dignity. In addition, healthcare professionals believe that customer benefits created by increased communications efforts are unlikely. In fact, some state that if consumers believe that healthcare is expensive now . . . just wait until the profession has to start covering the costs of its communications efforts. Needless to say, the jury is still out on who is correct. However, as time has passed and as competitive pressures among professional service providers have mounted, the use of marketing communications seems to be more acceptable in general.

10. *Professional providers have a limited marketing knowledge base.* As business students, many of the terms you take for granted, such as market segments, target markets, marketing mix variables, and differentiation and positioning strategies, are totally foreign terms to many service providers. Professional service providers are trained to effectively perform their technical duties. For example, lawyers attend law schools, physicians attend medical schools, dentists attend dental schools, and veterinarians attend veterinary schools. What do all these professional providers have in common when they go into practice for themselves? They all run businesses yet have no formal business educational backgrounds.

Due to a limited marketing knowledge base, their temptation is to develop the firm's communications mix in isolation, without regard to the firm's overall marketing strategy. Ultimately, the firm's communications mix should be consistent with targeted consumer expectations and synergistic with other elements in the marketing mix.

## > COMMUNICATIONS TIPS FOR PROFESSIONALS[16]

The following suggestions provide a guide for maximizing the potential of the service communication strategy.

## TURN CURRENT CLIENTS INTO COMPANY SPOKESPERSONS

Too often, service firms lose sight of their existing clients as they develop a communications mix with the sole purpose of attracting new business. A firm's existing client base is the heart of its business and represents a vast potential for additional revenue. Existing clients are a rich resource of further revenue and offer opportunities for business that can be generated without substantial promotional expenditures, without additional overhead, and frequently, without hiring additional personnel. By being constantly on the alert for suggestions and ideas and by discovering the clients' needs and responding to them in a professional and timely manner, professional service providers essentially win over clients, who, in turn, become a perpetual advertisement for the firm. Given the importance of personal sources of information in choosing among service alternatives, having existing clients who sing the praises of your firm to others is an invaluable resource.

## MAKE A POSITIVE FIRST IMPRESSION

Because of the **halo effect**, early stages of the service encounter often set the tone for consumer evaluations made throughout the service experience. As a result, providers must pay special attention to the initial interactions in the encounter because they are often the most important. First impressions are believed to often establish or deny relationships within the first four minutes of contact.[16] For example, telephone calls need to be answered promptly and politely. During a speech about service excellence, Tom Peters of *In Search of Excellence* fame reported his personal experience with telephone contact personnel at Federal Express. Mr. Peters reported that in 27 of 28 cases, FedEx operators answered the phone on or before the first ring. In fact, Mr. Peters admitted that FedEx may be 28 for 28 since he assumes that he misdialed and hung up the phone on the twenty-eighth event. Peters then redialed the number, and the phone was answered before the first ring.

*halo effect*
An overall favorable or unfavorable impression based on early stages of the service encounter.

Communication cues on which consumers base initial impressions include "yellow-page" advertisements, signage, and an easily accessible place of business. Once the client actually arrives, the firm's reception area should be a showplace, complete with tangible clues that reinforce the firm's quality image. Possible tangible clues in the reception area include the name of the firm and its service providers prominently displayed, furnishings that reflect the personality of the business, fresh flowers, a "brag book" that includes letters from happy customers, past company newsletters, provider profiles, and indications of the firm's involvement in the community. Finally, the reception area should be staffed by professional and pleasant customer contact personnel. Despite the importance of first impressions, many firms simply view their reception areas as waiting rooms, making little effort to enhance the aesthetics of these areas. In many cases, these areas are equipped with uncomfortable and unappealing furnishings and staffed by low-paid, poorly trained personnel.

A concierge plays an important role in projecting a professional image of a hotel because he/she is one of the first employees that many hotel guests first encounter as they plan their stay.

## CREATE VISUAL PATHWAYS THAT REFLECT THE FIRM'S QUALITY

The firm's printed image includes all printed communication to clients such as correspondence, annual reports, newsletters, and billings. It also includes printed material of general use, such as firm brochures, letterhead, envelopes, and business cards, as well as internal communications—from agendas to checklists, from memos to manuals. Printed materials create a **visual pathway** through which the professional image of the firm can be consistently transmitted.

**visual pathway**
Printed materials through which the professional image of the firm can be consistently transmitted, including firm brochures, letterhead, envelopes, and business cards.

From the first time the firm's business card is put into a prospective client's hand, through the first letter the client receives, and on through finished reports delivered to the client and final billings, the presentation of printed material is making an impression. With every piece of material the client receives, he or she subconsciously reacts to the quality of paper, reproduction, and binding with which the firm has produced it. And most of all, he or she is responding to the visual images the professional provider has chosen to represent the firm, starting with the logo.

Effective communication of the firm's logo assists the firm in establishing familiarity throughout the region in which it operates. In addition to identifying the firm, other primary goals of logo development are to simplify and explain the purpose of the organization. In essence, logo development can be viewed as creating a form of hieroglyphic symbol that enables others to quickly identify the professional firm. The logo is the service firm's brand.

Given the lack of a substantial marketing knowledge base, professional service providers should seriously consider engaging the advice of a communications professional. Graphic artists, ad agencies, and public relations firms are typical examples of communications specialists who work with a client to produce the kind of image that will give the firm the individual yet professional identity that successfully positions it in the marketplace. When a logo is designed, it can be printed in various sizes and in reverse. The various forms of the logo can then be easily applied to all manner and style of printed materials. Finally, the firm's choice of stock (paper), typeface, and kind of printing (engraving, offset, or thermograph) will complete the highly professional image of its printed material and create a visual pathway that consistently communicates quality to the client.

## ESTABLISH REGULAR COMMUNICATIONS WITH CLIENTS

Every letter sent to a client or a colleague is a potential promotional opportunity. Experts suggest taking advantage of this potential from the very beginning of the relationship with the client. Every new client should receive a special letter of welcome to the firm and a sample newsletter that conveys the firm's service concept. The use of standardized letters embossed with the firm's logo, which can be adapted for different circumstances such as welcome letters, thank-yous for referrals, and reminder letters of upcoming appointments, is also effective. Better yet, handwritten, personalized messages on the firm's notecards provide a personal touch.

The most important piece of regular communication with clients should be the firm newsletter. It can be as simple as an 8 1/2 -by-11 sheet, typed at the office and photocopied, or as elaborate as a small booklet, typeset and printed in color on quality stock. Some firms choose to make their newsletters informal bulletins; others prefer to make them polished publications. Regardless of the technique, the newsletter should always have a clean, professional appearance and be filled with information valuable to clients.

## DEVELOP A COMPANY BROCHURE

The company's brochure is a menu of the firm's service offering and should be the written showpiece. In addition to providing an overview of available services, firm brochures typically include the firm's history, philosophy, and profiles of personnel. To add to its flexibility, the brochure may be developed with flaps on the inside front and/or back covers for holding supplemental materials or other information that changes from time to time. Personnel profiles featuring printed photographs and biographies are likely candidates for materials that frequently change as employees move from firm to firm. The flaps for supplemental materials also provide the option to customize each brochure for particular clients who desire specific services and who will be dealing with specific personnel. The firm brochure is a prime opportunity for the professional service firm to project its uniqueness. Ultimately, the firm brochure should be the kind of product the firm can enthusiastically present to existing and prospective clients.

## PROJECT A PROFESSIONAL IMAGE

Last, but definitely not least, engendering respect and pride in the firm's capability does not stop with external promotion. In fact, it starts internally and generating a professional image for the benefit of firm staff can be as important as promoting that image to clients. Remember, the staff is in constant, direct contact with clients. Failure to effectively communicate with the firm's staff is readily apparent and quickly erases all other communication efforts to project a quality program.

## ✱ SUMMARY

This chapter has provided an overview of communications mix strategies as they apply to the marketing of services. Communications strategy is one of the key components of a firm's overall marketing mix. Its role is to inform, persuade, and/or remind consumers about the services being offered. The components of the communications mix include personal selling, media advertising, publicity and public relations, and sales promotion. The service firm's budget is allocated among each component of the communications mix. Depending on the target audience and the firm's objectives, some components of the mix will be utilized more often than others.

The objectives of a firm's communications mix often relate directly to the service offering's stage within the product life cycle. For instance, the content of communications during the introduction stage tends to be informational to create consumer awareness. As the service moves into the growth and maturity stages of its life cycle, the content of the communication tends to be informational and persuasive to help position the service among competing alternatives. The content of the communications mix switches to persuasive and reminder as the firm progresses through the maturity stage and into the decline stage.

A variety of special considerations that pertain to services must be addressed when developing the communications mix. These issues include mistargeted communications, the role of communications in managing consumer expectations, the effects of the communications mix on employees, and the conflicts many professional service providers face when attempting to allocate their time to marketing activities while being directly involved in the day-to-day operations of the firm.

## ✱ KEY TERMS

nonpersonal sources, 194
personal sources, 194
target markets, 194
positioning strategy, 195
communications mix, 196
personal selling, 196
media advertising, 196
publicity/public relations, 196
sales promotions, 196
type 1 service staff, 201

type 2 service staff, 201
type 3 service staff, 201
financial consequences, 203
social consequences, 203
performance consequences, 203
rational mathematician model, 204
mistargeted communications, 207
technical service quality, 207
halo effect, 217
visual pathway, 218

## ✱ REVIEW QUESTIONS

1. Discuss the options available for positioning and differentiating service firms.
2. Describe the strategic differences among the four elements of the communications mix.

3. Compare the communication skills necessary to conduct type 1, type 2, and type 3 service transactions.
4. What is the relevance of the rational mathematician model as it relates to developing communications strategy?
5. What problems are associated with mistargeted communications? Why do they occur?
6. Why should service employees be considered when developing communications materials?
7. Discuss how insurance companies make their services more easily understood.
8. What problems arise in turning professional service providers into proactive marketing personnel?
9. Discuss the concept of "visual pathways."

## ✱ NOTES

1. This section is adapted from John E. G. Bateson, *Managing Services Marketing*, 2nd ed. (Fort Worth, TX: The Dryden Press, 1992), pp. 393–401.
2. Adapted from Philip Kotler, *Marketing Management*, 9th ed. (Englewood Cliffs, NJ: Prentice Hall, 1997), pp. 279–305.
3. See, for instance, Louis E. Boone and David L. Kurtz, *Contemporary Marketing*, 8th ed. (Fort Worth, TX: The Dryden Press, 1995).
4. Based on a customer satisfaction study conducted by K. Douglas Hoffman for Rainmaker Marketing's North Carolina Lawyer Referral Service.
5. Adam Katz-Stone, "Web-Influenced Offline Sales Dwarf E-commerce," *Revolution*, Vol. 1 (5), (July 2000), pp. 8–9.
6. Bernard H. Booms and Jody L. Nyquist, "Analyzing the Customer/Firm Communication Component of the Services Marketing Mix," in *Marketing of Services*, James H. Donnelly and William R. George, eds. (Chicago: American Marketing Association, 1981), pp. 172–177.
7. This section is adapted from John E. G. Bateson, *Managing Services Marketing*, 3rd ed. (Fort Worth, TX: The Dryden Press, 1995), pp. 338–341.
8. This section has been modified from William R. George and Leonard L. Berry, "Guidelines for the Advertising of Services,"

*Business Horizons*, 24,4 (July–August 1981): pp. 52–56.
9. This section is adapted from John E. G. Bateson, *Managing Services Marketing*, 2nd ed. (Fort Worth, TX: The Dryden Press, 1992), pp. 397–399.
10. W. Earl Sasser and Stephen P. Albeit, "Selling Jobs in the Service Sector," *Business Horizons* (June 1976), p. 64.
11. William R. George and Leonard L. Berry, "Guidelines for the Advertising of Services," *Business Horizons*, 24,4 (July–August 1981): pp. 52–56.
12. Donna H. Hill and Nimish Gandhi, "Service Advertising: A Framework to Its Effectiveness," *The Journal of Services Marketing* 6,4 (Fall 1992), pp. 63–77.
13. This section adapted from Philip Kotler and Paul N. Bloom, *Marketing Professional Services* (Englewood Cliffs, NJ: Prentice-Hall, 1984), pp. 9–13.
14. Cyndee Miller, "Airline Safety Seen as New Marketing Issue," *Marketing News*, July 8, 1991, pp. 1, 11.
15. This section adapted from Jack Fox, *Starting and Building Your Own Accounting Business* (New York: John Wiley & Sons, 1994).
16. Leonard Zunin and Natalie Zunin, *Contact: The First Four Minutes*, (Los Angeles: Nash Publishing, 1972) IMAGES.

## CHAPTER 9

# MANAGING THE FIRM'S PHYSICAL EVIDENCE

## CHAPTER OBJECTIVES

*This chapter will provide you with an understanding of the importance of the service firm's physical evidence regarding customer perceptions of the quality of services provided.*

After reading this chapter, you should be able to:

- Appreciate the strategic role of physical evidence as it relates to the marketing of service firms.

- Outline the stimulus-organism-response (SOR) model.

- Discuss the major components of the servicescapes model.

- Describe the use of sensory cues when developing tactical design strategies.

- Compare design considerations for low- versus high-customer-contact firms.

*"From the customer's point of view, if they can see it, walk on it, hold it, step in it, smell it, carry it, step over it, touch it, use it, even taste it, if they can feel it or sense it, it's customer service."*

Kristen Anderson
and Ron Zemke

## > "BATTLE OF THE BEDS"

© AP / WIDE WORLD PHOTOS

The intangibility of the core service benefit often makes it difficult for customers to objectively evaluate the quality of service and/or compare service alternatives. As a result, customers rely on the physical evidence that surrounds the core benefit to assist in forming service evaluations. Hence, the effective management of physical evidence by service firms is key to establishing service differentiation.

Service differentiation through the purposeful use of physical evidence has long been exemplified by the lodging industry through the effective management of facility exterior, facility interior, and other tangibles associated with the hotel experience. Interestingly, the latest battleground in physical differentiation has become the bed itself. With the introduction of the "Heavenly Bed" in 1999, Westin Hotels ushered in a new movement in the hotel industry to "move away from the institutional feel of some rooms and give guests more luxurious accommodations." Westin was on a quest to build the best bed in the industry. The end result was a custom-made Simmons mattress decked out with down blankets, sheets with high thread counts, a comforter, a duvet, and five pillows— "enough to make other hotel beds feel like rock slabs." At first, rivals scoffed at Westin's new bedding strategy. First, the $30 million price tag seemed a bit extravagant and second the linens were white—"what was Westin thinking?" However, opinions changed quickly as Westin and the Heavenly Bed racked up multiple business rewards including "improved guest satisfaction, higher room rates, better revenue-per-available-room, and an avalanche of publicity." In addition, overall cleanliness scores increased even though Westin admits all they did extra was "add the bed." Since the Heavenly Bed's introduction, Westin has sold over 7,000 beds to its enamored customers. Westin's next move involved the introduction of Heavenly Cribs, which placed 2,000 new cribs in 300+ hotels at an investment of $1 million (note Westin does not refer to "costs" but "investments").

Given Westin's success, other hotels are taking the initiative and responding to the Heavenly Bed with their own luxury packages. Hotels, including Radisson and Hampton Inn, are investing thousands of dollars into new beds and bedding for their guests. Marriott International has perhaps undertaken the most ambitious investment in the "Battle of the Beds" with the replacement of 628,000 beds in 2005. Beds will be changed in eight different Marriott lodging brands including Fairfield Inn, Courtyard by Marriott, Renaissance Hotels, Marriott Hotels, and JW Hotels and Resorts. The project will cost an estimated $190 million and will use 30 million yards of fabric. JW Marriott Jr., Marriott CEO, notes, "This initiative draws on the finest designs and service traditions at our best hotels worldwide to position each of our brands as the most luxurious in their segment."

Marriott's intent is not to move out of their current market positions dominated by their eight lodging brands; however, Marriott wishes to be known as "best in class" in each of the various segments. This move is consistent with the message that is routinely delivered to Marriott's associates, "Marriott brands are about selling a rewarding experience, not just selling a hotel room. Our guests indicate that the room is their oasis, so we must ensure their oasis provides a thoroughly superior experience!"

Finally, in case you've ever wondered about America's sleep habits, the following statistics were found in the 2005 "Sleep in America Pool" conducted by the National Sleep Foundation:

- 6.8 average number of hours asleep, weeknights
- 7.4 average number of hours asleep, weekend nights

- 75 percent of respondents report symptoms of sleep disorder
- 61 percent of respondents sleep most nights with a significant other
- 12 percent of respondents sleep most nights with a pet
- 7 percent of respondents report using prescription sleep aids

Source: First draft provided by David Crews and Nick Reinig of Colorado State University; Matthew Creamer, "Marriott to Replace 628,000 Hotel Beds" accessed http://www.usatoday.com 2 May 2005; "Waking Up to the Marketing Potential of a Good Night's Sleep," *Advertising Age,* (April 18, 2005) 76, Issue 16, 16; No Author Listed, "Heavenly Bed for Babies," *Lodging Hospitality,* (September 15, 2001) 57, Issue 12, 9.

> ## INTRODUCTION

Managing the firm's physical evidence includes everything tangible, from the firm's physical facilities, to brochures and business cards, to the firm's personnel. A firm's physical evidence affects the consumer's experience throughout the duration of the service encounter. Consider the average consumer's restaurant experience.[1]

Prior to entering the restaurant, customers begin to evaluate it based on advertising they may have seen on television or in the phone book. As the consumer drives to the restaurant, the location of the restaurant, the ease with which the location can be found, the restaurant's sign, and the building itself all enter into the consumer's evaluation process. Similarly, the availability of parking spaces, the cleanliness of the parking lot, and the smells that fill the air once the customer steps out of the car affect consumer expectations and perceptions.

Upon entering, the restaurant's furnishings, cleanliness, and overall ambience provide further evidence regarding the quality of the ensuing experience. The appearance and friendliness of the firm's personnel and the ease with which customers can move about and find telephones and restrooms without asking also enter into the consumer's mind.

When seated at a table, the customer notices the stability and quality of the table and chairs, and the cleanliness of napkins, silverware, and the table itself. Additional evaluations occur as well: Is the menu attractive? Is it readable or crumbled and spotted with food stains from past customers? How are the wait-staff interacting with other customers? What do the other customers look like?

Once the meal is served, the presentation of the food is yet another indicator of the restaurant's quality. Consumers will make comparisons of the food's actual appearance and the way it is pictured in advertisements and menus. Of course, how the food tastes also enters into the customer's evaluation.

Upon completing the meal, the bill itself becomes a tangible clue. Is it correct? Are charges clearly written? Is the bill clean, or is it sopping wet with spaghetti sauce? Are the restrooms clean? Did the wait-staff personnel say thank-you and really mean it?

> THE STRATEGIC ROLE OF PHYSICAL EVIDENCE

Due to the intangibility of services, service quality is difficult for consumers to objectively evaluate. As a result, consumers often rely on the tangible evidence that surrounds the service to help them form their evaluations (see Table 9.1). The role of physical evidence in the marketing of intangibles is multifaceted. Physical evidence can fall into three broad categories: (1) facility exterior; (2) facility interior; and (3) other tangibles. Examples of the elements that compose the **facility exterior** include the exterior design, signage, parking, landscaping, and the surrounding environment. For example, the facility may be built on a mountainside, overlooking a lake. The **facility interior** includes elements such as the interior design, equipment used to serve the customer directly or used to run the business, signage, layout, air quality, and temperature. Other **tangibles** that are part of the firm's physical evidence include such items as business cards, stationery, billing statements, reports, employee appearance, uniforms, and brochures.[2]

*facility exterior*
The physical exterior of the service facility; includes the exterior design, signage, parking, landscaping, and the surrounding environment.

*facility interior*
The physical interior of the service facility; includes the interior design, equipment used to serve customers, signage, layout, air quality, and temperature.

*tangibles*
Other items that are part of the firm's physical evidence, such as business cards, stationery, billing statements, reports, employee appearance, uniforms, and brochures.

| TABLE 9.1 | THE IMPORTANCE OF PHYSICAL EVIDENCE |
|---|---|

*An organization's exterior appearance, interior design, and other tangibles create a package that surrounds the service. In a study of 1,540 hospitality-related service failures, 123 of the failures were attributed to problems associated with the hospitality firms' management of their physical evidence. Typical problems are described below.*

**Facility-Based Failures**
**Mechanical Problems:**
*Core Mechanical Problems* (e.g., core service is not available due to catastrophic mechanical problems such as airline engine problems)
*Mechanical Problems Relating to the Core* (e.g., core service is available; however, inoperative equipment relating to the core inconvenienced the customer such as computers, shower heads, toilets, heating and cooling equipment

**Cleanliness Issues:**
*Foreign Object (nonliving/nonhuman-related)* (e.g., foreign objects such as plastic, wood, and glass found in food or bedding)
*Foreign Object (human-related)* (e.g., foreign objects such as hair, blood, fingernails, and used band-aids found in food or bedding)
*Foreign Object (insect/animal-related)* (e.g., foreign objects such as ants, flies, mice, and worms found in food, bedding, or hotel room)
*General Cleanliness Issues* (e.g., hotel room or plane not cleaned or deteriorating conditions)
*Smells* (e.g., strange and/or offensive odors)

**Design Issues:**
*Poor Facility Planning* (e.g., undesirable view from room, sleeping quarters located next to hotel ballrooms and/or elevators, slippery walkways, or dangerous conditions)

Source: K. Douglas Hoffman, Scott W. Kelley, and Beth C. Chung (2003), "A CIT Investigation of Servicescape Failures and Associated Recovery Strategies," *Journal of Services Marketing*, 17 (4), 322–340.

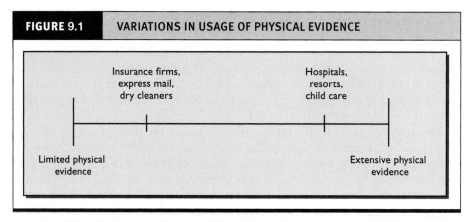

**FIGURE 9.1    VARIATIONS IN USAGE OF PHYSICAL EVIDENCE**

Insurance firms,
express mail,
dry cleaners

Hospitals,
resorts,
child care

Limited physical
evidence

Extensive physical
evidence

Source: Mary J. Bitner, "Servicescapes: The Impact of Physical Surroundings on Customers and Employees," *Journal of Marketing* 56,2 (April 1992), p. 60. Reprinted with permission of the American Marketing Association.

The extensive use of physical evidence varies by the type of service firm (see Figure 9.1). Service firms such as hospitals, resorts, and child-care facilities often make extensive use of physical evidence in facility design and other tangibles associated with the service. In contrast, service firms such as insurance and express mail drop-off locations use limited physical evidence. Regardless of the variation in usage, all service firms need to recognize the importance of managing their physical evidence in its role of:

- packaging the service;
- facilitating the flow of the service delivery process;
- socializing customers and employees alike in terms of their respective roles, behaviors, and relationships; and
- differentiating the firm from its competitors.[3]

For example, the Rainforest Cafe and other restaurants that are sometimes described as "museums with food" offer food as an interactive experience with the carefully managed physical evidence that comprises the dining environment. With an average floor space of 23,000 square feet, Rainforest Cafe venues feature aquariums, live parrots, a waterfall, a mechanical crocodile, fiberglass monkeys, a video screen, a talking tree, and a regularly-timed thunderstorm, complete with lightning. The environment theme features strongly in the chain's décor and products. The restaurants make a point of not serving beef from deforested land or fish caught in nets. The talking trees give messages about the environment to customers waiting in line. However, the restaurants place a great deal of focus on their core business, the food, and work to ensure quality in this area.[4]

The Rainforest Cafe purposely manages its servicescape to create a unique and interactive dining environment. The restaurant's servicescape includes waterfalls, geographically-themed music, life-like monkeys, and a wide variety of plant life.

## PACKAGING

The firm's physical evidence plays a major role in packaging the service. The service itself is intangible and, therefore, does not require a package for purely functional reasons. However, utilizing the firm's physical evidence to package the service does send quality cues to consumers and adds value to the service in terms of image development. Image development, in turn, improves consumer perceptions of service while reducing both levels of perceived risk associated with the purchase and levels of cognitive dissonance after the purchase.

The firm's exterior appearance, interior elements, and other tangibles create the package that surrounds the service. The firm's physical facility forms the customer's initial impression concerning the type and quality of service provided. For example, Mexican and Chinese restaurants often utilize specific types of architectural designs that communicate to customers their firms' offerings. The firm's physical evidence also conveys expectations to consumers. Consumers will have one set of expectations for a restaurant with dimly lit dining rooms, soft music, and linen tablecloths and napkins and a different set of expectations for a restaurant that has cement floors, picnic tables, and peanut shells strewn about the floor.

## FACILITATING THE SERVICE PROCESS

Another use of the firm's physical evidence is to facilitate the flow of activities that produce the service. Physical evidence can provide information to customers on how the service production process works. Examples include signage that specifically instructs customers; menus and brochures that explain the firm's offerings and facilitate the ordering process for consumers and providers; and physical structures that direct the flow of consumers while waiting, and barriers, such as counters at a dry cleaner, that separate the technical core of the business from the part of the business in which customers are involved in the production process.

## SOCIALIZING EMPLOYEES AND CUSTOMERS

*socialization*
The process by which an individual adapts to the values, norms, and required behavior patterns of an organization.

Organizational **socialization** is the process by which an individual adapts to and comes to appreciate the values, norms, and required behavior patterns of an organization.[5] The firm's physical evidence plays an important part in the socialization process by conveying expected roles, behaviors, and relationships among employees and between employees and customers. The purpose of the socialization process is to project a positive and consistent image to the public. However, the service firm's image is only as good as the image each employee conveys when interacting with the public.[6]

Physical evidence, such as the use of uniforms, facilitates the socialization of employees toward accepting organizational goals and affects consumer perceptions of the caliber of service provided. Studies have shown that the use of uniforms:

- aids in identifying the firm's personnel,
- presents a physical symbol that embodies the group's ideals and attributes,
- implies a coherent group structure,
- facilitates the perceived consistency of performance,
- provides a tangible symbol of an employee's change in status (e.g., military uniforms change as personnel move through the ranks), and
- assists in controlling the behavior of errant employees.[7]

Employee uniforms, such as those worn by a hotel's housekeeping staff, aid in identifying the hotel's personnel and assist employees in embracing the hotel's values, norms, and desired behavior patterns.

© JON FEINGERSH / CORBIS

One classic example of how tangible evidence affects the socialization process of employees involves women in the military. Pregnant military personnel were originally permitted to wear civilian clothing when pregnant in lieu of their traditional military uniforms. However, the military soon noticed discipline and morale problems with these servicewomen as they began to lose their identification with their roles as soldiers. "Maternity uniforms are now standard issue in the Air Force, Army, and Navy, as well as at US Air, Hertz, Safeway, McDonald's, and the National Park Service."[8]

## A MEANS FOR DIFFERENTIATION

The effective management of the physical evidence can also be a source of differentiation. For example, several airlines are now expanding the amount of leg room available for passengers.[9] In addition, the appearance of personnel and facilities often have a direct impact on how consumers perceive that the firm will handle the service aspects of its business. Numerous studies have shown that well-dressed individuals are perceived as more intelligent, better workers, and more pleasant.[10] Similarly, nicely designed facilities are going to be perceived as having the advantage over poorly designed facilities.

Differentiation can also be achieved by utilizing physical evidence to reposition the service firm in the eyes of its customers. Upgrading the firm's facilities often upgrades the image of the firm in the minds of consumers and may also lead to attracting more desirable market segments, which further aids in differentiating the firm from its competitors (see B2B Services in Action). On the other hand, note that too elaborate a facility upgrade may alienate some customers who believe that the firm may be passing on the costs of the upgrade to consumers through higher prices. This is precisely why many offices are decorated professionally, but not lavishly.

## THE SOR MODEL

The use of physical evidence to create service environments and its influence on the perceptions and behaviors of individuals is referred to as **environmental psychology**. The **stimulus-organism-response (SOR) model** presented in Figure 9.2 was developed by environmental psychologists to help explain the effects of the service environment on consumer behavior.[11] The SOR model consists of three components:

1. a set of **stimuli**,
2. an **organism** component, and
3. a set of **responses** or **outcomes**.

In a service context, the different elements of the firm's physical evidence, such as the exterior, interior design, lighting, and so on, compose the set of stimuli. The organism component, which describes the recipients of the set of stimuli within the service encounter, includes employees and customers. The responses of employees and customers to the set of stimuli are influenced by three basic emotional states: pleasure-

*environmental psychology*
The use of physical evidence to create service environments and its influence on the perceptions and behaviors of individuals.

*SOR (stimulus-organism-response) model*
A model developed by environmental psychologists to help explain the effects of the service environment on consumer behavior; describes environmental stimuli, emotional states, and responses to those states.

*stimuli*
The various elements of the firm's physical evidence.

*organism*
The recipients of the set of stimuli in the service encounter; includes employees and customers.

*responses (outcomes)*
Consumers' reaction or behavior in response to stimuli.

## > THE AIRBUS A380: THE WORLD'S LARGEST PASSENGER PLANE

One of the primary roles of a firm's physical evidence is to provide a means of differentiation among competing alternatives. A current example can be found in the B2B airline industry where European-based Airbus is attempting to differentiate its products from American-based Boeing. On April 27, 2005, Airbus unveiled its giant Airbus A380 as a direct attempt to increase passenger plane sales to the world's air carriers. According to French President, Jacques Chirac, "A new page in aviation history has been written. It is a magnificent result of European industrial cooperation."

The new jumbo jetliner, which weighs 308 tons, took Airbus 11 years to build and costs approximately $13 billion. Boeing had passed on making the new jumbo jet in favor of concentrating its business efforts on the construction of smaller, long-range jets like its Boeing 787 Dreamliner. However, Airbus believes that A380 improvements will reduce per-passenger costs by as much as 20 percent and is ideal for airlines flying between the world's airport hubs. Airbus has currently received 154 orders for the A380 from 15 different carriers including Virgin, Lufthansa, and Air France.

The Airbus A380 is huge! Due to enter service for Singapore Airlines in 2006, the A380 is 80 feet tall (equivalent to a seven-story building), 239 feet long, boasts a wingspan of

262 feet, and can fly approximately 8,000 nautical miles. In comparison, a Boeing 747 is 64 feet tall, 232 feet long, includes a wingspan of 211 feet, and flies 7,670 nautical miles. The Airbus A380 can carry up to 840 passengers on two decks or if preferred the space can be redesigned to include shops, a casino, and restaurant on the lower deck with passenger space maintained above.

© PIERRE VERDY/AFP/GETTY IMAGES

Source: Laurence Frost, "Biggest Bird Takes to the Sky: Airbus A380 Makes Aviation History with Maiden Flights," *The Coloradoan*, (Thursday, April 28, 2005). D8-D7. Laurence Frost is a writer for the Associated Press.

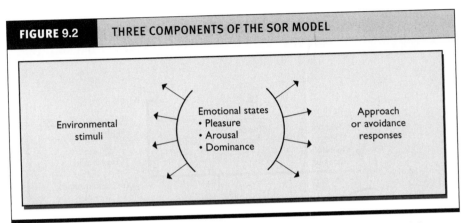

**FIGURE 9.2    THREE COMPONENTS OF THE SOR MODEL**

Environmental stimuli

Emotional states
• Pleasure
• Arousal
• Dominance

Approach or avoidance responses

Source: Adapted from Robert J. Donovan and John R. Rossiter, "Store Atmosphere: An Environmental Psychology Approach," *Journal of Retailing* 58 (Spring 1982), p. 42.

displeasure, arousal-nonarousal, and dominance-submissiveness. The **pleasure-displeasure** emotional state reflects the degree to which consumers and employees feel satisfied with the service experience. The **arousal-nonarousal** state reflects the degree to which consumers and employees feel excited and stimulated. The third emotional state, **dominance-submissiveness,** reflects feelings of control and the ability to act freely within the service environment. Ideally, service firms should utilize physical evidence to build environments that appeal to pleasure and arousal states, and avoid creating atmospheres that create submissiveness.

Consumer and employee responses to the set of environmental stimuli are characterized as **approach behaviors** or **avoidance behaviors.** Consumer approach and avoidance behaviors and outcomes can be demonstrated in any combination of four ways (employees exhibit similar behaviors):[12]

1. a desire to stay (approach) or leave (avoid) the service establishment
2. a desire to further explore and interact with the service environment (approach) or a tendency to ignore it (avoidance)
3. a desire to communicate with others (approach) or to ignore the attempts of service providers to communicate with customers (avoid)
4. feelings of satisfaction (approach) or disappointment (avoidance) with the service experience

## > THE DEVELOPMENT OF SERVICESCAPES[13]

The framework presented in Figure 9.3 is a more comprehensive SOR model that directly applies to the influence of the service firm's physical evidence on consumers' and employees' subsequent behaviors. The term **servicescapes** refers to the use of

**pleasure-displeasure**
The emotional state that reflects the degree to which consumers and employees feel satisfied with the service experience.

**arousal-nonarousal**
The emotional state that reflects the degree to which consumers and employees feel excited and stimulated.

**dominance-submissiveness**
The emotional state that reflects the degree to which consumers and employees feel in control and able to act freely within the service environment.

**approach/avoidance behaviors**
Consumer responses to the set of environmental stimuli that are characterized by a desire to stay in or leave an establishment, explore/interact with the service environment or ignore it, or feel satisfaction or disappointment with the service experience.

**servicescapes**
The use of physical evidence to design service environments.

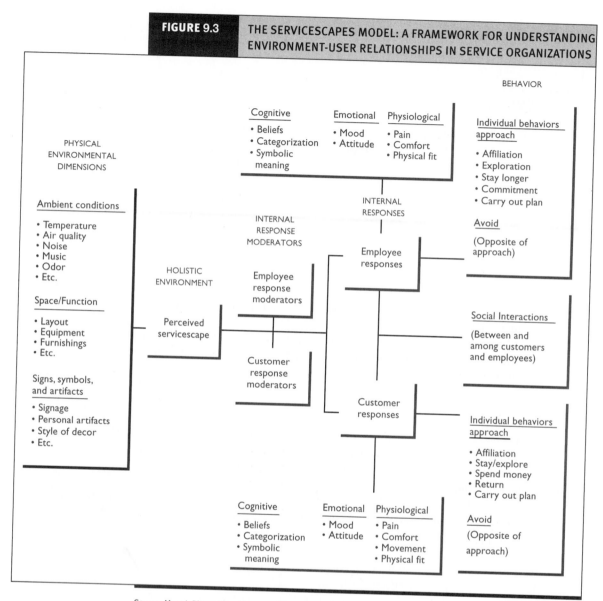

**FIGURE 9.3    THE SERVICESCAPES MODEL: A FRAMEWORK FOR UNDERSTANDING ENVIRONMENT-USER RELATIONSHIPS IN SERVICE ORGANIZATIONS**

Source: Mary J. Bitner, "Servicescapes: The Impact of Physical Surroundings on Customers and Employees," *Journal of Marketing* 60, no. 2 (April 1992), 60. Reprinted with permission of the American Marketing Association.

physical evidence to design service environments. Due to inseparability, the model recognizes that the firm's environment is likely to affect consumers and employees alike (see Global Services in Action). However, the facility should be designed to meet the needs of those individuals who spend the most time within the confines of the facility.

## GLOBAL SERVICES *IN ACTION*

### > | HONG KONG DISNEYLAND

Disneyland is a prime example of how a firm's servicescape differentiates it from competitors and packages the services within. Disneyland's servicescape has been purposely designed to reinforce its image as the Magic Kingdom. Adults and children alike are captivated by the sights and sounds that comprise the Disney environment. However, as Disneyland engages in its global expansion strategy into China, obstacles may lie ahead. One problem in particular is that Disneyland is undeniably Western!

Although the Magic Kingdom was first introduced into China in 1937 with the debut of "Snow White and the Seven Dwarfs," the Chinese government has been very cautious about opening the youth media to foreign companies. Generational, cultural, and economic divides are the roots of the problem. According to one concerned Chinese parent, "If [my son] receives too much Western culture, in the future he may not cherish family relations, forget his ancestors, and not go back to our hometown." Disney is not the only Western media product under scrutiny. Popular American television shows such as "Friends" are censored, and the Hollywood movie "Oceans Eleven" has been rejected from the DVD market since it portrays criminals in a positive light. More recent Disney releases such as "Mulan" have been forbidden in China for political reasons.

The economic divide between East and West also presents challenges. From Disney's viewpoint, expansion into China makes great economic sense. China has approximately 260 million children under the age of 15. In comparison, the total population (including children and adults) of the U.S. is 285 million. The $1.8 billion Hong Kong Park is expected to attract 5.6 million visitors annually of which 40 percent are expected to come from mainland China. Ticket prices are expected to be set at $38 for adults and $27 for children—a high price to pay in a country that boasts one of the world's highest savings rates of 40 percent. However, the kids may get the final say on whether Disney succeeds or fails. Most Chinese families have one child due to government edicts, and parents are willing to spoil their children.

Source: Don Lee, "Cost, Culture Deter Chinese from Theme Park: Generation Gap Apparent as Kids Embrace Opening of Hong Kong Disneyland," *The Coloradoan* (Sunday, May 1, 2005), E2. Don Lee is a writer for the *Los Angeles Times*.

## REMOTE, SELF-SERVICE, AND INTERPERSONAL SERVICES

Figure 9.4 presents a continuum of facility usage by service type. Some services, such as mail order, coupon-sorting houses, and telephone and utility services are described as **remote services**. In remote services, employees are physically present while

**remote services**
Services in which employees are physically present while customer involvement in the service production process is at arm's length.

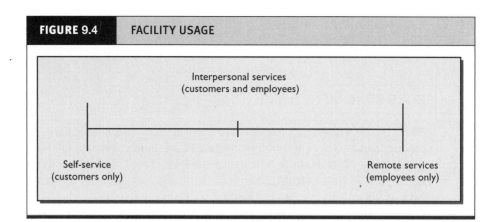

**FIGURE 9.4    FACILITY USAGE**

Interpersonal services
(customers and employees)

Self-service
(customers only)

Remote services
(employees only)

*self-services*
Service environments that are dominated by the customer's physical presence, such as ATMs or postal kiosks.

*interpersonal services*
Service environments in which customers and providers interact.

*ambient conditions*
The distinctive atmosphere of the service setting that includes lighting, air quality, noise, and music.

*space/function*
Environmental dimensions that include the layout of the facility, the equipment, and the firm's furnishings.

*signs, symbols, artifacts*
Environmental physical evidence that includes signage to direct the flow of the service process, personal artifacts to personalize the facility, and the style of decor.

customer involvement in the service production process is at arm's length. Consequently, facility design should facilitate the employees' efforts and enhance motivation, productivity, and employee satisfaction.

At the other end of the spectrum are services that customers can acquire on their own—**self-services**. Self-service environments are dominated by the customer's physical presence and include services such as ATMs, miniature golf courses, postal kiosks, and self-service car washes. The environment of self-service establishments should be constructed to enhance customer attraction and satisfaction.

In contrast to remote and self-service environments, many services such as restaurants, hospitals, hotels, banks, and airlines are **interpersonal services**, where the physical space is shared jointly by consumers and employees. The environment of interpersonal services should be developed with the needs of both parties involved and should facilitate the social interaction between and among customers and employees.

## PHYSICAL ENVIRONMENTAL DIMENSIONS

The servicescapes model depicted in Figure 9.3 begins by recognizing the set of stimuli that are commonly utilized when developing service environments. In broad terms, the set of stimuli include ambient conditions; space/function; and signs, symbols, and artifacts. **Ambient conditions** reflect the distinctive atmosphere of the service setting and include elements such as lighting, air quality, noise, and music. Environmental dimensions that pertain to the use of **space/function** include elements such as the layout of the facility, equipment, and the firm's furnishings. **Signs, symbols,** and **artifacts** include signage that directs the flow of the service process, personal artifacts, which lend character and individuality that personalize the facility, and the style of decor, such as southwestern, contemporary, or traditional.

## HOLISTIC ENVIRONMENT

The **holistic environment** portion of the servicescapes model pertains to the perceptions of the servicescape that employees and customers form based on the physical environmental dimensions. In other words, the holistic environment is a perceived overview or image of the firm based on the physical evidence, which is referred to in the model as the **perceived servicescape**. The perceived servicescape is difficult to precisely define, and perceptions of the same establishment will vary among individuals. Essentially, the perceived servicescape is a composite of mental images of the service firm's physical facilities.

Strategically managing the perceived servicescape aids in establishing a positioning strategy that differentiates the firm from competitors and ultimately influences the customer decision process when choosing among competing alternatives. The firm should develop the servicescape with its target market in mind. **Economic customers,** who make purchase decisions based on price, will avoid service establishments that appear too fancy or plush based on the perception that such an establishment will be a high-priced provider. Economic customers tend to be attracted to environments that are simple yet reflect quality and those that are clean and modern. Oil-change specialists such as the Jiffy Lube franchise use this type of environment. In contrast, **personalized customers** want to be pampered and attended to and are much less price sensitive when choosing among providers. Firms catering to personalized shoppers create environments that reflect the status their customers seek by investing more in items such as marble foyers, glass and brass fixtures, and furnishings that encourage customers to shop at a leisurely pace. Similarly, firms that service **apathetic customers,** who seek convenience, and **ethical customers,** who support smaller or local as opposed to larger or national service providers, should create their servicescapes accordingly.

## INTERNAL RESPONSE MODERATORS

The **internal response moderators** of the servicescapes model simply pertain to the three basic emotional states of the SOR model discussed earlier: pleasure-displeasure, arousal-nonarousal, and dominance-submissiveness. The three response moderators mediate the reaction between the perceived servicescape and customers' and employees' responses to the service environment. For example, if a customer desires to remain in a state of nonarousal and spend a nice, quiet evening with someone special, that customer will avoid bright, loud, and crowded service establishments and will be attracted to environments that are more peaceful and conducive to conducting conversation. Similarly, the employees' responses to the firm's environment will also be affected by their own emotional states. Sometimes employees look forward to engaging in conversations with customers. Other days, employees would just as soon minimize conversations and process customers as raw materials on a production line. Response moderators help explain why services are characterized by heterogeneity as the service varies from provider to provider, and even from day to day with the same provider.

**holistic environment**
Overall perceptions of the servicescape formed by employees and customers based on the physical environmental dimensions.

**perceived servicescape**
A composite of mental images of the service firm's physical facilities.

**economic customers**
Consumers who make purchase decisions based primarily on price.

**personalized customers**
Consumers who desire to be pampered and attended to and who are much less price sensitive.

**apathetic customers**
Consumers who seek convenience over price and personal attention.

**ethical customers**
Consumers who support smaller or local firms as opposed to larger or national service providers.

**internal response moderators**
The three basic emotional states of the SOR model that mediate the reaction between the perceived servicescape and customers' and employees' responses to the service environment.

## INTERNAL RESPONSES TO THE ENVIRONMENT

Theory asserts that customers and employees are exposed to the set of stimuli that make up the firm's perceived servicescape and the responses to these stimuli are moderated by emotional states. Customers and employees internally respond to the firm's environment at different levels—cognitively, emotionally, and physiologically.

### Cognitive Responses

**cognitive responses**
The thought processes of individuals that lead them to form beliefs, categorize, and assign symbolic meanings to elements of their physical environment.

**Cognitive responses** are the thought processes of individuals and, according to the model, include beliefs, categorization, and symbolic meaning. In the formation of **beliefs,** the firm's environment acts as a form of non-verbal communication and influences a consumer's beliefs about the provider's ability to perform the service. For example, if a professor's lectures are difficult to follow in class, a student may attribute this difficulty to the professor's inability to teach or may blame him/herself for an inability to learn the subject. Studies have shown that faced with this type of scenario, the physical environment influences consumers when they are attributing blame.[14] If the provider's office is in disarray, students are more likely to attribute poor service to the provider. Hence, physical evidence assists customers with beliefs about the provider's success, price for services, and competence. Employees form similar types of beliefs about the firm based on the overall perceived servicescape.

**beliefs**
Consumers' opinions about the provider's ability to perform the service.

**categorization**
Consumer assessment of the physical evidence and a quick mental assignment of a firm to a known group of styles or types.

**Categorization** is the second type of cognitive response. Bars and nightclubs operate within a number of environments. Some are high-class establishments, and others cater strictly to local clientele or specific market segments. The process of categorization facilitates human understanding at a quicker pace. Consumers assess the physical evidence and often quickly categorize new service establishments with existing types of operations. They then access the appropriate behavior script for the type of operation and act accordingly.

**symbolic meaning**
Meaning inferred from the firm's use of physical evidence.

Individuals also infer **symbolic meaning** from the firm's use of physical evidence. For example, if a nightclub features portraits of James Dean, Jimi Hendrix, Janice Joplin, Kurt Cobain, and others who have followed similar paths, the club evokes a symbolic meaning to its employees and customers. In this instance, the physical evidence may translate into a number of symbols, such as individuality, youthful success, shattered dreams, or other meanings, depending on individual interpretation. Symbolic meaning through the use of physical evidence aids in differentiation and positioning.

### Emotional Responses

**emotional responses**
Responses to the firm's physical environment on an emotional level instead of an intellectual or social level.

In addition to forming beliefs, individuals will also respond to the firm's physical environment on an emotional level. **Emotional responses** do not involve thinking; they simply happen, often inexplicably and suddenly. Specific songs, for example, may make individuals feel happy, feel sad, or recreate other past feelings that were associated with the particular piece of music. Scents have similar effects on individuals. Obviously, the goal of effective physical evidence management is to stimulate positive emotions that create atmospheres in which employees love to work and customers want to spend their time and money.

### Physiological Responses

In contrast to cognitive and emotional responses, **physiological responses** are often described in terms of physical pleasure or discomfort. Typical physiological responses involve pain and comfort. Environments in which music is played very loudly may lead to employee and customer discomfort and movement away from the source of the noise. The lack of a nonsmoking section may cause some customers difficulty in breathing and further discomfort. Instead of being arousing, environments that are brightly lit may cause eye discomfort. In contrast, a dimly lit restaurant may cause eye strain as customers struggle to read their menus. All these responses determine whether a customer will approach and explore the firm's offerings or avoid and leave the premises to minimize the amount of physiological discomfort. Because of the duration of time spent in the firm's facility, employees might find the physical environment particularly harmful if mismanaged. Adequate work space, proper equipment to get the job done, and appropriate ambient conditions such as temperature and air quality are directly related to employees' willingness to continue to work, their productivity while at work, their job satisfaction, and their positive interactions with co-workers.

*physiological responses*
Responses to the firm's physical environment based on pain or comfort.

## BEHAVIORAL RESPONSES TO THE ENVIRONMENT

### Individual Behaviors

As stated in the section on the fundamentals of the stimulus-organism-response (SOR) model, individual responses to environmental stimuli are characterized as approach and avoidance behaviors. In retail settings, the store's environment influences approach behaviors such as:

- shopping enjoyment,
- repeat visits,
- favorable impressions of the store,
- money spent,
- time spent shopping, and
- willingness of consumers to stay and explore the store.

In other instances, environmental stimuli have been purposely managed to discourage unwelcome market segments. For example, some U.S. convenience stores have cleverly used "elevator music" (e.g., Muzak—boring music) outside their stores to repel unwelcome neighborhood gangs that "hang out" in the store's parking lot and deter desired clientele from entering the store.

### Social Interactions

Due to the inseparability inherent in interpersonal services, the firm's servicescape should encourage interactions between employees and customers, among customers, and among employees. The challenge in creating such an environment is that often, what the customer desires, employees would prefer to forego so that they can complete their tasks with a minimum of customer involvement. Environmental variables such as

In contrast to the "community seating" of a Japanese steakhouse, traditional seating arrangements like those typical of a fine dining restaurant tend to limit the amount of social interaction between tables.

© AP / WIDE WORLD PHOTOS

physical proximity, seating arrangements, facility size, and flexibility in changing the configuration of the servicescape define the possibilities and place limits on the amount of social interaction possible.[15]

Consider the seating arrangements of a Japanese steakhouse, which combines different groups of customers at one table as opposed to traditional seating arrangements in which each party has its own table. Obviously, for better or worse, "community seating" at a Japanese steakhouse encourages interaction among customers. In addition, each table is assigned its own chef who actively interacts with the customers during the production process. Similar strides have been made in increasing consumer interaction at Max's and Erma's restaurants. Tables are numbered overhead and equipped with phones that enable customers to call one another. Oversized booths at Outback Steakhouse permit the wait-staff to actually sit at the customer's table while explaining the menu and taking dinner orders. This type of approach, while initially awkward to some customers who are not familiar with the practice (a modification to the traditional restaurant script), facilitates the amount of interaction between the wait-staff and their customers and yet permits them to stay within the traditional boundary of simply taking and delivering orders.

## > SPECIFIC TACTICS FOR CREATING SERVICE ATMOSPHERES

When developing the facility's atmosphere, the service firm must consider the physical and psychological impact of the atmosphere on customers, employees, and the firm's operations. Just as the firm cannot be all things to all people, the atmosphere developed will likely not appeal to all consumers. Therefore, firms should develop facilities with a particular target market in mind. Experts suggest answering the following questions before implementing an atmosphere development plan:[16]

1. Who is the firm's target market?
2. What does the target market seek from the service experience?
3. What atmospheric elements can reinforce the beliefs and emotional reactions that buyers seek?
4. How do these same atmospheric elements affect employee satisfaction and the firm's operations?
5. Does the suggested atmosphere development plan compete effectively with competitors' atmospheres?

Ultimately, individuals base their perceptions of a firm's facilities on their interpretation of sensory cues. The following section discusses how firms can utilize the senses of sight, sound, scent, touch, and taste in creating sensory appeal that enhances customer and employee attraction responses.[17]

## SIGHT APPEALS

The sense of sight conveys more information to consumers than any other sense and, therefore, should be considered as the most important means available to service firms when developing the firm's atmosphere. **Sight appeals** can be defined as the process of interpreting stimuli, resulting in perceived visual relationships.[18] On a basic level, the three primary visual stimuli that appeal to consumers are **size, shape,** and **colors.** Consumers interpret visual stimuli in terms of visual relationships, consisting of perceptions of harmony, contrast, and clash. **Harmony** refers to visual agreement and is associated with quieter, plusher, and more formal business settings. In comparison, **contrast** and **clash** are associated with exciting, cheerful, and informal business settings. Hence, based on the size, shape, and colors of the visual stimuli utilized and the way consumers interpret the various visual relationships, extremely different perceptions of the firm emerge. For example, consider how different target markets might respond to entering a Chucky Cheese restaurant for the first time. Some segments would find the environment inviting, while others might be completely overwhelmed by too much stimuli.

### Size Perceptions
The actual size of the firm's facility, signs, and departments conveys different meanings to different markets. In general, the larger the size of the firm and its corresponding physical evidence, the more consumers associate the firm with importance, power, success, security, and stability. For many consumers, the larger the firm, the lower the perceived risk associated with the service purchase. Such consumers believe that larger firms are more competent and more likely to engage in service recovery efforts when problems do arise. Still other customers enjoy the prestige often associated with conducting business with a larger, well-known, firm. On the flip side, other customers may view large firms as impersonal and uncaring and seek out smaller, niche firms that they view as more personal, intimate, and friendly. Hence, depending on the needs of the firm's target market, size appeals differently to different segments.

**sight appeals**
Stimuli that result in perceived visual relationships.

**size/shape/colors**
The three primary visual stimuli that appeal to consumers on a basic level.

**harmony**
Visual agreement associated with quieter, plusher, and more formal business settings.

**contrast/clash**
Visual effects associated with exciting, cheerful, and informal business settings.

### Shape

Shape perceptions of a service firm are created from a variety of sources, such as the use and placement of shelves, mirrors, and windows, and even the design of wallpaper. Studies show that different shapes arouse different emotions in consumers. Vertical shapes or vertical lines are perceived as "rigid, severe, and lend[ing] a masculine quality to an area. It expresses strength and stability . . . gives the viewer an up-and-down eye movement . . . tends to heighten an area, gives the illusion of increased space in this direction."[19] In contrast, horizontal shapes or lines evoke perceptions of relaxation and restfulness. Diagonal shapes and lines evoke perceptions of progressiveness, proactive-ness, and movement. Curved shapes and lines are perceived as feminine and flowing. Utilizing similar and/or dissimilar shapes in facility design will create the desired visual relationship of harmony, contrast, or clash. For example, the use of several different shapes in one area might be utilized for emphasis.[20]

### Color Perceptions

The color of the firm's physical evidence often makes the first impression, whether seen in the firm's brochure, the business cards of its personnel, or the exterior or interior of the facility itself (see E-Services in Action). The psychological impact of color upon individuals is the result of three properties: hue, value, and intensity. **Hue** refers to the actual family of the color, such as red, blue, yellow, or green. **Value** defines the lightness and darkness of the colors. Darker values are called **shades,** and lighter values are called **tints. Intensity** defines the brightness or dullness of the hue.

Hues are classified into warm and cool colors. Warm colors include red, yellow, and orange hues, while cool colors include blue, green, and violet hues. Warm and cool colors symbolize different things to different consumer groups, as presented in Table 9.2. In gen-eral, warm colors tend to evoke consumer feelings of comfort and informality. For example, red commonly evokes feelings of love and romance, yellow evokes feelings of sunlight and warmth, and orange evokes feelings of openness and friendliness. Studies have shown that warm colors, particularly red and yellow, are a better choice than cool colors for attracting customers in retail settings. Warm colors are also said to encourage quick deci-sions and work best for businesses where low-involvement purchase decisions are made.

In contrast to warm colors, cool colors are perceived as aloof, icy, and formal. For example, the use of too much violet may dampen consumer spirits and depress employ-ees who have to continuously work in the violet environment. Although cool colors do not initially attract customers as well as warm colors, cool colors are favored when the customer needs to take time to make decisions, such as the time needed for high-involvement purchases. Despite their different psychological effects, when used together properly, combinations of warm and cool colors can create relaxing, yet stimu-lating atmospheres.

The value of hues also psychologically affects the firm's customers. Offices painted in lighter colors tend to look larger, while darker colors may make large, empty spaces look smaller. Lighter hues are also popular for fixtures such as electrical face plates, air conditioning vents, and overhead speaker systems. The lighter colors help the fixtures blend in with the firm's environment. On the other hand, darker colors can be used to grab consumers' attention. Retailers are often faced with the problem that only 25 percent of their customers ever make it more than halfway into the store. Some

**hue**
The actual color, such as red, blue, yellow, or green.

**value**
The lightness and dark-ness of the colors.

**shades**
Darker values.

**tints**
Lighter values.

**intensity**
The brightness or the dullness of the colors.

## E-SERVICES *IN ACTION*

### > GOOGLE.COM'S SERVICESCAPE: WHEN LESS IS MORE

One of the secrets behind Google's success has been the thoughtful management of its own servicescape. The components of an online servicescape consists of the website's layout of text and graphics; colors; product depictions; use of flash media, streaming video and audio; and advertisements, just to name a few elements. In the early days of the Internet, it seemed like the fancier the website the better. Web designers were literally in a race to outdo one another for bragging rights. However, in the end, all that really mattered was whether the website effectively served customers.

Google's success story is extraordinary! Google entered the search engine market in 1998, long after its counterparts Yahoo and Excite. However, Google made three great decisions that eventually led to it being named Global Brand of the Year. First, Google found the right technology for the right price. The company's two young co-founders, Sergey Brin and Larry Page, built their own system from commodity hardware parts and were able to pack in eight times as much server power in the same space as competitors. Second, Google's search strategy is innovative. Instead of being based solely on key word searches, a Google search is based on the site's popularity. As a result, a Google search is directed more by human input than technology. The end result is that users typically receive more relevant information. Finally, Google.com provides an excellent example of how sometimes "less is more." Google uses simple graphics, allows no advertising on its home page, and within its website allows only banner advertisements without graphics. Consequently, Google's servicescape downloads faster than competitive offerings and is easier to read since it is less distracting.

As a testament to Google's effectiveness, the company performs 250 million searches on its 4 billion and growing Web pages a day. Customers can "google" in 88 languages and many customers are doing just that! Google is the fourth most visited U.S. website and is ranked in the top three in most European countries. In the last few years, Google's revenue growth and employee expansion rate have been in the triple digits. Today, it is estimated that Google powers 54 percent of all searches worldwide.

Source: Judy Strauss, Adel El-Ansary, and Raymond Frost, *E-Marketing*, Fourth Edition (Upper Saddle River, NJ: Pearson Prentice Hall, 2006), 241.

retailers have had limited success in attracting more customers farther into the store by painting the back wall in a darker color that attracts the customer's attention.

The intensity of the color also affects perceptions of the service firm's atmosphere. For example, bright colors make objects appear larger than do duller colors. However, bright colors are perceived as harsher and "harder," while duller colors are perceived as "softer." In general, children appear to favor brighter colors, and adults tend to favor softer tones.

| TABLE 9.2 | PERCEPTIONS OF COLOR | | | | |
|---|---|---|---|---|---|
| **Warm Colors** | | | **Cool Colors** | | |
| Red | Yellow | Orange | Blue | Green | Violet |
| Love | Sunlight | Sunlight | Coolness | Coolness | Coolness |
| Romance | Warmth | Warmth | Aloofness | Restfulness | Shyness |
| Sex | Cowardice | Openness | Fidelity | Peace | Dignity |
| Courage | Openness | Friendliness | Calmness | Freshness | Wealth |
| Danger | Friendliness | Gaiety | Piety | Growth | |
| Fire | Gaiety | Glory | Masculinity | Softness | |
| Sin | Glory | | Assurance | Richness | |
| Warmth | Brightness | | Sadness | Go | |
| Excitement | Caution | | | | |
| Vigor | | | | | |
| Cheerfulness | | | | | |
| Enthusiasm | | | | | |
| Stop | | | | | |

Source: Dale M. Lewison, *Retailing,* 4th ed. (New York: Macmillan, 1991), p. 277.

### The Location of the Firm

The firm's location is dependent upon the amount of customer involvement necessary to produce the service. While low-customer-contact services should consider locating in remote sites that are less expensive and closer to sources of supply, transportation, and labor, high-customer-contact services have other concerns. Typically, when evaluating locations for the firm, three questions need to addressed.

First, how visible is the firm? Customers tend to shop at places of which they are aware. The firm's visibility is essential in creating awareness. Ideally, firms should be visible from major traffic arteries and can enhance their visibility by facing the direction of traffic that maximizes visibility. If available, sites that are set back from the street (which permit customers to gain a broad perspective) while still remaining close enough to permit customers to read the firm's signs are preferable.

The second question about a location under consideration pertains to the compatibility of the site being evaluated with its surrounding environment. Is the size of the site suitable for the size of the building being planned? More importantly, what other types of businesses are in the area? For example, it would make sense for a law office specializing in healthcare matters to locate close to a major hospital, which is generally surrounded by a number of private medical practices as well.

The third question concerns whether the site is suited for customer convenience. Is the site accessible? Does it have ample parking or alternative parking options nearby? Do customers who use mass transit systems have reasonable access to the firm?

### The Firm's Architecture

The architecture of the firm's physical facility is often a three-way trade-off among the type of design that will attract the firm's intended target market, the type of design that maximizes the efficiency of the service production process, and the type of design that is affordable. The firm's architecture conveys a number of impressions as well as communicates information to its customers, such as the nature of the firm's business, the firm's strength and stability, and the price of the firm's services.

### The Firm's Sign

The firm's sign has two major purposes: to identify the firm and to attract attention. The firm's sign is often the first "mark" of the firm the customer notices. All logos on the firm's remaining physical evidence, such as letterhead, business cards, and note cards, should be consistent with the firm's sign to reinforce the firm's image. Ideally, signs should indicate to consumers the who, what, where, and when of the service offering. The sign's size, shape, coloring, and lighting all contribute to the firm's projected image.

### The Firm's Entrance

The firm's entrance and foyer areas can dramatically influence customer perceptions about the firm's activities. Worn carpet, scuffed walls, unprofessional artwork, torn and outdated reading materials, and unskilled and unkempt personnel form one impression. In contrast, neatly appointed reception areas, the creative use of colors, distinctive furnishings, and friendly and professional staff create a much different, more positive impression. Other tactical considerations include lighting that clearly identifies the entrance, doors that are easy to open, flat entryways that minimize the number of customers who might trip, nonskid floor materials for rainy days, and doors that are wide enough to accommodate customers with disabilities as well as large materials being transported in and out of the firm.

### Lighting

The psychological effects of lighting on consumer behavior are particularly intriguing. Our response to light may have started when our parents put us to bed, turned out the lights, and told us to be quiet and go to sleep. Through repetitive conditioning, most individuals' response to dimly lit rooms is that of a calming effect. Lighting can set the mood, tone, and pace of the service encounter. Consumers talk more softly when the lights are low, the service environment is perceived as more formal, and the pace of the encounter slows. In contrast, brightly lit service environments are louder, communication exchanges among customers and between customers and employees are more frequent, and the overall environment is perceived as more informal, exciting, and cheerful.

## SOUND APPEALS

**Sound appeals** have three major roles: mood setter, attention grabber, and informer. Proactive methods for purposely inserting sound into the service encounter can be accomplished through music and announcements. Music helps set the mood of the consumers' experience while announcements can be used to grab consumers' attention or to inform them of the firm's offerings. Sound can also be a distraction to the consumers' experience; consequently, sound avoidance tactics should also be considered.

**sound appeals**
Appeals associated with certain sounds, such as music or announcements.

| TABLE 9.3 | THE IMPACT OF BACKGROUND MUSIC ON RESTAURANT PATRONS | |
|---|---|---|
| **Variables** | **Slow Music** | **Fast Music** |
| Service time | 29 min. | 27 min. |
| Customer time at table | 56 min. | 45 min. |
| Customer groups leaving before seated | 10.5 percent | 12.0 percent |
| Amount of food purchased | $55.81 | $55.12 |
| Amount of bar purchases | $30.47 | $21.62 |
| Estimated gross margin | $55.82 | $48.62 |

Source: R. E. Milliman, "The Influences of Background Music on the Behavior of Restaurant Patrons," *Journal of Consumer Research* 13 (September 1986), p. 288; see also R. E. Milliman, "Using Background Music to Affect the Behavior of Supermarket Shoppers,"*Journal of Marketing,* Summer 1982, pp. 86–91.

### Music

Studies have shown that background music affects sales in at least two ways. First, background music enhances the customer's perception of the store's atmosphere, which in turn influences the consumer's mood. Second, music often influences the amount of time spent in stores.[21] In one study, firms that played background music in their facilities were thought to care more about their customers.[22]

Studies have shown that in addition to creating a positive attitude, music directly influences consumer buying behavior. Playing faster tempo music increases the pace of consumer transactions. Slowing down the tempo of the music encourages customers to stay longer. Still other studies have indicated that consumers find music distracting when considering high-involvement purchases, yet found that listening to music during low-involvement purchases made the choice process easier. Moreover, employees tend to be happier and more productive when listening to background music, which in turn leads to a more positive experience for customers.

Table 9.3 displays the impact of background music on consumer and provider behavior in a restaurant setting. As can be concluded by the numbers, the pace of service delivered and the pace of consumer consumption is affected by the tempo of the music. Although the estimated gross margin was higher when the restaurant played slow music, the restaurant should also consider the additional number of tables that would turn if faster-paced music was played throughout the day.

### Announcements

Another common sound in service establishments is the announcements made over intercom systems, such as to alert restaurant patrons when their tables are ready, to inform airline passengers of their current location, and to page specific employees within the firm. The professionalism in which announcements are made directly influences consumer perceptions of the firm. An example of a bizarre announcement made in a grocery store setting involved a male who over the intercom requested: "Red, what's the price on a box of so and so?" A female then responded for everyone in the store to hear: "Red, my ass!" If this type of announcement had been made in a doctor's or lawyer's office, consider how it would have reflected on the competence of the firm. Speaking of such incidents, now is probably a good time to discuss sound avoidance.

### Sound Avoidance

When planning the firm's facilities, it is as important to understand the avoidance of undesirable sounds as it is to understand the creation of desirable ones. Desirable sounds attract customers, and undesirable sounds distract from the firm's overall atmosphere. Within a restaurant setting, sounds that should be strategically masked include those emanating from kitchen, dish room, and restroom areas. Obviously, listening to a toilet flush throughout dinner does little to add to the enjoyment of the customer's dining experience. Other tactics for eliminating unwanted noise include installing durable hallway carpets to eliminate the distracting sounds of clicking heels, strategically placing loud central air conditioning units in areas away from those where the firm conducts the majority of its business, and installing lower ceilings and sound-absorbing partitions so that unwanted sounds can be reduced even further.

## SCENT APPEALS

The atmosphere of the firm can be strongly affected by scents, and the service manager should be aware of this fact. When considering **scent appeals,** as was the case with sound appeals, service managers should pay as much attention to scent avoidance as to scent creation. Stale, musty, foul odors affect everyone and are sure to create negative impressions about the firm. Poor ventilation systems that fail to remove odors and poorly located trash receptacles are common contributors to potential odor problems.

**scent appeals**
Appeals associated with certain scents.

On the other hand, pleasurable scents often induce customers to make purchases and can affect the perception of products that don't naturally have their own scent. For example, in one study conducted by Nike, customers examined pairs of gym shoes in two different rooms. One room was completely odor free, and the other was artificially permeated with a floral scent. Results of the study indicated that the floral scent had a direct positive effect on the desirability of the sneakers to 84 percent of the participants.[23] Although this particular example is related to a tangible product, it does seem to indicate that scents do influence consumer perceptions regarding products such as services that do not naturally smell on their own. Experts in scent creation note that a firm should smell like it's supposed to, according to target market expectations. Hospitals should smell clean and antiseptic, and perhaps older, established law firms should even smell a little musty.

## TOUCH APPEALS

The chances of a product selling increase substantially when the consumer handles it. But how does one touch an intangible product? Service firms such as mail-order retailers have a tangible component that can be shipped to customers. One of the reasons that non-store retailing now accounts for 10 percent of all retail sales and is increasing is the liberal return policies that were implemented to increase **touch appeals.** Spiegel, for example, will send the customer the merchandise for inspection, and if the customer

**touch appeals**
Appeals associated with being able to touch a tangible product or physical evidence of a service, such as shaking hands with service providers.

does not want it, the customer simply picks up the phone, notifies Spiegel, and places the returning product outside the door. Spiegel notifies UPS to pick up the package and pays for all costs associated with the return.

For purer services with a smaller tangible component, touch appeals can be developed through the use of "open houses" where the public has a chance to meet the people providing the service. Shaking hands and engaging in face-to-face communications with potential and existing customers is definitely a form of touch appeal. Clearly, firms engaged in creating touch appeals are perceived as more caring, closer to their customers, and genuinely concerned and interested in their customers' welfare.

## TASTE APPEALS

**taste appeals**
The equivalent of providing the customer with free samples.

**Taste appeals,** the final sensory cue, are the equivalent of providing the customer with samples. Within the service sector, the usefulness of taste appeals when developing service atmospheres is dependent upon the tangibility of the service. Service firms such as car washes, dry cleaners, and restaurants may use taste appeals to initially attract customers. While sampling the firm's services, the customer will have the opportunity to observe the firm's physical evidence and form perceptions regarding the firm and its performance capabilities. Consequently, firms that use samples should view this process as an opportunity rather than as catering to a bunch of people who want something for free.

> ## DESIGN CONSIDERATIONS FOR HIGH- VERSUS LOW-CUSTOMER-CONTACT SERVICE FIRMS[24]

One final topic that deserves special attention is the design considerations for low-customer-contact versus high-customer-contact firms. High-customer-contact firms include self-service and interpersonal services, while low-customer-contact firms include remote services. Depending on the level of contact, strategic differences exist regarding facility location, facility design, product design, and process design.

## FACILITY LOCATION

The choice location for the firm's service operation depends upon the amount of customer contact that is necessary during the production process. If customers are an integral part of the process, convenient locations located near customers' homes or workplaces will offer the firm a differential advantage over competitors. For example, with all other things being equal, the most conveniently located car washes, dry cleaners, and hairstylists are likely to obtain the most business.

In contrast, low-contact businesses should consider locations that may be more convenient for labor, sources of supply, and closer to major transportation routes. For example, mail-order facilities have little or no customer contact and can actually increase the efficiencies of their operations by locating closer to sources of supply and major transportation alternatives, such as close to interstate highways for trucking purposes or airports for overnight airline shipments. In many cases, these types of locations are less expensive to purchase or rent since they are generally in remote areas, where the cost of land and construction is not as expensive as it is inside city limits where other businesses are trying to locate close to their customers.

## FACILITY LAYOUT

In regard to the layout of the service operation, high-contact service firms should take the customers' physical and psychological needs and expectations into consideration. When a customer enters a high-contact service operation, that customer expects the facility to look like something other than a dusty, musty, old warehouse. Attractive personnel, clearly marked signs explaining the process, enough room to comfortably move about the facility, and a facility suited to bring friends and family to are among consumers' expectations. In contrast, low-contact facility layouts should be designed to maximize employee expectations and production requirements. Clearly, designing facilities for high-contact services is often more expensive than designing for their low-contact counterparts.

## PRODUCT DESIGN

Since the customer is involved in the production process of high-contact services, the customer will ultimately define that product differently from one produced by a low-contact service. In services such as restaurants, which have a tangible product associated with their service offering, the customer will define the product by the physical product itself as well as by the physical evidence that surrounds the product in the service environment. High-contact services that produce purely intangible products, such as education and insurance, are defined almost solely by the physical evidence that surrounds the service and by the thoughts and opinions of others.

In low-contact services, the customer is not directly involved in the production process, so the product is defined by fewer attributes. Consider our mail-order operation in which the customer never physically enters the facility. The customer will define the end product by the physical product itself (a pair of boots), the conversation that took place with personnel when ordering the boots, the quality of the mail-order catalog that featured the boots, the box in which the boots were packaged, and the billing materials that request payment.

## PROCESS DESIGN

In high-contact operations, the physical presence of the customer in the process itself must also be considered. Each stage in the process will have a direct and immediate effect on the customer. Consequently, a set of mini-service encounters and the physical evidence present at each encounter will contribute to the customer's overall evaluation of the service process. For example, a hotel guest is directly involved in the reservation process; the check-in process; the consumption process associated with the use of the hotel room itself; the consumption processes associated with the use of hotel amenities such as the restaurant, pool, and health club; and the check-out process. In contrast, since the customer is not involved with many of the production steps in low-contact services, their evaluation is based primarily on the outcome itself.

## ✳ SUMMARY

The effective management of physical evidence is particularly important to service firms. Due to the intangibility of services, consumers lack objective sources of information when forming evaluations. As a result, customers often look to the physical evidence that surrounds the service when forming evaluations.

A firm's physical evidence includes, but is not limited to, facility exterior design elements such as the architecture of the building, the firm's sign, parking, landscaping, and the surrounding environment of the firm's location; interior design elements such as size, shape, and colors, the firm's entrance and foyer areas, equipment utilized to operate the business, interior signage, layout, air quality, and temperature; and other physical evidence that forms customer perceptions, including business cards, stationery, billing statements, reports, the appearance of personnel, and the firm's brochures.

From a strategic perspective, the importance of managing the firm's physical evidence stems from the firm's ability to: (1) package the service; (2) facilitate the flow of the service delivery process; (3) socialize customers and employees alike in terms of their respective roles, behaviors, and relationships; and (4) differentiate the firm from its competitors.

From a theoretical perspective, the firm's environment influences the behavior of consumers and employees alike due to the inseparability of many services. When designing the firm's facilities, consideration needs to be given to whether the firm is a remote service, an interpersonal service, or a self-service. The subsequent design should reflect the needs of the parties who are dominating the service production process. Decisions about facility location, layout, product design, and process design in particular may result in different outcomes, depending on whether the customer is actively involved in the production process. Figure 9.3 illustrates the theoretical framework that helps us to further understand how individuals are affected by the firm's environmental dimensions, which ultimately leads to approach and/or avoidance behaviors.

Finally, numerous tactical decisions must be made when designing the firm's environment. Individuals base perceptions of the firm's services on sensory cues that exist in the firm's environment. Specific tactical decisions must be made about the creation and sometimes the avoidance of scent appeals, sight appeals, sound appeals, touch appeals, and taste appeals. The design and management of the firm's sensory cues are critical to the firm's long-term success.

# * KEY TERMS

facility exterior, 225
facility interior, 225
tangibles, 225
socialization, 228
environmental psychology, 229
SOR model, 229
stimuli, 229
organism, 229
response (outcome), 229
pleasure-displeasure, 231
arousal-nonarousal, 231
dominance-submissiveness, 231
approach behaviors, 231
avoidance behaviors, 231
servicescapes, 231
remote services, 233
self-services, 234
interpersonal services, 234
ambient conditions, 234
space/function, 234
signs, symbols, artifacts, 234
holistic environment, 235
perceived servicescape, 235
economic customers, 235

personalized customers, 235
apathetic customers, 235
ethical customers, 235
internal response moderators, 235
cognitive responses, 236
beliefs, 236
categorization, 236
symbolic meaning, 236
emotional responses, 236
physiological responses, 237
sight appeals, 239
size/shape/colors, 239
harmony, 239
contrast/clash, 239
hue, 240
value, 240
shades, 240
tints, 240
intensity, 240
sound appeals, 243
scent appeals, 245
touch appeals, 245
taste appeals, 246

# * REVIEW QUESTIONS

1. Discuss the strategic role of physical evidence.
2. Discuss the relevance of remote, self-service, and interpersonal services to facility design.
3. How should the servicescape of a firm that targets ethical shoppers be designed?
4. Discuss how internal response moderators relate to the characteristic of heterogeneity.
5. Discuss internal responses to the firm's environment.
6. What is the impact of music on customer and employee behavior?
7. Develop strategies for a service firm that would enhance the firm's touch and taste appeals.
8. Discuss the use of employee uniforms as physical evidence.
9. What are the major design differences between high-customer-contact and low-customer-contact services?

## ✳ NOTES

1. Kristen Anderson and Ron Zemke, *Delivering Knock Your Socks Off Service* (New York: AMACOM, 1991), pp. 27–30.

2. Mary Jo Bitner, "Servicescapes: The Impact of Physical Surroundings on Customers and Employees," *Journal of Marketing* 56 (April 1992), pp. 57–71.

3. Ibid.

4. Edgar Schein, "Organizational Socialization and the Profession of Management," *Industrial Management Review* 9 (Winter 1968), pp. 1–16.

5. http://www.rainforestcafe.com accessed 3 May 2005.

6. Michael R. Solomon, "Packaging the Service Provider," in Christopher H. Lovelock, *Managing Services Marketing, Operations, and Human Resources* (Englewood Cliffs, NJ: Prentice-Hall, 1988), pp. 318–324.

7. Ibid.

8. Ibid.

9. "Plane seats get bigger, cost more: Airlines betting fliers will pay extra for added legroom," *Denver Rocky Mountain News,* February 28, 2000, pp. 2A, 31A.

10. Ibid.

11. Avijit Ghosh, *Retail Management,* 2nd ed. (Fort Worth, TX: The Dryden Press, 1994), pp. 522–523.

12. Ibid.

13. Valerie A. Zeithaml and Mary Jo Bitner, *Services Marketing* (New York: McGraw Hill, 1996), p. 528.

14. Ibid, p. 531.

15. Ibid.

16. Philip Kotler, "Atmospherics as a Marketing Tool," *Journal of Retailing* (Winter 1973–1974), p. 48.

17. Dale M. Lewison, *Retailing,* 4th ed. (New York: MacMillan, 1991), pp. 273–283.

18. Ibid.

19. Kenneth H. Mills and Judith E. Paul, *Applied Visual Merchandising* (Englewood Cliffs, NJ: Prentice-Hall, 1982), p. 47.

20. Kenneth H. Mills and Judith E. Paul, *Create Distinctive Displays* (Englewood Cliffs, NJ: Prentice-Hall, 1974), p. 61.

21. J. Barry Mason, Morris L. Mayer, and J. B. Wilkinson, *Modern Retailing: Theory and Practice,* 6th ed. (Homewood, IL: Irwin, 1993), pp. 642–643.

22. Ronald E. Milliman, "Using Background Music to Affect the Behavior of Supermarket Shoppers," *Journal of Marketing* 46,3 (Summer 1982), pp. 86–91; see also Douglas K. Hawse and Hugh McGinley, "Music for the Eyes, Color for the Ears: An Overview," in *Proceedings of the Society for Consumer Psychology,* David W. Schumann, ed. (Washington, DC: Society for Consumer Psychology, 1988), pp. 145–152.

23. J. Barry Mason, Morris L. Mayer, and Hazel F. Ezell, Retailing, 5th ed. (Homewood, IL: Irwin), 1994.

24. Richard B. Chase, "Where Does the Customer Fit in a Service Operation?" *Harvard Business Review* (November–December 1978), pp. 137–142.

# CHAPTER 10

## PEOPLE ISSUES: MANAGING SERVICE EMPLOYEES

### CHAPTER OBJECTIVES

*The purpose of this chapter is to discuss the key issues that will help you understand the many challenges associated with managing employees within the service experience. Service business, by its very definition, is a people business and requires talented managers who can navigate the thin line between the needs of the organization, its employees, and its customers.*

After reading this chapter, you should be able to:

- Discuss the importance of contact personnel as boundary spanners.
- Explain the sources of conflict in boundary-spanning roles and the consequences of role stress.
- Define the concepts of empowerment and enfranchisement and understand the contingency empowerment approach.
- Describe the relevance of employee satisfaction as it relates to the service-profit chain.

*"I have never given away more than I got back!"*

Chairman Robert Wegman,
Wegmans Food Markets Inc.

Every year *Fortune Magazine* publishes its highly anticipated list of "The 100 Best Companies to Work For." The winner for 2005 may surprise you. It was not a dominant healthcare provider, a giant auto manufacturer, or the world's largest retailer—it was a grocery store! Wegmans—the best company to work for in America!

Who or what is a Wegmans? Wegmans is a privately held supermarket chain that employs over 30,000 employees in its 67 stores located in New York, Pennsylvania, New Jersey, and Virginia. Reported revenues for 2004 were $3.4 billion. Newer Wegmans stores boast 130,000 square feet, which makes Wegmans three times larger than the size of a typical supermarket. Wegmans' operating margins are double what the "big four" (Albertson's, Kroger, Safeway, and Ahold USA) earn, and sales per square foot are 50 percent higher than industry averages.

One of the key secrets to Wegmans' success has been its recognition that the grocery stores of tomorrow must become more than just a supermarket, and it cannot compete solely on price alone. The biggest challenge for supermarkets today is that there is no compelling reason to shop there anymore. Grocery stores are viewed as commodities—84 percent of customers believe that traditional grocers are all pretty much the same. As a result, nontraditional grocers such as club stores (Sams) and discounters (Wal-Mart and K-Mart) have been able to gain a stronghold in the market. In 2003, nontraditional grocers controlled 31.3 percent of the grocery market. According to industry experts, that number is expected to grow to nearly 40 percent by 2008. Traditional grocers have responded to the onslaught by cutting prices, which has further lowered already miniscule margins. Between 1999 and 2004, the four largest U.S. grocery chains (Albertson's, Kroger, Safeway, and Ahold USA) reported shareholder returns ranging from −49 to −78 percent. Labor unrest for several of these chains poses future challenges.

Wegmans has embraced the idea that in order to compete effectively with the mass merchandisers of the world grocery shopping should become a compelling experience. Employee comments reflect this notion: "We are taking customers to a place they have not been before." "Going there is not just shopping, it's an event." Creating the Wegmans experience has been the result of a keen combination of goods and services and hiring and retaining great personnel. Each Wegmans store boasts a huge selection of food products including amazing assortments of beautifully displayed produce, fresh-baked goods, and other specialty items such as a selection of over 500 cheeses. Other offerings within Wegmans include child play centers, a dry cleaner, a photo lab, a florist, a wine shop, a pharmacy, and a bookstore.

In addition to its compelling array of goods and services, much of the Wegmans experience is derived from its employees and its customers. Of the nearly 7,000 letters the company received in 2004, nearly half were requests by customers for Wegmans to open a new location in their town. Wegmans' customers are passionate about their grocery store, which is good news for Wegmans. Customers who are emotionally connected to their grocery stores spend on average 46 percent more than shoppers who are satisfied but do not share a bond with their local supermarket.

Wegmans' relationship with its employees is also legendary. Over the past 20 years, Wegmans has invested nearly $54 million in college scholarships to more than 17,500 full-time and part-time employees. The company promotes from within and new stores are populated by the best and brightest of existing employees. In addition, Wegmans listens to its employees. Wegmans' Chief of Operations half jokingly comments: "We're a

$3 billion company run by 16-year-old cashiers." Hourly wages and annual salaries are at the high end of the market. Wegmans' labor costs run approximately 16 percent of sales compared to the industry average of 12 percent; however, Wegmans' full-time employee turnover rate is 6 percent compared to the industry average of 19 percent. Moreover, nearly 6,000 Wegmans employees have ten years or more service with the firm. According to Chairman Robert Wegman: "I have never given away more than I got back." Clearly, Wegmans provides a tremendous example of how a company can excel through superior operations, legendary employee relations, and great customer service.

Source: Mathew Boyle, "The Wegmans Way," *Fortune,* (January 24, 2005), Vol. 151 (No. 2), pp. 62–68.

## > INTRODUCTION

Employee satisfaction and customer satisfaction are clearly related. Let's say it again another way: If you want to satisfy your customers, employee satisfaction is critical! The public face of a service firm is its contact personnel. Part factory workers, part administrators, part servants—service personnel often perform a complex and difficult job.[1] Despite their importance and the complexity of their activities, service personnel are often the lowest paid and least respected individuals in most companies, and often in society. For example, in the healthcare community, the individuals most responsible for patient care and patient perceptions of service quality received are the nurses. Who are the lowest paid and least respected individuals in the healthcare community? The nurses. In the education system, who is most responsible for the day-to-day education of and interaction with students? The classroom teachers. Who in the education system are the least paid and least respected individuals? The classroom teachers. The list goes on and on. Consider any service industry, and look to the individuals who are the most responsible for customer interactions and customer perceptions of quality delivered, and you will most likely see the lowest paid and least respected individuals in the company. It makes no sense!

It is little wonder, therefore, that service jobs often have extremely high levels of staff turnover. In one year, 119,000 sales jobs turned over within the retail network of the Sears Merchandise Group. The cost of hiring and training each new sales assistant was $900, or more than $110 million in total, a sum that represented 17 percent of Sears' 1989 income.[2]

Today, more than 45 million people representing 42 percent of the U.S. workforce are employed in selling food; selling merchandise in retail stores; performing clerical work in service industries; cleaning hospitals, schools, and offices; or providing some other form of personal service. These are occupations that accounted for most of the U.S. job growth over the last two decades. Yet, for the most part, these jobs are poorly paid, lead nowhere, and provide little, if anything, in the way of health, pension, and other benefits.[3] It's no wonder why *Business Week* recently investigated the issue: Why Service Stinks?"[4]

> | ## THE IMPORTANCE OF SERVICE PERSONNEL

This chapter highlights the importance of contact personnel to the service firm and explains their particular role in creating customer satisfaction. Strategically, service personnel are an important source of product differentiation. It is often challenging for a service organization to differentiate itself from other similar organizations in the benefits bundle it offers or its delivery system (see B2B Services in Action). For example, one extreme view is that many airlines offer similar bundles of benefits and fly the same types of aircraft from the same airports to the same destinations. Their only hope of a competitive advantage is, therefore, from the service level—the way things are done. Some of this differentiation can come from staffing levels or the physical systems designed to support the staff. Often, however, the deciding factor that distinguishes one airline from another is the poise and attitude of the service providers.[5] Singapore Airlines, for example, enjoys an excellent reputation due in large part to the beauty and grace of their flight attendants. Other firms that hold a differential advantage over competitors based on personnel include the Ritz Carlton, IBM, and Disney.[6]

Despite the strategic importance of personnel, it often seems that personnel, customers, and the service firm itself are in pursuit of different goals representing the classic confrontation between marketing, human resources, and operations. Inevitably, clashes occur that have profound long-term effects on how customers view the organization and how the service providers view customers in subsequent transactions. It is a self-perpetuating nightmare. Cynical service providers turn their clientele into "customers from hell," and nightmarish customers return the favor by eventually wearing down even the best service providers.[7]

According to one *Wall Street Journal* survey, when asked what irritated them the most about service personnel, approximately 1,000 customers had no problem voicing their major complaints. Answers most frequently mentioned on customer lists include the following:

1. Service personnel who say that they will show up at a particular time and fail to show up at all (40 percent).
2. Poorly informed personnel (37 percent).
3. Contact personnel who continue their personal phone calls while they wait on the customer (25 percent).
4. Personnel who pass customers off by saying "It's not my department" (25 percent).
5. Personnel who talk down to the customer (21 percent).
6. Personnel who can't explain how products work (16 percent).

In the book *At America's Service*, service personnel behaviors that irk customers the most mirrored similar themes. These unsavory behaviors have been classified into seven categories:

1. Apathy: What comedian George Carlin refers to as DILLIGAD—Do I look like I give a damn?
2. Brush-off: Attempts to get rid of the customer by dismissing the customer completely . . . the "I want you to go away" syndrome.

## B₂B SERVICES *IN ACTION*

### > PRIVATE BANKS: IT'S ALL ABOUT THE SERVICE

Strategically, service personnel are an important source of product differentiation. It is often challenging for a service organization to differentiate itself from other similar organizations in the benefit bundle it offers to its customers. Banks are one such product that to many customers is just another commodity product. However, some banks are using the personal touch to carve out a specialized niche in a crowded market space.

When is bigger not better? When smaller translates into more personal service, that's when! In a time where mergers and acquisitions spawn megabanks that find it difficult to provide personal service to its customers, private boutique banks such as PrivateBank & Trust, PrivateBancorp, Boston Private Financial Holdings, and Bryn Mawr Trust are filling the void. Case in point, Chicago developer Patrick F. Daly needed a loan to buy a shopping center but the big national bank that he usually dealt with couldn't track down necessary information fast enough, which jeopardized Daly's deal. Daly quickly called the bank that handled his personal finances, PrivateBank & Trust—a tiny little Chicago-based bank, and within 48 hours received a short-term signature loan for "tens of thousands of dollars." The bank's quick action saved Daly's shopping center deal and earned Daly's respect, "At Private Bank," he says, "they make it their business to know your business. They're just very responsive."

The so-called "small-fry" banks are making great strides in a territory usually reserved for banks that cater to clients who have investable assets exceeding one million. These smaller private banks are targeting attorneys, surgeons, and young "fast-trackers" who desire the personal touch from their bank. Many of these clients have household incomes in the $150,000 neighborhood with potential additional earnings growth; however, their existing banks treat them with indifference at best. Many of these fast-trackers have experienced the personal costs of the merger and acquisition craze of the banking industry—their bank doesn't know who they are anymore. As these traditional megabanks have lost touch with their smaller, but wealthy, clients, the smaller boutique private banks have more than willingly filled the void by providing the personal touch that is usually only reserved for the "uber-wealthy."

Source: Joseph Weber, "Personal Banking for the Merely Rich," *Business Week*, (May 3, 2004), Issue 3881, 121–123.

3. Coldness: Indifferent service providers who could not care less what the customer really wants.
4. Condescension: The "you are the client/patient, so you must be stupid" approach.
5. Robotism: Where the customers are treated simply as inputs into a system that must be processed.

6. Rulebook: Providers who live by the rules of the organization even when those rules do not make good sense.

7. Runaround: Passing the customer off to another provider, who will simply pass them off to yet another provider.

Unfortunately, customers experience service providers from *you-know-where* almost every day, and anecdotal evidence continues to mount indicating that dramatic improvements in the customer/provider relationship are slow in coming. For example, a colleague recently relayed the story of his attempt to order a ham and cheese sandwich with mayonnaise from the deli department of a local grocery store. The employee informed him that she could not fulfill his request because the deli was out of mayonnaise. (Gee whiz, lady, do you think you could get a new jar from aisle 2?)

## > SERVICE PERSONNEL AS BOUNDARY SPANNERS

**boundary-spanning roles**
The various parts played by contact personnel who perform dual functions of interacting with the firm's external environment and internal organization.

Service personnel often experience the pressures and tensions of their role as boundary spanners. As **boundary spanners**, service personnel perform the dual functions of interacting with both the firm's external environment and its internal organization and structure. In simpler terms, the boundary-spanning role has been defined as one that links an organization with the outside world.[8] Employees in boundary-spanning roles create these links for the organization by interacting with nonmembers of the organization. As such, boundary-spanning personnel have two main functions:

- information transfer, and
- representation.

Employees who directly interact with customers are referred to as boundary spanners. Boundary spanners occupy the dual role of organizational representative and information transfer agent. Boundary spanners transfer information from the organization to the customer and vice versa.

© PHOTODISC RED / GETTY IMAGES

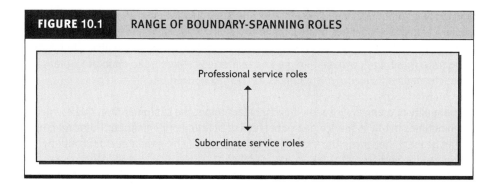

**FIGURE 10.1    RANGE OF BOUNDARY-SPANNING ROLES**

Professional service roles

↕

Subordinate service roles

Boundary spanners collect information from the environment and feed it back into the organization, and they communicate with the environment on behalf of the organization. Boundary-spanning personnel are also the organization's personal representatives.

Individuals who occupy boundary-spanning roles can be classified along a continuum that ranges from **subordinate service roles** to **professional service roles** (see Figure 10.1).[9] At one end of the continuum are the subordinate service roles that traditionally exist at the bottom of an organization. People who work in these roles work for service firms where the customers' purchase decision is entirely discretionary. They are subordinate to the organization and to the customer. Examples of subordinate service roles include waiters, bellmen, drivers, and others who operate at the very base of the organization and yet are the organization's primary contact personnel with the outside world.

Professional service roles occupy the position at the other end of the continuum. Professionals are also boundary spanners; however, their status is quite different from that of the subordinate provider. Due to their professional qualifications, professional service providers have a status that is independent of their place in the organization. Customers, or as they are more often called, clients, are not superior to professionals because clients acknowledge the professionals' expertise on which they wish to draw.

*subordinate service roles*
The parts played by personnel who work in firms where customers' purchase decisions are entirely discretionary, such as waitresses, bellmen, and drivers.

*professional service roles*
The parts played by personnel who have a status independent of their place in an organization due to their professional qualifications.

## SOURCES OF CONFLICT IN BOUNDARY-SPANNING ROLES

Employees who occupy boundary-spanning roles are often placed in situations that produce conflict and stress. Common sources of stress include person/role conflicts consisting of *inequality dilemmas*, *feelings versus behavior*, and *territorial conflicts*; organization/client conflicts; and interclient conflicts.

### Person/Role Conflicts

For services to operate successfully, both customers and contact personnel must conform to a script or role. Each must play his or her part. A **person/role conflict** indicates that playing such a role may be inconsistent with an individual's self-perception. Some customers may wish boundary spanners to be subservient, a role that an employee normally would not desire to play, especially with certain types of customers.

*person/role conflict*
A bad fit between an individual's self-perception and the specific role the person must play in an organization.

Boundary-spanning personnel often are called on to suppress their personal feelings and are asked to smile and be helpful while feeling miserable and aggressive; this is particularly the case for low-level staff.[10] Professionals are much more likely to be able to operate within their own self-image and to feel less obligated to maintain a pleasant "bedside manner." Person/role conflicts can be categorized into three types:

1. Inequality dilemmas. Although it is important to put the customer first, this can sometimes result in service personnel feeling belittled or demeaned. These feelings can be magnified if customers make a point of establishing their personal superiority over the server.
2. Feelings versus behavior. Contact personnel are required to hide their true feelings and present a "front" or "face" to the customer. This can result in role stress as the server does not identify with the role he or she is acting out.
3. Territorial conflict. Contact personnel will often try to establish their own personal space, which they can defend against clients and other servers. Trespassing on this space can lead to reactions that conflict with the server's own role.

### Organization/Client Conflicts

Contact personnel can sometimes receive conflicting instructions, one set from the client who wants a service performed in a particular way, the other from the organization that wants the service performed in a different way. This three-cornered fight among the customer, service, and organization must essentially be resolved by compromise. However, such compromise can, if mishandled, leave the server feeling badly treated. Conflicts between the demands of the organization and those of the client are the most common source of conflict for boundary-spanning personnel. Conflicts of this type arise when the client or customer requests services that violate the rules of the organization. Such a violation can be as simple as a request for a second bread roll in a restaurant or as complex as a request that a bus driver leave the established route to drop a passenger off at home.[11]

**organization/client conflicts**
Disagreements that arise when a customer requests services that violate the rules of the organization.

The reaction to the **organization/client conflict** is often related to the employee's role within the organization. Subordinate service personnel are often unable to change the rules and regulations of the company. Moreover, they are unable to explain why the rules and regulations exist in the first place. However, subordinate service personnel appear to be well aware of the rules and regulations that prevent them from giving good service. In many cases, when faced with an organization/client conflict, subordinate service personnel will side with the client and away from the organization to resolve the conflict. In contrast, professional service personnel, with their higher status and clearer understanding of the purpose of specific rules and regulations, are more able to control what happens.

### Interclient Conflicts

**interclient conflicts**
Disagreements between clients that arise because of the number of clients who influence one another's experience.

Conflicts between clients, or **interclient conflicts**, arise because many service delivery systems have a number of clients who influence one another's experiences. Because different clients are likely to have different needs, they tend to have completely different scripts for themselves, the contact personnel, and other customers. When customers do conflict, it is usually the boundary-spanning personnel who are asked to resolve the confrontation. For example, it is the waiter who is generally requested to ask another diner not to smoke in a nonsmoking section. Attempts to satisfy all of the clients all of the time can escalate the conflict or bring the boundary-spanning personnel into the battle. For example, a restaurant customer requesting speedy service and receiving it can cause complaints from other tables about the inequitable levels of service.

Employee reaction and effectiveness in resolving interclient conflicts appear to be once again related to the employee's role within the organization. Employees in subordinate roles start from the weakest position since they have low status with clients. Clients may simply disregard responses made by subordinate service providers. Professionals may face the same problems; for example, consider the patient in the hospital waiting room, demanding preferential treatment. In a case such as this, however, the professional can invoke his or her status and expertise to resolve the situation.

## THE IMPLICATIONS OF ROLE STRESS FOR BOUNDARY-SPANNING PERSONNEL

The consequences of conflict and stress produce dissatisfaction, frustration, and turnover intention in personnel (see E-Services in Action). When faced with potential conflict and stress in their jobs, employees attempt a variety of strategies to shield themselves. The simplest way of avoiding conflict is to avoid the customers. This is exemplified by the waiter who refuses to notice a customer who wishes to place an order. This strategy allows the employee to increase his or her personal sense of control over the encounter. An alternative strategy is to move into a people-processing mode,[12] where customers are treated as inanimate objects to be processed rather than as individuals. This reduces the requirement of the boundary-spanning personnel to associate or empathize with an individual.

Boundary-spanning personnel also employ other strategies to maintain a sense of control of the encounter. Physical symbols and furniture are often used to boost the employee's status and, hence, his or her sense of control.[13] In an extreme case, the employee may overact the role and force the customer into a subservient role, as is the case with some waiters and waitresses. Interestingly, a national restaurant franchise called Dick's Last Resort encourages employees to be overly demanding as part of their overall theme. In fact the restaurant's theme could easily be: "Dick's Last Resort...Where the Customer Is Always Wrong!"

An alternative strategy employees use to reduce organization/client conflict is to side completely with the customer. When forced to obey a rule with which they disagree, boundary-spanning personnel will proceed to list for the customer all the other things about the organization with which they disagree. In this way, employees attempt to reduce stress by seeking sympathy from the customer.

## REDUCING ROLE STRESS WITH MARKETING

Traditionally, marketing can either cause or reduce role stress. Marketing can, without making major strategic changes, help to reduce service employee stress levels, and it's in the firm's best interest to do so. Clearly, unhappy, frustrated, and disagreeing contact

## E-SERVICES *IN ACTION*

> **WHERE EMPLOYEES GO ONLINE TO SOUND OFF!**

We have all heard about customer complaint sites on the Internet. For example, unhappy United Airline customers can voice their complaints on http://www.untied.com and unhappy students can register their dissatisfaction on http://www.ratemy professor.com and many do just that! As of this writing, 558,559 professors from 4,596 schools have received over 3.5 million ratings with an additional 3,500 ratings or so being added every day. It would seem that with this much feedback being handed out by customers, turnabout—where employees get their chance to sound off against problematic customers—should be fair play.

Despite the old adage that the customer is never wrong, http://www.customerssuck.com gives employees the chance to vent their frustrations with customers. To date, over 500,000 people have visited the site. Visitors can subscribe to "The Customers Suck! Newsletter," chat with fellow customer service reps on the site's Message Boards, and contribute to moderated sites such as:

- At the Movies
  Stories from the film industry
- Customer Service Definitions
  Terms that should be used for customers who do certain things
- Coffee Shop Blues
  Stories about dealing with customers before they get their daily dose of caffeine
- The Real Cellular Craze
  Stories from those in the cellular/digital phone industry
- Loving the Library
  Stories from librarians
- Sick of Seniors
  The idea of a second childhood is apparently true
- Dealing with Drunks
  Customers are bad enough sober, but add a little alcohol...
- Customers Coming Clean
  Stories from customers who knew they screwed up
- Customers Being Bad to Other Customers
  When customers decided that for some reason they are the only customers who deserve respect in the store
- Disgruntled Employees Union!
  Other sites that deal with employees, customer service, etc.

Source: http://www.customerssuck.com accessed 23 May 2005.

personnel are visible to customers and will ultimately affect consumer perceptions of service quality.[14] Strategies such as ignoring the customer or simply processing the customer as a raw material through the service delivery system will most likely generate negative customer perceptions. Customers obviously do not like being ignored by waiters or treated as if they were inanimate objects. If contact personnel attempt to maximize their sense of control over their encounters, it will most likely be at the expense of the amount of control felt by customers. In addition, although customers may sympathize with a service provider's explanation that the organization stops them from providing excellent service, customers will still develop negative perceptions about the organization.

### Reducing Person/Role Conflicts

Marketing can reduce the conflict between the individual and the assigned role by simply being sensitive and by actively seeking input from employees about the issue. A promotional gimmick dreamed up at the head office may look great on paper. For example, a medieval-theme day in the hotel almost certainly will have great public relations value, but how will the staff feel when they are called upon to wear strange and awkward (not to mention uncomfortable) costumes? How will these costumes affect the employees' relationships with customers during the service encounter?

To improve the quality of service, a change in operating procedure may be needed. However, it is important to ensure that service providers are well trained in the new script. Should they not be, they may well become extremely embarrassed in the presence of customers. This situation can be aggravated if the new service is advertised in such a way that the customers are more aware of the new script than the staff.

### Reducing Organization/Client Conflicts

Similarly, marketing can help reduce conflicts between the organization and its clients. It is crucial, for example, that customer expectations be consistent with the capabilities of the service system. Customers should not ask for services the system cannot provide. Advertising is one of the main causes of inflated expectations as the temptation is to exaggerate claims in advertising to maximize the impact. Consider, for example, the advertisement that depicted a flight attendant reading a young child a story while the plane was in flight. A number of passengers took the advertisement literally, either because they believed it or because they could not resist the temptation, and called upon the flight attendants to read stories to their children.

### Reducing Interclient Conflicts

Conflicts between clients can be avoided if the clients are relatively homogeneous in their expectations. Due to the inseparability of services, customers often share their service experiences with other customers. Hence, successful service firms recognize the importance of effective segmentation, which minimizes the chances that two or more divergent groups will share the encounter simultaneously. As long as all the clients share the same script and expect the same standard of service, the chances of interclient conflicts are much reduced.

> ## THE IMPORTANCE OF HUMAN RESOURCES FOR SERVICE FIRMS

Personnel constitutes the bulk of the product of most service firms (see Global Services in Action). However, marketing theory is ill equipped to provide insights into the problem of where contact personnel fit into the hierarchy of the service firm. Human resources, by comparison, is a field of study focused on this and similar problems. Human resource policies are associated with the outcomes experienced by customers and the culture created within the service firm.[15]

*climate*
Employee perceptions of one or more organizational strategic imperatives.

Because service firms often involve the customer as a co-producer, they operate open systems, where the effects of human resource practices and policies as well as the organization's climate are visible to customers. **Climate** is defined as employee perceptions of one or more strategic imperatives. For example, a passion for service within the organization would lead to a climate that sets service as the key strategic imperative (see Tables 10.1 and 10.2). When service commitment is high, the service firm displays a passion for doing things directly related to the provision of service. Consider for example, employee comments from The Container Store, recently chosen by *Fortune Magazine* as the #1 Best Place to Work.[16]

- "I love this company because 'Customer Service is #1'!!...All customers can use our phones at any time."
- "We grew up with 'family values' and it's rare to find a company with the same values, philosophy, and foundation principles. Going to work is like going to a family reunion everyday."
- "Working for this company has made me a better person and certainly made the world a better, more organized place."
- "I miss everyone when I go on vacation."
- "I will never leave."

Employees speak often and favorably about the service delivery process and the product offered to consumers, as well as about the concern for and/or responsiveness of the firm to customer opinions. In addition, when service passion is strong, employees speak favorably about performance feedback, internal equity of compensation, training, and staff quality, which is communicated to customers throughout the service delivery process.

### CREATING THE RIGHT TYPE OF ORGANIZATION

Human resource management practices are the key drivers available to senior management for creating the type of organization that can be a source of sustainable competitive advantage. Often, however, front-line customer contact jobs are designed to be as simple and narrow as possible so that they can be filled by anyone—in other words, "idiot-proof" jobs. Employers place few demands on employees, selection criteria are minimal, and wages are low.

The result is the classic cycle of failure of the industrial model as discussed in Chapter 1. Fewer and less-knowledgeable contact personnel are available, and hence,

## GLOBAL SERVICES *IN ACTION*

### > DELL OFFSHORE TECH SUPPORT: LOST IN TRANSLATION

The interactions between a service firm's personnel and its customers define "moments of truth." Moments of truth represent the service firm's greatest opportunity for gains and losses. This is why employee selection and training are so important to service firms. One service firm that is currently struggling with this issue is Dell Inc. of Austin, Texas.

To outsource tech support offshore, or not, that is the question for Dell Inc. What began as a means for the company to cut costs, the offshoring of Dell's tech support to India, has become somewhat of a political incident. During the tech recession, Dell laid off nearly 5,700 workers. Most of these employees were tech support personnel working in Texas. Since this time, most of the growth in Dell's workforce has occurred in overseas call-centers based in India. To say the least, the average Texan is not too happy about this "motivated by cost-savings" turn of events.

Dell is now faced with the decision about whether to recall some of these lost jobs back to America. Dell customers have complained about the quality of support received from Indian-based call centers. Meanwhile, upset Indians are bristling at the thought that "their thick accents" and "scripted responses" have motivated Dell to move some of its tech support positions back to America. However, it does appear that Dell has done just this particularly for its large-scale corporate clients. In fact, delivering customer support from North American–based locations appears to have become a major selling point for Dell's corporate clients.

The offshoring of customer tech support has become a thorny issue. On the one hand, India provides the cost savings that drives Dell's value proposition. On the other hand, more and more corporate customers are shopping tech firms based on the issue of the location of technical support. In the meantime, many industry observers are wondering whether the quality of technical support has really declined due to its India-based location or whether Dell has become the victim of a well-organized email and bulletin board campaign that promotes protectionism. Commenting on Dell's dilemma, *The Economist* writes, "It may be its [Dell] customer service has become genuinely poorer as a result—though multi-regional, multi-racial America has its fair share of different accents, too. Which customers, after all, can claim happy experiences with Texan call centers?"

Source: Patrick, Thibodeau, "Offshore Tech Support Still Stirs Controversy," *Computerworld*, (May 2, 2005), Vol. 39, Issue 18, p. 7; "Lost in Translation," *The Economist*, (November 29, 2003), Vol. 369, Issue 8352, p58.

| TABLE 10.1 | DESCRIPTIONS OF STAFFING ISSUES IN FIRMS WITH A HIGH, MODERATE, AND LOW PASSION FOR SERVICE |
|---|---|

**High Passion for Service**
There is not enough staff to whom we can delegate responsibilities.
Management is running lean at the top.
There aren't enough people for cross training.

**Moderate Passion for Service**
There is nobody to replace someone who takes a vacation.
We have been reduced to a skeleton staff, but the work must still go out.
Unusually heavy workloads are our biggest problem.

**Low Passion for Service**
When people leave, they are not replaced.
Every day there is another staffing problem.
Our receptionist has so many duties she sometimes can't even answer the phone.

Source: Benjamin Schneider and David E. Bowen, *Winning the Service Game*, (Boston, MA: Harvard Business School Press, 1995), p. 130.

| TABLE 10.2 | DESCRIPTIONS OF TRAINING IN FIRMS WITH A HIGH, MODERATE, AND LOW PASSION FOR SERVICE |
|---|---|

**High Passion for Service**
There is cross-training in operations to improve service.
Seminars are held for both in-house personnel and customers.

**Moderate Passion for Service**
We can't learn other jobs because there is nobody here to relieve us while we are being trained.
Some people get terrific training; others get none.
We need more sales training.

**Low Passion for Service**
We have to go through hell to get permission to attend a training seminar.
No one is being trained to use the PCs; automation is occurring without the necessary training.
I'm taking a real estate course, and my company won't pay for it even though we are a
    mortgage bank.

Source: Benjamin Schneider and David E. Bowen, *Winning the Service Game*, (Boston, MA: Harvard Business School Press, 1995), p. 135.

the customer gets less and lower-quality help (see Table 10.3). Customers vent their feelings of impatience and dissatisfaction on the staff, which, in turn, demotivates the employees, especially the most conscientious ones, since they are already aware of the poor service they are being forced to give. The best staff leave and are replaced

| TABLE 10.3 | TEMP WORKER FACTS (U.S.) |
|------------|-------------------------|

- Temps earn an average of 40 percent less per hour than full-time workers.
- 55 percent do not have health insurance.
- 80 percent work 35 hours per week.
- 25 percent are under the age of 25.
- 53 percent are women; in the total workforce, 47 percent are women.
- 60 percent of the women have children under 18.
- 22 percent of the temp workforce is African-American; 11 percent of the total workforce is African-American.

Source: "Temporary Workers Getting Short Shrift," *USA Today*, April 11, 1997, p. B1.

with poorly trained recruits and the cycle continues. Current human resource theory is looking for ways to break out of the industrial model mindset, and, in particular, how to use empowerment and enfranchisement to break the cycle of failure.

## EMPOWERMENT AND ENFRANCHISEMENT

One of the most powerful tools for breaking free of the old logic is the use of employee empowerment and enfranchisement. **Empowerment** means giving discretion to contact personnel to "turn the front line loose." Empowerment is the reverse of "doing things by the book." **Enfranchisement** carries this logic even further by first empowering individuals and then coupling this with a reward system that recognizes people for their performance.

Rewarding employees is the most powerful way to encourage customer-oriented behaviors. Rewards can be extrinsic (e.g., pay) or intrinsic such as enjoying the job itself, receiving recognition from coworkers and supervisors, and/or accomplishing challenging and meaningful goals. Effective reward systems pass the seven tests listed below.[17] Interestingly, in many instances, pay alone does not pass these effectiveness tests.

*Availability*—Rewards must be available and substantial. Not having enough rewards or large enough rewards is likely to discourage desired behaviors rather than encourage them.

*Flexibility*—Rewards should be flexible enough that they can be given to anyone at any time.

*Reversibility*—If rewards are given to the wrong people for the wrong reasons, they should not be lifelong. Bonuses are better than pay increases that become lifetime annuities.

*Contingent*—Rewards should be directly tied to desired performance criteria.

*Visibility*—Rewards should be visible, and their value should be understood by all employees. For example, pay is not visible and is often shrouded in secrecy.

*Timeliness*—Not to say that employees are rats, but rats are trained to receive food pellets immediately following the execution of a desired behavior (e.g., pushing a bar). However, in this instance, employees are not that much different. Rewards should be given immediately following desired behaviors.

*empowerment*
Giving discretion to front-line personnel to meet the needs of consumers creatively.

*enfranchisement*
Empowerment coupled with a performance-based compensation method.

*Durability*—The motivating effects of a reward should last for a long time. The motivational effects of plaques and medallions last longer than the short-term effects of pay.

The most significant and successful enfranchisement programs have occurred in the field of retailing. Here, advocates argue that it can improve sales and earnings dramatically while at the same time require less supervision from corporate management. Perhaps the most commonly used example is Nordstrom, which pays salespeople a commission not only on what they sell but also on the extent to which they can exceed their superiors' projected sales forecasts. At the same time, Nordstrom's management frees salespeople of normal constraints and publicly celebrates associates' outstanding service accomplishments.

## WHEN TO EMPOWER AND ENFRANCHISE

No single solution exists to the problems encountered in managing contact personnel. Empowerment and enfranchisement do not always win out over the industrial-based models of management. Consider the examples of FedEx and UPS.

FedEx was the first service organization to win the coveted Malcolm Baldrige National Quality Award. Behind the blue, white, and red planes and uniforms are self-managed work teams, garnishing plans, and empowered employees seemingly concerned with providing flexible and creative service to customers with varying needs. In contrast, at UPS, we find turned-on people and profits, but we do not find empowerment. Instead we find controls, rules, a detailed union contract, and carefully studied work methods. UPS makes no promises that its employees will bend over backward to meet individual customer needs. However, what we do find are rigid operational guidelines, which help guarantee the customer reliable, low-cost service.[18]

### The Benefits

Empowerment clearly brings benefits. Empowered employees are more customer focused and are much quicker in responding to customer needs. They will customize the product or remix it in real-time.[19] Empowered employees are more likely to respond in a positive manner to service failures and to engage in effective service recovery strategies.

Employees who are empowered tend to feel better about their jobs and themselves. This is automatically reflected in the way they interact with customers. They will be genuinely warmer and friendlier. Empowerment, therefore, not only can reduce unnecessary service recovery costs, but also can improve the quality of the product.

If close to the front line, an empowered employee is in a position continuously exposed to both the good and the bad aspects of the service delivery system. This employee can be the key to new service ideas and may often be a cheaper source of market research than going to the customer directly.

### The Costs

Unfortunately, empowerment and enfranchisement do carry costs. The balance between benefits and costs determines the appropriateness of the approach. Empowerment increases the costs of the organization. A greater investment is needed in remuneration and recruitment to assure that the right people are empowered. A low-cost model of using inexpensive and/or part-time labor cannot cope with empowerment, so the basic labor costs of the organization will be higher.

If costs are higher, marketing implications also arise. By definition, an empowered employee will customize the product. This means that the service received will vary from one encounter to the next, depending on the employee. The delivery is also likely to be slower because the service is customized. Moreover, since customers are treated differently, other customers may perceive that some customers are receiving preferential treatment. Finally, empowered employees, when attempting to satisfy customers, sometimes give away too much and make bad decisions. For example, a bellman who notices that a businessman forgot his briefcase at the front desk should make every attempt to return the briefcase to its owner. However, tracking the owner to the airport and hopping on the next available flight to the owner's destination is far beyond the call of duty and worlds beyond what is economically feasible.

The balance of empowerment and enfranchisement, therefore, comes down to the benefit concept of the organization. A branded organization that guarantees consistency of product and service dare not empower for fear of the inconsistency that doing so would produce. For example, McDonald's would lose one of its key differential advantages if it empowered its employees.

An organization that competes on the basis of value driven by a low cost base cannot afford to empower because of the costs involved. Equally, a high-cost service organization using a nonroutine and complex technology almost certainly has to empower because its ability to use an industrial approach is severely limited.

## *LEVELS OF EMPOWERMENT*

As evidenced by the UPS and FedEx examples, empowerment is not for every firm. Firms can indeed be successful without fully empowering their employees. However, empowerment approaches vary by degree and include suggestion involvement, job involvement, and high involvement. Each of the three levels of empowerment fall along a continuum that ranges from control-oriented to involvement-oriented approaches (see Figure 10.2).

**Suggestion involvement** falls near the control-oriented point of the empowerment continuum. Suggestion involvement empowers employees to recommend suggestions for improving the firm's operations. Employees are not empowered to implement suggestions themselves but are encouraged to suggest improvements for formal review. Firms that utilize suggestion involvement typically maintain formal suggestion programs that proactively solicit employee suggestions. **Quality circles**, which often involve small groups of employees from various departments in the firm, are also utilized as brainstorming sessions to generate additional suggestions. Typical success stories of suggestion involvement programs include McDonald's, whose employees recommended the development of products such as the Big Mac, Egg McMuffin, and McBLT.

**Job involvement** typically falls in the middle of the empowerment continuum, between control-oriented and involvement-oriented approaches. Job involvement allows employees to examine the content of their own jobs and to define their role within the organization. Firms engaged in job involvement use teams of employees

*suggestion involvement*
Low-level empowerment that allows employees to recommend suggestions for improvement of the firm's operations.

*quality circles*
Empowerment involving small groups of employees from various departments in the firm who use brainstorming sessions to generate additional improvement suggestions.

*job involvement*
Allows employees to examine the content of their own jobs and to define their role within the organization.

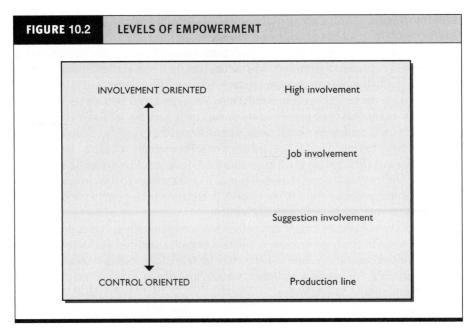

**FIGURE 10.2    LEVELS OF EMPOWERMENT**

INVOLVEMENT ORIENTED    High involvement

Job involvement

Suggestion involvement

CONTROL ORIENTED    Production line

Source: Adapted from David E. Bowen and Edward E. Lawler III, "The Empowerment of Service Workers: What, Why, How, and When," *Sloan Management Review* (Spring 1992), 31–39.

extensively for the betterment of the firm's service delivery system. In contrast to suggestion involvement, employees engaged in job involvement use a variety of skills, have considerably more freedom, and receive extensive feedback from management, employees, and customers. However, higher-level decisions and reward allocation decisions remain the responsibility of the firm's upper management.

**high involvement**
Allows employees to eventually learn to manage themselves, utilizing extensive training and employee control of the reward allocation decisions.

**High involvement** falls at the involvement-oriented end of the empowerment continuum. Essentially, the goal of high involvement is to train people to manage themselves. Extensive training is utilized to develop skills in teamwork, problem solving, and business operations. Moreover, employees control the majority of the reward allocation decisions through profit sharing and employee ownership of the firm. In sum, virtually every aspect of a high-involvement firm is different from those of a control-oriented firm.

## HOW MUCH TO EMPOWER: A CONTINGENCY APPROACH

When deciding among suggestion involvement, job involvement, and high-involvement empowerment strategies, the firm must consider several factors in order to select the correct strategy. Table 10.4 provides a rating system to help managers assess their particular situations. According to the table, managers should rate their firms on five contingencies:

1. the firm's basic business strategy,
2. its tie to the customer,

| TABLE 10.4 | THE CONTINGENCIES OF EMPOWERMENT | | |
|---|---|---|---|
| **Contingency** | **Production-Line Approach** | | **Empowerment** |
| Basic business strategy | Low cost, high volume | 1 2 3 4 5 | Differentiation, customized, personalized |
| Tie to the customer | Transaction, short time period | 1 2 3 4 5 | Relationship, long time period |
| Technology | Routine, simple | 1 2 3 4 5 | Nonroutine, complex |
| Business environment | Predictable, few surprises | 1 2 3 4 5 | Unpredictable, many surprises |
| Types of people | Theory X managers, employees with low growth needs, low social needs, and weak interpersonal skills | 1 2 3 4 5 | Theory Y managers, employees with high growth needs, high social needs, and strong interpersonal skills |

Source: David E. Bowen and Edward E. Lawler, III, "The Empowerment of Service Workers: What, Why, How, and When," *Sloan Management Review* (Spring 1992), pp. 31–39.

3. technology,
4. the business environment, and
5. types of leadership.

The **basic business strategy** of the firm pertains to whether the firm produces a standardized, low-cost, high-volume product or whether it produces a differentiated, customized, personalized product. As the product becomes more standardized, lower levels of empowerment are suggested. Production lining the service delivery system will make the system more efficient, thereby controlling costs and increasing the standardization of product produced.

The firm's **tie to the customer** refers to the type of relationship the firm has with its customers. If the relationship involves discrete transactions that occur over a short time period, control-oriented approaches should dominate. In contrast, if the customer-client relationship is long-term, such as that with an insurance agent, broker, or CPA, employees should be empowered to meet the individual needs of clients.

Similarly, if the **technology** utilized to carry out the firm's operations is simple and routine and the **business environment** within which the firm operates is predictable, then the costs associated with empowered employees outweigh the benefits. If, on the other hand, the technology is nonroutine and complex and the business environment is volatile, empowered employees are necessary for coping with client concerns and the constantly changing environment.

Finally, empowered employees need different kinds of leadership. Theory Y managers, who coach and facilitate rather than control and manipulate, are needed to work with employees who have high growth needs and strong interpersonal skills . . . the needs and skills of empowered employees. In contrast, firms governed by Theory

**basic business strategy**
A firm's fundamental approach as to whether it produces a standardized, low-cost, high-volume product or a differentiated, customized, personalized product.

**tie to the customer**
The degrees of involvement the firm has with its customers.

**technology**
The level of automation a firm utilizes.

**business environment**
The social, technological, and financial environment in which a firm operates and markets.

X managers believe that employees are working primarily to collect a paycheck. Theory X managers work best with employees who have low growth needs, low social needs, and weak interpersonal skills. Theory X managers fit best with control-oriented organizations.

The contingency approach, presented in Table 10.4, rates each of the five factors (basic business strategy, tie to the customer, technology, business environment, and types of people) on a scale from 1 to 5, where lower numbers favor a control-oriented approach and higher numbers favor an empowerment approach. Upon adding the scores of the five factors together, firms scoring in the 5–10 range are recommended to pursue a very control-oriented, production-line approach. Firms scoring in the 11–15 range are advised to implement a suggestion involvement strategy. Firms rating in the 16–20 range are urged to utilize a job involvement approach, and firms that score in the 21–25 range are encouraged to implement a high-involvement empowerment approach. The selection of empowerment strategy should be dependent upon the firm and the market in which it operates. Different types of firms have different needs.

## > PULLING IT ALL TOGETHER

Ultimately, the use of empowerment and enfranchisement is to break free from the shackles imposed by the industrial management model and move to values embraced by the market-focused management approach. As we introduced in Chapter 1, the market-focused management model champions the notion that the purpose of the firm is to service its customers. By following this approach, the service delivery process becomes the focus of the organization and the overall key to successfully differentiating the firm from its competition. People become the key to success.

Theory Y managers, who coach and facilitate rather than control and manipulate, thrive in work environments where employees have high growth needs and strong interpersonal skills.

© JON FEINGERSH / CORBIS

| TABLE 10.5 | BEST PERKS TO EMPLOYEES OF THE 100 BEST COMPANIES | | |
|---|---|---|---|
| **Perks** | **Number of Companies** | **Perks** | **Number of Companies** |
| Overnight dependent child care | 7 | Subsidized cafeterias | 64 |
| Free lunch (or other meals) | 15 | On-site ATM or banking service | 64 |
| Personal concierge service | 15 | Personal travel services | 68 |
| On-site child care | 31 | Elder-care resource and referral | 73 |
| Dry-cleaning service | 40 | Casual dress every day | 75 |
| Home-purchasing service | 44 | Relocation services | 83 |
| Adoption aid | 60 | Child care resource and referral | 83 |

Source: "The 100 Best Companies to Work For in America," *Fortune* 137, no. 1 (January 12, 1998), 88.

The market-focused management approach recognizes that employee turnover and customer satisfaction are clearly related. As a result, the recruitment and training of front-line personnel is emphasized. Pay is directly tied to performance throughout every level of the organization. Companies that compensate employees better than competitors often find that as a percentage of sales, their labor costs are actually lower than industry averages (see Table 10.5). The benefits of superior training and education programs are clear. Better-trained and better-paid employees provide better service, need less supervision, and are more likely to stay on the job. In turn, customers are more satisfied, return to make purchases more often, purchase more when they do return, and tell their friends of the positive experience.

## THE SERVICE-PROFIT CHAIN

The benefits of the market-focused management model are illustrated in the **service-profit chain** presented in Figure 10.3.[20] The links in the chain reveal that employee satisfaction and customer satisfaction are directly related. Employee satisfaction is derived from a workplace and job design that facilitates internal service quality. Hiring, training, and rewarding effective personnel are also major contributors to internal service quality.

Satisfied employees remain with the firm and improve their individual productivity. Hence, employee satisfaction is linked with increases in the firm's overall productivity and decreases in recruitment and training costs. Moreover, the increase in productivity coupled with a sincere desire to assist customers results in external service value. Employee attitudes and beliefs about the organization are often reflected in their behaviors. Given the customer's involvement in the production process, these behaviors are visible to the customer and ultimately influence the customer's satisfaction.

Customer satisfaction is directly related to customer loyalty, which is demonstrated through repeat purchases and positive word-of-mouth referrals to other customers. The net effects of customer retention are increased revenues and profitability for the firm.

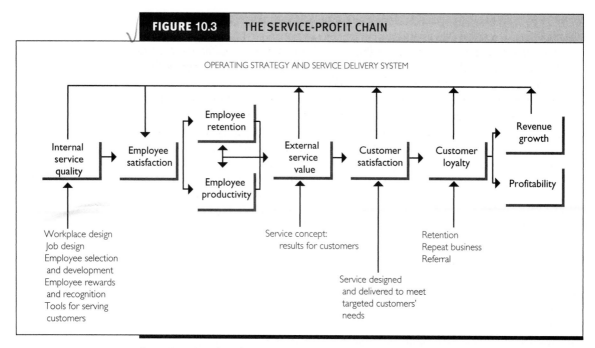

**FIGURE 10.3     THE SERVICE-PROFIT CHAIN**

OPERATING STRATEGY AND SERVICE DELIVERY SYSTEM

Internal service quality → Employee satisfaction → Employee retention / Employee productivity → External service value → Customer satisfaction → Customer loyalty → Revenue growth / Profitability

Workplace design
Job design
Employee selection
  and development
Employee rewards
  and recognition
Tools for serving
  customers

Service concept:
  results for customers

Service designed
  and delivered to meet
  targeted customers'
  needs

Retention
Repeat business
Referral

Source: James L. Heskett, Thomas O. Jones, Gary W. Loveman, W. Earl Sasser, Jr., and Leonard A. Schlesinger, "Putting the Service-Profit Chain to Work," *Harvard Business Review* (March–April 1994), 164–174. Reprinted by permission of *Harvard Business Review.* Copyright © 1994 by the President and Fellows of Harvard College.

Simultaneously, employees are also rewarded for their efforts. The outcomes associated with employee satisfaction—external service values, customer satisfaction, customer loyalty, revenue growth, and increased profitability reinforce the company's commitment for continually improving internal service quality. As the recipients of internal quality improvements and positive customer responses, employees directly experience the fruits of their efforts. Employee satisfaction is subsequently reinforced and the integrity of the service-profit chain is maintained.

The service-profit chain provides the logic behind the change in perspective which has led to the new services model. The major lessons to be learned by the chain are two-fold. First, a firm must satisfy its employees in order for customer satisfaction to become a consistent reality. Second, the chain proclaims the simple fact that service and quality pay off!

## ✱ SUMMARY

Successful service firms develop a seamless relationship among marketing, operations, and human resources. This chapter has focused on some of the human resource issues that must be considered when marketing services. Much has been written about the fact that, for many service firms, personnel constitute the bulk of their product. It is thus important that the place of personnel within the organization be understood. By drawing on the concepts of organizational behavior and, in particular, the concepts of boundary-spanning roles, empowerment, and enfranchisement, this chapter has provided a solid framework on which to develop the marketing implications of personnel as a key component of the firm's overall product offering.

As boundary spanners, service personnel perform the dual functions of interacting with both the firm's external environment and its internal organization and structure. Employees who occupy boundary-spanning roles are often placed in situations that produce conflict and stress. There are five common types of stress: inequality dilemmas, feelings versus behavior, territorial conflict, organization/client conflicts, and interclient conflicts.

Because service firms often involve the customer as a co-producer, they operate open systems, where the effects of human resource practices and policies as well as the organization's climate are visible to customers. Current human resource theory is looking for ways to break out of the industrial model mindset, and, in particular, how to use empowerment and enfranchisement to break the cycle of failure. When deciding among empowerment strategies, the firm must consider the following:

1. the firm's basic business strategy,
2. its tie to the customer,
3. technology,
4. the business environment, and
5. types of leadership.

The selection of empowerment strategy should be dependent upon the firm and the market in which it operates. Different types of firms have different needs. Ultimately, the use of empowerment and enfranchisement is to break free from the shackles imposed by the industrial management model and move to values embraced by the market-focused management approach. The benefits of the market-focused management model are illustrated in the service-profit chain. The major lessons to be learned by the chain are two-fold. First, a firm must satisfy its employees in order for customer satisfaction to become a consistent reality. Second, the chain proclaims the simple fact that service and quality pay off!

## ✳ KEY TERMS

boundary spanning roles, 256
subordinate service roles, 257
professional service roles, 257
person/role conflict, 257
organization/client conflict, 258
interclient conflicts, 258
climate, 262
empowerment, 265
enfranchisement, 265

suggestion involvement, 267
quality circles, 267
job involvement, 267
high involvement, 268
basic business strategy, 269
tie to the customer, 269
technology, 269
business environment, 269

## ✱ REVIEW QUESTIONS

1. Relate the concepts of intangibility, inseparability, heterogeneity, and perishability to the importance of personnel in the service firm.
2. What are boundary-spanning personnel? Discuss the five types of conflict that they generally encounter.
3. How can marketing be utilized to reduce the amount of stress and conflict experienced by boundary-spanning personnel?
4. In what types of organizations would it be best to avoid empowerment approaches?
5. In what type of organizations would it be best to implement a job-involvement empowerment approach?
6. Discuss the benefits and costs associated with empowerment and enfranchisement.
7. Discuss the relevance of employee satisfaction as it relates to the service-profit chain.
8. What is climate? Why is organizational climate of particular importance to service firms?
9. Define enfranchisement. Summarize the seven tests of reward effectiveness.

## ✱ NOTES

1. The first section of this chapter is based on Chapters 4 and 6 of John E. G. Bateson, *Managing of Services Marketing*, 3rd ed. (Fort Worth, TX: The Dryden Press, 1995).
2. Dave Ulrich et al., "Employee and Customer Attachment: Synergies for Competitive Advantage," *Human Resource Planning* 14,3 (1991), p. 89(15).
3. Leonard A. Schlesinger and James L Heskett, "The Service-Driven Service Company," *Harvard Business Review* (September-October, 1991), pp. 71–81.
4. Daine Brady, "Why Service Stinks?" *Business Week* (October 23, 2000), pp. 118–128.
5. This idea was originally suggested in a slightly different form in W. Earl Sasser, P. Olsen, and D. Daryl Wycoff, *Management of Service Operations: Text, Cases, and Readings* (Boston: Allyn and Bacon, 1978).
6. Philip Kotler, *Marketing Management*, 8th ed. (Englewood Cliffs, NJ: Prentice-Hall, 1994), p. 303.
7. Ron Zemke and Kristen Anderson, "Customers from Hell," *Training* (February 1990), pp. 25–29.
8. J. D. Thompson, "Organization and Output Transactions," *American Journal of Sociology* 68 (1967), pp. 309–324.

9. Boas Shamir, "Between Service and Servility: Role Conflict in Subordinate Service Roles," *Human Relations* 33,10, pp. 741–756.
10. See Arlie Hochshild, *The Managed Heart* (Berkeley, CA: University of California Press, 1983).
11. For example, see Jody D. Nyquist, Mary Jo Bitner, and Bernard Booms, "Identifying Difficulties in the Service Encounter: A Critical Incident Approach," in John Czepiel, Michael R. Solomon, and Carol F. Suprenant, eds., *The Service Encounter* (Lexington, MA: Heath, 1985), pp. 195–212.
12. Peter Klaus, "The Quality Epiphenomenon," in John Czepiel, Michael R. Solomon, and Carol F. Suprenant, eds., *The Service Encounter* (Lexington, MA: Heath, 1985), p. 15.
13. Charles T. Goodsell, "Bureaucratic Manipulation of Physical Symbols: An Empirical Investigation," *American Journal of Political Science XXI* (February 1977), pp. 79–91.
14. Benjamin Schneider, Jill K. Wheeler, and Jonathan F. Cox, "A Passion for Service: Using Content Analysis to Explicate Service Climate Themes," *Journal of Applied Psychology* Vol. 77, No. 5 (1992), pp. 705–716.

15. See Benjamin Schneider, "The Service Organization: Climate Is Crucial," *Organizational Dynamics* (Autumn 1980), pp. 52–65; and Benjamin Schneider and David E. Bowen, "The Service Organization: Human Resource Management Is Crucial," *Organizational Dynamics* (Spring 1993), pp. 39–52.

16. Daniel Roth, "My Job at the Container Store," *Fortune* (January 10, 2000) 141 (1), pp. 74–78.

17. Adopted from Benjamin Schneider and David E. Bowen (1995), *Winning the Service Game*, Boston, MA: Harvard Business School Press.

18. David E. Bowen and Edward E. Lawler, III, "The Empowerment of Service Workers: What, Why, How, and When," *Sloan Management Review* (Spring 1992), pp. 31–39.

19. Martin L. Bell, "Tactical Services Marketing and the Process of Remixing," in *Marketing of Services*, W. R. George and J. M. Donnelly, eds. (Chicago: American Marketing Association, 1986), pp. 162–165.

20. James L. Heskett, Thomas O. Jones, Gary W. Loveman, W. Earl Sasser, Jr., and Leonard A. Schlesinger, "Putting the Service-Profit Chain to Work," *Harvard Business Review* (March–April 1994), pp. 164–174.

## CHAPTER 11

# PEOPLE ISSUES: MANAGING SERVICE CONSUMERS

## CHAPTER OBJECTIVES

*The purpose of this chapter is to explore the special role of the service consumer. Due to the impact of inseparability, the consumer's role in service production can both facilitate and hinder the exchange process. Hence, it is critical to develop a strategic understanding of how the consumer can be effectively managed within the service encounter.*

After reading this chapter, you should be able to:

- Discuss strategies for managing consumer participation within the service encounter.
- Describe approaches that manage consumer waits.
- Explain appropriate methods for dealing with difficult customers.
- Understand the fundamental components of an electronic customer relationship management (CRM) system.

*"Use your good judgment in all situations. There will be no additional rules."*

Nordstrom, Inc., Employee Handbook

# > THE SAGA OF "YOURS IS A VERY BAD HOTEL"

© ROB BRIMSON / TAXI / GETTY IMAGES

What began as a customer complaint by two directors of a Web design firm from the Pacific Northwest, eventually became one of the most talked about PowerPoint presentations of the new millennium. The presentation, titled "Yours Is a Very Bad Hotel" (which can be easily googled on the Web), documents the fearless twosome's troubles with a major hotelier in Houston. The story begins as our two now somewhat famous hotel guests, Tom Farmer and Shane Atchison of Seattle, Washington, attempted to check in to their guaranteed hotel room at approximately 2 a.m. The desk clerk, believing that the two would never show up to claim their room, gave the room away several hours earlier. Tom and Shane pointed out to the desk clerk that the room was guaranteed with a credit card; however, the desk clerk was unimpressed and certainly unapologetic. As you might imagine, this particular service encounter went downhill from there.

Upon returning home to Seattle, Tom and Shane decided to voice their dissatisfaction with a cleverly derived PowerPoint presentation that poignantly expressed their dissatisfaction with the whole situation. Highlights of the presentation include the projected career path of the loathsome desk clerk and the rare chance that Tom and Shane would ever return to the hotel (which exceeded the chance that the earth would be ejected from the solar system by the gravitational pull of a passing star—1 in 2,200,000!). The original presentation was sent only to the hotel's general manager and front desk manager as well as two clients/friends and Shane's mother-in-law. The last slide of the presentation invited viewers to pass along the presentation as they saw fit. In retrospect, Tom and Shane expected 20 to 30 people would ever see the presentation. Thanks to the help of the Internet, little did they know how much their "customer complaint" slideshow would travel around the world.

According to the latest update, Tom and Shane had been contacted by nearly 2,500 people on six continents, including places as far away as Cairo and the Maldive Islands. Correspondents consisted primarily of hospitality professionals, marketing/public relations people, quality assurance managers, and business school professors. The vast majority of contacts were amused and/or sympathetic; however, approximately 2 percent referred to Tom and Shane as "jerks" or worse. One person recommended that Tom and Shane seek psychological counseling. In addition to the personal contacts Tom and Shane received, the hotel was also overwhelmed by inquiries to the point that it was affecting hotel operations. The story then took on a life of its own as *The Wall Street Journal, Forbes,* MSNBC, *Travel Weekly,* and *USA Today* got involved in the melee.

In the end, Tom and Shane turned down most opportunities to seek publicity and recommended that any compensation they received from the hotel for their troubles be donated to the hotel's hometown Toys for Tot's campaign in the hotel's name. The hotel has apologized to Tom and Shane and provided feedback on how their complaint had impacted training policies at the local and corporate levels to improve overbooking policies.

The lesson to be learned by all of this is that customers have the power to make or break any business. Customers are an integral part of the service encounter and their dissatisfaction can have disastrous consequences. Successful service marketers learn how to effectively manage their customers, correct mistakes when mistakes are made, and build trusting and lasting relationships with their customer base. Effective service marketers are not focused on the short-term sale, but are masters at building long-term relationships.

Source: hotels.about.com/b/a/032743.htm accessed 25 May 2005.

## > INTRODUCTION

Ultimately, the success of many service encounters depends upon how effectively the service firm manages its clientele. As mentioned in previous chapters, the service encounter can be viewed as a three-way fight for control among the customer, the employee, and the organization itself.[1] The procedures and systems established by the organization to balance this arrangement are not created simply to add to the bureaucracy of the encounter but are primarily put in place to ensure profitability.

Unlike the goods manufacturer, who may seldom see an actual customer while producing the good in a secluded factory, service providers are often in constant contact with their customers and must construct their service operations with the customer's physical presence in mind. This interaction between customer and service provider defines a critical incident. Critical incidents represent the greatest opportunity for both gains and losses in regard to customer satisfaction and customer retention.

During the customer's interaction with the service provider, the customer provides input into the service production process. As such, the customer often plays a key role in the successful completion of the service encounter. The customer's involvement in the production process may vary from (1) a requirement that the customer be physically present to receive the service, such as in dental services, a haircut, or surgery; (2) a need for the customer to be present only to start and stop the service, such as in dry cleaning and auto repair; and (3) a need for the customer to be only mentally present, such as in participation in college courses that are transmitted via the Internet. Each scenario reflects different levels of customer contact, and as a result each service delivery system should be designed differently.

The focus of this chapter is on four consumer management areas of particular importance:

1. the management of consumer participation in the service process;
2. the management of consumer waiting periods,
3. dealing with difficult customers—managing to keep your cool while those around you are losing theirs; and
4. an introduction to an electronic CRM system.

## > MANAGING CUSTOMER PARTICIPATION

Overall, as customer participation increases, the efficiency of the operation decreases. The customer's involvement in the production process creates uncertainties in the scheduling of production. For example, the customer has a direct impact on the type of service desired, the length of the service delivery process, and the cycle of service demand. Attempting to manage consumer participation in the production process with efficient operating procedures is a delicate art.

**co-produce**
Service produced via a cooperative effort between customers and service providers.

Increasing consumer participation in the service delivery process has become a popular strategy to increase the supply of service available to the firm and to provide a form of service differentiation. By allowing consumers to **co-produce** at least part of

© PETER CADE / STONE / GETTY IMAGES

Bank customers can co-produce some of their banking services by using the bank's ATM. In this instance, the ATM enhances customer convenience by increasing banking availability to 24 hours a day and extends the bank's services to hundreds of convenient locations. In turn, the ATM frees bank employees to serve other customers and reduces the cost of providing banking services.

their own service, contact personnel are freed to perform other duties, such as serving other customers or engaging in noncustomer-related activities (such as completing paperwork). Increasing customer participation is associated with a number of advantages and disadvantages. The primary advantage to the customer and the service firm is that customers can customize their own service and produce it faster and less expensively than if the firm had produced it. Customers who pump their own gas, make their own salads, and pick their own strawberries are classic examples. On the other hand, increased levels of customer participation are also associated with the firm's losing control of quality; increased waste, which increases operating costs; and customer perceptions that the firm may be attempting to distance itself from its customers.

When making the transition from a full-service to a self-service operation, the firm needs to be sensitive to the reasons the customer may prefer one format over another. Guidelines have evolved that help facilitate this transition and avoid insensitivity.[2]

## DEVELOP CUSTOMER TRUST

Efforts to increase customer participation throughout the production process should not be interpreted as the firm's way of distancing itself from the customer. The firm should provide information to the customer that explains why self-service opportunities are being provided and the potential customer benefits. When it is readily apparent that the only reason the firm is offering self-service options is to benefit the firm, customers will quickly flock to full-service competitors.

## PROMOTE THE BENEFITS AND STIMULATE TRIAL

The typical benefits associated with self-service are convenience, customization, and cost savings to the customer. Self-service gas stations provide a cost savings, self-service salad and dessert bars allow customers to customize their own salads and ice cream sundaes, and automatic teller machines provide 24-hour service and extend the bank's services to hundreds of convenient locations.

To promote new self-service options, customers may need an incentive to stimulate trial. For example, one bank purposely rigged its new ATM to sporadically distribute more cash than its customers requested to stimulate trial of the machine. The cash was used as a promotional tool and was free to the customer. The strategy was originally intended to make customers aware of the new ATM's location and to encourage older clientele, who traditionally resist change, to use the ATM. Soon after the promotion started, clever college students began withdrawing and redepositing their money over and over again to increase their chances to win extra cash. The grand prize of $500 was eventually rewarded to an elderly gentleman, who believed the ATM had made a mistake and attempted to return the money to the bank. It took bank employees several attempts to convince the man that this was his money to take and that it had not been withdrawn from his account.

## UNDERSTAND CUSTOMER HABITS

Part of the problem when transferring from full-service to self-service is that we tend to forget why customers might prefer using full-service options in the first place. Despite the convenience of ATMs, many customers like the personalization of dealing with a particular teller. Friendships and trust develop that cannot be replaced by machinery. In addition, many bank customers will use an ATM for withdrawals, but refuse to make deposits through the same ATM. The thought of handing over checks and cash to a machine seems to be too much of a risk for some customers.

## PRETEST NEW PROCEDURES

All new self-service options should be thoroughly pretested, not only by the firm's employees but particularly by customers who do not have the advantage of full information. For example, the British postal system attempted to enlist the help of its customers by requesting them to use extremely long zip codes when addressing envelopes. The plan was a disaster. The zip codes were far too long to remember, and the public basically vetoed any further development of the project by simply refusing to participate.

Pretesting helps in identifying and correcting potential problems before new procedures are fully introduced. In many instances, the company may have only one or two chances to prove to customers the benefits of self-service alternatives, many of which are often offered on the corporate website (see E-Services in Action). However, if the website and/or on-site processes are flawed and/or difficult to understand, the firm may lose its chance to convince customers of the advantages. For example, more customers might use ATMs if the screens did not face the sun and were easier to read, if the machines had not initially frequently "eaten" the customer's ATM cards, and if customers did not have to be gymnasts to use drive-through ATMs from their vehicles.

## E - S E R V I C E S  *IN ACTION*

> ## DEVELOPING AN EFFECTIVE WEB STRATEGY: THE 7Cs OF CUSTOMER INTERFACE

A customer's online experience progresses over time through four unique stages: (1) Functionality—"The site works well"; (2) Intimacy—"The site understands my particular set of needs"; (3) Internalization—"Visiting the site is part of my daily life"; and (4) Evangelism—"I love to tell others about the site." As the customer transitions through each stage, the experience moves from a general reaction (functionality) to a personal reaction (intimacy and internalization) to an outer-directed action (evangelism). In other words, as customers move through each of the stages, loyalty to the organization increases, purchasing intensifies, customers willingly provide more feedback, and customers are more likely to share their positive experiences with others. The challenge for marketers is how to transition customers through each of the stages within an online environment.

Effective Web designs incorporate the 7Cs of customer interface:

- *Context*—what is the look and feel of the screen-to-customer interface? Is the context purely functional dominant such as http://www.altavista.com or is it more aesthetic-dominant such as http://www.axis-media.com?
- *Content*—what is the digital matter posted on the website? Content includes the organization's offering mix (products, information) and multimedia mix (text, audio, and graphics).
- *Community*—the site should provide the means to build a closer relationship between the customer and the firm, and between customer and other customers (e.g., chat rooms).
- *Customization*—the site should have the ability to modify itself based on the customer's past usage behavior (personalization), or provide the ability for the customer to modify the site based on their own preferences (tailoring).
- *Communication*—the customer should be provided with multiple means to enable a dialogue between the website and its users. Examples include the posting of toll-free numbers, e-mail, self-help capabilities, on-line help desks, and the organization's mailing address.
- *Connection*—what other sites are connected to the main website? Connections can vary from destination sites such as http://www.nytimes.com (which has few connections to other sites) to a hub site such as http://www.drkoop.com (which provides a balance between internal and external (linked) content to a portal site such as http://www.ceoexpress (which provides almost exclusively links to other sites).
- *Commerce*—the site should be constructed so that customers can easily conduct transactions. Commerce involves all aspects of the interface supporting transactions such as order confirmation, shipping confirmation, easy payment options, order fulfillment, handling questions, and handling returns.

Each of the 7Cs should reinforce one another and be specifically designed with the organization's target market in mind as they transition through the four stages of the online experience.

Source: Rafi A. Mohammed, Robert J. Fisher, Bernard J. Jaworski, and Aileen Cahill, *Internet Marketing: Building Advantage in a Networked Economy,* (Boston, MA: McGraw-Hill Irwin, 2002), 622–624; Ron Zemke and Tom Connellan, *E-service,* New York, New York: AMACOM, 2001).

### UNDERSTAND THE DETERMINANTS OF CONSUMER BEHAVIOR

When considering consumer benefits of self-service alternatives, firms should understand the determinants of consumer behavior. Why would a customer use an ATM instead of a bank teller? Or why would customers like to select and cook their own steaks in a fine dining restaurant? The consumer benefits promoted by the firm should be defined by the customer. For example, customers who work shifts other than the traditional 8-to-5 slot enjoy the 24-hour accessibility of ATMs. Other customers may simply be in a hurry, and the ATM provides a faster means of service. At self-service cookeries, the experience of selection and preparation may facilitate social interaction and/or be ego driven.

### TEACH CONSUMERS HOW TO USE SERVICE INNOVATIONS

Many of today's self-service options are technology driven, and in many cases, customers are left to fend for themselves in attempts to use these new alternatives. An "on your own" approach does not exactly encourage customers to try new self-service methods. For customers to be taught, employees must first know how to use the technology themselves. Nothing will turn off customers faster than employees who have no idea how to use the new systems themselves.

### MONITOR AND EVALUATE PERFORMANCE

Finally, if a firm's self-service option enjoys an initial success, it should be continuously monitored and evaluated throughout the year. Does demand fluctuate? What are the possible causes? Has demand increased, decreased, or leveled off? What other services do consumers want self-service access to? Customer surveys and focus groups will not only define satisfaction with today's services but will also provide insight pertaining to the needs of tomorrow.

### > MANAGING CONSUMER WAITS

In addition to managing consumer participation, service managers are often faced with managing other customer-related challenges as well. Because production and

them? The typical service job included low pay, no career path, no sense of pride, and no training in customer relations. Automation also contributed to the problem. Replacing human labor with machines indeed increased the efficiency of many operating systems, but often at the expense of distancing customers from the firm and leaving customers to fend for themselves. Finally, over the years, customers have become tougher to please. They are more informed than ever, their expectations have increased, and they are more particular about where they spend their discretionary dollars.

Researchers in the field of consumer satisfaction clearly recognized the connection between the study of satisfaction and the consumer movement. The connection among the marketing concept, satisfaction, and consumerism continues to be one of the driving forces behind the study of customer satisfaction.

> ## THE IMPORTANCE OF CUSTOMER SATISFACTION

The importance of customer satisfaction cannot be overstated. Without customers, the service firm has no reason to exist. Every service business needs to proactively define and measure customer satisfaction. It is naïve to wait for customers to complain in order to identify problems in the service delivery system or to gauge the firm's progress in customer satisfaction based on the number of complaints received. Consider the following figures gathered by the Technical Assistance Research Program (TARP):[2]

- The average business does not hear from 96 percent of its unhappy customers.
- For every complaint received, 26 customers actually have the same problem.
- The average person with a problem tells 9 or 10 people. Thirteen percent will tell more than 20.
- Customers who have their complaints satisfactorily resolved tell an average of five people about the treatment they received.
- Complainers are more likely to do business with you again than noncomplainers: 54–70 percent if resolved at all, and 95 percent if handled quickly.

The TARP figures demonstrate that customers do not actively complain to service firms themselves. Instead, consumers voice their dissatisfaction with their feet, by defecting to competitors, and with their mouths, by telling your existing and potential customers exactly how they were mistreated by your firm. Based on the TARP figures, a firm that serves 100 customers per week and boasts a 90-percent customer satisfaction rating will be the object of thousands of negative stories by the end of a year. For example, if 10 dissatisfied customers per week tell 10 of their friends of the poor service received, by the end of the year (52 weeks) 5,200 negative word-of-mouth communications will have been generated.

The TARP figures are not all bad news. Firms that effectively respond to customer complaints are the objects of positive word-of-mouth communications. Although positive news travels at half the rate of negative news, the positive stories can ultimately translate into customer loyalty and new customers. A firm should also learn from the TARP figures that complainers are the firm's friends. Complainers are a free source of market information, and the complaints themselves should be viewed as opportunities for the firm to improve its delivery systems, not as a source of irritation.

## > WHAT IS CUSTOMER SATISFACTION/DISSATISFACTION?

Although a variety of alternative definitions exist, the most popular definition of customer satisfaction/dissatisfaction is that it is a comparison of customer expectations to perceptions regarding the actual service encounter. (Alternative definitions are provided in Table 12.1.)[3] Comparing customer expectations with their perceptions is based on what marketers refer to as the **expectancy disconfirmation model.** Simply stated, if customer perceptions meet expectations, the expectations are said to be **confirmed,** and the customer is satisfied. If perceptions and expectations are not equal, then the expectation is said to be **disconfirmed.**

Although the term disconfirmation sounds like a negative experience, it is not necessarily so. There are two types of disconfirmations. If actual perceptions were less than what was expected, the result is a **negative disconfirmation,** which results in customer dissatisfaction and may lead to negative word-of-mouth publicity and/or customer defection (see B2B Services in Action). In contrast, a **positive disconfirmation** exists when perceptions exceed expectations, thereby resulting in customer satisfaction, positive word-of-mouth publicity, and customer retention.

Every day, consumers utilize the disconfirmation paradigm by comparing their expectations with perceptions. While dining at a resort restaurant on the west coast of Florida, our waiter not only provided everything we requested but also was very good at anticipating needs. My three-year-old niece had had enough fun and sun for the day and was very tired. She crawled up into a vacant booth located directly behind our table and went to sleep. The waiter, noticing her absence from our table and on his own

*expectancy disconfirmation model*
Model proposing that comparing customer expectations to their perceptions leads customers to have their expectations confirmed or disconfirmed.

*confirmed expectations*
Customer expectations that match customer perceptions.

*disconfirmed expectations*
Customer expectations that do not match customer perceptions.

*negative disconfirmation*
A nonmatch because customer perceptions are lower than customer expectations.

*positive disconfirmation*
A nonmatch because customer perceptions exceed customer expectations.

| TABLE 12.1 | ALTERNATIVE SATISFACTION DEFINITIONS |
|---|---|
| Normative deficit definition | Compares actual outcomes to those that are culturally acceptable. |
| Equity definition | Compares gains in a social exchange—if the gains are inequal, the loser is dissatisfied. |
| Normative standard definition | Expectations are based on what the consumer believes he/she *should* receive—dissatisfaction occurs when the actual outcome is different from the standard expectation. |
| Procedural fairness definition | Satisfaction is a function of the consumer's belief that he/she was treated fairly. |

Source: Keith Hunt, "Consumer Satisfaction, Dissatisfaction, and Complaining Behavior." *Journal of Social Issues* 47, no. 1 (1991), 109–110.

## B 2 B   S E R V I C E S   *IN ACTION*

### > J. D. POWER & ASSOCIATES TO THE RESCUE

Tired of waiting in automated telephone queues? You're not alone. One recent call to Sears' award-winning customer service center to set up a service appointment was particularly frustrating. After waiting 30 minutes and 30 seconds in the queue, a customer was told by the customer service representative that his call would have to be transferred to another department. This was the second call to the service center for the same problem. The first time the appointment was made, Sears failed to appear or call. Adding to the frustration, the recorded message played while on hold, touted Sears' superior service record, and promoted a sale that had ended days before. This scenario and thousands like it, begs the question: *Is anyone listening?*

Customer relationship management systems code incoming callers based on their profitability and then route calls directly to customer service representatives or automated telephone queues based on the caller's code level. For customers, the minutes spent listening to the messages played in automated queues can seem like hours. Douglas Faneuil, the ex-Merrill Lynch Aide who testified in the Martha Stewart trial, lightened up the mood of the courtroom as he explained that Martha Stewart threatened to dump Merrill because she hated the company's hold music. Merrill Lynch, like General Motors, IBM, and Dell, plays classical music. Wal-Mart plays country, the Salvation Army plays hymns, and Microsoft callers listen to silence—apparently believing in this case "nothing" is better than "something."

To date, there are approximately 100,000 call centers worldwide. Realizing the need for a rating system, J. D. Power & Associates have begun evaluating call centers based on how long callers are kept on hold and how satisfied customers are when they hang up. The top 20 percent of performers will hold the designation "Certified by Power", the remainder of firms will receive feedback regarding how to improve their service. For Power, the call center market holds much potential. Company fees range from $20,000 to $100,000 per review. Interestingly, research already conducted by J. D. Power and Associates has not indicated any difference in service between onshore and offshore call centers.

---

Source: Brian Hindo and Ira Sager, "Your Call is Important," *Business Week,* (February 23, 2004), Issue 3871, 14; Brain Hindo and Ira Sager, "Call Centers from 'A' to 'F', " *Business Week,* Issue 3864, 13.

initiative, placed a white tablecloth over her to use as a blanket. This particular incident combined with other incidents throughout the evening lead to a positive disconfirmation of our expectations. That evening's great service reinforced the notion that with so much poor service all around, customers really do notice when the service is excellent.

## > THE BENEFITS OF CUSTOMER SATISFACTION

Although some may argue that customers are unreasonable at times, little evidence can be found of extravagant customer expectations.[4] Consequently, satisfying customers is not an impossible task. In fact, meeting and exceeding customer expectations may reap several valuable benefits for the firm. Positive word-of-mouth generated from existing customers often translates into more new customers. For example, consider the positive publicity generated for the firms listed in the Top 10 Most Admired Companies listed in Table 12.2. In comparison, as a potential employee, would you have any reservations about working for the Bottom 10? Satisfied current customers often purchase more products more frequently and are less likely to be lost to competitors than are dissatisfied customers.

Companies who command high customer satisfaction ratings also seem to have the ability to insulate themselves from competitive pressures, particularly price competition. Customers are often willing to pay more and stay with a firm that meets their needs than to take the risk associated with moving to a lower-priced service offering. Finally, firms that pride themselves on their customer satisfaction efforts generally provide better environments in which to work. Within these positive work environments, organizational cultures develop where employees are challenged to perform and rewarded for their efforts. Table 12.3 provides an example of the types of attributes that are key in building great corporate reputations and the companies that excel at particular key attributes.

In and of themselves, customer satisfaction surveys also provide several worthwhile benefits. Such surveys provide a formal means of customer feedback to the firm, which may identify existing and potential problems. Satisfaction surveys also convey the message to customers that the firm cares about their well-being and values customer input concerning its operations.[5] However, the placement of customer feedback forms by some companies makes customers wonder if they really want the feedback (see Figure 12.1).

Other benefits are derived directly from the results of satisfaction surveys. Satisfaction results are often utilized in evaluating employee performance for merit and

| TABLE 12.2 | AMERICA'S MOST ADMIRED COMPANIES | |
|---|---|---|
| | **The Top Ten** | **The Bottom Ten** |
| | 1. General Electric | 495. Humana |
| | 2. Microsoft | 496. Revlon |
| | 3. Dell Computer | 497. Trans World Airlines |
| | 4. Cisco Systems | 498. CKE Restaurants |
| | 5. Wal-Mart Stores | 499. CHS Electronics |
| | 6. Southwest Airlines | 500. Rite Aid |
| | 7. Berkshire Hathaway | 501. Trump Resorts |
| | 8. Intel | 502. Fruit of the Loom |
| | 9. Home Depot | 503. Amereco |
| | 10. LucentTechnologies | 504. Caremark Rx |

Source: Geoffrey Colvin, "America's Most Admired Companies, *Fortune,* 141, no. 4 (February 21, 2000), 108.

| TABLE 12.3 | EIGHT KEY ATTRIBUTES OF REPUTATION |
| --- | --- |

| Attributes | Most Admired Companies |
| --- | --- |
| 1. Innovativeness | Charles Schwab, Herman Miler |
| 2. Quality of management | General Electric, Omnicom Corp. |
| 3. Employee talent | Goldman Sachs, Cisco Systems |
| 4. Financial soundness | Microsoft, Intel, Cisco Systems |
| 5. Use of corp. assets | Berkshire Hathaway, Cisco, General Electric |
| 6. Long-term investment value | Microsoft, Home Depot, Cisco Systems |
| 7. Social responsibility | McDonald's, Du Pont, Herman Miler |
| 8. Quality of products/services | Omnicom Group, Philip Morris, UPS |

Source: Geoffrey Colvin, "America's Most Admired Companies, *Fortune*, 141, no. 4 (February 21, 2000), 110.

| FIGURE 12.1 | DELTA CUSTOMER FEEDBACK CARD FROM SKY MAGAZINE |
| --- | --- |

Source: Vicki Escarra, "We're Listening," *SKY*, (February, 2000), pp. 128–129.

According to the "We're Listening" section of Delta's in-flight magazine, *SKY*, ". . . becoming No. 1 in the eyes of our customers is the top priority in our goal to be the world's greatest airline." However, the "We're Listening" section and the customer feedback card are printed on pages 128 and 129 of the 150-page magazine. What are your impressions of the comment card?

compensation reviews and for sales management purposes, such as the development of sales training programs. Survey results are also useful for comparison purposes to determine how the firm stacks up against the competition. When ratings are favorable, many firms utilize the results in their corporate advertising.[6]

## > MEASURING CUSTOMER SATISFACTION

Measures of customer satisfaction are derived via indirect and direct measures. **Indirect measures** of customer satisfaction include tracking and monitoring sales records,

**indirect measures**
Tracking customer satisfation through changes in sales, profits, and number of customer complaints registered.

profits, and customer complaints. Firms that rely solely on indirect measures are taking a passive approach to determining whether customer perceptions are meeting or exceeding customer expectations. Moreover, if the average firm does not hear from 96 percent of its unhappy customers, it is losing a great many customers while waiting for the other 4 percent to speak their minds.

***direct measures***
The proactive collection of customer satisfaction data through customer satisfaction surveys.

**Direct measures** of satisfaction are generally obtained via customer satisfaction surveys. However, to say the least, customer satisfaction surveys are not standardized among firms. For example, the scales used to collect the data vary (e.g., 5-point to 100-point scales), questions asked of respondents vary (e.g., general to specific questions), and data collection methods vary (e.g., personal interviews to self-administered questionnaires). The following section discusses the use of various scales.

## THE SCALE OF 100 APPROACH

Some firms request customers to rate the firm's performance on a scale of 100. In essence, the firm is asking customers to give the firm a grade. However, the problems with this approach are readily apparent. Let's say that the firm scores an average of 83. What does the 83 mean—the firm received a B-? Does an 83 mean the same thing to all customers? Not likely. More importantly, what should the firm do to improve its satisfaction rating? The 83 does not provide specific suggestions for improvements that would lead to an increased customer satisfaction rating.

## THE "VERY DISSATISFIED/VERY SATISFIED" APPROACH

Other firms present customers with a 5-point scale, which is typically labeled utilizing the following format:

1. Very Dissatisfied
2. Somewhat Dissatisfied
3. Neutral
4. Somewhat Satisfied
5. Very Satisfied

Firms utilizing this format generally combine the percentage of "somewhat satisfied" and "very satisfied" responses to arrive at a satisfaction rating. Similarly, firms that utilize a 10-point scale with anchor points of "very dissatisfied" and "very satisfied" define customer satisfaction as the percentage of customers rating their satisfaction higher than 6. Although this approach provides more meaning to the satisfaction rating itself, it still lacks the diagnostic power to indicate specific areas of improvement. In other words, regardless of whether a firm uses a 100-point, 10-point, or 5-point scale, the interpretive value of the information is restricted by its quantitative nature. Qualitative information is needed to highlight specific areas of improvement. This is exactly the problem Federal Express encountered when it set up it first customer satisfaction measurement program. Initially, customer satisfaction was measured on a 100-point scale and transaction success was defined as whether the package actually arrived the next day. Upon further

| TABLE 12.4 | FEDEX'S "HIERARCHY OF HORRORS" |
|---|---|

1. Wrong day delivery (packaged delivered a day later than promised)
2. Right day late delivery (packaged delivered on the promised day, but after the promised deadline)
3. Pick-up not made (failure to make a pick-up on the day requested)
4. Lost package
5. Customer misinformed by Federal Express (mistaken or inaccurate information on rates, schedules, etc.)
6. Billing and paperwork mistakes (invoice errors, overcharges, missing proof-of-delivery documents)
7. Employee performance failures (courtesy, responsiveness, etc.)
8. Damaged packages

Source: AMA Management Briefing, *Blueprints for Service Quality: The Federal Express Approach* (New York: AMA Membership Publications Division, 1991).

qualitative examination, Federal Express determined that transaction success as defined by the customer was a much broader concept (see Table 12.4). The company now proactively improves its customer satisfaction ratings by continually improving upon those activities that were identified by its customer base—termed "The Hierarchy of Horrors."

## THE COMBINED APPROACH

The combined approach utilizes the quantitative scores obtained by the "very dissatisfied/very satisfied" approach and adds a qualitative analysis of feedback obtained from respondents who indicated that they were less than "very satisfied." Customers who indicate that they are less than "very satisfied" are informing the firm that the delivery system is performing at levels lower than expected. By prompting customers to suggest how the firm could perform better, the firm can then categorize and prioritize the suggestions for continuous improvement efforts.

The combined approach provides two valuable pieces of information. The quantitative satisfaction rating provides a benchmark against which future company satisfaction surveys should be compared. In addition, the quantitative rating provides the means of comparing the firm's performance against its competition. Complementing the quantitative rating, the qualitative data provides diagnostic information and pinpoints areas for improvement. Combining the qualitative and quantitative data outperforms either approach used alone.

## > UNDERSTANDING CUSTOMER SATISFACTION RATINGS

After a consultant conducted a customer satisfaction survey for a regional engineering firm, the results revealed to upper management were that the firm commanded an

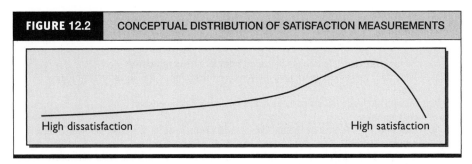

Source: Robert A. Peterson and William R. Wilson, "Measuring Customer Satisfaction: Fact and Artifact," *Journal of the Academy of Marketing Science* 20, 1 (1992), p. 61.

85 percent customer satisfaction rating. Immediately, upper management wanted to know whether 85 percent was a "good" satisfaction rating or not. To effectively utilize customer satisfaction ratings, it is necessary to understand the factors that may influence customer responses.

Despite the lack of standardization among satisfaction studies, they share one common characteristic. "Virtually all self-reports of customer satisfaction possess a distribution in which a majority of the responses indicate that customers are satisfied and the distribution itself is negatively skewed."[7] Figure 12.2 depicts the negatively skewed distribution of customer satisfaction results.

Typically, customer satisfaction ratings are fairly high. Table 12.5 displays a sample of customer satisfaction results across various industries. As can be viewed from the table, it is not unusual to see results in the 80–90 percent range. Repeated findings such as these have led some researchers to conclude that "to feel above average is normal."

## FACTORS INFLUENCING CUSTOMER SATISFACTION RATINGS

Satisfaction ratings may be influenced by numerous confounding factors that occur during the data collection process. The following section provides explanations for inflated satisfaction results and reinforces the notion that obtaining accurate measures of customer satisfaction is not an easily accomplished task.

### Customers Are Genuinely Satisfied
One possible reason for high satisfaction scores is simply that customers are satisfied with the goods and services they typically purchase and consume—that's why they buy these products from the firm in the first place! Intuitively, this makes good sense. If the majority of customers were neutral or dissatisfied, they would most likely defect to competitive offerings of goods and services. Of course, this explanation assumes that competitors in the market are better at providing goods and services than the original supplier (see E-services in Action).

**response bias**
A bias in survey results because of responses being received from only a limited group among the total survey population.

### Response Bias
Another possible explanation for inflated satisfaction results may be **response bias.** Some experts argue that the reason ratings are so high is that companies hear from only

| TABLE 12.5 | SAMPLING OF SATISFACTION RESULTS |
|---|---|

| Sample | Percentage Satisfied |
|---|---|
| British Airways customers | 85 |
| HMO enrollees | 92 |
| Sears' customers | 84 |
| Children's instructional programs/parents | 82 |
| Medical care | 84 |
| Clothing/and white goods/adults | 82 |
| Shoes/students | 83 |

Source: Robert A. Peterson and William R. Wilson, "Measuring Customer Satisfaction: Fact and Artifact," *Journal of the Academy of Marketing Science* 20, no. 1 (1992), 61.

satisfied customers. In contrast, dissatisfied customers do not believe that the firm's survey will do them any good; therefore, the questionnaire is discarded.

Other experts discount this explanation. Their argument is that it makes more sense for highly dissatisfied customers to express their opinion than it does for highly satisfied customers to do so. This position is supported by prior research, which indicates that dissatisfaction itself is more action oriented and emotionally intense than satisfaction.[8] Others argue that it is possible that highly dissatisfied customers and highly satisfied customers are more likely to respond than are those who are more neutral. Although these additional explanations are intriguing, they fail to explain the traditional response distribution depicted in Figure 12.2.

### Data Collection Method

A third explanation for inflated satisfaction scores is the **data collection method** used to obtain results. Prior research suggests that higher levels of satisfaction are obtained via personal interviews and phone surveys compared with results from mail questionnaires and/or self-administered interviews. In fact, studies indicate that as much as a 10-percent difference exists between questionnaires administered orally and self-administered questionnaires. The reason is that respondents to personal interviews and phone surveys may feel awkward expressing negative statements to other "live" individuals as opposed to expressing them anonymously on a self-administered questionnaire.

Research on data collection modes' effects on satisfaction ratings has produced some interesting results. The data collection mode does indeed appear to influence the level of reported satisfaction; however, the negatively skewed distribution of the satisfaction ratings remains unchanged, regardless of the data collection mode.

*data collection method*
The method used to collect information, such as questionnaires, surveys, and personal interviews.

### Question Form

The way the question is asked on the questionnaire, or the **question form,** has also been offered as a possible explanation for inflated satisfaction ratings. It does appear that the question's being asked in positive form ("How satisfied are you?") as opposed to

*question form*
The way a question is phrased, i.e., positively or negatively.

# E-SERVICES *IN ACTION*

## > HUMANIZING THE NET VIA INNOVATIVE E-SERVICE

What is e-service? Strictly speaking, *e-service* pertains to customer service support provided on the Net. E-service plays a critical role in online customer satisfaction. Ultimately, e-service humanizes the Net by providing various customer service activities while simultaneously reducing the online firm's operating costs. Examples include the following:

- *Electronic Order Confirmation*—Noted as one of the easiest and most cost-effective methods to increase customer satisfaction, electronic order confirmation notifies customers within seconds or minutes that their order has been received by detailing the item purchased, quantity selected, cost of the item, shipping charges, and order availability.
- *Package Tracking Services*—Once an order has been placed, effective e-tailers also notify customers when their purchases have been shipped and provide an expected delivery date. In addition, the best companies also provide package tracking identification numbers so that customers can track the physical movement of their purchases through a shipper's website (for example, FedEx or UPS).
- *Electronic Wallets*—According to one study, two-thirds of all shopping carts are left at the virtual checkout counter. Checking out online can be a lengthy process as customers enter their credit card information, phone numbers, billing address, shipping address, etc. Electronic wallets have been designed for repeat customers where the customer's credit card and desired shipping preferences are stored on the company's server and automatically appear when the customer places an order.
- *Co-browsing*—In order to facilitate the social aspects of online shopping, e-tailers that offer co-browsing opportunities enable users to access the same website simultaneously from two different locations. Live text boxes are also provided so that users can chat online while making their purchase decisions.
- *Live Text Chats*—In addition to enabling customer-to-customer communications, live text chats are also facilitating customer-to-e-tailer communications. Innovative outsourcing firms, such as liveperson.com, staff a number of major e-tailer's live text chats and respond to customer inquiries online, often in under 60 seconds.
- *Merchandise Return Services*—Twenty-five percent of all merchandise purchased online is returned and the rate is higher in some industries, such as apparel. Today, many e-tailers include Supply Return Authorizations with their shipments to facilitate the return process. Other e-tailers outsource their return activities to the United States Postal Service's E-Merchandise Return Service, which enables customers to print return labels from the e-tailer's website and drop returns off at the Post Office.
- *Collaborative Filtering*—This software program facilitates suggestive selling by monitoring the purchasing behavior of like-minded customers online and then suggesting

in real-time what other customers have purchased. For example, based on Customer A's past purchase behavior, Amazon.com will suggests to Customer A book titles of interest based on what others have purchased who also purchased the same title as Customer A.

Source: Rafi A. Mohammed, Robert J. Fisher, Bernard J. Jaworski, and Aileen Cahill (2002). *Internet Marketing: Building Advantage in a Networked Economy,* Boston, MA: McGraw-Hill Irwin. Zemke and Connellan, e-Service, AMACOM.

negative form ("How dissatisfied are you?") does have an impact on satisfaction ratings. Asking a question in the positive form appears to lead to greater reported levels of satisfaction than does posing the question in a negative form.

Table 12.6 presents results from a study about the effects of stating the same question in two forms. In one version, the question asked respondents "how satisfied" they were, and in the other version, the question asked "how dissatisfied" they were. Results reveal that 91 percent of respondents reported feeling "very" or "somewhat satisfied" when the question was stated in its positive form but only 82 percent when stated in the negative form. Similarly, 9 percent of respondents expressed that they were somewhat or very dissatisfied when asked in the positive form, compared with nearly 18 percent when asked in the negative form.

### Context of the Question

The **question context** may also affect the satisfaction rating. Question context effects pertain to the ordering of questions and whether questions asked earlier in a questionnaire influence answers to subsequent questions. For example, in a study concerning satisfaction with vehicles, asking a general satisfaction question (e.g., "In general, how satisfied are you with the products in your house?") prior to a specific vehicle satisfaction question (e.g., "How satisfied are you with your Saturn?") increased the tendency toward a "very satisfied" response for the specific question.

*question context*
The placement and tone of a question relative to the other questions asked.

| TABLE 12.6 | RESPONSES BY QUESTION FORM | |
|---|---|---|

| Response Category | Question Form | |
|---|---|---|
| | "Satisfied" | "Dissatisfied" |
| Very satisfied | 57.4% | 53.4% |
| Somewhat satisfied | 33.6% | 28.7% |
| Somewhat dissatisfied | 5.0% | 8.5% |
| Very dissatisfied | 4.0% | 9.4% |

Source: Robert A. Peterson and William R. Wilson, "Measuring Customer Satisfaction: Fact and Artifact," *Journal of the Academy of Marketing Science* 20, no. 1 (1992), 65.

### Timing of the Question

Satisfaction ratings may also be influenced by the **timing of the question** relative to the date of purchase. Customer satisfaction appears to be highest immediately after a purchase and then begins to decrease over time. Again, regarding automobile purchases, researchers have noted a 20-percent decline in satisfaction ratings over a 60-day period. It is not clear whether the initial ratings are inflated to compensate for feelings of cognitive dissonance or the latter ratings are deflated. Some consideration has been given that there may be different types of satisfaction measured at different points in time.

Another possible explanation is that satisfaction rates may decay over time as customers reflect upon their purchase decision. Prior research indicates that the influence of negative events, which are more memorable than positive events, carries more weight in satisfaction evaluations over time. Consequently, satisfaction surveys distributed longer after purchases provide respondents the opportunity to take retribution as they recall such negative events.

### Social Desirability Bias

**Social desirability bias** describes a respondent's tendency to provide information that the respondent believes is socially appropriate. In satisfaction surveys, some researchers argue that respondents tend to withhold critical judgment because to do otherwise would be socially inappropriate. This would explain high satisfaction ratings and the shape of the distribution of results. Although the explanation is intriguing, widespread empirical support is lacking.

### Mood

One more factor that could possibly influence customer satisfaction ratings is the mood of the customer while completing the survey. An abundance of research demonstrates the influence of positive mood states toward prosocial behaviors.[9] More specifically, prior research has shown that respondents in positive mood states make more positive judgments, rate products they own more favorably, tend to see the brighter side of things, and are more likely to rate strangers favorably. Hence, consumers in positive moods should give higher marks to service personnel and service firms than their neutral- or negative-mood counterparts.

> ## ARE CUSTOMER SATISFACTION SURVEYS WORTH IT?

Given the number of factors that may distort the "true" customer satisfaction ratings, one may wonder whether it is worth spending the time and money to measure satisfaction at all. Customer satisfaction ratings may fall under the category of the *Hawthorne effect,* that is, in and of themselves, satisfaction surveys might increase customer satisfaction regardless of the good or service being evaluated. Furthermore, due to the already high levels of customer satisfaction that already exist for most firms, it may not make sense to attempt to increase satisfaction levels across the board. However, two areas of satisfaction that do deserve special attention are (1) company attempts to maintain satisfaction over time to counter the decay effect, and (2) concentration on the tail of the satisfaction distribution—those customers who are dissatisfied. In and of themselves, satisfaction ratings cannot be interpreted with much meaning. Consequently, **benchmarking** with past satisfaction measures and comparisons with competition provide more meaningful feedback to companies.

*benchmarking*
Setting standards against which to compare future data collected.

All in all, despite all the possible complications and given the benefits derived from customer satisfaction, when firms use satisfaction surveys in conjunction with other measures, such as those described later in this chapter, the information provided is invaluable.

## > CUSTOMER SATISFACTION: HOW GOOD IS GOOD ENOUGH?

How much satisfaction is enough? At 98 percent, a company that completes 1,000 transactions per week upsets 20 customers per week, who tell 9 or 10 of their friends. Given this scenario, the bottom line translates into 200 negative stories per week and 10,400 negative stories per year. Although these numbers provide support for continuous improvements that enhance customer satisfaction ratings, we tend to forget that for every percentage of satisfaction improvement, very real investment costs are involved.

For example, if a firm currently boasts a 95-percent customer satisfaction rating, is it worth a $100,000 investment to improve satisfaction to 98 percent?[10] It depends. Pete Babich, the quality manager for the San Diego division of Hewlett-Packard, was faced with this exact question. Hewlett-Packard defines customer satisfaction as the customer's willingness to refer Hewlett-Packard products to friends. Hewlett-Packard has found that 70 percent of its purchases are made because of previous positive experiences with the product or referrals from others.

Although Babich found an abundance of anecdotal evidence that retaining customers was much less expensive than seeking out new customers, this information failed to answer his original question: Is it worth $100,000 investment to improve satisfaction to 98 percent? As a result, Babich proceeded to develop a customer satisfaction model that would predict market share changes over time as they related to customer satisfaction ratings.

The model is based on an algorithm that can easily be converted into a spreadsheet and that is built upon a number of assumptions. First, in this particular example, the model assumes a closed market of three firms that begin at period "zero" with equal market shares (i.e., 33.3 percent). The three firms offer comparable products and prices and compete for a growing customer base. Next, the model assumes that satisfied consumers will continue to buy from the same firm and that dissatisfied customers will defect to other firms in the market. For example, dissatisfied customers of Firm A will buy at Firm B or Firm C during the next time period. The length of the time period varies, depending on the product (e.g., eye exam versus lawn care).

The direction of customer defection depends upon the firm's market share. In other words, if Firm C's market share is higher than Firm B's market share, Firm C will obtain a higher share of Firm A's dissatisfied customers. This logic is based on the premise that dissatisfied customers will be more particular the next time around and will conduct more research and seek out referrals from others. In this case, due to Firm C's higher market share, Firm C would be the beneficiary of more positive referrals.

Results generated from the customer satisfaction model when given three different scenarios are presented in Figure 12.3. Panel (a) illustrates the scenario of how a firm

| FIGURE 12.3 | CUSTOMER SATISFACTION MODEL: THREE SCENARIOS |

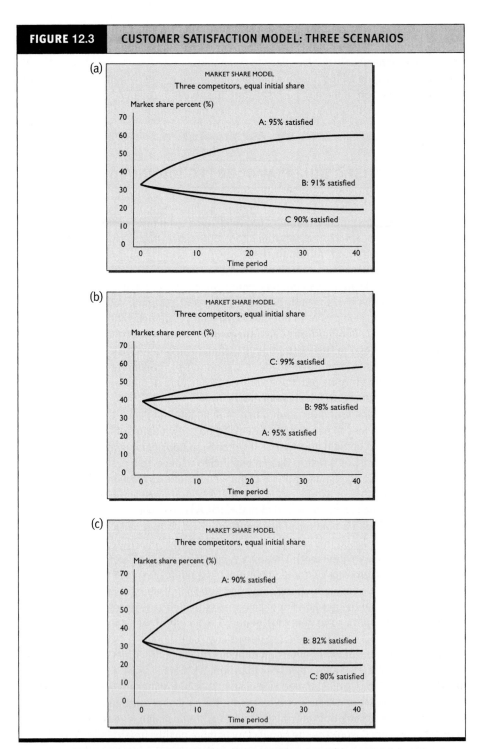

Source: Adapted from Peter Babich, "Customer Satisfaction: How Good Is Good Enough," *Quality Progress* (December 1992), pp. 65–67.

with a 95-percent customer satisfaction rating would stack up against firms commanding 90-percent and 91-percent customer satisfaction ratings. Clearly, the firm with 95-percent satisfaction dominates the market after 12 time periods. Panel (b) of the figure illustrates how that same firm with a 95-percent satisfaction rating would compete with firms commanding 98-percent and 99-percent ratings. In this scenario, the 95-percent firm controls less than 10 percent of the market after 24 time periods. This scenario dramatically illustrates the impact of the competition's satisfaction ratings.

Finally, Panel (c) illustrates the effect of customer satisfaction on market share at lower customer satisfaction levels. In this scenario, Firms A, B, and C command satisfaction ratings of 90 percent, 82 percent, and 80 percent, respectively. In essence, this panel illustrates the effect of increasing the dissatisfaction levels of Panel (a) by 2. In this scenario, Firm A once again achieves market dominance, but at a much faster rate.

What does Peter Babich's customer satisfaction model tell us? First, firms with higher customer satisfaction ratings make the firm more resistant to competitors' efforts to improve their market share. Secondly, if the firm knows what a 1-percent improvement in market share does for its bottom line, then comparing the 1-percent increase in market share to the investment needed to improve customer satisfaction gives the firm the necessary information to make a business decision. Finally, the model points out the necessity of knowing not only your own firm's satisfaction rating, but also your competitors'.

Should a firm invest $100,000 to improve customer satisfaction ratings from 95 percent to 98 percent? It depends upon several factors:

- the satisfaction ratings of the firm's competitors,
- the dollar investment necessary to increase customer satisfaction relative to the impact of increasing the firm's market share,
- the number of time periods required to recoup the investment, and
- the opportunity costs associated with other uses of the $100,000.

> ## DOES CUSTOMER SATISFACTION TRANSLATE INTO CUSTOMER RETENTION?

High satisfaction ratings do not necessarily mean that a firm is going to retain a customer forever.[11] In fact, according to one group of consultants, on average, 65 percent to 85 percent of customers who defect to competitors say they were "satisfied" or "very satisfied" with their former providers. Five criticisms of customer satisfaction research as they relate to customer retention provide insights into why firms with high satisfaction ratings may potentially lose customers. First, satisfaction research focuses on whether current needs are being met but fails to investigate customers' future needs. As customers' needs change, they will seek out a firm that best satisfies this new set of needs. Consequently, the progressive service firm must proactively engage in assessing its customers' future needs.

A second criticism of customer satisfaction research is that it tends to focus on registered complaints. According to the TARP figures presented earlier, many customers who defect never relay their complaints to an employee or the firm's management. Consequently, satisfaction research that examines only registered complaints overlooks a

H&R Block responded to its customers' growing need for convenience at tax time by providing three convenient methods for submitting tax information. Customers can meet face-to-face with a tax professional, skip a meeting and simply drop off their tax information and pick up their return when it's completed, or submit everything electronically and work with an online tax professional. By providing three methods for submitting tax information, H&R Block satisfied the tax needs of today's busy customers.

© TIM BOYLE / GETTY IMAGES

great deal of information. In addition, limiting research to only registered complaints most likely also overlooks many of the problems that need to be remedied in order to lower defection rates.

A third criticism is that customer satisfaction research tends to focus on global attributes and ignores operational elements. For example, firms often phrase questions in their customer satisfaction questionnaires using broad, global statements such as "The firm provides good service" and "The firm has good employees." Global statements such as these overlook the operational elements that make up these statements. Examples of operational elements that measure employee performance may include such items as eye contact, product knowledge, courteous actions, and credibility. Operational elements pertaining to good service might include the amount of time it takes to check in and check out at a hotel, the cleanliness of the facility, and the hours of operation. Utilizing global attributes instead of operational elements in surveys fails to provide the company with the information it needs for developing effective solutions to problems. Consider, for example, the operational usefulness of the Sheraton Hotels and Resorts Guest Satisfaction Survey conducted by J.D. Power and Associates, presented in Table 12.7.

A fourth criticism of customer satisfaction research is that it often excludes the firm's employees from the survey process. Employee satisfaction drives customer loyalty. Employees' perceptions of the service delivery system need to be compared with customers' perceptions. This process provides feedback to employees about the firm's performance and assists in ensuring that employees and customers are on the same wavelength. As internal customers, employees often contribute valuable suggestions for improving the firm's operations.

Finally, a fifth criticism is that some firms are convinced that customers may not know what they want and that sometimes ignoring the customer is the best strategy to follow, particularly when it comes to new product innovation.[12] Some believe that firms can go overboard listening to customers, thereby becoming slaves to demographics, market research, and focus groups. And, in fact, listening to customers often does discourage

**TABLE 12.7**    SHERATON HOTELS AND RESORTS GUEST SATISFACTION SURVEY

## SHERATON HOTELS & RESORTS GUEST SATISFACTION SURVEY

MAKE YOUR ANSWERS COUNT!    Correct Mark ☒ ☑

1. How likely are you to...

| | Very Likely | Somewhat Likely | Somewhat Unlikely | Very Unlikely |
|---|---|---|---|---|
| Return to this hotel if you are in the same area again? | ☐ | ☐ | ☐ | ☐ |
| Recommend this hotel to a friend or colleague planning to visit the area? | ☐ | ☐ | ☐ | ☐ |
| Stay at a Sheraton hotel again? | ☐ | ☐ | ☐ | ☐ |

2. How satisfied were you with...    **Outstanding** ←————————————————→ **Unacceptable**

| | | | | | | | | | |
|---|---|---|---|---|---|---|---|---|---|
| Your overall experience as a guest in this hotel | ☐ | ☐ | ☐ | ☐ | ☐ | ☐ | ☐ | ☐ | ☐ |
| The value for the price paid | ☐ | ☐ | ☐ | ☐ | ☐ | ☐ | ☐ | ☐ | ☐ |
| Cleanliness and maintenance of hotel | ☐ | ☐ | ☐ | ☐ | ☐ | ☐ | ☐ | ☐ | ☐ |
| Responsiveness of staff to your needs | ☐ | ☐ | ☐ | ☐ | ☐ | ☐ | ☐ | ☐ | ☐ |
| Knowledge of staff | ☐ | ☐ | ☐ | ☐ | ☐ | ☐ | ☐ | ☐ | ☐ |

**Check-in**

| | | | | | | | | | |
|---|---|---|---|---|---|---|---|---|---|
| Accuracy of reservation | ☐ | ☐ | ☐ | ☐ | ☐ | ☐ | ☐ | ☐ | ☐ |
| Speed/efficiency of check-in | ☐ | ☐ | ☐ | ☐ | ☐ | ☐ | ☐ | ☐ | ☐ |
| Staff friendliness at check-in | ☐ | ☐ | ☐ | ☐ | ☐ | ☐ | ☐ | ☐ | ☐ |

**Guest Room**

| | | | | | | | | | |
|---|---|---|---|---|---|---|---|---|---|
| Size of room | ☐ | ☐ | ☐ | ☐ | ☐ | ☐ | ☐ | ☐ | ☐ |
| Comfort of bed | ☐ | ☐ | ☐ | ☐ | ☐ | ☐ | ☐ | ☐ | ☐ |
| Room décor/furnishings | ☐ | ☐ | ☐ | ☐ | ☐ | ☐ | ☐ | ☐ | ☐ |
| Ability to work in guest room | ☐ | ☐ | ☐ | ☐ | ☐ | ☐ | ☐ | ☐ | ☐ |
| Cleanliness of guest room | ☐ | ☐ | ☐ | ☐ | ☐ | ☐ | ☐ | ☐ | ☐ |
| Maintenance of guest room | ☐ | ☐ | ☐ | ☐ | ☐ | ☐ | ☐ | ☐ | ☐ |
| Cleanliness of bathroom | ☐ | ☐ | ☐ | ☐ | ☐ | ☐ | ☐ | ☐ | ☐ |
| Bath/shower water pressure | ☐ | ☐ | ☐ | ☐ | ☐ | ☐ | ☐ | ☐ | ☐ |

**Hotel Services (If Used)**

| | | | | | | | | | | |
|---|---|---|---|---|---|---|---|---|---|---|
| Helpfulness of bell staff | ☐ | ☐ | ☐ | ☐ | ☐ | ☐ | ☐ | ☐ | ☐ | ☐ N/A |
| Hotel safety/security | ☐ | ☐ | ☐ | ☐ | ☐ | ☐ | ☐ | ☐ | ☐ | ☐ N/A |

**Food and Dining (If Used)**

| | | | | | | | | | | |
|---|---|---|---|---|---|---|---|---|---|---|
| Food quality | ☐ | ☐ | ☐ | ☐ | ☐ | ☐ | ☐ | ☐ | ☐ | ☐ N/A |
| Speed/efficiency of service | ☐ | ☐ | ☐ | ☐ | ☐ | ☐ | ☐ | ☐ | ☐ | ☐ N/A |
| Room service speed/efficiency | ☐ | ☐ | ☐ | ☐ | ☐ | ☐ | ☐ | ☐ | ☐ | ☐ N/A |

**Check-Out**

| | | | | | | | | | |
|---|---|---|---|---|---|---|---|---|---|
| Speed/efficiency of check-out process | ☐ | ☐ | ☐ | ☐ | ☐ | ☐ | ☐ | ☐ | ☐ |
| Accuracy of billing | ☐ | ☐ | ☐ | ☐ | ☐ | ☐ | ☐ | ☐ | ☐ |

3. Please rate...

| | | | | | | | | | |
|---|---|---|---|---|---|---|---|---|---|
| Delivery of Sheraton promise "I'll take care of you" | ☐ | ☐ | ☐ | ☐ | ☐ | ☐ | ☐ | ☐ | ☐ |
| This experience compared to other Sheraton hotels | ☐ | ☐ | ☐ | ☐ | ☐ | ☐ | ☐ | ☐ | ☐ |

4. Are you a member of the Starwood Preferred Guest Program?    ☐ Yes    ☐ No

5. If you are a member of the Starwood Preferred Guest Program, how satisfied were you with the benefits you received during your stay?    ☐ ☐ ☐ ☐ ☐ ☐ ☐ ☐ ☐    ☐ N/A

6. Please mark any problem you experienced during your stay. **(MARK ALL THAT APPLY)**

| | | | |
|---|---|---|---|
| ☐ Air conditioner/heater | ☐ Hotel maintenance | ☐ Reservation date | ☐ Room maintenance |
| ☐ Bathroom cleanliness | ☐ Noise | ☐ Reservation rate | ☐ Room readiness |
| ☐ Check-in | ☐ No reservation | ☐ Responsiveness of staff | ☐ Sink/tub/toilet |
| ☐ Guest room cleanliness | ☐ Number of towels | ☐ Room assignment | ☐ Other |

7. Did you contact anyone in the hotel to resolve the problem?    ☐ Yes    ☐ No

8. Was the problem resolved to your satisfaction?    ☐ Yes    ☐ No

9. Which of the following best describes the reason for your stay?    ☐ Business    ☐ Both Business/Leisure
☐ Leisure    ☐ Meeting/Conference

10. Your gender:    ☐ Female    ☐ Male

Please write in your e-mail address: |_|_|_|_|_|_|_|_|_|_|_|_|_|_|_|_|_|_|_|_|_|_|_|_|_|_|_|_|_|

Additional comments: _____

Please return in the enclosed envelope to: J.D. Power and Associates, 30401 Agoura Road, Suite 200, Agoura Hills, CA 91301

Source: J.D. Power and Associates, Agoura Hills, CA 91301.

truly innovative products. As evidence, 90 percent of so-called new products are simply line extensions of existing products.

Listening to customers does have its drawbacks. Customers often focus on current needs and have a difficult time projecting their needs into the future. In addition, consumers sometimes pick up cues from the person asking questions and attempt to answer questions in a direction that will please the interviewer. Other problems include the consumer being in a hurry, not fully understanding what is being asked, not wanting to be rude and so cheerfully agreeing with whatever is being asked, and most importantly, not making decisions using real money.

The list of products consumers initially rejected that went on to be huge successes is impressive. Products such as the Chrysler minivan, fax machines, VCRs, FedEx, CNN, Compaq PC servers, cellular phones, personal digital assistants, microwave ovens, and even Birdseye frozen foods were all rejected by customers during initial survey attempts. In contrast, products that surveyed customers indicated would be great successes, such as McDonald's McLean, KFC's skinless fried chicken, Pizza Hut's low-calorie pizza, and New Coke, among others, turned out to be flops.

The problem is not so much listening to what customers have to say as it is companies feeling paralyzed to make strategic moves without strong consumer support. Of course, customers should not be completely ignored. However, some marketers argue that the best consumer information is obtained through detached observation instead of through traditional survey techniques: "Ignore what your customers say; pay attention to what they do."[13]

---

## > CUSTOMER SATISFACTION: A CLOSER LOOK

So far, this chapter has provided a broad overview of customer satisfaction. The following section takes a closer look at customer expectations and how they relate to customer satisfaction and service quality assessments (see Global Services in Action). This section further defines customer satisfaction and provides the transition into the next chapter, which focuses solely on service quality issues.

### TYPES OF CUSTOMER EXPECTATIONS

At first glance, comparing expectations with perceptions when developing customer satisfaction evaluations sounds fairly straightforward. Expectations serve as benchmarks against which present and future service encounters are compared. However, this relatively simple scenario becomes a bit more confusing when you realize that there exist at least three different types of expectations.[14]

**Predicted service** is a **probability expectation** that reflects the level of service customers believe is likely to occur. For example, bank customers tend to conduct their banking business at the same location over time. Customers become accustomed to dealing with the same bank personnel and, over time, begin to anticipate certain performance levels. It is generally agreed that customer satisfaction evaluations are developed by comparing predicted service to perceived service received (see Figure 12.4).

*predicted service*
The level of service quality a consumer believes is likely to occur.

*probability expectation*
A customer expectation based on the customer's opinion of what will be most likely when dealing with service personnel.

## GLOBAL SERVICES *IN ACTION*

### > GLOBAL CUSTOMER SATISFACTION: THE INFLUENCE OF COLORS, NUMBERS, SMELLS, AND ANIMALS

Throughout the world, the case can be made that customer satisfaction is achieved by meeting and/or exceeding customer expectations. Consequently, increases in customer satisfaction may be strategically achieved by lowering customer expectations prior to arrival, and/or managing perceptions as the customer experiences the service encounter. However, the most complicated task of achieving global satisfaction is understanding the basis of different cultures' expectations and perceptions. Consider, for example, the differences in the meaning of colors, numbers, smells, and animals around the world.

Colors symbolize different ideas among the world's nations. Where white is the color of birth in the West, it symbolizes mourning in the East. In contrast, black is an everyday color in the East, but symbolizes death in the West. In fact, the color of mourning varies greatly around the word—purple in Brazil, yellow in Mexico, and dark red on the Ivory Coast. In America, green suggests freshness and good health; however, in countries with dense green jungles, green suggests disease. When projecting masculinity, blue is the color of choice in America and red is the manly color in the United Kingdom and France. Red is interpreted as a sign of good fortune in China but is associated with death in Turkey. If trying to project a more feminine image, pink is the most feminine color in America, but it is yellow that is more feminine in other parts of the world.

Service marketers must also carefully consider the meanings of smells, numbers, and animals when communicating with international markets. While the smell of lemon is associated with freshness in America, the same smell is associated with illness in the Philippines. In America, the number 13 is considered unlucky; however, the unlucky number in Japan is 4, and in Ghana, Kenya, and Singapore it is 7. In contrast, "lucky 7" is a common phrase in America. Finally, care should be taken when using animals to create various images. Although the owl may symbolize wisdom in America, it translates to bad luck in India (similar to a black cat in the U.S.). Moreover, a company might align itself with a fox to symbolize its intellect ("smart as a fox"), but in Japan that same company would be associated with witches.

Source: Jean-Claude Usunier and Julie Anne Lee, *Marketing Across Cultures*, 4th ed. (Harlow, England: Prentice Hall, 2005), 264.

**Desired service** is an **ideal expectation** that reflects what customers actually want compared with predicted service, which is what is likely to occur. Hence, in most instances, desired service reflects a higher expectation than predicted service. For example, our bank customer's desired service is that he not only receive his predicted service but that the tellers call him by his first name and enthusiastically greet him as he

*desired service*
The level of service quality a customer actually wants from a service encounter.

| FIGURE 12.4 | COMPARISON BETWEEN CUSTOMER EVALUATION OF SERVICE QUALITY AND CUSTOMER SATISFACTION |
| --- | --- |

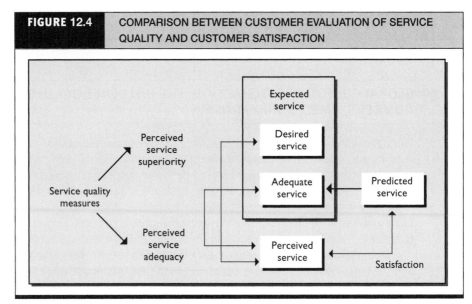

Source: Adapted from Valerie A. Zeithaml, Leonard L. Berry, and A. Parasuraman, "The Nature and Determinants of Customer Expectations of Service," *Journal of the Academy of Marketing Science* 21, 1 (1993), pp. 1–12.

**ideal expectation**
A customer's expectation of what a "perfect" service encounter would be.

**perceived service superiority**
A measure of service quality derived by comparing desired service expectations and perceived service received.

**adequate service**
The level of service quality a customer is willing to accept.

**minimum tolerable expectation**
A customer expectation based on the absolute minimum acceptable outcome.

**perceived service adequacy**
A measure of service quality derived by comparing adequate service and perceived service.

**zone of tolerance**
Level of quality ranging from high to low and reflecting the difference between desired service and adequate service; expands and contracts across customers and within the same customer, depending on the service and the conditions under which it is provided.

enters the bank. Comparing desired service expectations to perceived service received results in a measure of **perceived service superiority** (see Figure 12.4).

In contrast, **adequate service** is a **minimum tolerable expectation** and reflects the level of service the customer is willing to accept. Adequate service is based on experiences or norms that develop over time. For example, most adult consumers have dined at hundreds, if not thousands, of restaurants. Through these experiences, norms develop that consumers expect to occur. Hence, one factor that influences adequate service is predicted service. Encounters that fall below expected norms fall below adequate service expectations. Comparing adequate service with perceived service produces a measure of **perceived service adequacy**.

## THE ZONE OF TOLERANCE

Because services are characterized by heterogeneity, consumers learn to expect variation in service delivery from one location to the next and even with the same provider from one day to the next. Consumers who accept this variation develop a **zone of tolerance,** which reflects the difference between desired service and adequate service (see Figure 12.5). The zone of tolerance expands and contracts across customers and within the same customer depending on the service and the conditions under which the service is provided. Other factors, such as price, may influence the zone of tolerance. Typically, as the price increases, the customer's zone of tolerance decreases as desired service needs begin to dominate, and the customer becomes less forgiving of sloppy service.

Another interesting characteristic of the zone of tolerance is that desired service is less subject to change than adequate service. One way to picture the zone of tolerance is to compare it with a projector screen located at the top of a blackboard. The metal

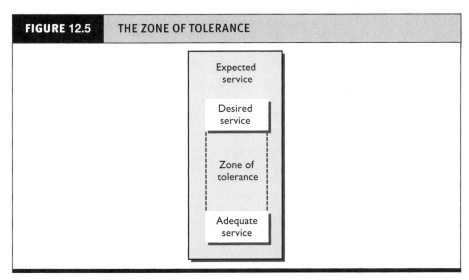

**FIGURE 12.5**     **THE ZONE OF TOLERANCE**

Expected
service

Desired
service

Zone of
tolerance

Adequate
service

Source: Valerie A. Zeithaml, Leonard L. Berry, and A. Parasuraman, "The Nature and Determinants of Customer Expectations of Service," *Journal of the Academy of Marketing Science* 21, 1 (1993), pp. 1–12.

The zone of tolerance tends to contract when the price of a service increases. For example, a customer who is having her hair styled at an expensive, upscale salon expects to be completely satisfied with the services provided. As the price of the service increases, so do the customer's expectations.

canister bolted to the wall that holds the screen represents the desired service level. The desired service level represents what the customer believes the ideal service firm should provide to its customers. Its movement is less subject to change than the rest of the screen. The screen itself represents the zone of tolerance, and the metal piece with the handle at the bottom of the screen represents the adequate service level. Adequate service fluctuates based on circumstances surrounding the service delivery process and changes the size of the zone of tolerance accordingly.

## FACTORS INFLUENCING SERVICE EXPECTATIONS: DESIRED SERVICE AND PREDICTED SERVICE

*enduring service intensifiers*
Personal factors that are stable over time and increase a customer's sensitivity to how a service should best be provided.

*derived expectations*
Expectations appropriated from and based on the expectations of others.

Desired service expectations are developed as a result of six different sources (see Figure 12.6). The first source, **enduring service intensifiers,** are personal factors that are stable over time and that increase a customer's sensitivity to how the service should best be provided. Two types of enduring service intensifiers include the customer's **derived expectations** and **personal service philosophies.** Derived expectations are created from the expectations of others. For example, if your boss requests that you find

### FIGURE 12.6    FACTORS INFLUENCING EXPECTED SERVICE

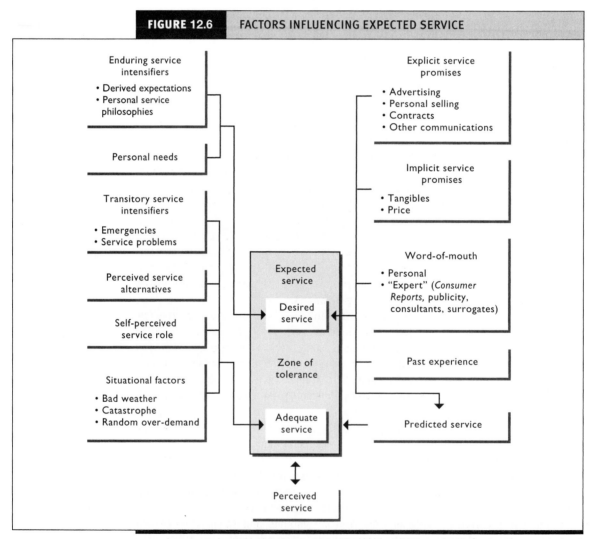

Source: Adapted from Valerie A. Zeithaml, Leonard L. Berry, and A. Parasuraman, "The Nature and Determinants of Customer Expectations of Service," *Journal of the Academy of Marketing Science* 21, 1 (1993), pp. 1–12.

someone to pressure-wash the office building, your expectations of the provider performing the job will most likely be higher than if you had hired the provider on your own initiative. In the attempt to satisfy your boss's expectations, your sensitivity to the caliber of service significantly increases.

**personal service philosophies**
A customer's own internal views of the meaning of service and the manner in which service providers should conduct themselves.

Similarly, the customer's personal service philosophies, or personal views of the meaning of service and the manner in which service providers should conduct themselves, will also heighten his or her sensitivities. Customers who work in the service sector are particularly sensitive to the caliber of service provided. These customers hold their own views regarding exactly how service should be provided; they want to be treated the way they believe they treat their customers.

The second factor influencing desired service expectations is the customer's own **personal needs,** including physical, social, and psychological needs. Simply stated, some customers are needier than others. Some customers are very particular about where they are seated in a restaurant, while others are happy to sit nearly anywhere. In a hotel, some customers are very interested in the hotel's amenities, such as the pool, sauna, dining room, and other forms of available entertainment, while others are simply looking for a clean room. This is one of the reasons that managing a service firm is particularly challenging. Customers have a variety of needs, and no two customers are alike in every way.

**personal needs**
A customer's physical, social, and psychological needs.

The other four factors that influence desired service expectations also influence predicted service expectations and include (1) explicit service promises, (2) implicit service promises, (3) word-of-mouth communications, and (4) past experience (see Figure 12.6).

**Explicit service promises** encompass the firm's advertising, personal selling, contracts, and other forms of communication. Due to the lack of a tangible product, consumers of services base their evaluations of the service on various forms of information available. The more ambiguous the service, the more customers rely on the firm's advertising when forming expectations. If a hotel stresses modern and clean rooms, customers expect the rooms to be exactly the way they were pictured in the advertisement. Similarly, if a builder states that a customer's new house will be completed in December, the customer takes this as the builder's promise, and the standard is established on which the customer will base subsequent evaluations.

**explicit service promises**
Obligations to which the firm commits itself via its advertising, personal selling, contracts, and other forms of communication.

**Implicit service promises** also influence desired service and predicted service. The tangibles surrounding the service and the price of the service are common types of implicit service promises. As the price increases, customers expect the firm to deliver higher-quality services. In the absence of a tangible product, the price becomes an indicator of quality to most consumers. For example, customers would probably have higher expectations for service at a higher-priced hair salon than they would for "Cheap Charley's Barber Shop." Similarly, if the tangibles surrounding a service are plush, customers interpret those tangibles as a sign of quality. In general, the nicer the furnishings of the service establishment, the higher customer expectations become.

**implicit service promises**
Obligations to which the firm commits itself via the tangibles surrounding the service and the price of the service.

**Word-of-mouth communications** also play an important role in forming customer expectations. As discussed in Chapter 4, customers tend to rely more on personal sources of information than on nonpersonal ones when choosing among service alternatives. Since services cannot be evaluated fully before purchase, customers view word-of-mouth information as unbiased information from someone who has been through the service experience. Sources of word-of-mouth information range from friends and family to consultants to product review publications such as *Consumer Reports.*

**word-of-mouth communications**
Unbiased information from someone who has been through the service experience, such as friends, family, or consultants.

**past experience**
The previous service encounters a consumer has had with a service provider.

Finally, **past experience** also contributes to customer expectations of desired and predicted service. Service evaluations are often based on a comparison of the current service encounter to other encounters with the same provider, other providers in the industry, and other providers in other industries. In the education system, student desired and predicted service expectations of instructors are likely to be based on past experience in other classes with the same instructor and on other classes with other instructors.

## FACTORS INFLUENCING SERVICE EXPECTATIONS: ADEQUATE SERVICE

Adequate service reflects the level of service the consumer is willing to accept and is influenced by five factors: (1) transitory service intensifiers, (2) perceived service alternatives, (3) customer self-perceived service roles, (4) situation factors, and (5) predicted service (see Figure 12.6).

### Transitory Service Intensifiers

**transitory service intensifiers**
Personal, short-term factors that heighten a customer's sensitivity to service.

In contrast to enduring service intensifiers, **transitory service intensifiers** are individualized, short-term factors that heighten the customer's sensitivity to service. For example, customers who have had service problems in the past with specific types of providers are more sensitive to the quality of service delivered during subsequent encounters. Another example is the need for service under personal emergency situations. Typically, consumers are willing to wait their turn to see a physician. However, under personal emergency conditions, consumers are less willing to be patient and expect a higher level of service in a shorter period of time. Hence, the level of adequate service increases, and the zone of tolerance becomes narrower.

### Perceived Service Alternatives

**perceived service alternatives**
Comparable services customers believe they can obtain elsewhere and/or produce themselves.

The level of adequate service is also affected by the customer's **perceived service alternatives.** The larger the number of perceived service alternatives, the higher the level of adequate service expectations, and the more narrow the zone of tolerance. Customers who believe that they can obtain comparable services elsewhere and/or that they can produce the service themselves expect higher levels of adequate service than those customers who believe they are not able to receive sufficiently better service from another provider.

### Self-Perceived Service Role

**self-perceived service role**
The input a customer believes he or she is required to present in order to produce a satisfactory service encounter.

As has been discussed on numerous occasions, the service customer is often involved in the production process and can directly influence the outcome of the service delivery system. When customers have a strong **self-perceived service role,** that is, when they believe that they are doing their part, their adequate service expectations are increased. However, if customers willingly admit that they have failed to complete forms or provide the necessary information to produce a superior service outcome, then their adequate service expectations decrease, and the zone of tolerance increases.

### Situational Factors

**situational factors**
Circumstances that lower the service quality but that are beyond the control of the service provider.

As a group, customers are not unreasonable. They understand that from time to time **situational factors** beyond the control of the service provider will lower the quality of service.

If the power goes out in one part of town around dinner time, restaurants in other parts of town will be overrun by hungry patrons. As a result, lengthy waits will develop as the service delivery system becomes backed up. Similarly, after a hurricane, tornado, or other natural disaster occurs, the customer's insurance agent may not be as responsive as under normal circumstances. When circumstances occur beyond the control of the provider and the customer has knowledge of these circumstances, adequate service expectations are lowered, and the zone of tolerance becomes wider.

### Predicted Service

The level of service consumers believe is likely to occur, is the fifth and final factor that influences adequate service expectations. **Predicted service** is a function of the firm's explicit and implicit service promises, word-of-mouth communications, and the customer's own past experiences. Taking these factors into consideration, customers form judgments regarding the predicted service that is likely to occur and set adequate service expectations simultaneously.

*predicted service*
The level of service quality a consumer believes is likely to occur

## THE LINK BETWEEN EXPECTATIONS, CUSTOMER SATISFACTION, AND SERVICE QUALITY

When evaluating the service experience, consumers compare the three types of expectations (predicted service, adequate service, and desired service) to the perceived service delivered. Customer satisfaction is calculated by comparing predicted service and perceived service. Perceived service adequacy, which compares adequate service and perceived service, and perceived service superiority, which compares desired service and perceived service, are measures of service quality (refer to Figure 12.4). Other major differences between service quality and customer satisfaction as well as issues related to service quality measurement are discussed in greater detail in Chapter 13.

## SUMMARY

Customer satisfaction research is one of the fastest growing areas in market research. Defined as a comparison of perceptions and predicted service expectations, customer satisfaction has been associated with such benefits as repeat sales, more frequent sales, increased sales per transaction, positive word-of-mouth communications, insulation from price competition, and pleasant work environments for employees. Customer satisfaction questionnaires send the signal to consumers that the firm cares about its customers and wants their input. In addition, data collected from questionnaires facilitates the development of employee training programs, identifies strengths and weaknesses in the firm's service delivery process, and provides information to be used in employee performance reviews and compensation decisions.

Firms use a variety of methods to track customer satisfaction. Moreover, a number of factors can dramatically increase or decrease the firm's satisfaction ratings. The main lessons to be learned are that (1) customer satisfaction surveys that collect qualitative and quantitative data are more useful than those that collect either qualitative or quantitative data alone; and (2) regardless of the methods used, such as the timing of the questions, the context of the questions, the data collection method, and a variety of other research issues, the firm must be consistent in its approach in order to make meaningful comparisons over time. Overall, customer satisfaction ratings tend to be negatively skewed, and responses indicating above-average performance tend to be the norm.

Despite its problems, customer satisfaction assessment is a valuable management exercise. However, firms should not attempt to increase their satisfaction ratings without carefully considering (1) the satisfaction ratings of competing firms, (2) the cost of an investment in increasing market share relative to the impact on the firm's bottom line, (3) the number of time periods it takes to recoup such an investment, and (4) the opportunity costs associated with the use of the firm's funds. Finally, one of the driving forces behind customer satisfaction is the customer's expectations. Three types of expectations and the factors influencing each type were presented. The three types of expectations form the basis for both customer satisfaction and service quality assessments, which are discussed in Chapter 13.

## ✳ KEY TERMS

expectancy disconfirmation
   model, 304
confirmed expectations, 304
disconfirmed expectations, 304
negative disconfirmation, 304
positive disconfirmation, 304
indirect measures, 307
direct measures, 308
response bias, 310
data collection method, 311
question form, 311
question context, 313
timing of the question, 314
social desirability bias, 314
benchmarking, 315
predicted service, 320
probability expectation, 320
desired service, 321
ideal expectation, 322

perceived service superiority, 322
adequate service, 322
minimum tolerable expectation, 322
perceived service adequacy, 322
zone of tolerance, 322
enduring service intensifiers, 324
derived expectations, 324
personal service philosophies, 325
personal needs, 325
explicit service promises, 325
implicit service promises, 325
word-of-mouth communications, 325
past experience, 326
transitory service intensifiers, 326
perceived service alternatives, 326
self-perceived service role, 326
situational factors, 326
predicted service, 327

## ✳ REVIEW QUESTIONS

1. Discuss the differences among a confirmation, a positive disconfirmation, and a negative disconfirmation.
2. What is meant by the description that most satisfaction scores are negatively skewed? Why does this score distribution occur?

3. Discuss how the form of a question may influence satisfaction scores.
4. Should a company always attempt to achieve 100-percent customer satisfaction?
5. Discuss the relationship between customer satisfaction and customer retention.
6. What are the drawbacks of listening to customers and assessing customer satisfaction?
7. Define and explain the relevance of the terms *predicted service, desired service,* and *adequate service* as they pertain to customer satisfaction and service quality.
8. What are the factors that influence customer expectations?

## ✱ NOTES

1. Robert A. Peterson and William R. Wilson, "Measuring Customer Satisfaction: Fact and Artifact," *Journal of the Academy of Marketing Science* 20, 1 (1992), p. 61.
2. Karl Albrecht and Ron Zemke, *Service America! Doing Business in the New Economy.* Homewood, IL: Business One Irwin, (1985), p. 6.
3. Keith Hunt, "Consumer Satisfaction, Dissatisfaction, and Complaining Behavior," *Journal of Social Issues* 47, 1, (1991), pp. 109–110.
4. Leonard L. Berry, A. Parasuraman, and Valerie A. Zeithaml, "Improving Service Quality in America: Lessons Learned," *Academy of Management Executive* 8, 2 (1994), p. 36.
5. Peterson and Wilson, "Measuring Customer Satisfaction," p. 61.
6. Peterson and Wilson, "Measuring Customer Satisfaction," p. 61.
7. Peterson and Wilson, "Measuring Customer Satisfaction," p. 62.
8. Marsha L. Richins, "Negative Word-of-Mouth by Dissatisfied Consumers: A Pilot Study," *Journal of Marketing* 47 (Winter 1983), pp. 68–78.
9. K. Douglas Hoffman, "A Conceptual Framework of the Influence of Positive Mood States on Service Exchange Relationships," in *Marketing Theory and Applications,* Chris T. Allen et al., eds. (San Antonio, TX: American Marketing Association Winter Educator's Conference), p. 147.
10. Adapted from Peter Babich, "Customer Satisfaction: How Good Is Good Enough," *Quality Progress* (December 1992), pp. 65–67.
11. Adapted from Michael W. Lowenstein, "The Voice of the Customer," *Small Business Reports* (December 1993), pp. 57–61.
12. Justin Martin, "Ignore Your Customer," *Fortune,* May 1, 1995, pp. 121–126.
13. Ibid, p. 126.
14. This section adapted from Valerie A. Zeithaml, Leonard L. Berry, and A. Parasuraman, "The Nature and Determinants of Customer Expectations of Service," *Journal of the Academy of Marketing Science* 21, 1 (1993), pp. 1–12.

## CHAPTER 13

# DEFINING AND MEASURING SERVICE QUALITY

## CHAPTER OBJECTIVES

*The major objectives of this chapter are to introduce you to the concepts of service quality, service quality measurement, and service quality information systems.*

After reading this chapter, you should be able to:

- Contrast service quality as it compares to customer satisfaction.
- Identify the gaps that influence consumer perceptions of service quality and discuss factors that influence the size of each service quality gap.
- Understand the basic concepts of SERVQUAL.
- Describe the components of a service quality information system.

*"It's just the little touches after the average man would quit that makes the master's fame."*

Orison Swett Marden, founder, *Success* magazine

# > THE MALCOLM BALDRIGE NATIONAL QUALITY AWARD

The most prestigious quality award within the United States is the Malcolm Baldrige National Quality Award. The award is named for Malcolm Baldrige who served as Secretary of Commerce during the Reagan administration for the period 1981–1987. Malcolm Baldrige was an innovator. During his seven-year tenure as Secretary of Commerce, Baldrige developed and implemented ground-breaking Administration trade policy with China, India, and the Soviet Union. In addition, he was recognized for his exceptional managerial excellence in improving the efficiency and effectiveness of government. Tragically, Baldrige was killed in a rodeo accident in 1987.

In honor of Malcolm Baldrige, the Malcolm Baldrige National Quality Award was signed into law on August 27, 1987 as Public Law 100–107. The Award is given to three enterprises in each of five business sectors that exhibit overall excellence in the areas of leadership, strategic planning, customer and market focus, information and analysis, human resource development, management, and business results. The five sectors include manufacturing, service, small business, education, and healthcare. More specifically, the fundamental reasons behind the Malcolm Baldrige National Quality Award can be found within the Findings and Purposes Section of Public Law 100–107 which state:

1. The leadership of the United States in product and process quality has been challenged strongly (and sometimes successfully) by foreign competition, and our Nation's productivity growth has improved less than our competitors' over the last two decades.
2. American business and industry are beginning to understand that poor quality costs companies as much as 20 percent of sales revenues nationally and that improved quality of goods and services goes hand in hand with improved productivity, lower costs, and increased profitability.
3. Strategic planning for quality and quality improvement programs, through a commitment to excellence in manufacturing and services, are becoming more and more essential to the well-being of our Nation's economy and our ability to compete effectively in the global marketplace.
4. Improved management understanding of the factory floor, worker involvement in quality, and greater emphasis on statistical process control can lead to dramatic improvements in the cost and quality of manufactured products.
5. The concept of quality improvement is directly applicable to small companies as well as large, to service industries as well as manufacturing, and to the public sector as well as private enterprise.
6. In order to be successful, quality improvement programs must be management-led and customer-oriented, and this may require fundamental changes in the way companies and agencies do business.
7. Several major industrial nations have successfully coupled rigorous private-sector quality audits with national awards giving special recognition to those enterprises the audits identify as the very best; and
8. A national quality award program of this kind in the United States would help improve quality and productivity by:
   a. helping to stimulate American companies to improve quality and productivity for the pride of recognition while obtaining a competitive edge through increased profits;
   b. recognizing the achievements of those companies that improve the quality of their goods and services and providing an example to others;

c. establishing guidelines and criteria that can be used by business, industrial, governmental, and other organizations in evaluating their own quality improvement efforts; and

d. providing specific guidance for other American organizations that wish to learn how to manage for high quality by making available detailed information on how winning organizations were able to change their cultures and achieve eminence.

Many organizations, such as Motorola, Inc., apply for the award with no intent of actually winning. Says Bob Barnett, Executive Vice President of Motorola, Inc: "We applied for the Award, not with the idea of winning, but with the goal of receiving the evaluation of the Baldrige Examiners. That [Baldrige] evaluation was comprehensive, professional, and insightful . . . making it perhaps the most cost-effective, value-added business consultation available anywhere in the world today." In the end, applicants for the award are thrilled to win the Malcolm Baldrige National Quality Award; however, win or lose, they find high value in the review process itself.

Source: "The Malcolm Baldrige National Quality Improvement Act of 1987 – Public Law 100–107" and "Biography of Malcolm Baldrige," http://www.quality.nist.gov accessed 31 May 2005; "Malcolm Baldrige National Quality Award" http://www.qualitymanagementsurvival.com accessed 31 May 2005.

> ## INTRODUCTION

One of the few issues on which service quality researchers agree is that service quality is an elusive and abstract concept that is difficult to define and measure.[1] This particular problem is challenging for academicians and practitioners alike. For example, traditional measures of productivity such as Gross Domestic Product (GDP) do not account for increases in service quality delivered. In fact, providing poor quality can actually increase the country's GDP.[2] If a mail-order company sends you the wrong product, the dollars spent on phone calls and return mailings to correct the mistake will add to the GDP.

Other governmental institutions, such as the Bureau of Labor Statistics (BLS), have attempted to account for increases in quality by adjusting the consumer price index. For example, if a car costs more this year than last but includes quality improvements such as an air bag, better gas mileage, and cleaner emissions, the BLS will subtract the estimated retail value of the improvements before calculating the consumer price index. However, the BLS does this for only a few industries and without the help of customers—the true evaluators of quality improvements. Efficiency measures are also of no help. A retail store that stocks lots of merchandise may please more customers and make more money while decreasing the firm's efficiency rating.

The productivity of education and government services is notoriously difficult to measure. Increases in quality, such as improving the quality of education and training government employees to be more pleasant throughout their daily interactions with the pubic, do not show up in productivity measures. However, it is readily apparent that increases in quality can have a dramatic impact on a firm's or industry's survival. As evidence, Japan did not simply bulldoze its way into U.S. markets by offering lower prices alone—superior quality relative to the competition at that time ultimately won customers over.

## > WHAT IS SERVICE QUALITY?

Perhaps the best way to begin a discussion of service quality is to first attempt to distinguish **service quality** measurement from customer satisfaction measurement. Most experts agree that customer satisfaction is a short-term, transaction-specific measure, whereas service quality is an attitude formed by long-term, overall evaluation of performance.

*service quality*
An attitude formed by a long-term, overall evaluation of a firm's performance.

Without a doubt, the two concepts of customer satisfaction and service quality are intertwined. However, the relationship between these two concepts is unclear. Some believe that customer satisfaction leads to perceived service quality, while others believe that service quality leads to customer satisfaction. In addition, the relationship between customer satisfaction and service quality and the way these two concepts relate to purchasing behavior remains largely unexplained.[3]

One plausible explanation is that satisfaction assists consumers in revising service quality perceptions.[4] The logic for this position consists of the following:

1. Consumer perceptions of the service quality of a firm with which he or she has no prior experience is based on the consumer's expectations;
2. subsequent encounters with the firm lead the consumer through the disconfirmation process and revised perceptions of service quality;
3. each additional encounter with the firm further revises or reinforces service quality perceptions; and
4. revised service quality perceptions modify future consumer purchase intentions toward the firm.

To deliver a consistent set of satisfying experiences that can build into an evaluation of high quality requires the entire organization to be focused on the task. The needs of the consumer must be understood in detail, as must the operational constraints under which the firm operates. Service providers must be focused on quality, and the system must be designed to support that mission by being controlled correctly and delivering as it was designed to do.

## > THE DIFFERENCE IN QUALITY PERSPECTIVES BETWEEN GOODS AND SERVICES

Service quality offers a way of achieving success among competing services.[5] Particularly, where a small number of firms that offer nearly identical services are competing within a small area, such as banks might do, establishing service quality may be the only way of differentiating oneself. Service quality differentiation can generate increased market share and ultimately mean the difference between financial success and failure.

Ample evidence suggests that the provision of quality can deliver repeat purchases as well as new customers. The value of retaining existing customers is discussed in much greater detail in Chapter 15. Briefly, repeat customers yield many benefits to the service organization. The cost of marketing to them is lower than that of marketing to new customers. Once customers have become regulars of the service, they know the script and are efficient users of the servuction system. As they gain trust in the organization, the level of risk for them is reduced, and they are more likely to consolidate their business with the firm. For example, insurance customers tend to move current policies to, and purchase new policies from, the one provider they feel serves their needs the best.

Goods manufacturers have already learned this lesson over the past decade and have made producing quality goods a priority issue. Improving the quality of manufactured goods has become a major strategy for both establishing efficient, smoothly running operations and increasing consumer market share in an atmosphere in which customers are consistently demanding higher and higher quality. Goods quality improvement measures have focused largely on the quality of the products themselves, and specifically on eliminating product failure. Initially, these measures were based on rigorous checking of all finished products before they came into contact with the customer. More recently, quality control has focused on the principle of ensuring quality during the manufacturing process, on "getting it right the first time," and on reducing end-of-production-line failures to zero. The final evolution in goods manufacturing has been to define quality as delivering the right product to the right customer at the right time, thus extending quality beyond the product itself and using external as well as internal measures to assess overall quality.

However, service quality cannot be understood in quite the same way. The servuction system depends on the customer as a participant in the production process, and normal quality-control measures that depend on eliminating defects before the consumer sees the product are not available. Consequently, service quality is not a specific goal or program that can be achieved or completed but must be an ongoing part of all management and service production on a daily basis.

## > DIAGNOSING FAILURE GAPS IN SERVICE QUALITY

Many difficulties are inherent in implementing and evaluating service quality. In the first place, perceptions of quality tend to rely on a repeated comparison of the customer's expectation about a particular service. If a service, no matter how good, fails repeatedly to meet a customer's expectations, the customer will perceive the service to be of poor quality. Second, unlike goods marketing, where customers evaluate the finished product alone, in services, the customer evaluates the process of the service as well as its outcome. A customer visiting a hairdresser, for example, will evaluate service not only on the basis of whether he or she likes the haircut, but also on whether the hairdresser is friendly, competent, and personally clean.

Conceptually, the service quality process can be examined in terms of gaps between expectations and perceptions on the part of management, employees, and customers (see Figure 13.1).[6] The most important gap, the **service gap**, is between customers' expectations of service and their perception of the service actually delivered. Ultimately, the goal of the service firm is to close the service gap or at least narrow it as far as possible. Consequently, examining service quality gaps is much like the disconfirmation of expectations model discussed in Chapter 12. However, remember that service quality

**service gap**
The distance between a customer's expectations of a service and perception of the service actually delivered.

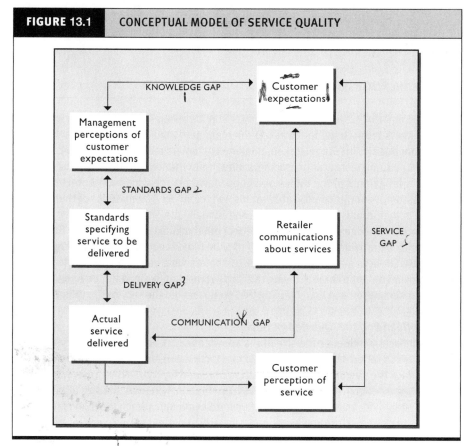

**FIGURE 13.1    CONCEPTUAL MODEL OF SERVICE QUALITY**

Source: Adapted from A. Parasuraman, Valerie Zeithaml, and Leonard Berry, "A Conceptual Model of Service Quality and Its Implications for Service Quality Research," *Journal of Marketing* 49 (Fall 1985), pp. 41–50.

focuses on the customer's cumulative attitude toward the firm, which is collected by the consumer from a number of successful or unsuccessful service experiences.

Before the firm can close the service gap, it must close or attempt to narrow four other gaps:

1. The **knowledge gap,** or the difference between what consumers expect of a service and what management perceives that consumers expect.
2. The **standards gap,** or the difference between what management perceives that consumers expect and the quality specifications set for service delivery.
3. The **delivery gap,** or the difference between the quality specifications set for service delivery and the actual quality of service delivery. For example, do employees perform the service as they were trained?
4. The **communications gap,** or the difference between the actual quality of service delivered and the quality of service described in the firm's external communications such as brochures and mass media advertising.

**knowledge gap**
The difference between what consumers expect of a service and what management perceives that consumers expect.

**standards gap**
The difference between what management perceives that consumers expect and the quality specifications set for service delivery.

**delivery gap**
The difference between the quality standards set for service delivery and the actual quality of service delivery.

**communications gap**
The difference between the actual quality of service delivered and the quality of service described in the firm's external communications.

Hence, the service gap is a function of the knowledge gap, the specifications gap, the delivery gap, and the communications gap. As each of these gaps increases or decreases, the service gap responds in a similar manner.

## THE KNOWLEDGE GAP

The most immediate and obvious gap is usually between what customers want and what managers think customers want. Often managers think they know what their customers want but are, in fact, mistaken. Banking customers may prefer security to a good interest rate. Some restaurant customers may prefer quality and taste of food over an attractive arrangement of the tables or a good view from the window. A hotel may think that its customers prefer comfortable rooms, when, in fact, the majority of them spend little time in their rooms and are more interested in on-site amenities.

When a knowledge gap occurs, a variety of other mistakes tend to follow. The wrong facilities may be provided, the wrong staff may be hired, and the wrong training may be undertaken. Services may be provided that customers have no use for, while the services they do desire are not offered. Closing this gap requires minutely detailed knowledge of what customers desire and then building that response into the service operating system.

### Factors Influencing the Knowledge Gap

**research orientation**
A firm's attitude toward conducting consumer research.

**upward communication**
The flow of information from front-line personnel to upper levels of the organization.

**levels of management**
The complexity of the organizational hierarchy and the number of levels between top management and the customers.

Three main factors influence the size of the knowledge gap. First, the firm's **research orientation,** which reflects its attitude toward conducting consumer research, can dramatically influence the size of the gap. Information obtained from consumer research defines consumer expectations. As the firm's research orientation increases, the size of the knowledge gap should decrease. The amount of **upward communication** is a second factor that influences the size of the knowledge gap. Upward communication refers to the flow of information from front-line personnel to upper levels of the organization. Front-line personnel interact with customers on a frequent basis, so they are often more in touch with customer needs than is top management. Consequently, as the flow of upward communication increases through the organization, the smaller the knowledge gap should become. Finally, the **levels of management** in the organization can also influence the size of the knowledge gap. As the organizational hierarchy becomes more complex and more levels of management are added, higher levels of management tend to become more distant from customers and the day-to-day activities of the organization. As a result, when the levels of management increase, the size of the knowledge gap tends to increase.

## THE STANDARDS GAP

Even if customer expectations have been accurately determined, the standards gap may open between management's perception of customer expectations and the actual standards set for service delivery, such as order processing speed, the way cloth napkins are to be folded, or the way customers are to be greeted. When developing standards, the firm should use a flowchart of its operations to identify all points of contact between it and its customers. Detailed standards can be written for (1) the way the system should operate, and (2) the behavior of contact personnel at each point in the system.

© MICHAEL MAHOVLICH / MASTERFILE

Every service firm must maintain certain standards in order to give customers a pleasant experience. For hotel employees, it may be acknowledging the customer on arrival, establishing eye contact, smiling, answering questions, and providing keys to the hotel room.

Hotel front-desk personnel, for example, may be trained to perform to specification in such areas as acknowledging the customer upon arrival, establishing eye contact, smiling, completing the proper paperwork, reviewing with the customer the available amenities, and providing the customer with keys to the room.

### Factors Influencing the Standards Gap

In many cases, management does not believe it can or should meet customer requirements for service. For example, overnight delivery of mail used to be thought of as an absurd possibility before Fred Smith and FedEx proved that, in fact, it could be done.

Sometimes management has no commitment to the delivery of service quality. Corporate leadership may set other priorities that interfere with setting standards that lead to good service. For example, a company's orientation toward implementing cost-reduction strategies that maximize short-term profits is often cited as a misguided priority that impedes the firm's progress in delivering quality services. Personal computer companies whose automated service hotlines reduce the number of customer service representatives employed are typical examples. In some instances, customers in need of service have been forced to remain on hold for hours before they could actually speak to a "real person." Hotlines were originally named to reflect the speed with which the customer could talk to the manufacturer. Now the name more appropriately reflects the customer's temper by the time he or she talks to someone who can actually help.

Sometimes there is simply no culture of service quality, and management genuinely fails to understand the issues involved. In other cases, management may wish to meet customer requirements but feel hampered by insufficient methods of measuring quality or by converting those measurements into standards. Because of the difficulties in attempting to write specifications for particular employee behaviors, some managers feel that quality measurement is not worth the effort.

## THE DELIVERY GAP

The delivery gap occurs between the actual performance of a service and the standards set by management. The existence of the delivery gap depends on both the willingness and the ability of employees to provide the service according to specification. For example, do employees wear their name tags, do they establish eye contact, and do they thank the customer when the transaction is completed?

### Factors Influencing the Delivery Gap

**willingness to perform**
An employee's desire to perform to his/her full potential in a service encounter.

One factor that influences the size of the delivery gap is the employee's **willingness to perform** the service. Obviously, employees' willingness to provide a service can vary greatly from employee to employee and in the same employee over time. Many employees who start off working to their full potential often become less willing to do so over time because of frustration and dissatisfaction with the organization. Furthermore, a considerable range exists between what the employee is actually capable of accomplishing and the minimum the employee must do in order to keep his/her job. Most service managers find it difficult to keep employees working at their full potential all the time.

**employee-job fit**
The degree to which employees are able to perform a service to specifications.

Other employees, no matter how willing, may simply not be able to perform the service to specification. Hence, a second factor that influences the size of the delivery gap is the **employee-job fit**. Individuals may have been hired for jobs they are not qualified to handle or to which they are temperamentally unsuited, or they may not have been provided with sufficient training for the roles expected of them. Generally, employees who are not capable of performing assigned roles are less willing to keep trying.

**role conflict**
An inconsistency in service providers' minds between what the service manager expects them to provide and the service they think their customers actually want.

Another common factor influencing the size of the delivery gap is **role conflict**. Whether or not the knowledge gap has been closed, service providers may still see an inconsistency between what the service manager expects employees to provide and the service their customers actually want. A waiter who is expected to promote various items on the menu may alienate some customers who prefer to make their own choices undisturbed. For example, how long does it take a McDonald's employee to finally realize that most customers really don't want an apple pie with their meal and are annoyed by the constant prompting? In some instances, customers even finish relaying their order by saying, "And no, I don't want an apple pie with that."

In more formal settings, persistent waiters may find customers retaliating by not leaving a tip. In other cases, the service provider may be expected to do too many kinds of work, such as simultaneously answering telephones and dealing with customers face to face in a busy office. If this kind of conflict continues to occur, employees become frustrated, gradually lose their commitment to providing the best service they can, and/or simply quit altogether.

Another contributor to the delivery gap is **role ambiguity**. Role ambiguity results when employees, due to poor employee-job fit or inadequate training, do not understand the roles of their jobs or what their jobs are intended to accomplish. Sometimes, too, they are even unfamiliar with the service firm and its goals. Consequently, as role ambiguity increases, the delivery gap widens.

A further complication for employees is the **dispersion of control,** the situation in which control over the nature of the service being provided is removed from employees' hands. When employees are not allowed to make independent decisions about individual cases without first conferring with a manager, they may feel alienated from the service and less a part of their job. Furthermore, when control over certain aspects of the service is moved to a different location, such as control over credit being removed from individual bank branches, employee alienation is bound to increase. Employees experience **learned helplessness** and feel unable to respond to customer requests for help. Consequently, as the dispersion of control increases, the delivery gap becomes wider.

Finally, the delivery gap may also suffer due to **inadequate support**, such as not receiving personal training and/or technological and other resources necessary for employees to perform their jobs in the best possible manner. Even the best employees can be discouraged if they are forced to work with out-of-date or faulty equipment, especially if the employees of competing firms have superior resources and are able to provide the same or superior levels of service with far less effort. Failure to properly support employees leads to a lot of wasted effort, poor employee productivity, unsatisfied customers, and an increase in the size of the delivery gap.

## THE COMMUNICATIONS GAP

The communications gap is the difference between the service the firm promises it will deliver through its external communications and the service it actually delivers to its customers (see Global Services in Action). If advertising or sales promotions promise one kind of service and the consumer receives a different kind of service, the communications gap becomes wider. External communicators are essentially promises the firm makes to its customers. When the communications gap is wide, the firm has broken its promises, resulting in a lack of future customer trust. A customer who orders a bottle of wine from a menu only to be told it is out of stock may feel that the offer held out on the menu has not been fulfilled. A customer who is promised delivery in three days but who then has to wait a week will perceive service quality to be lower than expected.

### Factors Influencing the Communications Gap

The communications gap is influenced primarily by two factors. The first, the propensity of the firm to **overpromise**, often occurs in highly competitive business environments as firms try to outdo one another in the name of recruiting new customers. The second factor pertains to the flow of **horizontal communication** within the firm. In other words, "Does the left hand know what the right hand is doing?" All too often, communications are developed at the firm's headquarters without conferring with service firms in the field. In some instances, new service programs are announced to the public by corporate headquarters before the local service firms are aware that the new programs exist. A lack

---

**role ambiguity**
Uncertainty of employees' roles in their jobs and poor understanding of the purpose of their jobs.

**dispersion of control**
The situation in which control over the nature of the service being provided is removed from employees' hands.

**learned helplessness**
The condition of employees who, through repeated dispersion of control, feel themselves unable to perform a service adequately.

**inadequate support**
A management failure to give employees personal training and/or technological and other resources necessary for them to perform their jobs in the best possible manner.

**overpromising**
A firm's promise of more than it can deliver.

**horizontal communication**
The flow of internal communication between a firm's headquarters and its service firms in the field.

## GLOBAL SERVICES *IN ACTION*

> ### THE COMMUNICATION GAP COMES TO DOMESTIC AND GLOBAL SERVICES

Findings from a research study conducted by the International Customer Service Association and e-Satisfy.com indicate that only 36 percent of the 50,000 e-shoppers that were surveyed report that they were satisfied with electronic commerce service. One of the primary service gaps appears to be in the area of communications. Customers report that they typically expect a reply to their e-mail requests within one hour; however, only 12 percent receive such a response, and only 42 percent of respondents were replied to within 24 hours.

A Rainer-Web index study of the Fortune 100 and FTSE 100 found that more than 2 in 5 U.S. and U.K. companies failed to reply to e-mail requests promptly. In fact 29 FTSE companies and 21 Fortune 100 could not be contacted at all from their websites. These companies included Marks & Spencer, Thames Water, GTE, and Intel. Of the companies contacted by e-mail, 15 FTSE and 20 Fortune 100 never replied. These types of results led the chairman of Rainer to comment: "All too often, companies focus on the content and look and feel of the site without considering its integration with existing customer contact systems. The result is [that these types of websites end up being] little more than corporate wallpaper."

Despite high levels of customer dissatisfaction with the quality of e-services offered by online firms, the number of offline businesses that will offer online shopping will double from last year. Customer participation in making online purchases is also continuing to grow at a rapid rate. Apparently, the zone of tolerance for acceptable service is wider for e-purchases than brick-and-mortar purchases. Customers realize that purchasing on the Web is new and that the ordering and delivery processes may not be perfect. Consequently, many online customers are willing to accept a certain amount of risk in exchange for potential cost savings (e.g., money and time) and appear more forgiving when perceptions fall short of expectations, at least for now.

Part of the problem in delivery quality e-services appears to be one of setting priorities. According to a recent study conducted by Retail Info Systems and Computer Sciences Corporation, order fulfillment was the most pressing issue for 40 percent of business respondents who participated in the study. Disturbingly, 35 percent of business respondents indicated that attracting visitors to their websites was top priority. The latter companies may eventually find that failing to provide quality e-services will sacrifice customer loyalty and long-term profitability. Internet analysts agree: "Companies need more than just a pretty website and email addresses. People who use this technology expect it to work, and if it doesn't it's frustrating."

Source: C. Brune, "E-business Misses the Mark on Customer Service," *Internal Auditor*, 57 (3), (June 2000), pp. 13–15; "Rainer: Top Companies Lax in Replying to Email," http://www.nua.ie/surveys (August 3, 2000).

of horizontal communication places an unsuspecting service provider in an awkward position when a customer requests the service promised and the provider has no idea what the customer is talking about.

## > MEASURING SERVICE QUALITY: SERVQUAL

Although measurements of customer satisfaction and service quality are both obtained by comparing perceptions to expectations, subtle differences between the two concepts are seen in their operational definitions. While satisfaction compares consumer perceptions to what consumers would normally expect, service quality compares perceptions to what a consumer should expect from a firm that delivers high-quality services. Given these definitions, service quality appears to measure a higher standard of service delivery.

A frequently used and highly debated measure of service quality is the **SERVQUAL** scale.[7] According to its developers, SERVQUAL is a diagnostic tool that uncovers a firm's broad weaknesses and strengths in the area of service quality. The SERVQUAL instrument is based on five service quality dimensions that were obtained through extensive focus group interviews with consumers. The five dimensions include *tangibles*, *reliability*, *responsiveness*, *assurance*, and *empathy*, and they provide the basic "skeleton" underlying service quality.

The SERVQUAL instrument consists of two sections: a 22-item section that records customer expectations of excellent firms in the specific service industry, and a second 22-item section that measures consumer perceptions of a particular company in that service industry (i.e., the firm being evaluated). Results from the two sections are then compared to arrive at "gap scores" for each of the five dimensions. The larger the gap, the farther consumer perceptions are from expectations, and the lower the service quality evaluation. In contrast, the smaller the gap, the higher the service quality evaluation. Customer expectations are measured on a 7-point scale with the anchor labels of "not at all essential" and "absolutely essential."[8] Similarly, customer perceptions are measured on another 7-point scale with anchor labels of "strongly agree" and "strongly disagree." Hence, SERVQUAL is a 44-item scale that measures customer expectations and perceptions regarding five service quality dimensions.

*SERVQUAL*
A 44-item scale that measures customer expectations and perceptions regarding five service quality dimensions.

### THE TANGIBLES DIMENSION

Because of the absence of a physical product, consumers often rely on the tangible evidence that surrounds the service in forming evaluations. The **tangibles dimension** of SERVQUAL compares consumer expectations and the firm's performance regarding the firm's ability to manage its tangibles. A firm's tangibles consist of a wide variety of objects such as carpeting, desks, lighting, wall colors, brochures, daily correspondence, and the appearance of the firm's personnel. Consequently, the tangibles component in SERVQUAL is two-dimensional—one focusing on equipment and facilities, the other focusing on personnel and communications materials.

The tangibles component of SERVQUAL is obtained via four expectations questions (E1–E4) and four perception questions (P1–P4). Keep in mind that the expectation

*tangibles dimension*
The SERVQUAL assessment of a firm's ability to manage its tangibles.

questions apply to excellent firms within a particular industry, while the perception questions apply to the specific firm under investigation. Comparing the perception scores to the expectation scores provides a numerical variable that indicates the tangibles gap. The smaller the number, the smaller the gap, and the closer consumer perceptions are to their expectations. The questions that pertain to the tangibles dimension are as follows:[9]

*not at all essential*                                    *absolutely essential.*

### Tangibles Expectations

E1. Excellent companies will have modern-looking equipment.
E2. The physical facilities at excellent companies will be visually appealing.
E3. Employees of excellent companies will be neat in appearance.
E4. Materials associated with the service (such as pamphlets or statements) will be visually appealing in an excellent company.

### Tangibles Perceptions

*Strongly agree*                                    *Strongly disagree*

P1. XYZ has modern-looking equipment.
P2. XYZ's physical facilities are visually appealing.
P3. XYZ's employees are neat in appearance.
P4. Materials associated with the service (such as pamphlets or statements) are visually appealing at XYZ.

## THE RELIABILITY DIMENSION

**reliability dimension**
The SERVQUAL assessment of a firm's consistency and dependability in service performance.

In general, the **reliability dimension** reflects the consistency and dependability of a firm's performance. Does the firm provide the same level of service time after time, or does quality dramatically vary with each encounter? Does the firm keep its promises, bill its customers accurately, keep accurate records, and perform the service correctly the first time? Nothing can be more frustrating for customers than unreliable service providers.

A constantly amazing observation is the number of businesses that fail to keep their promises. In many instances, the consumer is ready to spend money if only the service provider will show up and conduct the transaction as promised. As students, you may have experienced the reliability gap while attempting to have the local cable company install its services in your new apartment. Typically, the cable company will approximate the time at which the installer will come to your apartment in four-hour increments (e.g., morning or afternoon). In many cases, you may miss class or work waiting for the cable installer to arrive. All too often, the installer fails to show up during this time period and you must reschedule . . . missing yet more classes and/or time at work. Further aggravating this process is that you, the customer, must initiate the rescheduling process. Often the cable company offers no apology and provides little explanation other than, "Our installers are very busy."

Consumers perceive the reliability dimension to be the most important of the five SERVQUAL dimensions. Consequently, failure to provide reliable service generally translates into an unsuccessful firm (see B2B Services in Action). The questions used to assess the reliability gap are as follows:

## B2B SERVICES *IN ACTION*

### > | ISO 9000

What is ISO 9000? ISO 9000 consists of five international industrial standards (ISO 9000–9004) that are meant to provide quality assurances for purchasers of international products. Developed by the International Organization for Standardization in Geneva in 1987, ISO 9000 registers and certifies a manufacturer's quality assurance and quality control systems. Ultimately, ISO 9000 is a surrogate measure of a firm's reliability (typically named the most important dimension within SERVQUAL). Interestingly, ISO 9000 does not guarantee that the manufacturer produces quality products, but it does certify that the manufacturer implements quality processes. However, one would hope that a company that follows ISO 9000 quality standards would indeed produce quality products.

The need for ISO 9000 certification is a direct result of increasing global competition. Buyers who purchase from international sources of supply need assurances that suppliers are indeed reputable. This is particularly true in the European Union where the *EU Product Liability Directive* exerts pressure on all companies within the EU to be ISO 9000 certified. "The directive holds that a manufacturer, including an exporter, will be liable, regardless of fault or negligence, if a person is harmed by a product that fails because of a faulty component." Consequently, EU B2B purchasers want to be very careful about selecting sources of supply. Case in point, manufacturers of component parts in Japan and China are finding ISO 9000 certification to be an absolute necessity to conduct international business.

Recipients of ISO 9000 certification undergo a thorough audit process conducted by a third party that is authorized to conduct the certification process. All aspects of the audited firm are scrutinized including production processes, updating records, maintaining equipment, training employees, and handling customer relations. In the end, ISO 9000 lowers potential business-to-business purchasers' perceived risk and provides certified firms with a competitive edge in the marketplace.

Source: "ISO 9000 Quality – What is it?" http://www.strategosinc.com accessed 1 June 2005; "What is ISO 9000," http://www.qualitymanagmentsurvival.com accessed 1 June 2005; Philip R. Cateora and John L. Graham, *International Marketing*, 10th ed., (Boston, MA: Irwin McGraw-Hill, 1999), 289–301.

### *Reliability Expectations*

E5. When excellent companies <u>promise to do something by a certain time</u>, they will do so.

E6. When customers have a problem, excellent companies will <u>show a sincere interest</u> in resolving it.

E7. Excellent companies will perform the service right the <u>first time</u>.

cellent companies will provide their services at the time they promise to do so.
ellent companies will insist on error-free records.

343

*ty Perceptions*

. 5. When XYZ promises to do something by a certain time, it does so.
**P6.** When you have a problem, XYZ shows a sincere interest in solving it.
**P7.** XYZ performs the service right the first time.
**P8.** XYZ provides its services at the time it promises to do so.
**P9.** XYZ insists on error-free records.

## THE RESPONSIVENESS DIMENSION

*responsiveness dimension*
The SERVQUAL assessment of a firm's commitment to providing its services in a timely manner.

Responsiveness reflects a service firm's commitment to provide its services in a timely manner. As such, the **responsiveness dimension** of SERVQUAL concerns the willingness and/or readiness of employees to provide a service. Occasionally, customers may encounter a situation in which employees are engaged in their own conversations with one another while ignoring the needs of the customer. Obviously, this is an example of unresponsiveness.

Responsiveness also reflects the preparedness of the firm to provide the service. Typically, new restaurants do not advertise their "opening night" so that the service delivery system can be fine-tuned and prepared to handle larger crowds, thereby minimizing service failures and subsequent customer complaints. The SERVQUAL expectation and perception items that address the responsiveness gap are as follows:

*Responsiveness Expectations*

**E10.** Employees of excellent companies will tell customers exactly when services will be performed.
**E11.** Employees of excellent companies will give prompt service to customers.
**E12.** Employees of excellent companies will always be willing to help customers.
**E13.** Employees of excellent companies will never be too busy to respond to customer requests.

*Responsiveness Perceptions*

**P10.** Employees of XYZ tell you exactly when services will be performed.
**P11.** Employees of XYZ give you prompt service.
**P12.** Employees of XYZ are always willing to help you.
**P13.** Employees of XYZ are never too busy to respond to your requests.

*assurance dimension*
The SERVQUAL assessment of a firm's competence, courtesy to its customers, and security of its operations.

## THE ASSURANCE DIMENSION

SERVQUAL's **assurance dimension** addresses the competence of the firm, the courtesy it extends its customers, and the security of its operations. Competence pertains to the firm's knowledge and skill in performing its service. Does the firm possess the required skills to complete the service on a professional basis?

Courtesy refers to how the firm's personnel interact with the customer and the customer's possessions. As such, courtesy reflects politeness, friendliness, and consideration for the customer's property (e.g., a mechanic who places paper floor mats in a customer's car so as to not soil the car's carpet).

Security is also an important component of the assurance dimension. Security reflects a customer's feelings that he or she is free from danger, risk, and doubt. Recent robberies at ATM locations provide ample evidence of the possible harm that may arise at service locations. In addition to physical danger, the security component of the assurance dimension also reflects financial risk issues (e.g., will the bank fail) and confidentiality issues (e.g., are my medical records at the school's health center kept private). The SERVQUAL items utilized to address the assurance gap are as follows:

## Assurance Expectations

**E14.** The behavior of employees of excellent companies will instill confidence in customers.
**E15.** Customers of excellent companies will feel safe in their transactions.
**E16.** Employees of excellent companies will be consistently courteous with customers.
**E17.** Employees of excellent companies will have the knowledge to answer customer questions.

## Assurance Perceptions

**P14.** The behavior of employees of XYZ instills confidence in customers.
**P15.** You feel safe in your transactions with XYZ.
**P16.** Employees of XYZ are consistently courteous with you.
**P17.** Employees of XYZ have the knowledge to answer your questions.

## THE EMPATHY DIMENSION

Empathy is the ability to experience another's feelings as one's own. Empathetic firms have not lost touch with what it is like to be a customer of their own firm. As such, empathetic firms understand their customer needs and make their services accessible to their customers. In contrast, firms that do not provide their customers individualized attention when requested and that offer operating hours convenient to the firm and not its customers fail to demonstrate empathetic behaviors.

The SERVQUAL **empathy dimension** addresses the empathy gap as follows:

**empathy dimension**
The SERVQUAL assessment of a firm's ability to put itself in its customers' place.

## Empathy Expectations

**E18.** Excellent companies will give customers individual attention.
**E19.** Excellent companies will have operating hours convenient to all their customers.
**E20.** The employees of excellent companies give customers personal attention.

llent companies will have the customer's best interest at heart.
:mployees of excellent companies will understand the specific needs of their
»mers.

'erceptions

ves you individual attention.
is operating hours convenient to all its customers.
**P20.** XYZ employees give you personal attention.
**P21.** XYZ has your best interests at heart.
**P22.** Employees of XYZ understand your specific needs.

## CRITICISMS OF SERVQUAL

Since the development of the SERVQUAL instrument, it has received its share of criticism.[10] The major criticisms of the instrument involve the length of the questionnaire, the validity of the five service quality dimensions, and the predictive power of the instrument in regard to subsequent consumer purchases. The following discussion focuses on each of these issues and their respective importance to interpreting SERVQUAL results.

### Length of the Questionnaire

Combining the expectation and perception items of SERVQUAL results in a 44-item survey instrument. Opponents of the SERVQUAL instrument argue that the 44 items are highly repetitive and unnecessarily increase the questionnaire's length. Opponents further argue that the expectations section of the instrument is of no real value and that the perceptions (actual performance) section should be utilized alone to assess service quality.[11]

In response, the developers of SERVQUAL effectively argue that including the expectations section enhances the managerial usefulness of the scale as a diagnostic tool due to the gap scores developed for each dimension. Perception scores alone merely rate whether the respondent agrees or disagrees with each question. For example, Figure 13.2 provides a set of perception scores and SERVQUAL scores for a hypothetical

| FIGURE 13.2 | THE DIAGNOSTIC ADVANTAGE OF SERVQUAL SCORES |
|---|---|

The Diagnostic Advantage of SERVQUAL Scores

| Dimension | Perception Scores | SERVQUAL Scores |
|---|---|---|
| Tangibles | 5.3 | 0.0 |
| Reliability | 4.8 | −1.7 |
| Responsiveness | 5.1 | −1.0 |
| Assurance | 5.4 | −1.5 |
| Empathy | 4.8 | −1.1 |

firm. Utilizing this information for diagnostic purposes, perception scores alone would suggest placing an equal emphasis on improving the reliability and empathy dimensions. Incorporating expectations into the SERVQUAL score indicates that improving the reliability dimension should be the firm's top priority. Given that implementing service quality improvements requires a financial investment from the firm, maintaining the expectation section becomes valuable.

Creative suggestions have been made for maintaining the expectations component while at the same time reducing the questionnaire's length by 22 questions. Three approaches have been suggested: (1) On a single scale, ask respondents where they would rate a high-quality company and then where they would rate the firm under investigation; (2) utilize the scale's midpoint as the expected level of service from a high-quality company, and then rate the specific firm in relation to the midpoint above expectation or below; and (3) utilize the end point (e.g., 7 on a 7-point scale) as the expected level of a high-quality company, and rate the specific company relative to the high-quality company on the same scale. All three approaches provide alternatives for assessing customer perceptions and expectations while reducing the questionnaire's length.

### The Validity of the Five Dimensions

Another frequent criticism of the SERVQUAL instrument is that the five proposed dimensions of service quality—reliability, responsiveness, assurance, empathy, and tangibles—do not hold up under statistical scrutiny. Consequently, opponents of SERVQUAL question the validity of the specific dimensions in the measurement instrument.

SERVQUAL's developers argue that although the five dimensions represent conceptually distinct facets of service quality, they are interrelated. Hence, some overlap may exist (as measured by correlations) among items that measure specific dimensions. In particular, the distinction among the responsiveness, assurance, and reliability dimensions tends to blur under statistical scrutiny. However, when respondents are asked to assign importance weights to each dimension, results indicate that consumers do indeed distinguish among the five dimensions, as exhibited in Figure 13.3. According to

| FIGURE 13.3 | RELATIVE IMPORTANCE OF SERVQUAL DIMENSIONS AS REPORTED BY CONSUMERS |
|---|---|

| SERVQUAL Dimension Importance* | |
|---|---|
| Reliability | 32% |
| Responsiveness | 22% |
| Assurance | 19% |
| Empathy | 16% |
| Tangibles | 11% |

Source: Leonard L. Berry, A. Parasuraman, and Valerie A. Zeithaml, "Improving Service Quality in America: Lessons Learned," *Academy of Management Executive* 8, no. 2 (1994), 32–52.

*Consumers were asked to allocate 100 points among the five dimensions. The importance percentage reflects the mean point allocation for each dimension.

the developers of SERVQUAL, this ranking provides additional evidence of the dimensions' distinctiveness. For the statistical enthusiast, a variety of articles offering additional evidence and rationale supporting the viability of the five-dimensional framework is cited in the "Notes" section located at the end of this chapter.[12]

### The Predictive Power of SERVQUAL

The third major criticism of SERVQUAL pertains to the instrument's ability to predict consumer purchase intentions. Research has indicated that the performance (perceptions) section alone of the SERVQUAL scale is a better predictor of purchase intentions than the combined expectations-minus-perception instrument. As such, opponents of the SERVQUAL instrument conclude that satisfaction has a more significant effect on purchase intentions than does service quality. Consequently, they assert that managers need to emphasize customer satisfaction programs over strategies focusing solely on service quality.

The developers of SERVQUAL once again take issue with the preceding objections based on a variety of conceptual, methodological, analytical, and practical issues. Consequently, the jury is still out regarding this particular objection. From a managerial standpoint, perhaps the SERVQUAL proponents' most important counterpoint is the diagnostic value of the expectations-minus-perceptions approach. Based on information provided earlier, the developers of SERVQUAL make a convincing argument that incorporating customer expectations provides richer information than does examining the perceptions scores alone.

## > SERVQUAL: SOME FINAL THOUGHTS

### The Importance of Contact Personnel

The SERVQUAL instrument highlights several points that service providers should consider when examining service quality. First, customer perceptions of service are heavily dependent on the attitudes and performance of contact personnel. Of the five dimensions measured, responsiveness, empathy, and assurance directly reflect the interaction between customers and staff. Even tangibles depend partly on the appearance, dress, and hygiene of the service staff.

### Process Is as Important as Outcome

The manner in which customers judge a service depends as much on the service process as on the outcome. How the service is delivered is as important as the frequency and nature of the service. Consequently, customer satisfaction depends on the production of services as well as their consumption.

Viewing services as a process raises considerable difficulties for management when trying to write service quality standards. Standards can be examined either from the perspective of the consumer or from that of the operating system. Thus, a specification can be written based on consumers' ratings of the responsiveness of the organization. Unfortunately, although this is a quantitative measure, it does little to guide the behavior of operations managers and contact personnel.

### Consumer Perceptions Are Unpredictable

Ratings of service quality dimensions may be influenced by factors outside the control of the organization that may not be readily apparent to managers. For example, consumer moods and attitudes may influence ratings. Studies have shown that when rating services, consumers use a diverse variety of clues. A recent study shows that, even if a service firm generates a negative disconfirmation for a consumer, it may not be judged as delivering a poor level of satisfaction. Since they are part of the process, consumers may attribute failure to themselves or to factors outside the control of the firm. Such attributions are shown to depend on the physical characteristics of the service firm. For example, a tidy office setting leads negative attributions away from the firm, while a messy office generates attributions of dissatisfaction toward the firm.[13]

### Assessing the Criticisms of SERVQUAL

Finally, the criticisms of SERVQUAL should not be taken lightly. As is the case with most measurement scales, constructive criticism assists in the further development of improved measurement instruments. Moreover, concerns regarding measurement instruments should remind practitioners that firms should not "live or die" and make drastic decisions based solely on one measurement instrument's results. The value of measurement tools is that they provide management the opportunity to make a more informed decision.

Despite its opponents, SERVQUAL remains a frequently utilized instrument to assess service quality and is currently being modified to address service quality issues in e-business (see E-Services in Action). From the beginning, its developers have claimed that SERVQUAL is a useful starting point for measuring service quality and was never presented as "the final answer." The developers of SERVQUAL further contend that when used in conjunction with other forms of measurement, both quantitative and qualitative, SERVQUAL provides a valuable diagnostic tool for evaluating the firm's service quality performance. Overall, as was the case with satisfaction measures, SERVQUAL is most valuable when compared with a firm's own past service quality trends and when compared with measures of competitive service quality performance.

## > | SERVICE QUALITY INFORMATION SYSTEMS

A **service quality information system** is an ongoing research process that provides relevant data on a timely basis to managers, who utilize the data for decision-making purposes.[14] More specifically, service quality information systems utilize service quality and customer satisfaction measures in conjunction with other measures obtained at various points to assess the firm's overall performance. Components of a service quality information system include the following:

- reports on solicitation of customer complaints;
- after-sales surveys;
- customer focus group interviews;
- mystery shopping results;

*service quality information system*
An ongoing research process that provides relevant data on a timely basis to managers, who use the data in decision making.

## E-SERVICES *IN ACTION*

### > THE SEVEN DIMENSIONS OF E-QUAL

The importance of service quality in improving customer satisfaction and loyalty in traditional business settings has been established via SERVQUAL. The following recommendations are given for how consumers might evaluate online business via E-QUAL:

1. *Accessibility* Is the site easily found? This is measured by the number of search engines where a site is registered and by the number of links to related sites.
2. *Navigation* How easy is it to move around the site? A good rule-of-thumb is to be within three clicks of the information that is most desired by customers.
3. *Design and presentation* What is the image projected from the site? Design elements include colors, layout, clarity, and originality.
4. *Content and purpose* The substance (breadth) and richness (depth) of the site.
5. *Currency and accuracy* are important aspects of the "content" dimension. The strategic purpose of the site includes sites that are developed for an Internet presence (informational purpose) and online store fronts (revenue-producing purpose).
6. *Responsiveness* The company's propensity to respond to email messages. The collection of visitor information (i.e., cookies, guest book, contests, chat rooms, clubs, storybooks, auto-e-mail, and options to speak to customer representatives), and what the company does with this information.
7. *Interactivity, customization, and personalization* The hi-touch level of service provided. Interactivity, customization, and personalization relate to the empathy dimension of service quality. Amazon.com, for example, provides the quality of interaction and personalization that rivals traditional brick-and-mortar businesses.
8. *Reputation and security* Related to the assurance dimension of service quality, reputation and security pertain to consumer confidence issues. Consumer confidence is being built via proven encryption technologies.

Source: Kaynama, Shohreh A. (2000), "A Conceptual Model to Measure Service Quality of Online Companies: E-qual, in Developments in Marketing Science," Harlan E. Spotts and H. Lee Meadow, eds., *Proceedings of the Academy of Marketing Science*, Vol. 22, 46–51. For more information pertaining to online service quality see A. Parasuraman, Valerie A. Zeithaml, and Arvind Malhotra (2005), "E-S-QUAL: A Multiple-Item Scale for Assessing Electronic Service Quality," *Journal of Service Research*, Vol. 7, Issue 3, 213–234.

- employee surveys; and
- total market service quality surveys.

**customer research**
Research that examines the customer's perspective of a firm's strengths and weaknesses.

In general, service quality information systems focus on two types of research: customer research and noncustomer research. **Customer research** examines the customer's perspective of a firm's strengths and weaknesses and includes such measures as customer complaints, after-sales surveys, focus group interviews, and service quality surveys. In contrast, **noncustomer research** focuses on employee perspectives of the firm's strengths and weaknesses and employee performance (e.g., employee surveys and mystery shopping). In addition, noncustomer research examines how competitors perform on service (via total market service quality surveys) and serves as a basis for comparison.

*noncustomer research*
Research that examines how competitors perform on service and how employees view the firm's strengths and weaknesses.

## SOLICITATION OF CUSTOMER COMPLAINTS

The primary objectives of soliciting customer complaints are twofold. First, customer complaints identify unhappy customers. The firm's follow-up efforts may enable it to retain many of these customers before they defect to competitors. The second objective of soliciting customer complaints is to identify weaknesses in the firm's service delivery system and take the corrective actions necessary to minimize future occurrences of the same problem. Customer complaints should be solicited on a continuous basis.

The value of continuous customer feedback cannot be understated. Unfortunately, many firms address one complaint at a time and fail to analyze the content of the complaints as a group. The Chicago Marriott took 15 years to figure out that 66 percent of the calls to its customer service line concerned requests for an iron or ironing board.[15] As a result of learning this, the hotel redesignated $20,000 that had been earmarked for color televisions in guest bathrooms to purchase irons and ironing boards for the hotel. Interestingly, few, if any, customers had ever complained about the black-and-white televisions in the bathrooms. If the color televisions had been installed, we would have seen a classic example of a firm defining service quality on its own as opposed to listening to the voice of the customer. Chapter 14 takes an in-depth look at analyzing customer complaints and developing effective recovery strategies for use when service failures do occur.

## AFTER-SALES SURVEYS

As part of the service quality information system, **after-sales surveys** should also be conducted on a continuous basis. Since after-sales surveys pertain to discrete transactions, they are a type of satisfaction survey and, as such, are subject to the advantages and disadvantages of all customer satisfaction surveys discussed in Chapter 12. For example, after-sales surveys address customer satisfaction while the service encounter is still fresh in the customer's mind. Consequently, the information reflects the firm's recent performance but may be biased by the customer's inadvertent attempt to minimize cognitive dissonance.

*after-sales surveys*
A type of satisfaction survey that addresses customer satisfaction while the service encounter is still fresh in the customer's mind.

Although after-sales surveys can also identify areas for improvement, after-sales surveys are a more proactive approach to assessing customer satisfaction than is soliciting customer complaints. Many firms wait for customers to complain and then take action based on those complaints. Given the average customer's reluctance to complain, waiting for customer complaints does not provide the firm a "true" picture of its performance. The after-sales survey attempts to contact every customer and take corrective action if a customer is less than satisfied with his or her purchase decision.

## CUSTOMER FOCUS GROUP INTERVIEWS

*focus group interviews*
Informal discussions with eight to twelve customers that are usually guided by a trained moderator; used to identify areas of information to be collected in subsequent survey research.

Another important component of the service quality information system involves customer **focus group interviews.**[16] Focus group interviews are informal discussions with eight to twelve customers that are usually guided by a trained moderator. Participants in the group are encouraged to express their views and to comment on the suggestions made by others in the group. Because of the group interaction, customers tend to feel more comfortable, which motivates them to talk more openly and honestly. Consequently, researchers feel that the information obtained via focus group interviews is richer than data that reflects the opinions of a single individual.

Focus groups are probably the most widely used market research method. However, their primary purpose is to identify areas of information to be collected in subsequent survey research. Although the information provided by the group is considered valuable, other forms of research are generally necessary to confirm that the group's ideas reflect the feelings of the broader segment of customers. Advocates of service quality information systems believe that customer focus groups should be conducted on a monthly basis.

## MYSTERY SHOPPING

*mystery shopping*
A form of noncustomer research that consists of trained personnel who pose as customers, shop unannounced at the firm, and evaluate employees.

**Mystery shopping** is a form of noncustomer research that measures individual employee service behavior. As the name indicates, mystery shoppers are generally trained personnel who pose as customers and who shop unannounced at the firm. The idea is to evaluate an individual employee during an actual service encounter. Mystery shoppers

Focus groups can provide invaluable feedback to service firms. A roundtable format with participants and a facilitator helps identify areas that need to be improved, ways the service firm best meets the customers' needs, and other valuable information.

© ANDREAS POLLOK / TAXI/ GETTY IMAGES

evaluate employees on a number of characteristics, such as the time it takes for the employee to acknowledge the customer, eye contact, appearance, and numerous other specific customer service and sales techniques promoted by the firm.

Mystery shopping is a form of observation research and is recommended to be conducted on a quarterly basis. Results obtained from mystery shoppers are used as constructive employee feedback. Consequently, mystery shopping aids the firm in coaching, training, evaluating, and formally recognizing its employees.

## EMPLOYEE SURVEYS

Another vital component of the service quality information system is employee research. When the product is a performance, it is essential that the company listen to the performers. Too often, employees are forgotten in the quest for customer satisfaction. However, the reality is that employee satisfaction with the firm directly corresponds with customer satisfaction. Hence, the lesson to be learned by service firms is that if they want the needs of their customers to come first, they cannot place the needs of their employees last.

Conducted quarterly, **employee surveys** provide an internal measure of service quality concerning employee morale, attitudes, and perceived obstacles to the provision of quality services. Often employees would like to provide a higher level of quality service but feel that their hands are tied by internal regulations and policies. Employee surveys provide the means to uncover these obstacles so that they can be removed when appropriate. Moreover, employees are customers of internal service and assess internal service quality. Because of their direct involvement in providing service delivery, employee complaints serve as an early warning system; that is, employees often see the system breaking down before customers do.

*employee surveys*
Internal measures of service quality concerning employee morale, attitudes, and perceived obstacles to the provision of quality services.

## TOTAL MARKET SERVICE QUALITY SURVEYS

**Total market service quality surveys** not only measure the service quality of the firm sponsoring the survey but also assess the perceived service quality of the firm's competitors. When service quality measures such as SERVQUAL are used in conjunction with other measures, a firm can evaluate its own performance compared with previous time periods and with its competitors. Service quality surveys provide a firm with information about needed improvements in the service delivery system, plus measure the progress in making needed improvements that have been previously identified.

*total market service quality surveys*
Surveys that measure the service quality of the firm sponsoring the survey and the service quality of the firm's competitors.

Advocates of the service quality information system recommend that total market service quality surveys be conducted three times a year. However, as is the case with all the components of the service quality information system, the recommended frequencies are dependent upon the size of the customer base. Too frequent contact with the same customers can be an annoyance to them. On the other hand, conducting surveys too infrequently may ultimately cost the business its existence.

Overall, the service quality information system provides a comprehensive look at the firm's performance and overcomes many of the shortcomings of individual measures used in isolation. As with all measures, the information system's true value lies in the information it gives managers to help in their decision making. The measures should serve as a support system for decisions but not be the only inputs into the decision process. Managerial expertise and intuition remain critical components of every business decision. Ultimately, the key components that need to be built into every service quality system include the following:[17]

- *Listening*: Quality is defined by the customer. Conformance to company specifications is not quality; conformance to customers' specifications is. Spending wisely to improve service comes from continuous learning about expectations and perceptions of customers and manufacturers (see Figure 13.4).

| FIGURE 13.4 | QUALITY IMPROVEMENTS NEED FOCUS, NOT JUST $$$ |
| --- | --- |

Although adequate resource support is directly related to the successful implementation of service delivery systems, providing support without direction can be a huge waste of resources. For example, the United States leads the world in health care expenditures per capita, yet ranks thirty-seventh in terms of the quality of care provided to its citizens. The United States devotes 10 to 14 percent of national income to health care, with an average per-capita expenditure of $3,724; meanwhile, England spends 6 percent and is ranked eighteenth in the world.

### The most doesn't mean the best

A study of world health systems has found that the United States spends the most per person but ranked 37th for quality of service. Here are the top rankings for overall performance and spending.

**\* Indicates G-7 country, the seven richest countries in the world**

| Overall performance | Total spending, per capita | |
| --- | --- | --- |
| 1. France* | 1. **United States*** | $3,724 |
| 2. Italy* | 2. Switzerland | $2,644 |
| 3. San Marino | 3. Germany* | $2,365 |
| 4. Andorra | 4. France* | $2,125 |
| 5. Malta | 5. Luxembourg | $1,985 |
| 6. Singapore | 6. Austria | $1,960 |
| 7. Spain | 7. Sweden | $1,943 |
| 8. Oman | 8. Denmark | $1,940 |
| 9. Austria | 9. Netherlands | $1,911 |
| 10. Japan* | 10. Canada* | $1,836 |
| 18. United Kingdom* | 11. Italy* | $1,824 |
| 25. Germany* | 13. Japan* | $1,759 |
| 30. Canada* | 26. United Kingdom* | $1,193 |
| 37. **United States*** | | |

*Source: World Health Report 2000*                                                    AP

Source: Robert Cooke, "U.S. Leads in Health-Care Spending, but Not Quality," *Fort Collins Coloradoan*, June 21, 2000, p. B1.

- *Reliability*: Reliability is the core of service quality. Little else matters to a customer when the service is unreliable.
- *Basic Service*: Forget the frills if you cannot deliver the basics. American service customers want the basics; they expect fundamentals, not fanciness, and performance, not empty promises.
- *Service Design*: Reliably delivering the basic service that customers expect depends, in part, on how well various elements function together in a service system. Design flaws in any part of a service system can reduce the perception of quality.
- *Recovery*: Research shows that companies consistently receive the most unfavorable service quality scores from customers whose problems were not resolved satisfactorily. In effect, companies that do not respond effectively to customer complaints compound the service failure, thereby failing twice.
- *Surprising Customers*: Exceeding customers' expectations requires the element of surprise. If service organizations can be not only reliable in output but also surprise the customer in the way the service is delivered, then they are truly excellent.
- *Fair Play*: Customers expect service companies to treat them fairly and become resentful and mistrustful when they perceive that they are being treated otherwise.
- *Teamwork*: The presence of "teammates" is an important dynamic in sustaining a server's motivation to serve. Service team building should not be left to chance.
- *Employee Research*: Employee research is as important to service improvement as customer research.
- *Servant Leadership*: Delivering excellent service requires a special form of leadership. Leadership must serve the services, inspiring and enabling them to achieve.

© GETTY IMAGES

Because of their commitment to a total quality experience, British Airway's Club World has been completely redesigned in the style of a "lounge in the sky" to provide better service to its business travelers. The armchair-style seat converts into a flat bed at the touch of a button. The Club World Sleeper maximizes travelers' sleep time on board, allowing them to have a more restful journey.

## ✳ SUMMARY

This chapter has focused on defining and measuring service quality. The concepts of service quality and customer satisfaction, discussed in Chapter 12, are intertwined. In general, customer satisfaction can be defined as a short-term, transaction-specific measure. In turn, service quality is a long-term, overall measure. Another difference is that satisfaction compares perceptions to what customers would normally expect. In comparison, service quality compares perceptions to what customers should expect from a high-quality firm. Customer satisfaction and service quality assessments compliment each other. Satisfaction evaluations made after each service transaction help revise customers' overall service quality evaluations of the firm's performance.

Firms that excel in service quality do so by avoiding potential quality gaps in their delivery systems. Service quality gaps discussed in this chapter include knowledge, standards, delivery, and communication. Numerous managerial, marketing, and operational factors influence the size of each of these gaps. Ultimately, the goal of every firm is to minimize the service gap—the difference between customer perceptions and expectations. The service gap is a function of the knowledge, standards, delivery, and communication gaps and responds accordingly in the combined direction of the four gaps.

One popular method for assessing service quality is the SERVQUAL scale. The original SERVQUAL survey instrument consists of 44 questions that compare consumers' expectations to perceptions along five service quality dimensions—tangibles, responsiveness, reliability, assurance, and empathy. Gap scores for each of the five dimensions can be calculated by comparing consumer expectation and perception ratings. The SERVQUAL gaps indicate specific areas in need of improvement and assist the service firm in its continuous improvement efforts.

SERVQUAL is only one method to assess a firm's service quality. A service quality information system utilizes a variety of continuous measures to assess the firm's overall performance. The major components of such a system collect information about both customer and noncustomer research. Customer research methods include analyzing customer complaints, after-sales surveys, focus group interviews, and service quality surveys. Noncustomer research methods include employee surveys and mystery shopping.

In summary, service quality offers a means of achieving success among competing firms that offer similar products. The benefits associated with service quality include increases in market share and repeat purchases. Ultimately, the keys to delivering service quality are a detailed understanding of the needs of the consumer, service providers who are focused on providing quality, and service delivery systems that are designed to support the firm's overall quality mission.

## ✳ KEY TERMS

service quality, 333

service gap, 334

knowledge gap, 335

standards gap, 335

delivery gap, 335

communications gap, 335

research orientation, 336

upward communication, 336

## ✳ DISCUSSION QUESTIONS

1. What are the basic differences between customer satisfaction and service quality?
2. Explain how a manager might use the conceptual model of service quality to improve the quality of his/her own firm.
3. What factors contribute to the size of the knowledge gap?
4. How does the communication gap relate to success in e-business (see Services in Action)?
5. Discuss the basics of the SERVQUAL measurement instrument.
6. Develop specifications for the role of a "good student."
7. What are the criticisms of SERVQUAL? What are its developers' responses to these criticisms?
8. You have been hired by a firm to develop the firm's service quality information system. What are the components of this system?

## ✳ NOTES

1. J. Joseph Cronin, Jr., and Steven A. Taylor, "Measuring Service Quality: A Reexamination and Extension," *Journal of Marketing* 56 (July 1992), p. 55.
2. Thomas A. Stewart, "After All You've Done for Your Customers, Why Are They Still NOTHAPPY," *Fortune*, December 11, 1995, pp. 178–182.
3. Cronin, Jr., and Taylor, "Measuring Service Quality," pp. 60–63.
4. Ibid.
5. This section was adapted from John E. G. Bateson, *Managing Services Marketing*, 3rd ed. (Fort Worth, TX: The Dryden Press, 1995), pp. 558–565.
6. A. Parasuraman, Valerie A. Zeithaml, and Leonard L. Berry, "A Conceptual Model of Service Quality and Its Implications for Future Research," *Journal of Marketing* 49, (Fall 1985), pp. 41–50.
7. A. Parasuraman, Leonard L. Berry, and Valerie A. Zeithaml, "SERVQUAL: A Multiple-Item Scale for Measuring Customer Perceptions of Service Quality," *Journal of Retailing* 64, 1 (1988), pp. 12–40.
8. Parasuraman, Zeithaml, and Berry, "A Conceptual Model."
9. Scale items from A. Parasuraman, Leonard L. Berry, and Valerie A. Zeithaml, "Refinement and Reassessment of the SERVQUAL Scale,"

*Journal of Retailing* 67 (Winter 1991), pp. 420–450.

10. Cronin, Jr., and Taylor, "Measuring Service Quality," pp. 60–63.

11. A. Parasuraman, Valerie A. Zeithaml, and Leonard L. Berry, "Reassessment of Expectations as a Comparison Standard in Measuring Service Quality: Implications for Future Research," *Journal of Marketing*, 58 (January 1994), pp. 111–124.

12. See A. Parasuraman, Leonard L. Berry, and Valerie A. Zeithaml, "Refinement and Reassessment of the SERVQUAL Scale," *Journal of Retailing*, pp. 420–450; A. Parasuraman, Leonard L. Berry, and Valerie A. Zeithaml, "More On Improving Service Quality Measurement," *Journal of Retailing* 69, 1 (Spring 1993) pp. 1401; and A. Parasuraman, Valerie A. Zeithaml, and Leonard L. Berry, "Reassessment of Expectations as a Comparison Standard in Measuring Service Quality: Implications for Future Research," *Journal of Marketing* 58 (January 1994), pp. 111–124.

13. Mary Jo Bitner, "Evaluating Service Encounters: The Effects of Physical Surroundings and Employee Responses," *Journal of Marketing* (April 1990), pp. 42–50.

14. Leonard L. Berry, A. Parasuraman, and Valerie A. Zeithaml, "Improving Service Quality in America: Lessons Learned," *Academy of Management* Executive 8, 2 (1994), pp. 32–52.

15. Ibid., p. 33.

16. Adapted from Henry Assael, *Marketing Principles & Strategy*, 2nd ed. (Fort Worth, TX: The Dryden Press, 1993), p. 226; and Michael Levy and Barton Weitz, *Retailing Management*, (Homewood, IL: Irwin, 1992), p. 149.

17. Berry, Parasuraman, and Zeithaml, "Improving Service Quality," pp. 32–52.

# CHAPTER 14

## SERVICE FAILURES AND RECOVERY STRATEGIES

### CHAPTER OBJECTIVES

*The major objectives of this chapter are to introduce the concepts of service failures, consumer complaint behavior, service recovery strategies, and procedures for tracking and monitoring service failures and employee recovery efforts.*

After reading this chapter, you should be able to:

- Discuss the four different categories of service failure types.

- Explain customer complaining behavior, including the reasons customers do and do not complain and the outcomes associated with customer complaints.

- Describe the issues involved in mastering the art of service recovery.

- Understand the value of tracking and monitoring service failures and employee recovery efforts.

*"Don't fight a battle if
you don't gain anything
by winning."*

General George S. Patton, Jr.

© MILLER / E-VISUAL COMMUNICATION, INC.

In Part 3 of this text, we have addressed customer satisfaction and service quality issues as they pertain to assessing and improving service delivery processes. Another key management issue in this area involves tracking and analyzing service failures and designing recovery strategies that minimize customer defections. In many instances, excellent service companies utilize service failure analysis as a means to foresee the typical mistakes that are likely to occur and develop recovery strategies to offset their negative consequences. Of course, the primary goal is for service failures never to occur in the first place. However, given the nature of services, service failures do happen and customers do occasionally leave unhappy, never to be seen again.

Although most companies can reasonably predict where service may occasionally fall short, there are some instances that can never be foreseen. One such case involved WENDY'S International Inc. and "the-finger-in-the-chili-incident." In the spring of 2005, a Northern California woman claimed to bite into a one-and-a-half-inch-long finger while eating chili at a local WENDY'S restaurant. WENDY'S sales plummeted as news of the incident spread worldwide. The woman, while appearing on ABC's "Good Morning America" reported that: "knowing a human body part was in her mouth was disgusting." The woman then filed a lawsuit against WENDY'S International Inc. to recover damages.

WENDY'S response to the issue never wavered. First, company representatives traveled to the San Jose store where the incident occurred and verified that all of its employees had their fingers intact. They next went to the company's food suppliers for another digit inventory—all were in place. Voice stress analysis tests were given to employees and suppliers to determine their involvement in the incident—all suppliers and employees passed. Suspecting foul play, the company then publicly offered a $100,000 reward for information that would lead authorities to the source of the finger. In addition, a free "Junior Frosty" give-away to any customer who asked for one was planned as a way to get customers back in the stores. The give-away involved approximately 6,600 corporate and franchised WENDY'S that served an estimated 14 million ice cream treats in this "thank-you-for-your-understanding" gesture.

As a result of WENDY'S investigation of its own people and further findings that the woman and her family had previously sued at least a dozen other companies, increased scrutiny was directed towards the accuser who responded: "Lies, lies, lies, that's all I am hearing. They should look at WENDY'S. What are they hiding? Why are we being victimized again and again?" The woman eventually dropped her lawsuit, claiming the pressure associated with the whole incident had become too much to bear.

Over the next several weeks, WENDY'S $100,000 reward offer paid off as a tipster came forward to provide information leading to the source of the finger. As it turned out, the finger belonged to a co-worker of the accuser's husband who had severed the digit in the tailgate of his truck months earlier. The husband acquired the finger from the co-worker in return for a relinquished $50 debt. The accuser now faces charges of attempted grand theft in San Jose and further charges are being considered against the husband related to the WENDY'S incident.

Despite WENDY'S vindication, it came with a hefty price. The company estimates that it lost $2.5 million in sales over the incident. In addition, the company's promise to pay $100,000 to the tipster adds to the cost. However, WENDY'S had few alternative approaches available. Paying the woman off early to buy her silence would have been viewed as an admission of guilt. Advertising to the public that processes were in place to keep fingers out of WENDY'S food is not a viable marketing strategy. Relying on the public to believe the whole incident might be a hoax and giving the company the benefit of the doubt is unreliable. The only sound strategy was to defend the brand and hope the truth would eventually be made public and customers would return. WENDY'S sales are currently rebounding, but slowly. Time should help.

Source: Alan J. Liddle, "Tipster fingers hoax suspect as Wendy's awaits sales comeback." *Nation's Restaurant News*, (May 23, 2005), 39, Issue 21, p. 3, 208; Paul Winston, "Pointing the finger at the real culprit," *Business Insurance*, (May 23, 2005), 39, Issue 21, p. 6.

> ## INTRODUCTION

Despite the service firm's best efforts, service failures are inevitable. Planes are late, employees are rude or inattentive, and the maintenance of the tangibles surrounding the service is not always perfect. Don't give up! Developing an indifferent attitude or accepting service failures as a part of everyday business can be "the kiss of death." The secrets to success are to take a proactive stance to reduce the occurrence of **service failures** and to equip employees with a set of effective recovery tools to repair the service experience when failures do occur.

*service failures*
Breakdowns in the delivery of service; service that does not meet customer expectations.

The reason failures are inherent events in the service encounter are directly related to the unique characteristics that distinguish services from goods. Due to intangibility, customer comparison of perceptions to expectations is a highly subjective evaluation; consequently, not all customers are going to be satisfied. Due to heterogeneity, variations in the service delivery process are going to occur, and not every service encounter is going to be identical. Due to perishability, supply and demand match each other only by accident. Hence, service customers will experience delays from time to time, and service workers will occasionally lose their patience while attempting to appease an influx of anxious customers. Finally, inseparability places the service provider face-to-face with the customer, which provides a Pandora's Box of failure possibilities.

> ## TYPES OF SERVICE FAILURES

Service failures occur at **critical incidents** in the service encounter. Each service encounter is made up of numerous critical incidents, or "moments of truth," which represent the numerous interactions between the customer and the providing service firm. Critical incidents can range from human interactions, such as how the receptionist answers customer questions to human/servicescape interactions including, the comfort of a hotel bed or the ease of use of a self-service technology such as a bank's ATM or an airline's electronic check-in process. Critical incidents may positively or negatively impact the customer's service experience. Negative critical incidents result in service failures that require the service firm's attention to correct. The service firm's response to service failures greatly influences the customer's satisfaction and/or dissatisfaction and retention.

*critical incidents*
The moments of actual interaction between the customer and the firm.

| TABLE 14.1 | SERVICE FAILURE TYPES |
|---|---|
| **Primary Failure Type** | **Failure Subgroups** |
| Service Delivery System Failures | Unavailable Service |
| | Unreasonably Slow Service |
| | Other Core Service Failures |
| Customer Needs and Requests | "Special Needs" Customers |
| | Customer Preferences |
| | Admitted Customer Error |
| | Disruptive Others |
| Unprompted/Unsolicited Employee Actions | Level of Attention |
| | Unusual Action |
| | Cultural Norms |
| | Gestalt |
| Problematic Customers | Drunkenness |
| | Verbal and Physical Abuse |
| | Breaking Company Policies |
| | Uncooperative Customers |

Source: Adapted from Mary Jo Bitner, Bernard H. Booms, and Mary Stanfield Tetreault, "The Service Encounter: Diagnosing Favorable and Unfavorable Incidents," *Journal of Marketing* (January 1990), pp. 71–84; Mary Jo Bitner, Bernard H. Booms and Lois A. Mohr (1994), "Critical service encounters: the employee's viewpoint", *Journal of Marketing*, Vol. 58, October, pp. 95–106.

Although a firm may receive hundreds of customer complaints pertaining to perceived service failures throughout a year, ultimately these complaints (service failures) can be categorized into one of four main groups: (1) service delivery system failures; (2) failures relating to customer needs and requests; (3) failures relating to unprompted and unsolicited employee actions; and (4) failures relating to problematic customers (see Table 14.1).[1]

## SERVICE DELIVERY SYSTEM FAILURES

**system failures**
Failures in the core service offering of the firm.

**unavailable service**
Services normally available that are lacking or absent.

**unreasonably slow service**
Services or employees perceived by customers as being extraordinarily slow in fulfilling their function.

**other core service failures**
All remaining core service breakdowns or actions that do not live up to customer expectations.

Service delivery **system failures** are failures that relate directly to the core service offering of the firm. For example, airlines that do not depart on time, hotels that do not adequately clean their rooms, and insurance firms that do not process their claims are all guilty of service delivery system failures. In general, service delivery system failures consist of employee responses to three types of failures: (1) unavailable service, (2) unreasonably slow service, and (3) other core service failures. **Unavailable service** refers to services normally available that are lacking or absent. **Unreasonably slow service** concerns services or employees that customers perceive as being extraordinarily slow in fulfilling their function. Finally, **other core service failures** encompass all other core service failures. This category is deliberately broad to reflect the various core services offered by different industries such as financial services, healthcare, insurance, travel and tourism, retailing, and so on. Each has its own unique set of cores service issues (see E-Services in Action).

## E-SERVICES *IN ACTION*

### > E-FAILURES ONLINE

Consumer online spending, which reached $19 billion in 1999, doubled to $38 billion in 2000, and rose again by 46 percent to $54 billion in 2001. In 2002, 30 million, or roughly 15 percent of all Americans, purchased Christmas gifts via the Internet. In 2003, despite recession, terrorism, and war, consumer e-commerce spending was projected to hit $95 billion. In short, although all the hype surrounding the e-commerce revolution has subsided, the numbers are in and the e-commerce retail sector is booming and here to stay.

The phenomenal growth of the e-tail sector has not been without its unique troubles. One of the main issues arising repeatedly concerns the level of service provided during the course of electronic transactions. According to recent research, a comparison of offline to online failure types appears as follows:

| Failure Type | Brick and Mortar Failures Frequency (Percent) | E-tail Failures Frequency (Percent) |
|---|---|---|
| **Group 1. Response to Service Delivery System/Product Failure** | | |
| 1A. Policy Failure | 14.1 | — |
| 1B. Slow/Unavailable Service | 4.1 | 15.9 |
| 1C. System Pricing | 1.8 | 6.1 |
| 1D. Packaging Errors | 3.2 | 43.0 |
| 1E. Out of Stock | 2.4 | 2.9 |
| 1F. Product Defect | 33.3 | 12.2 |
| 1G. Hold Disaster | 2.3 | — |
| 1H. Alterations and Repairs | 4.2 | — |
| 1I. Bad Information | 5.1 | 5.3 |
| 1J. Website System Failure | — | 4.5 |
| Group 1 Total | 70.5 | 89.9 |
| **Group 2. Response to Customer Needs and Requests** | | |
| 2A. Special Order/Request | 6.5 | 3.2 |
| 2B. Customer Error | 1.5 | 3.2 |
| 2C. Size Variation | — | 3.7 |
| Group 2 Total | 8.0 | 10.1 |

| Group 3. Unprompted and Unsolicited Actions | | |
|---|---|---|
| 3A. Mischarged | 13.5 | — |
| 3B. Accused of Shoplifting | 0.8 | — |
| 3C. Embarrassments | 4.4 | — |
| 3D. Attention Failures | 2.9 | — |
| Group 3 Total | 21.6 | 0.0 |

Clearly, the speed of service and fulfillment issues (packaging errors) are key areas of concern for online retailers. Despite the problems, 73 percent of customers shopping online reported that they were satisfied with their experience. This compares to a 60 percent satisfaction rate for brick-and-mortar stores, and a 56 percent rate for catalog shopping.

Source: Lukas P. Forbes, Scott W. Kelley, and K. Douglas Hoffman "E-Loyalty and Satisfaction: A Typology of E-Commerce Retail Failures and Recovery Strategies," *Journal of Services Marketing*, forthcoming in 2005; Sterlicchi, John and Barbara Gengler, "E-tailers Costly Lessons, *Upside*", 12 (6), (June, 2000), pp. 195–200. For a best practices example of an e-return policy, go to Amazon.com at http://www.amazon.com accessed 4 June 2005.

## CUSTOMER NEEDS AND REQUESTS

*customer needs and requests*
The individual needs and special requests of customers.

*implicit needs*
Customer needs that are not requested but that should be obvious to service providers.

*explicit requests*
Customer needs that are overtly requested.

*special needs*
Requests based on a customer's special medical, psychological, language, or sociological difficulties.

*customer preferences*
The needs of a customer that are not due to medical, dietary, psychological, language, or sociological difficulties.

*customer errors*
Service failures caused by admitted customer mistakes.

The second type of service failure, **customer needs and requests,** pertains to employee responses to individual consumer needs and special requests. Consumer needs can be implicit or explicit. **Implicit needs** are not requested. For example, a disabled customer seated in a wheelchair should not be lead to an elevated booth in a restaurant. In contrast, **explicit requests** are overtly requested. A customer who asks for her steak to be cooked medium-rare and who would like to substitute mash potatoes for the baked potato listed on the menu is making explicit requests.

In general, customer needs and requests consist of employee responses to four types of possible failures: (1) special needs, (2) customer preferences, (3) customer errors, and (4) disruptive others. Employee responses to **special needs** involve complying with requests based on a customer's special medical, dietary, psychological, language, or sociological difficulties. Preparing a meal for a vegetarian would fulfill a "special request." Employee responses to **customer preferences** require the employee to modify the service delivery system in some way that meets the preferred needs of the customer. A customer request for a substitution at a restaurant is an example of a customer preference. An employee response to a **customer error** involves a scenario in which the failure is initiated by an admitted customer mistake (e.g., lost tickets, lost hotel key, forgot to tell the waitress to "hold the mustard"). Finally, employee responses to **disruptive others** require employees to settle disputes between customers, such as requesting patrons to be quiet in movie theaters or requesting that smoking customers not smoke in nonsmoking sections of a restaurant.

## UNPROMPTED / UNSOLICITED EMPLOYEE ACTIONS

The third type of service failure, **unprompted and unsolicited employee actions**, pertains to events and employee behaviors—both good and bad—that are totally unexpected by the customer. These actions are not initiated by the customer via a request, nor are they part of the core delivery system. Subcategories in this group include (1) level of attention, (2) unusual action, (3) cultural norms, (4) gestalt, and (5) adverse condition.

Within the failure group of unprompted or unsolicited employee action, the subcategory of **level of attention** refers to both positive and negative events. Positive levels of attention would occur when an employee goes out of his or her way to pamper a customer and anticipate the customer's needs. Negative levels of attention pertain to employees who have poor attitudes, employees who ignore a customer, and employees who exhibit behaviors consistent with an indifferent attitude.

The **unusual action** subcategory can also reflect positive and negative events. For example, a Domino's employee happened to see a family searching through the burnt-out remains of their house while making a delivery to another customer in the area. The employee reported the event to the manager, and the two immediately prepared and delivered pizzas for the family free of charge. The family was stunned by the action and never forgot the kindness that was extended toward them during their time of need. Unfortunately, an unusual action can also be a negative event. Employee actions such as rudeness, abusiveness, and inappropriate touching would qualify equally as unusual actions.

The **cultural norms** subcategory refers to actions that either positively reinforce cultural norms such as equality, fairness, and honesty, or violate the cultural norms of society. Violations would include discriminatory behavior, acts of dishonesty such as lying, cheating, and stealing, and other activities considered unfair by customers.

The **gestalt** subcategory refers to customer evaluations that are made holistically; that is, the customer does not describe the service encounter as discrete events but uses overall terms such as "pleasant" or "terrible." In our airline example, if the customer had not specified the individual failure events but had commented only, "It is almost unbelievable how poorly we were treated by the employees of your airline, almost a perfect negative case study in customer service," the complaint would be categorized as a gestalt evaluation.

Finally, the **adverse conditions** subcategory covers positive and negative employee actions under stressful conditions. If an employee takes effective control of a situation when all others around him/her are "losing their heads," customers are impressed by the employee's performance under those adverse conditions. In contrast, if the captain and crew of a sinking ship board the lifeboats before the passengers, this would obviously be remembered as a negative action under adverse conditions.

## PROBLEMATIC CUSTOMERS

The final service failure type involves instances where neither the employee nor the service firm is at fault for the service failure. In these situations, the cause of the service failure lies with the customer's own misbehavior. Service failures involving problematic

---

**disruptive others**
Customers who negatively influence the service experience of other customers.

**unprompted/unsolicited actions**
Events and employee behaviors, both good and bad, totally unexpected by the customer.

**level of attention**
Positive and/or negative regard given a customer by an employee.

**unusual action**
Both positive and negative events in which an employee responds with something out of the ordinary.

**cultural norms**
Service personnel actions that either positively reinforce or violate the cultural norms of society.

**gestalt**
Customer evaluations that are made holistically and given in overall terms rather than in descriptions of discrete events.

**adverse conditions**
Positive and negative employee actions under stressful conditions.

Problematic customers are one source of service failures. To avoid the problems associated with drunk and unruly fans, many professional baseball stadiums stop serving alcohol after the seventh inning.

© ANNIE GRIFFITHS BELT/CORBIS

**drunkenness**
An intoxicated customer's behavior adversely affects other customers, service employees, and the service environment in general.

**verbal and physical abuse**
A customer verbally or physically abuses either the employee or other customers.

**breaks company policies**
A customer who refuses to comply with policies that employees are attempting to enforce.

**uncooperative customer**
A customer who is generally rude, uncooperative, and unreasonably demanding.

customers include (1) drunkenness, (2) verbal and physical abuse, (3) breaking company policies, and (4) uncooperative customers. Problematic customer behavior involving **drunkenness** occurs when the intoxicated customer's behavior adversely affects other customers, service employees, or the service environment in general. In one airline incident, numerous members of a company sales group became intoxicated and began to expose themselves to other customers. The captain quickly cut off liquor sales, but the group continued to drink by opening their own personal bottles of liquor that were purchased at the duty-free shop before boarding.[2] **Verbal and physical abuse** refers to the customer verbally or physically abusing either the employee or other customers. For example, if a lover's quarrel breaks out in the middle of a restaurant and the couple begins screaming and/or hitting one another, this situation would qualify as verbal and physical abuse. A customer that **breaks company policies** refuses to comply with policies employees are attempting to enforce. For example, a queuing policy or a no substitution policy that is ignored by a customer would create a problematic situation. Finally, an **uncooperative customer** is one that is generally rude, uncooperative, and unreasonably demanding. Regardless of how the service employee attempts to appease this customer, the effort is typically futile. The customer simply will not be pleased.

## > CUSTOMER COMPLAINING BEHAVIOR

In a striking example of the impact of service failures, survey respondents were asked: "Have you ever gotten so upset at a store (or manufacturer) that you said, 'I'll never go into that store or buy that brand again,' and you haven't?" Researchers found that they had to limit respondents to relating only three incidents to keep the interview time reasonable. The oldest incident had happened more than 25 years ago, and 86 percent of the incidents were more than 5 years old. Apparently customers are not prone to "forgive and forget" when it comes to customer service failures!

The consequences of service failures can be dramatic. The vast majority of respondents in the survey (87 percent) indicated that they were still somewhat or very emotionally upset and were more upset about the treatment they received from employees than at the store or product performance. More than three-quarters of respondents indicated that they had engaged in negative word-of-mouth communications regarding the incident (46 percent claimed that they had told "lots of people"). Finally, true to form in what is typical consumer complaint behavior today, only 53 percent had voiced their complaint to the store, even though 100 percent defected to other firms.[3]

Most companies cringe at the thought of customers who complain, while other companies look at complaints as a necessary evil in conducting business (see Global Services in Action). The truth of the matter is that every company should encourage its customers to complain. Complainers are telling the firm that it has some operational or managerial problems that need to be corrected. Hence, complainers are offering the company a free gift, that is, they act as consultants and diagnose the firm's problems—at no fee. Moreover, complainers provide the firm with the chance to reestablish a customer's satisfaction. Complainers are more likely to do business with the firm again than are noncomplainers. Consequently, successful firms view complaints as an opportunity to satisfy unhappy customers and prevent defections and unfavorable word-of-mouth communications.[4]

It's not the complainers the company should worry about; it's the noncomplainers. Customers who do not express their complaints are already gone or ready to leave for the competition at any moment. In fact, 63 percent of dissatisfied customers who do not complain and who have purchased goods or services costing $1.00 to $5.00 will defect to a competitor. Even more disturbing is that as purchases exceed $100, the defection rate approaches 91 percent.[5]

Complaining is defined in *Webster's Third International Dictionary* as "expressing discontent, dissatisfaction, protest, resentment, or regret."[6] Complaining is different from criticism. Complaining expresses a dissatisfaction within the complainer, while criticism may be an objective and dispassionate observation about a person or object.

## TYPES OF COMPLAINTS

Based on past research in consumer psychology, complaints can be instrumental or noninstrumental.[7] **Instrumental complaints** are expressed for the purpose of altering an undesirable state of affairs. For example, complaining to a waiter about an undercooked steak is an instrumental complaint. In such a case, the complainer fully expects the waiter to correct the situation. Interestingly, research indicates that instrumental complaints make up only a small number of the complaints that are voiced every day.

In contrast, **noninstrumental complaints** are voiced without any expectation that the undesirable state will be altered. These kinds of complaints are voiced much more often than are instrumental complaints. For example, complaints about the weather such as, "It's too hot!" are voiced without any real expectation that conditions will change. Another type of noninstrumental complaint is an instrumental complaint that is voiced to a second party and not to the offending source. For example, complaining to a friend about your roommate being a "slob" is a noninstrumental complaint.

*instrumental complaints*
Complaints expressed for the purpose of altering an undesirable state of affairs.

*noninstrumental complaints*
Complaints expressed without expectation that an undesirable state will be altered.

## GLOBAL SERVICES *IN ACTION*

### > THE SNOWBALL EFFECTS OF NOT DEALING WITH CONSUMER COMPLAINTS

Complaint recognition and service recovery are important customer service issues for any type of firm whether it's a traditional goods manufacturer or a high-tech service operation. Failing to respond to customer complaints can become disastrous. Case in point, consider Japan's Mitsubishi Motors. For decades, Mitsubishi employees have apparently been going to great lengths to hide consumer complaints. Letters have been hidden in boxes, in changing rooms, behind lockers, and stashed in secret computer files. The primary reason for the cover-up appears to be cultural. On August 22, 2000, the company's president stood before the world press, took a deep sigh and an even deeper bow of apology, as he confessed to the company's systematic and deliberate attempts to avoid the recall of over 800,000 of its defective vehicles. "We were ashamed of reporting recalls," said the company's president, Katsuhiko Kawasoe.

The cost of the recall to the company is estimated to be in the tens of millions; however, the damage to its reputation and brand name may be much worse. DaimlerChrysler Corporation, which recently agreed to a 34 percent stake in Mitsubishi, is closely watching how the company responds to its admission of guilt.

Analysts blame the problem on the company's corporate culture of arrogance. Others note that Japan's reputation for excellence is quickly eroding due to its political leadership, and that the country is losing its confidence, strength, and momentum. Several other Japanese companies are also experiencing difficulties with the quality of their products, including Japan's Bridgestone Corp. and its subsidiary Firestone, which produced defective tires in the U.S.; Snow Brand Milk, which poisoned more than 15,000 of its customers; Kirin Beverage Company, which recently recalled over 600,000 cans of tomato juice; and careless accidents that occurred at the Tokiamura nuclear reactor.

Source: Mark Magnier and John O'Dell, "Mitsubishi Admits to Complaint Cover-up," *Coloradoan*, (August 23, 2000), pp. A1–A2.

**ostensive complaints**
Complaints directed at someone or something outside the realm of the complainer.

**reflexive complaints**
Complaints directed at some inner aspect of the complainer.

Complaints are also categorized as ostensive or reflexive. **Ostensive complaints** are directed at someone or something outside the realm of the complainer. In contrast, **reflexive complaints** are directed at some inner aspect of the complainer. Typically, complaints tend to be more ostensive than reflexive for two reasons. First, people generally avoid making negative comments about themselves so as not to reinforce negative self-esteem. Second, people seldom want to convey negative attributes about themselves to others.

## WHY DO CUSTOMERS COMPLAIN?

In the case of the instrumental complaint, the reason a customer complains is pretty clear. The complainer wants the undesirable state to be corrected. However, the reason is not so clear when it comes to noninstrumental complaints. Experts believe that noninstrumental complaints occur for several reasons. First, complaining serves a function much like the release of a pressure valve—it provides the complainer an emotional release from frustration. Complaints provide people with the mechanism for venting their feelings.

Complaining also serves as a mechanism for the complainer's desire to regain some measure of control. Control is reestablished if the complainer is able to influence other people's evaluations of the source of the complaint. For example, negative word of mouth spread by the complainer for the purpose of taking revenge on an offending business gives the complainer some measure of control through indirect retribution.

A third reason people complain to others is to solicit sympathy and test for consensus of the complaint, thereby validating the complainer's subjective evaluation of the events that led to the complaint. In other words, the complainer wants to know whether others would feel the same way under similar circumstances. If they would, the complainer then feels justified in having voiced the complaint.

Finally, complainers may complain simply to create an impression. As strange as it may seem, complainers are often considered to be more intelligent and discerning than noncomplainers.[8] The implication is that the complainer's standards and expectations are higher than those of noncomplainers.

## WHY DON'T CUSTOMERS COMPLAIN?

Compared to problems with goods, a greater percentage of problems with services are not voiced "because potential complainers do not know what to do or think that it wouldn't do any good."[9] This situation is directly attributable to the intangibility and inseparability inherent in the provision of services. Due to intangibility, evaluation of the service delivery process is primarily subjective. Consequently, consumers often lack the security of making an objective observation and may doubt their own evaluations.

Due to inseparability, customers often provide inputs into the process. Hence, given an undesirable outcome, customers may place much of the blame upon themselves for failing to convey to the service provider a satisfactory description of the level and type of service desired. In addition, inseparability encompasses the often face-to-face interaction between the customer and the service provider, and the customer may feel uncomfortable about complaining because of the physical presence of the provider.

Finally, many services are technical and specialized. Customers may not feel adequately qualified to voice a complaint for fear that they lack the expertise to evaluate the quality of the service. For example, do customers really know when their auto mechanic has completed everything they were billed for?

## COMPLAINING OUTCOMES

In general, complaining behavior results in three outcomes: voice, exit, and/or retaliation.[10] **Voice** refers to an outcome in which the consumer verbally communicates

*voice*
A complaining outcome in which the consumer verbally communicates dissatisfaction with the store or the product.

dissatisfaction with the store or the product. High voice means that the communication is expressed to the manager or someone higher in the organizational hierarchy than the actual provider. Medium voice occurs when the consumer communicates the problem to the person providing the service. Low voice occurs when the consumer does not communicate the problem to anyone associated with the store or product but may be relaying the problem to others outside the store.

**Exit,** the second type of complaining outcome, describes the situation in which a consumer stops patronizing the store or using the product. High exit occurs when the consumer makes a conscious decision never to purchase from the firm or buy the product again. Medium exit reflects a consumer's conscious decision to try not to use the store or product again if at all possible. Low exit means that the consumer does not change his or her purchasing behavior and continues to shop as usual.

The third type of complaint outcome is **retaliation**, the situation in which a consumer takes action deliberately designed to either damage the physical operation or hurt future business. High retaliation involves the situation where the consumer physically damages the store or goes out of his or her way to communicate to others negative aspects about the business. In medium retaliation, the consumer creates minor inconveniences for the store or perhaps tells only a few people about the incident. Low retaliation involves no retaliation at all against the store, perhaps consisting of only minor negative word of mouth.

Interestingly, the three complaining outcomes are not mutually exclusive and can be considered as three aspects of one behavior that may occur simultaneously. Experiencing high levels of all three outcomes simultaneously can result in explosive behavior. For example, "In one high-high-high example, the customer shouted his dissatisfaction at the clerk and the store manager, vowed never to buy at the store again, went out of the store, got in his car, and drove it in the front doors of the store through the checkout counter and between two lines of shelving, destroying everything in its path."[11] In contrast, a consumer who displays high-voice, low-exit, and low-retaliation behavior would typify a perpetual complainer who nevertheless continues to shop at the store as usual.

**exit**
A complaining outcome in which the consumer stops patronizing the store or using the product.

**retaliation**
A complaining outcome in which the consumer takes action deliberately designed to damage the physical operation or hurt future business.

> ## THE ART OF SERVICE RECOVERY

Complainers provide the firm with an opportunity to recover from the service failure. When the service is provided incorrectly the first time, an important but often forgotten management tool is the art of **service recovery**.[12] While some companies are great at delivering service until something goes wrong, other companies thrive on recovering from service failures and impressing customers in the process. Customers of service organizations often allow the firm one mistake.[13] Consequently, when a failure occurs, the customer generally provides the business with an opportunity to make amends. Unfortunately, many companies still drop the ball and further aggravate the customer by failing to take the opportunity to recover.

When the service delivery system fails, it is the responsibility of contact personnel to react to the complaint. The content and form of the contact personnel's response

**service recovery**
A firm's reaction to a complaint that results in customer satisfaction and goodwill.

determines the customer's perceived satisfaction or dissatisfaction with the service encounter.[14] Ironically, customers will remember a service encounter favorably if the contact personnel respond in a positive manner to the service failure. Hence, even though the service encounter included a service failure, the customer recalls the encounter as a positive event. In fact, a customer will rate performance higher if a failure occurs and the contact personnel successfully recover from the failure than if the service had been delivered correctly the first time. This phenomenon has been termed the **service recovery paradox.**

Experts in the area of service recovery recommend that in establishing service recovery as a priority and developing recovery skills, firms should consider the following issues.

*service recovery paradox* Situation in which the customer rates performance higher if a failure occurs and the contact personnel successfully recover from it than if the service had been delivered correctly in the first place.

## *MEASURE THE COSTS*

The costs of losing and the benefits of keeping existing customers as opposed to chasing new customers are substantial. In short, the costs of obtaining new customers are three to five times greater than those of keeping existing customers. Current customers are more receptive to the firm's marketing efforts and are, therefore, an important source of profit for the firm. In addition, existing customers ask fewer questions, are more familiar with the firm's procedures and employees, and are willing to pay more for services.

## *ACTIVELY ENCOURAGE COMPLAINTS*

Experts assert that actively encouraging complaints is a good way to "break the silence." Remember that complainers who actually voice their complaints to the source of the problem are the exception — most customers don't speak up. In fact, research indicates that the average company does not hear from 96 percent of its unhappy customers.[15] This doesn't mean that customers don't complain, only that they complain to friends and family rather than to the company. The average unhappy customer voices displeasure with a firm to 11 other people. If these 11 tell 5 other people, the firm has potentially lost 67 customers.[16] Strategies to encourage complaints include customer surveys, focus groups, and active monitoring of the service delivery process to ensure customer satisfaction throughout the encounter, before a customer leaves the premises.

## *ANTICIPATE NEEDS FOR RECOVERY*

Every service encounter is made up of a series of critical incidents, the points in the system where the customer and the firm interact. Firms that are effective in service recovery anticipate in advance the areas in their service delivery process where failures are most likely to occur. Of course, these firms take every step possible to minimize the occurrence of the failure in the first place, but they are prepared for recovery if delivery goes awry. Experts believe that firms should pay special attention to areas in which employee turnover is high. Many high-turnover positions are low-paying customer contact positions, and employees often lack motivation and/or are inexperienced in effective recovery techniques.

A good example of failing to anticipate a need for recovery might involve an airline that changed its flight schedule without notifying passengers. The airline should anticipate that this change will cause passengers problems with connecting flights.

## RESPOND QUICKLY

When a service failure does occur, the faster the company responds, the more likely that the recovery effort will result in a successful outcome. In fact, past studies have indicated that if the complaint is handled promptly, the company will retain 95 percent of its unhappy customers. In contrast, if the complaint is resolved in a less timely manner, the firm retains only 64 percent of unhappy customers.[17] Time is of the essence. The faster the firm responds to the problem, the better the message the firm sends to customers about the value it places on pleasing its customers. Why not give customers what they want, when they want it? Is it really worth it to the firm for employees to actively argue with customers?

One firm that learned this lesson the hard way involved a bank in Spokane, Washington. A customer who had millions of dollars in the bank's checking, investment, and trust accounts was denied having his parking validated because he "only" cashed a check as opposed to making a deposit. The customer was at a branch bank that was not his usual bank. After explaining the situation to the teller, who was unimpressed, and more loudly voicing his opinion to the branch manager, the customer drove to his usual bank and threatened to close his accounts if he did not receive a response from the bank's upper management by the end of the day. As incredible as it may seem, the call never came, and the customer withdrew $1 million the first thing next morning. This action did get the bank's attention, and the bank has been trying to recover ever since.[18]

## TRAIN EMPLOYEES

Expecting employees to be naturals at service recovery is unrealistic. Most employees don't know what to do when a failure occurs, and many others find making on-the-spot decisions a difficult task. Employee training in service recovery should take place on two levels. First, the firm must work at creating in the employee an awareness of customer concerns. Placing an employee in the shoes of the customer is often enlightening for an employee who has forgotten what it's like to be a customer of his or her own firm. For example, hospitals have made interns and staff dress in hospital gowns and had them rolled around on gurneys to experience some of the processes firsthand.

The second level of employee training, beyond developing an appreciation for customer needs, is defining management's expectation toward recovery efforts. What are acceptable recovery strategies from management's perspective? Effective recovery often means that management has to let go and allow employees to take risks, a transition that often leads to the empowerment of front-line employees.

By training employees and empowering them to respond to service failures, companies are more likely to overcome the service failure and regain customer confidence.

## EMPOWER THE FRONT LINE

Effective recovery often means that the employee has to bend the firm's rules and regulations—the exact type of activity that employees are trained not to do at any cost. Often the rules and regulations of the firm tie the hands of employees when it comes to effective recovery efforts, particularly in the area of prompt response. In many instances, firms require managerial approval before any effort to compensate a customer is undertaken. However, the manager is often engaged in other duties, which delays the response and adds to the frustration for both customer and employee.

## CLOSE THE LOOP

One of the most important activities in service recovery is providing feedback to the customer about how that customer's complaint made a difference. Customer-oriented firms that have a sound recovery strategy solve the customer's problem. However, firms that excel at recovery go the extra mile and reestablish contact with the customer for the purpose of informing the customer how their complaint will make a difference in the way operations are handled in the future. Incorporating the customer's complaint during a training session or developing new procedures to minimize future occurrences of the failure and communicating the impact of the complaint on the company to the customer closes the loop and win customers for life.

## > EVALUATING RECOVERY EFFORTS: PERCEIVED JUSTICE

Throughout the service recovery process, customers weigh their inputs against their outputs when forming recovery evaluations.[19] Inputs could be described by the costs associated with the service failure, including economic, time, energy, and psychic

*perceived justice*
The process whereby customers weigh their inputs against their outputs when forming recovery evaluations.

*distributive justice*
A component of perceived justice that refers to the outcomes (e.g., compensation) associated with the service recovery process.

*procedural justice*
A component of perceived justice that refers to the process (e.g., time) the customer endures during the service recovery process.

*interactional justice*
A component of perceived justice that refers to human content (e.g., empathy, friendliness) that is demonstrated by service personnel during the service recovery process.

(cognitive) costs. The sum of the inputs is compared to the sum of the outputs, which includes the specific recovery tactic (e.g., cash refund, apology, or replacement), the manner of personnel, the service policies developed to handle such situations, and the image associated with responsive organizations.

The customer's perception of whether the recovery strategy is just includes evaluations of the recovery process itself; the outcomes connected to the recovery strategy; and the interpersonal behaviors enacted during the recovery process. Accordingly, **perceived justice** consists of three components: distributive justice, procedural justice, and interactional justice.

**Distributive justice** focuses on the specific outcome of the firm's recovery effort. In other words, what specifically did the offending firm offer the customer to recover from the service failure, and did this outcome (output) offset the costs (inputs) of the service failure? Typical distributive outcomes include compensation (e.g., gratis, discounts, coupons, free upgrades, and free ancillary services); offers to mend or totally replace/reperform; and apologies.

The second component of perceived justice, **procedural justice**, examines the process that is undertaken to arrive at the final outcome. Hence, even though a customer may be satisfied with the type of recovery strategy offered, recovery evaluation may be poor due to the process endured to obtain the recovery outcome. For example, research has indicated that when implementing identical recovery strategies, those that are implemented "promptly" are much more likely to be associated with higher consumer effectiveness ratings and retention rates than their "delayed" counterparts.

**Interactional justice** refers to the manner in which the service recovery process is implemented and how recovery outcomes are presented. In other words, interactional justice involves the courtesy and politeness exhibited by personnel, empathy, effort observed in resolving the situation, and the firm's willingness to explain why the situation occurred.

A limited volume of research exists that specifically examines the influence of perceived justice on recovery strategy effectiveness. However, the bottom line is that the three components of perceived justice must be taken into consideration when formulating effective service recovery strategies. Deploying recovery efforts that satisfy distributive justice without consideration of customer procedural and interactional justice needs may still result in customer defections. If service firms are truly committed to the recovery process and retaining customers for life, all three aspects of perceived justice must be integrated into the service recovery process.

> ## SERVICE FAILURE AND RECOVERY ANALYSIS: A RESTAURANT INDUSTRY EXAMPLE[20]

The obvious benefit of service failure and recovery analysis is that management can identify common failure situations, minimize their occurrence, and train employees to recover from failures when they do occur (see B2B Services in Action). The example that follows is an actual study of service failures and recovery strategies in the restaurant industry.

## B2B SERVICES *IN ACTION*

### > THE SERVICE RECOVERY AUDIT

Service firms that wish to excel at service failure analysis and recovery may conduct an internal service recovery audit. The recovery audit directs the firm to think about the forces that drive its current failure and recovery management program (or lack thereof). The recovery audit consists of eight components: recovery culture, failure identification, failure attribution, recovery strategy, recovery implementation, monitoring, evaluating, and feedback. Ultimately, the recovery audit is a useful tool to continuously evaluate and enhance failure analysis and recovery efforts for the purpose of enhancing service excellence.

### *RECOVERY CULTURE COMPONENT:*

1. Does the leadership of the firm accept the notion that failures are a reality due to the nature of the business?
2. Does the leadership of the firm formally recognize the importance of having a recovery program in place?
3. Does the leadership provide employees the support necessary to effectively recover when failures occur?

### *FAILURE IDENTIFICATION COMPONENT:*

4. Does the organization know when a customer experiences a failure?
5. Are customers encouraged to notify the organization when a failure occurs?
6. Does the organization actively measure customer/employee satisfaction with the organization?
7. Are failures systematically collected and categorized?

### *FAILURE ATTRIBUTION COMPONENT:*

8. When a failure occurs, does the organization formally track the source (locus) of the problem?
9. When a failure occurs, does the organization formally track whether the problem is a random event (sporadic) or an event that is likely to repeat itself (chronic)?
10. When a failure occurs, does the organization formally track whether the organization had control over the cause of the problem?

## *RECOVERY STRATEGY COMPONENT:*

11. Does the organization have a preferred selection of recovery strategies?
12. Have preferred recovery strategies been discussed with front-line personnel?
13. Have preferred recovery strategies been discussed with the organization's customers?
14. Are different recovery strategies linked with specific types of failures and/or customers?

## *RECOVERY IMPLEMENTATION COMPONENT:*

15. Does the organization systematically measure the customer's satisfaction with the recovery implemented?
16. Does the organization systematically measure the customer's satisfaction with the process experienced to obtain the recovery implemented?
17. Does the organization systematically measure the customer's satisfaction with the human interaction (e.g., courtesy, empathy, professionalism) experienced during the recovery implementation?

## *MONITORING COMPONENT:*

18. Does the organization actively monitor the types of failures that occur to pinpoint areas for improvement?
19. Does the organization actively monitor failure attributions to more fully understand customer-perceived causes of failures?
20. Does the organization actively monitor recovery strategies selected by employees?
21. Does the organization actively monitor the outcome, process, and quality of inter-action after recovery has been implemented?

## *EVALUATION COMPONENT:*

22. Is the recovery program evaluated in terms of organizational goals?
23. Is the recovery program evaluated in terms of employee benefits (e.g., reduced role conflict and role ambiguity)?
24. Is the recovery program evaluated in terms of customer benefits (e.g., customer satisfaction)?

## *FEEDBACK COMPONENT:*

25. Are results obtained from the monitoring and evaluation components of the audit shared with employees for training and/or evaluation purposes?

Source: Gabriel R. Gonzalez, K. Douglas Hoffman and Thomas N. Ingram (2005), "The Sales Recovery Audit: A Tool for Enhancing Buyer-Seller Relationships," in *Proceedings of the National Conference in Sales Management*, C. David Shepherd, ed. Miami, FL., 20–22.

## THE VALUE OF TRACKING SERVICE FAILURES

As is the case in most service industries today, restaurant managers and service personnel are facing intensive customer service pressures now more than ever.[21] When a service failure does occur, the service provider's reaction can either reinforce a strong customer bond or change a seemingly minor distraction into a major incident. For example, an employee's indifferent reaction to a customer's complaint about cold french fries can cost a restaurant years of that particular customer's business and an abundance of negative word-of-mouth publicity. Consequently, it is imperative that managers have an established service recovery plan to overcome possible service failures.

Analyzing service failures and service recovery strategies is an extremely useful management tool.[22] In general, service failure analysis provides the type, frequency, and magnitude of various failures. By systematically categorizing consumer complaints, a hierarchy of criteria evolve that reflect the consumer's perspective of effective performance. This is a very important point. Typically, firms using measures such as FedEx's initial approach to measuring customer satisfaction defined performance based on measures developed internally.[23] However, performance should be measured based on what the customer, not upper management, perceives as important.

## THE VALUE OF ANALYZING SERVICE RECOVERY STRATEGIES

In addition to tracking service failures, analyzing service recovery strategies is equally enlightening. Service recovery analysis provides a sometimes alarming insight into:

- how personnel react to service failures,
- how consumers rate the effectiveness of the employee's recovery efforts, and
- the relationship between recovery strategies and customer retention rates.

Recent studies suggest that nearly half the responses to customer complaints actually reinforce a customer's negative feeling toward a firm.[24] Effective recovery strategies often require contact personnel to make decisions and to occasionally break company rules—the types of behaviors that many firms prohibit their employees from initiating. Contact personnel are often frustrated by rules and regulations that tie their hands and often prevent them from assisting a customer when needed. Furthermore, due to the lack of training in recovery efforts exhibited by most firms, many employees simply do not know how to recover from service failures. The result is a poor response or no response to customer complaints.

## THE RESTAURANT STUDY

This study was conducted by services marketing students and is a great example of the valuable managerial information that can be obtained by monitoring and tracking service failures. The example is presented in a series of steps that can be easily duplicated. We highly recommend this exercise to services marketing classes as a group project. Different groups may investigate different industries or specific businesses.

### Step 1: Developing The Questionnaire

An example of the questionnaire used to collect the data for this study is provided in the appendix to this chapter. The main objective of the questionnaire is to:

- identify and classify failures in the restaurant industry,
- assess customer perceptions of the magnitude of each failure,
- identify and classify recovery strategies utilized by restaurants to correct failures,
- assess customer perceptions of the effectiveness of each type of recovery,
- assess subsequent patronage behaviors that reflect restaurants' customer retention rates, and
- provide demographic information about respondents.

### Step 2: Data Collection

*critical incident technique*
A method of studying service failures by analyzing critical incidents described in story form by respondents.

*The critical incident technique*. The study utilized a data collection method referred to as the **critical incident technique** (CIT). The purpose of CIT in this study is to examine the sources of customer satisfaction and dissatisfaction regarding restaurant services. In essence, CIT is a qualitative approach to analyzing and categorizing critical incidents. The CIT analyzes the content of the critical incidents described by respondents in story form.

The actual critical incidents (or stories) for this study were recorded by students. Respondents were asked to report a restaurant service failure that was associated with a positive service recovery, as well as a service failure that was associated with a negative service recovery. Both scenarios were requested in order to identify recovery strategies that were effective as well as responses that were inadequate. Incidents associated with positive recovery strategies accounted for 49.6 percent of the sample, while 50.4 percent of the sample was associated with poor recoveries.

In addition, respondents were asked to do the following:

- rate the magnitude of the failure on a scale from 1 through 10, which ranges from trivial to serious;
- rate the effectiveness of the recovery strategy on a scale from 1 through 10, which ranges from poor to good;
- report changes in shopping behavior subsequent to the service failure attributed to the encounter; and
- provide demographic information on gender, education, and age. The data collection efforts resulted in the accumulation of 373 critical incidents.

### Step 3: Data Analysis

The critical incident technique is a qualitative approach to analyzing and categorizing critical incidents. More specifically, the CIT utilized in this study involved three steps:

1. *Identify the failure incident*. Initially, each of the 373 critical incidents was systematically categorized through a deductive sorting process into one of the three major failure groups discussed earlier in this chapter, (1) employee responses to service delivery system failures, (2) employee responses to implicit/explicit customer requests, and (3) unprompted and unsolicited employee actions.

2. *Identify failure subgroups within the three major groups.* This step involved classifying failures into subgroups within each of the three major failure groups noted earlier. This process resulted in the identification of 11 unique failure subgroups (five in Group 1; two in Group 2; and four in Group 3).
3. *Classify recovery strategies.* This step involved classifying the service recovery strategies within each failure subgroup. This process resulted in eight final service recovery strategies that are applicable to a variety of food service operations.

### Step 4: Establishing the Reliability of the Categories

An important procedure when categorizing data is to determine the reliability of the categories. Reliability simply refers to the issue of whether other researchers, given the same set of data, would assign each of the critical incidents to the same set of categories. To assess the reliability of the 11 failure subgroups and eight recovery strategies established through the sorting process in the study, an independent judge (such as a group member not involved in the original categorization) categorized each of the incidents included in the sample.

As a starting point to test for reliability, the critical incidents were presorted into the three main failure categories: (1) employee responses to service delivery system failures, (2) employee responses to implicit/explicit customer requests, and (3) unprompted and unsolicited employee actions. The independent judge was then presented with the 11 previously identified failure subgroups and asked to independently sort each failure incident into one of the 11 categories. In this example, the task resulted in agreement rates of 92 percent, 90 percent, and 90 percent. Typically, agreement rates of 70 percent or higher are regarded as acceptable for establishing reliability.

After establishing the reliability of the service failure categories, the independent judge's next task is to verify the reliability of the service recovery categories. Following a procedure similar to the one described earlier, the independent judge is given the stack of recovery strategies and the names of the eight categories of recovery strategies previously identified. The independent judge then compares his/her categorization efforts with the original results. For this study, the recovery agreement rate was 93 percent, and reliability was established for the recovery categories as well as for the failure categories.

### Step 5: Presenting the Results

*Demographic results.* Sample demographics revealed 42.5 percent of the respondents were male while 57.5 percent of the respondents were female. Regarding education, 68.2 percent of the respondents did not have college degrees; 21.7 percent had undergraduate degrees; and 10.1 percent had "some" or had completed graduate school. Results concerning the age of respondents revealed that 67.5 percent were 25 years old or younger; 14.1 percent were from 26 to 35; and 18.4 percent were 36 years of age or older.

Statistical tests were used in examining the relationships between demographics and restaurant type, failure type, recovery strategies, failure ratings, recovery ratings, and retention rates. Results revealed no statistically significant findings. These tests provide evidence that the findings, reported across different types of customers and across restaurant types, can be safely generalized.

*The failure categories: frequency and definition.* After carefully sorting the 373 critical incidents, the following restaurant service failure categories were developed and their reliability established. As described earlier in step 3, the incidents were first sorted into three main failure groups and then into subclass failures within each main failure group.

Group 1, "Employee Responses to Core Service Failures," accounted for 44.4 percent of all critical incidents. Core service failures included the following subclass categories (the frequency of occurrence expressed as a percentage of the total critical incidents is reported in parentheses):

*Product Defects* (20.9 percent): Food that was described as cold, soggy, raw, burnt, spoiled, or containing inanimate objects such as hair, glass, bandages, bag ties, and cardboard.

*Slow/Unavailable Service* (17.9 percent): Waiting an excessive amount of time and/or not being able to find assistance.

*Facility Problems* (3.2 percent): Cleanliness issues such as bad smells, dirty utensils, and animate objects found in food or crawling across the table (e.g., insects).

*Unclear Policies* (1.6 percent): Restaurant policies that were perceived as unfair by the customer (e.g., coupon redemption, form of payment).

*Out of Stock Conditions* (0.8 percent): An inadequate supply of menu items.

Group 2, "Employee Responses to Implicit/Explicit Customer Requests," accounted for 18.4 percent of the critical incidents. Implicit/explicit customer requests included the following subclass categories (the frequency of occurrence expressed as a percentage of the total critical incidents is reported in parentheses):

*Food Not Cooked to Order* (15.0 percent): The scenario in which the customer explicitly asks for the food to be prepared in a specific manner (e.g., medium rare, no mustard) and the request is not honored.

*Seating Problems* (3.4 percent): Involved seating smokers in nonsmoking sections and vice versa, lost or disregarded reservations, denial of request for special tables, and seating among unruly customers.

Group 3, "Unprompted/Unsolicited Employee Actions," accounted for 37.2 percent of the total critical incidents. Unprompted/unsolicited employee actions included the following subclass categories (the frequency of occurrence expressed as a percentage of the total critical incidents is reported in parentheses):

*Inappropriate Employee Behavior* (15.2 percent): Rudeness, inappropriate verbal exchanges, and poor attitudes that were associated with unpleasant behaviors.

*Wrong Orders* (12.6 percent): The delivery of an incorrect food item to the table, or in the case of fast food, packaging an incorrect food item that was not discovered until the customer was no longer on the restaurant premises.

*Lost Orders* (7.5 percent): Situations in which the customer's order was apparently misplaced and never fulfilled.

*Mischarged* (1.9 percent): Being charged for items that were never ordered, charging incorrect prices for items that were ordered, and providing incorrect change.

*The failure categories: magnitude and recovery.* In addition to developing the failure categories, we also recorded each respondent's perception of the magnitude of the failure. Respondents rated the magnitude of the failure on a scale from 1 (minor mistake) through 10 (major mistake). In addition, the average effectiveness of recovery for each failure was calculated on a scale from 1 (poor recovery) through 10 (good recovery). Magnitude and recovery rankings presented according to the failures' perceived severity are as follows:

| Failure Category | Magnitude | Recovery |
|---|---|---|
| 1. Seating Problems | 8.00 | 5.61 |
| 2. Out of Stock | 7.33 | 6.00 |
| 3. Facility Problems | 7.25 | 3.92 |
| 4. Inappropriate Employee Behavior | 7.12 | 3.71 |
| 5. Slow/Unavailable Service | 7.05 | 5.38 |
| 6. Lost Orders | 6.71 | 5.82 |
| 7. Product Defects | 6.69 | 6.21 |
| 8. Wrong Orders | 6.25 | 6.44 |
| 9. Unclear Policy | 6.16 | 6.33 |
| 10. Food Not Cooked to Order | 6.02 | 5.80 |
| 11. Mischarged | 5.86 | 7.71 |

*The recovery categories: frequency and definition.* In addition to categorizing the primary service failures in the restaurant industry, a second objective of this study was to utilize the critical incident technique to categorize employee response (recovery strategies) to the various service failures. The service recovery strategies resulting from the CIT approach are defined as follows (the frequency of occurrence expressed as a percentage of the total critical incidents is reported in parentheses):

*Replacement* (33.4 percent): Replacing the defective order with a new order.
*Free Food* (23.5 percent): Providing the meal, desserts, and/or drinks on a complimentary basis.
*Nothing* (21.3 percent): No action was taken to correct the failure.
*Apology* (7.8 percent): The employee apologized for the failure.
*Correction* (5.7 percent): Fixing the existing defective order as opposed to replacing the order with a new one as in replacement.
*Discount* (4.3 percent): Discounts were provided to customers for food items at the time of the incident.
*Managerial Intervention* (2.7 percent): Management in some way became involved and helped resolve the problem.
*Coupon* (1.3 percent): Discounts for food items purchased at the restaurant were provided to customers for use on their next visit.

*The recovery categories: perceived effectiveness and corresponding customer retention rates.* Respondents rated the effectiveness of each recovery on a scale from 1 (very poor) through 10 (very good). Recoveries ranked in declining order of effectiveness and their corresponding customer retention rates are as follows:

| Recovery Strategy | Effectiveness | Percent Retention Rate |
| --- | --- | --- |
| 1. Free Food | 8.05 | 89.0 |
| 2. Discount | 7.75 | 87.5 |
| 3. Coupon | 7.00 | 80.0 |
| 4. Managerial Intervention | 7.00 | 88.8 |
| 5. Replacement | 6.35 | 80.2 |
| 6. Correction | 5.14 | 80.0 |
| 7. Apology | 3.72 | 71.4 |
| 8. Nothing | 1.71 | 51.3 |

The customer retention rates revealed in this study suggest that it is possible to recover from failures, regardless of the type. Overall, customer retention for the incidents considered was above 75 percent. Even customers experiencing less-than-acceptable recoveries were still retained at a rate approaching 60 percent. However, in general, the statistical relationship between failure rating and recovery rating does indicate that as the magnitude of the seriousness of the failure increases, so does the difficulty in executing an effective recovery.

### Step 6: Developing Managerial Implications Based on Results

This research provides restaurant managers and employees with a list of service failures that are likely to occur in the restaurant industry as well as methods for effectively (and ineffectively) recovering from these failures when they occur. Managers should use this type of information when designing service delivery systems and procedures, establishing policies regarding service recovery, and selecting and training service personnel. Remarkably, approximately 1 out of every 4 service failures (23.5 percent) was met with no response by the offending firm. Unfortunately, other research has indicated that this "no response" rate is typical.[25]

The findings also suggest that it is difficult to recover from two failure types in particular. On a 10-point scale, failures associated with facility problems (failure 3) and employee behavior (failure 8) had mean recovery ratings of only 3.92 and 3.71, respectively. This amplifies the importance of providing the basics of service delivery well, as recovery from facility problems are particularly difficult. In addition, these findings provide evidence indicating the importance of employee training in the restaurant industry, as employee failures were difficult to effectively recover from as well. The mean recovery rating of all other failure types exceeded the midpoint on the 10-point scale.

The recovery findings provide information concerning the desirability of specific recovery strategies. For example, recoveries involving some form of compensation were rated most favorably. Compensation took the form of free food (recovery 1), discounts (recovery 2), and coupons (recovery 3). On a 10-point scale, these three recovery strategies had mean recovery ratings of 8.05, 7.75, and 7.00, respectively.

Several less effective recovery strategies were also identified. Based on recovery ratings, simply correcting a failure (recovery 6), apologizing (recovery 7), and doing nothing (recovery 8) seem to be less effective, as these recovery strategies had ratings of 5.14, 3.72, and 1.71, respectively.

As a result of this study and others like it that track service failure and recovery strategies, the categorization process reveals enlightening information about the particular industry's "hierarchy of horrors" and its sometimes feeble, sometimes admirable, attempts to recover from its failures. Managing service firms is a highly complex task. Exercises like this make this point abundantly clear.

## ✳ SUMMARY

The benefit of service failure and recovery analysis is that service managers can identify common failure situations, minimize their occurrence, and train employees to recover from them when they do occur. The value associated with developing effective service recovery skills is clear. Two-thirds of lost customers do not defect to competitors due to poor product quality but due to the poor customer service they received when problems occurred.

Many of today's service firms are great as long as the service delivery system is operating smoothly. However, once kinks develop in the system, many firms are unprepared to face unhappy customers who are looking for solutions to their problems. As evidence, nearly half the responses to customer complaints reinforce customers' negative feelings toward a firm. Consequently, firms that truly excel in customer service equip employees with a set of recovery tools to repair the service encounter when failures occur and customer complaints are voiced.

Customer complaints should be viewed as opportunities to improve the service delivery system and to ensure that the customer is satisfied before the service encounter ends. Customers voice complaints for a number of reasons, including the following: to have the problem resolved, to gain an emotional release from frustration, to regain some measure of control by influencing other people's evaluation of the source of the complaint, to solicit sympathy or test the consensus of the complaint, or to create an impression.

However, it's not the complainers who service firms should worry about, it's the people who leave without saying a word, who never intend on returning, and who inform others, thereby generating negative word-of-mouth information. A number of reasons explain why many consumers do not complain. Most simply, customers of services often do not know whom to complain to and/or do not think complaining will do any good. Other reasons consumers fail to complain are that (1) consumer evaluation of services is highly subjective; (2) consumers tend to shift some of the blame to themselves for not clearly specifying to the service provider their exact needs; (3) since many services are technical and specialized, many consumers do not feel qualified to voice their complaints; and (4) due to the inseparability of services, consumers may feel that a complaint is too confrontational.

Service failures generally fall into one of four main categories: (1) employee responses to core service failures such as slow service, unavailable service, and other core service failures; (2) employee responses to implicit/explicit customer requests such as special needs, customer preferences, customer error, and disruptive others; (3) unprompted/unsolicited employee actions, which include level of attention, unusual actions, cultural norms, gestalt evaluations, and employee actions under adverse conditions; and

(4) problematic customers including drunkenness, verbal and physical abuse, breaking company policies, and uncooperative customers.

Service recovery strategies are often industry specific, such as the restaurant example provided in the chapter. However, in general, responses to service failures can be categorized as two types: (1) responses to service failures that are attributed to the firm, and (2) responses to service failures that are attributed to customer error. Successful tactics for recovery from failures attributed to the firm include acknowledging the problem, making the customer feel unique or special, apologizing when appropriate, explaining what happened, and offering to compensate the customer. Successful responses to service failures attributed to customer error include acknowledging the problem, taking responsibility for the problem, and assisting in solving the problem without embarrassing the customer. Successful service recovery efforts such as these play an important role in customer retention.

## ✳ KEY TERMS

service failures, 361
critical incidents, 361
system failures, 362
unavailable service, 362
unreasonably slow service, 362
other core service failures, 362
customer needs and requests, 364
implicit needs, 364
explicit requests, 364
special needs, 364
customer preferences, 364
customer errors, 364
disruptive others, 365
unprompted/unsolicited employee
   actions, 365
level of attention, 365
unusual action, 365
cultural norms, 365
gestalt, 365

adverse conditions, 365
drunkenness, 366
verbal and physical abuse, 366
breaks company policies, 366
uncooperative customer, 366
instrumental complaints, 367
noninstrumental complaints, 367
ostensive complaints, 368
reflexive complaints, 368
voice, 369
exit, 370
retaliation, 370
service recovery, 370
service recovery paradox, 371
perceived justice, 374
distributive justice, 374
procedural justice, 374
interactional justice, 374
critical incident technique, 378

## ✳ DISCUSSION QUESTIONS

1. Define and discuss the subclass failures associated with the implicit/explicit request failure category.
2. Discuss the following types of complaints: instrumental, noninstrumental, ostensive, and reflexive.

3. What is the service recovery paradox? Provide an example based on your own personal experience.
4. Discuss the following types of failure outcomes: voice, exit, and retaliation.
5. What are the pros and cons of complaining customers?
6. Discuss how consumers evaluate a firm's service recovery efforts.
7. Give an overview of the steps, described in this chapter, necessary to track and monitor employee service failures and recovery efforts.

## ✳ NOTES

1. Mary Jo Bitner, Bernard H. Booms, and Mary Stanfield Tetreault, "The Service Encounter: Diagnosing Favorable and Unfavorable Incidents," *Journal of Marketing* (January 1990), pp. 71–84; Mary Jo Bitner, Bernard H. Booms and Lois A. Mohr (1994), "Critical service encounters: the employee's viewpoint", *Journal of Marketing*, Vol. 58, October, pp. 95–106.

2. Asra Q. Nomani, "In the Skies Today, A Weird New Worry: Sexual Misconduct," *Wall Street Journal*, (June 10, 1998), p. A1; Frances Fiorino, "Passengers Who Carry Surly Bonds of Earth' Aloft," *Aviation Week and Space Technology*, 149 (5), (December 28, 1998), p. 123.

3. H. Keith Hunt, "Consumer Satisfaction, Dissatisfaction, and Complaining Behavior," *Journal of Social Issues* 47,1 (1991), p. 116.

4. Mary C. Gilly, William B. Stevenson, and Laura J. Yale, "Dynamics of Complaint Management in the Service Organization," *The Journal of Consumer Affairs* 25,2 (1991), p. 296.

5. Oren Harari, "Thank Heaven for Complainers," *Management Review* (January 1992), p. 60.

6. Mark D. Alicke et al., "Complaining Behavior in Social Interaction," *Personality and Social Psychology Bulletin* (June 1992), p. 286.

7. Alicke, "Complaining Behavior," p. 287.

8. T. M. Amabile, "Brilliant but Cruel: Perceptions of Negative Evaluators," *Journal of Experimental Social Psychology* 19 (1983), pp. 146–156.

9. Gilly, Stevenson, and Yale, "Dynamics of Complaint Management," p. 297.

10. Hunt, "Consumer Satisfaction," p. 114.

11. Hunt, "Consumer Satisfaction," p. 115.

12. Adapted from Christopher W. L. Hart, James L. Heskett, and W. Earl Sasser, "The Profitable Art of Service Recovery," *Harvard Business Review* (July-August 1990), pp. 148–156.

13. James L. Heskett et al., "Putting the Service-Profit Chain to Work," *Harvard Business Review* (March–April 1994), p. 172.

14. Bitner, Booms, and Tetreault, "The Service Encounter," p. 321.

15. Karl Albrecht and Ron Zemke, *Services America* (Homewood, IL: Dow-Jones Irwin, 1985), p. 6.

16. Donna Partow, "Turn Gripes into Gold," *Home Office Computing* (September 1993), p. 24.

17. Albrecht and Zemke, *Services America*, p. 6.

18. Hart, Heskett, and Sasser, "The Profitable Art," p. 150.

19. This section adapted from K. Douglas Hoffman and Scott W. Kelley, "Perceived Justice Needs and Recovery Evaluation: A Contingency Approach," *European Journal of Marketing* 34, (2000), pp. 418–432.

20. Adapted from K. Douglas Hoffman, Scott W. Kelley, and Holly M. Rotalsky, "Tracking Service Failures and Employee Recovery Efforts," *Journal of Services Marketing* 9,2 (1995), pp. 49–61.

21. Eleena De Lisser, "Today's Specials Include Customer Satisfaction," *The Wall Street Journal*, June 7, 1993, p. B1.

22. Terry Vavra, "Learning from Your Losses," *Brandweek* 33,46 (December 7, 1992), p. 20(2).

23. American Management Association, *Blueprints for Service Quality: The Federal Express Approach*, (New York: AMA Membership Publication Division, 1991).

24. Hart, Heskett, and Sasser, "The Profitable Art," p. 150.

25. See Scott W. Kelley, K. Douglas Hoffman, and Mark A. Davis, "A Typology of Retail Failures and Recoveries," *Journal of Retailing* (Winter 1993), pp. 429–445; and K. Douglas Hoffman, Scott W. Kelley, and Laure M. Soulage, "Customer Defection Analysis: A Critical Incident Approach" (1994), working paper.

# APPENDIX

> | SAMPLE OF CRITICAL INCIDENT FORM

### I. Introduction/Purpose of Study

Have you ever been at a restaurant and received poor service?

We are conducting a study on service mistakes or failures made by restaurants and how restaurants recover when a service failure occurs. Would you be willing to participate in this study?

### II. Think of a time when you had an experience at a restaurant where a mistake was made and the restaurant tried to correct that mistake but did a POOR job of recovering. Please describe the nature of this service failure.

Where? _____

When? _____

What happened? _____
_____
_____
_____

What did the restaurant do to correct the failure? _____
_____
_____
_____
_____
_____

On a scale of 1 to 10, 1 being a MINOR MISTAKE and 10 being a MAJOR MISTAKE, how would you rate the severity of the mistake?

Minor Mistake                                                      Major Mistake

1    2        3        4        5        6        7        8        9        10

On a scale of 1 to 10, 1 being VERY POOR and 10 being a VERY GOOD how would you rate the efforts of the restaurant regarding the correction of the mistake?

Very Poor                                                          Very Good

1    2        3        4        5        6        7        8        9        10

Do you still patronize this restaurant?

_____ No, due to the service failure

_____ No, due to other reasons

_____ Yes

III. Think of a time when you had an experience at a restaurant where a mistake was made and the restaurant tried to correct that mistake but did a GOOD job of recovering. Please describe the nature of this service failure.

Where? _____

When? _____

What happened? _____

_____

_____

_____

What did the restaurant do to correct the failure? _____

_____

_____

_____

_____

_____

On a scale of 1 to 10, 1 being a MINOR MISTAKE and 10 being a MAJOR MISTAKE, how would you rate the severity of the mistake?

Minor Mistake                                                        Major Mistake

1     2        3         4         5         6        7        8        9        10

On a scale of 1 to 10, 1 being VERY POOR and 10 being VERY GOOD how would you rate the efforts of the restaurant regarding the correction of the mistake?

Very Poor                                                            Very Good

1     2        3         4         5         6        7        8        9        10

Do you still patronize this restaurant?

_____ No, due to the service failure

_____ No, due to other reasons

_____ Yes

## IV. Demographics

Sex (Categorical choices)
Education (Categorical choices)
Age (Categorical choices)

## CHAPTER 15

# CUSTOMER RETENTION

## CHAPTER OBJECTIVES

*The major objective of this chapter is to introduce you to the concept of customer retention.*

After reading this chapter, you should be able to:

- Discuss why the concept of customer retention has become increasingly important.
- Master successful tactics for retaining existing customers. Describe emerging customer retention programs.
- Explain defection management.

*"Who will testify to your existence during the last twelve months?"*

Tom Peters

© MICHAEL NAGLE / BLOOMBERG NEWS / LONDON

One recent innovation in loyalty marketing is the development of technologically-based loyalty devices. Examples include the Starbuck's Stored-Value card and Vail Resort's Colorado card. Loyalty devices offer convenience by enabling customers to conduct transactions both faster and easier than ever before. However, the real secret of their popularity for customers and marketers alike is their ability to create a sense of belongingness. Ruth P. Stevens, president of New York-based E-Marketing Strategy agrees, "They are a beautiful way to create a sense of belongingness. Other than the physical (and) practical benefits of saving time (and) convenience, you also get a feeling that, 'This is my store and I am a member of the club'."

Many loyalty devices are much like gift cards sold at major retailers. However, customers are able to reload their cards by accessing the sponsoring company's website, such as http://www.Starbucks.com, and bill their card replenishment amounts to their personal credit card numbers. Better yet, many of these cards such as the Colorado card (http://www.snow.com) can be tied directly to the customer's credit card account. In general, loyalty cards streamline the customer's payment activities. For example, Colorado cardholders pay a base fee for unlimited skiing at a number of Vail resort properties, including Arapahoe Basin, Breckenridge, Keystone, and Vail itself. In addition, since the Colorado card can be tied to the customer's credit card, it can also be used at numerous ski rental, merchandise, and food and beverage locations on the slopes.

Cardholders obtain several benefits by purchasing and using the Colorado card. First, the customer no longer has to stand in line to purchase a lift ticket. Colorado cardholders simply ski directly to the lift itself where a resort employee scans a bar code located on the Colorado card. Once scanned, the customer is then free to immediately begin their skiing experience. Essentially, the Colorado card removes cash from the skiing experience, which is a huge benefit to customers wearing cumbersome ski clothes. The Colorado card comes with six "Ski-with-a-Friend" tickets, which encourages Colorado cardholders to bring along their friends (who are able to purchase lift tickets at a discounted rate). Finally, cardholders are also rewarded Peak Points for using their Colorado card, which can be redeemed for free lift tickets and/or a variety of ski rental, merchandise, and dining discounts.

From a marketing perspective, a loyalty-based program offers a number of worthwhile benefits. First, it speeds up a necessary action—payment. Second, it provides novelty to the service experience and in some instances may be perceived as a "cool." For example, over 5 million customers have signed up for the Starbucks card since it was introduced in November of 2001. Flashing the card has become part of the Starbucks experience. As the name implies, loyalty cards facilitate customer retention and increase purchase amounts and purchase frequency. Scott Waltmann, a Merrill Lynch analyst for Starbucks notes, "The Starbucks card has a lot of usability—the average office worker may go downstairs for coffee two to three times a day. The card locks in the customer, because if they have a balance on the card, they're more likely to walk past another coffee purveyor to go to Starbucks."

Implementing a loyalty-based program does not come cheaply. Expenses include press releases and advertising, card reload costs, synchronizing the provider's inventory management system, and, of course, the cost of the scanning technology. However, nontechnologically-based loyalty cards are much less costly to implement. For example, a simple paper card such as a Buy-10, Get-One-Free card is a great example of a low-cost alternative that also builds customer loyalty. The beauty of any loyalty program is that it enhances the customer's overall experience through added convenience and a sense of belongingness.

Sources: Catherine Arnold, "Technology Reels 'em In," *Marketing News* (October 14, 2002). http://www.starbucks.com/card/default.asp accessed 6 June 2005; and http://www.snow.com accessed 6 June 2005.

## > INTRODUCTION

Depending on whom you ask within a service operation, you will likely discover that the various managers within a company evaluate the firm's value differently. The chief financial officer might offer a variety of impressive financial ratios that are great to use at cocktail parties, the operations manager will speak in terms of inventory and equipment, and the human relations manager will focus on the strengths of the firm's employees.[1] Although these measures are crucial to the firm's success, they all ignore the value of the customer.

This chapter focuses on the important concept of customer retention. Customer retention is a key strategy in today's leading-edge service firms and reflects a more futuristic outlook than does the concept of customer satisfaction. As discussed in Chapter 12, satisfaction measures assess the customer's current state of evaluation but fail to tap into the customer's set of changing needs. Consequently, additional measures that assess evolving customer expectations, the probability of future purchases with the firm, and the customer's willingness to conduct business with competitive firms are necessary in order to truly assess the firm's customer retention efforts.

## > WHAT IS CUSTOMER RETENTION?

*customer retention*
Focusing the firm's marketing efforts toward the existing customer base.

Simply stated, **customer retention** refers to focusing the firm's marketing efforts toward the existing customer base. More specifically, in contrast to seeking new customers, firms engaged in customer retention efforts work to satisfy existing customers with the intent of developing long-term relationships between the firm and its current clientele for the purpose of growing the business (see Figure 15.1).

Many examples of successful customer retention efforts are based on the firm's ability to redefine its existing business. Companies are challenging themselves, now more than ever before, to look at what the product really provides to their customers. Understanding consumer uses of the product and the steps required by consumers to obtain the product often leads to ideas that assist the firm in differentiating itself from its competition. Providing value-added services to the consumer reshapes the traditional and often confrontational supplier-customer relationship into more of a partnership.

For example, after rethinking its business, British Airways no longer views itself solely as a provider of air transportation.[2] As a result, the airline has revised its focus on first-class transatlantic customers to include improved services on the ground as well as in the air. Realizing that many of its customers would like to sleep through the night rather than eat huge meals followed by lavish desserts, accompanied by an endless supply of alcohol and bad movies, British Airways now provides its first-class passengers with the option of having dinner on the ground in its first-class lounge. Once on board, passengers are provided British Airways pajamas, real pillows, and a duvet to curl up in.

Once the plane has landed and after a good night's sleep, passengers are provided with breakfast on the ground as well as a shower and dressing room so that they can be fresh for the day's events. British Airways will even have passenger's clothes pressed

---

**FIGURE 15.1**   **NEW VS. OLD CUSTOMERS**

The leaky bucket depicted here portrays two companies. Each company is working hard to generate new customers each year and has managed to generated 10 percent more new customers per year, perhaps by developing new services or targeting new segments. However, not all of the customers acquired by the firm in a given year stay with the firm. The retention rate is not 100 percent; there is a "hole in the bucket." For company A, the "hole" is small, and the company loses only 5 percent of its customers each year. As a result, after 14 years company A has doubled the number of its customers. Company B has a bigger problem, because retention is 90 percent and the "hole in the bucket" is 10 percent. As a result, company B loses and gains customers at the same rate.

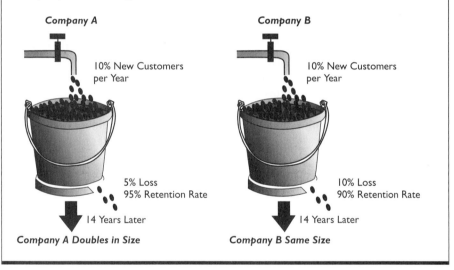

Source: John E.G. Bateson and K. Douglas Hoffman, *Managing Services Marketing*, 4th ed., Dryden Publishers: Fort Worth, TX, 1999.

---

while they are enjoying their breakfasts. With value-added services such as these, it is not surprising to learn that British Airways' profits have steadily increased.

## THE TREND TOWARD CUSTOMER RETENTION

Today's market is totally different than the ones U.S. marketers have experienced in the past. Competition is intense, and service and goods differentiation among competitors is minimal.[3] Let's face it, there is not a great deal of difference today among products, be they insurance companies, banks, or eye exams. Due to the relative parity among brand choices, consumer risk associated with switching brands has been drastically minimized. For example, consumers may be indifferent about the firm that holds their car insurance policy. Consequently, many consumers have forgone brand loyalty and selected the product that offers the best value—the best product at the best price.

*conquest marketing*
A marketing strategy for constantly seeking new customers by offering discounts and mark-downs and developing promotions that encourage new business.

Unfortunately, the majority of marketers today have reacted to this new environment of "brand parity" and "nonbrand loyalty" by constantly chasing new customers. Firms that are constantly seeking new customers are engaged in **conquest marketing**. Typical conquest marketing techniques include offering discounts and markdowns and developing promotions that encourage new business. Results obtained from conquest marketing are generally successful in the short run due to customers' lack of brand loyalty. The firm engaged in conquest marketing may even get a repeat purchase or two. However, as soon as the competition offers another "discount special," the firm loses many of the customers it previously attracted.

To this day, many companies spend the bulk of their marketing efforts on attracting new customers instead of on keeping the customers they already have. However, the long-term profitability of firms that utilize conquest marketing techniques is highly questionable. When one considers the cost of a sales promotion to attract customers, followed by sales at a discounted price, profits are minimal.

Even when conquest marketing techniques are successful, they sometimes lead to the demise of the firm. All too often, businesses are tempted to grow as fast as they can in order to increase their sales volume. However, because of the inseparability inherent in services, extensive growth of many service firms is commonly associated with a decrease in the quality of service provided.

As the firm continues to grow, the owner/provider will likely take on more of an administrative role, providing estimates, handling customer complaints, and managing employees. These additional duties result in the owner spending less time in the field attending to the original customer base. Consequently, the owner/provider might have to hire additional help, who may not provide the same level of service as the owner once delivered. Subsequently, customers may become disgruntled about the poor service and begin to look for alternatives.

Considering the costs associated with winning new customers, the only way to make a profit and avoid the continuous cycle of price discounts is to increase the lifetime spending of existing customers. "Customer retention is, therefore, far more important than customer attraction."[4] Given today's marketing environment, coddling existing clients makes good economic sense (see Global Services in Action).

## THE IMPORTANCE OF CUSTOMER RETENTION

Customer retention has become increasingly important because of several changes in the marketing environment.[5] First, in the United States, consumer markets are stagnant. The U.S. population for the next 50 years is predicted to grow at half the rate of the period from 1965 to 1990. As a result, there are fewer new customers to go around. Concurrent with the decrease in population growth, the once vibrant economic growth rate has suddenly begun to decline. There are not as many new customers as there once were, and those customers that exist are spending less.

Another reason customer retention has become important to today's marketers is the increase in competition (see E-Services in Action). Factors contributing to increased competition include the relative parity and lack of differential advantage of goods and services on the market, deregulated industries that now must compete for customers in

## GLOBAL SERVICES *IN ACTION*

### > PUTTING THE CUSTOMER FIRST: BMO BANK OF MONTREAL

One of the most interesting characteristics about companies that excel at customer retention is that at some point in the firm's evolution the overriding business philosophy changes from a product-centric to a market-centric orientation. BMO Bank of Montreal is a prime example of a financial institution that successfully navigated this transition. Most banks follow a product-centric approach by developing financial products and then attempting to convince customers that they really need them. BMO would call this a backward approach to doing business. In BMO's market-centric world, the customer should design the product.

BMO's transformation began with the bank's new credit card program called Mosaik. Mosaik allows customers to build their own credit card by specifying interest rates, card design, reward programs, and additional features such as travel protection and concierge services. According to Mark Fabian, senior manager of customer acquisitions and development, "When we decided to launch this [Mosaik], we really went in with a war-room mentality and looked at every aspect of the customer." In addition to customer and employee surveys, BMO marketing spent 18 months working in-house with decision support teams, customer experience teams, and operations and analytics teams to offer just the right product. Ultimately, the introduction of the Mosaik card reversed BMO's declining customer satisfaction trend and business hasn't been the same since. Given Mosaik's success, the company began to look at all of its financial products across all channels.

As a result of these efforts and many others like them, BMO increased its market share by 10 to 15 percent and new accounts have increased by 20 percent. More interestingly, customer defections have decreased by 30 percent, which translates into a yearly revenue savings of $38 million. BMO Bank of Montreal is now one of North America's largest financial institutions with $256 billion in assets and over 34,000 employees.

Source: Mila D'Antonio, "BMO Invests in a New Paradigm," *1to1 Magazine*, (January/February 2005), 14.

an open market, the growth of online alternatives, and accessible market information that is available to more firms, thereby minimizing informational advantages among competing firms. As a result of the increase in competition and the predominant use of conquest marketing techniques, firms are finding that retaining their current customer base is more challenging than ever.

Customer retention is also becoming increasingly important because of the rising costs of marketing. In particular, the cost of mass marketing, the primary tool of conquest marketers, has substantially increased. For example, the cost of a 30-second television

## E-SERVICES *IN ACTION*

> ### CUSTOMER RETENTION: OFFLINE VS. ONLINE

There is little doubt that online service firms such as Geico (insurance products) and E*Trade (brokerage services) have cut into the market shares of the traditional offline firms. However, in terms of customer retention, it's the brick-and-mortar firms with an online presence that are beating their pure online counterparts. Termed "bricks-and-clicks," firms that pursue a multichannel strategy appear to be winning the customer retention battle.

A recently published survey conducted by the Boston Consulting Group revealed that although "brick-and-click" sites were more likely to have a greater number of shopping carts abandoned (76 percent), 45 percent of their online revenues come from regulars. One explanation for the high abandonment rate is that users are simply collecting information before they trek off to a brick location. Hence, although the purchases were not made on the Web, they were Web-influenced—adding additional value to the firm's website. In comparison, pure online firms report that 30 percent of their revenues are from repeat purchasers. More impressive is the cost savings in acquiring customers. Many of the "brick-and-click" firms already have established brands. As a result, the average cost of acquiring an online customer is $31 compared to $82 for a pure online firm.

Why does it matter? When the financial markets began to reevaluate Internet stocks, stock prices became much more oriented toward bottom-line profits than reported revenues. This sent the dotcoms into a frenzy as they attempted to reorganize their budgets so that profits could be shown sooner than previously anticipated. Ad campaigns, customer service, and customer acquisition costs were reduced in the attempt to cut expenses. Getting the most out of the customers we have as opposed to trying to recruit as many customers as possible has now become a much higher priority.

Source: David Butcher, "You've Got You're Customer's, Now Milk 'em," *Revolution*, 1 (5), (July 2000), pp. 76–77; http://www.geico.com accessed 6 June 2005; and http://www.etrade.com accessed 6 June 2005.

spot in 1965 was $19,700. In contrast, a 2003 30-second Superbowl spot sold on average for $2,000,000!

Coupled with the increased cost of advertising has been the loss of the advertiser's "share of voice." Due to the shorter time period now allotted for individual commercials (the average length of commercials has decreased from 60 seconds, to 30 seconds, to 15 seconds), the number of commercials has increased by approximately 25 percent over the past ten years. Hence, firms are competing for attention in a medium that is constantly expanding. In addition, new forms of advertising have evolved, and consumer markets have become more fragmented, which further dilutes the chances of an advertiser's message reaching its intended target audience.

Interestingly, the growth of direct mail marketing in the 1980s is directly attributed to the high costs of mass marketing and subsequent heightened importance of customer retention efforts. Marketers became more selective about how and where their advertising dollars were spent. As a result, the databases built for direct marketing provided the means to identify current customers and track purchases. Subsequently, advertising to current customers became much more efficient than mass marketing in reaching the firm's target market.

Changes in the channels of distribution utilized in today's markets are also having an impact on customer retention. In many cases, the physical distance between producer and consumer is increasing. The growth of non-store retailing is a prime illustration of how the physical distance between the provider of products and the customer is changing. Transactions can be conducted by phone, mail order, or over the Internet, thereby limiting the physical contact between the provider and the customer. Firms engaged in customer retention efforts should beware of the old saying, "out of sight, out of mind," and realize that separation from the customer does not diminish their obligation to the customer.

Another change in the channel of distribution is the increasing use of market intermediaries, or "third parties," that assist in the transaction between provider and customer. In this scenario, the marketing intermediary becomes a surrogate provider and, as such, represents the firm that produces the product. Although the use of third parties and other market intermediaries increases the firm's market coverage, it can also adversely affect customer retention rates. For example, a travel agent who sells an airline's service may misrepresent the airline (e.g., flight times, seating arrangements, or connection times) and damage the relationship between the customer and the airline. Again, firms engaged in customer retention efforts must recognize that the physical distance between themselves and their customers does not minimize their responsibility.

Customer retention has also become increasingly important to firms because today's customers have changed. Typical consumers today compared with past generations are more informed about purchasing decisions, command more discretionary income, and are increasingly skeptical about the average firm's concern for their business. Consequently, firms that engage in customer retention practices are usually noticed by today's consumers and rewarded for their efforts via repeat sales.

## > THE BENEFITS OF CUSTOMER RETENTION

Some experts believe that customer retention has a more powerful effect on profits than market share, scale economies, and other variables commonly associated with competitive advantage. In fact, studies have indicated that as much as 95 percent of profits come from long-term customers via profits derived from sales, referrals, and reduced operating costs (see Figure 15.2).[6]

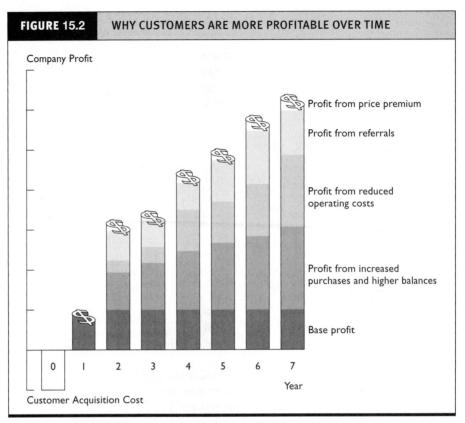

**FIGURE 15.2    WHY CUSTOMERS ARE MORE PROFITABLE OVER TIME**

Source: Adapted from Frederick F. Reichheld and W. Earl Sasser, Jr., "Zero Defections: Quality Comes to Services," *Harvard Business Review* (September–October 1990), p. 108. Copyright © 1990 by the President and Fellows of Harvard College.

## PROFITS DERIVED FROM SALES

One of the key benefits of customer retention is repeat sales (see Figure 15.3). In addition to the base profit derived from sales, profits are also acquired from increased purchase frequency and interest rates applied to higher balances on charge accounts (for firms that offer credit services). An added bonus of retaining existing customers is that existing customers are willing to pay more for a firm's offering. This occurs because customers become accustomed to the firm, its employees, and the manner in which the service is delivered. Subsequently, a relationship develops that lowers the customer's risk. In essence, repeat customers are willing to pay more for purchases and purchase more frequently in situations where the uncertainty of the outcome is lessened or removed. For example, credit card companies encourage their existing customers to use their credit cards when shopping online. One method to increase credit card usage is to promote the added value of guaranteed privacy. Visa's Zero Liability Policy, for example, provides the holder of any Visa credit or debit card 100 percent protection against fraud. Protecting shoppers against fraud is a good way to ease their privacy fears and to promote their credit card usage, but it is also good for consumers. According to Visa's new policy, if your

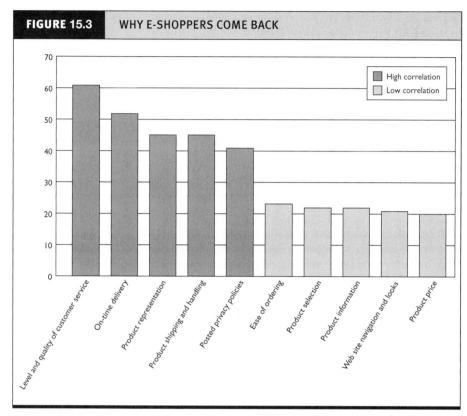

**FIGURE 15.3    WHY E-SHOPPERS COME BACK**

The correlation between online shoppers' ratings of merchants in selected categories and their likelihood of buying again from the same site (100 = perfect correlation; 0 = no correlation).

Source: BizRate.Com

credit card number is stolen while shopping online or in a store, you pay nothing (not even the traditional first $50). American Express also offers total protection for its customers making purchases online.[7]

Increasing customer retention rates can have a profound effect on a firm's profitability. For example, past studies have shown that a 5 percent increase in retention rate can translate into 85 percent higher profits for a branch bank, 50 percent higher profits for an insurance broker, and 30 percent higher profits for an auto-service chain.[8]

## PROFITS FROM REDUCED OPERATING COSTS

Past research has indicated that it costs three to five times less to keep a customer than to get a new one.[9] The trusting relationship that develops between customers and the firm makes existing customers more receptive to the firm's marketing efforts and, therefore, easier to sell new services to. This, in turn, lowers the cost of the firm's marketing efforts.

Overall, long-term customers tend to have lower maintenance costs. Existing customers become accustomed to the company, employees, and procedures; therefore, they ask fewer questions and have fewer problems and require less attention. The airlines price war that took place in the summer of 1992 presented a few unforeseen problems for the airlines. On one hand, the lower prices did achieve their desired effect—increased sales. Many of these sales, however, were to passengers who had never flown before and who were unfamiliar with ticketing practices, baggage handling, and typical airline behavior. Services such as complimentary beverages had to be explained to new passengers who were unfamiliar with the term "complimentary." In one instance, a passenger requested instructions on how to "roll down her window." The result of adding new customers to the mix was stressed-out and overworked flight attendants and lower-than-average quality service to existing customers.

## PROFITS FROM REFERRALS

Another benefit of customer retention is the positive word-of-mouth advertising generated by satisfied customers. Existing customers are necessary in order for a firm to develop a reputation that attracts new business. Satisfied customers often refer business to their friends and family, which, in turn, reinforces their own decision. As discussed in Chapter 4, personal sources of information are particularly important to services' consumers because of intangibility and the perception of increased risk associated with service purchases. New business attributed to current customer referrals can be dramatic. For example, a leading home builder in the United States has found that 60 percent of its business is based on referrals from past customers.[10]

## > CUSTOMER RETENTION TACTICS

Firms that embrace a defection management philosophy engage in customer retention tactics that should be routinely implemented on a per-customer basis. Unfortunately, prior research suggests that two-thirds of customers defect because they feel that companies are not genuinely concerned for their well-being. That's the bad news! The good news is that the opportunity exists to demonstrate to customers that the firm really cares about them. Because of the lack of consistent customer service that customers experience, firms that effectively communicate customer retention as a primary goal are noticed. Consequently, a firm's defection management efforts should serve to successfully differentiate the firm from its competitors. Effective tactics for retaining customers include the following practices.[11]

## MAINTAIN THE PROPER PERSPECTIVE

Managers and employees of service firms need to remember that the company exists to meet the needs and wants of its consumers. Processing customers like raw materials on an assembly line or being rude to customers is incredibly shortsighted. USAir employs the slogan: "The U in USAir starts with you, the passenger." Credos such as this affect customer expectations and reinforce to employees exactly where the firm's priorities lie.

Interacting with the public is not an easy task, and, unfortunately, employees occasionally fail to maintain the proper perspective. The same questions may have to be asked over and over, and not every customer is polite. Maintaining the proper perspective involves a customer-oriented frame of mind and an attitude for service. Employees need to remember that every customer has his or her own personal set of needs and that the customer's, not the employee's, expectations define performance.

## SET CUSTOMER RETENTION GOALS AND LINK GOALS TO THE BOTTOM LINE

MBNA America, a Delaware-based credit card company, improved its industry ranking from 38 to 4 and increased its profits by sixteen-fold. How did MBNA do it? The key to developing customer loyalty is to employ measures that monitor the firm's customer retention efforts. If you can measure it, you can manage it! Specific measures provide managers concrete targets on which to focus their efforts. In MBNA's case, the company tracks the average balance per card, plus 15 measures of customer satisfaction daily. MBNA further reinforces to employees the importance of customer retention through its reward structure. MBNA's employees earn up to 20 percent of their salaries in bonuses associated with customer retention efforts. MBNA employees talk with every customer who wishes to drop its services, and by doing so, they retain 50 percent of these customers.

How do MBNA's customer retention efforts affect the bottom line? MBNA's overall customer retention rate is 95 percent, and MBNA keeps its customers twice as long as industry averages. In fact, MBNA's retention rate of profitable customers, those who revolve their balances, is 98 percent. In addition, MBNA's credit losses due to bad debt are one-third to one-half lower than those of other companies. Moreover, MBNA customers use their cards more often and maintain higher balances—$2,500 compared with the industry average of $1,600.[12]

## REMEMBER CUSTOMERS BETWEEN CALLS

Contacting customers between service encounters is a useful approach in building relationships with the service firm. The key is in making customer contact sincere and personal. Typical approaches include sending birthday, get-well, and/or anniversary cards; writing personal notes congratulating customers for their personal successes; and keeping in touch with consumers concerning the performance of past services rendered and offering assistance if necessary. The goal of this tactic is to communicate to customers that the firm genuinely cares for their well-being.

## BUILD TRUSTING RELATIONSHIPS

Trust is defined as a firm belief or confidence in the honesty, integrity, and reliability of another person. In the service environment, three major components of trust are (1) the service provider's expertise, (2) the service provider's reliability, and (3) the service provider's concern for the customer. For example, one of the biggest obstacles that

| FIGURE 15.4 | CONFIDENTIALITY ISSUES ON THE WEB |
|---|---|

*Netscape summarizes online security threats as follows:*

- *Unauthorized access*: accessing or misusing a computer system to intercept transmissions and steal sensitive information.
- *Data alteration*: altering the content of a transaction—user names, credit card numbers, and dollar amounts—during transmission.
- *Monitoring*: eavesdropping on confidential information.
- *Spoofing*: a fake site pretending to be yours to steal data from unsuspecting customers or just disrupt your business.
- *Service denial*: an attacker shuts down your site or denies access to visitors.
- *Repudiation*: a party to an online purchase denies that the transaction occurred or was authorized.

Source: http://www.ecommerce.ncsu.edu accessed 10 June 2005. For more information see "The FBI's Top 10 Online Security Threats," http://insight.zdnet.co.uk/internet/security/0,39020457,39143773,00.htm accessed 10 June 2005.

keep consumers from purchasing products on the Internet is concern about confidentiality. Customers must trust that the sensitive financial and personal information that is transmitted to Web merchants is kept confidential. In turn, businesses must be certain that payment information collected from consumers over Web storefronts is indeed valid. Additional precautions must be taken by merchants to ensure that confidential consumer databases are not compromised by hackers or misused by malicious employees (see Figure 15.4). Generally speaking, strategies for building trust include the following:

- Protecting confidential information.
- Refraining from making disparaging remarks about other customers and competitors.
- Telling the customer the truth, even when it hurts.
- Providing the customer with full information—the pros and the cons.
- Being dependable, courteous, and considerate with customers.
- Becoming actively involved in community affairs.

## MONITOR THE SERVICE DELIVERY PROCESS

After the service has been requested, monitoring the service delivery process should be a key tactic in the firm's customer retention efforts. Due to the inseparability of services, the customer is involved in the delivery process. Although the customer's involvement may decrease the efficiency of the delivery process, vital information can be obtained regarding satisfaction levels prior to the final result of the service. Consequently, service providers that monitor the service delivery process are able to compensate for service inadequacies and influence customer perceptions of service quality prior to completion. Incidentally, this is not true in the manufacturing sector, where the customer has little or no input into the production process prior to the completed product.

Customers who use online banking services expect their transactions to be secure and safe. Banks build trusting relationships with customers by developing processes that ensure the safety and protection of a customer's money.

Obvious examples would involve a restaurant that regularly communicates with its customers throughout their meal or the owner of a firm who contacts a customer with questions about a recent purchase. Proactively seeking customer feedback throughout the process builds customer perceptions of trust and facilitates maintaining customers for life. Note, however, that asking for too much feedback can become an annoyance to the customer.

## PROPERLY INSTALL EQUIPMENT AND TRAIN CUSTOMERS IN USING THE PRODUCT

Proper installation and training customers saves a lot of headaches in the long run. Customers should not have to become frustrated over not understanding how to use something or, worse, improperly use the product, which may result in damage and further dissatisfaction. Simply dropping off the product and leaving customers to fend for themselves reinforces the idea that the company is not genuinely concerned for the customer's well-being.

## BE THERE WHEN YOU ARE NEEDED MOST

When a customer returns a product that is in need of service and repair, don't crawl under a rock and hide. Every firm should stand behind what it sells and ensure that each transaction is handled to the customer's satisfaction. Most customers are realistic and understand that nothing lasts forever. Many times customers are simply looking for advice and alternative solutions to problems and are not looking for someone to blame. Expressing a sincere concern for the customer's situation reinforces the firm's customer retention efforts.

## PROVIDE DISCRETIONARY EFFORT

Discretionary effort is behavior beyond the call of duty. It is the Procter & Gamble salesperson who voluntarily bags groceries at the grand opening of a new grocery store. It is the hotel that sends items misplaced by customers to their homes at no charge. It is the oil company that recognizes the special needs of its customers during difficult times (see Figure 15.5). Discretionary effort involves countless personal touches—the little things that distinguish a discrete business transaction from an ongoing relationship.

---

**FIGURE 15.5     AN EXAMPLE OF DISCRETIONARY EFFORT**

BP OIL COMPANY
101 PROSPECT AVENUE, WEST
CLEVELAND OH 44115

September 18, 1996

K DOUGLAS HOFFMAN
WILMINGTON NC 28409

RE: 04122

Dear K DOUGLAS HOFFMAN:

We are very concerned about the devastation from the recent hurricane in your area. We hope you have not been personally affected.

If you have, we know how disruptive and financially burdensome such a loss of property is. We'll be happy to give you additional time to pay any balance that may be due on your credit card account with no finance charges or late fees.

Just write a short note at the bottom of this letter to let us know how you wish to extend payment over the next few months. Or, you may call us toll free at 1-800-883-5527 to work out an arrangement.

We realize this is a small gesture but we wanted to offer a helping hand to you as one of our valued customers.


BP Oil Company

Credit Card Account Number: 04122

Payment Plan:

_____
_____
_____
_____
_____
_____
_____
_____

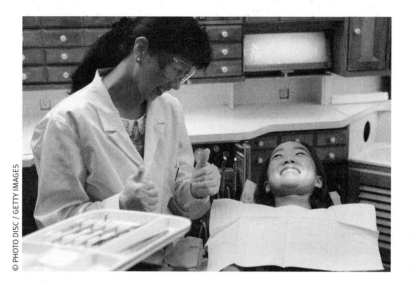

© PHOTO DISC / GETTY IMAGES

Recognizing the fear many patients face during a dental procedure, some dentists take extra measures, or provide discretionary effort, to ensure their comfort. Relaxing music, a slower pace, and willingness to "talk a patient through a procedure" are simple yet effective methods for reducing anxiety and demonstrating the dentist's willingness to improve the dentist-patient relationship.

## *IS IT ALWAYS WORTHWHILE TO KEEP A CUSTOMER?*

Although saving every customer at any cost is a controversial topic and opinions are divided, some experts believe that the customer is no longer worth saving under the following conditions:[13]

- The account is no longer profitable.
- Conditions specified in the sales contract are no longer being met.
- Customers are abusive to the point that it lowers employee morale.
- Customer demands are beyond reasonable, and fulfilling those demands would result in poor service for the remaining customer base.
- The customer's reputation is so poor that associating with the customer tarnishes the image and reputation of the provider.

Other experts believe that although these criteria are valid, a more appropriate strategy is to retreat but keep the lines of communication open. Overall, retention efforts should focus on retaining the most profitable customers. Although zero defection is an admirable goal worth pursuing, the investment in customer retention and service recovery programs may not be economically justified in every case. Moreover, it is argued that focusing too heavily on customer retention efforts can harm the firm in the long run if customer acquisition and development efforts are completely overlooked in the process.[14]

## > EMERGING CUSTOMER RETENTION PROGRAMS

Several relatively new marketing programs have surfaced that typify the recent interest in customer retention strategies, such as frequency marketing, relationship marketing, aftermarketing, service guarantees, and defection management. The discussions that follow illustrate the importance of customer retention within each of these programs.

## FREQUENCY MARKETING

**frequency marketing**
Marketing technique that strives to make existing customers purchase more often from the same provider.

The primary goal of **frequency marketing** is to make existing customers more productive.[15] Consequently, customer retention is a critical component in frequency marketing efforts. In short, frequency marketing combines the use of data collection, communications, recognition, and rewards to build lasting relationships.

The first step in implementing a frequency marketing program is to collect data on the firm's best customers and to determine their level of relationship with the firm. The level of relationship pertains to the number of different services the customer purchases. For example, bank customers may have a relationship with their bank not only through checking accounts, but also through savings accounts, car loans, investments, or a home mortgage.

The next step is to communicate with customers on a personal level. Communications need to be interactive to the point that customers can ask questions and establish a relationship with the firm and action-oriented in that the firm's communications incite customers to respond. Personal communications demonstrate to customers that the firm recognizes the importance of their patronage. When reward programs are developed that prompt customers to act, the communications become action-oriented. Perhaps the most successful frequency marketing programs of all time are the frequent-flier programs. Airlines such as American, Continental, Delta, Northwest, Southwest, TWA, United, and USAir have developed frequent flyer programs designed to reward passengers for flying with one airline. Passenger loyalty is rewarded with credit for "miles," which can be redeemed for discounted fares, free flights, and upgraded seating from coach to first class.

In addition to appealing to the pleasure traveler, frequent-flier programs are the easiest way for airlines to compete for business travelers who often travel 10 to 12 times a year or more. Due to the nature of their activities, business travelers often book flights at the last minute and pay higher fares than pleasure travelers. To attract the more profitable business flier segment, most airlines now assign their best customers, customers who fly more than 25,000 to 30,000 miles a year, to premium memberships that include reservation hotlines, early boarding, bonus mileage, and frequent upgrade privileges.[16]

The frequent-flier programs have become so popular that they are now referred to as the "Green Stamps of the 1990s." In addition to redeeming miles for airline-associated discounts, miles are increasingly being redeemed for things other than flights, such as free nights at hotels, savings bonds, restaurant meals, cruises, and merchandise from a variety of retailers. This new way to redeem miles is accompanied with new ways to earn the miles as well. Other businesses, such as credit card and telephone companies, have signed on with the airlines and typically pay an airline two cents per mile to help retain their own customers as well as attract new ones. Travel experts report that frequent-flier program members earn, on average, 40 percent of their miles without flying and redeem 10 percent of their miles for things other than free trips.[17]

## RELATIONSHIP MARKETING

Another relatively new marketing term that typifies the newfound interest in customer retention efforts is relationship marketing. **Relationship marketing** is the union of customer service, quality, and marketing. More specifically, the relationship marketing perspective takes place on two levels: macro and micro.[18] At the macro level, firms engaged in relationship marketing recognize that the marketing activity impacts customer markets, employee markets, supplier markets, internal markets, and influencer markets (such as financial and government markets). Simultaneously, at the micro level, relationship marketing recognizes that the focus of marketing is changing from completing the single transaction and other conquest marketing practices to building a long-term relationship with existing customers.

*relationship marketing*
Marketing technique based on developing long-term relationships with customers.

Proponents of relationship marketing believe that their firm's products will come and go; consequently, the real unit of value is the long-term relationship with the customer. For example, construction and agricultural equipment manufacturer John Deere & Co. measures its success in terms of generations of farming families who have used its products. Baxter International, a $9 billion healthcare products and services company, has also embraced the relationship marketing concept.[19] Baxter International actually offers to share the business risk with some of its customers by jointly setting sales and cost reduction targets and sharing the savings or extra expenses.[20]

Overall, relationship marketing emphasizes the importance of customer retention and a concern for quality that transcends departmental boundaries. Relationship marketing broadens the definition of the customer from final consumer to all the groups (e.g., suppliers, employees, and influencer markets) that are integral components in bringing the good or service to the marketplace. Efforts to retain the relationship with all these types of customers are at the core of the relationship marketing concept.

## AFTERMARKETING

A third marketing concept that embraces customer retention efforts is aftermarketing.[21] **Aftermarketing** emphasizes the importance of marketing efforts after the initial sale has been made. Aftermarketing techniques include the following:

*aftermarketing*
Marketing technique that emphasizes marketing after the initial sale has been made.

- Identifying customers and building a customer database so that customers can be easily contacted after the sale has been completed.
- Measuring customer satisfaction and continuously making improvements based on customer feedback.
- Establishing formal customer communication programs, including newsletters that convey information on how the company is using customer feedback in its continuous improvement efforts.
- Creating an aftermarketing culture throughout the firm that reinforces the importance of maintaining a relationship with the customer after the initial sale.

An industry that has made some of the biggest strides in aftermarketing is the automobile industry. Customers are frequently contacted by sales and service personnel after a vehicle has been purchased or after service has been completed on a vehicle. Generally, customers have been very impressed by the dealer's concern in an industry that has historically focused on the quick sell.

Weyerhaueser, the paper giant, has taken aftermarketing even farther by requiring some of its employees to actually work at their client's operations sites for a week. One aftermarketing success story involved the placement of a bar code on newsprint rolls the company regularly shipped to its consumers. Weyerhaueser employees in the field noticed that the bar code would regularly stick to its customers' high-speed presses. The problem was solved by merely moving the bar code a few inches. Weyerhaueser later found that other customers had experienced similar problems but had never complained. Placing employees in the field to see personally how customers use the company's products has been beneficial for both Weyerhaueser and its customers.[22]

## SERVICE GUARANTEES

One of the most innovative and intriguing customer retention strategies to be developed in recent years is the service guarantee.[23] Although guarantees in and of themselves are not particularly new, they are new with respect to services, particularly professional services. Overall, service guarantees appear to facilitate three worthwhile goals:

1. reinforce customer loyalty,
2. build market share, and
3. force the firm offering the guarantee to improve its overall service quality.

As discussed in Chapter 13, service quality consists of five dimensions: reliability, responsiveness, assurance, empathy, and tangibles. Although each dimension is a crucial component of the service delivery process, experts contend that "customers value reliability above all other dimensions." Consequently, a firm's efforts to enhance its reliability may serve to significantly differentiate the firm from its competitors.

In theory, the offering of a service guarantee to customers should assure customers that the firm is reliable. Simply stated, reliability is "the ability to perform the service dependably and accurately." The service guarantee lowers the risk generally assumed by service customers by "overcoming client concerns about the highest value for the money."

In general, successful guarantees are unrestrictive, stated in specific and clear terms, meaningful, hassle free when invoked, and quick to be paid out. On the other hand mistakes to avoid when constructing a guarantee include (1) promising something that is trivial and normally expected, (2) specifying an inordinate number of conditions as part of the guarantee, and (3) making the guarantee so mild that it is never invoked.

### Types of Guarantees

In general, there are three types of guarantees: (1) the implicit guarantee, (2) the specific result guarantee, and (3) the unconditional guarantee. The discussion that follows briefly describes each type of guarantee and the trade-offs associated with it.

The **implicit guarantee** is essentially an unwritten, unspoken, guarantee that establishes an understanding between the firm and its customers. Although the guarantee is not specified, customers of firms that offer implicit guarantees are ensured that the firm is dedicated to complete customer satisfaction. Consequently, a partnership spirit is developed between the firm and its customers based on mutual trust and respect.

*implicit guarantee*
An unwritten, unspoken guarantee that establishes an understanding between the firm and its customers.

The trade-offs associated with an implicit guarantee strategy are intriguing. On the positive side, because the guarantee is implicit, no explicit specifications state exactly what the firm will do should the guarantee need to be invoked. Consequently, the service firm can tailor the payout of the guarantee to fit the magnitude of the service failure. Hence, an implicit guarantee may not result in an all-or-nothing type of arrangement. Other benefits associated with the implicit guarantee strategy are that (1) it avoids the appearance of a tacky marketing ploy compared with an explicit guarantee; and (2) it avoids stating publicly the possibility that the firm on occasion may not fulfill its promises. In sum, an implicit guarantee is thought to be the "classy" way of pursuing a guarantee strategy.

An implicit guarantee also has its drawbacks. Since an implicit guarantee is unspoken and unwritten, "a firm pursuing an implicit guarantee strategy has to earn its reputation by repeated acts of goodwill communicated to potential clients via word of mouth, a time-consuming process."[24] Hence, an implicit guarantee does little to differentiate a firm early in its business life cycle. In addition, because the guarantee is implicit, new customers may be unaware of the firm's stance on customer satisfaction and may not bring problems to the firm's attention.

Another type of guarantee is a specific result guarantee. A **specific result guarantee** is considered milder than an explicit unconditional guarantee as "the conditions for triggering the guarantee are narrower and well defined, and the payouts are less traumatic."[25] In contrast to an unconditional guarantee, which covers every aspect of the service delivery process, a specific result guarantee applies only to specific steps or outputs.

*specific result guarantee*
A guarantee that applies only to specific steps or outputs in the service delivery process.

On the positive side, specific result guarantees are most easily applied to quantitative results. For example, FedEx guarantees overnight delivery. Moreover, by guaranteeing a specific result as opposed to an overall guarantee, the firm may be able to state its commitment to a particular goal more powerfully. On the negative side, a specific result guarantee may appear weak compared with an unconditional guarantee, and customers may perceive this as the firm's lack of confidence in its own abilities.

An **unconditional guarantee** is the most powerful of the three types of guarantees. The unconditional guarantee "in its pure form promises complete customer satisfaction, and, at a minimum, a full refund or complete, no-cost problem resolution for the payout."[26] In general, offering unconditional guarantees benefits the firm in two ways. First, the firm benefits from the effect that the guarantee has upon customers. More specifically, customer-directed benefits associated with unconditional guarantees include the following:

*unconditional guarantee*
A guarantee that promises complete customer satisfaction, and at a minimum, a full refund or complete, no-cost problem resolution.

- Customers perceive that they are getting a better value.
- The perceived risk associated with the purchase is lower.
- The consumer perceives the firm to be more reliable.
- The guarantee helps consumers decide when comparing competing choices; consequently, the guarantee serves as a differential advantage.

- The guarantee helps in overcoming customer resistance toward making the purchase.
- The guarantee reinforces customer loyalty, increases sales, and builds market share.
- A good guarantee can overcome negative word-of-mouth advertising.
- The guarantee can lead to brand recognition and differentiation; consequently, a higher price can be commanded.

The second benefit of the unconditional guarantee is directed at the organization itself. A necessary condition for a firm to offer an unconditional guarantee is that it must first have its own operations in order. If not, the payouts associated with an unconditional guarantee will eventually bankrupt the firm. Organization-directed benefits of offering unconditional guarantees include the following:

- The guarantee forces the firm to focus on the customer's definition of good service as opposed to the firm's own definition.
- In and of itself, the guarantee states a clear performance goal that is communicated to employees and customers.
- Guarantees that are invoked provide a measurable means of tracking poor service.
- Offering the guarantee forces the firm to examine its entire service delivery system for failure points.
- The guarantee can be a source of pride and provide motivation for team building within the firm.

As with the other types of guarantees, a number of risks are associated with unconditional guarantees. First, guarantees may send a negative message to some customers, thereby tarnishing the image of a firm that offers a guarantee. Some customers may ponder why the firm needs to offer the guarantee in the first place. For example, customers may consider whether the guarantee is because of failures in the past or out of desperation for new business. Another drawback to unconditional guarantees involves the actual payout when the guarantee is invoked. Customers may be too embarrassed to invoke the guarantee; consequently, the guarantee may actually motivate customers not to complain. Other potential problems associated with the payout involve the amount of documentation the firm requires in order to invoke the guarantee and the time it takes for the actual payout to be completed.

### Minimizing the Risk of a Payout

Obviously, the primary purpose of a guarantee is to communicate to customers that the firm believes in what it provides and that it is committed to customer satisfaction. Ideally, firms that employ a guarantee strategy will seldom have the guarantee invoked. Firms implementing a guarantee strategy can minimize the event of a payout by:

- fully understanding the customer's needs prior to service delivery;
- tracking and monitoring the firm's performance throughout the service delivery process;
- limiting the payout so that it pertains to the key activities and not to minor details (e.g., the firm is not refunding the entire amount of the project just because the doughnuts were stale at one of the meetings);

- specifying up front who has the authorization to approve a payout (i.e., upper management or contact personnel); and
- specifying prior to service delivery the amount involved in the payout.

### The Payout

When a guarantee is invoked, the question then turns to the amount of the **payout**. While a full refund or double the customer's money back in some instances may make sense, these types of refunds may be out of proportion for small mistakes. In general, the amount of the payout ultimately should depend upon the cost of the service, the magnitude of the service failure, and the customer's perception of what is fair.

In 1989, the Hampton Inn chain offered an unconditional guarantee to its customers.[27] "The policy states that any guest who has a problem and is not satisfied by the end of the stay will receive one night's stay at no charge." Incidentally, the guarantee is paid out when the guest settles the account and is not a voucher for a future stay. The impact of the guarantee has been overwhelmingly positive. Employees immediately took notice and responsibility for correcting potential service problems. Moreover, overall quality standards in the hotel have noticeably changed. As a result, employee morale has increased, and employee turnover has decreased.

During the first few months of the program, fewer than one-tenth of 1 percent of customers invoked the guarantee. By 1991, only 7,000 guests, representing $350,000 in sales, had used the guarantee. Of the guests who have invoked the guarantee, 86 percent say they will return, and 45 percent had already done so. The CEO of Hampton Inn believes that these numbers prove that most guests will not take unfair advantage of the guarantee, and this fact coupled with the positive impact on employee morale has meant that the guarantee has had a very positive effect on the firm's bottom line.

*payout*
The amount of money or resolution a service firm spends in order to fulfill an invoked guarantee.

### Professional Service Guarantees

As a final note, guarantees as they relate to professional services deserve special consideration.[28] Experts in the area of guarantees believe that guarantees are most effective for professional service providers under the following conditions:

- *Prices are high*. Professional service prices easily approach the five- and six-figure range. Guarantees may alleviate some of the risk associated with such costly decisions.
- *The costs of a negative outcome are high*. Simply stated, the more important the decision and the more disastrous a negative outcome, the more powerful the guarantee.
- *The service is customized*. As opposed to standardized services, where outcomes are fairly certain, customized services are accompanied by a degree of uncertainty. The guarantee helps to alleviate some of the risk associated with the uncertainty.
- *Brand recognition is difficult to achieve*. It is difficult to successfully differentiate professional services. For example, an eye exam or dental services are fairly consistent from one provider to the next. In cases like these, the unconditional service guarantee may successfully differentiate the service from the competition.
- *Buyer resistance is high*. Due to the expense of many professional services and the uncertainty of the outcome, buyers of professional services are highly cautious. An unconditional guarantee may help in overcoming customer reservations and help close the sale.

## > | DEFECTION MANAGEMENT

*defection management*
A systematic process that actively attempts to retain customers before they defect.

Another way of increasing the customer retention rate is by reducing customer defections. The concept of defection management has its roots in the total quality management (TQM) movement. **Defection management** is a systematic process that actively attempts to retain customers before they defect. Defection management involves tracking the reasons that customers defect and using this information to continuously improve the service delivery system, thereby reducing future defections. Cutting defections in half doubles the average company's growth rate. Moreover, reducing the defection rate by even 5 percent can boost profits 25 percent to 85 percent, depending on the industry (see Figure 15.6).[29]

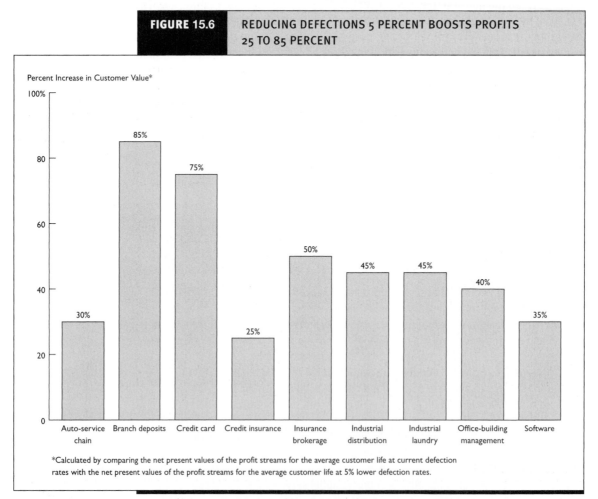

| **FIGURE 15.6** | **REDUCING DEFECTIONS 5 PERCENT BOOSTS PROFITS 25 TO 85 PERCENT** |

*Percent Increase in Customer Value\**

*\*Calculated by comparing the net present values of the profit streams for the average customer life at current defection rates with the net present values of the profit streams for the average customer life at 5% lower defection rates.*

Source: Frederick F. Reichheld and W. Earl Sasser, Jr., "Zero Defections: Quality Comes to Services," *Harvard Business Review* (September–October 1990), p. 110. Copyright © 1990 by the President and Fellows of Harvard College.

## *ZERO DEFECTS VERSUS ZERO DEFECTIONS*

Since the acceptance of total quality management by the manufacturing sector, the guide to follow has been the **zero defects model**. Although appropriate within the manufacturing sector, where specifications can be identified well ahead of production, the zero defects model does not work well in the service sector.[30]

Service customers carry specifications in their minds and can only approximate their desires to a service provider. For example, customers often show hairstylists pictures of a desired hairstyle and request a similar style for themselves. The picture is an approximation of a desired result—it does not specify exact lengths to be cut nor specific degree of curve for curls.

Another obstacle to applying the zero defects model in the service sector is that each consumer has his or her own set of expectations and corresponding specifications. As one hairstylist stated, "They [some consumers] come in here with two spoonfuls of hair and expect to leave here looking like Diana Ross!" Consequently, specifications that are available in the service sector frequently cannot be standardized for all customers. As a result, the service provider must be able to adapt to each set of expectations on the spot.

Because of the unique properties of the service delivery system, the zero defects model used in the manufacturing sector is out of touch with the realities of the service sector. A more appropriate philosophy for service firms would be **zero defections**. In contrast to the "defect pile" of unsellable goods for the manufacturing sector, the "defection pile" in the services sector consists of customers who will not come back.

*zero defects model*
A model used in manufacturing that strives for no defects in goods produced.

*zero defections*
A model used by service providers that strives for no customer defections to competitors.

## *THE IMPORTANCE OF DEFECTION MANAGEMENT*

Businesses commonly lose 15 to 20 percent of their customers each year.[31] In some industries, the rate is much higher. For example, the cable television industry loses in excess of 50 percent each year,[32] the cellular phone industry experiences turnover at a rate of 30 percent to 45 percent per year,[33] and customer defections in the pager industry range from 40 to 70 percent annually.[34] Reducing customer defections is associated with immediate payoffs. In the credit card industry, for example, a 2 percent decrease in defections has the same net effect on the bottom line as a 10 percent decrease in cost (see Figure 15.7).[35]

Another reason that monitoring customer defections is important is the disturbing possibility that customer defection rates may not be directly associated with customer satisfaction ratings.[36] One would think that satisfied customers would be easily retained. Although the idea is intuitively appealing, receiving high satisfaction marks from current customers does not necessarily translate into undying customer loyalty. On average, 65 to 85 percent of defectors say they were satisfied or very satisfied with their former provider.[37] Why, then, do customers defect (see B2B Services in Action)?

## *DEFECTOR TYPES*

Customers defect for a variety of reasons.[38] **Price defectors** switch to competitors for lower priced goods and services and are probably the least loyal of any customer type.

*price defectors*
Customers who switch to competitors for lower priced goods and services.

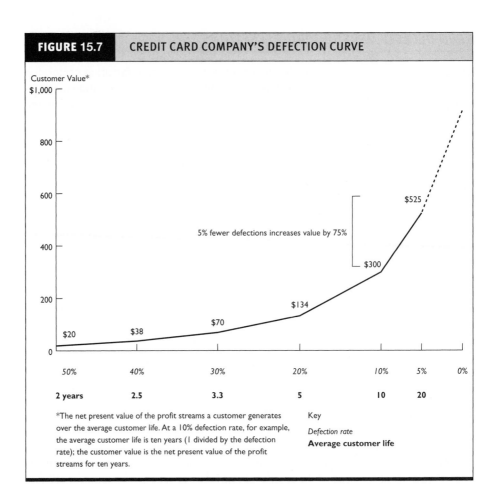

**FIGURE 15.7    CREDIT CARD COMPANY'S DEFECTION CURVE**

Customer Value*

5% fewer defections increases value by 75%

$525

$300

$134

$70

$38

$20

50%    40%    30%    20%    10%    5%    0%

2 years    2.5    3.3    5    10    20

*The net present value of the profit streams a customer generates over the average customer life. At a 10% defection rate, for example, the average customer life is ten years (1 divided by the defection rate); the customer value is the net present value of the profit streams for ten years.

Key

*Defection rate*

**Average customer life**

Source: Frederick F. Reichheld and W. Earl Sasser, Jr., "Zero Defections: Quality Comes to Services," *Harvard Business Review* (September–October 1990), p. 109. Copyright © 1990 by the President and Fellows of Harvard College.

Many businesses that pursue a customer retention philosophy are willing to sacrifice price defectors to avoid constantly discounting their own products and services. In particular, firms that differentiate themselves from competitors based on factors such as reliability, responsiveness, empathy, assurance, and the effective management of the tangible evidence that surrounds the service are generally able to retain customers without constantly discounting their products.

*product defectors*
Customers who switch to competitors who offer superior goods and services.

**Product defectors** switch to competitors who offer superior goods and services. As such, product defectors are the most difficult to bring back to the fold once they leave. For example, it is difficult to imagine returning to a provider of inferior service once a superior provider is found. The secret to minimizing product defectors is to not become complacent with today's successes and ignore the changing needs of customers. Innovations and continuous improvement are critical in the battle of retaining product defectors.

*service defectors*
Customers who defect due to poor customer service.

**Service defectors** defect due to poor customer service. Contrary to other defector types, firms that are plagued by service defectors are actually providing existing customers with reasons to take their business elsewhere. Inadequately informed

## B 2 B  S E R V I C E S  *IN  ACTION*

> ### YOU'RE GREAT, BUT IT'S OVER!

Although intuitively higher levels of customer satisfaction would be expected to be associated with higher levels of customer retention, the relationship does not always necessarily exist. Based on a survey of 767 business executives who purchase pensions and health insurance products for their firms, customer satisfaction is not necessarily the "holy grail" of customer retention. Although 75 percent of the executives claimed to be satisfied with their current financial service supplier, 66 percent reported that they were planning to find an alternative source for their financial services needs. According to industry experts, what seems to be lacking are the personal relationships that bind suppliers and customers. Other clues indicating that a break-up may be imminent include that only 49 percent of purchasers thought their suppliers were highly ethical, and only 28 percent believed that the supplier treated their own customers well. Even among their own members, fewer than 50 percent of financial service companies claimed to be loyal to their providers.

The shaky link between customer satisfaction and customer loyalty also exists in B2C markets. Consider the following cases where (1) customers are not satisfied yet they are retained; and (2) customers are satisfied yet they defect to competitive offerings.

#### Low Satisfaction/High Retention

- Regulated monopoly or few substitutes (e.g., hospitals, airlines)
- Dominant brand equity (e.g., Microsoft)
- High cost of switching (e.g, physicians, financial institutions)
- Proprietary technology (e.g., Microsoft)

#### High Satisfaction/Low Loyalty

- Commodity products or little or no differentiation (e.g., rental cars)
- Consumer indifference (low involvement) (e.g., car wash, drycleaner)
- Many substitutes (e.g., lawn care service)
- Low costs of switching (e.g., trash collection services)

Source: Pallavi Gogoi and Ira Sager, "I Love You—But I'm Leaving You," *Business Week* (July 21, 2003) Issue 3842, 10; K. Douglas Hoffman and John E. G. Bateson, *Essentials of Services Marketing*, 2nd ed., (Thomson South-Western: Mason, Ohio, 2001).

personnel, unfulfilled promises, and unacceptable employee behavior are typical reasons customers flee to the competition. Service failures like these, combined with inadequate employee responses to those failures, can lead to service defections. While other defector types are primarily externally driven, service defectors leave as a result of problems with the internal operations of the firm.

*market defectors*
Customers who exit the market due to relocation or business failure.

*technological defectors*
Customers who switch to products outside the industry.

*organizational defectors*
Customers who leave due to political consider-ations inside the firm, such as reciprocal buy-ing arrangements.

**Market defectors** exit the market because of relocation or business failure reasons. Customers, both individuals and businesses, who move out of the market area would be considered market defectors. Similarly, companies that go out of business and are no longer in the market for goods and services are market defectors.

**Technological defectors** switch to products outside the industry. Typical examples of technological defections include the switch from lamp oil to electricity and from rail to air transportation. As is the case with product defections, technological defections may occur due to the complacency of the firm. Successful firms are often lulled into a false sense of security and fail to react to technological developments outside their own industry. For example, the manufacturers of vinyl albums who were caught off guard by the development and consumer acceptance of the compact disk lost much of their busi-ness through technological defections.

**Organizational defectors** result from political considerations inside the firm. In some instances, organizational defections will occur due to reciprocal buying arrange-ments. For example, an engineering firm may switch its paper products purchasing to a firm that sells the brand of paper products marketed by the pulp and paper mill that re-tains the engineering firm's services. In other instances, organizational defections may occur as the result of friendships that develop through civic clubs, country clubs, and a variety of other social and business gatherings.

## THE DEFECTION MANAGEMENT PROCESS

Although customer defections are frustrating for many firms, defection rates are mea-surable and manageable.[39] Defections indicate where profits are heading as well as spe-cific reasons why customers are leaving. Information obtained by analyzing defections can assist firms in reaching the goal of continuous improvement.

The key to defection management is the creation of a zero defections culture within the firm. Everyone in the firm must understand that zero defection is a primary goal of the organization. To establish this primary goal, the firm's first step in the defection management process is communicating to its employees the importance of retaining current customers and the benefits obtained by reducing defections. The earlier discus-sions in this chapter outline the importance and benefits of customer retention that should be conveyed to employees.

The zero defections goal communicated to employees must have supporters at all levels, starting at the top of the organization. It is critical that upper management lead by example and that managers "walk what they talk." Managers who talk customer ser-vice in employee meetings and then bad-mouth customers in the backroom will never successfully implement a zero defections culture within their firm.

The second step in creating a zero defections culture is to train employees in defec-tion management. Defection management involves (1) gathering customer information; (2) providing specific instructions about what to do with the information; (3) instructing employees in how to react to the information; and (4) encouraging employees to respond to the information.

The third and perhaps most critical step in the defection management process is to tie incentives to defection rates. Simply stated, if the firm truly values reducing defections, the reward structure should reinforce customer retention efforts. Firms such as MBNA, as mentioned earlier, are dedicated to customer retention and have developed reward systems consistent with their customer retention efforts. It is MBNA's policy to talk with every customer who wishes to drop its services. MBNA's employees earn up to 20 percent of their salaries in bonuses associated with customer retention efforts. As a result of the reward structure and these extra communication efforts with customers, MBNA retains 50 percent of customers who call with the intention of ending the relationship.[40] Another great example is State Farm Insurance. State Farm agents receive the same commission for securing renewals as they do for signing up new customers.[41] As a company, State Farm recognizes the value of customer retention and rewards employees for their customer retention efforts.

Finally, firms successful in defection management also carefully consider creating switching barriers that discourage defections.[42] A customer switching banks is subjected to the time-consuming task of closing one account at the old bank, opening a new account at the new bank, and sometimes paying for new checks to be printed. Switching to a new dentist may require the cost of new x-rays, and switching to a new physician may translate into completing extensive patient information forms and enduring an extensive physical exam. The key to successfully implementing switching barriers is to develop low entry barriers and non-manipulative, yet high exit barriers.

Overall, the key to defection management is the realization that customer defections are measurable and manageable. Too often, firms simply write off customers who no longer request their services. Defection management focuses on retaining customers before they defect and determining the reasons for defections when they do occur. Therefore, defectors are a valuable source of information regarding the firm's operations, its employees, and its future.

## ✳ SUMMARY

Due to stagnant markets, increased competition, the rising costs of marketing, changes in channels of distribution, and the ever-changing needs of consumers, the concept of customer retention has increased in importance. Customer retention refers to focusing the firm's marketing efforts toward its existing customer base. Hence, in contrast to seeking new customers, firms engaged in customer retention efforts work to satisfy existing customers in hope of further developing the customer-provider relationship.

Customer retention is associated with a wide variety of benefits, including the profits derived from initial and repeat sales, the profits from reduced operating costs, and the profits from referrals. Typically, existing customers make more efficient use of the supply of service available and often prefer to stay with one provider over long periods of time to reduce the risk associated with service purchases.

A number of effective customer retention tactics were presented in this chapter. These strategies include maintaining the proper perspective and remembering that the company exists to serve the needs of its customers; maintaining contact with customers between service encounters; building trust between the firm and its customers; monitoring the

416 PART 3 Assessing and Improving Service Delivery

service delivery process; properly installing products and training customers in how to use the products they purchase; being available when problems occur; and being willing to expend discretionary effort when needed.

Not all customers may be worth keeping. In general, however, firms focusing their efforts on customer retention programs such as frequency marketing, relationship marketing, aftermarketing, service guarantees, and defection management have found their efforts to be worthwhile and highly profitable.

---

## ✳ KEY TERMS

customer retention, 390
conquest marketing, 392
frequency marketing, 404
relationship marketing, 405
aftermarketing, 405
implicit guarantee, 407
specific result guarantee, 407
unconditional guarantee, 407
payout, 409

defection management, 410
zero defects model, 411
zero defections, 411
price defectors, 411
product defectors, 412
service defectors, 412
market defectors, 414
technological defectors, 414
organizational defectors, 414

---

## ✳ DISCUSSION QUESTIONS

1. Why has conquest marketing become an acceptable form of business for many of today's firms?
2. Discuss the problems associated with conquest marketing.
3. Discuss the steps associated with frequency marketing as they relate to frequent-flier programs.
4. How have changes within service distribution channels impacted customer retention?
5. Discuss the distinction between zero defects and zero defections.
6. How do service defectors differ from other defector types?
7. Is it always worthwhile to retain a customer?
8. Discuss the characteristics of successful guarantees.
9. What are the trade-offs associated with utilizing implicit guarantees?

# ✳ NOTES

1. Robert E. Wayland and Paul M. Cole, "Turn Customer Service into Customer Profitability," *Management Review* (July 1994), pp. 22–24.

2. Rahul Jacob, "Why Some Customers Are More Equal than Others," *Fortune*, September 19, 1994, pp. 218, 220.

3. Terry G. Vavra, *AFTERMARKETING: How to Keep Customers for Life through Relationship Marketing* (Homewood, IL: Business One Irwin, 1992), pp. 2–6.

4. Vavra, *AFTERMARKETING*, p. 1.

5. Ibid., pp. 2–6.

6. Michael W. Lowenstein, "The Voice of the Customer," *Small Business Reports* (December 1993), pp. 57–61.

7. Carol Schultz, "Something for Today," Colorado State University Cooperative Extension Service, (July/August 2000), p.2.

8. Frederick F. Reichheld and W. Earl Sasser, Jr., "Zero Defections: Quality Comes to Services," *Harvard Business Review* (September–October 1990), pp. 105–111.

9. Barry Farber and Joyce Wycoff, "Customer Service: Evolution and Revolution," *Sales and Marketing Management* (May 1991), pp. 44–51.

10. Reichheld and Sasser, "Zero Defections," p. 107.

11. Larry Armstrong, "Beyond May I Help You?" *Business Week/Quality* (1991), pp. 100–103; Ron Zemke, "The Emerging Art of Service Management," *Training* (January 1992), pp. 37–42; Frederick F. Reichheld and W. Earl Sasser, Jr., "Zero Defections: Quality Comes to Services," *Harvard Business Review* (September–October 1990), pp. 105–111; and Rahul Jacob, "Why Some Customers Are More Equal than Others," *Fortune*, September 19, 1994, p.218.

12. Adapted from Barton A. Weitz, Stephen B. Castleberry, and John F. Tanner, Jr., *Selling: Building Partnerships* (Homewood IL: Irwin, 1992), pp. 330–340.

13. "Is Customer Retention Worth the Time, Effort and Expense," *Sales and Marketing Management* 143,15 (December 1991), pp. 21–22.

14. Wayland and Cole, "Turn Customer Service," p. 24.

15. Richard Barlow, "Building Customer Loyalty through Frequency Marketing," *The Bankers Magazine* (May/June 1990), pp. 73–76.

16. Jim Ellis, "Frill-Seeking in the Clouds," *Business Week*, September 13, 1993, pp. 104–105.

17. Adam Bryant, "Airlines' Frequent-Flier Miles Not Just for Flying Anymore," *Sunday Star-News*, August 21, 1994, p. 10A.

18. Martin Christopher, Adrian Payne, and David Ballantyne, *Relationship Marketing* (Oxford: Butterworth-Heinemann, 1991).

19. Jacob, "Why Some Customers," p. 222.

20. Ibid., p. 215.

21. Vavra, *AFTERMARKETING*, p. 1.

22. Jacob, "Why Some Customers," p. 222.

23. Adapted from Christopher W. L. Hart, Leonard A. Schlesinger, and Don Maher, "Guarantees Come to Professional Service Firms," *Sloan Management Review* (Spring 1992), pp. 19–29.

24. Ibid., p. 29.

25. Ibid., p. 28.

26. Ibid., p. 20.

27. "Service Guarantees Yield Surprising Results," *The Cornell H.R.A. Quarterly* (February 1991), pp. 14–15.

28. Hart, Schlesinger, and Maher, "Guarantees Come," p. 20.

29. Reichheld and Sasser, "Zero Defections," p. 110.

30. Ron Zemke, "The Emerging Art of Service Management," *Training* (January 1992), pp. 37–42.

31. Reichheld and Sasser, "Zero Defections," p. 108.

32. "How Five Companies Targeted Their Best Prospects," *Marketing News*, February 18, 1991, p. 22.

33. *The Cellular Telephone Industry: Personal Communication* (Silver Spring, MD: Herschel Shostack Assoc., 1992), p. 122.

34. *The Pager Industry: ProNet Annual Report*, 1989.

35. Reichheld and Sasser, "Zero Defections," p. 108.

36. Lowenstein, "The Voice," p. 57.

37. Patricia Sellers, "Keeping the Buyers," *Fortune* (Autumn/Winter 1993), pp. 56–58.

38. Glenn DeSouza, "Designing a Customer Retention Plan," *The Journal of Business Strategy* (March/April 1992), pp. 24–28.

39. Reichheld and Sasser, "Zero Defections," p. 105.

40. Larry Armstrong, "Beyond May I Help You?," *Business Week/Quality* (1991), pp. 100–103.

41. Sellers, "Keeping the Buyers," p. 58.

42. DeSouza, "Designing," p. 27.

## CHAPTER 16

# PUTTING THE PIECES TOGETHER: CREATING THE SEAMLESS SERVICE FIRM

## CHAPTER OBJECTIVES

*The purpose of this chapter is to tie together the information presented in this book. In order to provide service excellence, the individual components of the firm must act in unison to create a "seamless" organization. The firm will not act as one if the current culture of the organization is based on departmentalization and functionalism. Consequently, creating and supporting a customer-focused organizational culture is critical. Finally, by conducting a service audit, a seamless service culture is fostered, as personnel throughout the organization come to appreciate the challenges faced and the contributions made by everyone involved in the firm's final service delivery effort.*

After reading this chapter, you should be able to:

- Compare and contrast the concept of seamlessness to departmentalization and functionalism.
- Discuss the historical weakness of marketing in service firms.
- Explain the basic concepts of the three-tiered model of service firms.
- Explain what is meant by the firm's culture and discuss the four methods that facilitate cultural change.
- Discuss the basic components of a service audit.

*"What is needed now is to surround these individuals with the system—a logically and tightly connected seamless set of interrelated parts that allows people to perform their jobs well."*

Benjamin Schneider and
David E. Bowen

# > AN EXTRAORDINARY HOSPITALITY EXPERIENCE: THE KATITCHE POINT GREAT HOUSE

© STEVE BLY / STONE / GETTY IMAGES

Tired of the same old vacations in the same old hotels? The Katitche Point Great House, strategically located on the island of Virgin Gorda in the British Virgin Islands (BVI), will put a definitive end to your vacation blues. In fact, as you stand on the panoramic horizon pool deck, the word "blue" takes on an entirely new meaning. Go to http://www.katitchepoint.com and you'll see what we mean as the blue shades of pool water, the Caribbean, and the skyline provide a servicescape beyond compare.

The British Virgin Islands are a paradise in and of themselves. Part of the Lesser Antilles, which boasts the most beautiful sailing waters in the world, the BVI is the world's playground for water recreation. The island of Virgin Gorda (Fat Virgin) is best known for the BVI's most stellar natural attraction called "The Baths." The Baths, located on the southern side of Virgin Gorda, are the result of volcanic activity that took place thousands of years ago where huge granite boulders were strewn along Virgin Gorda's southern coastline. The boulders, which often lie upon one another, formed grottos and pools that are now a major tourist attraction for hikers, snorkelers, and scuba divers. In contrast to the sandy beaches of the southern section, the northern half of Virgin Gorda is mountainous with peaks reaching nearly 1,400 feet above sea level. Located on a narrow strip of land between the best of what Virgin Gorda has to offer is the Katitche Point Great House.

The Katitche Point Great House is a compound of sorts, or more pleasantly described as a "small holiday village." The "village" comfortably sleeps 8 to 10 people consisting of a three-level, pyramid-shaped main house, four large bedroom suites each complete with their own bathroom suite and private verandahs, and a large separate master bedroom suite complete with sitting room and a deep soaking tub that is built into the rocks next to a Koi pond. In all, the Katitche Point Great House is comprised of 22,000 spacious square feet of living space that offer unobstructed panoramic views of the Caribbean in all directions.

Built in 2000, Katitche Point has received many accolades. *Elle* magazine ranked the Katitche Point Great House as the 8th best "deluxe holiday home around the globe." *Vogue* magazine included Katitche Point in a special section of its magazine called "Destination Dreamland" and referred to the property as "a private paradise." The United Kingdom's version of *The Travel Channel* featured Katitche Point in a 10-minute segment on its "Cool Caribbean" series and called the Great House "the most stunning villa they've ever seen." *Barefoot Traveler* featured the Great House's Viking Kitchen and called Katitche Point "the best that life has to offer." These comments and many more like them serve as Kititche Point's primary promotional strategy, which is backed up by the website and reinforced by positive word-of-mouth testimonials from fortunate guests.

So, what is the price of this level of luxury? Given the villa's limited capacity and tremendous accommodations, a week's stay at the Katitche Point Great House is not inexpensive. Rates start at $17,500 per week for the full facility during the off-season and peak over the Christmas and New Year's season at $26,000 a week. For those who do not require the separate master bedroom suite, prices are reduced by $5,000 per week. A special honeymoon package is also offered for $6,600 per week based on availability. All rates include full maid service from 8 a.m. to 4 p.m., pool maintenance, laundry service, and a gardener! Gourmet chef and masseuse services are also available upon request for additional fees. Although expensive, the Katitche Point Great House offers a once-in-a-lifetime experience for its guests who will never forget this unimaginable holiday destination.

---

Source: http://www.katitchepoint.com and http://www.b-v-i.com/baths.htm, accessed 11 June 2005 and the good fortune of personal experience.

> | # INTRODUCTION

*seamless service*
Services that occur with-
out interruption, confu-
sion, or hassle to the
customer.

Creating a **seamless service** organization means providing services without interruption, confusion, or hassle to the customer.[1] Seamless service firms manage to simultaneously provide reliable, responsive, competent, and empathetic services and have the
facilities and resources necessary to get the job done. Seamlessness applies not only to
the provision of services but also to service recovery efforts pertaining to core system
failures, implicit/explicit customer requests, and employee behavior.

Seamlessness thrives on tightly connected interrelated parts within the service delivery
system. Functionalization and departmentalization kill seamlessness. For example, consider
the following three memos sent to a young manager of a branch bank on the same day:[2]

*From the marketing department:*

We shortly will be launching a new advertising campaign based on the friendliness of our staff. This is in direct response to the increasingly competitive
marketplace we face. Please ensure that your staff members deliver the
promises we are making.

*From the operations department:*

As you are aware, we are facing an increasingly competitive marketplace and, as
a result, our profits have come under pressure. It is crucial, therefore, that we
minimize waste to keep our costs under control. From today, therefore, no
recruitment whatsoever will be allowed.

*From the human resources department:*

Our staff members are becoming increasingly militant. This is due, in large part,
to the availability of alternative employment with our new competitors. We
currently are involved in a particularly delicate set of negotiations and would be
grateful if you could minimize any disruptions at the local level.

These instructions from the three different departments obviously conflict with one
another. To obey the operations department means no recruitment and, therefore, an
increase in the workload of contact personnel. The increased workload will most likely
be a hot topic during labor negotiations and could be disastrous for the human
resources department. Finally, the increased workload, in all probability, will have a negative effect on staff morale. Given the inseparability of the service, the staff's low morale
will be visible to customers and will negatively affect customer satisfaction levels.

If this particular branch bank is marketing-oriented, the young manager will
attempt to trade off the three sets of instructions, giving added weight to the marketing
department's instructions. It should be stressed that, in service firms, it is nearly impossible to be totally marketing-oriented. Customers cannot be given everything they want
because of the constraints imposed by the firm's service delivery system. For example,
in a restaurant setting, every customer cannot be seated and served immediately upon
arrival due to seating and available service (personnel) constraints.

If this branch is operations-oriented, added weight will be given to the operations department's set of instructions. The young manager may relay marketing's request to the vice-president of operations and ask for clarification. The operations vice-president, in turn, may fire off an abusive memo to her counterpart in marketing. The memo may ask why marketing was sending memos directly to the branches at all and suggest that in the future, all other requests made by marketing should be cleared by operations.

Firms that continue to cling to functional and departmental mindsets are often besieged by internal conflict as departments compete against one another for resources instead of pulling together to provide exceptional service. Seamlessness is "tooth-to-tail" performance—a term commonly used in the armed forces. "The personnel out front in the trenches need to be backed up with coordinated supplies, information resources, personnel reinforcements, and so on."[3] Similarly, the primary efforts of the service firm should focus on the service delivery process and on the personnel providing customer services.

The conflict that often occurs among marketing, operations, and human resources is not personal.[4] It is a result of their different cultures, which are functions of each department's goals, planning horizons, departmental structure, people-management systems, and the specific individuals in each department. For example, marketing tends to have a longer planning horizon, is less rigidly and hierarchically organized, and tends to reward innovation and creativity compared with its operations counterparts.

In comparison with goods-producing firms, turf wars among departments are more prevalent in service firms due to lack of inventories. Inventories, which provide a buffer between marketing and operations in goods-producing firms, are for the most part nonexistent in service firms. In a service firm, production and consumption often occur simultaneously in a real-time experience.

## > THE HISTORICAL WEAKNESS OF MARKETING IN SERVICE FIRMS[5]

Service firms often find themselves in a three-cornered fight among marketing, operations, and human resources (see Figure 16.1.) Somehow, marketing always seems to lose this fight since marketers tend to have less influence in service companies than in goods companies.

At this point, it is necessary to understand the differences among marketing orientation, the marketing function, and the marketing department. **Marketing orientation**

*marketing orientation*
A firm's view toward planning its operations according to market needs.

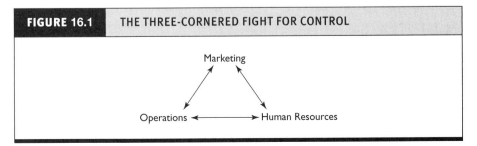

| **FIGURE 16.1** | **THE THREE-CORNERED FIGHT FOR CONTROL** |
|---|---|

Marketing

Operations ←→ Human Resources

Source: John E. G. Bateson, *Managing Services Marketing: Text and Readings*, 3rd ed. (Fort Worth, TX: The Dryden Press, 1995).

*marketing functions*
Tasks such as the design of a product, its pricing, and its promotion.

*marketing department*
The formal department in an organization that works on the marketing functions of the company.

*customization/ customer contact matrix*
A table that illustrates the variety of relationships between marketing and other functions within the organization.

means that a firm or organization plans its operations according to market needs (see Global Services in Action). The objectives of the firm are to satisfy customer needs rather than merely to use production facilities or raw materials.[6] Marketing orientation is clearly an attitude that puts the customer's needs first in any trade-off. Firms do not necessarily have a formal marketing department in order to have a marketing orientation.

**Marketing functions** in a firm include tasks such as the design of the product, pricing, and promotion. Decisions in these areas are made in order for the organization to operate, but they need not necessarily be made by people with marketing titles nor by individuals in a formal **marketing department**—the department that traditionally works on marketing functions in the company.

In a typical goods company, the distinctions among marketing orientation, marketing functions, and marketing department are not necessary. They are, however, necessary in service firms, where a formal marketing department may not exist. Because the service product is an interactive process, it may be more appropriate to leave the different functional decisions to different departments.

The variety of relationships between marketing and other functions within the organization can be illustrated by the **customization/customer contact matrix** depicted in Figure 16.2. One axis of the matrix relates directly to the degree of contact the firm has with its customers. The higher the level of customer contact, the higher the level of inefficiency because of the uncertainty introduced by customers. This idea is based largely on the concept of inseparability and the participation of consumers in the service delivery process. The second axis relates to the amount of customization of the service available to consumers. Once again, we would expect the "low" state to be preferable for efficiency purposes as it would allow the service delivery system to operate as a production line free from outside influences. A variety of businesses are introduced into the cells to illustrate how the matrix is used.

For example, a travel agency can operate in a number of cells simultaneously. Booking an airline ticket by telephone for a business traveler fits into the low/low cell. But the same travel agency could just as well operate in a different cell if it also maintained a retail operation. From within the retail operation, both high and low customization are possible, depending on whether the customer is a business traveler wanting a ticket or a vacationer planning a multi-stop European trip.

From an operations perspective, the ideal cell is the low/low cell. In this cell, the degree of customization is minimized so that large parts of the organization can be isolated and run like any other manufacturing plant.[7] In addition, the level of customization is also minimized so that the operating system is focused on a limited range of output and its efficiency increased.[8] A move into this cell, however, can have major implications for marketing. Customers may be seeking contact and customization and be willing to pay a premium for them.

A top-quality French restaurant might fit into the high/high cell. Compared with McDonald's, this is a different business with a different formula (but, interestingly, the target segment may be the same person on a very different occasion). The loss of efficiency implied by the high/high cell is compensated for by the price that can be charged.

The importance of the matrix and this discussion is to show how different cells suggest alternative roles and places for the marketing departments of firms operating within them. Two contrasting examples are the provision of legal services by a traditional law firm and by a franchised firm such as Hyatt Legal Services.

# GLOBAL SERVICES *IN ACTION*

> ## ETHNIC MARKETING

Lessons learned from global marketing are now being turned inward in the form of domestic ethnic marketing. Within the U.S., changes in our demographic and ethnicity composition continue to impact societal values and subsequent marketing efforts. According to the 2000 U.S. Census, minority markets, now more accurately termed *emerging markets*, account for approximately 80 million of the 281 million Americans. Emerging markets now represent more than half the population of America's largest cities. By 2005, emerging market populations are expected to exceed majority populations in California, Hawaii, New Mexico, Texas, and the District of Columbia. In 2010, one-third of the U.S. population is forecasted to be composed of African-American, Latino, Asian-American, and Native American populations. By 2050, America's emerging markets will likely surpass the majority population throughout the U.S.

Due to the rapid growth of emerging markets in the U.S., there has been a growing interest in ethnic marketing in recent years. Emerging markets including Latinos, African-Americans, and Asian-Americans account for nearly 13 percent, 12 percent, and 4 percent of the U.S. population, respectively. The purchasing power of these three groups combined is forecasted to be a trillion-dollar growth market. As a result, half of the Fortune 100 companies have established marketing programs geared toward emerging markets.

Best practice guidelines for successfully attracting and retaining emerging markets include the following:

- Discover the insights of your target market and observe all cultural cues with respect to emotions, numbers, letters, and colors.
- Work with agencies that specialize in ethnic marketing from the beginning of the project. Do not expect a product concept that is already developed to be successful.
- Hire employees from the ethnic backgrounds you are targeting.

- Employees should have appropriate in-language skills.
- Point-of-purchase in-language materials should be available.
- Ethnic mystery shoppers should be used to test in-language services available.
- Offer training in cultural competency to all employees so they know how to respond to people from different cultures.

Experts in the field of ethnic marketing believe that failure to follow these fundamental steps will at worst offend and at best demonstrate that your firm was too lazy to really understand the unique needs and wants of emerging markets.

Source: Janet Bigham Bernstel, "Courting Culturally Diverse Customers," *Bank Marketing*, (October, 2000), Vol. 32, Issue 10, 32–37; Daniel Joelson, "U.S. Financial Firms Cater to Latinos," *Bank Technology News*, (March 2001), 14 (3); Bonnie McGreer, "Banks Focus on Minority Merchants," *American Banker* (May 7, 2001), 166 (87); Rodney Moore, "1-To-1 An Ethnic Star," *Advertising Age*, (October 29, 2001), 72 (44); Geng Cui, "Marketing to Ethnic Minority Consumers: A Historical Journey (1932–1997)," *Journal of Macromarketing*, (June 2001), 21 (1); and John Kerrigan, "Playing to Hispanics Garners Rewards," *Marketing News*, (July 22, 2002), 20.

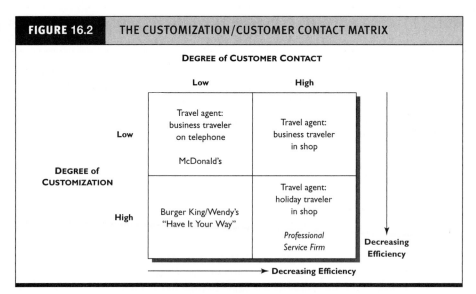

Source: John E. G. Bateson, *Managing Services Marketing: Text and Readings*, 3rd ed. (Fort Worth, TX: The Dryden Press, 1995).

Operationally, the traditional firm will fit into the high/high cell in the matrix. The firm's attorneys will be in intensive contact with clients and will customize each service to meet the needs of each individual client. Except for routine cases, there will be little opportunity for economies of scale in this type of legal firm.

From a marketing point of view, the service product in the high/high cell often is created in the client's offices, away from the home firm of the attorney. In such situations, it is clear that a central marketing department has little influence over the final product and that most of the marketing needs to be delegated to the field offices, if not to the individual attorneys themselves. The selling function is done by consultants or professionals, so that, too, must be delegated.

The alternative is a firm such as Hyatt Legal Services. This firm represents a clear attempt to move the operating system away from the inefficiency of the high/high cell toward the low/low or, at least, the high contact/low customization cell. By reducing the types of cases handled, operations can be simplified and economies of scale generated. These economies, in turn, can be passed on to the customer through lower fees.

The marketing implications of moving the operation from a high/high cell to a more standardized outcome are relatively straightforward. The service is branded in order to add value for the consumer in a market that traditionally is not heavily branded. The firm depends on systematization and, from an operations point of view, implies centralization. We therefore would expect to find a strong centralized marketing department as well. Clearly, many service firms do not operate in the low/low cell of the matrix, even though they may wish to do so. For many service firms, therefore, the traditional combination of marketing functions in a marketing department breaks down. The result is that there is no strong marketing group to drive a marketing orientation in the organization. The weakness of the marketing function is compounded by the strength of the operations group and the linkages between them.

> ## MOVING BEYOND DEPARTMENTALIZATION AND FUNCTIONALIZATION: THE THREE-TIERED MODEL OF SERVICE FIRMS[9]

Seamless service is based on a **three-tiered model** of the service organization (see Figure 16.3). Traditionally, organizations are sliced by functions such as marketing, human resources, and operations management. In contrast, the three-tiered model consists of a customer tier, a boundary tier, and a coordination tier. Success is based on the effective management and integration of the three tiers.

*three-tiered model*
A view of service organizations that reconfigures traditional departmental functions into a customer tier, a boundary tier, and a coordination tier.

### THE CUSTOMER TIER

As we have discussed throughout this book, attracting and retaining customers is the lifeblood of every service organization. Without customers, the service firm has no reason to exist. The **customer tier** focuses on customer expectations, needs, and competencies. To provide seamless service, management must have a deep understanding of each of these areas from the customer's perspective (see Figure 16.4).

*customer tier*
The tier in the three-tiered model that focuses on customer expectations, needs, and competencies.

**Expectations** have been discussed throughout this book and are an integral component in developing customer satisfaction evaluations. As firms have realized the importance of customers, experts believe that businesses now have a fairly good understanding of their customers' expectations but not necessarily of their customers' needs and competencies. At a minimum, service firms must meet customer expectations in order to provide customers what they want, when they want it, and where they want it so that the firms can strategically differentiate themselves from competitors and stay in the service game.

*expectations*
Consumer expectations pertaining to the service delivery process and final outcome.

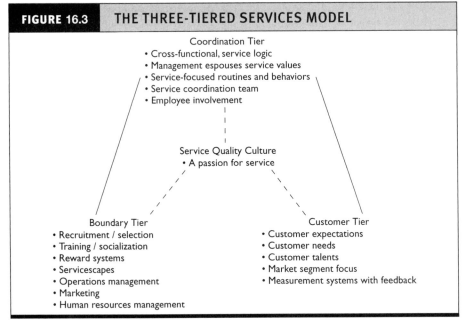

**FIGURE 16.3    THE THREE-TIERED SERVICES MODEL**

Coordination Tier
• Cross-functional, service logic
• Management espouses service values
• Service-focused routines and behaviors
• Service coordination team
• Employee involvement

Service Quality Culture
• A passion for service

Boundary Tier
• Recruitment / selection
• Training / socialization
• Reward systems
• Servicescapes
• Operations management
• Marketing
• Human resources management

Customer Tier
• Customer expectations
• Customer needs
• Customer talents
• Market segment focus
• Measurement systems with feedback

Source: Benjamin Schneider and David E. Bowen, *Winning the Service Game* (Boston: Harvard Business School Press, 1995), 244. Copyright © 1990 by the President and Fellows of Harvard College.

---

**FIGURE 16.4**    **THE TEN COMMANDMENTS OF CUSTOMER SERVICE**

1. **Bring 'em back alive.** . . . Ask customers what they want and give it to them again and again.
2. **Systems, not smiles.** . . . Saying please and thank you doesn't ensure you'll do the job right the first time, every time. Only systems guarantee that.
3. **Underpromise, overdeliver.** . . . Customers expect you to keep your word. Exceed it.
4. **When the customer asks, the answer is always yes.** . . . Period.
5. **Fire your inspectors and customer relations department.** . . . Every employee who deals with clients must have the authority to handle complaints.
6. **No complaints, something's wrong.** . . . Encourage your customers to tell you what you're doing wrong.
7. **Measure everything.** . . . Baseball teams do it. Football teams do it. Basketball teams do it. You should too.
8. **Salaries are unfair.** . . . Pay people like partners.
9. **Your mother was right.** . . . Show people respect. Be polite. It works.
10. **Japanese them.** . . . Learn how the best really do it; make their systems your own. Then improve them.

Source: Paul B. Brown and Carl Sewall, *Customers for Life* (New York: Bantam, 1998).

---

*needs*
Security, esteem, and justice; often unrecognized as needs by customers themselves.

**Needs** are distinguished from expectations in that customers are generally aware of their expectations but are often unaware of what they need. Chapter 10 provided ample examples of products that met with great success such as minivans, personal computers, and cellular phones, despite early customer research indicating that customers did not feel a need for these products. Service experts believe that firms must deliver three key customer needs in order to deliver service excellence:[10]

1. Security: the need to feel secure and unthreatened by physical, psychological, or economic harm.
2. Esteem: the need to feel that one's self-esteem is maintained and enhanced by others.
3. Justice: The need to feel fairly and justly treated.

Examining and understanding customer needs is the foundation of building a competitive strategy that differentiates the firm from its competitors and of providing service excellence.

*competencies*
The contributions customers bring to the service production process.

**Competencies** are the contributions customers bring to the service production process. Service firms that excel look beyond their employees as their only human resources. Throughout much of this book, we have discussed the consumer's involvement in the service delivery process. The customer influences the type and length of demand and often is a major determinant in the success or failure of the final outcome. Consequently, appealing to the "best customers" can be a source of competitive advantage.

For example, Dayton Hudson, the retailer, pursued a strategy that specifically targeted customers who spent more than $1,500 per year in their stores. By involving these customers in designing a program that would attract and retain their business, a special card was developed that entitled the holder to special discounts, free alterations, gift wrapping, free parking, and presale sales days. The information for designing the program was obtained through survey data, which consisted of more than 2,000 detailed responses from targeted clientele.[11]

## THE BOUNDARY TIER

While the customer tier deals with customer expectations, needs, and competencies, the **boundary tier** concerns itself with the individuals who interact with the customers—the boundary spanners. The boundary tier is where the customer meets the organization and where the critical incidents or "moments of truth" occur (see E-Services in Action). Service personnel in the boundary tier must be more flexible, communicative, able to deal with stress, and willing to take initiative than their manufacturing counterparts. To the customer, personnel in the boundary tier *are* the organization and occupy a two-way communication role—from the organization to the customer, and from the customer back to the organization.

  The key to successfully navigating the boundary tier is to avoid the "human resources trap." This trap makes the fatal flaw in judgment of placing the full burden of "moments of truth" upon boundary-spanning personnel. The firm's nonpersonnel services, such as the physical facility, the accuracy and timeliness of billing, and all the support staff who enable the boundary personnel to perform their jobs, must be in place and working together in order for the firm to provide seamless service. Ultimately, boundary personnel are only as good as the service delivery system that supports their efforts.

*boundary tier*
The tier in the three-tiered model that concerns itself with the individuals who interact with the customers—the boundary spanners.

## THE COORDINATION TIER

The **coordination tier** is the responsibility of upper management and involves coordinating the activities that help integrate the customer and boundary tiers (see Figure 16.5). Management's most important concerns pertain to (1) defining a target market and developing a strategy for effectively attracting this market; (2) ensuring that the boundary tier has the support necessary to meet the expectations and needs of the customer tier; and (3) ensuring that the expectations and needs of boundary-tier personnel are also being met.

  The primary challenge of the coordination tier is to get the various departments within the organization to work with one common goal in mind—serving the customer. Before attempting to integrate the various departments of the firm, it is important to understand that each department is driven by its own **internal logic**—implicit and explicit principles that drive organizational performance.[12] Each department's logic is internally focused on departmental needs and creates seams in the service delivery process. For example, consider the logic behind the following functions: operations management, marketing, and human resources.

  **Operations logic** is driven by the goal of reducing or containing costs through mass production or the use of advanced technologies. Operations and marketing are often in conflict with each other, which creates seams in service delivery. While marketing is concerned with identifying and understanding customer needs and providing goods and services that meet those needs, operations is concerned with how these products and

*coordination tier*
The tier in the three-tiered model that coordinates activities that help integrate the customer and boundary tiers.

*internal logic*
Implicit and explicit principles of individual departments that drive organizational performance.

*operations logic*
The reasoning that stresses cost containment/reduction through mass production.

# E-SERVICES *IN ACTION*

> ## RATEMYPROFESSORS.COM

Ratemyprofessors.com is an opportunity for students to turn the tables on their professors. Instead of professors grading students, ratemyprofessors.com provides the means for students to grade their professors. Ultimately, the site allows students to take advantage of the knowledge gained from previous students' experiences. Students can use this information to guide their instructor selections when alternatives are available. To date, ratemyprofessors.com contains over 3.5 million ratings of over half a million instructors from 4,600 colleges and universities. New ratings are posted at the rate of three to four thousand a day.

In addition to its rating service, ratemyprofessors.com offers a number of other services to its users. One service posted on its main menu is a collection of what the site designers call "Funny Ratings." These ratings are selected quotes from some very creative students who felt less than happy about their professors. So, here we go, the TOP 20 Funniest Ratings include the following:

20. You can't cheat in her class because no one knows the answers.
19. His class was like milk; it was good for two weeks.
18. Houston, we have a problem. Space cadet of a teacher, isn't quite attached to Earth.
17. I would have been better off using the tuition money to heat my apartment last winter.
16. Three of my friends got A's in his class and my friends are dumb.
15. Emotional scarring may fade away, but that big fat F on your transcript won't.
14. Evil computing science teaching robot who crushes humans for pleasure.
13. Miserable professor—I wish I could sum him up without foul language.
12. Instant amnesia walking into this class. I swear he breathes sleeping gas.
11. BORING! But I learned there are 137 tiles on the ceiling.
10. Not only is the book a better teacher, it also has a better personality.
9. Teaches well, invites questions, and then insults you for 20 minutes.
8. This teacher was a firecracker in a pond of slithery tadpoles.
7. I learned how to hate a language I already know.
6. Very good course, because I only went to one class.
5. He will destroy you like an academic ninja.
4. Bring a pillow.
3. Your pillow will need a pillow.
2. If I was tested on her family, I would have gotten an A.
1. She hates you already.

Source: http://www.ratemyprofessors.com, accessed 11 June 2005.

| FIGURE 16.5 | SOUTHWEST AIRLINES' ELEVEN PRIMARY ATTITUDES |
|---|---|

*We are not an airline with great customer service. We are a great customer service organization that happens to be in the airline business.*

*Colleen Barrett, Southwest Airlines executive*

1. Employees are number one. The way you treat your employees is the way they will treat your customer.
2. Think small to grow big.
3. Manage in the good times for the bad times.
4. Irreverence is okay.
5. It's okay to be yourself.
6. Have fun at work.
7. Take the competition seriously, but not yourself.
8. It's difficult to change someone's attitude, so hire for attitude and train for skill.
9. Think of the company as a service organization that happens to be in the airline business.
10. Do whatever it takes.
11. Always practice the Golden Rule, internally and externally.

Source: Kevin Freiberg and Jackie Freiberg, *Nuts! Southwest Airlines' Crazy Recipe for Business and Personal Success* (Austin, TX: Bard Press, 1996).

services will be produced and delivered. In essence, marketing is concerned with the management of demand, while operations is concerned with the management of supply. Marketing attempts to focus on meeting demand in the most effective manner in terms of product form, location, price, and promotions, while operations is primarily concerned with meeting demand in the most cost-effective manner. Typical goals of operations management and marketing concerns regarding these goals are displayed in Figure 16.6.

The major challenge for operations in a service setting is the involvement of customers in the production process. Compared with raw materials in a pure manufacturing setting, customers are unpredictable and decrease the efficiency of the delivery system. Operations would like to remove the customer from the production process as much as possible, while marketing promotes the importance of the customer in the production process. Consequently, operations and marketing must establish a point of equilibrium between the variety and depth of products marketing would like to offer and the cost effectiveness of meeting that demand through efficient operations.

While operations management is internally focused, marketing is externally focused on meeting the expectations and needs of consumers. Ideally, the **marketing logic** is to provide customers with options that better enable the service offering to meet individual consumer needs. Although ideal for customers, providing numerous options leads to serious cost inefficiencies in a firm's operations.

In addition to often being in conflict with operations, marketing may also find itself in conflict with human resources, creating additional seams in service delivery. For example, marketing would like to staff all personnel positions with individuals who, in addition to being technically competent, possess strong interpersonal skills that enable the organization to better communicate with its customers. Marketing would argue that hiring personnel

*marketing logic*
The reasoning that stresses providing customers with options that better enable the service offering to meet individual needs.

| FIGURE 16.6 | OPERATIONS AND MARKETING PERSPECTIVES ON OPERATIONAL ISSUES |
|---|---|

| Operational Issues | Typical Operation Goals | Common Marketing Concerns |
|---|---|---|
| Productivity improvement | Reduce unit cost of production | Strategies may cause decline in service quality |
| Make-versus-buy decisions | Trade off control against comparative advantage and cost savings | "Make" decisions may result in lower quality and lack of market coverage; "buy" decisions may transfer control to unresponsive suppliers and hurt the firm's image |
| Facilities location | Reduce costs; provide convenient access for suppliers and employees | Customers may find location unattractive and inaccessible |
| Standardization | Keep costs low and quality consistent; simplify operations tasks; recruit low-cost employees | Consumers may seek variety, prefer customization to match segmented needs |
| Batch-versus-unit processing | Seek economies of scale, consistency, efficient use of capacity | Customers may be forced to wait, feel "one of a crowd," be turned off by other customers |
| Facilities layout and design | Control costs; improve efficiency by ensuring proximity of operationally related tasks; enhance safety and security | Customers may be confused, shunted around unnecessarily, find facility unattractive and inconvenient |
| Job design | Minimize error, waste, and fraud; make efficient use of technology; simplify tasks for standardization | Operationally oriented employees with narrow roles may be unresponsive to customer needs |
| Learning curves | Apply experience to reduce time and costs per unit of output | Faster service is not necessarily better service; cost saving may not be passed on as lower prices |
| Management of capacity | Keep costs down by avoiding wasteful under-utilization of resources | Service may be unavailable when needed; quality may be compromised during high-demand periods |
| Quality control | Ensure that service execution conforms to predefined standards | Operational definitions of quality may not reflect customer needs, preferences |
| Management of queues | Optimize use of available capacity by planning for average throughput; maintain customer order, discipline | Customers may be bored and frustrated during wait, see firm as unresponsive |

Source: © 1989 by Christopher H. Lovelock. Reprinted with permission from Christopher H. Lovelock. Christopher H. Lovelock, "Managing Interaction Between Operations and Marketing and Their Impact on Customers," in Bowen et al. (eds.) *Service Management Effectiveness* (San Francisco: Jossey Bass, 1990), p. 362.

who have well-developed interpersonal skills in addition to being technically competent is a bonus. In turn, human resources would argue that obtaining and keeping highly trained and personable personnel is much more expensive than hiring people who simply adequately perform their roles in the organization. Furthermore, human resources will point out that certain market segments can be served by personnel who are simply civil with customers and who perform their duties adequately. This point is valid. Does the customer really want a McDonald's worker to engage the customer in a lengthy conversation about the weather, community happenings, and family matters, or would the customer rather have a simply civil employee take the order and deliver the food in a speedy manner? Moreover, the food is more likely to be less expensive when provided by adequate, as opposed to superior, personnel because of the savings in labor costs.

**Human resources logic** is to recruit personnel and to develop training that enhances the performance of existing personnel. In the service encounter, operations, marketing, and human resources are inextricably linked. Figure 16.7 depicts the link between operations and human resources. This figure, which compares the degree of customer contact with production efficiency, reveals that the perfect service employee does not exist. Characteristics of the "right employee" depend on the characteristics of the particular job in question. Some employees will need to be people oriented, while others will need to be more task oriented to process "things" instead of "people."

The importance of service firm personnel as they interact with customers throughout the service delivery process highlights the link between human resources and marketing. In services, human resources are the only source of quality control. Consequently, the hiring, training, and reward structures developed by human resources will ultimately play a major role in how employees interact with the firm's customers.

Despite the opportunity to make major contributions to the firm's overall service effort, human resources departments are often stuck in their own production orientation and have difficulty getting their own acts together, let alone helping the organization provide superior service. Human resources production-oriented activities include mistakes such as using the same employee evaluation forms for everyone in the firm even though the jobs may be very different, conducting canned employee training programs that never change from year to year, and using generic employee selection procedures for a variety of jobs that actually require different skill sets. In contrast, service-oriented

*human resources logic*
The reasoning that stresses recruiting personnel and developing training to enhance the performance of existing personnel.

| **FIGURE 16.7** | **LINK BETWEEN OPERATIONS AND HUMAN RESOURCES** |

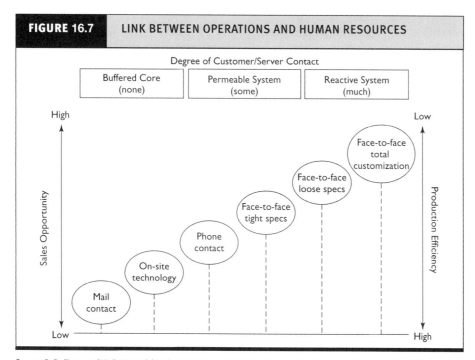

Source: R. B. Chase and W. E. Youngdahl, "Service by Design," *Design Management Journal* 9 (Winter 1992), 12. Adapted from R. B. Chase and N. J. Aquilano, *Production and Operations Management: A Lifecycle Approach* (Homewood, IL: Irwin, 1991).

human resources programs would be co-designed and co-taught with relevant managers, and evaluation forms would be thought of as coaching and evaluating devices rather than as rating forms used solely for compensation decisions. Overall, the service-oriented human resources department would work much more closely with its customers—the firm's employees—and form an ongoing, interactive, long-term relationship in pursuit of supporting those who serve the firm's final consumers.

> ## BUILDING THE SERVICE LOGIC THROUGH CULTURAL CHANGE

**culture**
The shared values and beliefs that drive an organization.

The service logic stitches the departmental and functional seams together in order to help the firm provide flawless service. However, before this can happen, the firm's organizational **culture** must be customer focused (see B2B Services in Action). The firm's culture reflects the shared values and beliefs that drive the organization—the formally written, the unwritten, and actual occurrences that help employees understand the norms for behavior in the organization. In short, organizational culture establishes the "dos and don'ts" of employee behavior and provides the basis on which various employee behaviors can coalesce.[13]

Figure 16.8 presents a simple framework for considering the options available when implementing cultural change in the service organization.[14] The figure suggests that culture is internally linked to and partly an outcome of three organizational components: structure, systems, and people. **Structure** relates to the formal reporting channels normally represented in an organizational chart (such as front-line employees reporting to middle managers, who report to regional managers, who report to national managers, who report to the chief executive officer).

**structure**
The formal reporting hierarchy normally represented in an organizational chart.

**systems**
People-management systems of control, evaluation, promotion, and recognition.

The **systems** component of the framework refers to the people-management systems utilized for control, evaluation, promotion, and recognition. Evaluation and promotion systems include both formal and informal components. For example, management by objectives would be a formal component, while "What do I really have to do around here to get noticed?" would be an informal part of the system. Recognition systems focus on formal and informal rewards as well, ranging from formal rewards such as company trips to informal "pats on the back" such as lunch with the boss.

The other two major components of the culture framework are the people who work in the organization and the firm's current culture. Creating a more customer-focused organization can be accomplished by altering any one of the four components: structure, systems, people, and culture, individually or together.

### CHANGING CULTURE THROUGH STRUCTURE

The organization's culture is a function of its structure. Changing culture through structure, however, is a slow process because in many instances, it takes years to successfully implement an organizational change in structure. In the effort to create a more customer-focused organization, two approaches to changing the culture through structure have been tried: (1) utilizing the marketing department as a change agent; and (2) restructuring the firm around the servuction system model.

## B2B SERVICES *IN ACTION*

### > | STATE FARM INSURANCE: BUILDING A MARKETING CULTURE

In its 99th year of existence, State Farm Insurance, the largest insurer of homes and automobiles in the U.S., was attempting to make a radical transformation within its corporate culture. For almost 100 years the company had been operating on a sales culture where it attempted to sell insurance products that the company had already developed. As the company approached its 100th year of operation, State Farm's management team recognized the importance of strategic and marketing planning in achieving its future growth objectives. By switching from a sales-oriented to a marketing-oriented culture, the firm was essentially transforming its business philosophy from "selling what we make" to "making what we can sell."

The transformation to a marketing culture was accomplished on a number of fronts including changing the structure of the company, hiring a champion, implementing new systems, and changing the culture directly by offering training programs that educated employees about the nature of the new business philosophy. Changing the structure of the company was completed by creating a marketing department within State Farm. As amazing as it may seem, the company had not had a formal marketing department throughout its previous 99-year history. By creating a marketing department, the corporate level of State Farm was signaling to its employees and agents that marketing had taken on a new sense of importance within the State Farm family. In addition to creating a marketing department, State Farm created a new and highly visible management position to lead the department—Vice President of Marketing. Once again this move signaled the importance of marketing's new role and the Vice President of Marketing was charged with the responsibility of leading the new transformation.

State Farm also facilitated the culture transformation by putting reward systems in place that would facilitate the adoption of the new marketing culture. State Farm wanted its agents to develop marketing plans for each agency. However, State Farm's current contract with its agent did not specifically require this activity. Consequently, State Farm created its "Select Agent" program, which designated those agents that participated in marketing planning. One of the major perks of being designated a Select Agent was the inclusion of the agent's name at the end of State Farm's television advertising. Hence, even though numerous agents may be in a given area, only Select Agents would be listed at the conclusion of any State Farm regional television advertisements. Finally, corporate-wide marketing training programs were instituted so that all employees truly understood the difference between a sales orientation and a marketing orientation. By implementing all four culture change initiatives simultaneously, State Farm substantially increased the rate of transformation and dramatically increased its odds of success.

---

Source: http://www.statefarm.com, accessed 11 June 2005; and personal experience.

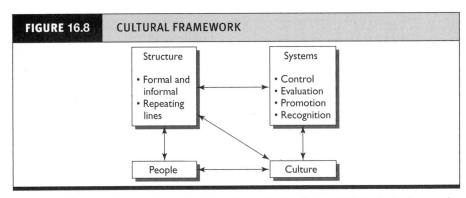

FIGURE 16.8    CULTURAL FRAMEWORK

Source: John E. G. Bateson, *Managing Services Marketing: Text and Readings* (Fort Worth, TX: The Dryden Press, 1995).

### Marketing Department as Change Agents

Marketing departments can be created in order to simply change the current orientation of the firm by creating a customer advocate within the organization. There is a real danger in this approach, however. Once the marketing department has been created, other departments may quickly transfer the complete responsibility for customer satisfaction to the marketing department.[15] Moreover, this transfer is likely to create open warfare among departments in the organization.[16]

Consider again the logic of the operations and the marketing departments. Operations departments, by their very nature, tend to be cost driven. Their focus is on evaluating the operation to find costs to save and procedures to simplify. This outlook tends to have a short time horizon. Marketing, by comparison, is looking for product enhancements in order to create a competitive advantage. The creation of such an advantage is not something that firms can expect to achieve in the short run.

The coordination of conflicting departments such as marketing and operations often requires the use of unconventional management techniques. To mesh the logic of the different groups and to allow them to understand one another, a number of strategies have been suggested by organizational-behavior theory. **Interfunctional task forces** are a classic way of forcing individuals with diverse viewpoints to work together and to develop a better understanding of one another's perspectives. In the same way, **interfunctional transfers** can create informal networks of individuals from different departments who understand and trust one another.

For example, operations managers who are promoted to run a marketing department will face initial problems. Their orientation is toward operations, but their new roles require a marketing perspective. If such a transfer can be achieved successfully, the result is usually a general manager who makes rational and clear trade-offs between operations and marketing. Moreover, it also creates a marketing person who has direct contacts in the operations group and who can overcome many of the traditional barriers to change.

Once the organization has achieved a strong customer orientation, the marketing department can shrink. For example, in the early 1980s, many professional service firms created marketing departments in this way. The departments focused on advertising but also on research and customer-satisfaction surveys. The result was a shift in the culture of the firm and the recognition of the importance of the customer's needs and expectations.

*interfunctional task force*
Problem-solving group in which individuals with diverse viewpoints work together and develop a better understanding of one another's perspectives.

*interfunctional transfers*
Moving, via promotion or transfer, an employee from one organizational department to another to foster informal networks among departments.

### Restructuring around the Servuction Model

A number of service firms have explicitly or implicitly restructured around the servuction model. For example, one major airline has all departments that have direct customer contact report to the head of marketing. Only engineering and the flight crew (pilots) report to the head of operations. Combining all customer-contact departments with the marketing group has reversed the arguments from, "It will cost too much; it is inefficient," to, "The customer needs this; how can we make it happen?"

## CHANGING CULTURE THROUGH SYSTEMS

The firm's culture is also a function of the systems put into place that control, evaluate, promote, and recognize the firm's personnel. A number of approaches have been used to change culture through these systems. Some firms, for example, have started to give bonuses to managers at all levels based upon the firm's customer satisfaction scores. The firm's overall research effort can be tailored to measure satisfaction down to the branch level, and managers can be rewarded for improved scores. Unfortunately, the problem with this approach is that only part of the customer's satisfaction is under the control of management. The customer's expectations can be raised by competitive offerings, and satisfaction scores can drop as a consequence.

Another approach has been to introduce revenue into branch manager targets. A major New York bank wanted to change the retail branch manager orientation from one of considering only costs and security to one of considering customers first. The bank introduced a revenue-based performance evaluation system. For the first time, managers had to worry about where the customers came from and had to stop thinking of them as "people who made a mess of my branch." Early successes by a few managers produced interesting results. Up to 20 percent of managers left the company, claiming that this was not what they were hired to do. The balance of the managers woke up the bank's sleeping central marketing department to demand help in getting more customers. The long-term result of the change in the system was an increase in customers as well as in bad debt. The managers had discovered that money is an easy product to sell, and the bank had discovered it needed to revamp its credit control function.

Planning systems can also be used to change the orientation of companies. Formal marketing planning can drive organizations through the logic of marketing and can force them to develop an understanding of consumers' needs. Such planning exercises can eventually become "mind-numbing," but for the first two or three cycles, the process can be educational for all personnel involved. This approach is all the more powerful if combined with training and/or direct attacks on culture.

## CHANGING CULTURE THROUGH PEOPLE

Outsiders increasingly are being brought into the marketing departments of service firms to try to change the orientation. Such an approach must be supplemented with the development of training programs inside the firm. Operations people need to be trained in marketing, and marketing people need to understand all the areas discussed in this book.

## CHANGING CULTURE DIRECTLY

Culture-change programs are becoming increasingly popular. These programs range from broad-scale educational activities to highly empowering personnel in order to re-engineer the firm's entire service delivery process around the customer. Figure 16.9 provides a simple way to categorize such activities. Along one axis is the nature of the groups used. Mixed groups are cross-sectional or interdepartmental; family groups can be a department or a naturally occurring group based on process, such as all the individuals involved in loading a particular flight with passengers. The second axis deals with the level of empowerment given to employees. Low levels of empowerment imply that individuals will change their behavior but that the group will have no authority to change the processes and systems of the organization. High-level empowerment implies an ability to change the organization during the event or series of events. The slogans in the cells represent the hypothetical titles of such change programs, which often involve one or more meetings.

**putting the customer first**
The element of the culture change initiative that teaches personnel to put the customer first.

The top left cell refers to **putting the customer first** programs that take place in mixed groups within the organization. Seated together in sessions, personnel are lectured to and motivated to put the customer first. Through role playing, they are encouraged to recognize the importance of customers and change their behavior accordingly.

These types of programs can be very successful. To be successful, however, the new behavior needs to be reinforced on the job. If management and front-line personnel do not share the same level of enthusiasm and dedication toward the goal of creating a customer-oriented organization, the value of the lessons learned can be wiped out within hours. Without commitment to change, the new behaviors learned will be trivialized by colleagues, the old behaviors will be reinstated quickly, and the value of the program will be a total loss.

**orientation change**
The element of the culture change initiative that teaches "families" of personnel to reinforce one another on the job.

The top right cell, **orientation change**, overcomes these problems by processing personnel by family groups whose members can reinforce one another on the job. Both cells, however, focus on changing attitudes and individual behaviors. Changing organizational processes and systems are not part of these programs. This potentially produces role conflict as desired individual behaviors are inhibited by organizational constraints, such as the physical environment or the current operating system.

| FIGURE 16.9 | CATEGORIZING CULTURE CHANGE INITIATIVES | |
|---|---|---|

| Empowerment | Group | |
| | Mixed | Family |
|---|---|---|
| Low | "Putting the Customer First" | "Orientation Change" |
| High | "Change the Way You Work" | "Change the Way We Work" |

Source: John E. G. Bateson, *Managing Services Marketing: Text and Readings*, 3rd ed. (Fort Worth, TX: The Dryden Press, 1995).

**Change the way you work**, in the lower-left cell, draws on the empowerment ideas described in detail in Chapter 10. It implies active empowerment of the personnel attending the program. Personnel are allowed to break the rules in the context of serving their customers. Because of the mixed group, however, this type of initiative is focused on the individual rather than on process-level empowerment.

The lower-right cell, **change the way we work**, refers to initiatives that draw on many of the ideas in this book. Groups are in families and can be asked to flowchart their activities. They can then be asked to re-engineer the process to better serve their customers. The level of excitement in such groups is matched only by the anxiety of their bosses. Empowerment at this level really does place the boss in the role of coach and facilitator, and that is exactly what the boss's role should be. In creating a seamless organization, it is not management's job to force or dictate to employees to deliver service excellence. "Management's job is to put together a system that actually makes it possible to deliver quality service."[17]

*change the way you work*
The element of the culture change initiative that allows personnel to break the rules in the context of serving their customers.

*change the way we work*
The element of the culture change initiative that teaches personnel to flowchart their activities and to re-engineer the process to better serve their customers.

## THE TACTICAL QUESTIONS RELATING TO SEAMLESSNESS: CONDUCTING A SERVICE AUDIT[18]

One helpful approach in creating a seamless organization involves conducting a service audit that addresses a number of questions. The **service audit** directs the firm to think about the forces that drive its current profits and suggests strategies that have been discussed throughout this book that lead to competitive differentiation and long-term profitability. Moreover, the active involvement of front-line and top management personnel in conducting the audit facilitates the change in culture necessary to make the transition from the traditional industrial management approach to an employee- and customer-focused, service-oriented approach.

*service audit*
A series of questions that forces the firm to think about what drives its profits and suggests strategies for competitive differentiation and long-term profitability.

### THE SERVICE AUDIT: THE PROFIT AND GROWTH COMPONENT

- *How does the firm define customer loyalty?* Traditional measures of customer loyalty involve repeat sales, purchase frequency, and increases in amounts purchased. The firm also needs to consider the depth of the relationship. For example, the depth of a customer's banking relationship would be defined by types of transactions and accounts such as savings, checking, certificates of deposit, car loans, home mortgages, savings bond programs, safety deposit box rentals, and so on.
- *Does the firm measure profits from referrals?* Customer loyalty and satisfaction should also be measured in terms of the customers' willingness to refer the firm to friends, family, and colleagues. Given the importance consumers place upon personal sources of information when selecting from among competing services, encouraging referrals or at least creating an atmosphere where customers freely inform others of the firm's services is crucial.
- *What proportion of the firm's development funds are spent on retaining customers as opposed to attracting new ones?* As discussed in Chapter 15, the benefits of customer retention are clear. Current customers generate referrals, are less expensive to

A service audit provides information that helps a firm improve its service orientation. A service audit for a golf course, for example, may address questions about customer loyalty by learning how frequently customers golf and the number of times they dine at the restaurant and make purchases at the pro shop.

© ARTHUR TILLEY/TAXI/GETTY IMAGES

market to, purchase more services more frequently, are knowledgeable about the firm's operating system and, therefore, are more efficient users of the system, and are a great source of information about how the firm can better serve its targeted markets. Unfortunately, under traditional models of management, firms spend the majority of their resources on obtaining new customers while neglecting their existing customers.

- **When customers do not return, do we know why?** Service firms that excel pursue the bad news as well as the good. Traditionally, customer satisfaction assessments are obtained from current customers, who tend to rate the firm toward the more positive end of the scale. Uncovering the reasons customers defect reveals potentially fatal flaws in the firm's service delivery system that other customers have yet to discover and of which the firm may have been unaware. Consequently, contacting customers who have defected provides the firm with the opportunity to make improvements. Moreover, contacting customers who defect makes a positive impression that the firm cares about its customers and may actually lead to recapturing some lost customers.

## THE SERVICE AUDIT: THE CUSTOMER SATISFACTION COMPONENT

- **Is customer satisfaction data collected in a systematic manner?** In Chapters 12 and 13, we discussed a number of methods for assessing customer satisfaction and service quality. The key to successful measurement is consistency so that current assessments can be compared with past benchmarks. Satisfaction measurement should also occur on a regular basis and not only when problems arise. Catching minor problems early through periodic customer satisfaction surveys enables the firm to adjust the service delivery system before major gaps in service occur.

- *What methods are utilized to obtain customer feedback?* The service quality information system discussed in Chapter 13 reveals a number of important methods of obtaining customer feedback on a variety of issues. The active solicitation of customer complaints, after-sale surveys, customer focus-group interviews, mystery shopping, and total market service quality surveys should be used in conjunction with employee surveys. Too often, employees are left out of traditional customer feedback loops even though they are exposed to vast amounts of information about customers' daily interactions with the firm.
- *How is customer satisfaction data used?* Is the information used at all, or is it stuffed in the bottom drawer of a manager's desk? Customer satisfaction data needs to be shared with employees who provide the service. Front-line employees should feel they are an active part of the firm's overall goals and take pride in improvements in customer satisfaction scores. The data should reveal company strengths that can be used for promotional purposes and weaknesses that can be corrected through training programs or by redesigning the service system itself.

## THE SERVICE AUDIT: THE EXTERNAL SERVICE VALUE COMPONENT

- *How does the firm measure value?* One key to providing superior customer service is to define service value from the customer's perspective. Traditional approaches define value internally and frequently miss what is really important to customers. Remember, buyers' perceptions of value represent a trade-off between the perceived benefits of the service to be purchased and the perceived sacrifice in terms of the total costs to be paid.
- *How is information on customer perceptions of the firm's value shared within the company?* Keeping customer information in the hands of top management does little to improve the service effort on the front line. By sharing information about customer perceptions with the front line, the employees become sensitized to the behaviors and outcomes that are really important to customers. Improvements made in these specific areas should increase customer satisfaction scores. Similarly, sharing the information with operations, marketing, and human resources personnel should assist each area in understanding the customer's perception of the entire service delivery process.
- *Does the firm actively measure the gap between customer expectations and perceptions of services delivered?* Once customer perceptions are obtained, a comparison with customer expectations is vital in assessing customer satisfaction. Customer perceptions alone do not tell the full story. This point was made particularly clear in Chapter 13 regarding the SERVQUAL scale. Perception scores alone merely reflect whether customers agree with the statement, not whether what they are evaluating is really important to them. Including expectation measures increases the managerial usefulness of the information. Given that making improvements often involves a financial investment, comparing expectations to perceptions assists the firm in allocating resources to the most appropriate areas.
- *Is service recovery an active strategy discussed among management and employees?* Although many firms will spend vast amounts of time and effort to deliver the service right the first time, little discussion centers on appropriate courses of action for

employees to take when things do not go according to plan. Consequently, employees are left to fend for themselves while dealing with unhappy customers, and it is apparent that employees often do a poor job in service recovery efforts. Chapter 14 stresses the benefits of both service failure and service recovery analysis. Actively tracking failures and recoveries identifies failure points in the system and allows the firm to minimize their occurrence by training employees in service recovery techniques.

## THE SERVICE AUDIT: THE EMPLOYEE PRODUCTIVITY COMPONENT

- *How does the firm measure employee productivity?* If the firm does not measure what it really believes is important, employees will never pay attention to it. In addition, if productivity is measured simply in terms of output and outcomes and not by the behaviors used to achieve these outcomes, the firm may actually be rewarding employees for anticustomer-oriented activities. For example, the employee may be very curt with one customer so that a quick sale can be transacted with another customer who already knows what he or she wants. Service productivity measures such as timeliness, accuracy, and responsiveness need to be developed to reinforce these types of customer-oriented behaviors.

## THE SERVICE AUDIT: THE EMPLOYEE LOYALTY COMPONENT

- *Does the firm actively pursue strategies to promote employee loyalty?* Employee loyalty to the organization is often visible to customers and directly influences customer evaluations of the firm. When employees feel more positive about the firm, customers feel more positive about the services the firm delivers. Preaching that employees are the firm's most important asset and then laying off employees in large numbers during periods of downsizing sends a hypocritical message to both employees and customers.
- *Does the firm set employee retention goals?* Although rarely is 100 percent the correct level, employee retention saves the firm funds in terms of recruiting and training costs. Additionally, customers prefer the continuity of interacting with the same personnel over time so much that the firm's personnel may be its key differential advantage over competitors. When service personnel do leave, their regular customers often seek them out at their new places of employment.

## THE SERVICE AUDIT: THE EMPLOYEE SATISFACTION COMPONENT

- *Are employee satisfaction measures linked to customer satisfaction measures?* Employee satisfaction is linked to increases in productivity and external service value. External service value is linked to customer satisfaction and the additional benefit of customer loyalty. The net effects of customer loyalty are increased revenues and profitability for the firm. The outcomes associated with employee satisfaction—external service values, customer satisfaction, customer loyalty, revenue growth, and increased profitability—provide feedback and reinforce the company's internal service quality and employee satisfaction.

- *Are customer and organizational needs considered when hiring?* Southwest Airlines invites panels of customers to help select flight attendants. Customers are so sold on the idea that some take off time from their own work schedules to be on the selection team. Hiring people with good job skills is important in manufacturing. Hiring people with good job skills and good interpersonal skills is vital in services.

- *Are employee reward programs tied to customer satisfaction, customer loyalty, and quality of employee performance?* Service firms wishing to enhance the customer focus of their employees must implement behavior-based reward systems that monitor employee activities and evaluate employees on aspects of their job over which they have control. Traditional, outcome-based reward systems often discourage the development of long-term relationships with the firm's customers in pursuit of short-term profitability.

## THE SERVICE AUDIT: THE INTERNAL SERVICE QUALITY COMPONENT

- *Are employees aware of internal and external customers?* The ideal service firm should work seamlessly as a team. Each member of the team should understand fully how individual performance affects the performance of other team members as they provide superior service to external customers. Consequently, employees need to understand that the firm's external customers are not the only ones who are depending on their efforts.

- *Do employees have the support necessary to do their jobs?* Does the firm just talk about providing superior service, or does it talk about it and back up it with the support necessary to get the job done right? Over the past few years, Taco Bell, a fast food franchise, has emerged as a firm with some fairly progressive service strategies. Personnel are supported by the latest advances in information technology, self-managing team training, effective food service equipment, and work scheduling that enhances employee performance.

## THE SERVICE AUDIT: THE FIRM'S LEADERSHIP COMPONENT

- *Does the firm's leadership help or hinder the service delivery process?* Service personnel frequently find that even though they want to provide good service, their hands are tied by overbearing, conservative, upper-management types. Frequently, upper management is far removed from the front line of the operation and has lost touch with the realities associated with daily service interactions. The leaders of successful firms act as enablers, coaches, and facilitators, and they are participatory managers who listen to employees and encourage creative approaches to solving old problems.

- *Is the firm's leadership creating a corporate culture that helps employees as they interact with customers?* Top management sets the tone and provides the resources that support personnel who interact with customers. The links in the service-profit chain discussed in Chapter 10 reveal that employee satisfaction and customer satisfaction are directly related. Top management's job, therefore, is to create an organization culture in which employees thrive.

## THE SERVICE AUDIT: THE MEASUREMENT RELATIONSHIP COMPONENT

- *How do the preceding measures of service performance in the service audit relate to the firm's overall profitability?* The preceding components of the audit provide strategic measures that aid the provision of superior service. Ideally, the contribution of each measure should be related to the firm's bottom line. Relating these measures to the firm's overall profitability provides a resounding message throughout the company that service and quality pay!

## ✳ SUMMARY

In pursuit of service excellence, the individual departments and functions of the firm must act in unison to create a seamless organization. The firm will not act as one if the current focus of the organization is on departmental and functional needs. The three-tiered model of service firms offers an alternative view of how the organization should focus its efforts by segmenting the operation into a customer tier, a boundary tier, and a coordination tier. The goal is to have those in the coordination tier work in harmony with personnel in the boundary tier so that customers experience seamless service.

Creating and supporting a customer-focused organizational culture is critical when developing a seamless operation. The firm's culture drives employee behavior and directly influences the quality of the firm's service delivery system and subsequent consumer evaluations of the firm's service effort. Firms can change the existing culture of the organization by changing the firm's structure, people-management systems, and/or key personnel, or they can change the culture directly through broad-based educational activities or re-engineering the firm's entire service delivery process.

Finally, by conducting a service audit, a seamless service culture is fostered as organizational personnel throughout the organization come to appreciate the challenges faced and the contributions made by everyone involved in the firm's final service delivery effort. The service audit deals directly with such issues as profit and growth, customer satisfaction, external service value, employee productivity, employee loyalty, employee satisfaction, internal service quality, leadership, and measures that assess the impact of each of these issues on the firm's bottom line.

The service audit also provides a framework for combining the materials that are discussed throughout this book. In closing, we hope that this book has helped develop your understanding of the special challenges involved in the marketing and management of service operations. With challenge comes opportunity, and as you well know, there are plenty of opportunities in the business community to make the service encounter a more productive and pleasant experience for everyone involved—customers and employees alike. The time has come to make a difference and we look forward to writing about the difference you made in future editions of this book.

## ✳ KEY TERMS

seamless service, 420
marketing orientation, 421
marketing function, 422
marketing department, 422
customization/customer
   contact matrix, 422
three-tiered model, 425
customer tier, 425
expectations, 425
needs, 426
competencies, 426
boundary tier, 427
coordination tier, 427
internal logic, 427

operations logic, 427
marketing logic, 429
human resources logic, 431
culture, 432
structure, 432
systems, 432
interfunctional task force, 434
interfunctional transfers, 434
putting the customer first, 436
orientation change, 436
change the way you work, 437
change the way we work, 437
service audit, 437

## ✳ DISCUSSION QUESTIONS

1. Discuss seamlessness as it relates to "tooth-to-tail" performance.
2. Discuss the fight for control among marketing, operations, and human resources personnel.
3. Define the following terms: marketing orientation, marketing functions, and marketing department. Why is it necessary to distinguish among these terms when discussing service firms? Relate your answer to the customization/customer contact matrix.
4. Discuss each tier of the three-tiered model of service firms separately and then as a combined unit.
5. What is the importance of organizational culture?
6. Explain the relevance of interfunctional task forces and interfunctional transfers as they relate to corporate culture.
7. Discuss the four approaches to directly changing culture as presented in the text.
8. What are the key components of a service audit?

## ✳ NOTES

1. Benjamin Schneider and David E. Bowen, *Winning the Service Game* (Boston: Harvard Business School Press, 1995), pp. 1–16.
2. This section adapted from John E. G. Bateson, *Managing Services Marketing*, 3rd ed. (Fort Worth, TX: The Dryden Press, 1995), pp. 636–645.
3. Schneider and Bowen, *Winning the Service Game*, p. 199.
4. Bateson, *Managing Services Marketing*, pp. 636–645.
5. Ibid.
6. C. Gronroos, "Designing a Long-Range Marketing Strategy for Services," *Long Range Planning* 13 (April 1980), p. 36.
7. R. B. Chase, "Where Do Customers Fit in a Service Operation?" *Harvard Business Review* 56, 6 (November-December 1978), pp. 137–142.

8. W. Skinner, "The Focused Factory," *Harvard Business Review* 52, 3 (May–June 1974), pp. 113–121.

9. Schneider and Bowen, *Winning the Service Game*, pp. 1–16.

10. Ibid.

11. Ibid, p. 43.

12. Jane Kingman-Brundage, William R. George, and David E. Bowen, "Service Logic-Achieving Essential Service System Integration," *International Journal of Service Industry Management*, 6, 4 (1995), pp. 2–40. (forthcoming)

13. Cynthia Webster, "What Kind of Marketing Culture Exists in Your Service Firm? An Audit," *The Journal of Services Marketing* 6, 2 (Spring 1992), pp. 54–67.

14. Bateson, *Managing Services Marketing*, pp. 636–645.

15. Gronroos, "Designing a Long-Range Marketing Strategy," p. 36.

16. C. H. Lovelock, E. Langeard, J. E. G. Bateson, and P. Eiglier, "Some Organizational Problems Facing Marketing in the Service Sector," in J. Donnelly and W. George, eds., *Marketing of Services* (Chicago: American Marketing Association, 1981), pp. 148–153.

17. Schneider and Bowen, *Winning the Service Game*, p. 8.

18. This section was adapted from James L. Heskett, Thomas O. Jones, Gary W. Loveman, W. Earl Sasser, Jr., and Leonard A. Schlesinger, "Putting the Service-Profit Chain to Work," *Harvard Business Review*, (March–April 1994), pp. 165–174.

# PART | 4

# CASES

## CASES FOR PART ONE

## CASES FOR PART TWO

## CASES FOR PART THREE

# EMMY'S AND MADDY'S FIRST SERVICE ENCOUNTER

August 16, 1995. Our day began at 5:20 A.M. Hurricane Felix was predicted to hit the Carolina coast by the end of the afternoon, and I, like most of the other folks in southeastern North Carolina had spent much of the previous day preparing the house for the upcoming storm. However, my wife and I had one extra concern that the others did not. My wife was six months pregnant with twins, and the prospect of spending lots of time in the car in the attempt to remove ourselves from harm's way was not particularly attractive. We had decided to wait until after my wife's doctor appointment at 9:00 A.M. to make a decision on whether we should leave or stay at home and ride out the storm. We never made it to the doctor appointment.

At 5:20 A.M., I was awakened by the fear in my wife's voice. Her water had broken, and the twins that were due on November 16 had apparently made up their collective minds that they were going to be born 13 weeks early. As first-time parents, we understood that our next move would be to go to the hospital; however, we were unsure as to the best mode of transportation given our particular situation. We had been informed by doctors that multiple-birth pregnancies were high-risk pregnancies and that every precaution should be taken. We quickly called the hospital and asked for advice. The hospital suggested that my wife take a shower, shave her legs, and pack some essentials and that it would be appropriate for us to drive ourselves to the hospital. Too stressed out to take any chances, we passed on the shower advice, quickly threw some things together, and drove to the hospital immediately.

## * THE EMERGENCY DEPARTMENT

Upon our arrival at the hospital, we drove to the emergency entrance, and I quickly exited the car to find a wheelchair. I was immediately confronted by a security guard who had been previously engaged in a casual conversation with another gentleman. I was

Source: Originally printed as: K. Douglas Hoffman, "Rude Awakening," *Journal of Health Care Marketing*, Summer 1996, 16 (2), 14–22.

informed that I could not leave my car in its current position. In response, I informed the security guard that I needed a wheelchair and would move the car after I was able to move my wife inside. The security guard pointed his finger in the direction of the wheelchairs. I grabbed the first wheelchair I could get my hands on and headed back out the sliding doors to assist my wife. At this point, the security guard informed me that I had grabbed a juvenile-sized wheelchair. I headed back inside and grabbed a much larger wheelchair. I returned to the car, assisted my wife into the wheelchair, and headed back inside. The security guard, while continuing with his other conversation, instructed me to leave my wife with the triage nurse in the emergency department so that I could move my vehicle. I said goodbye to my wife and went to move the vehicle. When I returned, the security guard informed me that they had taken my wife to the maternity ward, located on the third floor.

My wife's encounter with the triage nurse was apparently short and sweet. The triage nurse had called for an orderly to move my wife to the maternity ward. On her way to the third floor, the orderly asked my wife whether she was excited about having the baby. She responded that she was scared to death because she was only six months pregnant. The orderly replied that there was "no way [she was] having a baby that early that [would] survive."

## ✳ THE MATERNITY WARD

As I exited the elevator on the third floor, I headed for the nurses' station to inquire about my wife's current location. I was greeted by several smiling nurses who escorted me to my wife's room. On my way to the room, I met another nurse who had just exited my wife's room. This nurse pulled me aside and informed me of the orderly's remarks. She continued on to assure me that what he said was not only inappropriate, but more importantly, inaccurate. She also informed me that my wife was very upset and that we needed to work together to help keep her calm. This particular nurse also informed us that she herself had given birth to a premature child, who was approximately the same gestational age as ours, a couple of years earlier.

By this time, it was between 6:00 and 6:30 A.M. The resident on duty entered the room and introduced himself as Dr. Baker. My wife gave me this puzzled and bewildered look. The clinic where my wife is a patient consists of five physicians who rotate their various duty assignments. Dr. Baker is one of the five. However, Dr. Baker was 30 to 40 years older than the resident who had just introduced himself as Dr. Baker. What had happened was that the resident was nervous and had introduced himself as Dr. Baker rather than as Dr. Baker's assistant. Realizing his mistake, he embarrassingly reintroduced himself and informed us that Dr. Baker was the physician on call and that he was being contacted and kept informed of my wife's condition.

The resident left the room and soon reappeared with an ultrasound cart to check the positions of the babies. This time he was accompanied by a person I assumed to be the senior resident on duty. For the next 30 minutes or so, I watched the junior resident attempt to learn how to use the ultrasound equipment. He consistently reported his findings to us in sentences that began with, "I think. . . ." Several times during this period my wife voiced her concern over the babies' conditions, and the location of Dr. Baker. We were reassured by the residents that Dr. Baker was being kept informed and were told that being upset was not going to help the babies' conditions. After about 30 minutes, I informed both residents that despite their advice for us to stay calm, they were not exactly instilling a lot of confidence in either one of us. The senior resident took over the ultrasound exam at this time.

Dr. Baker arrived at the hospital somewhere between 7:00 and 7:30 A.M. He apologized for not being there earlier and mentioned that he was trying to help his wife prepare for the ensuing hurricane. Sometime during this same time period, it was shift-change time for the nurses and also for Dr. Baker. New nurses were now entering the room, and now Dr. Johnson was taking over for Dr. Baker. By approximately 8:00 A.M., Dr. Baker had pulled me aside and informed me that after conferring with Dr. Johnson, they had decided that if my wife's labor subsided, she would remain in the hospital for seven to ten days, flat on her back, before they would deliver the babies. It was explained that with each passing day, the babies would benefit from further development. The lungs were of particular concern.

Upon being admitted to the maternity floor, my wife had immediately been hooked up to an EKG to monitor contractions. Due to the small size of the babies, the contractions were not severe. However, as far as my wife and I could tell, the interval between contractions was definitely getting shorter. Being first-time parents, we were not overly alarmed by this since we figured we were in the hospital and surrounded by health-care providers.

Between 8:00 and 8:30 A.M., two other nurses entered the room with lots of forms for us to complete. Since we were having twins, we needed duplicates of every form. The forms covered the basics: names, addresses, phone numbers, social security numbers, and insurance information. All the same questions that the hospital had sent to us weeks earlier, which we had completed and returned. The nurses asked us the questions, we supplied the information, and they wrote the responses.

By 8:30 A.M., Dr. Baker was informing me that due to one of the baby's breach position, they would deliver the babies by caesarean section. Wondering whether the schedule had been moved up from a week to ten days, I asked when he thought this would be happening. He replied: "In the next hour or so." He then commented that labor had not subsided and that Dr. Johnson would be delivering the babies.

As my wife was being prepared for the operating room, I stood in the hallway outside her room. I noticed another physician limping down the hall with one foot in a cast and a crutch underneath one arm. He stopped outside my wife's room and began to examine her medical charts. He introduced himself as Dr. Arthur (he had broken his foot while attempting to change a tire). Dr. Arthur was the neonatologist, which meant nothing to me at the time. I eventually figured out that my wife had her set of doctors and that my unborn children had their own set of health-care providers. Dr. Arthur asked to speak to my wife and me together. This is when he told us that 90 percent of babies such as ours survive and that 90 percent of those survivors develop normally. He was a calm, pragmatic individual who encouraged us to ask questions. He continued to explain that the babies would spend their next few months in the hospital's Neonatal Intensive Care Unit (NICU) and that if all went well, we could expect to take them home within two weeks of their due date (November 16, 1995).

By 9:00 A.M., all hell had broken loose. My wife had dilated at a quicker pace than had been anticipated . . . the contractions had indeed been occurring at more frequent intervals. Some orderlies and nurses grabbed my wife's bed and quickly rolled her down the hall to the delivery room. I was thrown a pair of scrubs and told to put them on. I was further told that they would come back and get me if they were able. For 10 to 12 very long minutes, I sat on a stool in an empty hospital room by myself, watching The Weather Channel track Hurricane Felix. The volume on the television had been muted, and the only thing I could hear was a woman screaming from labor in the next room. Suddenly, a nurse popped her head in the door and said that a space had been prepared for me in the delivery room.

## ✳ THE DELIVERY ROOM

As I entered the delivery room, I was overwhelmed by the number of people involved in the process. Myself included, I counted 12 "very busy" people. I was seated next to my wife's head. She had requested to stay awake during the procedure. My wife asked me whether the man assisting Dr. Johnson was the junior resident. Sure enough, I looked up to see the junior resident wearing a surgical gown and mask with a scalpel in his hand. I lied and told her, "No."

Suddenly, we realized that we had not finalized our choices for names. Somehow, what we couldn't decide despite months of discussion, we decided in 30 seconds. Our first baby girl, Emma Lewis (Emmy), was born at 9:15 A.M. Emmy weighed 2 pounds and was 14.5 inches long. Our second baby girl, Madeline Stuart (Maddy), was born at 9:16 A.M. and weighed 2 pounds, 2 ounces, and also measured 14.5 inches long. Both babies were very active at birth, and their faint cries reassured my wife and I that they had at least made it this far.

Upon being delivered from their mother, the babies were immediately handed to Dr. Arthur and his staff, who had set up examination stations in the delivery room. Each baby had her own team of medical personnel, and I was encouraged by Dr. Arthur, who hopped on one foot across the delivery room, as I watched him examine the girls. The neonatal staff examining the girls "ooohed and aaahed," and almost in a competitive manner compared measurements about which baby had better vitals in various areas. Dr. Arthur then suggested that I follow the girls to the Neonatal Intensive Care Unit (NICU) to watch further examinations. He also made sure that my wife got a good look at both babies before they were wheeled out of the delivery room in their respective incubators. My wife and I said our goodbyes, and I was told I could see her again in the recovery room in about 20 to 30 minutes.

## ✳ THE RECOVERY ROOM

The recovery room and the delivery room are contained within the maternity ward on the third floor of the hospital. The NICU is located on the fourth floor, which is designated as the gynecological floor. The staff on the third floor is geared for moms and babies. The staff on the fourth floor, outside the NICU, is geared for women with gynecological problems.

After receiving the "so far, so good" signals from both my wife's and my babies' doctors, I was permitted to rejoin my wife in the recovery room. It was a basic hospital room with the exception that a nurse was assigned to the room on a full-time basis. One of the hospital volunteers from the maternity floor had taken pictures of each of the babies and taped them to the rails of my wife's hospital bed. The nurses of the third floor maternity ward asked my wife whether she would like a room on the fourth floor so that she could be closer to her babies when she was ready to start walking again. She agreed and spent the next four days in a room on the fourth floor.

Hurricane Felix stayed out to sea and moved up the coastline, missing us completely.

## ✳ THE FOURTH FLOOR

My wife's private room on the fourth floor was small, dingy, and dirty. From an emotional standpoint, the staff on the fourth floor were not prepared to deal with our situation. In fact, one nurse, after discussing the situation with my wife, asked whether we were going to have the babies transported to a major university medical center three hours away.

My wife's quality of care on the fourth floor was sporadic. Some of the nurses were good and some were inattentive . . . slow to respond to the patient's call button and blaming nurses on other shifts when medications and other scheduled or promised care (e.g., providing the patient with a breast pump) were not provided on a timely basis. Although it might seem trivial to many, the breast pump represented my wife's primary contribution to the care of her babies. It was the only thing she could control. Everything else was out of her hands. My wife was instructed to begin pumping as soon as she felt able, yet due to her location away from the maternity ward, obtaining a breast pump was difficult and became a sore point for my wife.

After receiving a courtesy call by the hospital's patient representative, my wife expressed her concerns. Shortly thereafter, personnel were changed, the quality of care improved, and we were moved to a much larger room on the third afternoon.

## ✳ THE NEONATAL INTENSIVE CARE UNIT

The NICU (pronounced "nick-u") is located in an isolated area of the fourth floor. The primary purpose of the NICU is to provide care for premature babies and for full-term babies requiring special care. The number of babies cared for each day throughout our stay typically averaged 12.

Emmy and Maddy spent approximately seven weeks in the NICU. The staff made every effort to explain the purpose of every piece of machinery and every tube that seemed to cover the babies' bodies. I was repeatedly told that I could and should ask questions at any time and that the staff understood that it was an overwhelming amount of information. Hence, it was understandable and acceptable to ask the same questions day after day. The staff had made signs welcoming each of the babies in bright neon colors and taped them above each of their stations. For ease of access, the girls had not yet been placed in incubators. They laid in what looked like large in/out baskets with raised borders. We celebrated weeks later when they finally had enough tubes removed so that they could be moved into incubators . . . what we called "big-girl beds."

During the first three days, I walked into the NICU to find baby quilts at each of the girls' stations. A local group called Quilters by the Sea had sewn the quilts; apparently they regularly provide the quilts for infants admitted to the NICU. For some reason that I still cannot explain today, the fact that someone outside the hospital who I did not know cared about my girls touched me deeply. The signs the staff had made and the babies' patchwork quilts humanized all the machines and tubes. Somehow, I was no longer looking at two premature infants . . . I was looking at Emmy and Maddy.

Throughout the girls' stay in the NICU, the quality of care delivered was primarily exceptional. The staff not only excelled at the technical aspects of their jobs but also were very good in dealing with parents. Some of the personal touches included numerous pictures of each of the girls for us to take home, homemade birthday cards with pictures from the girls for Mom and Dad on their birthdays, baby stickers on their incubators, and notes of encouragement from staff when a milestone, such as when weighing 3 pounds, was achieved. We arrived one day and found pink bows in the girls' hair. The nurses even signed Emmy's and Maddy's names on the foot cast worn by the baby boy in the next incubator.

Parental involvement in the care of all the infants was encouraged, almost demanded. I had somehow managed to never change a diaper in my life (I was 35 years old). I was threatened, I think jokingly, that the girls would not be allowed to leave the NICU until I demonstrated some form of competency with diaper changes, feedings, and baths. The primarily female staff made me feel at times that my manhood was at stake if I was not able to perform these duties. Personally, I think they all wished they'd had the same chance to train their husbands when they'd had their own babies. I am now an expert in the aforementioned activities.

As for the babies' progress, some days were better than others. We celebrated weight gains and endured a collapsed lung, blood transfusions, respirators, alarms caused by bouts with apnea and bradycardia, and minor operations. Throughout the seven weeks, many of the staff and three neonatologists became our friends. We knew where one another lived, we knew about husbands, wives, boyfriends, and kids. We also heard a lot about the staff's other primary concern . . . scheduling.

## ✳ THE GROWER ROOM

Sometime after the seventh week, we "graduated" from the NICU and were sent to the Grower Room. The Grower Room acts as a staging area and provides the transition between the NICU and sending the babies home with their parents. Babies who are transferred to the Grower Room no longer require the intensive care provided by the NICU but still require full-time observation. As the name indicates, the Grower Room is for feeding and diaper changing, administering medications, and recording vital statistics . . . basic activities essential for the growth and development of infants. The Grower Room held a maximum of four infants at any one time.

The Grower Room was located in a converted patient room located in the back corner of the second floor, which is designated as the pediatric floor of the hospital. In general, the Grower Room was staffed by one pediatric nurse and visited by the neonatologists during rounds. As parents who were involved in the care of their babies, being transferred to the Grower Room meant that we had to establish new relationships with another set of health-care providers all over again.

Compared with the "nurturing" culture we had experienced in the NICU, the Grower Room was a big letdown. One of the first nurses we were exposed to informed us that the nurses on the second floor referred to the Grower Room as "The Hole," and that sooner or later they all had to take their turn in "The Hole." We asked the reasons for such a name, and the nurse explained that because the room was stuck back in the corner, the rest of the staff seldom allowed the "grower nurse" to take a break, and because of the constant duties involved, the grower nurse could never leave the room unattended. It was also explained that some of the nurses simply did not feel comfortable caring "for such small little babies." We quickly found that this attitude had manifested itself in a lack of supplies specifically needed for smaller babies, such as premature-sized diapers and sheepskin rugs inside the incubators.

Furthermore, it became quickly apparent that friction existed between the NICU and the Grower Room. The Grower Room was very hesitant to request supplies from the NICU and on several occasions would delay informing NICU that an occupancy existed in the Grower Room. The reason for delay was so that the Grower Room nurse could catch up on other duties and avoid having to undertake the additional duties involved in admitting new patients. The "successful delay" would pass on these activities to the nurse taking the next shift. Apparently, the friction was mutual, since one of the nurses in the NICU commented to us on the way out of the NICU, "Don't let them push you around down there. If you don't think they're doing what they should, you tell them what you want them to do."

When the Grower Room was in need of supplies for our babies and others, I (on more than one occasion) volunteered to ask for supplies from the NICU. Although my foraging attempts were successful, I definitely got the feeling that there was some reluctance on both sides for me to do this. I suspected that the Grower Room nurses did not want to ask for any favors, and the NICU staff felt that it was not their job to keep the Grower Room stocked with supplies. Moreover, I suspect that the NICU and the Grower Room operate from different budgets. Stocking the Grower Room is not one of the objectives of the NICU's budget. However, from my side, my babies needed supplies, and I did not care about either department's budget.

After a few dark days, we established new relationships with the Grower Room personnel and became very involved with the care of our babies. After spending seven weeks in the NICU, we felt more familiar with each baby's personal needs than some of the Grower Room staff were. Recognizing our level of involvement, most of the staff looked forward to our visits since it meant less work for them. By now, we had learned to ask lots of questions, to doublecheck that medications had been provided, and to develop a working relationship with Grower Room personnel. Looking back, it was almost as we and the Grower Room staff trained each other. At the conclusion of our Grower Room experience, my wife and I felt that we had met some good people, but also that the quality of the experience was far lower than what we had grown accustomed to in the NICU.

# * NESTING

Once the babies had "graduated" from the Grower Room, our last night in the hospital was spent "nesting." Friends of ours joked that this must have involved searching for twigs, grass, and mud. The nesting rooms were located on the second floor of the hospital, in the same general location as the Grower Room. Nesting allows the parents and the babies to spend a night or two together in the hospital before they go home. During the nesting period, parents are solely responsible for all medications, feedings, and general care of the infants. The nesting period allows the parents to ask any last-minute questions and to smooth the transition from, in our case, nine weeks of hospital care to multiple infant care at home.

The nesting room itself was a small patient room that consisted of one single bed and a fold-out lounge chair. By now, the babies had been moved from their incubators to open, plastic bassinets that were wheeled into the room with us. Each baby remained attached to a monitor that measured heart and breathing rates. To say the least, space was limited, but for the first time in nine weeks, the four of us were alone as a family.

Throughout the 22 hours we nested, we were frequently visited by neonatologists, nurses who continued to take the babies' vital signs, the babies' eye doctor, social workers who were assigned to all premature baby cases, hospital insurance personnel, and a wonderful discharge nurse who was in charge of putting everything together so that we could get out the door. Nine weeks to the day after we had entered the hospital, we took our two 4-pound babies home.

# * CASE QUESTIONS

1. Develop a molecular model for this hospital.
2. Using the Servuction model as a point of reference, categorize the factors that influenced this service encounter.
3. How do the concepts of inseparability, intangibility, and heterogeneity apply to this case?
4. Discuss corrective actions that need to be taken to ensure that subsequent encounters run more smoothly.
5. How would you measure customer satisfaction in this situation?

# * EPILOGUE

As of August 1996, Emmy and Maddy both weighed approximately 18 pounds and appeared to be in good overall health. One of the NICU nurses we met at the hospital helps us out in our home on a regular basis, and we have kept in touch with many of the NICU staff as well as with Dr. Arthur. The charges for our hospital stay were more than $250,000. This bill did not include any of the physicians' (e.g., neonatologists, eye doctors, surgeons, or radiologists) charges. Emmy recently returned to the hospital for a cranial ultrasound, which is an outpatient service (the results were negative for brain bleeds, and Emmy is fine). Despite her previous lengthy stay in NICU, we once again had to provide the hospital with all the insurance information one more time. Ironically, the only information the out-patient service had about Emmy was that her "responsible party" was Maddy.

In terms of our overall experience, we are thankful for the lives of our babies and for the health of their mother. We are particularly grateful to the staff of the NICU and to Dr. Arthur. Emmy and Maddy celebrated their 10th birthday on August 23rd, 2005. They both requested gift certificates from Limited Too and Starbucks!

# CASE | 2

# MANAGING THE SERVICE EXPERIENCE: *"POLICE GAS MILE HIGH FANS"*

**HEADLINE: THE DENVER POST**

It's football season once again sports' fans, and it's yet another opportunity to demonstrate the difficulty of managing the service encounter. Like most service encounters, a football game is a shared experience as other fans can greatly impact the level of enjoyment an individual derives from the event. This particular game between Colorado State University (CSU) and the University of Colorado (CU) at Mile High Stadium (the home of two-time defending Super Bowl Champions—the Denver Broncos) was no different. . . . except for the fact that the game ended in a police action where fans were doused with pepper spray and tear gas. Hence, the headline: *"Police Gas Mile High Fans."*

    *ESPN's Sport's Center* reported the story approximately as follows: At the request of the Denver Broncos, police dressed in riot gear marched down the sidelines with four minutes left in the game to the Colorado State University student section to protect the field and the goal posts. (CSU was in the process of upsetting its long-time intrastate rival CU to the tune of 41–14 and there were not many CU fans remaining in the stands at this point. The police were informed that CSU students were planning on storming the field). In response to the armed police presence, CSU students began pelting the police with everything from ice filled soft drink cups to the occasional can of corn and chili. In response to the pelting and the attempt by a handful of students to take the field, the Denver police began pepper spraying the offending students and then eventually launching tear gas canisters into the stands to dissuade others from charging the field. In response to the gassing, most fans hurriedly headed for the exits while others threw the tear gas canisters that had landed in the stands back on the field aiming for the police. By the time the melee was over, fans young and old, the CSU pep band, players and coaches, the police and the media were all suffering from the effects of tear gas. The reputations of the CSU fans and the Denver police were both tarnished by the event.

## ✳ WHAT TO DO NEXT YEAR?

Now it's your turn! Currently, there is much talk about whether the CSU/CU game should even be played at Mile High Stadium. In fact, the Mayor of Denver, the Denver police and members of both schools' administrations are meeting this week to discuss the future venue for this game. For years, the game had been played at each school's home campus and this was only the second time the teams had met in Denver (the inaugural meeting was the year before). Below is listed a number of factors that might aid you in the decision of 1) Should the two teams continue to meet at Mile High Stadium; and 2) If so, how would you manage this encounter so everyone doesn't leave crying again?

- Beer was sold at the game and tailgating was permitted in the Parking lot starting at 12:00 P.M. The game began at 5:00 P.M.
- Playing the game at Mile High featured the game as a Colorado Event instead of as a campus event. The last two games have been sell-outs. Seating at Mile High is approximately 76,000 fans, while seating at CSU is approximately 36,000 fans.
- Since the game has been played at Mile High, the two respective colleges have been less involved in the management of the game itself. When games are played on campus, each school manages traffic flow, parking, crowd control, etc. . . .
- The University of Colorado's locker room was located beneath the CSU student section.
- The Denver police have repeatedly used pepper spray and tear gas on sports fans in other situations including post-game celebrations of the Avalanche and Broncos championship games.
- A chain-link fence stood between the field and the stands.
- College students on a number of campuses are becoming less intimidated by police.
- The Denver Broncos organization and the police denied earlier reports that the Broncos had requested police to protect the field and the goal posts.
- Prior to kick-off, CU was ranked 14th nationally. In contrast, CSU was picked to finish sixth in the newly formed Mountain West Conference.
- National television coverage dictates when the game is played and the additional revenues generated by coverage contribute greatly to the schools' athletic funds.
- Fans sitting in the alumni section at the game stated: "There was no way to escape, no warning (about the tear gas or mace), there was no way to help friends."[1]
- The CSU band director was inundated with pepper spray while attempting to help injured students. The spray permeated his uniform, blinded him and began to burn his skin. "I asked the event staff for help but no one was responding. I told the band to start running up the seats and get out as fast as they could."[2]
- The Denver police department continues to avidly defend its actions in response to drunken and overzealous fans. While many have criticized the action taken by police, many others credit the police for preventing a potential riot.

## ✳ CASE QUESTIONS

1. What would your recommendation be? Continue to play at Mile High or stay on campus?
2. If the game continues at Mile High, what suggestions would your provide?
3. Do you think that the fact that the fans who were originally targeted by police were college students as opposed to a "traditional adult population" factored into the actions taken by the police?
4. What unique steps does your school take to manage the sporting event experience?

## ✳ NOTES

1. Lyle, L'Shawn, "Students Express Anger," *The Rocky Mountain Collegian*, Vol. 108 (12), September 8, 1999, p. 1.
2. Olson, Eric, "CSU Band Members Speak Out Against Denver PD," *The Rocky Mountain Collegian*, Vol. 108 (12), September 8, 1999, p. 1.

# CASE | 3

# THE NEW YORK CITY ARBORETUM

It was a rainy morning in early November 1990, as Mary Saxon, Vice-President of External Affairs for the New York City Arboretum (NYCA), steered her car onto the Bronx River Parkway and made her way to work from her home in Pelham. "How appropriate," she thought, "that the weather is so gloomy. Could this be a preview of the rest of my life?" Yesterday, at the November board meeting, Mary had presented the decision to start charging for admission to the Arboretum. However, instead of building cooperation and buy-in for the plan, her presentation had fractionalized the employees and board members even more. Mary knew she needed buy-in from all employees to make the switch from free entrance to paying admission a success. She also knew that the Arboretum would need additional funding for initiatives to attract more visitors (and earned revenues) to the Arboretum, and the board's support was integral to raising these additional funds. If her programs failed, the Arboretum would not be able to generate enough revenue to continue operating. If this were to happen, drastic cuts in operating hours, educational programs, and personnel would be undertaken, dramatically changing the scope and mission of the Arboretum.

Had she done the right thing by announcing her decision in yesterday's meeting, or should she have approached the issue differently? She had to come up with a plan for building consensus and support for her program.

She was also concerned about the reaction of the Arboretum's external constituents. In particular, she was concerned about how the community boards in the surrounding neighborhoods would react. The local community had already protested strongly against other decisions the Arboretum had made. And certain Arboretum employees represented another challenge: there was a group, informally represented by the editor of *Arboretum Magazine* (a monthly science and botany magazine published by the NYCA), opposed to the "commercialization" of the Arboretum. Because this group had access to the New York area press, what might have been simply a pesky internal protest had the potential to be aired in public. What would be the best way to manage the Arboretum's communications to its constituents?

Source: This case was prepared by Esther da Silva and Todd Huntley under the supervision of Professor Brian Wansink as a basis for class discussion rather than to illustrate either effective or ineffective handling of the administrative situation, Copyright 1993 by Professor Brian Wansink, Amos Tuck School of Business Administration, Dartmouth College, Hanover NH 03755. All rights reserved. No part of this publication may be reproduced, stored in a retrieval system, or transmitted in any form or by any means without permission.

# ✳ HISTORY OF THE NEW YORK CITY ARBORETUM

The New York City Arboretum was founded as a botanical research and public education institution in 1891. Located on a 250-acre tract of land in the Bronx near the New York Zoological Park, it contained educational facilities, display gardens, the largest botanical library in North America, an extensive herbarium (for the cataloguing of dried plant species), a turn-of-the-century conservatory, and scientific research laboratories. The Arboretum also offered 480 educational courses a year—from gardening for children to the art of bonsai—to some 19,500 amateurs and professionals.

Over the years, the Arboretum's mission expanded from botany and horticulture to include environmental education and community gardening programs. James Hastings, who joined the Arboretum as president in 1980, felt that the Arboretum should take a more activist stance. He established the Millbrook, New York-based Institute for Ecosystem Studies, devoted to studying and preventing environmental deterioration. He also founded the Institute of Economic Botany, which is devoted to conserving the tropical rain forests and to finding new plant sources of food, fuel, and medicine. The Institute of Economic Botany has conducted field studies in South American rain forests in conjunction with the National Cancer Institute, studied use of herbal remedies with a Mayan shaman in Belize, and worked with the Brazilian government to develop new sources of fuel and vitamin C.

## FUND RAISING

Although the Arboretum was funded primarily by the city and the state, donations from the private sector became increasingly important, beginning when NYC funding was cut back in the late 1960s and accelerating when the city faced bankruptcy in the 1970s. Arboretum President Hastings proved particularly adept at attracting donations. He augmented the board with CEOs from companies such as Chase Manhattan Bank and General Foods and helped raise $51.7 million during his nine-year tenure.

Closer connections with corporations generated additional fund-raising venues. For example, Chase Manhattan matched every new individual membership ($35) 100 percent.

# ✳ THE NYCA IN 1989: AN ABUSED TREASURE

Although the Arboretum was intended to function as a living museum of horticultural and natural beauty, its appearance was very much like a park. Consequently, visitors to the Arboretum tended to treat the grounds as they would, say, Central Park in Manhattan. The formal display gardens (such as the Rockefeller Rose Garden and the Daffodil/Daylily walk) were maintained by experienced gardeners but were often not in pristine condition due to abuse from visitors. Some visitors picked flowers, while others harvested the produce from the Arboretum's vegetable gardens and fruit trees. On weekend days one's first view of the Arboretum's glorious Grand Esplanade was often the sight of families grilling on portable hibachies on the lawn among the towering trees.

The Arboretum grounds also included some natural areas, such as the Forest. Due to the Arboretum's large size and its proximity to troubled neighborhoods, some of these natural areas had become strewn with litter and frequented by drug dealers and users.

## ✳ ARBORETUM VISITORS

The Arboretum drew visitors from the surrounding neighborhoods as well as from Manhattan and other parts of New York City, Westchester County, Connecticut, and New Jersey. These visitors could be divided into two groups: the neighbors and the non-Bronx visitors. The two groups had different motives for visiting the Arboretum.

People from the neighborhood viewed the Arboretum as their local park and their "back yard" (density of housing was high in this area of the Bronx, so most dwellings did not have yards of their own). These visitors used the Arboretum for walking their dogs, giving their children a large space in which to run, and respite from steaming apartments on hot summer days. For this group of people the Arboretum was an integral part of the neighborhood and an important part of their lives.

Non-Bronx visitors were by nature different because they had to plan a special outing to the Arboretum. As a NYC Arboretum board member noted: "People don't just drop in on the Bronx." These visitors often came with high expectations (raised by frequently placed stories in the NYC media) and admired the manicured display gardens, the Victorian conservatory, the library's collection of botanical illustrations, and the rare orchids on display. This group also came for special events such as the New York Orchid Show and the blooming of Azalea Way. These non-Bronx visitors also composed the majority of those taking classes and attending seminars.

## ✳ EFFORTS TO CLEAN UP THE ARBORETUM

With the arrival of Grant Longet as president of the Arboretum in the summer of 1989 came new guidelines and rules for Arboretum visitors. Longet's goal was to make the Arboretum a premier visitor attraction, one that would be revered like the Metropolitan Museum of Art. To that end he began a campaign to clean up the grounds and add visitor amenities. In addition, he brought in talented individuals from industry and other cultural institutions to run the various visitor-oriented departments. Included in Longet's summer 1989 upgrading program were the banning of picnics on the grounds, the elimination of dog walking inside the Arboretum, the closing of all internal roads to vehicular traffic (in order to make the grounds more pedestrian-friendly), and preliminary plans to add two diesel-powered trams in the spring of 1990 to provide internal transportation for those not wanting to walk.

## THE REACTION

These initiatives caused an uproar among the Arboretum's constituencies. Neighborhood groups were incensed by the decision to ban dog walking and picnics and used their local community boards to contact state legislators. There were also organized protests at the main gate (though small, they were still quite visible and therefore potentially damaging), and Kent Lorby, Director of Marketing and Public Relations, estimated that on average 5 protest letters and 25 phone calls were received per day during the two-week period immediately following the implementation of the policies. Some of these protests dealt with the fact that the policies had been changed abruptly, without consulting the people who would be affected by them. But most protesters were simply irate that the activities had been banned.

There was also dissension from non-Bronx visitors, but their ire tended toward the revoking of driving privileges on Arboretum roadways. Especially disconcerting were the protests from members of the elderly community who claimed that they would be forced to stop visiting the Arboretum if they had to walk through its collections rather than driving. This complaint was easier to mitigate than the others because Longet had already secured funding for trams that would shuttle Arboretum visitors between the entrance and the Old Mill restaurant (on the far side of the property).

Among both Bronx and non-Bronx visitors were Arboretum members. Many members upset by the policy changes were threatening to forgo renewing their memberships, potentially resulting in revenue shortfalls for 1990. In addition, many Arboretum employees were second-guessing Longet's decisions and management style. Already Kate Pierpont, *Arboretum Magazine* editor, had spoken with *New York Times* garden columnist Linda Yang about "Longet's grand scheme to take the Arboretum away from the people."

Despite all the opposition to Longet's policies, there was very little effect on their implementation. Longet did reopen the River Gate (adjacent to the Zoo) as a concession to the community, but all other policy changes remained. As a result, the Arboretum's appearance improved dramatically. No negative articles were published in any of the influential New York publications, and visitation seemed to be on par with that of previous years.[1]

## ✳ FURTHER ARBORETUM ENHANCEMENTS: 1990

Having weathered the storm in 1989 and with Mary Saxon aboard, Longet launched yet another round of changes to enhance the visitor experience at the Arboretum. In the spring, as planned, the tram became operational. Because the gift to purchase the tram did not include an endowment to cover operating expenses, a fee of 50 cents was charged for each one-way trip made between the Herbarium and the Old Mill restaurant.

Longet also hired architect Hugh Hardy to design additional recreational structures (an outdoor cafe opposite the Herbarium and a gazebo tram stop) and coordinate a comprehensive Arboretum signage program. Hardy was nationally known for his preservation work[2] and was able to generate publicity for new projects he undertook. In addition, a new Arboretum Shuttle, providing transportation from Manhattan direct to the Arboretum, had been put into operation.[3] Longet had privately raised more than a million dollars for the project, called the Spring 1990 Initiative, and it was completed on time in May 1990. For the first time in the Arboretum's history there were internal transportation and food services available on both sides of the property.

## ADVERTISING AND PUBLIC RELATIONS

The new additions created legitimate "news" for the Arboretum and an aggressive public relations campaign was begun, supplemented by advertising (the initial budget was set at $50,000) for which private donations had been solicited. The Arboretum staff developed a print and entitled "People Grow Here, Too," which ran in the *New York Times* Weekend section and on billboards inside Metro North Commorer Railroad trains and stations. Since advertising funds were dependent on donations, advertising on a regular basis was nearly impossible. This was in stark contrast with the Bronx Zoo's $1,000,000 advertising budget and assistance from a prominent Madison Avenue advertising agency.

In addition to these communications, the Arboretum enjoyed a donation from *Town & Country Magazine* in the form of a yearly supplement called *The New York Arboretum Journal*. This was a glossy magazine devoted entirely to the Arboretum. It described projects and improvements underway at the Arboretum and featured key employees and board members, as well as photo collages of attendees at the Arboretum's social events and board meetings. This supplement was distributed free of charge to all *Town & Country* subscribers.

## MARY SAXON

Mary Saxon joined the NYC Arboretum in September 1989, as Vice President of External Relations. She had previously been the Special Events Director at the New York Public Library and was lured to the Arboretum by Longet (with whom she had worked at the library). At the Arboretum, Mary was responsible for all the departments with which outside visitors to the Arboretum came into contact: Marketing, Visitor Services, Volunteers, Membership, Special Events, Public Relations, Tours, and Retailing. Even though she had been there only a short time, Mary had become increasingly frustrated with her position at the Arboretum. She had given up a very prestigious position to tackle the problems of a neglected public garden in a disadvantaged part of the city. Although she was excited about the prospect of "making a difference," she also wondered whether she had made the right decision to leave the library.

## THE DECISION TO CHARGE ADMISSION

Following the direction of Grant Longet, Mary had formulated an admissions plan with the help of Kent Lorby and his marketing staff. After parking their cars, visitors would have to enter the Arboretum grounds through one of three gates. (Access would be limited by an interior fence that ran just inside the Arboretum's perimeter. Due to a mandate from Longet to have the admission plan running in the spring in 1991, construction of the fence had already begun.) Because of the Arboretum's state charter, it was forbidden to require a fee of visitors. But the solicitation of donations was allowed; Mary's plan was to have a visitor host at each pedestrian entrance to the Arboretum asking for specific donations of $3.50 for adults and $2.50 for children. This plan was modeled on the one in use by the Metropolitan Museum of Art and had been presented to and endorsed by Longet.[4]

## THE BOARD MEETING: NOVEMBER 1990

One of the most challenging, and frustrating, aspects of Mary's position at the Arboretum was the constant struggle to get agreement about policy changes from the staff and the board members; the brouhaha surrounding the charging of admission was typical. Some constituents refused to acknowledge that there *was* a budget problem, proposing instead increased lobbying of city and state agencies for funding. Others clearly recognized that rising operating costs and decreasing public funding made it imperative that the Arboretum increase its earned revenues in order to avoid a budget deficit.[5]

To assure general acceptance of the decision to charge admission, Mary had prepared a plan for her presentation at the November board meeting. First, she would point out the Arboretum's dire financial position, underlining the need for increased revenues. Then she would bring up the decision to request donations at the Arboretum entrance, pointing to the Metropolitan Museum of Art as an example of successful execution of this strategy. The admission fee discussion would then provide a natural segue to the construction of the fence already underway.

The board meeting was well attended—roughly 20 board members were present, and approximately 10 employees (including Kate Pierpont, some gardeners, and Pat Holmberg, VP: Science) had elected to attend as well.[6] Mary looked at the audience assembled and quickly reviewed the key points of her message. Then she took a deep breath and began her presentation.

### Mary Saxon:
As you've heard from Grant and from our Finance VP, Joan Roar, the Arboretum faces difficult times. This year we will surely have a budget deficit. Next year we anticipate state and city funding to diminish further, and there is no reason to believe that our Development office will be able to generate more private funding. It is therefore imperative that the Arboretum put in place a plan to generate earned revenue.

### Mobee Weinstein, Curator of the Fern Collection:
Mary, I'd like to ask a question about the construction that's going on. There are rumors that a fence is being built. If this is true, the horticulture staff is very disturbed. We'd like to hear what's going on.

### Mary Saxon:
Yes, Mobee, it is true that a fence is being built, and that is to facilitate the collection of earned revenue. The plan that we have developed—and Kent will present the details of it in just a moment—will allow us to solicit a donation from each and every visitor to the Arboretum.

**Grant Longet:**
Allow me to interject, Mary. We did a study using last year's visitor figures and compared those to total revenues generated by the Arboretum for the year. What we found was that total revenues from parking, the conservatory, the rock garden, and the Arboretum's rent on the restaurant concessions averaged to only 12 cents per visitor. This is unacceptable.

**Board Member 2:**
But where is it written that we should be expecting anything from our visitors? This institution was founded for the public, and that is who we should continue to serve. The motion that visitors should be exploited for revenue is absurd.

**Board Member 3:**
Now, Shelby, that worked very well when the Arboretum was flush with donated funds, but those days are over. The reality is that we are running a business here. Granted, we are not trying to take profits. But we are providing entertainment and education, and the users must contribute toward these operations.

**Board Member 4:**
Yeah, but at the same time, won't charging a fee drive down the number of visitors? In my experience, as price goes up, demand goes down. How can we be sure that we'll attract enough visitors to realize a gain?

**Mary Saxon:**
Well, that's part two of our plan. To ensure that we keep attracting visitors to the Arboretum, we'll have to step up our marketing efforts. For example, we could run the "People Grow Here, Too" ad again.

**Board Member 4:**
Excuse me, Mary. We're looking at what could potentially be a significant downturn in visitation and all you want to do is run that print ad again? I don't know much about marketing for nonprofit, but if all General Foods did was run a print ad every once in a while, we would not be selling much Maxwell House coffee.

**Kent Lorby:**
Well, we'd supplement the advertising with public relations. Some articles in the *New York Times* Weekend section will generate a lot of interest.

**Board Member 4:**
That's what the Arboretum always does. I can't imagine that would be enough to overcome the drop in visitation you'll see.

Mary felt a headache coming on, and she was beginning to panic. The meeting was not progressing at all the way she had planned. She had not really given much thought to the marketing communication plan yet and was not prepared to go into much detail.

**Grant Longet:**
The issue of whether or not the Arboretum needs to raise revenues is not debatable. This institution is at risk. We as a group can either be the stewards of its demise, or we can anticipate the worst and plan to mitigate it. I have asked Mary Saxon and her staff to put together a plan to do just that. Let's take a look at the plan.

**Kent Lorby:**
I've brought in a map showing the new fence. As you can see, the fence runs from the administration building to the laboratory and has three distinct entrances. At each of these entrances will be a booth with a cash register and a visitor host who will ask each visitor for a suggested donation of $3.50 for adults and $2.50 for children. This host will also distribute a color map of the grounds and will direct the visitor to the gardens of interest on that particular day. There will also be a similar booth and visitor host at the Fordham Gate. The River Gate is rarely used and, therefore, will not be manned.

**Mobee Weinstein:**
But what about the Arboretum's charter? I thought we couldn't legally charge admission.

**Kent Lorby:**
That's right. This is a suggested donation.

**Kate Pierpont:**
I think this is just a way to discriminate against the neighbors who really use the Arboretum. You know most of the community visitors cannot afford to pay that kind of money. And the fence looks disgusting on our beautiful lawn. The Arboretum has already suffered through the addition of those gazebos and that awful cafe. We have too many man-made things in the Arboretum already.

**Mary Saxon:**
We have to offer such amenities in order to attract more visitors. Restrooms and a cafe are the least that we should offer.

**Pat Holmberg:**
Why do we want to actively encourage people to visit? This place was perfect when nobody came. It was quiet and peaceful and the people who really appreciated plants had a chance to enjoy them. Now there are people all the time. Science is the backbone of this institution, but some people are trying to turn it into Disneyland. Perhaps we need to consider closing off part of the property and reducing the horticultural headcount.

**Rick Muggieto:**
I'm not disputing the Arboretum's scientific preeminence, Pat, but the institution has always had a strong horticulture component. Closing down part of the property

would be a tragedy. As it is, the horticultural staff is too small to really do the Arboretum's mission as a leading institute of horticulture much justice.

**Board Member 1:**

I agree that we need to take steps to raise revenue, but $3.50 and $2.50 seems excessive. That would mean that a family of four would pay $12 to get in, $4 to park, $4 to take a round-trip tram ride, and another $12 to go to the conservatory. That's total of $32.

**Grant Longet:**

Mary and her staff will work out the pricing details; there will probably be family discounts to bring the net fee down.

**Kate Pierpont:**

If the Arboretum is in such dire shape, why don't we eliminate some of the tertiary expenditures like the tram and advertising? An institution like the Arboretum should not have to advertise; cutting advertising would save us $50,000.

**Board Member 2:**

If we are cutting tertiary programs, we'd better look at the Education division. That area is bleeding money.

**Grant Longet:**

I see that we are out of time. The tram is waiting outside the Administration building to take the board members on a tour of the perennial garden. I move that the meeting be adjourned.

With that, those assembled left the room. Mary heard individual board members discussing the issues as they filed out, but there appeared to be no consensus. Equally ambiguous was the reaction among the employees who had attended the meeting. "I've done nothing here to further our cause," thought Mary. She had expected some opposition, but not the widely divergent views on whether the Arboretum even needed visitors. "Sometimes it feels like we don't even belong to the same organization," she muttered to herself. She wondered whether she had handled this issue correctly and what she could do in the future to get everybody on the same side.

As Mary maneuvered her car into a parking spot at the Arboretum, she reviewed in her mind the key events of the past two years. She was still irritated about yesterday's attack on her marketing efforts. Everyone at the Arboretum had liked the print ad, and although she had no measurements of visitorship, it *seemed* like more people were coming to the Arboretum. She was sure that running the ad again, with public relations backup, would result in a similar increase. She walked back to her office pondering what to do next.

## * CASE QUESTIONS

1. Identify the key issues faced by the New York City Arboretum.
2. Provide three alternative solutions for each of the key issues faced by the New York City Arboretum.
3. Discuss the pros and cons of each alternative solution provided.
4. Provide an overall recommendation for the New York City Arboretum and justify your answer.

## * NOTES

1. No formal annual visitor count had been undertaken at the Arboretum until Longet implemented one in 1989. Up to that point visitation was reported at "over a million," but was, in fact, suspected to be around 300,000 people per year.
2. Previous New York City work had included the restaurant kiosks in front of the New York Public Library and the restoration of Bryant Park in midtown Manhattan.
3. The shuttle made three round trips daily between Manhattan and the Arboretum (with drop-off/pick-up points at The Museum of Natural History and the Metropolitan Museum of Art). The Shuttle used the Henry Hudson Parkway and traversed Riverdale, thereby eliminating visual exposure to blighted areas of the Bronx.
4. The Met used an elaborate entrance system composed of imposing arches, turnstiles, and signage with specific donation amounts to imply that visitors were expected to donate. Many visitors to the Met believed that the museum *did* charge admission when, in fact, a donation was optional.
5. Earned revenues were funds gained through parking, which had been charged since the sixties, admission to the Conservatory and the Rock Garden, education department tuition, and group tours.
6. It was in the Arboretum's charter that all board meetings were open to employees, but only recently had employees taken advantage of this provision.

# AIRLINES ATTEMPTING TO GET A "LEG UP" ON THE COMPETITION

In its biggest move since the introduction of business class over two decades ago, major airline carriers are now considering offering consumers more legroom. Airlines who are offering more legroom are hoping that this added perk will provide a differential advantage that is valued by consumers and subsequently will lead to higher profits. Consumers like Harry Dodge, a retired oil services company owner, agrees . . . "I have taken some transcontinental flights and developed some painful cramps in my legs. I swore I would never fly again. This extra room in coach will make a big difference for me."

Two of the major corporations leading the charge are United Airlines and American Airlines; however, their mutual goal of increasing profits is obtained through different routes.

## ✱ UNITED'S STRATEGY

United is dividing its coach section of the airplane into two classes—premium (referred to as Economy Plus) and economy. Passengers wanting the extra legroom will have to pay for it. For example, a United Flight from New York to Chicago would cost $1602 for First Class, $1094 for Economy Plus, and $324 for the cheapest economy fare. However, even passengers who do not want to pay for the extra legroom may be affected. By increasing the amount of space between the rows of seats, planes will now have fewer rows and fewer seats. Consequently, fewer economy seats will be available (best guess estimates are that United will reduce its economy seating by 5%) and customers will have to pay an additional 20% for the next available discount fare. In addition, some airlines are considering increasing the baggage-weight limit for higher-paying passengers, thereby, reducing the limits for baggage and carry-ons for budget passengers.

United is betting on the continuation of a booming economy and that passengers will be willing to pay for the extra legroom. It also feels that by creating the Economy Plus

Source: "Plane seats get bigger, cost more: Airlines betting fliers will pay extra for added legroom," *Denver Rocky Mountain News*, February 28, 2000, pp. 2A, 31A.

class, the airline can serve more Business Class customers. Business travelers only purchase 20 percent of all airline tickets but account for over 50% of the industry's profits. United is hoping that by attracting more business travelers it will rely less on budget travelers whose fares do not always cover the costs of running an airline.

United's strategy evens the playing field in the sense "you get what you pay for." On many of today's flights a business traveler seated in coach who had to book a flight on short notice may have paid triple of what the budget passenger paid who is seated next to them. Richard Branson of Virgin Atlantic agrees . . . "Why should someone pay full-coach fare and get the same exact service as someone who paid $99 for the same ticket? There is no other industry where that happens."

## * AMERICAN'S STRATEGY

American airlines is currently implementing a $70 million plan that refurbishes its fleet by providing "economy passengers more legroom than they have had on any domestic carrier in 20 years." American's strategy is to remove two rows of seats in coach cabins (each row takes up 37 inches) and provide each of the remaining 21 rows in a typical Boeing 737 with 3 extra inches. The extra room is provided at no additional charge. Samuel Buttrick, an airline analyst at Paine-Webber, calls this approach . . . "a big win for consumers . . . but it's not a way to increase profitability. What's good for the customer is not always good for the airline industry." Upon completion of the refurbishment project, American Airlines will have 6.4% fewer economy seats.

American believes by offering the additional room at no cost its airline will become the number one choice for budget-minded consumers. According to American's Mike Gunn, executive vice president for marketing and planning . . . "By having a better product throughout coach, we think that we will be the first call that discount travelers make. We also expect to attract more business travelers who are willing to pay a higher-yielding fare."

## * COMPETITIVE REACTION

British Airways is also increasing its legroom and is following a strategy similar to United by creating two different classes of coach section seats. Their premium coach seats will be called "World Traveler Plus." British Airways has yet to announce how its newest seating section will be priced.

Continental Airlines has characterized the latest moves made by British Airways, United Airlines and American Airlines as "fads." According to Gordon M. Bethune, CEO of Continental Airlines, "We believe at Continental in giving people what they will pay for . . . and at the end of the day, many passengers want to pay the cheapest air fare. There's more to a good product than a few inches of extra legroom. That's a dumb approach by a bunch of mediocre airlines."

Other carriers, such as Delta Air Lines, are taking a "wait and see" attitude and like Delta are selecting to evaluate "various options" before jumping into anything too hastily. According to a recent Delta passenger survey, the most important criteria passengers consider when selecting an airline are flight schedule, price, and frequent flyer miles. The president of Air Travelers Association, David S. Stempler, agrees . . . "seat size and the quality of meals are way down the list." Many other industry consultants are unsure whether the move to more legroom will be adopted universally across the industry.

## * CASE QUESTIONS

1. Survey 3 fellow students and 3 businesspeople and ask them to list and rank the top 5 criteria they consider when booking flights. Is legroom a consideration?
2. Referring back to the text (Chapter 4) and the managerial implications of multi-attribute models, how are United, American, and British Airways attempting to influence consumer decision making?
3. Discuss the fundamental differences in pricing strategy between United and American. Which pricing strategy is superior?
4. Discuss the reaction by competitive airlines. If you managed Delta Air Lines, what would you do?

# CASE | 5

# THE CASE OF JIM BAKKER AND PTL

Jim Bakker created PTL, a Christian-oriented syndication network, in 1977. Prior to that time, Bakker had spent seven years working for the Christian Broadcast Network (CBN) owned by Pat Robertson. Bakker was not well educated in theology; he had dropped out of North Central Bible College after only three semesters. However, he was a natural on television, where he preached seed-faith and prosperity theology. These theological philosophies had originated with Oral Roberts in the 1940s and by the 1980s were widely embraced by most evangelists.

The seed-faith philosophy taught that if the believers served and gave to God, they would be rewarded by God with an abundance of material needs. Prosperity theology, also known as "health and wealth theology," asserted that God wanted the whole man, including his finances, to be healed. Those practicing prosperity theology recommended that believers pray for a specific outcome or object. Indeed, Bakker recommended that if his supporters prayed for a camper, they should specify the color; otherwise, they were asking God to do their shopping.

Bakker, then, did not preach hard work, saving, and responsible planning. Instead, he subscribed to the belief that the Spirit willed financial miracles as well as the actions of Its followers. Bakker sermonized only on the love of God and ignored the topic of sin. This religious philosophy apparently appealed to a wide cross-section of middle-class Americans, as Bakker's congregation grew rapidly. Only 20 percent of Bakker's supporters came from his own Assemblies of God Pentecostal faith; the remainder came from other Pentecostal denominations, other Protestant denominations, and the Roman Catholic Church. Their contributions and support made PTL one of the three wealthiest and most popular media ministries in the nation. Consequently, by 1984, PTL served 1,300 cable systems of 12 million homes and had accumulated $66 million in revenues and $86 million in assets. PTL also had 900 people on the payroll and enormous operating expenses and debt.

Source: This case written by Judy A. Siguaw, Associate Professor of Marketing, Cornell University, and K. Douglas Hoffman, Professor of Marketing, Colorado State University.

Bakker often prayed, with his television audience, for the financing of specific projects, an evangelical university, a PTL show in Italy or Brazil, or the "Christian Disneyland" labeled Heritage USA. When the money for these projects poured in from viewers, however, Bakker would use the funds for something else because that was the way he had been moved by the Spirit. Because of this style of financial management, PTL debts mounted.

Thus, it was in 1983 that Bakker conceived the idea of selling lifetime partnerships for donations of $1,000 or more. The lifetime partnerships entitled the contributors to three free nights of lodging and recreation at Heritage USA for the remainder of their lives—a package previously valued at $3,000. The funds from the lifetime partnerships were to be designated for completion of construction at Heritage USA. Unfortunately, Bakker sold lifetime partnerships to more donors than he could accommodate at Heritage USA. Further, as the number of lifetime partnerships sold escalated, contributions to the general PTL fund diminished. In order for PTL to continue, funds from the lifetime partnerships had to be diverted for everyday operating expenses. Consequently, construction on the lodging facilities at Heritage USA were never completed.

Bakker's followers were aware of where their contributions were being channeled. *The Charlotte Observer* regularly reported the financial actions of PTL and the Heritage USA construction cost overruns as well as Bakker's purchases, which included three vacation homes, gold-plated bathroom fixtures, an air-conditioned doghouse, and vast amounts of clothing and jewels. Indeed, Bakker would display the headlines on television to demonstrate the hostility of the press. His followers never wavered. They supported and even endorsed Bakker's materialistic lifestyle and promise of financial miracles. After all, Bakker was only acting out what he preached—a religion with standards of excess and tenets of tolerance and freedom from accountability. As a televangelist, he was free to preach what he pleased, and people were free to listen or not. No one coerced monetary contributions from Bakker's supporters—they willingly sent in funds and did not hold Bakker accountable for the disbursement of those funds.

Further, the government was aware of Bakker's actions. Bakker and his PTL operation were extensively investigated in separate incidences by the Federal Communication Commission, the Justice Department, and the Internal Revenue Service beginning in 1979. Even though the agencies had substantial evidence of misconduct involving millions of dollars, no efforts were made to stop Bakker, and none of the agencies moved toward indictment.

Bakker was allowed, indeed, encouraged in his behavior because he personified the culture of the eighties. No government agency or public outcry arose to stop him until after Bakker, fearing reprisal concerning his affair with Jessica Hahn, resigned from PTL. Bakker's actions could hardly be called covert because they had taken place in plain sight, exemplifying the religious philosophy he and his followers had daily espoused.

In 1987, almost a decade after noting apparent misconduct in the operations of PTL, the federal government charged Jim Bakker with 24 counts of fraud and conspiracy, alleging that Bakker had bilked his supporters.

## ✳ CASE QUESTIONS

1. What service properties inherent in religious groups contribute to consumer vulnerability?
2. Which types of moral philosophies could be argued to be the basis for Bakker's actions?
3. What are the ethical issues involved?
4. What factors, other than moral philosophies, may have influenced the ethical behavior of Jim Bakker?
5. What have been the consequences of Bakker's actions?
6. What strategies would you suggest to help control future abuses by other religious leaders?

## ✳ REFERENCES

Henry G. Brinton, "Pray TV," *The Washington Monthly* (April 1990), pp. 49–51; Charles Colson, "The Pedestal Complex," *Christianity Today*, February 5, 1990, p. 96; Frances Fitzgerald, "Reflections: Jim and Tammy," *The New Yorker*, April 23, 1990, pp. 45–48; and Kim A. Lawton, "The Remnants of PTL," *Christianity Today*, October 6, 1989, pp. 36–38.

# FOR INNOVATIVE SERVICE, RUN FOR THE BORDER

While the vast majority of other food franchises have remained in the traditional management mode by focusing on more advertising, more promotions, more new products, and more new locations, Taco Bell has been focusing on the customer. Taco Bell believes that the company should be organized to support what the customer truly values . . . the food and the service delivery system.

Unlike other food franchises, Taco Bell has shifted its operation from manufacturing to assembly. Backroom tasks such as cleaning heads of lettuce, slicing tomatoes, shredding cheese, and making taco shells has been outsourced to other operations. As a result, labor's primary focus is now on serving customers as opposed to preparing food. In contrast, much of the remainder of the industry is expanding its on-site food manufacturing operations by offering products such as freshly baked biscuits and pizzas. Firms pursuing this strategy have complicated their operations and have placed their emphasis on production as opposed to service delivery.

Other changes within Taco Bell's operations have included a total revamping of the firm's managerial hierarchy. This change has translated into managers who coach and counsel rather than direct and control. In addition, a renewed emphasis on selecting and training public contact personnel has also occurred. An investment in advanced technology has also helped move Taco Bell and its employees to the forefront. Unlike other companies that utilize technology to monitor, control, and sometimes replace their employees, Taco Bell provides technology to employees as a resource to assist them in their duties.

Taco Bell has also recognized the importance of employee morale and loyalty to customer perceptions of service quality. To enhance employee morale, Taco Bell offers frontline employees higher-than-average wages compared with those throughout the rest of the industry. Moreover, because of a generous bonus system, managers are able to make 225 percent more than their competitive counterparts. Such actions have not only

Source: Leonard A. Schlesinger and James L. Heskett, "The Service-Driven Service Company," *Harvard Business Review* (September–October 1991), pp. 71–81. Reprinted by permission of *Harvard Business Review*. Copyright © 1991 by the President and Fellows of Harvard College.

improved employee morale but have also resulted in lower employee turnover rates and an improved caliber of recruits.

Taco Bell's training efforts are also unique. Managers are encouraged to spend half their time on developing employees in areas such as communication, empowerment, and performance management. As a result, the majority of Taco Bell employees now feel they have more freedom, more authority to make decisions, and more responsibility for their own actions.

Overall, the consequences of Taco Bell's restructuring efforts to improve its service delivery systems have been overwhelmingly positive. In times of stagnant market growth for the rest of the industry, sales growth at company-owned Taco Bells has exceeded 60 percent, and profits have increased by more than 25 percent per year. In comparison, McDonald's U.S. franchises have increased their profitability during this same period at a rate of 6 percent. What makes the 25 percent increase in profits even more amazing is that Taco Bell has decreased the price on most menu items by 25 percent! Strategies such as these have led to value-oriented perceptions of Taco Bell that surpass competitive offerings.

## ✳ CASE QUESTIONS

1. In order to provide seamless service, service firms must balance the needs of their operations, marketing, and human resource departments. Discuss how improvements at Taco Bell have been shared by these three departments.
2. How do the actions taken by Taco Bell relate to the various components of the service-profit chain presented in Chapter 10?

# WESTIN HOTELS IN ASIA: GLOBAL DISTRIBUTION

The Westin Stamford & Plaza Hotel is a five star business, and an Incentives, Conventions and Meetings (ICM) hotel in the heart of Singapore. It opened in 1986 with over 2,000 rooms and 70,000 square feet of meeting and banquet space. The hotel had been enjoying high occupancy rates of above 80% until mid-1997, benefiting from Singapore's position as an Asian business and ICM hub. Its sister hotels, The Westin Banyan Tree in Bangkok and The Westin Philippine Plaza in Manila, were similarly blessed with high occupancies and buoyant markets just prior to June 1997. The economic crisis that hit Asia in mid-1997, however, took the wind out of the Asian markets. Business and ICM arrivals into the three countries declined by some 10% to 25% in 1998. The three Westin hotels saw their occupancies fall by 10% to 20%, as well as a sharp decline in average room rates. To compound things, the pre-crisis economic boom had seen a proliferation of five star hotel developments in the three cities. Travel management trends in Asia were also undergoing rapid changes. Many of the hotels' corporate clients were not local companies but multi-national corporations (MNCs), which were increasingly centralizing their purchases of travel-related services at overseas corporate headquarters, giving them more bargaining power.

In view of the shrinking market conditions, intense competition, and changing travel management trends, the three Westin hotels in Asia had to critically reassess their own marketing and distribution strategies. A new opportunity presented itself in late 1997, when Westin's parent company, Starwood Hotels & Resorts Worldwide Inc., acquired ITT Corporation, which owned the Sheraton Hotels & Resorts, St. Regis Luxury Collection, Four Points Hotels, and Caesars World brands of hotels and casino. This acquisition made Starwood the largest hotel and gaming company in the world, with over 650 hotels in 73 countries employing more than 150,000 employees. Uppermost in the mind of Vice President Operations for the three Westin Hotels, David Shackleton, was the need to leverage on the size and global marketing strength of Starwood, to develop new business for his

*"No Boundry, No Limits"*

Mission statement of Starwood Hotels & Resorts Worldwide Inc., parent company of the Westin Hotels.

hotels and gain market share from the competitors. Further information on Westin and Starwood can be found at www.westin.com and www.starwood.com.

## ✳ TRADITIONAL MARKETING AND DISTRIBUTION STRATEGIES

Up until the recent five years, local companies, local MNC offices, and local travel agents in Asia were the key decision makers, negotiating rates with the local hotels and selecting venues for corporate meetings, company incentives, company social functions, and making hotel reservations for their overseas guests. The marketing and distribution strategies of the three Westin hotels in Asia were thus predominantly focused on the local markets, and sales team efforts were concentrated on servicing and cultivating local decision makers. Well-staffed reservation departments were also important, as direct bookings with the hotels via fax and phone were the preferred method of making reservations.

Advertising and promotional (A&P) activities, to build brand awareness and reach the end customer for the three Westin hotels, were also highly decentralized at individual properties and rarely coordinated across sister hotels. As A&P expenses can be prohibitive, individual hotels tended to target their campaigns at the local market and allocated only a limited proportion of their budgets to overseas advertising.

Moreover, since each individual property was responsible for its own cost and revenue figures, each hotel would focus its sales and marketing efforts on selling its own rooms and facilities. There was minimal cross-selling of other Westin hotels worldwide. In other words, there was no cost effective and concerted effort by all Westin hotels in reaching out to the travelers.

## ✳ TRAVEL MANAGEMENT TRENDS

However, as travel decisions are being made increasingly closer to the travel dates, decisions about hotel choice and the actual reservations are made closer to the customer. The traditional approach of relying on one's local offices or travel agents takes too long. Hence, hotels that can provide their global customers easier and faster access will have a competitive edge.

Local secretaries' and the individual business traveler's power to select hotels have also been diluted. The three Westin hotels in Asia saw an increasing trend of their multinational corporate clients centralising their global hotel room rate negotiations at corporate head office, in order to reduce cost through global volume purchasing and to increase bargaining power. Corporate travelers can only select a hotel that is on the approved listing. The change in corporate travel policies and practices is a result of management's concern with their rising travel and entertainment (T&E) costs. *The 1991 American Express Survey of Business travel management* reported that 60 percent of the 1,564 companies surveyed agreed that rising T&E costs is one of management's top concerns.

Corporate clients were also increasingly turning to travel management companies (TMCs) for a total travel solution. The TMCs, such as American Express and Carlson Wagon Lit, are able to handle all airline, hotel and other travel arrangements. They use mainly global distribution systems (GDSs, global reservation systems containing extensive information on airfares, hotel rates, etc.) such as Galileo, Sabre, and Amadeus, for hotel reservations. The Westin Stamford & Plaza in particular had seen an increase in the number of reservations coming in via the GDSs. This reservation channel brings in about 27% of the hotel's transient (non-group) revenue. Even wholesale travel agents, who had traditionally booked directly via fax and phone, were increasingly turning to the use of GDS to improve efficiency and obtain instant confirmation.

On this issue, Mr. Shackleton said, "This trend of centralising travel management is not new in the United States, Europe, nor Australia, but we in Asia are just beginning to feel the impact. Many MNCs have now organised their home grounds and are extending their centralised management and purchase of travel services to their Asian offices. With the Asian economic crisis dampening demand from large traditional markets like Japan, Indonesia, Malaysia and Hong Kong, we certainly need to grow our markets out of the United States, Europe, and Australia. We need to reassess our marketing and distribution strategies in order to align ourselves with these changes and to be effective in reaching out to these decision makers overseas. Competition among the international hotel chains is very keen. Once we have been selected onto a corporate listing, the battle is far from over. We still have to incentivise the travel managers overseas to select our hotels in Asia over Hyatt, Marriot, and the Shangri-Las, who are also listed. The individual business travelers can still choose among hotels on the approved list. Another development is that meeting and conference planners increasingly need a quick turnaround in exploring possible destinations, checking meeting space and room availability, and finally negotiating the piece of business. Our current process takes days or weeks and is becoming unacceptable to demanding clients."

## ✱ STARWOOD'S GLOBAL MARKETING AND DISTRIBUTION STRATEGIES

Since Starwood's acquisition of the ITT corporation in late 1997, a key issue had become to examine how Starwood and its individual properties, such as the Westin, could leverage on Starwood's size, geographic coverage, and brand diversity.

### GLOBAL SELLING AND CROSS SELLING

Roberta Rinker-Ludloff, Vice President of Starwood Global Sales, quoted Henry Ford, "Coming together is the beginning. Keeping together is the progress. Working together is success." Starwood's strategy had comprised of global selling, cross-selling, and improving customer service.

Starwood had formed over 30 global sales offices (GSOs) around the world to manage customer relationships with key global accounts. These GSOs provided a one-stop solution to corporate travel planners, wholesalers, meeting planners, incentive houses, and mega travel organizations by addressing all accommodation issues including global room rate negotiations, corporate meetings, and events planning at any of Starwood's 650 hotels worldwide.

Besides the GSOs, each hotel had its own sales team. With over 2,000 sales managers from individual properties making sales calls and meeting clients daily, how could Starwood produce synergy and leverage on these activities? Team Hot was the answer – a new program to harness the tremendous power of cross-selling across its 650 hotels in an efficient and automated way. Team Hot provided incentives for hotel sales and catering managers to cross-sell other resorts and hotels under the Starwood umbrella. Program participants needed to anticipate their clients' accommodation and catering needs outside of their own hotel, and then send the lead to the relevant property(s) via the Internet. For leads that resulted in confirmed business, participants received points redeemable for airline tickets, room nights, and other rewards. Starwood aimed to generate an additional US $225 million in revenue in 1999 through Team Hot.

Overseas guests no longer wanted to make long distance calls to hotels for reservations, preferring to call a local toll-free telephone number instead. Starwood had set up nine central reservation offices (CROs) worldwide to provide one-stop total customer service for the guests, including hotel reservations worldwide, enrollment and redemption of Starwood's loyalty program, and general customer service. With the toll-free numbers, guests only needed to remember one number to book any Starwood hotel.

## TECHNOLOGY AND AUTOMATION

Whether it's the individual customer, the travel agent or corporate travel planner, all prefer and are likely to stay with hotels that are easy and quick to book, provide immediate response to customer queries, and have rates that are reasonably competitive and up-to-date. Traditional booking methods via direct faxes and phone calls to the hotel were fast on the decline, as they were cumbersome and required customers to remember multiple phone and fax numbers. Meeting and conference planners increasingly needed quick turnaround and prompt servicing. Starwood used technology and automation to improve the quality of customer service and efficiency. The emphasis was on automating reservations and information provision to the customer.

Starwood's Internet capabilities were continuously upgraded, and cutting edge concepts such as electronic brochures were being pioneered and tested. Individual and corporate clients could gain instant access to information on the facilities and amenities provided by any of the 650 Starwood hotels, and could make online reservations and payment, all at a click of the mouse. Corporate clients could even book their own confidential negotiated rates through the Internet. The Internet has had great potential in creating value to both travelers and hotels. The revenue from bookings through Starwood's Web sites had increased 280% in 1998 and over US $48m worth of meeting leads had already been received through the Web sites in the first nine months of 1998.

Starwood had also developed its own internal central reservation system called Starlink. Starlink contained up-to-date property information and data on rates and availability for each of the 650 hotels, and fed the information interactively to all the major global distribution systems (GDSs). Seamless interface between Starlink and the GDSs ensured that all Starwood hotel services were instantly available and up-to-date at over 400,000 travel agents worldwide.

Starwood had also enlisted the help of technology to make their mobile global sales force more responsive to corporate clients. Its corporate travel information system software enabled the global sales manager to negotiate worldwide corporate rates with clients and print/sign the contracts all in one visit. The global sales force automation software would soon allow the notebook-armed global sales managers to negotiate and close group deals all in a single day. GSOs could check hotel availability, propose pricing, explore alternative dates, negotiate the contracts, close the business deal, and immediately book guest and meeting rooms. It is a system designed to give all necessary information at a manager's fingertips and certainly to impress the client.

## CONCERTED MARKETING EFFORT

Individual properties also needed to create more awareness in overseas markets. To share the burden of high advertising and marketing costs, Starwood hotels clustered together and shared advertising space. Certain rates and promotions were also branded across all hotels within a chain in order to facilitate global advertising. All Westin hotels in Asia Pacific, for example, offered advance purchase discounts that have been branded as the Westin Valuestays Promotions.

## ✳ ALIGNING INDIVIDUAL HOTELS TO STARWOOD

How can the three individual hotels in Asia leverage on the marketing muscles of Starwood to help them address the trend of centralized corporate purchasing for hotel services and to grow their markets from the United States, Europe, and Australia?

With over 650 properties to sell, and Asia being in recession, it would not be surprising if very little of the global sales efforts was being spent to promote hotels in Asia to Americans and Europeans. To compound things, many of the global sales managers and central reservation agents were heritage Sheraton, and were thus not well acquainted with the Westin hotels. David Shackleton believed that the first priority would be to restructure the sales and marketing teams at his hotels to align them with the global Starwood marketing structure. Hence, besides traditional relationship marketing to the local companies and corporate secretaries, the hotel sales and marketing teams were now tasked to also 'market' their individual properties to the GSOs and CROs. Each hotel sales manager was responsible for cultivating close working relationships with specific global sales managers. Hotel sales managers needed to prioritize and discuss their global sales objectives with the GSOs, and ensure that all leads provided by them were followed up promptly. The hotel reservation and distribution marketing managers needed to ensure that property information, rates, and availability were constantly kept up-to-date in all the various distribution systems such as Starlink, the Internet, and the GDSs. Monthly reports on local sales and marketing activities were provided to the GSOs via electronic media. Hotel promotional collaterals were regularly distributed to the GSOs and CROs to heighten their awareness of the three Westin properties. Familiarization trips were also being planned for the GSO and CRO managers to acquaint them with the hotel service experience and enable them to sell the hotels more effectively.

| EXHIBIT 1 | COMPARISON OF FREQUENT FLYER CONVERSION RATIOS ACROSS HOTEL LOYALTY PROGRAMMES | | | |
| --- | --- | --- | --- | --- |
| | **Starwood Preferred Guest** | **Hilton Honors** | **Hyatt Gold Passport** | **Marriot Rewards** |
| Frequent Flyer conversion ratio (for most airlines) | 1 point =1 airline mile | 10,000 points = 1,500 airline miles <br> 20,000 points = 3,500 airline miles <br> 50,000 points = 10,000 airline miles | 3 points = 1 airline mile | 10,000 points = 2,000 miles <br> 20,000 points = 5,000 miles <br> 30,000 points = 10,000 miles |

## ✳ CASE QUESTIONS

1. Apart from the preferential rates and good service, what other strategies can Starwood hotels employ to encourage selection and loyalty from corporate travel managers and event planners?
2. Even after corporate travel managers have selected and negotiated with individual hotel chains, the individual corporate traveler can still choose among the various chains listed in his company's directory. How can Westin and the other Starwood brands differentiate themselves from other hotel chains and make themselves the top choice of the corporate traveler?
3. In the long term, would it be more effective for the three Westin hotels in Asia to focus their distribution strategy on intermediaries (travel agent or corporate travel managers), or should they employ multi-channel distribution strategies?
4. What are the key challenges facing the three hotels in its move to leverage on Starwood's marketing and distribution programs?

## ✳ NOTES

1. Jochen Wirtz is an Associate Professor with the Department of Marketing, Faculty of Business Administration, National University of Singapore. Jeannette Ho Pheng Theng is an MSc student with the Department of Marketing and Director of Revenue Management at The Westin Stamford & Westin Plaza Hotels in Singapore.

The authors greatly acknowledge the generous support in terms of time, information and feedback provided on earlier drafts of this case by David Shackleton, Vice President Operations, Central Region for Starwood Asia Pacific, and Philip Ho, Managing Director Distribution and Revenue Management Asia Pacific. Furthermore, the authors would like to acknowledge the assistance of Cindy Kai Lin Koh and Sim Liew Lien in writing up the case.

# "THE PROUD SPONSORS OF . . ."

~Prometrix, Inc.*

Steve Knight, one of the three principals of Prometrix, Inc., was anxious about the future of this young Macintosh computer consulting company. Since their recent awareness-building campaign, Prometrix had signed on only a small percentage of the companies that had requested information or that had requested bids.

Steve was determined to come up with a new approach to closing more deals on long-term contracts. His fellow principals were becoming nervously aware of the stagnation the company was experiencing at this fragile stage. They all seemed to be running out of ideas about what their problems were and what they could do about them.

## * COMPANY HISTORY

*I'm beginning to think we've plateaued, Colin. We're converting the same percentage of our leads into clients, but the number of leads is drying up. And we're just not pushing the right buttons to generate new ones. Things have been okay until now. But we've got to start expanding our (client) base in a hurry . . . especially those buying full-service contracts.*

*Steve Knight*
*Director of Business*
*Development*

The idea for Prometrix began long before Steve joined the company. The founder, Colin Laing, had grown up in Austria and had attended a top technical university. Upon graduation he joined Brustrich Ltd., an established software development company. He quickly gained a reputation as a bright, talented programmer who was especially adept at learning new programming languages. Unfortunately, the highly regulated and structured working environment of an Austrian business continually frustrated Colin, who had many new product ideas that never gained the attention of upper management.

Since starting his own business in Austria was next to impossible due to government constraints, he left to earn his MBA at the University of California at Berkeley. After graduating with honors, Colin moved to Kansas City to be close to family and friends who had settled in the area. One of these relatives, Colin's uncle, was a talented ophthalmologist, Felix Paplardein. Having gained prominence through many years of personal sacrifice, Felix was sympathetic towards Colin's ambitions to start his own company, and he agreed to consider investing in it upon the presentation of a sound business plan.

To generate some income in the meantime, Colin made a living by doing freelance specialty programming for local small businesses. It was through this work that he met several key individuals who would prove to be instrumental in the formation of his own company. Leslie West and Steve Knight were working as independent Macintosh computer consultants when they met Colin and became friends. Steve was an electrical engineer by training and a Kansas City native who had numerous contacts with smaller businesses in the area. Leslie had earned her masters in computer science from Purdue and moved to Kansas City in 1989. Although they generally worked as individuals, their talents were complementary and they often joined forces to take on larger system projects as their talents were complementary.

## ✳ A COMPANY IS BORN

While attending business school, Colin came to the conclusion that starting a general purpose software company involved too much risk and required more capital than he could realistically expect to raise. He considered specialty software, but concluded he did not have enough expertise in a specific area to develop top-flight programs. Instead he envisioned a computer consulting firm that would provide a full range of services, including small-scale database programming and training for users.

Colin had a gut feel for the number of businesses that could benefit from such services. Knowing that this was not the basis for a new business idea, he studied the Kansas City business market and found most to be users of computers, many of which were Apple Macintoshes. Feeling comfortable with this foundation, he decided to move ahead. In the fall of 1991, Colin invited Leslie and Steve to dinner at the Plaza Club to present his plans for a new business and to ask them to consider joining him. He explained that it would involve a substantial financial commitment from each of them (around $35,000), in return for a large share in the company. Given that all three were experts with Macintosh computers, the company would specialize only in Macs, and would provide programming and standalone support.

Steve felt that Colin had defined the company's mission too broadly. It seemed that they would be coming at the market from too many different approaches, and that this would harm personal service as the number of clients increased. Steve's concerns were laid to rest, however, when it was agreed to that (1) the company would be formed only when money was available to hire qualified technical personnel, and (2) the company would provide system support in only the following areas:

- Software consulting and database programming
- Network configuration
- Online and on-site support
- Software training

These areas were finally agreed on as they best addressed all client concerns, and provided an incentive for buying a total service package.

It was not an easy decision for Leslie and Steve. After all, $35,000 was a sizable sum of money, and they would be able to draw a salary only when the company began to make a reasonable profit. If the business were successful, however, there would be considerable earnings potential. After giving it some thought, both decided to go with Colin's offer.

Felix Paplardein made good on his promise to put up $100,000, and each principal contributed $35,000. Bank financing of $80,000 was secured. This money would be used for incorporation fees, salaries for the technicians, and operating expenses such as office rent, supplies, and phone service. On October 12, 1991, Prometrix was officially incorporated as a subchapter C corporation, and the office doors opened on October 13th (see Exhibit 1).

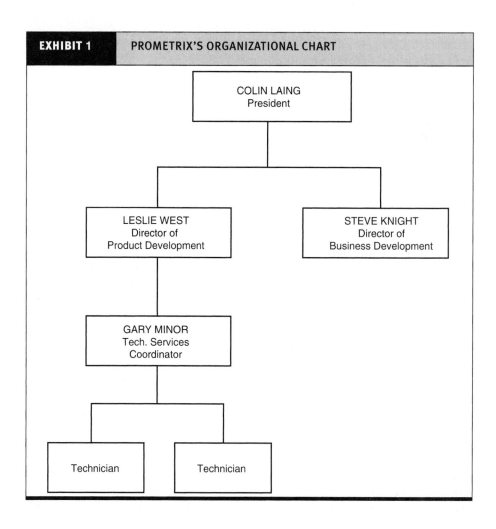

**EXHIBIT 1     PROMETRIX'S ORGANIZATIONAL CHART**

- COLIN LAING — President
  - LESLIE WEST — Director of Product Development
    - GARY MINOR — Tech. Services Coordinator
      - Technician
      - Technician
  - STEVE KNIGHT — Director of Business Development

## ✱ THE FIRST FEW WEEKS

As the first days passed, the office was full of expectation as new prospects were signed onto the service. The first four clients had been lined up through existing contacts of the principals before the company was formed.

In subsequent weeks, new clients were signed on, usually referrals from the first clients. These new clients shared the same basic needs, and they were more than satisfied as the service was exactly as promised. The referring clients had communicated the services' advantages and benefits that they had experienced. This word-of-mouth would sustain Prometrix for weeks to come.

These first clients tended to be experienced users of computers, or at least fast learners. Once the client was up and running, Prometrix found itself simply making the standard monthly service call, routinely upgrading software, and occasionally answering questions of the users. As one technician put it:

> Once in a while we'll go on a call to fix a major machine or software malfunction, but usually we just take care of the normal upgrades and system add-ons.

## ✱ THE PRODUCT

Prometrix had deliberately decided to provide only services, not hardware or software sales. For this reason, they could be seen by the client as an objective, knowledgeable third party who would be able to recommend the most effective configuration of hardware and software available.

Prometrix planned to provide different services for companies in different stages of their computer system development. For a client who did not yet own any computers, Prometrix would spend time assessing the needs of the company through personal interviews and observation. Next, they would recommend an integrated system of hardware and software that best fit the current and expected needs of the client. At this point, the *client* would order the machines and software themselves from an authorized Apple dealer (which had close ties with Prometrix).

Once the system was up and running, Prometrix would offer an appropriate version of its standard package, the Prefix Services. These services came with pre-determined fees, but they offered the flexibility to effectively assist a wide variety of Macintosh users.

The Prefix Services were aimed at making Prometrix an integral part of the client's computer operations, and they were the backbone of Prometrix's offering because they generated a substantial and a continuous revenue stream.

The showcase feature of the Prefix Services was HelpLink, a service that enabled Prometrix to walk a client through unfamiliar computing functions over the phone lines, using sophisticated software. Appendix A includes a copy of the brochure that Prometrix gives to inquiring parties. It describes the company in its own words, explaining the Prefix Services (diagnostics, configuration, preventive maintenance, telephone support, and HelpLink), and providing a description of the benefits for the client.

Although the Prefix Services can be tailored to the client by eliminating unnecessary services, the brochure does not state it in plain terms. The principal working with the client was able to negotiate these changes (and the associated price reductions) without obtaining approval from any other principal.

## ✳ THE PROMETRIX ORGANIZATIONAL STRUCTURE

Prometrix consisted of the principals and a support staff of three highly skilled technicians led by the Technical Service Coordinator, Gary Miner. It was up to the technical staff to maintain the services to existing clients. The three principals were primarily involved in the initial consultation for new clients and in establishing new business (business development).

Exhibit 1 gives the organizational structure and job titles of each of the three principals and technical personnel. Colin held the position of President and performed most of the administrative functions. Leslie was named Director of Product Development, and Steve, Director of Business Development.

As Director of Product Development, Leslie continually reviewed the effectiveness of the Prefix Services and worked to develop new services that would better serve the customer and keep Prometrix at the forefront of its field.

Steve, as Director of Business Development, described the way he viewed his role in the company:

> I want to establish Prometrix as a well-known name in the business community . . . a name synonymous with excellent service. Once this is done, the selling will become easier as Prometrix will have its reputation behind it. Businesses need to be aware of us as a profit-enhancing alternative to maintaining their own computer systems.

## ✳ REVIVING THE BUSINESS

Prometrix's present client base had been developed primarily through contacts and Word-of-Mouth (WOM). The first clients were medium-sized businesses that had established prior working relationships with the principals. Subsequent clients tended to be smaller in size.

Leads for small companies were much easier to come by. They tended to be managed by more entrepreneurial types who (1) used more Macs than established businesses, and who (2) were thought to be more willing to try a service like Prometrix's if the benefits could be clearly illustrated.

Prometrix found that the leads it was getting were increasingly from smaller companies. In Steve's words:

> It just makes sense. We're not sure exactly what the numbers are, but you have to figure that there are many more small companies than medium-sized ones. And, they're usually very young, just like us. When you're that small, getting business is the number-one priority, not fooling around with your computer system. That's what we're here for.
>
> Our full service may be overkill for most of these companies, but we can start them off with a very basic system and add features as they grow. We'll have already made plans for adapting their system to match their changing needs. No worry on their part; their system will always be able to handle their load.

Steve had been pondering a new thrust intended to increase awareness of Prometrix, and thus, the number of inquiries. He decided to bring Leslie and Colin together for a meeting to discuss some of his concerns and to bring up some of the questions that stuck in his mind:

> We know we need to expand our client base, but do we want to do this by generating more inquiries, or by getting some kind of list and calling them?
>
> It seems that a cold call would be less productive because it's important that the prospective client be interested in what we offer before we have much of a chance to sell to them. Inquiries are inherently self-selecting . . . we know we at least have our foot in the door.

Leslie responded by saying:

> I agree up to a point. We need to build awareness about Prometrix that will make our prospects more open to our pitch because they've at least heard of us before. They need to know we're not a trendy, fly-by-night organization. Having said this, I think that medium-sized companies may be our best bet—they have more money to spend and are less likely to get scared away by price.

Colin joined in:

> I don't know about medium-sized companies. It may look like they are our most stable clients, but look at how we got them . . . we already had personal contacts there through our past work. No medium-sized company has ever made a serious inquiry on its own.
>
> The little firms are more eager to grow. They're young and lean and mean, and they're open to new and different ideas that will make them some bucks. Besides that, there are so many more small companies than medium-sized ones. Also, keep in mind that the founder or president of a small company, the one who writes the checks, is going to be a heck of a lot easier for us to get hold of. We need to sell a long-term service like ours at the top.

## ✳ MARKET ANALYSIS

### *THE MAKEUP OF KANSAS CITY BUSINESSES*

Steve knew that Colin had looked at the potential market for their services, but he also knew of Colin's tendency to get blinded by ambition. He decided the only way to confirm what was really out there was to do some more thorough research on businesses in the Kansas City area. He wanted to know exactly how many companies were in business, their relative size, and what percentage of those used Macintosh computers.

To determine the size distribution of companies, he went to the Kansas City Area Chamber of Commerce. The Chamber provided a list of companies based in Kansas City along with their revenues and number of employees. This list included members of the Chamber as well as non-member corporations and partnerships.

Determining what firms used Macs proved more difficult as this information was held in the records of individual Apple dealers and magazine publishers. Apple would not release warranty card return information.[1] Steve decided to buy the regional subscription lists of *MacWeek* and *MacUser*, thinking this would provide the best representation of the metro area Macintosh owners.

Exhibit 2 breaks down the businesses by number of employees and revenues and details whether or not they use Macintosh computers. The results confirmed what his gut feel was—most Macintosh users were small companies.

| EXHIBIT 2 | MARKET RESEARCH DATA OF KANSAS CITY COMPANIES | |
| --- | --- | --- |
| **By Number of Employees:** | **Percent of Businesses in This Range** | **Percent of Range using Macs** |
| 1 to 5 | 35% | 59% |
| 6 to 15 | 29% | 48% |
| 16 to 50 | 20% | 51% |
| 51 to 100 | 8% | 36% |
| 101 to 500 | 5% | 21% |
| 500+ | 3% | 23% |
| | 100% | |
| **By Revenue ($):** | **Percent of Businesses in This Range** | **Percent of Range using Macs** |
| <100,000 | 33% | 60% |
| 100k to 500k | 25% | 49% |
| 500k to 3 Mln | 21% | 52% |
| 3 Mln to 10 Mln | 9% | 33% |
| 10 Mln to 30 Mln | 8% | 28% |
| 30 to 100 Mln | 3% | 20% |
| 100 Mln + | 1% | 18% |
| | 100% | |

It became clear that there just were not that many companies in the medium range of $3 million to $30 million in revenues. Seventy-nine percent of companies did less than $3 million per year while only 17% were in the medium range.

## DIFFERENCES IN COMPANY TYPES

The small companies (<$3 million or <100 employees) were structured very differently compared to the medium-sized companies. The small companies usually consisted of a founder/president and a couple of other officers supported by a small staff. The computing needs of these companies were not complex (from one to four machines), but the important thing was that whatever system they used, it needed to be expandable for it to be useful as the company grew.

The medium-sized companies tended to have larger systems (five to 50 machines) and included networked configurations with file servers. There was more immediate opportunity for Prometrix to add value with their service. These companies tended not to have staff assigned to maintaining the computer network, but there always seemed to be someone who became known as the "computer person." This person was seldom authorized to purchase such a system, but often the decision maker (the office manager or possibly the president) would consider this person a good enough solution to justify putting off the procurement of professional computer consulting support.

Armed with this information, Steve concluded that a fresh outside perspective might shed new light on this quandary, so he called a local university professor, Brian MacKenzie, whom Steve had heard speak at a local chapter meeting of the American Marketing Association. Steve asked:

> I'm really struggling with how to approach this. We need clients who will stay with us for the long-term and who will also subscribe to a fairly complete package of services.

After asking a series of questions, McKenzie replied:

> Given the breakdown of the types of businesses in Kansas City, it seems obvious that you need to go where the customers are. You've been experiencing a fall-off in inquiries, but that just might be due to your clients' WOM having reached its limits. Assuming your product is acceptable to a significant size of the market, you are looking at either an awareness issue or a persuasion issue.

This was all Steve needed to hear to reinforce what he and his colleagues had discussed previously. Prometrix needed to embark on an awareness-building campaign, within a reasonable budget.

## * THE AWARENESS-BUILDING CAMPAIGN

Colin, Leslie, and Steve planned an intensive retreat at Colin's home the following Saturday to brainstorm the campaign. It was agreed that awareness would help generate leads which could eventually be converted into clients. In the meeting, each would contribute their own ideas about how to accomplish this, but in the end Colin would have the final say. The future of Prometrix would be determined in the next few months, and more pressure was being put on the three principals by both Felix Paplardein's interest in the company's performance, and the fact that the bank note, though an interest-only loan, was barely being serviced.

At the retreat, Colin favored short-term volume in an effort to avoid cash problems and maintain their good reputation:

> Our immediate goal, as we've all agreed, is to build our client base. At this point in time, we really need to attract all potential users of our service. Once we attain a critical mass of clientele, we can begin to get a little more selective about whom we target with our publicity efforts.
>
> I think we should also follow up with a direct mailing to the companies on the subscription list that Steve purchased. That will give them our number and a description of our services to hold onto—something that will reinforce what they heard in our ad. To save money, we'll use the same pamphlet we've been using (shown in Appendix A), but we'll add a cover letter for a more personal touch. Like they say, "the brochure tells, and the letter sells."

As Leslie sat listening to Colin's ideas, she felt the need to offer a more effective course of action. She explained:

> I like the idea of following up with a letter. After all, who knows how much attention they'll be paying to our ad when they hear it. Maybe they'll recognize us next time they hear our name, but it's all the better if they have one of our brochures to hold on to.

Steve had been feeling like they were on the right track, but was uneasy about the logistics of it all:

> I'm behind the basic logic of using direct mail advertising. But I think that a simultaneous direct mailing would be best. I mean maybe we should even send one out just before the ads stop airing. I think it would be beneficial for the recipients of our direct mailing to hear about us on radio at the same time they're reading about us—there's more intensity and reinforcement that way.
>
> Another idea I had was to try and gain some publicity through charity events. I had a past client contact me about designing a flyer for the Kansas City Hoops Fest.[2] In exchange for the design, she offered to place our logo on the back of the t-shirts that are worn by the teams and sold at the concession stands. There are a lot of corporate sponsors there, so it's another way of building awareness and goodwill.

Over the next couple of weeks, the radio commercial (see Exhibit 3) and cover letter (see Exhibit 4) were prepared. The radio spot was run for three weeks. Fifteen-second spots ran during the morning rush hour ("drive time") and once during mid-morning on

---

**EXHIBIT 3**    **FIFTEEN-SECOND RADIO SPOT**

At Prometrix, we know what it means to wait for a computer system to add value to a company's operations. We also know how much value is lost to downtime and equipment malfunctions.

Let us help you make the most of your Macintosh. Whether you use your Macintosh in isolation or as part of a network, we can help you select the best combination of hardware and software for your needs.

We also keep you up and running with monthly visits, training, and online assistance. Give Prometrix a call today at 364–1100 and start unleashing the full potential of your Macintosh.

---

**EXHIBIT 4**    **COVER LETTER SENT IN THE DIRECT MAILING**

Dear Fellow K.C. Businessperson:

Let us take this opportunity to introduce ourselves. Here at Prometrix, we are dedicated to helping customers get the most from their Macintosh computer systems. As a Mac user, we're sure you've had times when you've thought that maybe your system isn't doing all it can for you. Well, it doesn't have to be that way.

Our business is to assist you with your business. We do this by helping you get the most out of the computer equipment you presently own in addition to working with you to configure your system for the future. We'll take the time to learn not only your computer system, but your business as well.

Macintosh is all we do; we're experts in the field. Give us a call at 913/555-3905 anytime, even after hours. Put our experience to work for you.

Sincerely,

Colin Weigel, Director of Business Development

Enclosure

---

98.1 KUDL, 94.5 KMBR, and 94.1 KIXX, all popular, unobtrusive top 40 stations that were also played as background music in many stores and offices. On Tuesday of the last week, the direct mailing was sent out.

The Kansas City Hoops Fest went as planned, and over 1,600 t-shirts were given away or sold. In addition to the Hoops Fest, Prometrix also received exposure (in trade for some basic services) in various other events including the 50th anniversary ball of the Kansas City Philharmonic and the Kansas City Chiefs fan appreciation night, where their name appeared repeatedly on the scoreboard and was announced over the public address system.

## ✱ RESULTS OF THE AWARENESS CAMPAIGN

### *RESPONSE*

It did not take long for Prometrix to realize that they had struck gold with their efforts. By the second week, the office was receiving two to three calls per day, and that number doubled the following week. Because Steve was eager to see what kinds of companies were calling and what prompted them to call, he instructed anyone who received an inquiry to log this information about the company.

Inquiries came in steadily for about two weeks after the ad stopped running. Then they trailed off. After another two weeks had gone by, only about one or two calls per day were coming in.

A few calls came in from each charity event during which Prometrix received publicity. By and large, the response from the events was not impressive, and most inquiries were from other sponsors of the event.

Exhibit 5 provides a breakdown of the companies that inquired into Prometrix as a result of the awareness campaign. The overwhelming majority of respondents were small companies that were unaware that a service such as Prometrix's existed until they heard the radio ad. After a short telephone conversation briefly describing the service, about a third were still interested enough to set up an appointment to discuss further what Prometrix had to offer. Most of these conversations were with the founder or general manager.

Of the medium-sized companies that responded, over half requested an initial consultation. The contact person was most frequently a person who was heavily involved with the computer system on a day-to-day basis and who had the most to gain from being a subscriber. Again, the overwhelming majority cited the radio ad as the medium that prompted them to call.

| EXHIBIT 5 | BREAKDOWN OF BUSINESSES RESPONDING TO AWARENESS CAMPAIGN | |
|---|---|---|

| Company Size | Percent of Respondents | Percent of Respondents in Each Size Category Requesting an Initial Consultation |
|---|---|---|
| <100,000 | 28% | 65% |
| 100k to 500k | 23% | 62% |
| 500k to 3 Mln | 16% | 55% |
| 3 Mln to 10 Mln | 11% | 46% |
| 10 Mln to 30 Mln | 9% | 44% |
| 30 to 100 Mln | 7% | 43% |
| 100 Mln + | 6% | 40% |
| | 100% | 51% |

A few Kansas City branches of large corporations made inquiries, but once they learned that Prometrix consisted of only six people, they usually looked for an excuse to end the conversation.

The public events Prometrix sponsored generated only a few insignificant calls. The exception was the publicity that followed the Hoops Fest. The *Kansas City Business Journal*, a local business magazine widely read by managerial professionals, wrote an article spotlighting each corporate sponsor of the Hoops Fest, including Prometrix. The company spots, two short paragraphs each, highlighted how long they had been doing business in Kansas City, their product or service, and their address and telephone number. This article was written as a civic service to promote corporate sponsorship of charitable organizations. This write-up generated a number of calls from office managers of fairly well-known medium-sized companies. Of the four serious calls they received, two resulted in signed service contracts.

## CONVERSION

In assessing the entire awareness campaign, all six people in the Prometrix organization were initially enthusiastic, but that enthusiasm was short-lived.

Once the calls came in and an initial consultation was scheduled, either Colin, Leslie, or Steve would go on site to explain the service and try to either close the deal or at least arrange for another visit. The results of these short meetings were turning out to be quite predictable. With the smaller companies, the manager was usually impressed with the service—in fact, it was often more comprehensive than they had imagined. However, when the subject of price arose, the manager typically stated that they wanted the service but did not know if they could afford it.

By specifically underscoring how the system would be a net saver of money, Prometrix could sometimes close the deal, even if they ended up selling a more basic package. The profitability of the basic package was marginal at best, but it was thought that as the customer gained experience and satisfaction with Prometrix, the customer would soon upgrade as their needs grew.

The medium-sized companies seemed a little more enthusiastic over the phone. In the initial visit, Prometrix usually dealt with the top technical person who had taken the initiative to contact Prometrix in the first place. He or she was usually interested in most of Prometrix's services, and even when price was raised, enthusiasm did not seem to be dampened.

This person was often easily sold on the product, but progress hit a wall when Prometrix left and relied on him or her to follow through with their promise to sign on to the service. When contacted again, Prometrix was either told that funding could not be secured or were given some other excuse as to why they changed their mind. Only a couple of these medium-sized companies were signed over a three-week period.

## ✳ WHERE FROM HERE?

Steve was frustrated and discouraged. So much effort had gone into generating dozens of leads and they resulted in only a few quality long-term contracts. The radio ads seemed to have done their job extraordinarily well, but the direct mailing, which was really supposed to do the pre-consultation selling job, was rarely mentioned by inquirers. He summed up his feelings this way:

> *Companies all around the city know who we are now. We've visited with dozens of them and almost universally they rave about what we have to offer. So, what's the bottom line? They just don't buy.*
>
> *Sure, it's sometimes hard to visualize how our product makes a company money, but I'm confident that we do a pretty darn good job of communicating this to the people with whom we sit down and talk.*
>
> *We know that when we reach a certain size we'll have to add a sales force, but right now we can't even do the personal selling job necessary to close a deal. I'm not sure what else we can do.*

## ✳ CASE QUESTIONS

1. Identify the key issues faced by Prometrix, Inc.
2. Provide three alternative solutions for each of the key issues faced by Prometrix, Inc.
3. Discuss the pros and cons of each alternative solution provided.
4. Provide an overall recommendation for Prometrix, Inc. and justify your answer based on course material.

## ✳ NOTES

1. These lists were made up of only the buyers/users who have done business with a dealer or subscribed to a magazine. Each entity had its own different list. Apple was the only company to have a comprehensive owner/user list.
2. The Kansas City Hoop Fest was a large three-on-three basketball tournament held in the streets of downtown. It lasted about a week and was the subject of much publicity, including nightly spots on the evening news.

**\* APPENDIX**

# Prometrix.

## What is Prometrix?

Prometrix is a programming and consulting services company. We specialize in Apple Macintosh® and integrating it with other computers.

■ Our Macintosh consulting services can begin before your company purchases new systems or expands existing systems. Our recommendations are based exclusively on meeting your requirements—we don't sell computer systems.

We can show you the ins and outs of computer networks and communications. We can test new combinations of hardware and software for definitive answers about how you can share information on the Mac, as well as with PC compatibles, mainframe and minicomputers. Count on your com-

dled projects ranging from purchase order systems to Point of Purchase systems to visitor center scheduling systems. Depending on the job, we utilize 4th Dimension® multiuser relational database from Acius® Inc. and FileMaker® multiuser database from Claris®. We also do special projects with Wingz from Informix®, with Resolve™ and HyperCard® from Claris and with several mainframe connectivity packages. See the special section on the back page for more information.

■ Keeping your systems running optimally means more than replacing the rare broken part. Smooth operation primarily depends on software configuration. Subscribe to our Prefix Services for a monthly preventive maintenance check of all the systems in your office; exhaustive reports and telephone answers to all your questions, including something really exciting: Prometrix HelpLink— *We're there in sixty seconds...* See page three for more information about Prefix Services.

■ Getting up to speed can be straight forward for many tasks on the Macintosh. When you need extra help,

## Where Does Prometrix Work?

We work locally with clients all over Kansas City. Our central office location (in the Fairway Offices complex, at the Roe Avenue exit of I-35) was carefully selected for optimum access to most of the metro area.

■ Downtown KCMO is about 12 minutes from here; Corporate Woods about 14. That's important because we can come out to see you quickly, working on *your* system, getting *your* jobs done.

*Continued on Page Two*

*Inside*

## INTRODUCING PROMETRIX

**How to reach us at Prometrix...**

*Continued from Front Page*

■ Need quick answers to your questions over the phone? Our *local* phone number means *local* phone charges.

## How does Prometrix get the job done?

The job: make your work go as smoothly as possible. Here's how.

■ Perform continuous preventive maintenance to head off problems before they happen, and to plan for orderly enhancements.

■ Replace numerous off-the-shelf programs with a single custom program in cases where it could help you handle a job faster and more completely.

■ Help you exchange information effortlessly within/between your offices and your clients with easy-to-use electronic mail, computer faxes and file transfers.

■ Answer the regular quick questions with a single, local phone call to help you get right back to work.

■ Resolve complex problems in a hurry—we can be standing next to you *electronically* in about a minute. You may call it a miracle, or a real life saver. Or you can call it *Prometrix HelpLink.*

■ Make you more self-sufficient with the right tools and training.

## Why would you need Prometrix?

We could start with the same old 'save time and money.' Instead...

■ We can help your company get work done faster. Few have time to explore all the features available in even a single program. Undoubtedly, a few of them would help productivity; some would not. Call on our experience to sort them out.

■ What could be more consistent than a single, local phone call? Get to know us once. Hear a familiar voice. See a familiar face. You won't be retelling your entire life story to four different technicians during four different long distance phone calls.

We'll know you, your computer experience level, areas of emphasis, and non-computer background.

We'll know your system, exactly how it's configured and the interac-

tions between various programs—we keep an electronic version of your monthly Prefix analysis report online for fast lookups (see more about Prefix Services on page three).

We'll know your situation, including your turn-around requirements, how the various players in your office interact, and the directions you are headed with computer systems.

We offer consistent professional business practices and high ethics—we have appropriate charges for services, we conform to your company's purchasing and billing procedures and we're confidential and reliable on every project.

■ Our skills are specialized in Macintosh. We have broad and deep technical knowledge in-house, as well

*Continued on Back Page*

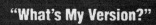

**"What's My Version?"**

## Get Full Time Help Without Extra Staff

## Prefix
### SERVICES

We're there in sixty   seconds...

Many companies have one, maybe two computer-saavy people who handle all the computer matters for the rest of the office. Usually they can't devote the necessary time for the computers and still get all their regular work done. It all adds up to a lot of frustrated people.

Prometrix can serve as your full time computer resource with no extra staff. We do this thing for a living, utilizing what we learn everyday to help your computer people be much more saavy.

■ First we run comprehensive diagnostics where all of your systems are vigorously interrogated over the network to find any unusual/unsatisfactory/unsavory configurations, including any computer viruses. We return concise printed reports along with our recommendations.

■ Next, we configure your systems the way you want them, making approved changes to file organization and to system and application software to get optimum performance. We do general cleanup of the mouse and disk drives, install standard computer virus protection software, and collect all file 'fragments' on your disk drives and put them back together for faster opening, saving and moving.

■ Then we help you keep everything running smoothly with regular preventive maintenance visits every month, including in-depth reports. See the special inset to the left for samples.

■ Ask us anything. Complete telephone support is included. It only takes one local phone call.

■ Show us anything. We can be standing next to you *electronically* in about a minute with Prometrix HelpLink. We can see your screen on our screen, help you with your mouse using our mouse, and type in text from our keyboards, and it's all done *over a phone line.*

■ Special consulting needs can be handled quickly and at a 35% discount for subscribers to our Prefix Services. ◆

## Three

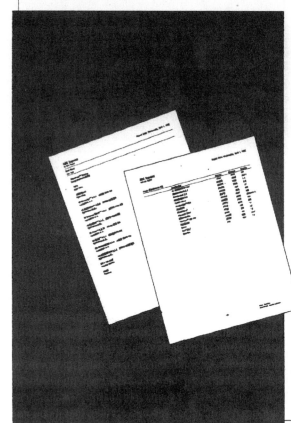

*Continued from Page Two*

as a wide array of resources for additional information. We do this full-time, for a living, keeping abreast of what's new and what works, and what's pertinent to you.

■ We translate Technical to Human— everyday English is spoken here (or German, if you like). You just won't hear us throwing techno-jargon around.

## Who is Prometrix?

Prometrix is incorporated in the state of Kansas by experienced Macintosh specialists. We have long-term local Kansas City roots, with family-owned businesses located here, combined with international roots for a global perspective. Our people resources include:

■ Four full-time staff people with combined experience of 20 years general Macintosh, 14 years custom database design, 8 years general PC, 15 years professional consulting, and 5 years electronic systems maintenance. Our formal educations include Journalism, Computer Science, Electrical Engineering, Electronics Maintenance and Psychology.

■ Two contract people with combined experience of 10 years general Macintosh, 8 years custom database design, 8 years application and utility programming, 5 years professional consulting and 7 years computer systems maintenance.

We have established track records of many years and proven solutions, with the accompanying enthusiastic references.

4330 Shawnee Mission Parkway, Suite 227
Shawnee Mission, Kansas 66205

*Printed on 100% Recycled Paper*

# CASE | 9

# ELECTRONIC BANKING SERVICES: HIGH-TECH, LOW-TOUCH?

## ✳ PROFILE OF A HIGH-TECH BANK

MeritaNordbanken is one of the leading financial services groups in the Nordic and Baltic Sea. With Finland and Sweden as its base, the Group develops and markets a broad range of financial products and services for private individuals, companies, institutions, and the public sector (see the organizational chart in appendix).

The customer base comprises about 6.5 million private individuals and more than 400,000 companies and institutions, which are serviced through 735 branch offices and 1,000 Swedish post offices. Customers also have access to an extensive network of bill payment ATMs and cash dispensers. Almost 2 million customers use MeritaNordbanken's network banking services, which include its telephone bank and PC/Internet bank.

MeritaNordbanken's vision is to assist its customers to grow by acting as their leading banking partner, the best supplier of electronic banking services and the most cost-effective financial service institute.

## ✳ EXPLAINING THE IMPORTANCE OF NETWORK-BANKING

The Internet has revolutionized the way that businesses operate and the financial world has not been spared. Financial services and online banking services are among the industries that flourished rapidly from an estimated US$240 million to US$22 billion by the turn of the century. Internet banking, online share trading, online mortgage and insurance services are all recording phenomenal growth. Online financial transactions have a clear cost advantage compared to traditional transactions. A brief look at MeritaNordbanken personnel data illustrates this point:

Source: Contributed by Stephan Martin, MBA candidate, Helsinki School of Economics and Business Administration.

| Number of employees at MeritaNordbanken | | |
|---|---|---|
| | 31-Dec-98 | 31-Dec-97 |
| Retail operations | 14,171 | 14,824 |
| Asset management | 238 | 196 |
| Corporate | 1,312 | 1,214 |
| Markets | 615 | 656 |
| Central staff units (incl. service units) | 2,096 | 2,063 |
| Banking operations, total | 18,399 | 18,986 |
| Real estate | 270 | 381 |
| Subsidiaries (other subsidiaries and companies in temporary ownership) | 1,130 | 1,239 |
| MeritaNordbanken Group, total | 19,799 | 20,606 |

(Source: http://www.merita.fi)

The figures of MeritaNordbanken's personnel from 1997 to 1998 have declined by 653 employees in retail operations (the front-line staff of banks) and by 807 for the whole group. This reduction in the number of personnel is illustrative of the cost-savings generated by the rapid development of online banking services of the MeritaNordbanken Group.

In parallel to the development of the Internet is the development of electronic commerce (e-commerce). One of the most critical elements enabling e-commerce is the banking and financial service sector. Where e-commerce has developed the banking and credit facilities are the major enablers of payment facilities for online transactions. To a large extent, e-commerce transaction relies on the intermediary role of banks, credit card companies and other financial institutions, which must be interconnected. Banks, thus, provide also an infrastructure that links local and national businesses with global banking network. Banks also give consumers, small businesses and local communities access to financial resources and services that will allow them to participate in e-commerce.

Another aspect that illustrates the growing importance of Internet banking services is the increased automation of data-entry and integration of systems within organizations which is eliminating data redundancy and errors due to data manipulations. These improvements are believed to help raise productivity in organizations.

Finally, the ability to provide better consumer service is also underlined as one of the factors contributing to the development of online banking. Direct communication with customers enable businesses to tailor their products and services to the individual preferences of their customers. Witness of this phenomenon is the proliferation of web sites providing individualization and personalization capacities to their online visitors. Businesses may provide their customers with personalized information and additional services that help them retain the loyalty of their customers. Customers also benefit from the ability to seek information and eventually shop, pay their bills, consult their accounts, transfer money, etc., at any time or day.

## ✳ INTERNET BANKING AT MERITANORDBANKEN

In a recent statement, available on the bank web site, Hans Dalborg, the Chief Executive Officer of the MeritaNordbanken group declared: "We have clearly exceeded our Internet banking goals for 1999, and we are ready to move forward. MeritaNordbanken is the number one bank in the world in terms of monthly log-ons, and we plan to stay at the top."

Services through data networks are deeply rooted in the MeritaNordbanken Group. They began in 1982 with automatic telephone payments and were expanded to PC services in 1984, GSM (cellular network) in 1992, the Internet in 1996 and TV in 1998. Today, almost all banking services can be carried out over the Internet.

By late 1998, the bank counted half a million customers using its data networks. The customer base today has grown to 1.1 million. Monthly log-ons to the Solo services on the Internet amount to 3 million. Nearly 4 million bills are paid via the Internet every month and the figure is constantly growing. The proportion of share purchase and sale orders and mutual fund transactions over the net has periodically reached 61 per cent and 10 per cent, respectively, in Finland. The growth of online banking is believed to carry on even further in the foreseeable future:

---

**Internet banking goals for 2000/2001**

5 million log-ons per month
6 million bill payments per month
2 million Internet banking clients (early 2001)

---

(Source: http://www.merita.fi )

## ✱ HOW NETWORK SERVICES CREATE CUSTOMER VALUE

Network services make it possible to handle routine items such as payments as well as sophisticated services regardless of the time or location, with various types of technical tools. Customers can save time and money and receive reports that provide a much better overview of assets, loans, cash flow and transactions.

"Customers with an Internet connection are more satisfied with their bank than other customers, which illustrates that customer value is appreciated," says Bo Harald, the Executive Vice President.

Customer value also arises through a growing service content, clarity, user-friendliness and volume-tolerating reliability.

## ✱ INTERNET SOLO SERVICES: A CUSTOMER PERSPECTIVE

The Finnish Bank has a simple interface and is available in three languages (Finnish, Swedish and English). The benefit for prospective customers is that one can test the online banking service with the training function. Interested customers may experience directly the types of services offered by the online bank by logging in with a generic customer number and password.

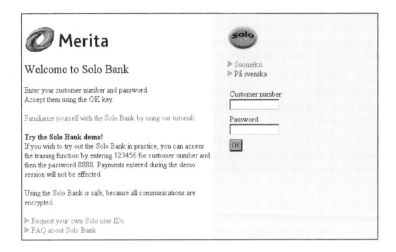

The Internet bank service provides a rapid overview of all the user accounts (current, investments and even loans). By clicking on any of these accounts, the user can have a detailed list of all debits and credits that occurred from each of his accounts as well as the name of the payee or payer. Transactions can be set both in Euros and Finnish Marks.

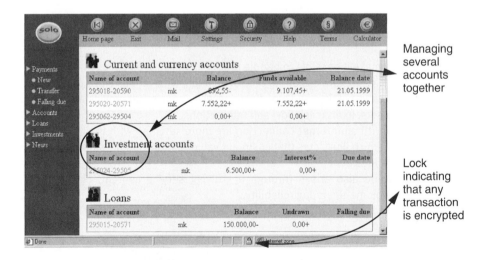

Furthermore, the online bank permits users to invest in high interest accounts or directly on the stock and bond market. However, some of the instructions on how to proceed are still not available in English.

Merita bank also offers the ability to pay bills online. The online payment form is simple and user-friendly. It requires the account number of the recipient and its name.

A unique reference number is inserted and the user enters the due date as well as the amount of the bill. There is an option which allows users to receive a receipt for a small fee.

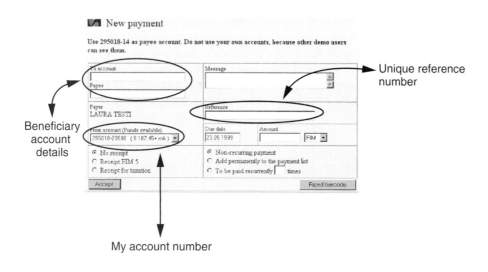

Basic online services such as account monitoring and payments are available to Merita customers for about 120 marks a year (about $20). More complicated services (share trading, lending, investments) are available for an additional 540 marks a year (about $45) plus an additional charge for each buying and selling transaction.

The bank also displays clearly its policy with matters regarding security of transactions and the protection of customer data. Encryption software is used to protect data sent across networks and the little lock logo at the bottom of the browser attests that it is doing so.

For customers who do not have access to the Internet at home, the physical bank has several PCs at the disposition of its customers. These are also used to train and educate customers to use the bank's system. It is not uncommon to see an elderly customer alongside an employee teaching the basics of Internet banking.

Finally, a telephone number is provided to customers who wish to contact an employee should they face any problems during their online experience.

## ✳ FUTURE PROSPECTS

Strong of its advance in terms of network banking services, MeritaNordbanken continues its progression by adding further services via the Internet. For example, up to 16% of credit applications are currently sent to the bank via the Internet. This trend, explains

Bo Harald, is "something which has revolutionized the old thinking that personal service is always indispensable in negotiations on household loans."

In addition to new services, Merita is pioneering the use of the latest technologies for its wireless banking services. Basically, the bank plans to offer all services currently available with the online Solo services directly to its customers' mobile phones. A WAP- (Wireless Application Protocol) enabled mobile telephone can be used for account and credit card transaction monitoring, account-to-account transfers and bill payments. It also enables shopping at MeritaNordbanken's virtual marketplace, the Solo Mall, already familiar to Internet banking customers. All these services will be free of charge until the end of February 2000. Thereafter a monthly charge of FIM 4.00 will be introduced. Stock trading will be the next service to be made available via WAP phones.

## ✳ CASE QUESTIONS

1. Analyze the impact of internet banking on the components of the services marketing mix.
2. Is the servuction model still a valid framework to explain a customer's experience?
3. Evaluate the role of customers as partial employees.
4. How should future services be promoted?

**APPENDIX**

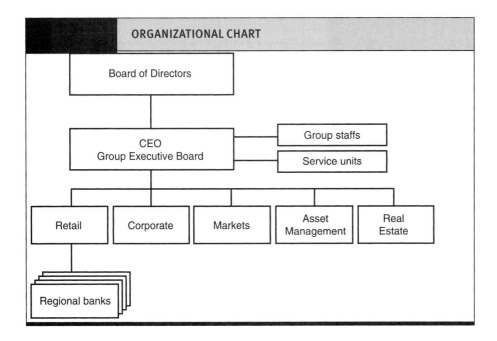

ORGANIZATIONAL CHART

Board of Directors

CEO
Group Executive Board

Group staffs

Service units

Retail | Corporate | Markets | Asset Management | Real Estate

Regional banks

# O'KEEFE ASSOCIATES

The partner meeting of O'Keefe Associates,[1] a preeminent management consulting firm, had gotten underway and Kevin O'Keefe, the founding father of the firm, had just announced that he would be removing himself from all decision-making positions. He would be passing control of the firm to its vice-presidents, the new partners of the firm.

Recent events had made this departure inevitable, and it had been expected for some time. Despite this, Aviva Katz felt a lump form in her throat, and she quickly reached for the glass of Dom Perignon in front of her. In her haste, she knocked it clean across the shining mahogany into the lap of Henning Amelung who, even as he felt the wetness permeate his clothes, directed his gaze calmly at her, kind of waiting for an apology. She had half a mind to not offer one but decided to leave personal battles for another day, for today belonged to Kevin O'Keefe, the patriarch who had started the firm 18 years ago. She gestured an apology to the unruffled Henning and her mind started to churn. Kevin's departure meant that the vice-presidents had to quickly regroup and decide the immediate fate of the firm. The consulting industry had been declining for the past two years, and O'Keefe Associates had born the brunt of the downturn due to their connection with a recent, well-publicized lawsuit. The right moves now could stem client erosion, reverse reputation damage, and set the firm on the course to rejuvenation; the wrong moves would mean a slow demise.

> *I've watched this firm grow just like I've watched my own children, and perhaps with as much love and care. This makes the decision I face even more difficult. But like most painful decisions, it is inevitable.*

## ✳ BRIEF HISTORY OF O'KEEFE

Kevin O'Keefe had stepped into the management consulting world with the start-up Boston Consulting Group (BCG). Industry watchers and insiders attributed his meteoric rise within BCG to an undying commitment to deliver to his clients' bottom line. He succeeded in consistently doing so by coming up with unorthodox ideas and ensuring that his recommendations were implementable. In 1971 he left BCG with three of his

---

Source: Copyright©1996 by Professor Brian Wansink.

colleagues to form O'Keefe Associates. In an interview at a later date, he gave the following reason for his move: "Paul [another O'Keefe founding father] and I were bringing in about half the revenue for the firm. We operated independently and, over time, drifted away from everyone at BCG. Finally, my entrepreneurial urge got the better of me and I decided to start O'Keefe Associates."

Kevin had built a strong reputation for himself. His clients openly commended him. He earned the respect of colleagues and competitors after creating the highly effective O'Keefe Model for strategy formulation, which was first published in the Harvard Business Review and won the award for the year's best article. When he moved out on his own, his clients decided to continue retaining him. At the same time, three of his colleagues: Paul Vivek, John Hartmann, and Ted Chesner decided to join him. They decided to split up the ownership of the firm based on the projected revenues each could bring. Consequently, Kevin held 37 percent ownership, Paul 33 percent, and John and Michael, 15 percent each.

O'Keefe Associates focused on high-level corporate and business-unit strategy consulting and shied away from industry specialization. Charging the highest billing rates in the industry, they introduced the concept of relationship consulting[2] and focused on a single client in each industry. In return, they asked that their clients not engage any other consulting firm. This one-to-one relationship set the firm apart in the industry and gave CEOs the assurance that their company's secrets and strengths would not be exposed to potential and existing competitors.

Each of the partners had the potential to be a powerful rainmaker at most firms in the industry; together they formed a powerhouse. They leveraged Kevin's reputation and warm personality very effectively with clients as well as with potential recruits at the top three business schools in the United States. As a start-up that promised to reach stellar heights, O'Keefe Associates attracted the topmost talent at schools. As a consulting firm that brought a unique proposition to the table, they attracted Fortune 500 clients from all industries. The result was the perfect high-growth formula, and by 1980, a mere nine years after its birth, O'Keefe Associates had registered itself on the radar of the bigger, more established consulting firms.

As it grew, O'Keefe Associates won friends as well as enemies. While about 80 percent of clients had nothing but praise for them, others felt they had been poorly served. In response to a question asking for their opinion of the firm, respondents had this to say:

> O'Keefe has the brightest talent in the industry. Moreover, their people are not snobs like most consultants are. They mix well with our employees, come up with truly innovative out-of-the-box ideas, and work at convincing all levels of our hierarchy. They know how to address bottom-line concerns and they know how to produce bottom-line results. If I were stranded on a remote desert island, the one thing I'd want with me is an O'Keefe consultant.

> *CEO of a Fortune 500 chemicals company*

> O'Keefe may be good intellectually, but they have been inconsistent in dealing with us. Some of the advice they gave us set the company back 10 years. Once

when I needed support to defend one of their recommendations to my CEO, they just did an about-face on me, like they had never made the recommendation! They leave me with the feeling that they would do anything to save their own necks!

*SBU Manager of a Fortune 500 manufacturer*

One of the probable reasons for this variation in quality of service was the growth rate: O'Keefe could not grow its people into experienced consultants fast enough to serve the needs of the entire client base. As a result, some clients suffered. Business media, which thrives on reporting the out-of-the-ordinary, picked up on stories disgruntled clients had to tell. The ensuing bad press hurt O'Keefe's image and, by many accounts, they managed to survive only because clients found it impossible to change consultants due to contractual obligations and costs involved in getting new consultants up to speed. Over the next two years or so, the founding partners worked hard at avoiding similar embarrassment by building good relations with the media, convincing clients with success stories to speak out, and implementing rigorous recruiting and training procedures. Their efforts at improving quality and cleaning up the image of the firm worked, and they were able to continue commanding the highest billing rates in the industry.

## ✳ O'KEEFE'S ORGANIZATION

O'Keefe Associates was organized like most other partnerships. After inception, part of the firm's ownership was given to employees via the Employee Stock Ownership Plan (ESOP), primarily as an incentive for them to help the firm grow. The four founding fathers continued to hold most of the equity in the firm, and vice-presidents held the rest (about 10 percent). The 27 vice-presidents, all officers of the firm, reported to the partners and managed the activities of 68 managers while having complete responsibility for relationships with two to seven clients (depending on the size of the clients). Managers were responsible for one to three cases that were staffed by senior associates, associates, and research associates (RAs). Senior associates helped in conducting the case while assuming responsibility for case modules.[3] Associates managed case modules. RAs helped case teams analyze data and came up with helpful insights. They were high-performing undergraduates, while associates were the top graduates of the three most highly rated business schools in the country. A typical case team was made up of one vice-president, one manager, two senior associates, four associates, and two RAs. Turnover among associates and RAs was high, with about 50 percent of recruits staying on till the three-year mark, at which they made senior associate. Senior associates made manager within about two years. Managers who showed an aptitude for managing client relationships were promoted to vice-president after about three years. Base compensation at all levels was high (an associate started at $70,000 a year plus a $30,000 sign-up bonus) and above industry norms. Top performers earned annual bonuses of up to about 50 percent of the base salary.

# * THE MANAGEMENT CONSULTING INDUSTRY

Although the management consulting industry can be entered easily by engaging any one client, it is one of the toughest service industries to survive in. The following characteristics explain why.

Consultants face the toughest business problems. Consulting firms have high billing rates, and each engagement costs the client a lot of money and other resources. Consequently, businesses tend to call in consultants if they offer innovative solutions (e.g., CSC Index's reengineering, BCG's Matrix) or if the management is perplexed about a certain problem. Problems that perplex upper management are tough to solve, since the upper management of large businesses is made up of very bright people.

Convincing management about recommendations is an arduous task. As mentioned earlier, senior management is made up of bright people who have known their business and industry well for many years. As a result, all recommendations have to be thoroughly supported, and all levels of the client's hierarchy have to buy in to them.

In many cases, it is difficult to measure results. The nature of the problems is such that it is difficult to discern the impact of a recommended solution. The result of adopting a recommended strategy may not be visible for years. Observed outcomes could be the result of factors other than the recommendation. Even when the result can be distinctly identified, it is impossible to tell whether a better recommendation could have been made. This also leads to difficulty in discerning the quality of advice.

Good employees are hard to come by. Employees are the largest constituent of the costs incurred by a consulting firm and are the factor that allows a firm to distinguish itself. Consequently, the recruiting process is rigorous and expensive (see Exhibit 1). Also, since many firms end up competing for the same people, recruitment yields[4] are lower than in other industries.

It is difficult to retain employees. After expending a great number of resources on recruiting, consulting firms face the challenge of retaining employees. This is primarily because consultants lead high-pressure lives plagued with immovable deadlines and consequently long hours. Many recruits burn out quickly, while others leave due to lifestyle issues.

Consultants are always viewed as expendable. If profits come under severe pressure, businesses will first dispense with consultants. This can lead to consulting firms' facing costs without getting revenues; this pressures them to cut costs by laying off employees. This action not only results in the loss of superior resources but also creates a poor reputation for future recruiting efforts.

It is important to be differentiated, clearly positioned, and well reputed. Only distinguishable firms are consistently able to attract talented employees as well as clients; others succumb to vagaries of the economy or to competition.

The management consulting industry can be divided into five categories.[5] These categories are the following:

1. Pure strategy advisors: These are small firms that provide high-cost advice to corporate and business-unit management (O'Keefe belongs in this category). The competition is strong, though gentlemanly. These firms compete for the topmost talent and compensate their employees extremely well. Their costs are consequently the highest

| EXHIBIT 1 | THE CONSULTING RECRUITING PROCESS |
|-----------|-----------------------------------|

Consulting firms have a rigorous recruitment process. This process is also costly since employees have to be pulled off cases to visit campuses to conduct interviews and select candidates. Candidates selected on campus then visit the office of the hiring firm and are interviewed by more employees. The following is an excerpt from a guide to interviewing with consulting firms.

Most consulting firms conduct case interviews. The primary purpose of these interviews is to get an idea of how well you break a problem down and then logically try to solve it. Due to the nature of the interview they also get to see how you think on your feet and how well you keep your composure. At times, they also get to see how quickly you bounce back after making mistakes.

In addition to problem-solving ability, interviewers make judgments about your ability to work in teams and lead at client sites. Usually, the last question the interviewer has to answer on the evaluation form is, "Would you like this person to be on your team tomorrow?"

Consulting firms recruit through a multi-round process. Some firms have three rounds, while others have only two. In the first round, you interview with one person, and in subsequent rounds you have back-to-back interviews with two to three people. Each of these interviews ranges from 30 to 45 minutes.

In addition to other factors, doing well at case interviews requires skill. Like all other skills, this one can be learned by practice.

### ANATOMY OF A CASE INTERVIEW

An interview typically begins with 10 minutes of resume-based discussion. During this, the usual set of questions (why consulting, etc.) are asked. Following this, the interviewer presents a business case and asks you general/specific questions. Your analysis will probably be guided in the direction your interviewer wants you to go, so do not ignore comments or instructions. With each additional insight, the interviewer will probe deeper and push you to the next issue. While there is no right answer to any case, you will generally be expected to take a stand (state a hypothesis) at the end of the case. You should base this stand on what your analysis reveals, any assumptions you want to make, and any input the interviewer gives you. The following are examples of case questions:

An overseas construction firm wants to establish its presence in a growing regional U.S. market. What advice would you give it?

A major airline is considering acquiring an existing route from Tokyo to New York. How can it determine whether the route is a good idea?

An Israeli travel agent has been extremely successful. His primary source of revenue is customers who fly to and from the United States. He manages to fill up over two planeloads on a daily basis. Given his success, he is considering buying an aircraft and plying the U.S.-Tel Aviv route himself. What advice would you give him?

How would you compare the airline industry with the baby food industry? In which would you invest your own money?

Source: Copyright©1996 by Professor Brian Wansink.

among all segments. Examples of this category are The Boston Consulting Group, LEK Partnership, and Bain & Company.

2. Traditional management consultants: These firms consult in all areas and are somewhat diversified in that sense. They offer strategy consulting services as well as advice in functional areas. These are large in size, and competition between them is keen but polite. Examples are Booz, Allen & Hamilton, McKinsey & Co., and Arthur D. Little.

3. Accounting firms (Big 6): These firms are recent entrants looking for new sources of revenue. They have well-established client relationships due to their accounting services and are now trying to leverage these relationships. Traditionally, these firms dealt in functional areas such as accounting and information services. Through acquisitions of specialist strategy boutiques and in-house expansion, they are now encroaching on the territory of management consultants. Competition among these firms is high, and costs are relatively low. Examples are Andersen Consulting, Coopers & Lybrand, and Deloitte Touche.

4. Human resource firms: These are mid-sized firms designing compensation packages for clients. Their costs are low since they do not recruit at top business schools. Competition in this category is intense. Examples are Sibson & Co., and Johnson & Higgins.

5. Specialized firms: These firms advise clients in specialized areas (e.g., financial services). Their costs are at a level between those of accounting firms and traditional firms. This category includes sole practitioners (college professors, retired executives, etc.). Competition in this category is fierce. Examples are Oliver Wyman & Co., and Marketing Corporation of America (MCA).

The management consulting industry enjoyed spectacular success and grew at the rate of about 20 percent annually through the last decade.[6] This boom had attracted many new entrants. A downturn in the U.S. economy started the current decline two years ago. Financially strapped clients started terminating engagements prematurely, and recent entrants started falling like ninepins. New engagements were being given to the lower-priced accounting firms.[7] Faced with global competition and technological changes, clients looked for help from specialists, and the demand for the services of generalists crashed. The industry began to consolidate, with outside buyers recognizing an opportunity to buy several firms and merge them. Summarily, the industry was experiencing change like it had never experienced before, and the foreseeable future did not seem to promise any stability.

## * CUSTOMERS

O'Keefe's clients were CEOs or divisional heads of Fortune 500 companies seeking advice on strategy formulation or implementation. They engaged O'Keefe because they looked for top-quality advice and an exclusive relationship. Client business units typically had revenues greater than $100 million since smaller operators could not afford O'Keefe's billing rates.

Customers for the management consulting industry cut across all industries and come in all shapes and sizes. Some require ongoing advice, while others call in consultants on an "as needed" basis. Matters on which they need advice range from corporate strategy to operational improvement. Some clients have substantial in-house capability to implement recommendations, while others need ongoing support and help during implementation. Without variation, all customers pay top dollar and demand top performance.

## ✴ RECENT OCCURRENCES AT O'KEEFE ASSOCIATES

The last two years had brought rough times to O'Keefe Associates. The decline in the consulting market resulting from the economy-wide decline had forced clients to cut engagements and stretch receivables to the maximum. This placed tremendous financial pressure on O'Keefe, but the company was able to handle it reasonably well by finding new clients. However, as the market decline commenced, an employee at the Canadian office was named as a co-defendant in a lawsuit brought by client shareholders against client management for undervaluing a recent divestiture.

The lawsuit was fairly complicated. In it, the shareholders claimed that some senior managers were part owners of the closely held acquiring firm. By undervaluing the divestiture, management had cheated shareholders for personal gain. The O'Keefe consultant claimed he was innocent and had no knowledge of any wrongdoing. His name was finally dissociated from the lawsuit, but only after he had agreed to testify against client management. The scandal had been well publicized by the popular and business press, and O'Keefe's reputation had been badly damaged. Moreover, the Canadian client had engaged 40 O'Keefe consultants, who were suddenly left without a case to work on. The loss in revenue and poor market conditions had forced O'Keefe to lay off 65 employees.

The story did not end there. The firm was also in deep financial trouble. During the growth years (O'Keefe revenues grew at about 40 percent annually), the firm's financial needs had been met through internally generated cash and limited bank borrowing. Seeing the steady, low-debt-burden growth of the firm, the founding partners had decided to cash in on their success by selling their holdings to the ESOP. To compensate them, the ESOP had to borrow heavily from various banks, and this placed a heavy debt burden on the firm. In the current downturn, it became impossible for the firm to meet its debt commitments: it was brought to the verge of declaring bankruptcy. Rumor also had it that Kevin O'Keefe had conducted negotiations to sell the firm to an outside buyer but that they had been unable to see eye to eye.

Facing the combined onslaught of reduced business and financial distress, O'Keefe had no choice but to cut costs further. A second round of layoffs was followed by a third. The crisis that ensued had finally forced Kevin O'Keefe to step down as managing director. It had also been decided that the firm would restructure its debt after the founding fathers agreed to revalue the firm and return some of the money they had taken from the ESOP. Consequently, the debt burden would become somewhat more manageable. Challenges that still faced the vice-presidents were

The Canadian lawsuit and financial trouble had severely hurt the firm's reputation among current and potential clients. Consequently, there was a danger of losing more clients without gaining any.

The skeletal staff remaining was barely able to service the needs of clients. Experienced consultants had been retained, but associates and RAs (who had been laid off) were sorely needed. However, the layoffs had hurt O'Keefe's reputation on college campuses, and potential recruits were largely ignoring the firm.

Remaining consultants were insecure in their positions, and morale was low. There was a danger that many more would leave very soon if nothing were done to address their concerns. Those leaving first would probably be the best since they would be in high demand.

The departing leadership had left a void, and the firm needed to establish direction quickly.

## ✱ O'KEEFE NOW

Following Kevin's departure, the first order of business for the new partners was to elect a new leader for the firm. The partner meeting for this election had been scheduled already, and the two vice-presidents that were expected to be nominated for managing director were Aviva Katz and Henning Amelung. The following profiles characterize these two well.

### *AVIVA KATZ*

Aviva was one of the earliest employees of O'Keefe Associates. Prior to attending Harvard Business School, she was a nurse with the U.S. Army. She had dazzled professors and fellow students at Harvard with her intellectual prowess and sharp wit. During her summer job at O'Keefe, she was convinced that she wanted to come back and share in and contribute to the success of the firm. Once there, she had quickly won the confidence of the founding fathers and had built a strong client base in the consumer products area. Through the late seventies and early eighties, Aviva was the top revenue earner for the firm. More recently, she had cut back on work hours to spend more time with her family. Aviva was well respected and fondly liked by most colleagues. For many, she was the ideal choice for managing director.

### *HENNING AMELUNG*

The descendant of a wealthy German family, Henning Amelung had graduated from the Amos Tuck School and joined the firm in 1981. Within the first two years he had distinguished himself and won accolades for creative solutions that helped in turning around some steel industry clients. Seeing his penchant for finance, Kevin O'Keefe had allowed him to start a venture capital subsidiary, which turned out to be a super success. While Henning drew respect from colleagues and clients, he had a reputation for being a ruthless driver of case teams. One RA had this to say about his experience working with Henning:

> Its almost as though you are a piece of machinery. Your feelings do not exist, you are tireless, and you respond without questioning. That's how he treats you. I was

told when I joined that vacation is considered sacred by all at O'Keefe and by and large I have found that to be true. But Henning considers nothing sacred except the directions he gives you. If I'm assigned to another case with him, I'm quitting!

Henning was an extremely hard worker and expected others to follow suit. His entrepreneurial success, "nose for the money," and drive made him a strong candidate for managing director.

## AVIVA'S PLATFORM

Aviva was acutely aware that in making their choice for managing director, partners would consider the nominee's views about the future strategy of the firm. Consequently, she was confident she would win since she felt her stick-to-historical-strengths perspective was more popular. Salient aspects of this viewpoint were:

Maintain the one-client-per-industry offering. This had helped in setting the firm apart from the rest of the industry and had helped their initial growth. No other firm had built this capability, and it promised O'Keefe a competitive advantage.

Remain general management consultants. The firm had built a reputation for being generalists and had the talent pool to support that position. Specialization in functional or industry areas means (a) building expertise in them, probably by hiring experienced people,[8] and (b) dealing with functional management instead of top management that O'Keefe had customarily dealt with.

Maintain a wide geographical presence. During its high-growth years, O'Keefe had expanded nationwide and internationally by establishing offices in 16 cities. This had been done to (a) be closer to clients to create a stronger partnership with them and (b) reduce travel requirements for employees. Many partners felt that both issues were extremely important and that O'Keefe should not change this position in any way.

While Aviva espoused these views, she had heard from colleagues that Henning's view was markedly different and was based on the premise that the firm's situation would not improve without radical change. He felt that O'Keefe's strategy had been appropriate for entry and initial growth but that now it had to adapt to the times and the competitive environment. Hearsay had it that his views were

O'Keefe should accept more than one client per industry. In the past, they had turned away business to honor their one-client-per-industry policy, and there was no telling how much revenue had been forgone. Some partners felt that in the current situation, they could not afford to be picky and turn away more business.

O'Keefe should be general management consultants with specialized strengths in some areas. Specialization was important as the market demand was heading in that direction. But there were very few general management firms left in the marketplace, and while there was a temporary lull in demand, many industry watchers expected it to bounce back. Keeping the general management strength would mean carrying some employees and partners without adequate business to keep them busy. Building specialization would mean training senior staff and hiring experienced people.

Operations should be consolidated geographically; service coverage should be maintained. Since prestigious firms buy or rent prestigious office space, O'Keefe's lease and mortgage payments were astronomical. Although most internal services were centralized in Washington, D.C., some office staff and services were required to support each location. The current level of business in most offices did not justify maintaining them.

Aviva realized that Henning's perspective was not altogether without merit; however, she was confident that the majority of partners wanted the firm to continue doing what it knew best. She was sure that the discussion about respective platforms prior to the vote would position her well. There was, however, the possibility of the group's digressing to the issue of the firm's reputation. In the recent past, Aviva had been very vocal about her stand on this issue and had discovered, much to her surprise, that the majority opposed her views. While she had tried to tone down her stand on the issue, a complete about-face would not have reflected well on her. Besides, she did feel very strongly about her beliefs. She advocated that

O'Keefe must rebuild its reputation through high-quality advice and renewed commitment to client bottom lines, much the way it had done in the past. The resulting favorable word-of-mouth will ensure reestablishment of O'Keefe's reputation.

To regain high visibility in a positive light, O'Keefe's partners and employees should publish their work in business periodicals and journals, form alliances with prominent universities, and encourage employees to become involved in community services.

Under no circumstances should O'Keefe increase starting salaries to become more attractive on campuses. This would be self-defeating since potential recruits would see this as a sign of weakening reputation.[9] Besides, this would necessitate revising salaries for all employees, resulting in higher cost when the firm least needed them.

She was sure that Henning saw the merit in her position on the reputation issue. Her sources had informed her, though, that he had opportunistically aligned himself with the perceived majority, which favored

Undertaking a concerted advertising effort via advertisements indicating that O'Keefe was still a strong player. Placed in eminent business periodicals, these would emphasize O'Keefe's past successes and current strengths by quoting clients. They would assert that O'Keefe's had always focused on bottom-line results. Such a strategy had recently been executed by Andersen Consulting with significant success.

Actively promoting positive word-of-mouth. This could be done by targeting champion CEO(s) and offering O'Keefe's services with a guarantee or at concessional terms. Champions would be high-profile entrepreneurs or executives who are quoted in the media often and are respected for their opinions.

Offering new recruits higher starting salaries and bonuses. Money was a strong motivator, and there would be a salary level beyond which recruits would have a very hard time declining offers. O'Keefe's weakened reputation was no secret; not raising salaries was not going to fool anyone.

Aviva was critical of these views, especially the aggressive promotion of word-of-mouth. Arranging for a quid pro quo with senior level executives was unthinkable. Even if one were arranged, how could O'Keefe offer guarantees? In case of success stories, how could they be sure that O'Keefe would get desired exposure? She just did not think these ideas were implementable, and even if they were, she felt they would not go down well with clients.

The partners' meeting was still about an hour away, and Aviva decided to go get some coffee. When she returned she found Michael Silfen, a rising star and currently a manager, waiting for her. Aviva was Michael's mentor[10] and had also worked with him in the past. They shared a strong, positive relationship.

Hi, Michael! What can I do for you?

Hi, Aviva, Something's come up and I need your advice, that is if you have the time.

I have a few minutes. What's up?

Well, it's like this. A headhunter cold-called me about two weeks age. We struck up a conversation, and to cut a long story short, I have received a very, very attractive offer from a competitor. I'm torn between memories of the good times and the sheer frustration of being here now. Any ideas about what I should do?

Aviva heaved a quiet sigh. This was going to be a long evening, and the battle had already begun.

---

## ✳ CASE QUESTIONS

1. Identify the strengths and weaknesses and the opportunities and threats that are faced by O'Keefe Associates.
2. Who will be voted managing director?
3. What should the firm's strategy be going forward?
4. How should the firm handle its reputation problem?
5. What should Aviva say to Michael Silfen? If you were in his shoes, would you take the competitor's job offer?

## ✳ NOTES

1. O'Keefe and O'Keefe Associates have been used synonymously.
2. Relationship consulting means that the client and the consulting firm maintain an ongoing relationship as opposed to having a relationship for the term of an engagement only.
3. Managers usually divided a case assignment into related tasks known as case modules.
4. Recruitment yield is defined as the ratio between the number of recruits accepting the firm's offer to the total number of offers given out by the firm. At 66 percent, O'Keefe's ratio was one of the highest in the industry.
5. Shankar Suryanarayanan, "Trends and Outlook for US Consulting," *Journal of Management Consulting* 5, 4(1989), pp. 4–5.
6. Ibid.
7. Ibid.
8. This would be a marked departure for O'Keefe. Prestigious firms traditionally hired fresh MBAs and groomed them to fit the firm's culture. Although there had been instances of competitors' relaxing this rule, many within O'Keefe were quite opposed to doing so.
9. While high salaries were important to recruits, many surveys had shown that firm reputation and prestige were the topmost considerations.
10. O'Keefe had a mentoring system in which new associates were assigned to mentors, usually vice-presidents. These mentors advised mentees on matters regarding performance, social adjustment, and career planning.

# PASSENGER-INDUCED TURBULENCE

The service encounter is often a shared experience where customers can have a profound impact on each other's overall experience. Nowhere is this more evident than sharing an airplane with hundreds of "other customers." During the late 1990s and continuing into the 2nd millennium, the popular press has been full of stories that describe incidents of "air rage" or "passenger-induced turbulence." Areas known to contribute to disruptive behavior include alcohol abuses, sexual misconduct, smoking in nonsmoking areas, failure to follow boarding instructions, violating carry-on baggage restrictions, and a variety of other confrontations dealing with lapses in creature comforts, crew training, and food quality.

Clearly, the airlines are concerned and are part of the problem. During the summer of 2000, the CEO of United Airlines publicly apologized to the airline's customers during United's stalled contract negotiations with employees. Numerous flights were canceled or delayed. United admitted on television commercials that their airline had failed to deliver on its basic promise—to service its customers. The voice of the customer is being heard loud and clear as customers are letting the airlines know when violations of customer service occur. Air traveler complaints are up 25%, and the number of incidents involving passengers interfering with flight crews has more than tripled over the last ten years. However, the airlines themselves are not totally to blame for what's going on in the skies up above. Clearly, some customers are out of control.

One of the more recent problems deals with increasing numbers of passengers performing sex in their seats or in airplane restrooms. "It's unihibited up there these days," says psychologist Christina Lawrence, a former United Airlines flight attendant. Airline consultant, Agnes Huff, agrees . . . "People used to be discreet. But more and more passengers these days are pushing the limits." In one case involving a South African Airways jumbo jet, a couple disrobed and began having sex in full view of other customers. Flight attendants summoned the captain who was quoted as saying . . . "this plane is not a shag

---

Source: Asra Q. Nomani, "In the Skies Today, A Weird New Worry: Sexual Misconduct," *Wall Street Journal* (June 10, 1998), p. A1; Frances Fiorino, "Passengers Who Carry Surly Bonds of Earth' Aloft," *Aviation Week and Space Technology* 149 (5), (December 28, 1998), p. 123.

house!"—South African slang for bordello. In another incident, numerous members of a company sales group became intoxicated and began to expose themselves to other passengers. One couple, who was part of the group, consummated their office romance on the plane while being cheered on by other members of the group. The captain cut-off liquor sales, but the group continued to drink by opening their own personal bottles of liquor that were purchased at the duty-free shop before boarding. In yet another incident, the flight attendant of a Delta airlines flight felt compelled to knock on the door of the plane's bathroom. Inside a Southern California woman was having sex with her boyfriend. After the passenger responded that she would be out "in a second," the frustrated flight attendant began citing federal rules that do not allow the plane to land unless all passengers are seated.

The policing of customer misconduct aboard planes is a tricky issue. According to one flight attendant, "At 37,000 feet, you don't have the option of throwing people out like you can in a cocktail lounge."

## ✳ CASE QUESTION

1. As the airline's Training Director, how would you instruct employees to handle situations that involve disruptive customers?

# MEASURING CUSTOMER SATISFACTION: THE FEDEX APPROACH

When Federal Express first opened its doors on April 17, 1973, it shipped eight packages, seven of which were trial runs addressed from one Federal Express employee to another. No one had any idea that this event marked the birth of an entire industry—overnight mail or parcel delivery. Particularly inspiring to college students is that Fred Smith, the CEO of FedEx, had sketched out the early details of the operation in an undergraduate paper at Yale University. The paper was given a grade of "C." By 1990, the company was generating $7 billion in annual sales revenue and controlled 43 percent of the air express mail market.

FedEx has two ambitious goals: 100 percent customer satisfaction with every interaction and transaction, and 100 percent performance on every package handled. In its early days, Federal Express defined service quality as the percentage of packages delivered on time. After cataloging complaints for many years, it had become apparent that percentage of on-time delivery was an internal measure of service quality and did not necessarily reflect absolute service quality by customer standards.

The customer's definition of service quality, which included eight service failures to be avoided, became known as the "Hierarchy of Horrors" and included (1) wrong-day delivery; (2) right day, late delivery; (3) pick-up not made; (4) lost package; (5) customer misinformed by FedEx; (6) billing and paperwork mistakes; (7) employee performance failures; and (8) damaged packages. Based on these categories generated by customer complaints, it was readily apparent that on-time delivery was not the only measure important to FedEx customers.

In addition to categorizing customer complaints, FedEx measures service quality by tracking 12 service quality indicators every day, both individually and in total. Moreover, the firm conducts numerous customer research studies each year in five major categories: (1) service quality studies, conducted quarterly, of four market segments: base business that is phoned to FedEx, U.S. export customers, manned-center customers, and

Source: Briefing Staff, Blueprints for Service Quality: The Federal Express Approach, AMA Management Briefing (American Management Association: New York, 1991). Reprinted by permission of the publisher. 1991 American Marketing Association. All rights reserved.

drop-box customers; (2) 10 targeted customer studies, conducted semiannually, that contact customers who have had an experience with one of 10 specific FedEx processes such as customer service, billing, and invoice adjustments; (3) FedEx center comment cards, which are collected and tabulated twice a year and used as feedback to the managers of each center; (4) customer automation studies of FedEx's 7,600 largest customers, representing 30 percent of the company's total package volume, who are equipped with automated systems that permit package tracking and a variety of other self-service activities; and (5) the Canadian customer study conducted yearly, which is the single most frequent point of destination for FedEx packages shipped outside the United States.

How successful is FedEx? In monetary terms, its success has been history making. FedEx was the first company in U.S. history to top $1 billion in revenues within its first 10 years of existence. Customer satisfaction ratings at FedEx are also legendary. The highest quarterly rating of customer satisfaction achieved thus far has been a 94 percent "completely satisfied" rating from customers on a 5-point scale that ranges from "completely dissatisfied" to "completely satisfied." Most firms combine "somewhat satisfied" and "completely satisfied" responses when calculating customer satisfaction ratings, but not at FedEx. Due to achievements such as these and many others, FedEx is a recipient of the Malcolm Baldrige National Quality Award.

## * CASE QUESTIONS

1. According to the case, FedEx has two ambitious goals: 100 percent customer satisfaction with every interaction and transaction, and 100 percent performance on every package handled. Using information provided in the text, should FedEx spend the money necessary to achieve these two goals?
2. Based on information provided in this case and within this chapter, discuss whether FedEx uses qualitative or quantitative methods to assess customer satisfaction. Provide specific examples of the type(s) of question(s) used.
3. What are the advantages and disadvantages of using solely quantitative measures of customer satisfaction?
4. What are the advantages and disadvantages of using solely qualitative measures of service quality?
5. What are the advantages of using qualitative and quantitative measures in combination?

# ROSCOE NONDESTRUCTIVE TESTING

After nine months, Grover Porter, president of Roscoe Nondestructive Testing, Inc. (Roscoe) was beginning to question the success of his new quality improvement program (QIP). Initiated in March 1991, the QIP had produced substantial increases in recent customer satisfaction surveys; however, none of that satisfaction seemed to be fueling a return to growth in either revenue or number of clients. Porter anticipated Roscoe's second down year in a row as the company continued to lose major customers, and he was eager to reestablish the growth that had preceded the last two years of decline.

It was hard to believe that the cyclical downturn in the pulp and paper industry had pushed the boiler inspection business to competing solely on price. Porter still felt that there was room in the industry for a quality service at a fair price, but the ineffectiveness of the QIP had prompted Porter to reconsider adjusting Roscoe's pricing structure.

## ✳ THE NONDESTRUCTIVE TESTING INDUSTRY

Nondestructive testing (NDT) involves the examination of materials to discover microscopic cracks, corrosion, or malformation, using inspection techniques that do not damage the material under scrutiny. Common inspection techniques include the use of x-rays, ultrasonics, and electrical eddy currents.

NDT is used in a wide variety of applications, including the examination of aircraft parts, tanks and vessels of various shapes and sizes, and welds of all kinds. Roscoe primarily uses ultrasonic thickness measuring devices to determine the thickness of metal plating.

NDT technicians are certified by area of expertise (e.g., ultrasonic) and accumulated skill and experience (Levels I–III). Technicians certified in more than one inspection

---

Source: This case was prepared by Brian Wansink and Eric Cannell as a basis for class discussion rather than to illustrate either effective or ineffective handling of an administrative situation.

technique are a treasured resource in most firms. They were generally employed by four types of companies:

1. Mom and pop labs usually employ less than 25 people and provide a single type of inspection service to a small number of customers. These firms are the low-cost providers and are quite willing to bid at cost simply to keep busy. Many are often tied to a single client who wields considerable control over pricing and delivery.

2. Nationwide companies have labs around the country and a high degree of name recognition. These firms also provide inspection services to a large number of different industries; however, individual offices usually serve a narrow segment of the market.

3. Specialty firms target very narrow market segments that require specific needs. These firms make large capital investments in the latest inspection equipment and employ the highest-skilled technicians. Barriers to entry into these specialized markets are high, so specialty firms have traditionally achieved high levels of profitability.

4. While much larger than the mom and pop labs, regional firms lack the name recognition and market strength of the nationwide companies. These firms employ up to 150 technicians and have the resources to tackle the largest inspection jobs. Roscoe is a regional firm, operating primarily in the central southern part of the United States.

All in all, management of NDT firms has been historically uninspired, driven mainly by owner-operators who managed to survive the lean years.

## ✳ HISTORY OF ROSCOE

Roscoe was founded in 1973 by Hans Norregaard in Roscoe, Louisiana. After 30 years as an NDT technician, Norregaard decided to set up shop for himself amidst many of the pulp and paper mills located in western Louisiana. Roscoe focused on the inspection of large boilers, a service designed to monitor the corrosion of the boiler walls. Inspections conducted every two to three years provided mills with sufficient warning to replace weakened, corroded plates in boiler walls before a catastrophic accident occurred.

In 1980, Norregaard sold the company to National Inspection Services (NIS) for $1.75 million. NIS was a subsidiary of Swanson Industries, a large diversified holding company. At that time, NIS brought in Chad Huerlmann (a Harvard MBA) to manage the company. Huerlmann was eager to run a small business and viewed the Roscoe acquisition as a great opportunity.

The company continued well for four years, until the pulp and paper industry bottomed out again. Hampered by misguided directives and burdened by corporate overhead, Roscoe's low-cost position no longer protected it from the growing price pressure facing NDT companies in the pulp and paper industry. Also, Huerlmann failed to establish an effective relationship with the technicians in the company, and many resigned or left the NDT industry altogether. By 1984, Swanson Industries decided to divest of NIS altogether, and Roscoe was once again up for sale.

At that time, Hans Norregaard and a long-time business associate, Grover Porter, decided to get back into the NDT business. Together, they bought back Roscoe for about 35 cents on the dollar. They were convinced that by offering an improved inspection service for a fair price, they could rebuild the company's reputation and good fortunes.

After dismissing Huerlmann, Hans and Grover began building a new management team for Roscoe. A new controller, Jane Bottensak, was hired away from MQS Inspection. Ted Witkowski, a staff Professional Engineer (PE) out of Texas A&M, who had previously worked for Exxon, was also taken on. Both men thought Ted would bring some much-needed technical backbone to the company. Also, long-time technician, Ed Brown, was promoted to operations manager. Finally, Roscoe began recruiting technicians from the best vocational tech schools in the country.

In 1987, Hans Norregaard retired, and Grover Porter became president. Roscoe was back on track.

In 1990, Roscoe encountered a downturn in both revenues and customers. Many mills simply decided not to release bids as often as they used to. While Roscoe always lost some contracts to lower bidders, Porter felt the recent slowdown in the pulp and paper industry exacerbated Roscoe's situation by forcing mills to be more cost conscious. Still, Porter felt that there must be room for the services that Roscoe offered:

> Hans and I have put together a great management team over the last three years and our technicians are some of the best in the industry. Roscoe offers an efficient, quality inspection service and we feel that we can price accordingly.

However, the recent loss of established customers caused Grover Porter to question the validity of Roscoe's purported "high-quality" service.

## ✱ CUSTOMER PROFILES

Although boiler inspections in pulp and paper mills have been standard practice for many years, mills differed widely on the representative who interacted with Roscoe's inspection team. This contact could be almost anyone from the plant manager down to a purchasing agent. The following descriptions illustrate many of the problems that have plagued Roscoe recently.

George McDonald at the Franklin Paper Company was a typical plant manager who reigned over his plant like a king over his castle. As any other plant manager, McDonald was primarily concerned about controlling costs and was hostile to the idea of boiler inspections in general. Since inspections could be conducted only during plant shutdowns, McDonald was unhappy about the lost production time:

> Besides the $85,000 inspection fee, my plant is idle during the two days it takes your team to complete the job. At 750 tons per day, I pay an additional opportunity cost of over $330,000 every day you are in my plant. A boiler will last 20 years without exploding and if it wasn't for corporate HQ, I would never bother with the inspections. Besides, the only thing that I ever get out of it is an "OK" and a pile of figures that I can't make head nor tail of.

International Paper's plant in Longview, Texas, was one of the few clients that maintained their own NDT department. As with other mills, the department consisted of only one retired NDT technician who interacted with service providers like Roscoe. Bob Kapala typified the kind of NDT person often found in paper mills. He was friendly and eager to help but was actually often more of a hindrance. The last thing a technician wanted was someone looking over his shoulder all the time.

After the inspection was completed, Bob would combine the recent inspection data with a pile of past data and attempt to find trends in corrosion patterns. The fact that different inspection firms provided data in different formats complicated Bob's task.

Jim Bulgrin at the Rockton Paper Mill in Texarkana, Texas, presented a different problem. Bulgrin, a recent graduate of Georgia Tech, had been hired into the mill's engineering services department seven months ago. As one of Roscoe's team supervisors described him, Bulgrin was "as wet behind the ears as a newborn calf." But he was eager to learn and was on top of every detail.

Problems arose when Jim noticed that thickness readings on one section of a boiler were considerably greater than when inspected two years before. After confronting the technicians, who ended up getting very angry, Jim eagerly reported the discrepancy to his boss. It was later discovered that a new plate had been welded onto the boiler in that area, but Roscoe lost the contract with Rockton.

Pulp mill supervisors, like Billy Dunlap at the Lufkin Pulp Mill, were Roscoe's most common contact inside a mill. Dunlap has been cajoling his boiler along for the past 15 years and did not take easily to anyone mistreating his "baby."

Finally, the inevitable contact is the purchasing representative who files the paperwork with accounting. Lucy Boyle in purchasing at Lufkin was never happy about processing paperwork relating to inspection services:

> Corporate headquarters requires us to file additional paperwork for one-time expenses greater than $50,000. With inspection fees well over $75,000, I end up processing over three times more paperwork than normal. My life doesn't return to normal until the mill goes back on-line.

## ✳ A PRELUDE TO ACTION

In January 1991, while attending the Nondestructive Testing Managers Association meeting in Las Vegas, Grover Porter was still struggling with the question of what defined a quality service. As it turned out, one of the speakers in the New Business Segment of the conference presented a talk on the components of service quality. And in that same month, a number of articles describing quality improvement programs at major aerospace inspection firms ran in both the ASNT and AWS Journals.[1]

At the monthly staff meeting in February, Porter discussed his concerns regarding the level of service provided by Roscoe. "As you all know, we've lost a bunch of accounts in the last few months. I suspect our service quality is not what it should be, and I've been thinking about a quality improvement program. If we don't do something soon, we may be forced to reduce our fees."

Bottensak, the controller, nodded her head in agreement and commented that something had to be done. "Let's go for it! None of us need reminding that 1990 was a bad year, but it looks like this year will be even worse. That's not great for our bonuses!"

Ted Witkowski, the staff PE, and Ed Brown, the operations manager, were extremely skeptical. Ted explained, "Look, we have the best-trained technicians out there with top-of-the-line equipment. They make some mistakes now and then, but when a boiler inspection requires 20,000 readings, that will happen. Besides, the mill has to look at the readings over an entire area and not just a single point. It's not reasonable to inspect every point twice. The mills couldn't afford the cost or the downtime."

After further discussion, Porter suggested that they first conduct a short customer survey to determine whether there were any areas for improvement. No one resisted the idea, so Porter spent the weekend composing the survey, and Bottensak pulled together a mailing list of Roscoe customers from the last five years. On Monday morning, 357 surveys were dropped in the mail.

## ✳ THE SURVEY RESULTS

By the first week of March, Porter had collected 82 responses. With only three responses returned in the last four days, Porter felt his sample was as big as it was going to get and asked Jane Bottensak to aggregate the results into a single report (Exhibit 1). The next morning, Jane walked into Porter's office with a grin:

> Grover, look's like we got something here. I ignored 11 of the responses since they obviously knew nothing about our work. I reckon those surveys didn't even reach the right contact in the mills. Anyway, that left 71 responses. I pulled all the results together to determine the frequency distributions and from what I can see it seems our people skills need work. Even our office staff could use some improvement.

Porter was surprised that the accuracy of inspection data and time to completion rated so highly, considering that business was so tough these last months. But then he recalled that the speaker at the NDTMA Conference last month emphasized the importance of the people aspect in service quality.

Unfortunately, Roscoe did not attract the type of people blessed with an abundance of social grace. The environment around a boiler is not pleasant. There is constant noise, grime, and heat. And if there was a reason to climb inside the boiler, the technician found himself struggling through cramped areas with his equipment and his flashlight. Once out, his clothing and equipment were coated with a black muck that not even Ultra-Tide could remove. Thus, while technicians survived the conditions on-site, they did not necessarily do so quietly.

At the March staff meeting, Porter announced his plans for Roscoe's Quality Improvement Program.

| EXHIBIT 1 | ROSCOE CUSTOMER SATISFACTION SURVEY (MARCH 1991) |
|---|---|

Dear Roscoe Customer,

In an effort to provide you with the best inspection service possible, we would like your opinion of Roscoe and the people who work for us. Simply check the appropriate column on the survey and drop it in the mail within the enclosed stamped envelope. Your cooperation is truly appreciated.

Grover Porter
President

| Questions | Poor | Below Average | Average | Above Average | Excellent |
|---|---|---|---|---|---|
| **On-Site Inspection Team** | | | | | |
| Accuracy of inspection data | 1.3% | 5.9% | 15.3% | 34.7% | 42.8% |
| Time to complete inspection | 2.9 | 4.8 | 8.4 | 45.6 | 38.3 |
| Knowledge of technicians | 1.5 | 11.5 | 25.6 | 33.3 | 28.1 |
| Willingness to make an extra effort | 24.6 | 26.0 | 23.6 | 13.5 | 12.3 |
| Courtesy of technicians | 26.1 | 30.3 | 18.7 | 16.2 | 8.7 |
| Degree of individualized attention | 17.6 | 29.6 | 38.2 | 9.9 | 4.7 |
| Willingness to make an extra effort | 13.7 | 30.1 | 42.9 | 8.3 | 5.0 |
| Conveys trust and confidence | 9.2 | 28.3 | 34.7 | 23.8 | 4.0 |
| Organization of team supervisor | 4.2 | 25.6 | 37.2 | 29.9 | 3.1 |
| **Accounting Department** | | | | | |
| Accuracy of billing | 3.4 | 8.3 | 16.1 | 55.8 | 16.4 |
| Promptness of billing | 9.8 | 43.9 | 21.7 | 16.5 | 8.1 |
| Courtesy of staff | 6.9 | 24.7 | 38.6 | 13.5 | 16.3 |
| Willingness to help | 22.7 | 25.6 | 38.1 | 8.9 | 4.7 |
| **Overall Performance of Roscoe** | | | | | |
| Ability to deliver the promised service | 2.7 | 15.6 | 18.5 | 39.4 | 23.8 |
| Variety of services that meet your needs | 2.3 | 13.2 | 48.8 | 26.5 | 9.2 |
| Overall service value for your money | 12.7 | 34.1 | 43.2 | 7.8 | 2.2 |

Recorded percentages are the frequency distribution of 71 responses compiled by Jane Bottensak, RNDT's controller. An average was taken for respondents who checked adjacent ratings (i.e., poor and below average).

## ✳ THE QUALITY IMPROVEMENT PROGRAM

The three elements that Porter decided to include in the QIP were initial training, a bonus reward system, and customer surveys at the conclusion of every job. He recognized that the QIP had to be more than a one-shot deal to be successful and felt that the proposed combination of training, surveys, and bonuses would establish the lasting, fundamental changes Roscoe needed.

Training was provided by ABS Consultants of Madison, Wisconsin, who specialized in teaching customer contact skills for industrial service companies. Training consisted of guided roundtable discussions and role playing, through which technicians and office staff explored not only customers' perceptions of Roscoe, but also their perceptions of the customers as well.

ABS also had Ed Brown put together some services guidelines that went beyond the traditional level of service. Brown explained one aspect of the guidelines:

> For example, while on-site, we need to emphasize constant visual inspection of the customer's plant and equipment. If a technician sees some insulation hanging off a section of piping, we expect that person to make a note in his report to the client. It doesn't take much time, and our customers appreciate the extra effort.

Technicians also earned bonus points that were cashed out at the end of the year for $25 per point. Every time a client requested a particular technician to be part of the on-site inspection team, that person received a bonus point. Also, after each job, the client filled out a customer satisfaction survey. At the end of the year, the surveys were ranked, and for each instance that a technician's team was in the top 5 percent, that technician received a bonus point.

Porter also gave a cash bonus to technicians who passed their certification tests and advanced a level. Achieving Level II earned a $150 cash bonus, while reaching Level III earned $500, as this was the most difficult level to achieve. Finally, the customer satisfaction surveys were compiled monthly and the statistics displayed in the shop area.

## ✴ ANOTHER DISAPPOINTING YEAR

Jane Bottensak wrapped up her part of the December staff meeting:

> Well, as I predicted, 1991 is going to be a disappointing year. Revenues were down again and profits were negligible. However, our performance wasn't as bad as I expected, so maybe the quality improvement program was more successful than I thought. But, I think we will still need to reevaluate our fee structure for the coming year.

Ted Witkowski agreed that the program was a success and commented that Roscoe had a record number of technicians certified at Levels II and III. Even Ed Brown conceded that customer satisfaction ratings had improved dramatically over the second half of 1991 (Exhibit 2):

> Most of the experienced technicians are excited about the program. They have been around Roscoe a number of years and have established their families in the area. On the other hand, some of the younger folks have not committed as easily. Part of that is the fact that less-experienced workers get smaller bonuses, on average. But, also, the younger technicians are more mobile and easily move from company to company. Overall, our work force is providing a better service to the customer.

However, regardless of how well the quality improvement program increased customer satisfaction, unless it could support new growth in the company, Grover Porter could only deem the program a failure.

| EXHIBIT 2 | ROSCOE CUSTOMER SATISFACTION SURVEYS (NOVEMBER 1991) | | | | |
|---|---|---|---|---|---|
| Questions | Poor | Below Average | Average | Above Average | Excellent |
| **On-Site Inspection Team** | | | | | |
| Accuracy of inspection data | 1.0% | 4.2% | 2.1% | 24.8% | 55.9% |
| Time to complete inspection | 1.4 | 6.3 | 7.1 | 60.0 | 25.2 |
| Knowledge of technicians | 0.9 | 12.1 | 20.5 | 37.4 | 29.1 |
| Willingness to make an extra effort | 11.9 | 18.2 | 36.5 | 27.8 | 5.6 |
| Courtesy of technicians | 9.3 | 8.9 | 55.3 | 16.3 | 10.2 |
| Degree of individualized attention | 2.1 | 16.7 | 45.9 | 30.1 | 5.2 |
| Willingness to make an extra effort | 9.8 | 17.6 | 40.3 | 30.4 | 1.9 |
| Conveys trust and confidence | 3.8 | 22.7 | 39.8 | 30.6 | 3.1 |
| Organization of team supervisor | 0.0 | 11.9 | 31.8 | 44.7 | 11.6 |
| **Accounting Department** | | | | | |
| Accuracy of billing | 1.5 | 10.4 | 19.6 | 44.2 | 24.3 |
| Promptness of billing | 13.5 | 33.4 | 25.6 | 18.5 | 9.0 |
| Courtesy of staff | 7.9 | 17.8 | 33.4 | 35.1 | 5.8 |
| Willingness to help | 8.6 | 29.4 | 30.3 | 24.6 | 7.1 |
| **Overall Performance of Roscoe** | | | | | |
| Ability to deliver the promised service | 0.0 | 13.2 | 23.1 | 44.2 | 19.5 |
| Variety of services that meet your needs | 7.4 | 13.5 | 56.1 | 15.3 | 7.7 |
| Overall service value for your money | 10.2 | 31.2 | 47.1 | 11.5 | 0.0 |

Compilation of 17 customer satisfaction surveys for inspections completed during November 1991. An average was taken for those respondents who checked adjacent ratings.

In light of the continued downturn in the pulp and paper industry, Porter felt resigned to restructure the company's pricing policies. And that would mean big changes for Roscoe.

## CASE QUESTIONS

1. Evaluate Roscoe's progress with the quality improvement program.
2. Evaluate Roscoe's customer survey.
3. With respect to the QIP and the survey, is Roscoe doing all it can do?
4. Who is Roscoe's customer?
5. What price changes should Roscoe make?
6. Using the Service Quality Gap Model as a point of reference, which gaps appear to be the largest for Roscoe . . . knowledge, specifications, delivery, and/or communications?

## NOTES

1. Trade journals of the American Society of Nondestructive Testing and the American Welding Society.

# IS THIS ANY WAY TO RUN AN AIRLINE?

The following letters are detailed accounts of an actual service encounter and the company's response to the service failures.

July 23, 200x

Dear Customer Service Manager:

Through the Carolina Motor Club my wife and I booked round-trip first-class and clipper-class seats on the following World Airlines flights on the dates indicated:

> 1 July World Airlines 3072 Charlotte to Kennedy
> 1 July World Airlines 86 Kennedy to Munich
> 21 July World Airlines 87 Munich to Kennedy
> 21 July World Airlines 3073 Kennedy to Charlotte

We additionally booked connecting flights to and from Wilmington and Charlotte on Trans Air flights 263 (on 1 July) and 2208 (on 21 July).

The outbound flights 3072 and 86 seemed pleasant enough, especially since World Airlines had upgraded our clipper-class seats on flight 86 to first class. However, mid-flight on 86 we discovered that we had been food poisoned on flight 3072, apparently by the seafood salad that was served in first class that day (it seemed warm to us and we hesitated to eat it but unfortunately did so anyway). My wife was so ill that, trying to get to the restroom to throw up, she passed out cold, hitting her head and, we discovered over the next few days, apparently damaging her back. The flight attendants were very concerned and immediately tried to help her, but there was nothing they could do except help her clean herself up and get the food off her from the food trays she hit. In addition to the nausea and diarrhea, she had a large knot on her head and headaches for several days. Her lower back has been in constant pain ever since. I, too, was very ill for several days. A nice start for a vacation! But it gets worse.

During the long layover between flights at Kennedy, there was a tremendous rainstorm, and our baggage apparently was left out in it, a situation that we discovered

Source: Richard A. Engdahl and K. Douglas Hoffman, "World Airlines: A Customer Service Air Disaster," in Carol A. Anderson, *Retailing: Concepts, Strategy, and Information* (Minneapolis/St. Paul: West, 1993), pp. 215–218.

when we arrived at our first night's lodging and discovered ALL of our clothing was literally wringing wet. In addition, four art prints we were bringing as gifts for friends were ruined.

The return flights were better only in that we did not get poisoned; instead we did not get fed! Flight 87 out of Munich was apparently short-handed and due to our seating location, the flight attendant who had to do double duty always got to us last. We had to ask for drinks; there were no hot towels left for us; the meals ran out and we were given no choice but an overdone piece of gray meat with tomato sauce on it. We tasted it, but it was odd tasting and given our experience on flight 3072, we were afraid to eat it.

Flight 87 was delayed in boarding due to the slowness in cleaning the aircraft (according to an announcement made) and also due to the late arrival of the crew. In addition, the flight was further delayed due to a heavy rainstorm, which backed up traffic for takeoff. However, had the flight boarded on time it would have not lost its takeoff priority and could likely have taken off two hours sooner than it did. We might have been able to make our connection in Charlotte. Onboard the flight, the plane was the dirtiest and in the most disrepair of any aircraft I have ever flown on—peeling wall coverings, litter on floor, overhead bins taped shut with duct tape, etc. As a first-class passenger I asked for some cold beer while we were waiting for the rest of the passengers to board; it was warm. We were quite hungry, having not eaten much in the past 12 hours, and asked for some peanuts; there were none; the plane had not been stocked. I asked for a pillow and blanket for my wife; there was none. What a great first-class section! There were only three flight attendants for the whole plane, and I felt sorry for the pregnant one who had to do double duty in first class and the rear cabin. She was very sympathetic to the poor conditions; I don't see how you keep employees when they are treated like that.

Due to the excess delay at Kennedy, flight 87 was very late and we could not make our connection from Charlotte to Wilmington. As it turned out, we would have barely been able to make it if the flight had been on time because World Airlines had changed not only the flight numbers but also the flight times on the Kennedy-Charlotte leg of our journey—AND WE WERE NEVER NOTIFIED OF THIS CHANGE UNTIL WE ARRIVED AT THE AIRPORT! I deplaned in Raleigh to try to alert the people meeting us in Wilmington that we would not be in that night; however, it was too late and they had already gone to the airport. The gate attendant at Raleigh assured me that World Airlines would put us up for the night in Charlotte, so I returned to the plane. However, when we arrived in Charlotte, the World Airlines representative refused to take care of us stating that, since we had not booked the Wilmington-Charlotte portion of our trip through World Airlines, "it is not our problem." Furthermore, he tried to wash his hands of it, saying we had an "illegal connection" due to the times between flights and that he wouldn't provide lodging and meals. After I pointed out to him at least three times that the connection was not illegal when booked and World Airlines changed its flight times without notifying us, and further made it clear that not only was I not going to go away, but that there was going to be a lot more said about the matter, he finally capitulated and gave us a voucher.

After traveling for 24 hours, receiving lousy service, poor food, no amenities, it is a real pleasure to run into an argumentative SOB like your agent in Charlotte. He should be fired!!! As first-class passengers we have been treated like cattle! But, it does not end here.

Upon arriving in Wilmington the next morning, only two of our four bags arrived with us. We had to initiate a baggage trace action. Our missing bags were finally delivered to our house around 3:00 p.m. on 23 July. And SURPRISE, they were left out in the rain at Kennedy again and EVERYTHING was so wet that water poured out of the pockets. I poured water out of the hairdryer. All of our paper purchases, maps, guide books, photos, souvenir brochures, etc. are ruined. I don't know yet if the dryer, radio, electric toothbrush, voltage converters, etc., will work—they are drying out as this is being written. In addition, my brand new bag now has a hole in the bottom of a corner where it was obvious that World Airline baggage handlers dragged it on the tarmac (obviously a water-logged dufflebag-size piece of luggage is too heavy to lift).

As near as I can figure, we have lost at least a roll of color prints (irreplaceable); approximately $100.00 in travel guides and tour books, many souvenir booklets, brochures, menus, etc.; $100.00 in art prints; $50.00 in damage to luggage; an unknown amount in electronics that may not work; a lot of enjoyment due to pain and suffering resulting from illness and injury (bill for x-rays enclosed); and all sense of humor and patience for such inexcusable treatment by an airline.

If there is to be any compensation for what we have suffered it should be in monetary form. There is no recapturing the lost time and pleasure on the vacation. The art, books, etc. (except for the photos) can be replaced . . . assuming we should make such a trip again. But if we do, you can be assured we would not choose World Airlines.

In closing, I am particularly angry and adamant about this whole fiasco as we wanted this vacation to be special and treated ourselves to the luxury of first-class treatment . . . which we got everywhere except on World Airlines . . . it is almost unbelievable how poorly we were treated by your airline, almost a perfect negative case study in customer service. I have purposely tried to mention every little nit-picky thing I can recall because I want you to realize just how totally bad this whole experience has been!

In disgust,
J. Q. Customer

---

## ✱  WORLD AIRLINE'S RECOVERY STRATEGY

The following is World Airline's actual response to the customer's letter. The first letter was written by the Claims Manager, and the second by the Customer Relations Manager.

September 25, 200x

Dear Mr. and Mrs. Customer:

This letter confirms the settlement agreed upon during our phone conversation just concluded.

Accordingly, we have prepared and enclosed (in duplicate) a General Release for $2,000.00. Both you and your wife should sign in the presence of a Notary Public, have your signatures notarized, and return the Original to this office, keeping the copy for your records. As soon as we receive the notarized Release, we will forward our draft for $2000.00.

Again, our sincerest apologies to Mrs. Customer. It will be most helpful for our Customer Relations staff if you included with the Release copies of all available travel documents.

Very truly yours,
Claims Manager

October 12, 200x

Dear Mr. Customer:

Let me begin by apologizing for this delayed response and all of the unfortunate incidents that you described in your letter. Although we try to make our flights as enjoyable as possible, we obviously failed on this occasion.

Our claims manager informs me that you have worked out a potential settlement for the matter regarding the food poisoning. We regret you were not able to enjoy the food service on the other flights on your itinerary because of it. I assure you that such incidents are a rare occurrence and that much time and effort is expended to ensure that our catering is of the finest quality.

Fewer things can be more irritating than faulty baggage handling. Only in an ideal world could we say that baggage will never again be damaged. Still, we are striving to ensure baggage is handled in such a way that if damage should occur, it will be minimized.

Flight disruptions caused by weather conditions can be particularly frustrating since, despite advanced technology, accurate forecasts for resumption of full operations cannot always be obtained as rapidly as one would wish. These disruptions are, of course, beyond the airlines' control. Safety is paramount in such situations and we sincerely regret the inconvenience caused.

We make every reasonable effort to lessen the inconvenience to passengers who are affected by schedule changes. Our practice is, in fact, to advise passengers of such changes when we have a local contact for them and time permits. We also try to obtain satisfactory alternative reservations. We are reviewing our schedule change requirements with all personnel concerned and will take whatever corrective measures are necessary to ensure that a similar problem does not arise in the future.

You made it clear in your letter that the interior of our aircraft was not attractive. We know that aircraft appearance is a reflection of our professionalism. We regret that our airplane did not measure up to our standards since we place great emphasis on cabin maintenance and cleanliness. Please be assured that this particular matter is being investigated by the responsible management and corrective action will be taken.

As tangible evidence of our concern over your unpleasant trip. I have enclosed two travel vouchers, which may be exchanged for 2 first-class tickets anywhere that World Airlines flies. Once again, please accept our humble apology. We hope for the opportunity to restore your faith in World Airlines by providing you with completely carefree travel.

Sincerely,
Customer Relations Manager

 **EPILOGUE**

World Airlines filed for bankruptcy within 24 months after this incident.

✱  **CASE QUESTIONS**

1. Categorize the failures that occurred above utilizing the three failure categories depicted in Figure 14.1, page 362.
2. What is your assessment of the firm's recovery efforts based on the concepts of distributive, procedural and interactional justice?

# CASE | 15

# THE OPTICAL SHOP

**7:00 A.M. — THE UPCOMING AGENDA**

It was 7:00 A.M. Monday morning as Christopher Connor, M.D. sat in his office reviewing the agenda for a 7:30 staff meeting. The issues on the agenda were difficult and contentious, and Chris wondered if the group could do them justice in the hour before he was due in surgery. As director of primary care for the Eye Clinic at the Dartmouth Hitchcock Medical Center (DHMC), the Optical Shop had been "his baby" since its inception a year and a half ago. Now that the baby had learned to walk, it needed guidance to chart its role in the future direction of the Eye Clinic — a role that could push the Eye Clinic in totally new directions.

Chris looked again at the four items on the agenda:

## 1. OPTICAL SHOP BROCHURE

First up, a proposal to enclose a brochure "introducing" the Optical Shop with the confirmation letters for every appointment at the Eye Clinic. While this seemed like a great way to generate traffic for the Shop, Chris wondered how competing optometrists and opticians — many of whom referred patients to the specialists at the Clinic — would react to this bid for their patients' eyewear business. Chris looked again at the initial draft of the brochure (see Exhibit 1). While the text and format had been designed to avoid direct confrontation with rival opticians, he wondered whether either the message and the brochure itself fit the Clinic's objectives.

| EXHIBIT 1 | DARTMOUTH-HITCHCOCK OPTICAL SHOP |
|-----------|----------------------------------|

**Located off the Rotunda on Level 4**

**Open Monday – Friday**
9:00 A.M. – 5:30 P.M.

**(630) 650-2050**

The Dartmouth-Hitchcock Optical Shop specializes in prompt service and superior quality eyewear at reasonable prices. We sell eyewear for the whole family and carry a full selection of prescription eyewear

- sunglasses
- contact lenses
- sports and safety glasses
- children's glasses
- accessories

**A Service of the Section of Ophthalmology
of The Hitchcock Clinic**

If there are any questions regarding your prescription, our staff is able to communicate with your Hitchcock eyecare provider quickly and easily.

**Frames**

The Optical Shop displays several hundred contemporary and traditional frames for all ages and lifestyles. Some of our designer frames include Giorgio Armani, Liz Claiborne, and Ralph Lauren. All of our eyeglass frames are warranted for at least one year.

**Lenses**

We offer the most current designs and materials for your lenses, including glass, plastic and polycarbonate, scratch resistant coatings, UV absorbing filters, and assorted colors and shades.

**Sunglasses**

We sell prescription and non-prescription sunglasses by many designers, including Vuarnet and Ray-Ban.

**Eye Exams**

For your convenience, an optometrist sees patients in the Optical Shop by appointment. This member of the Section of Ophthalmology provides complete eye exams and contact lens fittings and follow-ups.

| EXHIBIT 1 | DARTMOUTH-HITCHCOCK OPTICAL SHOP (CONT'D) |
|---|---|

### Contact Lenses

Contact lenses can be an excellent alternative to eyeglasses for many people. Optical Shop staff can answer any questions you have regarding contact lenses and can arrange an appointment for you to see our optometrist. We provide a full range of contact lens services, including fitting, wearing instructions, follow-up, insurance, and replacements.

### Do I need an eye exam before I buy glasses?

Many people feel that as long as they are seeing well with their glasses everything is okay. Unfortunately that's not always the case. Your eyes, like the rest of your body, undergo gradual changes as you grow older. However, your eyes rarely hurt when something is wrong. Undesirable changes in your eyes can occur that will not adversely affect vision in the early stages. This is the case with glaucoma, cataracts, and complications caused by high blood pressure and diabetes. Your eye doctor normally checks for symptoms of these conditions to detect problems before they affect your vision.

Visit your eye doctor on a regular schedule and if you have and questions about when you need to be seen, contact your eye doctor's office.

**Please call us with your questions at**
**(603) 650-2050.**

## 2. PROPOSAL TO ADD A SECOND OPTOMETRIST

The second agenda item posed the same dilemma, but with an added twist. Putting a second optometrist on staff promised to increase the Optical Shop's business by as much as 50 percent, but much of the business it added would come at the expense of optometrists in the surrounding towns. More than this though, the Eye Clinic had always been known for tertiary eye care (especially glaucoma, cataracts, diabetic retinopathy, and macular degeneration). Chris wondered, how far did the Section want to push into primary care?

Should it strive to compete with local optometrists for "well eye care"? Most of all, was the Optical Shop in a position to compete for these patients given its unique clinical setting and the restrictions of its tax-exempt status? If so, would the added volume and mix of customers reopen the discussion of an on-site lab that had been tabled two years ago?

## 3. WRITTEN GUARANTEE

Third, the staff planned to discuss the possibility of an explicit, written guaranty for all eyewear provided by the Shop. While the topic of a written guarantee had come up in casual conversation a number of times, there had never been a formal discussion of the issue among the staff. From these casual conversations, Chris knew that many of his colleagues were uncomfortable with the message and implications of providing a written guarantee. However, the more Chris thought about it, the more he felt that a guarantee would be in keeping with the Shop's goals and mission. He also knew that a guarantee could provide a valuable feedback mechanism and an opportunity to differentiate the Shop from local competitors. For that reason, he decided to put the issue on the agenda. People had been dancing around this idea long enough. Chris felt they needed to discuss it and come to a decision.

## 4. NEW BUSINESS

Chris knew that if all of the proposals on the agenda were implemented, other things at the Shop would also need to change. But what?

It was 7:25. Maybe his colleagues had some answers.

## ✳ HITCHCOCK BACKGROUND

Founded in 1893, the Mary Hitchcock Memorial Hospital had served as the teaching hospital for the Dartmouth Medical School for 100 years. Offering the most sophisticated and comprehensive medical care between Boston and Burlington, DHMC's reputation and staff of renowned specialists drew patients from 2400 square miles of northern New England for everything from coronary by-pass surgery to annual physicals.

For most of its 100 years, the hospital and the Hitchcock Clinic (the largest private practice of doctors in the State) had expanded in a hodgepodge of buildings just north of the Dartmouth campus. By 1991, however, this patchwork of buildings no longer served the needs of the area or the hospital, and a new $218 million state-of-the-art medical center was constructed on a 225-acre wooded tract three miles to the east. In addition to the hospital and doctor's offices for the Clinic, the 1.2 million square foot medical center (the largest building in New England north of Boston) included an enclosed mall and rotunda with space for 15 retail stores. It was in this space—off the fourth floor rotunda—that the Eye Clinic (a/k/a "the Section") opened an optical dispensary.

Bethany Kieley, the Section's clinical-administrative liaison, explained the impetus behind the shop.

> *Dr. Connor was specifically interested in the idea of an optical dispensary as an extension of the service the Section provides to patients. Primarily, his motivation was to provide continuity and control of our patients' eye-care needs from beginning to end. He felt that far too often our patients were returning with complaints*

*about their vision, only to have us find that the glasses, not the prescription, were at the root of the problem. Secondly, although the Clinic's tax status does not allow it to make "profits" per se, Dr. Connor saw an opportunity to add to the Section's revenues and income.*

*The administration was a hard sell in some ways, but an easy sell in other ways. Literature searches showed that it could be a very profitable extension. In private practice settings, optical dispensaries are big money-makers.*

*The other physicians, on the other hand, were quite skeptical. Because of their profitability and complaints from patients about outrageous prices, optical dispensaries have traditionally been viewed by physicians as "less than ethical." Consequently, there was a real hesitation from the other physicians about getting into something that could be perceived by patients as just a plan to make more money.*

Although the other physicians had become more accepting of the Shop as time passed, Bethany knew that many remained hesitant about mentioning it as part of their routine with patients. For some, it was an issue of "selling" something to their patients. For others, it was a matter of becoming comfortable with the operation itself.

*They want to be in control and yet it is something they can't control. They have to trust Gary and Kathy to produce a product that will be good. And yet, they don't know anything about making the product or what makes it good, really. Technically, they understand it. They know how a pair of glasses works and that the measurements have to be right and that kind of thing. But in terms of how that actually happens, they understand enough to be nervous. They are getting better. Dr. Connor talks to them a lot about what goes on up there. How they do it, the lab and the frame manufacturers they use, the prices they are charging, and comparative information. So they are getting more comfortable with it. But it is taking a long time.*

As a consequence of his peers' reluctance to promote the Shop with patients, Chris Connor felt the need to "take the matter out of their hands" by including a brochure about the Shop with all appointment confirmations.

## MISSION

When the Optical Shop first opened, the Eye Clinic believed it would be a significant moneymaker. First year revenues were expected to total $709,000 and operating profit was projected to exceed $250,000. Several weeks after its grand opening, however, it became apparent that the Shop would not be as successful as originally planned. The projections, which had been made prior to hiring an optician, had been based on the number of patients seen in the Eye Clinic, not the number of prescriptions written by the doctors. Since the Clinic's ophthalmologists wrote relatively few prescriptions, the Section found that the Shop's revenues had been overestimated by a factor of two. The bottom line, meanwhile, hovered around breakeven.

Although the optician hired to run the Shop believed growth and profit were still the most important measures of the Shop's success (in his opinion, no other measures made sense), the rest of the Eye Clinic shifted its focus away from these measures when it became apparent that the Shop would not be a big profit contributor.

Instead, the doctors and the administrators focused on their other reasons for opening the Shop—to "extend the service" the Section furnished to patients, and to provide "continuity of care" between their patients' eyecare provider and the eyewear provider. As Chris Connor explained:

> Our primary mission is service. Our secondary mission is profit. I want my patients to be happy and taken care of; even if that means returning their money in full and them going elsewhere to get their glasses made, I want them to leave satisfied. Now and then, when I hear they are not, it is upsetting to me. I don't want to hear from my patients six months later that they are not happy with the glasses they got upstairs. The second thing I want is to be sure we always have trained people up there. I want them to be happy and enjoy their job because body language communicates that attitude to the patients.
>
> When I was out in private practice, the practitioners were always at the whim of the neighborhood optical shop or the neighborhood optician. We would try to develop a good working relationship with them, but there are so many areas where problems can occur, there are so many variables where slip-ups can be made in making glasses, that patients will often blame the primary care provider and not the optician—or vice versa. Patients are then stuck running between two establishments trying to get the problem solved.

Despite his focus on service to the patients, Chris felt mounting pressure to increase both the number of patients using the Shop and the Shop's profits (which remained near breakeven). Finances were tightening at the hospital and management had recently announced plans to reduce staff (mostly through early retirement, attrition, and layoffs). Y.B. Rhee, the Clinic COO, regularly inquired about the performance of the Shop. Also, quarterly bonuses for the doctors in the Eye Clinic were based on the Section's profits, which included the operations of the Shop. By "extending the service" to more patients, increasing profits, and generating positive patient feedback, Chris hoped to convince his skeptical colleagues that opening an optical dispensary had been "the right thing" to do. (See Exhibit 2 for the Hitchcock Clinic Mission Statement and Vision Statement.)

## OPERATIONS

The Optical Shop occupied 500 square feet of retail space off the fourth floor rotunda, one level above the Eye Clinic. Although Chris and the administration had hoped to put the shop next to (or across from) the Eye Clinic to increase its visibility and make its connection to the Eye Clinic clear, this had not been possible in the construction of the facility. Consequently, many patients continued to believe that the shop was an independent third-party dispensary, rather than part of the Eye Clinic. (The shop's neighbors included a travel agency, a pharmacy, and the service desk for a local auto dealer.) At the back of

| EXHIBIT 2 | MISSION STATEMENT OF THE HITCHCOCK CLINIC: A DOCUMENT IN EVOLUTION |
|-----------|---------------------------------------------------------------------|

The Hitchcock Clinic exists to serve the health care needs of our patients. We intend to provide effective, efficient, accessible, affordable health care, in a trusting environment, with compassionate respect for individual human values.

We seek to improve our understanding for the causes, courses, treatments, and prevention of disease. Our commitment includes both academic research under the aegis of Dartmouth College and Dartmouth Medical School and continuous Clinic-wide reassessment and improvement of our daily work.

We desire to share our knowledge where it does good: with the Dartmouth-Hitchcock community of students, trainees and colleagues, and with competitors, legislators, regulators, schools, and the public at large.

We wish for ourselves the satisfactions of participating together in meaningful work in a collegial atmosphere and of experiencing personal and professional growth.
We acknowledge the necessity to work within resources constraints. Although we cannot do everything, what we choose to do we will do well.

Adopted by the Board of Trustees
February 22, 1992

### OUR VISION OF DHMC

DHMC and its component entities—Dartmouth Medical School, the Hitchcock Clinic, Mary Hitchcock Memorial Hospital, the Matthew Thornton Health Plan, and the White River Junction, VT, Veterans Administration Hospital—are committed to excellence in health care, education, and research.

We are developing a comprehensive, integrated health care system serving New Hampshire and the adjacent northern New England states, and intend to make that system a premier resource for the region. The achievement of that objective will depend importantly on the provision of health care noted for exceptional quality, responsiveness, and accessibility and the delivery of that care at a competitive price.

Our growing role in health care will be accompanied by further development of our programs of education and research. We are an academic health center and we wish to be one of the best in the nation, the preeminent such center in northern New England, and a major contributor to the reputation of Dartmouth College.

Our missions in education and research differentiate us from other excellent but non-academic health service systems. Similarly our service mission differentiates us from the non-clinical programs at Dartmouth and other colleges and universities.

While private in structure, we are public in purpose. Our commitment to public service on statewide, regional, and national levels is essential to the vitality, character, and support of our educational and research objectives.

The connection between DHMC and Dartmouth College is mutually beneficial, and will contribute greatly to DHMC's ability to move into the top echelon of academic health centers nationally.

Reflecting DHMC's belief that quality, effectiveness, and cost containment in health care can best be achieved through integration, the health care we offer will be provided primarily through our own physician groups, hospitals, and managed care programs. DHMC is committed to serving all residents of the region who request such service. The strategic benefits of integration will be realized through adherence to a common vision, coordinated program planning, coordinated resource allocation, and the coordinated delivery of health care.

DHMC's activities in education, research, and service require adequate financial resources, and the development of those resources represents an important undertaking. Revenues must be sufficient to cover operating expenses, to build financial strength, and to provide for continuing investment renewal. We cannot do everything, but the things we do must be done well. It is essential that we adhere firmly to that principle in the years ahead.

the store was an office (which included a repair bench) and an examining room for the Clinic's optometrist, Peter Lapre, O.D. (Dr. Lapre spent roughly half of his time there and half of his time examining patients in the Clinic.) The majority of the space was taken up with display cases, dispensing tables, and a reception desk/cash register.

The shop carried all the major frame manufacturers, including Safilo, Luxotica (several lines), American Optical, and Zeiss, plus "designer" frames like Calvin Klein, Polo, Armani, Anne Klein, and Laura Ashley. Prices ranged from a low of $70 to as much as $200. If a customer came in without a doctor's prescription, their old prescription could be read from their existing glasses using the "lensometer." Once the prescription had been determined, the customer could chose to use their existing frames or a select new frame. Either Gary Nevers, the manager, or Kathy Delaney, an optical assistant, would offer to help the customer with advice on fit, fashion, style, durability, and other features (i.e. spring hinges and various coatings). Customers varied widely in their need and desire for advice. After a frame was chosen, various measurements needed to be taken (i.e., pupilary distance and placement of the "line" for bifocals), before the frame and the prescription were sent to New Hampshire Optical (the wholesale lab that ground the lenses). Turnaround time averaged 3 to 5 days for a normal order, but "rush" orders could be processed in as little as 24 hours using express shipping (at no charge). At times, if there was a delay at the lab or if there was an error that required a set of lenses to be remade, Kathy would drive half-way to New Hampshire Optical (located 60 miles away in Concord) to pick up a customer's order from one of their lab technicians. Overall, however, Gary felt comfortable with the quality of service New Hampshire Optical provided.

> They know what I expect and that's what they are going to give me. And if they don't, they are going to get it back. I'm sure they have other customers who will accept what I don't accept, and vice versa. When you have been doing business with someone day-in and day-out, you know what they will take and what they won't take.

Gary had been an optician for over 15 years, working previously at a wholesale/retail optical dispensary 100 miles away in Burlington. The dispensary, owned by a group of local optometrists, had struggled and folded after the manager died, resulting in Gary's move to DHMC. Over the years, Gary had maintained a professional relationship with New Hampshire Optical and was instrumental in their selection as the wholesale lab for the Clinic. There had been some discussion at the outset of installing a lab in the shop to grind standard prescriptions (but which would continue to rely on an outside vendor for complicated orders like "no-line" bifocals, high-index lenses, and "prism" lenses).[1] While several job candidates argued that turnaround time (a major advantage of an on-site lab) was critical to the success of an optical dispensary, several others, including Gary, argued that turn-around time and lens fabrication were less important than the "fit" of the frames and the accuracy of the prescription and the measurements. Gary also felt that customers who had been wearing glasses for many years expected to wait a few days for their prescription. While the Shop was eventually constructed without a lab, some of the Eye Clinic staff felt that they had never done a thorough analysis of the costs and benefits of an in-store lab. Given the changes being proposed for the Shop, some felt it would be a good time to reexamine the issue.

In addition to fitting and measuring frames, the Shop also dispensed and trained people in the use of contact lenses, scheduled appointments and received patients for the optometrist (all functions previously handled by the Clinic staff), repaired frames and adjusted their fit (a time-consuming service but, by industry custom, a free service, regardless of where the frames were purchased), and sold accessories like sunglasses and Croakies. Kathy also spent a considerable amount of time satisfying the complex auditing, reporting, and administrative procedures required by the Clinic's bureaucracy. Frequently, she felt these procedures interfered with the demands of the retail environment.

Administratively, The Hitchcock Clinic was divided into Responsibility Centers (e.g., orthopedics, internal medicine, and ophthalmology). Doctors received quarterly incentive bonuses based on their Center's operating performance versus budget. While Ophthalmology separately tracked the revenues and expenses of the Optical Shop, results for the Optical Shop were rolled into the Ophthalmology Responsibility Center for reporting to Clinic Administration and for bonus calculations. Technicians, secretaries, and Optical Shop staff did not qualify for bonuses or incentive money.

Each doctor went through a Clinic "appointment" process (or "reappointment" process) every two years. This consisted of a questionnaire touching on research activities, teaching activities, financial performance, and anything else pertinent to their activities as a professional. Also, at the time of (re)appointment, each physician's name was sent to the other physicians in the Clinic for comments and feedback. Otherwise, there was no formal system of performance review for doctors. The Clinic's other employees received either a "clinical" or an "administrative" evaluation, depending on the nature of their position. Gary and Kathy received administrative evaluations, which focused on such things as communication, teamwork, interpersonal relationships, and knowledge of their assigned tasks.

Like most optical dispensaries, the Shop did not directly accept Medicaid, Medicare, or private insurance (because of restrictions regarding the type and quality of frames they would cover and the lack of profit opportunity), but would accept payment from the customer and submit a statement to the insurer on his or her behalf.

## COMPETITION

Because there were no other optical dispensaries in the medical center, Gary felt that the Optical Shop had no true competitors. However, several optical dispensaries in the town of Hanover and the shopping area of West Lebanon (each about three miles away from the medical center campus) continued to attract DHMC employees and Eye Clinic patients as well as patients of local optometrists. Most of these dispensaries were owned by an optometrist (who dispensed glasses in the waiting area) or maintained a referral relationship with a nearby optometrist. Their frame selection was pretty much the same as at DHMC, with some tailoring to the particular clientele they attracted. For example, Hill Opticians in downtown Hanover attracted many more college students and young people than DHMC Optical. (Gary felt this was because young people had fewer medical needs and were less likely to come to the medical center.) Pearle Vision in West Lebanon competed mostly on price and on the quick turnaround provided by its in-store lab.[2] (Gary believed that most Optical Shop customers had gone to Pearle before the Optical Shop opened.) Powerhouse Optical also competed on price, mostly by giving a 20 percent discount to businesses, including employees of DHMC.[3]

Although the Optical Shop's prices were competitive with the *non-sale* prices of its competitors, Bethany Kieley explained that the Shop had a hard time conveying this message to customers.

> *Part of what makes it so difficult is that the Hitchcock Clinic as a whole has a reputation of being the most expensive provider of healthcare in the area. And that is probably rightfully so. So people have a hard time believing that our optical shop—up here in this expensive space—is going to give a better deal than the shop down the street. We are hoping that some internal marketing will help, but we can't be real specific. We don't want to say, "Compare glasses A from the Hitchcock Clinic—higher quality, reasonable price—with glasses B from 'Acme Opticians'—low quality, terrible price." That is not the image we feel comfortable projecting for the Clinic, the Shop, or the Section.*

By virtue of its location at the Clinic, however, the Shop tended to see a greater mix of complex cases than surrounding competitors, making price somewhat less of a factor in the buying decision.[4]

## MARKETING

Customers of the Optical Shop came from any of several sources. Patients and employees of DHMC comprised the largest group, totaling up to 70 percent of the Shop's business. Some of these employees were also patients of the Eye Clinic, others used off-site optometrists and came to the Optical Shop because of convenience. (The wait for an appointment with Dr. Lapre, the Clinic's only optometrist, ran as long as 4 weeks compared with a few days for some local optometrists.) Most Optical Shop customers who came from the Clinic (up to 60 percent of the Shop's total business) were patients of Dr. Lapre. The Clinic's 7 ophthalmologists (specialists in glaucoma, cataracts, etc.) seldom performed refractions themselves (since this was not their area of expertise), instead referring patients to Dr. Lapre (or to one of the technicians if Dr. Lapre was booked) for post-operative refractions. About 30 percent of Dr. Lapre's work came through these specialists, and their referrals tended to comprise most of the complicated refractions he performed. The remainder of his patients were more or less "standard" primary care cases.

Dr. Lapre had come to the Clinic at about the same time as the new medical center opened as part of the Eye Clinic's expansion into primary care.[5] Despite pleasure with his success attracting patients, however, the Section was concerned about the growing length of his patient backlog. For this reason, and in recognition of the volume of business Dr. Lapre drove through the Optical Shop, the Clinic was considering a proposal to add another optometrist. These plans included adding another exam room in the Optical Shop, or splitting the two optometrists between an exam room in the Eye Clinic and the existing exam room in the Optical Shop. Although the doctors believed that it presented a "less professional" appearance to perform exams in the back of the Optical Shop, records indicated that sales revenue jumped dramatically when Dr. Lapre performed exams there.

The specialists in the Eye Clinic received many of their referrals from optometrists in the surrounding towns. When this was the case, the patient's file would be coded with a blue stripe as a signal for the ophthalmologist to refer the patient back to that doctor for post-treatment refraction. Then, depending on whether that doctor also dispensed glasses (or if the patient had a relationship with another optical dispensary) the Optical Shop might or might not attract their business.

Because of DHMC's "pull" from the surrounding region, patients came to the Eye Clinic for primary and tertiary care from distances of up to 100 miles. For many of these patients, even those living at great distances, it was not uncommon to purchase glasses from the Optical Shop and to return several days later to pick them up. Gary believed that the doctor's recommendation had the most powerful influence on where people got their prescription filled. As he explained, "If the doctor hands them a prescription and says, 'You can get this filled upstairs,' they will do it, even if they used to get glasses elsewhere." Another important influence was the powerful and prestigious reputation of The Hitchcock Clinic. However, because of its location among the medical center's other retail stores, many customers and patients remained unaware of the Shop's affiliation with the Clinic.[6] Finally, especially for DHMC employees, convenience played an important role in the choice of an optical dispensary. (DHMC employed 4000 people whose eyewear needs accounted for as much as 30 percent of the Shop's business.)

Because of its tax-exempt status, the Clinic was prohibited from recruiting clients just for the Optical Shop. This precluded advertising, "sales," or even a Yellow Pages listing under "Optical." Instead, the Clinic had to limit itself to "internal marketing" (to existing patients of the hospital or the Clinic).[7] These efforts included locating Dr. Lapre in the Optical Shop part-time, a sign and a small display case of frames in the waiting room of the Eye Clinic, ophthalmologists' mention of the shop in their routine with patients (which some doctors were still reluctant to do), and now a proposal to mail brochures to incoming patients. Word-of-mouth was also a powerful internal marketing tool (especially among employees).

## * CUSTOMER FOCUS

### *QUALITY*

The Optical Shop had never done a survey of customer satisfaction or expectations, but those involved with the Shop each had their own beliefs about quality and patients' perceptions of quality.

Dr. Connor:
Because of technical limitations and the vagaries of each patient's physiology, Chris Connor believed that "education" had perhaps the most significant influence on a patient's perception of quality. The eye doctor, he felt, had to manage each patient's expectation of what glasses could do and had to respond rapidly if the product failed to deliver on those expectations.

*Probably no other product has as much influence on a patient's psyche as glasses. If glasses aren't right, it is extremely upsetting to the patient. If your shoes aren't quite right, you will take them back. You are not going to get angry about them. Patients get angry when their glasses are made incorrectly. Glasses are something you count on to receive information from the world.*

*I think the patient's perception of quality occurs over a period of time. Their initial impression will be what the world looks like when they first put on the glasses. If their doctor has told them when he hands them their prescription that it will take at least two weeks to get used to the glasses, then adaptation shouldn't be an issue. After that, if the patient calls back and is told to go two more weeks, quality drops off.*

*You have to handle problems immediately. A rapid program to correct mistakes would be in a patient's perception of good quality. I would almost like to see what I call a "glasses emergency" for patients who need to see the optometrist right away because of problems with their glasses.*

*If you have a cataract growing, your vision is going to change. Sometimes patients have the perception that the glasses are ruining their eyes. This goes back to the eyecare provider. He needs to explain that the glasses you get today may not work in six months. Quality and education really go hand-in-hand.*

*This is a business in which you will never have 100 percent satisfaction because there are so many idiosyncrasies in terms of fitting glasses. The patient has a perception of what they think they should look like in glasses, and it may go beyond what can actually be done for them.*

*The patient can judge quality immediately when they pick the glasses up if they fit well on their face, if they look good, and (if they wait a few weeks for their eyes to adjust) whether they can see well. Further down the road, they judge quality by whether the glasses hold-up. Then it all comes back to communication and understanding their eyes. It is the eyecare provider's job to do that.*

*The most common complaints we hear are 1) our turnaround time is too slow, and 2) the glasses have to be remade. Sometimes, the glasses aren't right because of the patients—they weren't concentrating enough during their eye exam. But in the majority of cases, the mistakes occur somewhere after the patient leaves, either the way the prescription was written by the doctor, the measurements taken in the Shop, or the way the glasses were ground at the lab.*

Gary Nevers:

Gary, meanwhile, believed that quality could best be measured by whether customers accepted the product. "If they accept what you present," he stated, "then you have met their expectations."

*Everybody wants their glasses yesterday. It used to be price, quality, and service. Most customers want a lower price, but they don't understand that a $120 frame really is better than a $70 frame. They don't appreciate how* *long-lasting the parts are, how interchangeable the parts are, or the reputation of the manufacturer.*

Most manufacturers offered a standard one-year warranty on their frames. Lenses were warranted at the discretion of the optician. If a customer needed to have lenses remade because of an inaccurate prescription, most optical shops would remake the glasses for free to maintain goodwill with the referring doctor.

## FEEDBACK

Although it had never conducted a formal survey of its customers, there was general consensus within the Eye Clinic that the Optical Shop was serving its patrons well. Bethany Kieley's comments reflected the opinion of most of the staff:

> *I think truly they are doing an excellent job right now, even though I can't tell you how. Still, I know of no employee who has gone there thinking they'll check it out who has left to buy somewhere else. The feedback to physicians is excellent. Kathy and Gary are honest with patients. If there is a service they can't provide, they help them find someone who can. I was up there when somebody needed a special screw. Gary called a couple of jewelry stores to see if they could help and off they went knowing they could get the service. I think it reflects very positively that we are willing to know a) our limitations and b) not just to say, "No, sorry, we can't help you." We continue to foster a collaborative relationship with people who aren't even our customer but potentially will be. In that regard, I think it is truly a sign of the staff and their sort of instinct for how to keep people happy even if they aren't able to give them what they want today.*

## ✱ 8:15 — EYE CLINIC CONFERENCE ROOM

As Chris Connor looked around the conference room, it was obvious that there was going to be very little consensus among his colleagues either about the issues on the agenda or about the role of the Optical Shop and primary eye care in the Eye Clinic's strategy.

To begin the meeting, Gary and Chris argued that *adding another optometrist* would increase revenues, reduce Dr. Lapre's backlog, and give the Section some measure of slack to experiment with the concept of a "glasses emergency." Dr. Morse and Dr. Welsh, however, expressed skepticism about the wisdom of delving further into primary eye care. In their opinion, the mission of the Section was to be the region's expert center for specialty, tertiary eye care. Though they now felt comfortable with Gary and Kathy and with the idea of dispensing eyewear to provide post-operative "continuity of care," they questioned whether competition with local optometrists for "well eye care" —either through the proposed *brochure* or the addition of a *second optometrist*—was an appropriate part of the Eye Clinic's mission. Besides, they asked, how would the Optical Shop cope with increasing volume? Would the staff still be able to provide the level of care required for complex cases if the shop was packed with customers? What about the reaction of local optometrists who referred patients to them and to the other specialists at the Clinic?

Then there was the question of a *guarantee*. While Chris felt there should be some type of guarantee for the "seeing" part of the glasses (as opposed to just breakage or defects in materials), even he was concerned that an explicit guarantee might give customers the impression that problems happened frequently. Gary took the position that the manufacturers' one-year warranty on frames and the Shop's generous policy for lens "remakes" made an explicit guarantee unnecessary. Dr. Lapre, meanwhile, indicated that he always instructed patients to "call him" if they had trouble with their glasses. When they did, he would often follow-up with a free exam. Still, he thought, an explicit guarantee would be dangerous:

> *Many people are very surprised when I tell them there will be no charge for the visit. But I think it pays to be very careful with expressing warranties and saying, "Okay, if you have any problem with these glasses, I will recheck them at no charge." I think that from a business standpoint it would be unwise to say that to people. There is a significant percentage of the population that will beat that to death.*

Gary agreed,

> *If we offer a guarantee, people will take advantage of it. They might not come back for a new pair of glasses, but they will come back with nuisance complaints which can't be solved. Let's face it, people's glasses are never going to be perfect. As it is, half of our time is spent doing "adjustments" for walk-ins. A guarantee will just make things worse.*

It was 8:25 and Chris had to leave for surgery. As he prepared to close the meeting, he wondered what he should do next. The Section had a great service to offer its patients and the community. The Shop had to move forward. Why couldn't his colleagues agree?

## ✳ CASE QUESTIONS

1. Identify the key issues faced by the Optical Shop.
2. Provide three alternative solutions for each of the key issues faced by the Optical Shop.
3. Discuss the pros and cons of each alternative solution provided above.
4. Provide an overall recommendation for the Optical Shop and justify your answer based on course material.

---

**\*  NOTES**

1. A lab to grind single-vision lenses cost between $40,000 and $50,000.
2. Pearle could promise one hour turnaround on "standard" lenses, but took much longer to grind complicated prescriptions.
3. The Optical Shop offered neither employee discounts nor payroll deduction for DHMC personnel, but Gary was fighting with Clinic administration to add these benefits.
4. For example, Dr. Morse, the pediatric specialist, occasionally required glasses for children with Down's Syndrome and various birth defects as well as for neo-natal cases.
5. Previously, the Clinic had one part-time optometrist.
6. Establishing a clear connection between these two organizations was a major priority for Dr. Connor in the year ahead.
7. However, few people in the area had not been a patient of DHMC at some time.

# PRIMULA PARKROYAL HOTEL – POSITIONING & MANAGING FOR TURNAROUND

Primula Parkroyal Kuala Terengganu (PPR), a hotel on the east coast of peninsular Malaysia, was going through a strategic change exercise after a new management took over in 1996. In June 1997, Rodney Hawker, PPR's General Manager, was working on the 1998 marketing plan for the hotel. As input into this marketing plan, he needed to decide what target customer segments to focus on, and how the hotel should be positioned to compete effectively with other hotels in Kuala Terengganu as well as with hotels in other destinations. The Asian financial crisis was beginning to unfold with dropping arrival numbers. The situation was further aggravated by the intense competition from the many new resorts and hotels that had mushroomed in the state during the past four years. Furthermore, PPR's service levels and staff morale needed to be improved. Behind this backdrop, Hawker had the objective of reinstating the hotel's position as the premier quality hotel in Kuala Terengganu.

## ✳ MANAGEMENT TAKE-OVER AND REFURBISHMENT

The hotel is located on a beach off the South China Sea in Kuala Terengganu, the capital of Terengganu, a northeastern state of peninsular Malaysia. Terengganu is an oil-rich

Copyright © 1999 by Aliah Hanim M. Salleh, and Jochen Wirtz. The authors retain all rights. Not to be reproduced or used without written permission from one of the authors. This case was prepared as the basis for class discussion rather than to illustrate effective or ineffective handling of an administrative situation. Primula Parkroyal has approved this case for publication with disclosure of the hotel's name.

*Aliah Hanim M. Salleh is Associate Professor of Marketing, Faculty of Business Management, Universiti Kebangsaan Malaysia, 43600 UKM, Bangi, Selangor, Malaysia, Fax: +60-3-8293163, E-mail: aliah@pkrisc.cc.ukm.my. Jochen Wirtz is an Associate Professor, Department of Marketing, Faculty of Business Administration, National University of Singapore, 17 Law Link, Singapore 117591, Tel: +65-8743656, Fax: +65-7795941, E-mail: fbawirtz@nus.edu.sg; http://www.nus.sg. The case authors gratefully acknowledge Rosiati Ramli, Zakiah M. Mohamed and Zaleha Abd. Shukor, who together with the main author, interviewed all personalities in this case and drafted an earlier version in Bahasa Melayu. The data gathering was funded by a Universiti Kebangsaan Malaysia research grant for a case research project, headed by Dr. Nik Rahimah Nik Yacob, and the write-up was partially funded by the National University of Singapore. Finally, the authors like to acknowledge the valued assistance of Sim Siew Lien for assisting in writing the case.

state with a population of about 850,000, comprising mostly Malay Muslims. PPR was one of the first four-star hotels to be built along the eastern coast of peninsular Malaysia in the 1980s. As of 1997, PPR had a total equity of RM[1] 1.6 million, and total assets of RM 3.1 million. However, being owned by a state government agency, it incurred millions of RM in accumulated losses, and the state government aimed at making the hotel profitable as well as at improving the state's tourism infrastructure.

In March 1996, Southern Pacific Hotel Corporation (SPHC) took over PPR's management. SPHC had won a "12-plus five-year contract" to manage the hotel, after successfully outbidding several other large hotel management operating companies from the Asia-Pacific region. Hawker asserted that a unique factor favoring SPHC's interest in PPR was Terengganu's unspoiled beaches, waterfalls, lakes and untapped potential as an attractive tourist destination in Malaysia. This was seen relative to Penang and Langkawi, both of which were expected to reach saturation as tourist destinations. PPR was also the only hotel in Kuala Terengganu which enjoyed both a resort image (with its beach location) as well as a business image, being so close to town.

In managing the strategic change of the hotel, SPHC focused on the following key priorities: upgrading the quality of the hotel's physical facilities, re-marketing and positioning the hotel, training staff, and changing the work culture. Permodalan Terengganu Berhad (PTB), the Terengganu state government's investment arm, became the new owner just before this management take-over. Under the terms of a profit-sharing agreement between PTB and SPHC, PTB financed an initial RM 11m to be used for physically upgrading and refurbishing the hotel. In recognising the need to motivate its staff to deliver quality services, rebuilding a new staff canteen was the first renovation work done. Other work included renovating 72 guestrooms in the double-story wing with access to the beach, and 150 deluxe rooms in the hotel's eleven-story tower block. A new tea lounge was opened adjoining the reception area and coffee house facing the beach. The entire swimming pool area was also re-landscaped, befitting a world-class business resort hotel.

## ✳ COMPETITION

Table 1 shows PPR's main competitors in the vicinity of Kuala Terengganu, and Table 2 presents their market shares. The tables show PPR's strong position in terms of positioning (i.e., excellent city and beach front location), quality of service and facilities (the only four-star hotel). This strong positioning also translated into a 41.7% share revenue of the total market in Terengganu.

## ✳ MARKET SEGMENTS

PPR reached the following target segments: commercial guests (30.1% of room nights), individual travellers (29%), government (17.1%), conference (13.7%), and tour groups and sports (15.2%) [Table 3]. Table 4 shows the food and beverage (F&B) revenues by segment for May 1997. An internal report indicated that PPR enjoyed a lion's share

| TABLE 1 | COMPARATIVE CHARACTERISTICS OF PRIMULA PARKROYAL VERSUS COMPETITORS | | | |
|---|---|---|---|---|
| | Sutra Beach Resort | Seri Malaysia | Permai Park Inn | Primula Parkroyal |
| Location | 38km from town centre; beach front | In town | 5km from town centre | 3km from town centre; beach front |
| No. of Rooms | 120 chalets/rooms | 145 rooms | 131 rooms | 150 deluxe rooms, 27 suites & 72 guest/family rooms |
| Affiliation/owner | SPR Management | Gateway Inn Management | Kemayan Resorts | SPHC/Permodalan Terengganu Bhd. |
| Market Segment Mix | Private, Corporate, Government, Groups | Groups, Private, Government | Corporate, Government, Travel Agents/Tour Groups | Corporate, Government, Travel Agents/Tour Groups |
| Service Positioning | 3.5-star deluxe resort, medium priced | 2.5-star "value-for-money" budget hotel chain | 3-star Town hotel "Bed & breakfast" image | 4-star beach cum business resort |
| Occupancy Rate for 1997 (est.) | 40% | 55% | 50% | 49% |
| Rooms Sold: 1997 (est.) | 16,790 | 30,113 | 23,908 | 44,805 |
| Average Room Rate (RM): 1997 (est.) | 125.00 | 80.00 | 92.00 | 137.91 |
| F&B Outlets/ Conference Facilities | • *Merang* Restaurant<br>• *R-U Tapai* Lounge<br>• Conference Hall (350 pax)<br>• Karaoke Lounge | • *Sekayu* Café (A-la carte menu except Sunday & Friday)<br>• Lunches | • Café-in-the-Park<br>• Conference Hall (250 pax) | • *Bayu*-Lounge<br>• Cascade Grill<br>• *Rhusila* Coffee House<br>• 1 Ballroom<br>• 7 Meeting Rooms |
| Physical Facilities & Services | • Business Centre<br>• Tennis Court<br>• Souvenir Shop<br>• Swimming Pool | • Business Centre<br>• Swimming Pool<br>• Shopping Arcade<br>• Gymnasium<br>• Tea/Coffee-making facilities in rooms | • Retail Stores | • Business Centre<br>• *Koko Nut Klub*<br>• Swimming Pool<br>• Health Centre<br>• Tennis & Volleyball<br>• Iron & Ironing<br>• Board & Tea/Coffee-making facilities in rooms |

Source: Primula Parkroyal internal reports and authors' observations during site visits.

| TABLE 2 | MARKET SHARE AMONG COMPETING HOTELS/RESORTS: MARCH–DECEMBER 1996 | | | | | | | |
| --- | --- | --- | --- | --- | --- | --- | --- | --- |
| | | | | | | | Actual Share | |
| Hotel | No. of Rooms | Capacity (Room nights/year) | Rooms Sold | Occupancy Rate (%) | Average Room Rate | Room Revenue (RM) | % Rooms | % Revenue |
| Primula Parkroyal | 247 | 75,582 | 34,453 | 46 | 130.04 | 4,480,268 | 34.2 | 41.7 |
| P. Park Inn | 131 | 40,086 | 18,039 | 45 | 87.81 | 1,478,369 | 17.9 | 13.8 |
| Seri Malaysia | 150 | 45,900 | 24,327 | 53 | 68.33 | 1,743,781 | 24.1 | 16.2 |
| Sutra Beach Resort | 100 | 30,600 | 10,710 | 35 | 116.00 | 1,242,360 | 10.6 | 11.5 |
| Tanjung Jara Beach | 115 | 35,190 | 13,372 | 38 | 135.00 | 1,805,220 | 13.2 | 16.8 |
| Total | 743 | 227,358 | 100,901 | 44.38 | 106.54 | 10,749,998 | 100.0 | 100.0 |

Source: Primula Parkroyal 1997 Business Plan.

of the commercial market in Terengganu, giving it a higher average yield than its competitors. This report forecasted a 16.8% growth in this segment for 1998.

Guests of SPHC hotels in the Asia-Pacific region could obtain special discounts and other privileges through the Pacific Privilege Card membership program. This Pacific Privilege market was PPR's largest supporter in its private (individual travelers) segment. While this program was low-yielding, it produced volume. The private segment was anticipated to become the hotel's biggest segment over time. PPR planned to increase its share with a "low-season promotion drive" and intensive customer database marketing.

The conference market was primarily supported by the Malaysian government. This segment was projected to increase by 30%. A sales executive based in Kuala Lumpur and Kuala Terengganu was in charge of promoting PPR as a conference destination focusing on the government segment. To cushion reductions in government spending due to the Asian crisis, promotions were mostly targeted at senior departmental officers, who were less severely restricted in their hotel choice.

## * ROOM SALES

According to Cik[2] Norshidah, one of three sales personnel working in the Marketing and Sales Department, sales were conducted by SPHC's Kuala Lumpur head office, which collectively promoted the Parkroyal chain. Room sales were the responsibility of the Rooms Division, headed by Clive Murray. As rooms can be sold at steep discounts, SPHC used both occupancy rates and average room rates to measure the yield of its rooms. Adlin Masood headed the Public Relations Department, which planned and executed cultural, sports, and social events and the hotel's public relations activities throughout the year. Adlin's work supported not only room sales, but helped bring in the crowds for the F&B outlets, as well as servicing the conference and tour group guests.

Out of RM 11.7m in total operating revenue planned for 1997, RM 6.18m were expected to come from room revenues (Table 3). 77% of room revenues were planned to be net contribution, which compared to an actual net contribution of 70% for the time

| TABLE 3 | SUMMARY OF ROOM REVENUES FOR JANUARY – DECEMBER 1997 (PLANNED) |
|---|---|

| | 1997 Budget |
|---|---|
| No. of rooms available | 90,885 |
| No. of rooms occupied | 44,805 |
| Occupancy (%) | 49.3 |
| Average tariff (RM) | 137.91 |

| Customer Segment | Rooms Occupied RM | Rooms Occupied % | Average Tariff RM | Room Revenue RM |
|---|---|---|---|---|
| Commercial: | | | | |
| • Corporate | 8,590 | 19.2 | 153.10 | 1,315,100 |
| • Corporate conference | 2,270 | 5.1 | 126.09 | 286,220 |
| • Others | 2,615 | 5.8 | 148.51 | 388,350 |
| Subtotal Commercial | 13,475 | 30.1 | 147.66 | 1,989,670 |
| Private: | | | | |
| • Rack | 255 | 0.6 | 227.88 | 58,110 |
| • FITs | 9,555 | 21.3 | 149.15 | 1,425,100 |
| • Other discounts | 3,165 | 7.1 | 125.42 | 396,950 |
| Subtotal Private | 12,975 | 29.0 | 144.91 | 1,880,160 |
| Others: | | | | |
| • Govt. – govt. FITs | 7,190 | 16.0 | 135.69 | 975,600 |
| • Conference | 3,860 | 8.6 | 137.05 | 529,000 |
| • Sports | 1,625 | 3.6 | 117.05 | 190,200 |
| • Embassies & others | 515 | 1.1 | 185.00 | 17,575 |
| • Tour groups | 5,165 | 11.6 | 115.57 | 596,900 |
| Subtotal Others | 18,355 | 40.9 | 130.05 | 2,309,275 |
| Total | 44,805 | 100.0 | 137.91 | 6,179,105 |

Source: Primula Parkroyal internal management report.
Note: FIT stands for frequent independent travellers.

from January to May 1997. A breakdown of room and F&B revenues for each customer segment for May 1997 is provided in Table 4.

PPR's beach location fronting the South China Sea made it vulnerable to seasonal fluctuations of demand. During peak holiday periods of June, July, and August, the occupancy rate was expected to reach 62%–63%, (with average room rates of RM 143). In contrast, demand could go as low as 31%–34% (with average room rates dipping to RM 125) in the off-peak monsoon season of December, January and February (Table 5). During the peak season, the occupancy rate could reach 100% on weekends and public holidays.

According to Hawker, PPR's occupancy rate had not increased very much since the management take-over. Table 5 compares the 1997 planned occupancy and average room rates against 1996 figures. The sales and marketing expenses for January to May 1997 are shown in Table 6.

| TABLE 4 | ROOM AND F & B REVENUES BY SEGMENT FOR MAY 1997 | | | | |
|---|---|---|---|---|---|

| Customer<br>Segment | No. of<br>Clients | Room-<br>Nights | % | Room<br>Revenue<br>(RM) | F&B<br>Revenue<br>(RM) |
|---|---|---|---|---|---|
| **Commercial:** | | | | | |
| • Corporate | 658 | 489 | 11.00 | 77,074.71 | 13,357.82 |
| • Corporate-conferences | 970 | 488 | 10.59 | 50,938.76 | 5,847.02 |
| **Subtotal Commercial** | **1628** | **977** | **21.59** | **128,013.47** | **19,204.84** |
| | | | | | |
| **Private:** | | | | | |
| • Private individuals | 1268 | 729 | 15.83 | 107,169.69 | 27,796.45 |
| • Other discounts | 907 | 593 | 12.87 | 41,342.11 | 13,030.61 |
| **Subtotal Private** | **2175** | **1322** | **28.70** | **148,511.80** | **40,827.06** |
| | | | | | |
| **Government-related:** | | | | | |
| • Govt. conferences | 1176 | 625 | 13.57 | 62,940.12 | 17,587.53 |
| • Govt. groups | 16 | 8 | 0.17 | 1,080.00 | 0.00 |
| • Government | 650 | 437 | 9.49 | 65,298.63 | 9,087.21 |
| • Embassies | 9 | 5 | 0.11 | 790.00 | 584.33 |
| **Subtotal Govt-related** | **1851** | **1075** | **23.34** | **130,108.75** | **27,259.07** |
| | | | | | |
| **Others:** | | | | | |
| • Tour groups | 807 | 359 | 7.79 | 36,284.53 | 2,830.95 |
| • Tour agents | 195 | 110 | 2.39 | 13,593.87 | 6,679.12 |
| • Sports | 1192 | 521 | 11.31 | 44,159.38 | 17,661.43 |
| • Internal use | 228 | 165 | 3.58 | 0.00 | 734.26 |
| • Daily use | 0 | 0 | 0.00 | 1,165.00 | 288.53 |
| • Long-term use | 101 | 73 | 1.58 | 8,863.60 | 1,471.52 |
| • Employee offers | 7 | 5 | 0.11 | 0.00 | 97.12 |
| **Subtotal Others** | **2530** | **1233** | **26.76** | **104,066.38** | **29,762.93** |
| Total | 8184 | 4607 | 100.00 | 510,703.40 | 118,063.90 |

Source: Primula Parkroyal internal management report.

## * HOTEL OPERATIONS

PPR's business was organised into two main departments, which operated as separate profit centres: the Room Division, which included the Front Office Operation, and the Food and Beverage Department.

## *ROOM DIVISION & FRONT OFFICE OPERATIONS*

The hotel's Front Office operations were managed by Encik[3] Radi. This department was responsible for managing room reservations and setting room prices, as well as for arranging every activity their guests engaged in throughout their stay. The department received room reservations either directly from individual guests, tour operators, or event

| TABLE 5 | MONTHLY AVERAGE ROOM OCCUPANCY RATES JANUARY–DECEMBER 1997 (PLANNED) | | | |
|---|---|---|---|---|
| | 1997 | | 1996 | |
| Month | Occupancy (%) | Average Rate (RM) | Occupancy (%) | Average Rate (RM) |
| January | 31.3 | 125.22 | Not Available | Not Available |
| February | 33.8 | 125.44 | Not Available | Not Available |
| March | 43.0 | 135.85 | 26.9 | 134.47 |
| April | 51.8 | 135.70 | 43.6 | 123.42 |
| May | 58.6 | 140.87 | 46.6 | 142.23 |
| June | 63.0 | 142.66 | 47.9 | 127.04 |
| July | 62.3 | 142.97 | 49.8 | 122.29 |
| August | 60.2 | 143.47 | 56.4 | 128.03 |
| September | 58.3 | 143.08 | 31.6 | 131.25 |
| October | 56.5 | 141.52 | 51.6 | 132.20 |
| November | 38.3 | 134.93 | 47.4 | 131.36 |
| December | 36.4 | 125.07 | 35.3 | 126.64 |

Source: Primula Parkroyal internal management report.

| TABLE 6 | SALES AND MARKETING EXPENSES (COST CENTRE) |
|---|---|

| Sales and Marketing Expenses | Jan–May 1997(TLM) |
|---|---|
| Salaries & related expenses | 70,216 |
| Staff benefits | 11,987 |
| Promotional expenses | 50,261 |
| Other expenses | 92,027 |
| **Total Expenses** | **224,491** |

Source: Primula Parkroyal internal management report.

sponsors. Other functions of the department included managing the reception counter and room services, porter and concierge services, and recreational support. The Room Division's Income Statement is shown in Table 7, with the main cost item being staffing (21.1% of gross room revenue).

Encik Radi was fully aware that personal interactions with his Front Office staff were the key drivers of guest satisfaction. He strongly believed that his staff needed to be developed and trained to increase service levels, especially as no formal Front Office training had been conducted since 1992 under the previous management. Radi felt that job rotation, for example, between reception and reservation personnel, as well as cross-training (in other Malaysian Parkroyal hotels), could be carried out to develop skills and enrich jobs. Also, there was a need to motivate and retain his Front Office staff, to contain the high turnover rates in the department. He noted that staff motivation was low and turnover and absenteeism were high. Radi had 35 Front Office staff at the end of 1997.

| TABLE 7 | INCOME STATEMENT FOR ROOMS DIVISION (PROFIT CENTRE) | |
|---|---|---|

| Room P&L from Jan–May 1997 | | RM | % of Revenue |
|---|---|---|---|
| Room Income | | 1,827,807 | 100.0 |
| Staff Expenses | | | |
|   Salaries & Wages | 212,565 | | 11.6 |
|   Overtime | 9,129 | | 0.5 |
|   Employee Benefits | 165,216 | | 9.0 |
| Subtotal: Staff Expenses | | 386,910 | 21.1 |
| Other Expenses | | 161,242 | 8.9 |
| Total Expenses | | 548,152 | 30.0 |
| Net Contribution | | 1,279,655 | 70.0 |

Source: Primula Parkroyal internal report.

Another key area of concern was to manage room capacity more effectively. In particular, the occupancy rate had to be increased throughout the year, but especially so during the low seasons (the monsoon months). Also, since 83% of the hotel's room nights were currently occupied by Malaysians, Radi believed that more efforts should be made to attract Malaysian tour groups, rather than tying up high promotional expenses in attempting to bring in more foreign tourists.

## FOOD AND BEVERAGE DEPARTMENT

Harry Thaliwal, a Malaysian with a Swiss qualification in hotel management, was appointed the F&B manager. Previously, he was attached to Parkroyal properties in Sydney and Kuala Lumpur. With 75 staff reporting to him, Thaliwal was responsible for the kitchen, four F&B outlets, conference facilities, and banquet services.

In general, F&B outlets contribute about 30–35% of a hotel's operating revenue. In the past, lunch buffets were offered only when the occupancy rate was considered high enough to sustain it. Thaliwal saw the potential to attract locals and other tourists not residing at PPR to the hotel for the breakfast, lunch, tea, and dinner/supper buffets, served throughout the day. With the introduction of a new set of menus for the buffets, PPR managed to attract a significant number of non-hotel guests, which pushed its F&B's contribution to over 50% of total operating revenue. 60% of the F&B clientele were non-hotel guests; 20% of breakfast buffets, 40% of lunch and dinner buffets, and 90% of the "high tea" and supper buffets were consumed by guests not residing at the hotel. The department's P&L statement is presented in Table 8.

As banquet services accounted for about 50% of F&B revenue, more effective planning and marketing of the hotel's banquet services, F&B outlets, and conference rooms were planned. To facilitate more efficient booking of banquets, Thaliwal introduced a system for managing event scheduling, and ruled that all requests on quotations were to be answered within 24 hours of a client's inquiry. Also, on-the-job training of the chefs and their cross training with Kuala Lumpur's Parkroyal were conducted. This was necessary,

| TABLE 8 | PROFIT AND LOSS STATEMENT FOR FOOD & BEVERAGE (PROFIT CENTRE) |
|---|---|
| **P&L Food & Beverage (Jan–May 1997)** | **RM** |
| Revenues | 1,809,670 |
| Less cost of goods sold | (679,517) |
| **Gross Revenues** | **1,130,153** |
| Expenses | |
| Total Wages | 460,314 |
| Employee Benefits | 230,285 |
| Other Expenses | 193,293 |
| **Total Expenses** | **883,892** |
| Net Profit (Loss) | 246,261 |

Source: Primula Parkroyal internal report.

as the menus had not been changed for the past twelve years before the management change.

Thaliwal also observed that a significant number of waiters and waitresses were reluctant to interact with foreign guests, mostly caused by a lack of confidence in their English language proficiency. Also, an adequate sense of urgency to respond to guests' requests had to be instilled. Improving service standards had become a key challenge. Viewing customer complaints seriously, Thaliwal introduced lucky draws to encourage guests to fill in comment cards as a continuous system of soliciting customer feedback. Analyses of customer comments were made regularly to keep service standards in line with the guests' expectations.

Thaliwal implemented many changes targeted at upgrading service quality. They included restructuring of job positions by promoting several staff to supervisory levels, enriching jobs by deploying staff for both room service and reception duty, and cutting manpower and energy costs by merging the coffee house and bar operations. Thaliwal also replaced a karaoke lounge located at the hotel rooftop with a banquet room, as the former was under-utilized and was incurring losses.

Thaliwal also implemented a proper inventory and storage system for hotel supplies (including food and beverage items). The system was designed to ensure that there are sufficient supplies, particularly of fresh produce, to meet the daily needs of all F&B outlets, and to avoid excessive overstocking of certain room supplies. The use of kitchen supplies was tightly controlled by himself and the Chief Chef. The ordering process for new hotel supplies also needed revamping. Thaliwal terminated all contracts requiring tenders for food and room supplies. Also, tenders for hotel supplies were now open every six months, in contrast to the previous system of once in three months. The suppliers of food and room materials were evaluated on price, quality, and services rendered.

Upon the request of PTB, which ran all its operations based on Islamic principles, income from alcoholic beverages was treated separately from income from other hotel operations. As Table 9 illustrates, the special accounting treatment was made to 'cleanse'

| TABLE 9 | PROFIT FROM LIQUOR SALES |
|---|---|

| Profit from Liquor Sales (May 1997) | RM |
|---|---|
| **Revenue** | |
| Liquor sales | 21,295 |
| Less cost (33.27% of liquor sold) | (7,085) |
| **Gross Revenue** | **14,210** |
| **Expenses** | |
| Management/License Fees (2% of liquor revenue) | 426 |
| Portion of F&B Expenses Relating to Liquor Sales (4.6% of F&B expenses) | 9,071 |
| **Total Expenses** | **(9,497)** |
| Liquor profit (GOP) | 4,713 |
| Deduct: Incentive Fee (6% of GOP) | (283) |
| **Transfer to Liquor Profit Reserve** | **4,430** |

Source: Primula Parkroyal internal report.

the hotel revenues (Islamic principles prohibit profiteering from the sale of liquor). Therefore, PTB's share of the profit generated from alcoholic beverages was not absorbed into PTB's group profits. Instead, this portion was given on a yearly basis to Baitulmal, a public welfare agency.

## ✳ HUMAN RESOURCE DEVELOPMENT

SPHC appointed Encik Rohaizad as the manager of the human resources department (HRD) three months after the management take-over. He found himself in the following situation: low levels of staff training, absence of staff exposure to other hotels' operations and services, and high absenteeism (Table 10). Rohaizad saw changing the work culture as his top priority, with the need to instill service orientation and a high level of work ethics across the ranks. Staff size was trimmed from 350 to 315 after the management take-over.

To upgrade skills and advance career development, training programs were conducted at three levels. At the preliminary stage, knowledge of the hotel's service offerings, and training targeted at instilling service orientation and higher work ethics were conducted. Next, customer complaint handling and related skills training was done. Lastly, for middle management and above, specific courses, such as management accounting and industrial relations, were conducted. Despite the training, changing work culture and attitude remained imperative. For instance, during the last rainy season, among the ten employees that were sent to the Penang-Parkroyal Hotel for cross-training, four returned before the training was completed.

Besides problems with employees' work attitude, Rohaizad also found difficulty in recruiting hotel personnel in the predominantly Muslim state. This was possibly due to

| TABLE 10 | HUMAN RESOURCE STATISTICS (JULY–DECEMBER 1996) | | | | | |
|---|---|---|---|---|---|---|
| | July | Aug | Sep | Oct | Nov | Dec |
| Employee strength | 292 | 304 | 305 | 301 | 305 | 308 |
| Days absent | 65 | 66 | 128 | 78 | 88 | 125 |
| Employee turnover | 24 | 17 | 6 | 13 | 9 | 3 |
| New employees | 17 | 30 | 8 | 7 | 12 | 6 |

Source: Primula Parkroyal's HRD's records.

the Muslim religious code that prohibits Muslims from serving or consuming alcoholic drinks. Rohaizad believed that the people's low level of awareness of the various employment benefits, such as free meals and transport to and from work, also contributed to their reluctance to work in the hotel/catering industry. Rohaizad had conducted career lectures and participated in exhibitions aimed at Terengganu youths and secondary school graduates, to search for new personnel.

Hawker pondered over the formulation of the 1998 business plan. The worsening economic crisis made it crucial for Hawker to decide on the positioning of the hotel, to identify PPR's primary target segments, as well as develop strategies that could smoothen the severe seasonal demand fluctuations. Also, work attitudes and culture of staff had to be critically assessed should a high quality positioning be desired.

## ✱ CASE QUESTIONS

1. What should PPR's positioning be to differentiate it from its competitors?
2. What should be its target markets for the coming year(s)? Should they be the same for peak and off-peak seasons?
3. How could PPR improve room revenue during all seasons?
4. What are PPR's key challenges to achieve its target positioning and improve room revenues?
5. What actions would you recommend PPR to take over the next 12 months?

The following Web sites may provide useful information for the case analysis:

- Primula Parkroyal - http://www.sphc.com.au/hotels/parkroylal/pprimula.html
- Asia Travel Hotels and Resorts Reservation Service – http://asiatravel.com/malaysia/primula/index.html
- Introduction to Terengganu – http://terengganu.gov.my/intro.htm
- Information on Tourism in Malaysia – http://tourism.gov.my/
- Malaysia Home Page – http://www.visitmalaysia.com
- SPHC Home Page – http://www.sphc.com.au

---

## * NOTES

1. RM = Malaysian Ringgit, Malaysia's currency. The exchange rate was US $1 = RM 3.8 at the end of 1998.
2. Cik is the Malay equivalent of the title Miss.
3. Encik is the Malay equivalent of the title Mr.

---

**EXHIBIT 1    PRIMULA PARKROYAL CALENDAR OF EVENTS**

| 1998 Proposed Activities | Reasons for Proposed Activities | Special Occasions |
|---|---|---|
| January<br>Convention packages special | | • New Year's Day<br>• Hari Raya Puasa |
| February<br>Chinese New Year special<br>Convention Packages Special | | • Chinese New Year |
| March<br>Malay Foods Festival | | • End of Ramadan |
| April<br>Cultural Fest | | • Hulu Terengganu Cultural Fest |
| May<br>Cultural Fest<br>Sports Extravaganza<br>Family Packages Special<br>Turtle Viewing Season | | • Terengganu Theatre Festival<br>• Dungun Cultural Fest<br>• National Taekwondo Championship<br>• Beach carnival<br>• Attracting families on vacation |
| June<br>Sports Extravaganza<br>Family Packages Special<br>Cultural Fest<br>Fishing competitions<br>Turtle Viewing Season | | • Marang Cultural Fest<br>• Squid Fishing Fiesta<br>• Boat and Marina Show<br>• Attracting families on vacation |
| July<br>Sports Extravaganza<br>Cultural Fest<br>Turtle Viewing Season | | • Terengganu Beach Games<br>• Kemaman Cultural Fest |
| August<br>Sports Extravaganza<br>Cultural Fest<br>Turtle Viewing Season | | • Kenyir Kayak Regatta<br>• Terengganu Literary Week<br>• International Long Boat Race |
| September<br>Sports Extravaganza<br>Cultural Fest<br>Lantern Festival<br>Turtle Viewing Season | | • Beach Festival '98<br>• Terengganu Gathering of Performing Arts<br>• Mid Autumn Festival |
| October<br>Sports Extravaganza | | • Cultural Gathering<br>• Terengganu Open Traditional Dance Competition |

*Continued*

| EXHIBIT 1 | PRIMULA PARKROYAL CALENDAR OF EVENTS (CONT'D) |
| --- | --- |

November

Conventions Packages Special
Family Packages Special

- Crafts, Arts & Textiles Expo
- Batik & Craft Festival
- Attract families on vacation

December

Magic Show
Convention Packages Special

Family Packages Special
Christmas Promotion

- School holiday treat for children
- Christmas
- Attract families on vacation

Legend:

 Monsoon season

 Turtle viewing season

 School holidays

 Peak periods

# Glossary

## A

**activity time** The time required to perform one activity at one station.

**activity-based costing** Costing method that breaks down the organization into a set of activities, and activities into tasks, which convert materials, labor, and technology into outputs.

**adequate service** The level of service quality a customer is willing to accept.

**adverse conditions** Positive and negative employee actions under stressful conditions.

**aftermarketing** Marketing technique that emphasizes marketing after the initial sale has been made.

**after-sales surveys** A type of satisfaction survey that addresses customer satisfaction while the service encounter is still fresh in the customer's mind.

**ambient conditions** The distinctive atmosphere of the service setting that includes lighting, air quality, noise, and music.

**anticipating** Mitigating the worst effects of supply and demand fluctuations by planning for them.

**apathetic customers** Consumers who seek convenience over price and personal attention.

**applications-on-tap** E-service that is available for rent on the Internet.

**approach/avoidance behaviors** Consumer responses to the set of environmental stimuli that are characterized by a desire to stay in or leave an establishment, explore/interact with the service environment or ignore it, or feel satisfaction or disappointment with the service experience.

**arousal-nonarousal** The emotional state that reflects the degree to which consumers and employees feel excited and stimulated.

**ASPs** Application service providers—those who provide aps-on-tap.

**assurance dimension** The SERVQUAL assessment of a firm's competence, courtesy to its customers, and security of its operations.

**automation** Replacing tasks that required human labor with machines.

## B

**Bad-Mouth Betty** The type of customer who becomes loud, crude, and abusive to service personnel and other customers alike.

**basic business strategy** A firm's fundamental approach as to whether it produces a standardized, low-cost, highvolume product or a differentiated, customized, personalized product.

**beliefs** Consumers' opinions about the provider's ability to perform the service.

**benchmarking** Setting standards against which to compare future data collected.

**benefit concept** The encapsulation of the benefits of a product in the consumer's mind.

**benefit-driven pricing** A pricing strategy that charges customers for services actually used as opposed to overall "membership" fees.

**blueprinting** The flowcharting of a service operation.

**bottlenecks** Points in the system at which consumers wait the longest periods of time.

**boundary tier** The tier in the threetiered model that concerns itself with the individuals who interact with the customers—the boundary spanners.

**boundary-spanning personnel** Personnel who provide their services outside the firm's physical facilities.

**boundary-spanning roles** The various parts played by contact personnel who perform dual functions of interacting with the firm's external environment and internal organization.

**breaks company policies** A customer who refuses to comply with policies that employees are attempting to enforce.

**buffering** Surrounding the technical core with input and output components to buffer environmental influences.

**business environment** The social, technological, and financial environment in which a firm operates and markets.

**business ethics** The principles of moral conduct that guide behavior in the business world.

## C

**capacity sharing** Strategy to increase the supply of service by forming a type of co-op among service providers that permits co-op members to expand their supply of service as a whole.

**categorical imperative** Asks whether the proposed action would be right if everyone did it.

**categorization** Consumer assessment of the physical evidence and a quick mental assignment of a firm to a known group of styles or types.

**change the way we work** The element of the culture change initiative that teaches personnel to flowchart their activities and to re-engineer the process to better serve their customers.

**change the way you work** The element of the culture change initiative that allows personnel to break the rules in the context of serving their customers.

**climate** Employee one or more organizational strategic imperatives.

**code of ethics** Formal standards of conduct that assist in defining proper organizational behavior.

**coding** Categorizing customers based on how profitable their business is.

**cognitive dissonance** Doubt in the consumer's mind regarding the correctness of the purchase decision.

**cognitive moral development** A model of ethical development that proposes individuals progress through six stages of ethical development.

**cognitive responses** The thought processes of individuals that lead them to form beliefs, categorize, and assign symbolic meanings to elements of their physical environment.

**commercial cue** An event or motivation that provides a stimulus to the consumer and is a promotional effort on the part of the company.

**communications gap** The difference between the actual quality of service delivered and the quality of service described in the firm's external communications.

**communications mix** The array of communications tools available to marketers.

**competencies** The contributions customers bring to the service production process.

**complementary services** Services provided for consumers to minimize their perceived waiting time, such as driving ranges at golf courses, arcades at movie theaters, or reading materials in doctors' offices.

**complementary** The result of negative cross-price elasticity in which the increasing price of one service decreases the demand for another service.

**complexity** A measure of the number and intricacy of the steps and sequences that constitute a process.

**confirmed expectations** Customer expectations that match customer perceptions.

**conflict of interest** The situation in which a service provider feels torn between the organization, the customer, and/or the service provider's own personal interest.

**conquest marketing** A marketing strategy for constantly seeking new customers by offering discounts and markdowns and developing promotions that encourage new business; the pursuit of new customers as opposed to the retention of existing ones.

**consequentialism** A type of ethical decision making that assesses the morality of decisions based on their consequences.

**consumer decision process** The three-step process consumers use to make purchase decisions; includes the prepurchase stage, the consumption stage, and the postpurchase evaluation stage.

**consumer management** A strategy service personnel can implement that minimizes the impact of inseparability, such as separating smokers from nonsmokers in a restaurant.

**consumption process** The activities of buying, using, and disposing of a product.

**contact personnel** Employees other than the primary service provider who briefly interact with the customer.

**contrast/clash** Visual effects associated with exciting, cheerful, and informal business settings.

**convergent scripts** Employee/consumer scripts that are mutually agreeable and enhance the probability of customer satisfaction.

**coordination tier** The tier in the threetiered model that coordinates activities that help integrate the customer and boundary tiers.

**co-produce** Service produced via a cooperative effort between customers and service providers.

**corporate culture** The general philosophy of a company that guides decisions, actions, and policies of the company.

**corrective control** The use of rewards and punishments to enforce a firm's code of ethics.

**cost drivers** The tasks in activitybased costing that are considered to be the "users" of overhead.

**creative pricing** Pricing strategies often used by service firms to help smooth demand fluctuations, such as offering "matinee" prices or "earlybird specials" to shift demand from peak to nonpeak periods.

**critical incident** A specific interaction between a customer and a service provider; the moment of actual interaction between the customer and the firm.

**critical incident technique** A method of studying service failures by analyzing critical incidents described in story form by respondents.

**cross-price elasticity** A measure of the responsiveness of demand for a service relative to a change in price for another service.

**cultural differences** Differences in standards of behavior from one culture to another.

**cultural norms** Service personnel actions that either positively reinforce or violate the cultural norms of society.

**culture** The shared values and beliefs that drive an organization.

**customer errors** Service failures caused by admitted customer mistakes.

**customer needs and requests** The individual needs and special requests of customers.

**customer participation** A supply strategy that increases the supply of service by having the customer perform part of the service, such as providing a salad bar or dessert bar in a restaurant.

**customer preferences** The needs of a customer that are not due to medical, dietary, psychological, language, or sociological difficulties.

**customer relationship management (CRM)** The process of identifying, attracting, differentiating, and retaining customers where firms focus their efforts disproportionately on their most lucrative clients.

**customer research** Research that examines the customer's perspective of a firm's strengths and weaknesses.

**customer retention** Focusing the firm's marketing efforts toward the existing customer base.

**customer tier** The tier in the three-tiered model that focuses on customer expectations, needs, and competencies.

**customization** Taking advantage of the variation inherent in each service encounter by developing services that meet each customer's exact specifications.

**customization/customer contact matrix** A table that illustrates the variety of relationships between marketing and other functions within the organization.

## D

**data collection method** The method used to collect information, such as questionnaires, surveys, and personal interviews.

**decoupling** Disassociating the technical core from the servuction system.

**defection management** A systematic process that actively attempts to retain customers before they defect.

**delivery gap** The difference between the quality standards set for service delivery and the actual quality of service delivery.

**deontology** A type of ethical decision making in which the inherent rightness or wrongness of an act guides behavior, regardless of the outcome.

**derived expectations** Expectations appropriated from and based on the expectations of others.

**desired service** The level of service quality a customer actually wants from a service encounter.

**dichotomization** of wealth The rich get richer and the poor get poorer.

**Dictatorial Dick** The type of customer who assumes superiority over all personnel and management.

**differential association** A theory that proposes ethical decision making is greatly influenced by significant others.

**direct measures** The proactive collection of customer satisfaction data through customer satisfaction surveys.

**disconfirmed expectations** Customer expectations that do not match customer perceptions.

**dispersion of control** The situation in which control over the nature of the service being provided is removed from employees' hands.

**disruptive others** Customers who negatively influence the service experience of other customers.

**distributive justice** A component of perceived justice that refers to the outcomes (e.g., compensation) associated with the service recovery process.

**divergence** A measure of the degrees of freedom service personnel are allowed when providing a service.

**divergent scripts** Employee/consumer scripts that "mismatch" and point to areas in which consumer expectations are not being met.

**dominance-submissiveness** The emotional state that reflects the degree to which consumers and employees feel in control and able to act freely within the service environment.

**drunkenness** An intoxicated customer's behavior adversely affects other customers, service employees, and the service environment in general.

**dual entitlement** Cost-driven price increases are perceived as fair, whereas, demand-driven price increases are viewed as unfair.

## E

**economic customers** Consumers who make purchase decisions based primarily on price.

**efficiency pricing** Pricing strategies that appeal to economically minded consumers by delivering the best and most cost-effective service for the price.

**Egocentric Edgar** The type of customer who places his or her needs above all other customers and service personnel.

**egoist** An individual who subscribes to a subclass of teleology in which acceptable actions are defined as those that benefit the individual's self-interest as defined by the individual.

**emotional responses** Responses to the firm's physical environment on an emotional level instead of an intellectual or social level.

**empathy dimension** The SERVQUAL assessment of a firm's ability to put itself in its customers' place.

**employee socialization** The process through which an individual adapts and comes to appreciate the values, norms, and required behavior patterns of an organization.

**employee surveys** Internal measures of service quality concerning employee morale, attitudes, and perceived obstacles to the provision of quality services.

**employee-job fit** The degree to which employees are able to perform a service to specifications.

**empowerment** Giving discretion to front-line personnel to meet the needs of consumers creatively.

**enduring service intensifiers** Personal factors that are stable over time and increase a customer's sensitivity to how a service should best be provided.

**energy costs** The physical energy spent by the customer to acquire the service.

**enfranchisement** Empowerment coupled with a performance based compensation method.

**environmental psychology** The use of physical evidence to create service environments and its influence on the perceptions and behaviors of individuals.

**e-service** An electronic service available via the Net that completes tasks, solves problems, or conducts transactions.

**ethical customers** Consumers who support smaller or local firms as opposed to larger or national service providers.

**ethical vigilance** Paying close attention to whether one's actions are "right" or "wrong," and if ethically "wrong" asking why you are behaving in that manner.

**ethics** A branch of philosophy dealing with what is good and bad and with moral duty and obligations; the principles of moral conduct governing an individual or group.

**evaluation of alternatives** The phase of the prepurchase stage in which the consumer places a value or "rank" on each alternative.

**evoked set** The limited set of "brands" that comes to the consumer's mind when thinking about a particular product category from which the purchase choice will be made.

**exit** A complaining outcome in which the consumer stops patronizing the store or using the product.

**expansion preparation** Planning for future expansion in advance and taking a long-term orientation to physical facilities and growth.

**expectancy disconfirmation model** Model proposing that comparing customer expectations to their perceptions leads customers to have their expectations confirmed or disconfirmed; the model in which consumers evaluate services by comparing expectations with perceptions.

**expectations** Consumer expectations pertaining to the service delivery process and final outcome.

**explicit requests** Customer needs that are overtly requested.

**explicit service promises** Obligations to which the firm commits itself via its advertising, personal selling, contracts, and other forms of communication.

**external search** A proactive approach to gathering information in which the consumer collects new information from sources outside the consumer's own experience.

## F

**facility exterior** The physical exterior of the service facility; includes the exterior design, signage, parking, landscaping, and the surrounding environment.

**facility interior** The physical interior of the service facility; includes the interior design, equipment used to serve customers, signage, layout, air quality, and temperature.

**factories in the field** Another name for multisite locations.

**fail points** Points in the system at which the potential for malfunction is high and at which a failure would be visible to the customer and regarded as significant.

**fairness** The characteristics of just treatment, equity, and impartiality.

**financial consequences** The perceived monetary consequences of a purchase decision by a consumer.

**financial risk** The possibility of a monetary loss if the purchase goes wrong or fails to operate correctly.

**fixed costs** Costs that are planned and accrued during the operating period regardless of the level of production and sales.

**flat-rate pricing** A pricing strategy in which the customer pays a fixed price and the provider assumes the risk of price increases and cost overruns.

**focus group interviews** Informal discussions with eight to twelve customers that are usually guided by a trained moderator; used to identify areas of information to be collected in subsequent survey research.

**focused factory** An operation that concentrates on performing one particular task in one particular part of the plant; used for promoting experience and effectiveness through repetition and concentration on one task necessary for success.

**forward buying** When retailers purchase enough product on deal to carry over until the product is being sold on deal again.

**Freeloading Freda** The type of customer who uses "tricks" or verbal abuse to acquire services without paying.

**frequency marketing** Marketing technique that strives to make existing customers purchase more often from the same provider.

# G

**gestalt** Customer evaluations that are made holistically and given in overall terms rather than in descriptions of discrete events.

**goods** Objects, devices, or things.

# H

**halo effect** An overall favorable or unfavorable impression based on early stages of the service encounter.

**hard technologies** Hardware that facilitates the production of a standardized product.

**harmony** Visual agreement associated with quieter, plusher, and more formal business settings.

**heterogeneity** A distinguishing characteristic of services that reflects the variation in consistency from one service transaction to the next.

**high involvement** Allows employees to eventually learn to manage themselves, utilizing extensive training and employee control of the reward allocation decisions.

**holistic environment** Overall perceptions of the servicescape formed by employees and customers based on the physical environmental dimensions.

**honesty** The characteristics of truthfulness, integrity, and trustworthiness.

**horizontal communication** The flow of internal communication between a firm's headquarters and its service firms in the field.

**hue** The actual color, such as red, blue, yellow, or green.

**human resources logic** The reasoning that stresses recruiting personnel and developing training to enhance the performance of existing personnel.

**Hysterical Harold** The type of customer who reverts to screaming and tantrums to make his or her point.

# I

**ideal expectation** A customer's expectation of what a "perfect" service encounter would be.

**image value** The worth assigned to the image of the service or service provider by the customer.

**implicit guarantee** An unwritten, unspoken guarantee that establishes an understanding between the firm and its customers.

**implicit needs** Customer needs that are not requested but that should be obvious to service providers.

**implicit service promises** Obligations to which the firm commits itself via the tangibles surrounding the service and the price of the service.

**inadequate support** A management failure to give employees personal training and/or technological and other resources necessary for them to perform their jobs in the best possible manner.

**indirect measures** Tracking customer satisfaction through changes in sales, profits, and number of customer complaints registered.

**industrial management model** An approach to organizing a firm that focuses on revenues and operating costs and ignores the role personnel play in generating customer satisfaction and sustainable profits.

**industrialization** Mechanized or automated services that replaced human labor with machines.

**inelastic demand** The type of market demand when a change in price of service is greater than a change in quantity demanded.

**information search** The phase in the prepurchase stage in which the consumer collects information on possible alternatives.

**inseparability** A distinguishing characteristic of services that reflects the interconnection among the service provider, the customer involved in receiving the service, and other customers sharing the service experience.

**instrumental complaints** Complaints expressed for the purpose of altering an undesirable state of affairs.

**intangibility** A distinguishing characteristic of services that makes them unable to be touched or sensed in the same manner as physical goods.

**intangible dominant** Services that lack the physical properties that can be sensed by consumers prior to the purchase decision.

**intensity** The brightness or the dullness of the colors.

**interactional justice** A component of perceived justice that refers to human content (e.g., empathy, friendliness) that is demonstrated by service personnel during the service recovery process.

**interclient conflicts** Disagreements between clients that arise because of the number of clients who influence one another's experience.

**interfunctional task force** Problem-solving group in which individuals with diverse viewpoints work together and develop a better understanding of one another's perspectives.

**interfunctional transfers** Moving, via promotion or transfer, an employee from one organizational department to another to foster informal networks among departments.

**internal logic** Implicit and explicit principles of individual departments that drive organizational performance.

**internal response moderators** The three basic emotional states of the SOR model that mediate the reaction between the perceived servicescape and customers' and employees' responses to the service environment.

**internal search** A passive approach to gathering information in which the consumer's own memory is the main source of information about a product.

**interpersonal services** Service environments in which customers and providers interact.

**invisible organization and systems** That part of a firm that reflects the rules, regulations, and processes upon which the organization is based.

**job involvement** Allows employees to examine the content of their own jobs and to define their role within the organization.

**knowledge gap** The difference between what consumers expect of a service and what management perceives that consumers expect.

**learned helplessness** The condition of employees who, through repeated dispersion of control, feel themselves unable to perform a service adequately.

**level of attention** Positive and/or negative regard given a customer by an employee.

**levels of management** The complexity of the organizational hierarchy and the number of levels between top management and the customers.

**lexicographic approach** A systematic model that proposes that the consumer makes a decision by examining each attribute, starting with the most important, to rule out alternatives.

**linear compensatory approach** A systematic model that proposes that the consumer creates a global score for each brand by multiplying the rating of the brand on each attribute by the importance attached to the attribute and adding the scores together.

**long-term contracts** Offering prospective customers price and non-price incentives for dealing with the same provider over a number of years.

**market defectors** Customers who exit the market due to relocation or business failure.

**market-focused management model** A new organizational model that focuses on the components of the firm that facilitate the firm's service delivery system.

**marketing department** The formal department in an organization that works on the marketing functions of the company.

**marketing functions** Tasks such as the design of a product, its pricing, and its promotion.

**marketing logic** The reasoning that stresses providing customers with options that better enable the service offering to meet individual needs.

**marketing myopia** Condition of firms that define their businesses too narrowly.

**marketing orientation** A firm's view toward planning its operations according to market needs.

**materialismo snobbery** Belief that without manufacturing there will be less for people to service and so more people available to do less work.

**maximum output per hour** The number of people that can be processed at each station in one hour.

**media advertising** A one-way communications tool that utilizes such media as television and radio to reach a broadly defined audience.

**minimum tolerable expectation** A customer expectation based on the absolute minimum acceptable outcome.

**mistargeted communications** Communications methods that affect an inappropriate segment of the market.

**mixed bundling** Price-bundling technique that allows consumers to either buy Service A and Service B together or purchase one service separately.

**molecular model** A conceptual model of the relationship between tangible and intangible components of a firm's operations.

**monetary price** The actual dollar price paid by the consumer for a product.

**moral philosophies** The principles or rules service providers use when deciding what is right or wrong.

**multi-site locations** A way service firms that mass produce combat inseparability, involving multiple locations to limit the distance the consumers have to travel and staffing each location differently to serve a local market.

**mystery shopping** A form of noncustomer research that consists of trained personnel who pose as customers, shop unannounced at the firm, and evaluate employees.

# N

**needs** Security, esteem, and justice; often unrecognized as needs by customers themselves.

**negative disconfirmation** A nonmatch because customer perceptions are lower than customer expectations.

**niche positioning strategy** A positioning strategy that increases divergence in an operation to tailor the service experience to each customer.

**noncustomer research** Research that examines how competitors perform on service and how employees view the firm's strengths and weaknesses.

**noninstrumental complaints** Complaints expressed without expectation that an undesirable state will be altered.

**nonpeak demand development** A strategy in which service providers use their downtime to prepare in advance for peak periods or by marketing to a different segment that has a different demand pattern than the firm's traditional market segment.

**nonpersonal sources** Communication channels that are considered impersonal, such as television advertising or printed information; sources such as mass advertising that consumers use to gather information about a service.

**nonsystematic evaluation** Choosing among alternatives in a random fashion or by a "gutlevel feeling" approach.

# O

**offshoring** The migration of domestic jobs to foreign host countries.

**one-sided blueprint** An unbalanced blueprint based on management's perception of how the sequence of events should occur.

**operations logic** The reasoning that stresses cost containment/ reduction through mass production.

**opportunity** An occasion in which a chance for unethical behavior exists.

**organism** The recipients of the set of stimuli in the service encounter; includes employees and customers.

**organization/client conflicts** Disagreements that arise when a customer requests services that violate the rules of the organization.

**organizational defectors** Customers who leave due to political considerations inside the firm, such as reciprocal buying arrangements.

**organizational image** The perception an organization presents to the public; if well known and respected, lowers the perceived risk of potential customers making service provider choices.

**organizational relationships** Working relationships formed between service providers and various role partners such as customers, suppliers, peers, subordinates, supervisors, and others.

**organizational structure** The way an organization is set up regarding hierarchy of authority and decision making.

**orientation change** The element of the culture change initiative that teaches "families" of personnel to reinforce one another on the job.

**ostensive complaints** Complaints directed at someone or something outside the realm of the complainer.

**other core service failures** All remaining core service breakdowns or actions that do not live up to customer expectations.

**outsourcing** The purchase and use of labor from a source outside the company.

**overpromising** A firm's promise of more than it can deliver.

## P

**part-time employees** Employees who typically assist during peak demand periods and who generally work fewer than 40 hours per week.

**past experience** The previous service encounters a consumer has had with a service provider.

**payout** The amount of money or resolution a service firm spends in order to fulfill an invoked guarantee.

**penetration strategy** A positioning strategy that increases complexity by adding more services and/or enhancing current services to capture more of a market.

**perceived justice** The process whereby customers weigh their inputs against their outputs when forming recovery evaluations.

**perceived service adequacy** A measure of service quality derived by comparing adequate service and perceived service.

**perceived service alternatives** Comparable services customers believe they can obtain elsewhere and/or produce themselves.

**perceived service superiority** A measure of service quality derived by comparing desired service expectations and perceived service received.

**perceived servicescape** A composite of mental images of the service firm's physical facilities.

**perceived-control perspective** A model in which consumers evaluate services by the amount of control they have over the perceived situation.

**perfect-world model** J. D. Thompson's model of organizations proposing that operations' "perfect" efficiency is possible only if inputs, outputs, and quality happen at a constant rate and remain known and certain.

**performance consequences** The perceived consequences of a consumer's purchase decision should the service perform less than 100 percent effectively.

**performance risk** The possibility that the item or service purchased will not perform the task for which it was purchased.

**perishability** A distinguishing characteristic of services in that they cannot be saved, their unused capacity cannot be reserved, and they cannot be inventoried.

**person/role conflict** A bad fit between an individual's selfperception and the specific role the person must play in an organization.

**personal needs** A customer's physical, social, and psychological needs.

**personal selling** The two-way element of the communications mix in which the service provider influences a consumer via direct interaction.

**personal service philosophies** A customer's own internal views of the meaning of service and the manner in which service providers should conduct themselves.

**personal sources** Communication channels that are considered personal, such as a face-to-face encounter; sources such as friends, family, and other opinion leaders that consumers use to gather information about a service.

**personal values** The standards by which each person lives in both a personal and professional life.

**personalized customers** Consumers who desire to be pampered and attended to and who are much less price sensitive.

**personnel value** The worth assigned to the service-providing personnel by the customer.

**physical cue** A motivation, such as thirst, hunger, or another biological cue, that provides a stimulus to the consumer.

**physical evidence/tangible clues** The physical characteristics that surround a service to assist consumers in making service evaluations, such as the quality of furnishings, the appearance of personnel, or the quality of paper stock used to produce the firm's brochure.

**physical risk** The possibility that if something does go wrong, injury could be inflicted on the purchaser.

**physiological responses** Responses to the firm's physical environment based on pain or comfort.

**plant within a plant (PWP)** The strategy of breaking up large, unfocused plants into smaller units buffered from one another so that each can be focused separately.

**pleasure-displeasure** The emotional state that reflects the degree to which consumers and employees feel satisfied with the service experience.

**positioning strategy** The plan for differentiating the firm from its competitors in consumers' eyes.

**positive disconfirmation** A nonmatch because customer perceptions exceed customer expectations.

**predicted service** The level of service quality a consumer believes is likely to occur.

**price bundling** The practice of marketing two or more products and/or services in a single package at a single price.

**price defectors** Customers who switch to competitors for lower priced goods and services.

**price discrimination** Charging customers different prices for essentially the same service.

**principle of utility** The behavior that produces the most good for the most people in a specific situation.

**probability expectation** A customer expectation based on the customer's opinion of what will be most likely when dealing with service personnel.

**problem awareness** The second phase of the prepurchase stage, in which the consumer determines whether a need exists for the product.

**procedural justice** A component of perceived justice that refers to the process (e.g., time) the customer endures during the service recovery process.

**process time** Calculated by dividing the activity time by the number of locations at which the activity is performed.

**product defectors** Customers who switch to competitors who offer superior goods and services.

**product** Either a good or a service.

**product value** The worth assigned to the product by the customer.

**production-line approach** The application of hard and soft technologies to a service operation in order to produce a standardized service product.

**product-line pricing** The practice of pricing multiple versions of the same product or grouping similar products together.

**professional service roles** The parts played by personnel who have a status independent of their place in an organization due to their professional qualifications.

**psychic costs** The mental energy spent by the customer to acquire the service.

**psychological risk** The possibility that a purchase will affect an individual's self-esteem.

**publicity/public relations** A one-way communications tool between an organization and its customers, vendors, news media, employees, stockholders, the government, and the general public.

**putting the customer first** The element of the culture change initiative that teaches personnel to put the customer first.

**quality circles** Empowerment involving small groups of employees from various departments in the firm who use brainstorming sessions to generate additional improvement suggestions.

**quantization** The breaking down of monolithic services into modular components.

**question context** The placement and tone of a question relative to the other questions asked.

**question form** The way a question is phrased, i.e., positively or negatively.

**rational mathematician model** A model that assumes consumers are rational decision makers using a choice matrix of attributes, brand or company scores, and importance weights.

**rationing** Direct allocations of inputs and outputs when the demands placed on a system by the environment exceed the system's ability to handle them.

**red-lining** The practice of identifying and avoiding unprofitable types of neighborhoods or types of people.

**reflexive complaints** Complaints directed at some inner aspect of the complainer.

**relationship marketing** Marketing technique based on developing long-term relationships with customers.

**relationship pricing** Pricing strategies that encourage the customer to expand his/her dealings with the service provider.

**relativism** A type of ethical decision making in which the correctness of ethical decisions is thought to change over time.

**reliability dimension** The SERVQUAL assessment of a firm's consistency and dependability in service performance.

**remote services** Services in which employees are physically present while customer involvement in the service production process is at arm's length.

**research orientation** A firm's attitude toward conducting consumer research.

**reservation price** The price a consumer considers to capture the value he or she places on the benefits.

**reservation system** A strategy to help smooth demand fluctuations in which consumers ultimately request a portion of the firm's services for a particular time slot.

**response bias** A bias in survey results because of responses being received from only a limited group among the total survey population.

**responses (outcomes)** Consumers' reaction or behavior in response to stimuli.

**responsiveness dimension** The SERVQUAL assessment of a firm's commitment to providing its services in a timely manner.

**retaliation** A complaining outcome in which the consumer takes action deliberately designed to damage the physical operation or hurt future business.

**reward systems** The methods used by an organization to evaluate and compensate employees.

**role ambiguity** Uncertainty of employees' roles in their jobs and poor understanding of the purpose of their jobs.

**role conflict** An inconsistency in service providers' minds between what the service manager expects them to provide and the service they think their customers actually want.

**role congruence** The property of actual behaviors by customers and staff being consistent with their expected roles.

**routing** Directing incoming customer calls to customer service representatives where more profitable customers are more likely to receive faster and better customer service.

# S

**sales promotions** A one-way communications tool that utilizes promotional or informational activities at the point of sale.

**satisfaction-based pricing** Pricing strategies that are designed to reduce the amount of perceived risk associated with a purchase.

**scale of market entities** The scale that displays a range of products along a continuum based on their tangibility.

**scent appeals** Appeals associated with certain scents.

**script norms** Proposed scripts developed by grouping together events commonly mentioned by both employees and customers and then ordering those events in their sequence of occurrence.

**script theory** Argues that rules, mostly determined by social and cultural variables, exist to facilitate interactions in daily repetitive events, including a variety of service experiences.

**seamless service** Services that occur without interruption, confusion, or hassle to the customer.

**search** The ability and ease in which information can be sought.

**selection and training** A strategy that minimizes the impact of inseparability by hiring and educating employees in such a way that the customer's service experience is positive and the employees are properly equipped to handle customers and their needs.

**selective agreement** A method of dealing with a dissatisfied customer by agreeing on minor issues in order to show that the customer is being heard.

**self-perceived service role** The input a customer believes he or she is required to present in order to produce a satisfactory service encounter.

**self-services** Service environments that are dominated by the customer's physical presence, such as ATMs or postal kiosks.

**service audit** A series of questions that forces the firm to think about what drives its profits and suggests strategies for competitive differentiation and long-term profitability.

**service cost per meal** The labor costs associated with providing a meal on a per-meal basis (total labor costs/maximum output per hour).

**service defectors** Customers who defect due to poor customer service.

**service economy** Includes the "soft parts" of the economy consisting of nine industry supersectors.

**service failures** Breakdowns in the delivery of service; service that does not meet customer expectations.

**service gap** The distance between a customer's expectations of a service and perception of the service actually delivered.

**service imperative** Reflects the view that the intangible aspects of products are becoming the key features that differentiate the product in the marketplace.

**service providers** The primary providers of a core service, such as a waiter or waitress, dentist, physician, or college instructor.

**service quality** An attitude formed by a long-term, overall evaluation of a firm's performance.

**service quality information system** An ongoing research process that provides relevant data on a timely basis to managers, who use the data in decision making.

**service recovery** A firm's reaction to a complaint that results in customer satisfaction and goodwill.

**service recovery paradox** Situation in which the customer rates performance higher if a failure occurs and the contact personnel successfully recover from it than if the service had been delivered correctly in the first place.

**service value** The worth assigned to the service by the customer.

**services** Deeds, efforts, or performances.

**servicescape** All the nonliving features that comprise the service environment; the use of physical evidence to design service environments.

**SERVQUAL** A 44-item scale that measures customer expectations and perceptions regarding five service quality dimensions.

**servuction model** A model used to illustrate the factors that influence the service experience, including those that are visible to the consumer and those that are not.

**shades** Darker values.

**sharing** Making accessible key customer information to all parts of the organization and in some cases selling that information to other firms.

**shortage** The need for a product or service due to the consumer's not having that particular product or service.

**sight appeals** Stimuli that result in perceived visual relationships.

**significant others** Supervisors, peers, subordinates, customers, and others who influence a service provider's behavior.

**signs, symbols, artifacts** Environmental physical evidence that includes signage to direct the flow of the service process, personal artifacts to personalize the facility, and the style of decor.

**situational factors** Circumstances that lower the service quality but that are beyond the control of the service provider.

**size/shape/colors** The three primary visual stimuli that appeal to consumers on a basic level.

**smoothing** Managing the environment to reduce fluctuations in supply and/or demand.

**social consequences** The perceived consequences of a consumer's purchase decision among the consumer's peers or the public in general.

**social cue** An event or motivation that provides a stimulus to the consumer, obtained from the individual's peer group or from significant others.

**social desirability bias** A bias in survey results because of respondents' tendencies to provide information they believe is socially appropriate.

**social risk** The possibility of a loss in personal social status associated with a particular purchase.

**socialization** The process by which an individual adapts to the values, norms, and required behavior patterns of an organization.

**soft technologies** Rules, regulations, and procedures that facilitate the production of a standardized product.

**SOR (stimulus-organism response) model** A model developed by environmental psychologists to help explain the effects of the service environment on consumer behavior; describes environmental stimuli, emotional states, and responses to those states.

**sound appeals** Appeals associated with certain sounds, such as music or announcements.

**space/function** Environmental dimensions that include the layout of the facility, the equipment, and the firm's furnishings.

**special needs** Requests based on a customer's special medical, psychological, language, or sociological difficulties.

**specialization positioning strategy** A positioning strategy that reduces complexity by unbundling the different services offered.

**specific result guarantee** A guarantee that applies only to specific steps or outputs in the service delivery process.

**standardization** To produce a consistent service product from one transaction to the next.

**standards gap** The difference between what management perceives that consumers expect and the quality specifications set for service delivery.

**stations** A location at which an activity is performed.

**stimuli** The various elements of the firm's physical evidence.

**stimulus** The thought, action, or motivation that incites a person to consider a purchase.

**structure** The formal reporting hierarchy normally represented in an organizational chart.

**subordinate service roles** The parts played by personnel who work in firms where customers' purchase decisions are entirely discretionary, such as waitresses, bellmen, and drivers.

**substitutes** The result of positive cross-price elasticity in which the increasing price of one service increases the demand for another service.

**suggestion involvement** Low-level empowerment that allows employees to recommend suggestions for improvement of the firm's operations.

**switching costs** Costs that accrue when changing vendors.

**symbolic meaning** Meaning inferred from the firm's use of physical evidence.

**system failures** Failures in the core service offering of the firm.

**systematic evaluation** Choosing among alternatives by using a set of formalized steps to arrive at a decision.

**systems** People-management systems of control, evaluation, promotion, and recognition.

## T

**tangible dominant** Goods that possess physical properties that can be felt, tasted, and seen prior to the consumer's purchase decision.

**tangibles dimension** The SERVQUAL assessment of a firm's ability to manage its tangibles.

**tangibles** Other items that are part of the firm's physical evidence, such as business cards, stationery, billing statements, reports, employee appearance, uniforms, and brochures.

**target markets** The segments of potential customers that become the focus of a firm's marketing efforts.

**targeting** Offering the firm's most profitable customers special deals and incentives.

**taste appeals** The equivalent of providing the customer with free samples.

**technical core** The place within an organization where its primary operations are conducted.

**technical service quality** An objective, measurable level of performance produced by the operating system of the firm.

**technological defectors** Customers who switch to products outside the industry.

**technology** The level of automation a firm utilizes.

**teleology** A type of ethical decision making in which an act is deemed morally acceptable if it produces some desired result.

**third parties** A supply strategy in which a service firm uses an outside party to service customers and thereby save on costs and personnel.

**three-tiered model** A view of service organizations that reconfigures traditional departmental functions into a customer tier, a boundary tier, and a coordination tier.

**tie to the customer** The degrees of involvement the firm has with its customers.

**time costs** The time the customer has to spend to acquire the service.

**timing of the question** The length of time after the date of purchase in which questions are asked.

**tints** Lighter values.

**total market service quality surveys** Surveys that measure the service quality of the firm sponsoring the survey and the service quality of the firm's competitors.

**touch appeals** Appeals associated with being able to touch a tangible product or physical evidence of a service, such as shaking hands with service providers.

**transitory service intensifiers** Personal, short-term factors that heighten a customer's sensitivity to service.

**two-sided blueprint** A blueprint that takes into account both employee and customer perceptions of how the sequence of events actually occurs.

**type 1 service staff** Service staff that are required to deal with customers quickly and effectively in "once only" situations where large numbers of customers are present.

**type 2 service staff** Service staff that deal with numerous, often repeat customers in restricted interactions of somewhat longer duration.

**type 3 service staff** Service staff required to have more highly developed communication skills because of more extended and complex interactions with customers.

## U

**unavailable service** Services normally available that are lacking or absent.

**unbundling** Divesting an operation of different services and concentrating on providing only one or a few services in order to pursue a specialization positioning strategy.

**unconditional guarantee** A guarantee that promises complete customer satisfaction, and at a minimum, a full refund or complete, nocost problem resolution.

**uncooperative customer** A customer who is generally rude, uncooperative, and unreasonably demanding.

**unfulfilled desire** The need for a product or service due to a consumer's dissatisfaction with a current product or service.

**unprompted/unsolicited actions** Events and employee behaviors, both good and bad, totally unexpected by the customer.

**unreasonably slow service** Services or employees perceived by customers as being extraordinarily slow in fulfilling their function.

**unusual action** Both positive and negative events in which an employee responds with something out of the ordinary.

**upward communication** The flow of information from front-line personnel to upper levels of the organization.

**utilitarianist** An individual who follows a subclass of teleology in which acceptable behavior is defined as that which maximizes total utility—the greatest good for the greatest number of people.

**value** The lightness and darkness of the colors.

**variable costs** Costs that are directly associated with increases in production and sales.

**verbal and physical abuse** A customer verbally or physically abuses either the employee or other customers.

**visual pathway** Printed materials through which the professional image of the firm can be consistently transmitted, including firm brochures, letterhead, envelopes, and business cards.

**voice** A complaining outcome in which the consumer verbally communicates dissatisfaction with the store or the product.

**volume-oriented positioning strategy** A positioning strategy that reduces divergence to create product uniformity and reduce costs.

**willingness to perform** An employee's desire to perform to his/her full potential in a service encounter.

**woofs** "Well-off older folks," that segment of the population that controls 77 percent of the nation's assets and 50 percent of its discretionary income.

**word-of-mouth communications** Unbiased information from someone who has been through the service experience, such as friends, family, or consultants.

**Z**

**zero defections** A model used by service providers that strives for no customer defections to competitors.

**zero defects model** A model used in manufacturing that strives for no defects in goods produced.

**zone of tolerance** Level of quality ranging from high to low and reflecting the difference between desired service and adequate service; expands and contracts across customers and within the same customer, depending on the service and the conditions under which it is provided.

# Index

# T